Developmental Psychology

McGRAW-HILL SERIES IN PSYCHOLOGY

HARRY F. HARLOW, *Consulting Editor*

BARKER, KOUNIN, AND WRIGHT · Child Behavior and Development
BEACH, HEBB, MORGAN, AND NISSEN · The Neuropsychology of Lashley
VON BÉKÉSY · Experiments in Hearing
BLUM · Psychoanalytic Theories of Personality
BROWN · The Psychodynamics of Abnormal Behavior
BROWN AND GHISELLI · Scientific Method in Psychology
CATTELL · Personality
CRAFTS, SCHNEIRLA, ROBINSON, AND GILBERT · Recent Experiments in Psychology
DEESE · The Psychology of Learning
DOLLARD AND MILLER · Personality and Psychotherapy
DORCUS AND JONES · Handbook of Employee Selection
FERGUSON · Personality Measurement
FERGUSON · Statistical Analysis in Psychology and Education
GHISELLI AND BROWN · Personnel and Industrial Psychology
GRAY · Psychology Applied to Human Affairs
GRAY · Psychology in Industry
GUILFORD · Fundamental Statistics in Psychology and Education
GUILFORD · Psychometric Methods
GUILFORD · Personality
HAIRE · Psychology in Management
HIRSH · The Measurement of Hearing
HURLOCK · Adolescent Development
HURLOCK · Child Development
HURLOCK · Developmental Psychology
KARN AND GILMER · Readings in Industrial and Business Psychology
KRECH AND CRUTCHFIELD · Theory and Problems of Social Psychology
LEWIN · A Dynamic Theory of Personality
LEWIN · Principles of Topological Psychology
LEWIS · Quantitative Methods in Psychology
MAIER AND SCHNEIRLA · Principles of Animal Psychology
MILLER · Language and Communication
MISIAK AND STAUDT · Catholics in Psychology: A Historical Survey
MOORE · Psychology for Business and Industry
MORGAN AND STELLAR · Physiological Psychology
PAGE · Abnormal Psychology
REYMERT · Feelings and Emotions
SEASHORE · Psychology of Music
SHAFFER AND LAZARUS · Fundamental Concepts in Clinical Psychology
SIEGEL · Nonparametric Statistics: For the Behavioral Sciences
STAGNER · Psychology of Personality
TOWNSEND · Introduction to Experimental Method
VINACKE · The Psychology of Thinking
WALLEN · Clinical Psychology: The Study of Persons
WATERS, RETHLINGSHAFER, AND CALDWELL · Principles of Comparative Psychology
ZUBEK AND SOLBERG · Human Development

John F. Dashiell was Consulting Editor of this series from its inception in 1931 until January 1, 1950. Clifford T. Morgan was Consulting Editor of this series from January 1, 1950 until January 1, 1959.

Developmental Psychology

ELIZABETH B. HURLOCK, Ph.D.

Associate in Psychology, The Graduate School

University of Pennsylvania

Second Edition

McGRAW-HILL BOOK COMPANY, INC.

New York   Toronto   London   1959

TO MY DAUGHTERS

Daryl and Gail

Preface

The span of time from conception to death is a long one for the average American of today. During his lifetime he will change not only in size, proportions, appearance, and bodily functions, but also in attitudes, interests, and patterns of behavior. While it is true that all people are different and that the way they change differs according to their innate capacities and environmental influences, there is a fundamental, underlying pattern that is much the same for all. A presentation of this pattern is the main objective of this book.

To understand a person at any stage of his development, it is necessary to know what went before and what is likely to happen in the future. This cause-and-effect relationship may best be seen by getting a bird's-eye view of the person throughout his life span. From a practical point of view, this is important because it will help to dispel any delusion the person may have that this behavior or that attitude "doesn't count." When one takes a look at life from the beginning to the end, it becomes readily apparent that what the person does at one age leaves an impression on his attitudes and future activities which may never be completely eradicated.

The purpose of this book is to give as complete a picture of the developmental changes of the total life span of the normal human being as is possible within the covers of one book. In addition, possible causes of deviations from the normal pattern of development will be suggested, based on the findings of experimental studies. Because of the tremendous amount of research that has been done on each age level, this is a more gigantic task than one may realize. Indeed, the matter of selection has proved to be an even greater problem in the revision than in the 1953 edition of this book since the growing interest in developmental psychology has led to more extensive research.

As with all revisions of college textbooks, certain major changes have been made in this edition. In the area of subject matter, more emphasis has been placed on cultural influences and on social-class influences within the culture. Recent studies in psychology, sociology, and gerontology, as well as anthropological research, have turned the spotlight on such influences and have revealed the role they play in producing individual differences. This point of view, implemented by these new research studies, is strongly emphasized throughout the book.

Since this book appeared in its original form, gerontologists have been going downward in the age scale to investigate the typical problems and behavior patterns of the older adult years, or "middle age," as it is commonly referred to in the American culture. Because there is now adequate material available to present a fairly complete picture of what happens to the individual in middle age, it was decided to treat this period as a separate stage in the developmental span rather than include it in the chapters on old age, as was done in the original edition. As a result, two chapters on middle age have been added.

To keep the number of the chapters within the limit of the standard college semester, the chapter "The 'Mature' Adult," which appeared in the original text, has been eliminated. However, important information from this chapter has been included in the chapter "Late Adolescence" with the hope that the student will be able to see whether the development characteristic of late adolescence, namely, preparation for adult life, has been achieved.

The major revision in the format has been to limit the references mainly to studies that have appeared since the late 1940s and to place them at the ends of the chapters in which they are discussed. Limiting the references to recent studies does not mean that these studies were considered better than the older ones in the same areas; it was simply a practical way of reducing the number of references. Nor were the studies included in the references selected necessarily because they seemed the best, but rather because, in most cases, they contained reviews of earlier studies in the same area, thus making it possible for a student who is interested in obtaining a more complete picture of a particular pattern of behavior at a specific age level to trace the older studies through the references given.

To facilitate the reading of the text, the names of the researchers whose studies are reported have been omitted. Instead, a number has been used to identify the study as it is reported in the bibliography at the end of each chapter. It is believed that this change will eliminate the break in the reader's train of thought and avoid giving him the impression that he is being "bogged down" by a long list of names.

It is hoped that, from a study of the chapters covering adulthood, middle age, and old age, the reader will derive a true appreciation of the importance of the earlier years of the life span, the foundation years. It is further hoped that the emphasis placed on cultural influences at every period of the life span will leave the reader with the impression that the human being is truly a product of both his heredity and his environment —a point of view which has gained widespread acceptance among psychologists, sociologists, and anthropologists in recent years.

Elizabeth B. Hurlock

Contents

» 1 «

Growth and Decline

Developmental psychology is the branch of psychology that studies the development of the human being from conception to death, with emphasis on the changes that take place during the different periods in the life span. At first, interest in the study of development was limited to school children. Later, interest spread to those of preschool ages, and still later to the newborn infant and the prenatal period. Shortly after World War I, research studies of the adolescent years began to appear in increasingly large numbers, and since World War II, more and more attention has been focused on adulthood and the latter years of the life span [32*]. As late as 1933, however, Miles pointed out, "Maturity, later maturity, and senescence are still a realm for folklore, anecdote, and personal impression" [43].

Studies of different periods of life have been motivated by the need to solve some of the practical problems associated with those ages. Research in the area of childhood, for example, was designed first to throw light on educational problems and, later, on problems relating to child-training methods. Interest in studying the newborn infant came largely from a desire to know what the birth equipment of the human being is as the starting point for his training. The practical problems of marital adjustment and the effects of broken homes on children have motivated extensive research in the period of adulthood. Because an increasing number of people are now living to be sixty years of age and older and must face new personal and social problems, another area of research

---

* A bibliography is given at the end of each chapter.

has opened up in recent years. Finally, the latest focus of research attention, middle age, is the outgrowth of the realization that good adjustment in the latter years of life has its foundation in the success with which the individual adjusts to the physical and psychological changes that normally occur in his middle years.

Obstacles to Study. Despite both popular and scientific interest in the different periods of the life span, research has been hindered by difficult and, at times, insuperable obstacles. Getting representative samplings of *subjects* has been relatively easy among school children and college students. In the case of the newborn infant, on the other hand, there is often strong parental objection on the grounds that the infant is so delicate that he might be permanently harmed if subjected to scientific investigation. Getting information from adults at any age level is extremely difficult because many refuse to be interviewed or tested. This is especially true of upper-class women and lower middle-class men and women [22]. This difficulty increases with advancing age, which is why so many of the studies relating to the latter years of life have been made on men and women living in institutions, people who unquestionably are not representative of the general population. Many middle-aged and elderly people are hesitant about being tested because they do not want to know, or let others know, what they have suspected—that they are "slipping."

Finding a satisfactory *method* for studying development has likewise proved to be a stumbling block to research. Developmental changes can be traced most successfully by longitudinal studies of the same individuals over the life span, for only in that way is it possible to know if the changes that are reported are changes in the individuals themselves or the result of differences in sampling, a source of error inherent in the more commonly used cross-sectional approach. Comparisons of old people with young adults, for example, show them to have fewer interests than the young adults. But this may be because the old people grew up at a time when fewer recreations, such as movies, sports, radio, and television, were available and when home duties gave them less time to cultivate interests. Thus, what appears to be a decline in interests with age may be only a difference in interests between two groups with different cultural and environmental backgrounds [34]. In recent years, studies using the longitudinal method have appeared in larger numbers, but the time, effort, and money required to make such studies have militated against widespread usage. The most extensive and best known of the studies using the longitudinal approach is Terman's genetic study of genius, which traces the development of a group of individuals from preschool days to middle age [57].

THE LIFE SPAN

The length of the life span varies from individual to individual, from culture to culture, and from time to time in the history of the world. Today, American men and women, on the average, live longer than men and women of any other country. Changes in fertility, due to birth control, and in mortality, due to improved medical treatment, have resulted in an increase at the upper age levels [59]. Within our nation, women as a group outlive men. In age groups above sixty-five years, the ratio of men to women is now 85.7 to 100 [46]. The excess of females over males in the upper age brackets is shown in Figure 1.

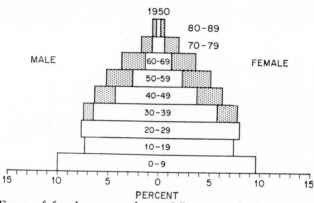

FIG. 1. Excess of females over males at different age levels. (*From C. Tibbitts and H. D. Sheldon, Introduction: a philosophy of aging. Ann. Amer. Acad. pol. soc. Sci., 1952, 279, 1–10. Used by permission.*)

Although it is impossible to predict how long a given individual will live, there is evidence that the length of his life span is influenced by hereditary endowment. In some families, longevity prevails; in others, a shorter life span is characteristic. Improved prenatal and postnatal care and feeding, modern medical methods, accident-prevention measures, habits of work, rest, ambition, the speed at which a person lives, the ability to adjust to stress and strain, climate, sex, the age of the mother at the time of the individual's birth, and a host of other factors have been found to influence life expectancy [27, 59].

Periods in Life Span. Regardless of how short or long the total life span may be, it falls into stages or periods. As Feldman has pointed out, "Human life proceeds by stages. The life periods of the individual are no less real and significant than the geographical ages of the earth or the evolutionary stages of life. . . . Each stage is distinguished by a dominant feature, a leading characteristic, which gives the period its coherence, its unity, and its uniqueness" [15]. Each period in the life span, according to Lawton, has "its own problems of adjustment. These age periods are related, not in surface story since the problems change; it is the method of attacking these problems which is likely to remain the same. Throughout the life span, people develop techniques of handling each of their difficulties. Some of these techniques are suitable and efficient, others are inappropriate and wasteful, or a method may be suitable for one age period and not another" [38].

The life span, when divided according to the forms of development predicted for each age, has been found to have eleven periods, and the remaining chapters of this book will present the characteristic development for each of these periods. The periods and their approximate ages are:

Prenatal: conception to birth.
Infancy: birth to the end of the second week.
Babyhood: end of the second week to end of the second year.
Early childhood: two to six years.
Late childhood: six to ten or twelve years.
Puberty or preadolescence: ten or twelve to thirteen or fourteen years.
Early adolescence: thirteen or fourteen to seventeen years.
Late adolescence: seventeen to twenty-one years.
Early adulthood: twenty-one to forty years.
Middle age: forty to sixty years.
Old age or senescence: sixty years to death.

DEVELOPMENTAL CHANGES

Development means a progressive series of changes in an orderly, coherent pattern. It is a "process in which the internal physiological changes and the psychological processes stimulated by them are integrated (or responded to) in a way which enables the individual to master further, and anew, environmental stimulations. . . . There are two periods in life when changes of the organism put the individual's capacity to master these changes to a test—puberty and the climacteric" [4]. As Gesell has stressed, "Development is more than a concept. It can be observed, appraised, and to some extent even 'measured' in three major manifestations: (a) anatomic, (b) physiologic, (c) behavioral. . . . Behavior signs, however, constitute a most comprehensive index of developmental status and developmental potentials" [19].

In order to exist and function, the organism must make continuous changes throughout life. These changes occur in the continuous replacement of cells, tissues, fluids, and chemical constituents of the organism, as well as in the emotions, behavior, and personality pattern. Some of the changes are in a state of developing; some are at their peak, and some in their decline [39]. There are two essentially antagonistic processes in development which take place simultaneously throughout life—*growth* or evolution and *atrophy* or involution. Both begin at conception and end at death. In the early years, growth predominates, even though atrophic changes occur as early as embryonic life, as in the atrophy of the gill clefts in the mammalian embryo. In the latter part of life, atrophy predominates, though growth continues as is shown in the growth of hair and in cellular replacements [12]. With aging, some parts of the body and mind change more than others. Thus, the individual is not the same biologic age all over. Atrophy may come from disease, deterioration, poor food, infection, or excessive wear and tear [51].

The human being is never static. From the moment of conception to the time of death, he is changing. The change from a microscopically small speck to an individual who measures from 5 feet or less to 6 feet or more and weighs somewhere between 85 and 250 pounds occurs in a fifth or less of the entire life span. To show how rapid the development is at first, increases in weight may be used as a criterion. From fertilization to birth, weight increases 11 million times. After birth, increases continue at a progressively slower rate until the late teens or early twenties when growth comes to a standstill. Increase in strength continues from birth to approximately twenty-five years of age and remains at about the same point from twenty-five to forty-five or fifty-five years, after which it decreases slowly or rapidly, owing to retrogression [9].

Physical development does not necessarily mean increase in size. There are modifications of the composition of the body taking place constantly. In the baby, for example, gain in weight comes partly from increase in neural, glandular, and muscle tissue; in childhood, the gain comes principally from bone and muscle tissue; while in the adult years, the gain is from an accumulation of fat tissue [40]. Changes in bodily size and functioning are accompanied by changes in mental capacity. For a half or more of the life span, there is a gradual but ever-perceptible increase in capacity, thus enabling the individual to adjust himself with greater and greater skill to his environment. Then, at varying times from the middle to the latter part of the life span, a period of contraction or decline starts. As a rule, physical decline precedes mental.

Typically, the pattern of human life is that of a bell-shaped curve, rising abruptly at the start, then flattening out to some extent during the middle years, only to decline slowly or abruptly toward the closing years of the life span. At no time can this pattern be represented by a straight line, though plateau periods of short or long duration may be found in the curves for different capacities. As Kahn and Simmons have pointed out,

Man never stands still in his development. All his organs and functions show curves of capacity achievement rather than plateaus. The brain gains and loses weight, basal metabolism reaches a peak and declines, endocrine functions flourish and fade, the powers of taste and the capacity to experience pain and pleasure vary in intensity. There is a rise and fall of physical energy in terms of both force and speed of action: sexual powers wax and wane. Intelligence and related mental functions develop and decline, and there appear to be shifts in interests and attitudes. The skeleton is delicately sensitive to the processes of age and accurately records them. In fact, no organ or function of man has yet been found in which an "age determinant" does not exist [29].

Awareness of Changes. In spite of the fact that changes of a physical or psychological sort are constantly taking place, the individual may not be aware of them. In childhood, puberty, and even early adolescence, when changes occur so rapidly that new adjustments are constantly necessary, the individual is attentive to these changes. Likewise, in senescence, when the downward movement begins to speed up, the individual is aware of the fact that his health is "failing" and that his mind is "slipping." These changes necessitate constant readjustments in the scheduled pattern of his life. He must slow down as the incapacities and infirmities of old age catch up with him.

While the changes of old age are at a much slower pace than the changes of childhood and adolescence, they still require readjustments on the individual's part. Because these readjustments can be made more slowly than developmental changes, they may not be recognized by others or even by the individual himself. Furthermore, because they are unwelcome and suggest to the individual that his life is drawing to a close, he is likely to shut his eyes to them as long as he can or to minimize their severity. Developmental changes, by contrast, are welcome. The child likes to feel that he is growing up and, as a result, he eagerly welcomes each new change which brings him nearer and nearer to the longed-for goal of maturity with its rights, privileges, and independence.

SIGNIFICANT FACTS ABOUT DEVELOPMENT

Studies of development have revealed certain fundamental and predictable facts so important to the understanding of the pattern of development that they are worthy of serious attention. These facts are:

Childhood Is the Foundation Period of Life. During the early years of life, attitudes, habits, and patterns of behavior are established which will determine, to a large extent, how successfully the individual will be able to adjust to life as he grows older. From the study of adolescents, it has become apparent that "the foundation and most of the framework of the human action system are laid down in the first decade" [21]. Because of the plasticity of his physical and nervous structures, the human child is capable of learning and can develop more varied types of adjustment than are possible in animals.

Numerous studies of adolescents, as well as young and old adults, have emphasized the importance of childhood as the foundation period for different physical and psychological traits. Studies of obesity, for example, have revealed that overweight adults are the product of eating habits established early in life and of overprotection during their childhood years. Similarly, the role which the child plays in the family and in the peer group will determine whether he develops into a leader or a follower. People who are "self-bound" have had childhood experiences which have made them incapable of affectionate interchange with others. The limited interests of middle-aged and elderly people today are due not to mental deterioration but rather to the lack of opportunity to develop a wide range of interests when they were children [34].

The *basic personality pattern* of the individual, the "personality configuration which is shared by the bulk of the society's members as a result of the early experiences which they have in common," is set during the early years of life [31]. In fact, personality traits of men and women in later life have been found to be so similar to those of their childhood days that they can readily be identified even by strangers [53]. Studies of child guidance clinic records of men who were later admitted to mental hospitals show that, as children, these men had symptoms of withdrawal, shyness, listlessness, excesive daydreaming, and seclusiveness, and that they had few relations with others and showed little interest in others [17]. On the other hand, well-adjusted children, with few exceptions, develop into well-adjusted adolescents and adults.

Attitudes toward members of the opposite sex and adjustment in marriage have been found to be profoundly influenced by early interpersonal experiences in the home and in the peer group [44]. Serious behavior problems seldom arise abruptly in adolescence or adulthood but trace their origin to maladjustment in the early years. Delinquent behavior in adolescence results from methods of meeting frustration that were established early in life [48]. Indeed, boys who will later become delinquent can be identified as early as six years of age [58].

The foundations laid in the early years of life are the result of *child-training methods*, whether authoritarian or democratic, of *cultural values* passed on through parents, teachers, and peers, of the *atttiude of the parents* toward the child and their relationships with him, of the *ordinal position* of the child in the family and his relationships with his siblings, and of *emotional deprivation* due to separation from the mother during the early years of life. Despite the fact that the foundations are laid during the early years, changes can and do occur as the life cycle progresses. Early patterns are not, therefore, unchangeable, but they are usually persistent because the individual continues to view the world and to react to it under the guidance of these early developed patterns [16].

Development Comes from Maturation and Learning. The second fundamental fact about human development is that it comes from both maturation and learning. *Learning* means development that comes through exercise and effort on the individual's part. *Maturation* is the "net sum of the gene effects operating in a self-limited life cycle" [19]. It is the unfolding of traits inherent in the individual. Studies of large groups of children of different age levels to see whether, under different environmental conditions, similarities of behavoir appear at approximately the same ages, have given us some clues as to whether a trait that was supposed to be a product of maturational influences actually was, or whether similarities in teaching methods have brought about these similarities.

Attempts to control the environment of the individual so as to prevent him from having an opportunity to learn have been few in number but have provided significant findings. The elimination of opportunities for practice in reaching, sitting, and standing, for example, has shown little influence on the development of these abilities [14]. In *phylogenetic* functions, or functions common to the race, such as crawling, creeping, sitting, and walking, training is of little importance, while in *ontogenetic* functions, or functions which are specific to the individual, such as roller skating, swimming, or tricycle riding, training is essential to the acquisition of the skill [41].

Maturation and learning are interrelated causes of development, the one aiding or retarding the other. Maturation provides the raw material for learning and determines the more general patterns and sequences of the individual's behavior. The increase with age of parent-child similarities in physical and mental development gives evidence of the existence of an hereditary core responsible for these similarities [55]. However, although external forces influence the maturational process without effort on the individual's part, traits potentially present will not develop to their maximum without motivation and self-direction.

The patterns of behavior developed through learning will be determined largely by *cultural influences*. Through child training in the home and through social pressures from the peer group and society in general, patterns of behavior approved by the cultural group are being learned throughout life. Within a cultural group, social class values are learned by the individual, and these influence the pattern of his personality and the form of his behavior. Unfavorable environmental influences may retard the individual's development or keep traits potentially present from developing to their maximum.

Three important facts emerge from our present knowledge of the interrelationship of maturation and learning as the causes of development. First, because humans are capable of learning, which is untrue of many of the animal species, variation is possible. Individual differences in personality, attitudes, interests, and patterns of behavior come not from maturation alone but from maturation and learning [65]. Second, maturation sets limits beyond which development cannot progress even with the most favorable learning methods and the strongest motivation on the part of the learner. As Gesell has pointed out, innate capacity for growth "is a gift of nature. It can be guided, but it cannot be created; nor can it be transcended by an educational agency" [18].

And, finally, the interrelation between maturation and learning establishes a "timetable" for learning. The individual cannot learn until he is ready. *Developmental readiness* is the "individual's state of preparedness with some one or more areas of functioning" [6]. This is the "teachable moment when the task should be learned" [23]. If the "teachable moment" has not arrived, forcing the child to learn will not only lead to failure on the child's part and wasted time and effort for the teacher, but it will result in negativistic, resistant behavior which will militate against successful learning when the child is ready [6]. As Wishik has emphasized in relation to teaching, "It is not so much *what* we do as *when* we do it" [65].

Delaying the opportunity to learn, by either underestimating the child's ability or harboring misconceptions or cultural biases concerning the "right time" to learn, may lead to a lack of interest in learning when the opportunity is given. Motivation will thus lag to the point where learning is hindered [23].

Development Follows a Definite and Predictable Pattern. Every species, whether animal or human, has a characteristic pattern of development which is normal for the species. Although individual differences exist within a species, these differences are, for the most part, slight and do not appreciably influence the general trend of development. Studies of the prenatal development of humans have shown that the pattern there is definite and predictable, just as it is throughout the course of postnatal life [18]. By observing a group of individuals over a number of years, it is possible to see the genetic sequences in different areas of development and to note similarities in the patterns of development from one individual to another.

In *physical development,* there are many evidences of the orderly, predictable pattern of growth. During prenatal life, the pattern of development follows the *cephalocaudal sequence,* which means that improvements in structure as well as in control of different areas of the body come first in the head region, then in the trunk, and last, in the leg region. The same sequence is found in postnatal development. Not only do the structures in the head region develop sooner than those in the leg region, but motor control comes first in the upper areas of the body and last in the lower areas [20].

Studies of puberty changes show that the pattern of development is regular and predictable for the two sexes. Not only do the sex organs of boys and girls grow and become functionally mature in much the same manner for all individuals of a given sex, but the secondary sex characteristics also appear in a patterned order; furthermore, growth in body size proceeds at a predictable rate while these sexual changes are taking place. At middle age, when the sex life comes to a close with the

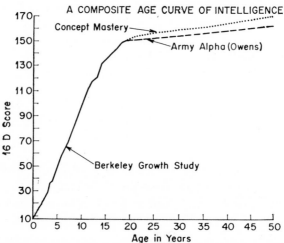

Fig. 2. Intellectual growth from birth to fifty years. (*From N. Bayley, On the growth of intelligence. Amer. Psychologist, 1955, 10, 805–818. Used by permission.*)

menopause in women and the climacteric in men, there is ample evidence that individuals are following a pattern that is similar for all members of the same sex: that is, a slowing down of the sexual functions accompanied by a lessening in sexual desire, and finally, an end of both. As old age approaches, the process of deterioration likewise follows a pattern of structural change that is similar for all people.

Longitudinal studies have revealed that maturing *intellectually* is a "dynamic succession of developing functions, with the more advanced and complex functions in the hierarchy depending on the prior maturing of earlier, simpler ones. . . . It is a complex of separately timed, developing functions" [2]. The pattern of intellectual growth up to fifty years of age, for a group of gifted individuals, is illustrated in Figure 2. This pattern shows little change after twenty years but a slight rise up to fifty years. In the pattern of intellectual development, memory precedes reasoning, with abstract reasoning following concrete. With age, there is a significant increase in test scores on practical judgment, information, disarranged sentences, and synonym-antonym [47].

In behavioral development, there is ample evidence of a common pattern in all individuals. In the development of motor skills such as block building, writing, and drawing, in emotional behavior, in smiling and laughing, in learning to speak, in social behavior, in falling in love, in reading, and in arithmetic, similar patterns for all children have been found. Patterns in the development of the meaning of time, rules, money, and sex and racial differences have been reported. A characteristic pattern has also been found in the child's identification with another person and his consequent modification of behavior to resemble that person. Changes in goals with age follow a predictable pattern as do interests. These patterns will be discussed in subsequent chapters.

The pattern of human development is *continuous*. From the moment of conception to the time of death, changes are taking place, sometimes rapidly and sometimes slowly. As a result, what happens at one stage of development carries over and influences the following stages. Unhealthy attitudes developed in childhood, for example, have been found to be at the root of much of the unhappiness and poor adjustment at middle and old age. Within the pattern of development, there is a marked *correlation* between physical and mental development. The growth pattern for symbolic behavior, for example, follows the pattern of biologic growth [24]. There is a definite relationship between the level of sexual maturity and the pattern of behavior for children of the same age, with early maturers differing markedly from late maturers. As Gesell has pointed out, "The products of growth are envisaged as a fabric in which threads and designs are visible" [20].

Even though all individuals follow much the same pattern of development, the *rate* of development varies from individual to individual. Three distinct rates have been found: consistent progress, a generally progressive trend with intermittent pauses, and generally progressive trends with periods of regression. The second type, a progressive trend with intermittent pauses, has been found to be the most common [65]. Because rates of development differ, all children of the same age have not reached the same point of physical or mental development [5] (see Figure 3). Nor do all individuals decline physically or mentally at the same rate. Some are as old at fifty years as others who are a decade or more older than they. In the same individual, different physical and mental traits develop at different rates and reach their mature levels at different ages. Different rates of decline have likewise been observed for different physical and mental traits. Most individuals, however, are con-

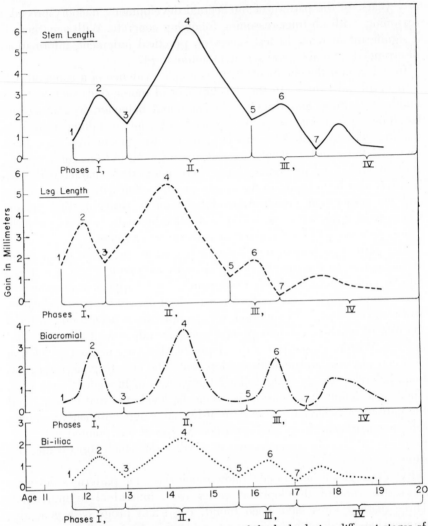

FIG. 3. Rhythm of growth in different parts of the body during different stages of sexual maturing. (*From H. R. Stolz and L. M. Stolz, Somatic development of adolescent boys. New York: Macmillan, 1951. Used by permission.*)

sistent in the rate of development and show a trend toward earliness or lateness in reaching critical periods in the growth cycle [21].

Irregularity of the rates of development, especially when pronounced, leads to many adjustment problems. The "superior-immature child," whose intellectual development has advanced more rapidly than his physical development, thus causing him to be immature in total functioning, is likely to find himself socially unacceptable to older groups, and this will affect his social adjustment [21]. A premature ending of the sexual life, through an early menopause, will result in physical and mental changes normally found in individuals of older ages. Atypical development, at any age and in any area of development, as well as in periods of total development, causes manifestations which affect the individual's adjustment unfavorably [11].

Implications. Knowing that development proceeds in an orderly, predictable way for all individuals is of great practical value. It is now possible to set up standards in the form of age-height, age-weight, mental-age, or social-development age scales to know what to anticipate in the developmental level of a given individual at any chronological age. And, because all children conform to a greater or lesser extent to a pattern of development, it is also possible to predict with a fair degree of accuracy what one can expect of a given child at a given age. The practical importance of this is great. No longer is it necessary to adopt a "wait-and-see" policy in the training and education of children, as it was in the past. This puts education and child training on a firmer foundation than it ever has been before.

Knowing what to expect and when to expect it avoids the tendency to expect too much or too little of a child at a given age. When too much is expected of a child, he soon develops feelings of inadequacy because he realizes that he is falling below adult expectations. It is equally bad to expect too little of a child. When this happens, it stifles the child's motivation to do what he is capable of doing and, at the same time, builds up feelings of resentment toward the individual or individuals who do things for him when he would like to be independent of adult help.

There is another important advantage in knowing what to expect of a child at a given age. This is the correct timing of training and the introduction of incentives to stimulate the child's development. When, for example, the child is ready to learn to read, that is the psychological moment to begin formal instruction in reading. It is also the time to turn the child's attention to pictures, stories, and books, so that he will develop the necessary motivation to learn the skills that are needed to be able to read to himself. In the absence of correct timing, there is a tendency to begin training in reading too soon or too late.

It is equally important to the child to be prepared ahead of time for the development of new physical features, new interests, or new abilities, thus enabling him to prepare himself psychologically for them. Perhaps the best illustration of this is in the case of physical and mental changes which come with sexual maturity. When the child knows ahead of time about menstruation or nocturnal emissions, about uneven growth of facial features which may make the nose seem proportionately too large at first, or about the new urges that come with the maturing of the sex organs, he is able to face these changes without the emotional tensions that are almost inevitable when these changes come suddenly and un-expectedly. While not all tensions of childhood, adolescence, maturity, or even old age will necessarily disappear just because the individual knows about these changes ahead of time, there is every reason to believe that some of the tensions will be minimized and the adjustments made more easily if foreknowledge of what to anticipate is given.

One of the most comprehensive and useful standards for measuring development is Havighurst's series of "Developmental Tasks" for different age levels. According to Havighurst, a *developmental task* is "a task which arises at or about a certain period in the life of the individual, successful achievement of which leads to his happiness and to success with later tasks, while failure leads to unhappiness and difficulty with later tasks." Some tasks arise mainly as a result of physical maturation, such as learning to walk; others develop primarily from the cultural pressures of society, such as learning to read; and still others grow out of the personal values and aspirations of the individual, such as choos-ing and preparing for a vocation. In most cases, however, developmental tasks arise from these three forces working together.

The tasks for each major developmental period may be summarized as follows [23]:

Developmental Tasks of Infancy and Early Childhood

Learning to walk.
Learning to take solid foods.
Learning to talk.
Learning to control the elimination of body wastes.
Learning sex differences and sexual modesty.
Achieving physiological stability.
Forming simple concepts of social and physical reality.
Learning to relate oneself emotionally to parents, siblings, and other people.
Learning to distinguish right and wrong and developing a conscience.

Developmental Tasks of Middle Childhood

Learning physical skills necessary for ordinary games.
Building wholesome attitudes toward oneself as a growing organism.
Learning to get along with age-mates.
Learning an appropriate sex role.
Developing fundamental skills in reading, writing, and calculating.
Developing concepts necessary for everyday living.
Developing conscience, morality, and a scale of values.
Developing attitudes toward social groups and institutions.

Developmental Tasks of Adolescence

Accepting one's physique and accepting a masculine or feminine role.
New relations with age-mates of both sexes.

Emotional independence of parents and other adults.
Achieving assurance of economic independence.
Selecting and preparing for an occupation.
Developing intellectual skills and concepts necessary for civic competence.
Desiring and achieving socially responsible behavior.
Preparing for marriage and family life.
Building conscious values in harmony with an adequate scientific world-picture.

Developmental Tasks of Early Adulthood

Selecting a mate.
Learning to live with a marriage partner.
Starting a family.
Rearing children.
Managing a home.
Getting started in an occupation.
Taking on civic responsibility.
Finding a congenial social group.

Developmental Tasks of Middle Age

Achieving adult civic and social responsibility.
Establishing and maintaining an economic standard of living.
Assisting teen-age children to become responsible and happy adults.
Developing adult leisure-time activities.
Relating oneself to one's spouse as a person.
Accepting and adjusting to the physiological changes of middle age.
Adjusting to aging parents.

Developmental Tasks of Later Maturity

Adjusting to decreasing physical strength and health.
Adjusting to retirement and reduced income.
Adjusting to death of spouse.
Establishing an explicit affiliation with one's age group.
Meeting social and civic obligations.
Establishing satisfactory physical living arrangements.

All Individuals Are Different. Although all individuals follow a definite and predictable pattern of development, each individual has his own distinct style of doing so. Some develop in a smooth, gradual, step-by-step fashion, while others move in spurts; some show wide swings, while others show only slight ones [21]. As Frank has stated it, the life career of an individual is a "broad highway along which every individual must travel. . . . Each individual, with his unique heredity and nurture (including prenatal) will travel along that highway at his or her own rate of progress and will attain the size, shape, capacity, and developmental status which are uniquely his or her own at each stage of the life career" [16] (see Figure 4).

The fact that all individuals are different has, in recent years, been so definitely proved by measurements with tests of all kinds that now there is no question or doubt about it. As Gesell has pointed out, "The range of individual differences is as wide as humanity itself" [21]. How much or how little individuals vary among each other has not as yet been proved as definitely or conclusively as the fact that they do differ. There are definite indications, however, that there are fewer differences in physical structure than in intellectual capacity. Personality differences, on the other hand, are far more marked than either physical or intellectual differences, and differences in special aptitudes seem to be the most marked of all.

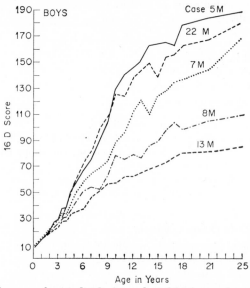

Fig. 4. The life span of an individual is a broad highway along which each individual travels in his own way and at his own speed. (*Based on individual curves of intelligence for five boys, one month to twenty-five years. From N. Bayley, On the growth of intelligence. Amer. Psychologist, 1955, 10, 805–818. Used by permission.*)

Individual differences are due partly to differences in hereditary endowment and partly to environmental influences. Even when the environment is similar, individuals react differently to it because of the differences in their make-ups. As Carlson and Stieglitz have explained, "We are what we are today, to a great degree, because of what happened to us in our yesterday, and no two people have had identical sequences of yesterdays. Furthermore, the effect of all these experiences increases with age, because they accumulate" [12]. There are many factors in the individual's life which are responsible for bringing about differences in his physical and mental structure, the most important of these including such environmental factors as food, climate, health conditions, opportunities for learning, motivation to learn, social relationships, codes of behavior set up by the social group to which the individual belongs, and the strength of social approval or disapproval.

Not only are the patterns of physical and mental growth for each child unique in that they often deviate from the patterns of other children, but these patterns also vary from the child's own past history. As Bayley has emphasized, "It is a rare child who follows the same course in all of the observed variables through all of his growth" [3]. Throughout the years of growth, structures and functions develop and become differentiated from each other at different rates and reach maturity at different times. This is true of mental as well as physical development. Thus, the pattern of development for each individual is unique [2, 3].

From a practical point of view, it is important to know that individuals are different, because it means that no two persons can be expected to react in the same manner to the same environmental stimuli. One can never predict with accuracy how an individual will react to a situation, even when there is ample information about his hereditary abilities. Furthermore, in dealing with people, methods that bring success when applied to one may bring failure when applied to another. It is impossible, under such conditions, to lay down rules of behavior that will prove to be successful in handling different people, even when they are of the same age level. Children having the same mental age, for example, will not necessarily be ready to read or do other types of school work at the same time [13]. And, finally, individual differences are significant because they are responsible for individuality in personality make-up, which not only makes people interesting, but makes social progress possible.

Each Phase of Development Has Characteristic Traits. Because all traits develop in their own way and at their own rate, it is understandable that, at different ages, certain traits will stand out more conspicuously than others. In babyhood, for example, the major development consists of gaining control over the muscle patterns of the body. In adolescence, on the other hand, social adjustments to members of the opposite sex and adjustments to adult standards of behavior dominate the developmental pattern. Adjustment to physical and mental decline, to changed patterns of living, of work, and of social life, dominate the latter years of the life span.

The developmental pattern is marked by periods of *equilibrium* and *disequilibrium,* which alternate in accordance with the principle of reciprocal neuromotor interweaving. During periods of disequilibrium, the child displays behavior patterns which may be judged as "problem" behavior. At these times, tensions, indecisions, insecurities, and similar forms of problem behavior are commonly observed [25]. But these behavior difficulties are not individual aberrations. Rather, they are predictable and characteristic of the age level. Of course, children may not all show the same behavior at the same ages. Children who mature early, for example, show the characteristic behavior of periods of disequilibrium before those who mature later [21].

Genetic studies have revealed the ages when disequilibrium usually occurs. During the preschool years of 2 to 6, periods of disequilibrium are commonly found at $2\frac{1}{2}$, $3\frac{1}{2}$, and $5\frac{1}{2}$ years. In the older child, a period of disequilibrium usually accompanies the onset of puberty, at 11 years. At these times, there is evidence that the child is "loosening up" and "snapping old bonds." Between the periods of disequilibrium are periods of equilibrium, when the child is "in focus" and when his behavior indicates better adjustment in the form of cooperation, friendliness, sympathy, affection, and helpfulness [21].

While it is unquestionably true that some stages of growing up are marked by more difficult behavior than others, there is no stage when the characteristic behavior is not "problem behavior" if judged by adult standards. "Immature" is frequently used to describe children who incur adult displeasure. Sleep problems, such as bed refusal, waking at night, calling out, or early morning wakening, are especially annoying to parents and are commonly found during the first three years of life [26]. The elementary school child's carelessness about his work and his appearance, his daydreaming and indifference to school work, and his vocal aggressions, as seen in shouting and name calling, are normal at that age, especially among children of the lower social classes [30].

Only when an individual's behavior is atypical for his age and leads to poor adjustment may it justly be referred to as "problem behavior." In most instances, such behavior is infantile in that it is characteristic of an earlier age level. The child has not "learned to act his age" either because no one has taught him how to do so or because he derives more satisfaction from infantile behavior than from more mature behavior. Aggressiveness and destructiveness are perfectly normal and to be expected in the earlier stages of the individual's development. But if such behavior continues or reemerges at a later date, when society has decreed that it should long since have been successfully modified or repressed, the child is then labeled "delinquent."

Studies of normal growth patterns have revealed that many of these difficult, unsocial, and often hard-to-understand forms of behavior which appear at different times during the years of growing up will gradually wane and disappear, only to be replaced by other forms of behavior as difficult to understand and live with as the ones that have just been outgrown. However, it is never safe to assume that all difficult behavior will disappear as the child grows older. Such behavior may be a danger signal of possible future trouble and should not be disregarded. When it persists beyond the age in which it is normally found, difficult behavior suggests that the individual's needs, both personal and social, are not being satisfactorily met.

There Are Traditional Beliefs about Individuals of Different Ages. These traditional beliefs, often called "old wives' tales," are beliefs that are passed down from one generation to another and accepted uncritically by each subsequent generation. Sometimes these beliefs relate to behavior and sometimes to physical make-up, abilities, and personality patterns. The latter are known as *stereotypes*, which are generally used to signify negatively valued judgments about an individual or a group. Although there is no justification for believing that all "old wives' tales" are completely false, few of them bear up under the scrutiny of scientific investigation. The belief, for example, that the only child is "different" in his psychological make-up is widespread, and yet studies of young adults have revealed no real personality differences between only and non-only children [10].

Traditional beliefs influence the individual's attitudes and behavior, both toward others and toward himself. Parents who accept the belief that they will "spoil the child if they spare the rod," discipline their children by corporal punishment even when their better judgment tells them that it is unfair to the child to do so. Similarly, stereotypes regarding groups with different religious and racial origins lead to prejudice and discrimination. Traditional beliefs about the roles of men and women or "father" and "mother" are learned early in life, being transmitted by the family which trains the child in the folkways of the group, and as a result are uncritically accepted. Thus in our culture, the commonly held stereotypes relating to middle and old age lead to the unfavorable treatment of individuals in the latter years of their lives. Some stereotypes lead to favorable attitudes and treatment, as in the case of the stereotype of the business man. Most stereotypes, however, are unfavorable and lead to unfavorable attitudes and treatment [50].

Individuals themselves tend to accept the cultural stereotype of the group with which they are identified, and this, in turn, influences their self-concepts. There are many stereotypes of racial and nationality minorities which are ascribed to by society and frequently accepted by minority-group members as applying to themselves. Furthermore, certain professions and occupations are believed to have in their groups individuals with characteristic "personality types," as the "crafty politician," the "absent-minded professor," or the "emotionally unstable artist" [7]. The fact that scientists are thought of as "eggheads" or "longhairs" has been suggested as one of the influences in keeping high school students from planning to enter the sciences as a life career [42]. Stereotypes set roles for individuals of a given group, and the adjustment of these individuals is then affected by how well they conform to the cultural pattern assigned to their group by society. This is well illustrated in the case of men and women in middle or old age who, according to the cultural stereotypes, are nearly "through" or "reaching the end." Acceptance of these stereotypes by the individuals is not only responsible for much of the unhappiness in the latter years of life, but is an important factor in physical and mental decline [36].

The seriousness of traditional beliefs lies in the fact that they are held to, even in the face of contradictory evidence, and thus continue to influence the behavior of people. A preparental educational program was found to change parents' attitudes from authoritarian to permissive child care in certain areas, for example, but there was resistance to change in areas relating to discipline, feeding, toileting, and sleep, areas in which traditional beliefs are especially strong [56]. Mothers who reported food-refusal problems in their children were advised to try permissive feeding. Some tried this method but rejected it after a few trials. In a group of 57 mothers, only 8 adopted permissive feeding as a customary procedure [8]. Because twins are traditionally considered to be alike, there is a tendency for parents to treat them as such. This is, without question, an important factor in maintaining and increasing twin similarities [28].

HAPPY AND UNHAPPY AGES IN THE LIFE SPAN

Childhood is, traditionally, the "happy age of life" because it is a carefree time. Likewise, there is a belief that with the approach of the end of life, the individual is happy not only because age releases him from many of the burdens and responsibilities imposed upon younger people, but also because the individual can look back over his life and say, "Well done." But happiness, as experimental studies have revealed, depends not upon the chronological age of the individual, his intellectual level, his socioeconomic status, the religious group with which he is identified, or any similar factor. It is dependent upon the *adjustment* of the individual to the role he plays in life. There are two opposing sets of forces which determine how satisfactorily or unsatisfactorily the individual will make this adjustment. The first emerges from the individual himself and includes his needs, purposes, and desires; the second consists of the demands, expectations, and pressures from the individual's social environment. Adjustment means integrating one's own needs, purposes and desires with the purposes of one's social group. If he can do this, the individual will be well adjusted and all concerned will be happy.

However, because the individual's needs, purposes, and desires change from age to age, there is no guarantee that a person who is well adjusted at one age will be well adjusted at another. A study of goals during the adult years has revealed that marriage is the goal of most women in their twenties, but few after thirty have this goal. Instead, they emphasize professional advancement, as do married men. Interest in or planning for retirement rarely comes before the forties [35]. Furthermore, successful adjustment to one social group does not guarantee successful adjustment to another. While an individual may make good adjustments in a group where certain of his outstanding traits are admired, he will not make good adjustments in another group unless he conforms to the cultural pattern of that group [63].

At any age, happiness depends on the adequacy of one's emotional adjustment. The difference between well and poorly adjusted people is in the quantity and intensity of their negative attitudes. In the well-adjusted, negative attitudes are expressed less often and with less intensity but with more focus and direction than in the poorly adjusted [45]. Furthermore, adjustment is influenced by the individual's attitude toward an age period, and this, in turn, is influenced by childhood experiences and stereotypes. Because childhood experiences and stereotypes relating to middle-aged and elderly people are generally unfavorable, most people have unfavorable attitudes toward those periods of life and, as a result, make poor adjustments to them [33].

The individual's own age colors his interpretation of happiness at different life periods, since the meaning of happiness varies at different ages according to the values the individual assigns to them. Thus the young child who thinks of happiness in terms of freedom may regard adulthood as happy. For the adult with many responsibilities, "carefree" childhood may be looked upon as the happiest age. There is a tendency to regard ages already passed as more favorable for happiness than one's own age [62].

One very common cause of unhappiness throughout the major part of life is the individual's *unrealistic concept* of himself. He believes he has greater capacities than he actually has or than other people recognize in him, and because of this unrealistic self-concept, he expects greater success than he is capable of achieving and more acceptance from people than his behavior would warrant. As a result, he feels out of place, misunderstood, and mistreated—feelings that certainly are not conducive to happiness. To be well adjusted and, in turn, happy, the individual must have a realistic concept of himself. He must be aware of his strong qualities and achievements as well as of his weaknesses and failures.

As the individual's needs, desires, and goals change with different ages, different methods are needed to achieve good adjustment. At every age, however, the methods used by the individual may be limited by his physical or mental capacity, or by restrictions from the social group

[52]. In adolescence, girls have been found to be happier than boys, because boys feel more pressures toward goals and accomplishments than girls do. Girls, by contrast, are more protected and have fewer pressures placed on them. In addition, they are given more help and encouragement by their parents to achieve their goals than are boys, whose demands for independence force them to make their own adjustments [64]. In the middle- and old-age periods of life, obstacles to the achievement of satisfaction, such as poor health, waning vigor, reduced income, idleness from retirement status, and many other changes in the individual's pattern of living, result in difficulties in adjustment and subsequent unhappiness. Only when hopes and ambitions can be achieved and when there is freedom from worry and overburdening responsibility can the individual be happy [62].

Retrospective Reports. The best way to find out when people think they have been happy or unhappy is to ask them. This cannot be done with any degree of accuracy while the individual is living through a particular period of his life span. But in retrospect he can get a clearer perspective and can see how one stage in his life compares with another. Like all retrospective studies, this is subject to error because of forgetfulness and the tendency to minimize some events that were mildly unhappy when they occurred and to exaggerate the severity of the unhappiness of others. On the whole, the tendency is to think of childhood as the happiest of all periods. As Rosenzweig and Rosenzweig have emphasized, "The golden days of childhood, as they appear in the conventional reminiscence of adults, are more consistent with fantasy than with fact. The myths of all races similarly portray the childhood of man as a paradise" [49].

However, although childhood is remembered as a happy age, it is not free from memories of unhappy experiences, most of which center around the home and the family. Later, when the child goes to school, where more demands are made on him, and when he meets more environmental obstacles, he has many memories of feelings of inadequacy and insecurity. Home and family becomes less important with each passing year; nevertheless, there are unhappy memories of friction with family members, of feelings of guilt when parental expectations were not met, and of feelings of being unloved and unwanted [1, 54, 60].

Retrospections covering the whole life span show how great the happiness is at different ages. In one study, single men and women reported that they were happiest when young. Those who were married, divorced, or separated, by contrast, said they were happiest when married and when their children were in the home. In middle and old age, happiness centers around the home and children. When the individual is deprived of either or both, he is unhappy [37]. Negative attitudes toward the older ages may be a projection of the individual's present adjustment and the acceptance of cultural stereotypes of the older ages [61].

Significance of Unhappiness. It is obvious that the average individual experiences as many if not more periods of unhappiness than of happiness. Even babyhood, the happiest of all ages, has its moments of sorrow. This is evidenced in the baby's cries when he is frustrated in his attempts to do something or to gain the attention of someone. Periods of physical discomfort or pain likewise bring him momentary unhappiness.

The significant fact about the unhappiness that prevails so generally throughout the life span of the human individual is that it affects the individual's attitudes and, in turn, leaves its mark on his personality. In addition, it reduces his efficiency in whatever work he may undertake. Whether he be a school child, a factory worker, or a business executive, his chances of making the most of his potentialities are greatly reduced by his unhappy mental state.

While unhappiness is inevitable at some time during the life span of every individual, much of the unhappiness that individuals of all ages experience could be reduced if they had more healthy attitudes about themselves, their achievements, their families, and society in general. Healthy attitudes depend upon a realistic concept of self. The individual who sees himself as he actually is, not as he would like to be or as his family and friends expect him to be, will be able to face life far more realistically than will the individual whose concept of self has been distorted by wishful thinking.

BIBLIOGRAPHY

1. Barschak, E.: Happiness and unhappiness in the childhood and adolescence of a group of women students: a comparative study of English and American girls. *Brit. J. Psychol.*, 1952, 43, 129–140.
2. Bayley, N.: On the growth of intelligence. *Amer. Psychologist*, 1955, 10, 805–818.
3. Bayley, N.: Individual patterns of development. *Child Develpm.*, 1956, 27, 45–74.
4. Benedek, T.: Climacterium: a developmental phase. *Psychoanal. Quart.*, 1950, 19, 1–27.
5. Bloomers, P., L. M. Knief, and J. B. Stroud: The organismic age concept. *J. educ. Psychol.*, 1955, 46, 142–150.
6. Blum, L. H.: Pediatric practice and the science of child development. *Nerv. Child*, 1952, 9, 233–241.
7. Borg, W. R.: The effect of personality and contact upon a personality stereotype. *J. educ. Res.*, 1955, 49, 289–294.
8. Brim, O. G.: The acceptance of new behavior in child rearing. *Hum. Relat.*, 1954, 7, 473–491.
9. Bühler, C.: The course of life as studied in biographies. *J. appl. Psychol.*, 1935, 19, 405–409.

10. Burke, M. O.: A search for systematic personality differentiae of the only child in young adulthood. *J. genet. Psychol.*, 1956, 89, 71–84.
11. Caplan, H.: The role of deviant maturation in the pathogenesis of anxiety. *Amer. J. Orthopsychiat.*, 1956, 26, 94–107.
12. Carlson, A. J., and E. J. Stieglitz: Physiological changes in aging. *Ann. Amer. Acad. pol. soc. Sci.*, 1952, 279, 18–31.
13. Cornell, E. L., and C. M. Armstrong: Forms of mental growth patterns revealed by reanalysis of the Harvard growth data. *Child Develpm.*, 1955, 26, 169–204.
14. Dennis, W.: Infant development under conditions of restricted practice and minimum social stimulation. *Genet. Psychol. Monogr.*, 1941, 23, 143–189.
15. Feldman, S.: Origins of behavior and man's life-career. *Amer. J. Psychol.*, 1941, 54, 53–63.
16. Frank, L. K.: Genetic psychology and its prospects. *Amer. J. Orthopsychiat.*, 1951, 21, 506–522.
17. Frazee, H. E.: Children who later became schizophrenic. *Smith Coll. Stud. soc. Wk*, 1953, 23, 125–149.
18. Gesell, A.: Growth potentials of the human infant. *Sci. Mon., N.Y.*, 1949, 68, 252–256.
19. Gesell, A.: Developmental pediatrics. *Nerv. Child*, 1952, 9, 225–227.
20. Gesell, A.: The ontogenesis of infant behavior. *In* L. Carmichael, *Manual of child psychology*, 2d ed. New York: Wiley, 1954. Pp. 335–373.
21. Gesell, A., F. L. Ilg, and L. B. Ames: *Youth: the years from ten to sixteen.* New York: Harper, 1956.
22. Havighurst, R. J.: Problems of sampling and interviewing in studies of old people. *J. Geront.*, 1950, 5, 158–167.
23. Havighurst, R. J.: *Human development and education.* New York: Longmans, 1953.
24. Hodges, A.: A developmental study of symbolic behavior. *Child Develpm.*, 1954, 25, 277–280.
25. Ilg, F. L., J. Learned, A. Lockwood, and L. B. Ames: The three-and-a-half-year-old. *J. genet. Psychol.*, 1949, 75, 21–31.
26. Illingworth, R. S.: Sleep problems in the first three years. *Brit. med. J.*, 1951, 1, 722–728.
27. Ingle, D.: The tempo of aging. *Today's Hlth*, 1956, May, p. 14.
28. Jones, H. E.: Perceived differences among twins. *Eugen. Quart.*, 1955, 2, 98–102.
29. Kahn, E., and L. W. Simmons: Problems in middle age. *Yale Rev.*, 1940, 29, 349–363.
30. Kaplan, L.: The annoyances of elementary school teachers. *J. educ. Res.*, 1952, 45, 649–665.
31. Kardiner, A.: *The psychological frontiers of society.* New York: Columbia Univer. Press, 1945.
32. Kelly, E. L.: Consistency of the adult personality. *Amer. Psychologist*, 1955, 10, 659–681.
33. Koch, H. L.: The relation of certain family constellation characteristics and the attitude of children toward adults. *Child Develpm.*, 1955, 26, 13–40.
34. Kuhlen, R. G.: Social change: a neglected factor in psychological studies of the life span. *Sch. and Soc.*, 1940, 52, 14–16.
35. Kuhlen, R. G., and G. H. Johnson: Changes in goals with increasing adult years. *J. consult. Psychol.*, 1952, 16, 1–4.
36. Kuhlen, R. G., and E. Luther: A study of the cultural definition of the prime of

life, middle age, and old age, and of attitudes toward the old. *J. Geront.*, 1949, 4, 324.

37. Landis, J. T.: What is the happiest period of life? *Sch. and Soc.*, 1942, 55, 643–645.

38. Lawton, G.: *New goals for old age.* New York: Columbia Univer. Press, 1943.

39. Linden, M. E., and D. Courtney: The human life cycle and its interruptions. *Amer. J. Psychiat.*, 1953, 109, 905–915.

40. Macy, I. G., and H. J. Kelly: Body composition in childhood. *Hum. Biol.*, 1956, 28, 289–308.

41. McGraw, M. B.: *Growth: a study of Johnny and Jimmy.* New York: Appleton-Century-Crofts, 1935.

42. Michael, D. N.: Scientists through adolescent eyes: what we need to know, why we need to know it. *Sci. Mon., N.Y.*, 1957, 85, 135–140.

43. Miles, W. R.: Age and human ability. *Psychol. Rev.*, 1933, 40, 99–123.

44. Milner, E.: The childhood bases of marital adjustment. *Phylon*, 1950, 11, 263–269.

45. Moustakas, C. E.: Emotional adjustment and the play therapy process. *J. genet. Psychol.*, 1955, 86, 79–99.

46. New York Times Report: Women increase majority in U.S. *The New York Times*, 1956, Nov. 12.

47. Owens, W. A.: Age and mental abilities: a longitudinal study. *Genet. Psychol. Monogr.*, 1953, 48, 3–54.

48. Rich, G. J.: Childhood as a preparation for delinquency. *J. educ. Sociol.*, 1954, 27, 404–413.

49. Rosenzweig, S., and L. Rosenzweig: Aggression in problem children and normals as evaluated by the Rosenzweig Picture Frustration Study. *J. abnorm. soc. Psychol.* 1952, 47, 683–688.

50. Saenger, G., and S. Flowerman: Stereotypes and prejudicial attitudes. *Hum. Relat.* 1954, 7, 217–238.

51. Shock, N. W.: Gerontology (later maturity). *Annu. Rev. Psychol.*, 1951, 2, 353–366.

52. Shock, N. W.: Aging and psychological adjustment. *Rev. educ. Res.*, 1952, 22, 439–456.

53. Smith, M. E.: A comparison of certain personality traits as rated in the same individuals in childhood and fifty years later. *Child Develpm.*, 1952, 23, 159–180.

54. Smith, M. E.: Childhood memories compared with those of adult life. *J. genet. Psychol.*, 1952, 80, 151–182.

55. Smith, M. E.: Mental test ability in a family of four generations. *J. genet. Psychol.*, 1954, 85, 321–335.

56. Stott, L. H., and M. P. Berson: Some changes in attitudes resulting from a pre-parental education program. *J. soc. Psychol.*, 1951, 34, 191–202.

57. Terman, L. M., and M. H. Oden: *The gifted child grows up.* Stanford, Calif.: Stanford Univer. Press, 1947.

58. Thompson, R. E.: A validation of the Glueck social prediction scale for proneness to delinquency. *J. crim. Law Criminol.*, 1952, 43, 451–470.

59. Tibbitts, C., and H. D. Sheldon: Introduction: a philosophy of aging. *Ann. Amer. Acad. pol. soc. Sci.*, 1952, 279, 1–10.

60. Tuckman, J., and I. Lorge: The best years of life: a study in ranking. *J. Psychol.*, 1952, 34, 137–149.

61. Tuckman, J., and I. Lorge: Old people's appraisal of adjustment over the life span. *J. Pers.*, 1954, 22, 417–422.

62. Tuckman, J., and I. Lorge: Perceptual stereotypes about life adjustments. *J. soc. Psychol.*, 1956, 43, 239–245.
63. Tuddenham, R. D.: Studies in reputation. I. Sex and grade differences in school children's evaluations of their peers. II. The diagnosis of social adjustment. *Psychol. Monogr.*, 1952, 66, No. 1.
64. Wilson, F. M.: The best in life at any age. *Ment. Hyg., N.Y.*, 1955, 39, 483–488.
65. Wishik, S. M.: The importance of "timing" in child health supervision. *Child Develpm.*, 1950, 21, 51–60.

» 2 «

How Life Begins

Life begins at the time of conception. The first major developmental period in the human life span is a relatively short one of approximately nine months, which extends from the moment of conception to the time of birth. This period is important for two reasons: first, because what the individual will ultimately be is largely determined at that time and, second, because there is proportionally greater growth and development taking place during this period than at any other time throughout the individual's entire life.

CARRIERS OF HEREDITY

The true carrier of heredity is the *gene*, a minute particle within the human sex cell which is passed on from parent to offspring. The gene is found in combination with other genes in a stringlike formation within each *chromosome*. It has been estimated that there are approximately 3,000 genes in each chromosome [57]. "Sex-linked" characters, such as color blindness, hemophelia, and hereditary baldness, are produced by the genes responsible for determining sex. Generally, they skip a generation and are transmitted by the male, through the female, to a male [54].

Each fertilized germ cell, or zygote, contains 24 pairs of chromosomes, one from each pair coming from the father and the other from the mother. This is illustrated in Figure 5. Each chromosome in turn contains genes from the parent from which it originated. But, because the combination of genes is a matter of chance, it is impossible to predict what the physical and mental characteristics of a child will be, even

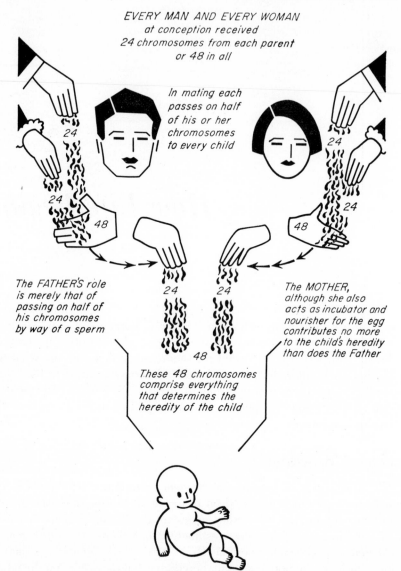

EVERY MAN AND EVERY WOMAN
at conception received
24 chromosomes from each parent
or 48 in all

In mating each passes on half of his or her chromosomes to every child

24

24

48

24

24

48

The FATHER'S role is merely that of passing on half of his chromosomes by way of a sperm

24   24

48

The MOTHER, although she also acts as incubator and nourisher for the egg contributes no more to the child's heredity than does the Father

These 48 chromosomes comprise everything that determines the heredity of the child

FIG. 5. The hereditary process. (*From A. Scheinfeld, The new you and heredity. Philadelphia: Lippincott, 1950. Used by permission.*)

when the traits of his parents are known. Furthermore, because there are so many possible chromosome and gene combinations, it is understandable that siblings (brothers and sisters) within a family are likely to be very different from one another in physical as well as in mental traits. Only in the case of identical twins is there an identical genetic make-up.

Sex Cells. The maternal and paternal germ cells are developed in the reproductive organs, the *gonads*. The male germ cells, the *spermatozoa* (singular, *spermatozoon*), are produced in the male gonads, the *testes,* while the female germ cells, the *ova* (singular, *ovum*), are produced in the female gonads, the *ovaries*. Ova and spermatozoa differ from each other in the following five ways:

1. The spermatozoon is one of the smallest cells of the body, while the ovum is one of the largest. The ovum is approximately 0.1 millimeter in diameter, as contrasted with a diameter of approximately 0.05 millimeter in the case of the spermatozoon. The ovum is about the size of a period on a page, while it has been estimated that it would take 300,000,000 sperms to fit into a teaspoon.

2. The ovum contains yolk which can be used to nourish a new individual should the ovum be fertilized. The spermatozoon contains no yolk, which is why the spermatozoon is so much smaller than the ovum.

3. The ovum is round and has no means of locomotion within itself. By contrast, the spermatozoon is elongated with a fine, hairlike tail which can be lashed back and forth to enable the spermatozoon to swim through the semen in which it is found. A healthy spermatozoon can swim an inch in about an hour and can continue at this speed for about 2 days. The ovum, by contrast, is dependent upon the contractions of the tissues by which it is surrounded for locomotion.

4. Normally only one ovum is ripened every menstrual cycle of approximately 28 days, while several hundred million spermatozoa develop every 4 or 5 days [57].

5. In the ovum, there are 24 matched chromosomes. In only one half of all spermatozoa are there 24 matched chromosomes. In the other one half of the spermatozoa, there are 23 matched pairs and one unmatched pair of chromosomes. This difference in the male chromosomes is responsible for sex determination.

THE BEGINNING

Before new life can begin, the sex cells from which the new individual will develop go through three preliminary stages of development. These are *maturation, ovulation,* and *fertilization.*

Maturation is chromosome reduction through cell division in which one chromosome from each pair goes to a subdivided cell which, in turn, splits lengthwise and forms two new cells. The mature cell, which contains only 24 chromosomes, is known as a *haploid cell.* Both male and female cells must become mature before they can unite to form a new individual. Maturation of sex cells does not occur until sex maturity has been attained, following the onset of puberty in both boys and girls. In the case of the spermatozoon, there are four new cells, the *spermatids,* each of which is capable of fertilizing an ovum. In the division of the ovum, one chromosome from each pair is pushed outside the cell wall and forms a *polar body.* Three polar bodies are formed in the process of division. Unlike the spermatids, the polar bodies cannot be fertilized, while the fourth cell, the *ovum,* can. If, however, the ovum is not fertilized, it disintegrates and passes from the body with the menstrual flow.

Division of the chromosomes during the maturational process is a matter of chance. Any possible combination of chromosomes from the male and female may be found in a new cell after division. This explains the "skipping of a generation" in a given trait. It has been estimated that there are 16,777,216 possible combinations of the 24 chromosomes from the male and the 24 from the female sex cells [50]. That is why children of the same family, except in the case of identical twins, are often so different in their physical and mental characteristics. It also means that it is impossible to predict what the physical and mental characteristics of a child will be, even when one knows his parents, grandparents, and other near relatives.

Ovulation is the process of escape of one mature ovum during the menstrual cycle. It has been estimated that in the follicles of the female ovaries there are approximately 30,000 immature ova when the girl reaches sexual maturity. Only about 400 of these ova mature during the female reproductive period, from the onset of puberty, at approximately thirteen years, until the onset of the menopause, in the forties or early fifties. It is believed that the two ovaries alternate in producing a ripe ovum during each menstrual cycle of 28 days. After being released from one of the follicles of the ovary, the ovum finds its way to the open end of the Fallopian tube nearest the ovary from which it has been released. Once it enters the tube, it is propelled along the tube by a combination of factors: cilia, or hairlike cells which line the tube; fluids composed of *estrogen* from the ovarian follicle and a mucus from the lining of the tube; and rhythmic, progressive contractions of the walls of the tube [48].

When the female menstrual cycle is normal, lasting for approximately 28 days, ovulation occurs between the 5th and 23d day of the cycle, with the average on the 11.8th day. Even in the same woman, variations from one cycle to another are common. There are also marked individual differences from one woman to another and in the same woman from one menstrual cycle to another in the time during which the ovum remains in the tube. The time varies from 2 to 7 days, with an average of 3 days [14, 48].

Fertilization, or conception, normally occurs while the ovum is in the Fallopian tube. More specifically it is generally believed that fertilization takes place within 12 to 36 hours and usually within the first 24 hours after the ovum has entered the tube [48, 57]. During coitus, or sexual intercourse, spermatozoa are deposited at the mouth of the uterus. Through strong hormonic attraction, they are drawn into the tubes where they are aided in making their way up the tubes by rhythmic muscular contractions. It is believed that a healthy sperm cell can be in the female sex organs for 24 to 36 hours before losing too much of its energy to reach the ovum and penetrate its outer wall [48].

After the spermatozoon has penetrated the ovum, the surface of the ovum changes so that no other spermatozoon can enter. Contrary to popular belief, twins are not formed by two spermatozoa entering the same ovum. After the sperm cell penetrates the wall of the ovum, the nuclei from the two cells, each containing 24 chromosomes, approach each other. There is a breakdown in the membrane surrounding each nucleus and this allows the two nuclei to merge. Thus the species number of chromosomes, 48, is restored, half coming from the male and the other half from the female cell.

Conception can be regarded as the most important single moment of the individual's life, because what happens then will determine the whole course of his future life. Three significant things are determined at that moment. They are:

1. *Hereditary Endowment.* With the fusion of the chromosomes from the male and female cells, the newly formed individual's hereditary endowment is established. As Kuhlen and Thompson have pointed out, "Every individual's supply of genes, the bearers of hereditary factors, is given him once and for all and inalterably at conception" [35]. These genes are assorted by chance during the maturation of the cells from the male and female and carry traits from the ancestors on both sides. Thus every newly created individual is unique, though he will resemble in certain physical and mental traits his parents, grandparents, and other more remote ancestors.

Because heredity places limits beyond which the individual cannot go, even with the most favorable environmental conditions, the best teaching methods, and the strongest personal motivation, it is apparent that the determination of his hereditary endowment is of crucial importance to the pattern of his future development. With favorable conditions in the prenatal and postnatal environments, and with strong motivation on the individual's part, the physical and mental traits he has inherited will develop to their maximum potentials but they can go no further.

2. *Sex Determination.* There are many traditional beliefs concerning the control of the sex of a child. Because in almost all civilized cultures men have been given places of greater importance than women, it is the wish of practically every man and woman to have a son and heir. There have been many theories as to how this can be done. The most common of the traditional practices are to regulate the time of conception to coincide with the period of the menstrual cycle when it is believed that a male offspring will result, to eat a protein-heavy diet to guarantee a boy and a diet heavy in starches and sweets if a girl is wanted, or to

drink certain alkaline potions regularly during pregnancy to produce a boy and acid ones to produce a girl.

In spite of scientific evidence to the contrary, many people still believe that it is within their power to control the sex of their offspring. The effects of such a belief are more serious than most people realize. When parents are convinced that they can produce an offspring of the sex they want, they are generally bitterly disappointed when the child turns out to be of the opposite sex. This disappointment may wane and disappear in time, but it frequently leaves its imprint upon the parents' attitudes toward the child. Furthermore, many men feel that it is the woman who has the power to control the sex of her child and, if she does not produce an offspring of the sex her husband wants, his attitude toward her may be seriously affected.

Since the turn of the century, there has been ample scientific evidence to disprove all the traditional beliefs and practices relating to sex control. It is now reliably proved that neither parent has any control whatsoever over the sex of the child. Whether the child turns out to be a boy or a girl is purely a matter of chance. As for the mother's being to blame if the child is not of the desired sex, that belief has also been disproved. If it were possible for either parent to control the child's sex, that power would be in the hands of the father, not the mother. It is from his germ cells that the types of chromosomes that produce male and female offspring come.

In the human species, there are two kinds of spermatozoa: those with 23 matched chromosomes and one small Y sex chromosome and those with 23 matched chromosomes and one large X sex chromosome. Thus, each spermatozoon contains a total of 24 chromosomes. The spermatozoon with the Y chromosome is somewhat smaller in size and differs in shape from the spermatozoon with the X chromosome. There are equal numbers of these two types of spermatozoa, because they have resulted from the splitting of the spermatids during maturation. The difference in chromosome make-up does not occur in ova, all of which have 23 matched plus one large X sex chromosome.

Should an ovum be fertilized by a spermatozoon containing the X sex chromosome, the result is a female offspring. A male offspring is produced by the union of an ovum with a spermatozoon containing the small Y sex chromosome (see Figure 6). Sex determination is entirely a matter of chance. Which type of spermatozoon, the male-producing or the female-producing, will reach the ovum first and penetrate it cannot be controlled. Once the union of the male and female cells has occurred, nothing can be done to change the sex of the newly formed individual.

According to statistics, there are 105 to 106 male offspring born for every 100 females, a ratio which is seen also in abortions and premature births [5, 39]. This slight discrepancy in the law of chance has been explained in various ways, the most plausible explanation being that because the spermatozoon bearing the Y chromosome (the male-producing)

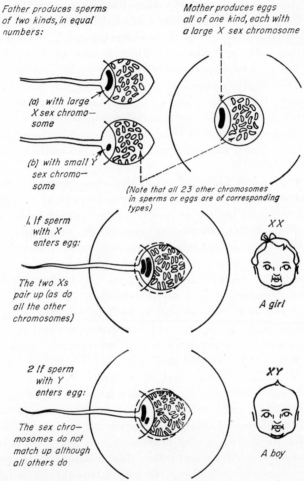

Father produces sperms of two kinds, in equal numbers:

Mother produces eggs all of one kind, each with a large X sex chromosome

(a) with large X sex chromo—some

(b) with small Y sex chromo—some

(Note that all 23 other chromosomes in sperms or eggs are of corresponding types)

1, If sperm with X enters egg:

The two Xs pair up (as do all the other chromosomes)

X X

A girl

2 If sperm with Y enters egg:

The sex chro—mosomes do not match up although all others do

X Y

A boy

FIG. 6. How sex is determined. (*From A. Scheinfeld, Women and men. New York: Harcourt, Brace, 1943. Used by permission.*)

is slightly lighter, it is able to move more swiftly than the heavier spermatozoon bearing the X chromosome (the female-producing) and, as a result, has a slightly better than fifty-fifty chance of reaching the ovum first and fertilizing it.

Tradition holds that there are more boys born during wartime than girls. The explanation given for this is that nature is compensating for the disruption of the normal sex ratio brought about by war. Data from a number of countries involved in World War II, however, show that the sex ratio did not change appreciably during the years of the war as compared with the years immediately preceding or following the war [41]. Nor is there any evidence that families can and do have only children of one sex [42, 54]. The traditional belief that young fathers produce more male offspring than older fathers is not borne out by evidence from scientific studies [6]. There is some evidence that families in the higher socioeconomic levels produce more male offspring than families of the lower socioeconomic levels, but this may be merely a statistical error due to sampling [7]. This same explanation applies to the reports that men in the "masculine" occupations have a higher percentage of male offspring than those in the "female" occupations. In fact, there is no conclusive evidence that sex is determined by anything but chance [18].

The sex of the individual influences the whole pattern of his development from the moment of birth. *Cultural pressures* from parents, teachers, the peer group, and society at large will be applied to the child with increasing force with each passing year to develop attitudes and behavior patterns that are sexually appropriate to the cultural group. The child who learns to behave in a way that is considered "appropriate" for his sex is assured of social acceptance; the child who fails to conform is subjected to criticism and social ostracism [25]. The *learning experiences* of the individual are determined by his sex. In the home, at school, and in play groups, the child is given an opportunity to learn what members of his or her sex consider appropriate. The boy who, for example, learns to play as girls play is labeled a "sissy" just as the girl is classed as a "tomboy" if she plays boys' games and sports [52].

The most important influence stemming from the sex of the individual is the *attitude of parents* toward the child. Studies of sex preferences for offspring have revealed that the traditional preference for a boy, especially for the first-born, still persists. If only one child is born, there is a strong preference for a son rather than a daughter. However, when there are several children, the preference is usually for a family composed of children of both sexes in approximately equal numbers [3, 16].

Strong preferences for a child of a given sex have marked influences on parental attitudes, which in turn affect the parent's behavior toward the child and his relationships with the child. Mothers, who frequently have a preference for boys, may try not to show favoritism, but there is a tendency for them to be more severe with their daughters than with their sons. The father's treatment of the child is likewise affected by whether or not the child is of the sex he had hoped for [51].

Parental attitudes are often intensified by the traditional belief that the sex of the unborn child can be accurately *predicted*. Many of the methods of prediction are a part of our folklore and are not only inaccurate but often ludicrous. Others are based on scientific methodology, as in the case of tests of the fetal heartbeat, X-ray studies of the ossification of the fetal bones, analysis of the mother's saliva, and analysis of cells from the amniotic fluid, but none has, to date, proved to be accurate enough to be used for prediction [43, 49]. The seriousness of *believing* that sex can be accurately predicted lies in the fact that parental disappointment will be greatly intensified should the child not be of the preferred sex after it has been predicted to be.

3. *Number of Offspring.* While normally the human female produces one ripe ovum every menstrual cycle, it sometimes happens that two ova are ripened and released simultaneously. When this happens, and when both ova are in the Fallopian tubes at the same time, there is a very good chance that both will be fertilized. This fertilization is not by one spermatozoan but by two, and the result will be *nonidentical*, biovular, or fraternal twins. Because the chromosomes and genes of the two zygotes from which they develop are not the same, the twins will lack similarity in physical and mental make-up. They may be of the same or of opposite sex. Like their heredity, their prenatal environment is different. Each has its own placenta, sac, and umbilical cord. In reality, nonidentical twins are not twins but simultaneous pregnancies.

If, however, only one ovum is ripened and released, the offspring will be a *singleton* unless the zygote splits into two or more distinct parts in the early stages of cell cleavage. If the latter occurs, each part will then develop into a complete individual and the result will be *identical* or uniovular twins, triplets, or other multiple births. Because they have originated from the same zygote, the offspring from this type of fertilization will have exactly the same assortment of chromosomes and genes and will therefore closely resemble each other in all their hereditary traits and will always be of the same sex. They have one placenta and are enclosed in one sac, though each has its own umbilical cord. In rare cases, the division of the zygote is incomplete and the result is then a pair of *siamese twins*.

Triplets, quadruplets, and other larger numbers of multiple births may be of three types: identical, in that all have come from the same zygote; identical and nonidentical; or siblings, each having come from a separate fertilized ovum. While not definitely proved, there was evidence to show that in the case of the Dionne quintuplets, six embryos started to develop independently as a result of the division of cells of the zygote. Only five of them reached maturity, the sixth having aborted [8].

The larger the number of offspring, the less frequent is the occurrence.

It has been estimated that *twins* occur once in every 87 births; triplets, once in every 7,500 births; quadruplets, once in every 658,000 births; and quintuplets, once in every 57,000,000 births. One-third of all twins are identical. Twins constitute 2.19 per cent of all babies, though the rate is reduced to 1.9 per cent by mortality during the first year of life. After the first year, there is no significant difference between the mortality of twins and non-twins [1]. Among Negroes, multiple births are more frequent than among whites, and more frequent among whites than among members of the yellow race. Nonidentical twins are more frequent than identical in the lower socioeconomic groups [36].

What causes multiple births is still unknown. While there is no evidence that all multiple births "run in the family," there is some evidence that nonidentical twinning is influenced by a hereditary tendency transmitted through either the male or the female. Identical twins, by contrast, seem to occur sporadically without a hereditary basis [50]. Uniovular twinning may result from hormonal disturbance, such as the slow secretion of folliculin, which prevents ovulation. Or, it may be due to an inherent tendency of the ovum to divide before the reduction division, thus causing two separate ova [13]. Maternal age has little effect on uniovular twinning. However, up to the age of thirty-eight years, there has been found to be a definite increase in liability to biovular twinning, with a rapid decline after that age. For a woman who has produced multiple births, there is a ten times greater probability of subsequent multiple maternity than for the average woman [56]. Women who have given birth to nonidentical twins show, subsequently, a greater frequency in producing identical twins than is true of the general population [13].

IMPLICATIONS. Whether the individual is a singleton or one of multiple births will have a tremendous influence on the pattern of his development both before and after birth. The hereditary foundations for his development will, in fact, be affected. With identical hereditary endowments, for example, there will be greater similarities in physical and mental development, which may give rise to personality patterns not found in individuals who have markedly dissimilar hereditary endowments.

In the *prenatal* period of development, the individual must share with one or more individuals the space nature has provided for one. While the uterine walls are capable of expansion, there is a limit to the amount of expansion that can take place. As a result, there will be less space for each of the multiple births than there is for a singleton, and this will limit the amount of fetal activity possible. This, in turn, will be a handicap to normal development of the fetal muscles. Furthermore, when the combined size of multiple births reaches that of a normal full-term fetus, there is likely to be a premature birth [26]. The larger the number of multiple births, therefore, the greater the likelihood of prematurity and the shorter the period for prenatal development. As a result, more cases of multiple births fail to survive than is true of singletons. Those who do survive are subjected to many of the unfavorable influences of prematurity [2]. (See pages 60–63 for a discussion of effects of prematurity.)

In the postnatal environment, the *attitudes of parents* and the *child-training methods* they use are different for singletons and multiple births, thus affecting further the patterns of their development. Mothers sometimes reject twins because they are "ashamed" or because twins make "too much work." Most parents, however, have favorable attitudes toward the twins but feel that they should share the same postnatal environment, just as they shared the same prenatal environment. Therefore, twins are treated as if they belonged together, are dressed alike, and are expected to share the same friends. Whether identical or nonidentical, twins of the same sex are subjected to more similar treatment than twins of both sexes [32, 40].

The effects of prenatal and postnatal environmental influences have been extensively studied in the case of twins and triplets. These have revealed a developmental lag in physical, mental, motor, and speech development in the case of multiple births, some of which is compensated for as development progresses to older ages. However, there are such marked individual differences between singletons, twins, and triplets that it would be incorrect to say that multiple birth per se causes a developmental lag or that twins and triplets are always inferior to singletons [22, 29, 31, 38].

The common practice of keeping twins and triplets together affects their *social development*. In the preschool years, there is a tendency for them to be competitive for adult attention, to imitate one another's behavior, and to be more dependent upon each other for companionship than on outsiders [10, 29]. As they grow older, sibling rivalry and competition and feelings of inferiority develop. Because each individual feels that he lacks independence and is being compared with his twin in all his achievements, he experiences frustrations. Furthermore, as is true of all social relationships, one individual is likely to usurp the role of leader and force the other into the role of follower. This affects social relationships with outsiders [10]. Even the dating experiences and marital adjustments of twins are likely to be different from those of singletons [33, 40].

The *personality development* of twins has been found to be markedly affected by the closeness of their association. In personality traits, identical twins are not much more alike than nonidentical twins [22, 31]. It is difficult for identical twins to develop individuality because it is often impossible for them to distinguish between themselves and their twins, even though they may delight in the attention they attract. This lack of a feeling of individuality frequently leads to frustrations, conflicts, and aggressive reactions which leave their mark on the personality pattern [33, 40].

Difficulties in Fertilization. Conditions are not always favorable to fertilization. When these conditions persist month after month, a state of *sterility* is said to exist. Failure to produce an offspring may be due to a number of unfavorable conditions, the three most important of which are:

1. An unfavorable condition in the female reproductive organs, such as excessive acidity of the vaginal secretions which kills the spermatozoa, or obstruction in the Fallopian tubes, due to inflammation or some foreign substance.
2. An unfavorable condition of the ovum due to poor health, malnutrition, glandular or vitamin deficiency, or old age in the woman.
3. An unfavorable condition of the spermatozoa due to poor health, malnutrition, vitamin or glandular deficiency, or old age in the man [15, 48].

As a result of female glandular deficiencies, especially of the pituitary gland, the normal female menstrual cycle may be interfered with. This usually results in the lengthening of the normal 28-day period. The ripened ovum is, therefore, delayed in its release from the follicle in the ovary or it remains longer than the usual time in its passage down the Fallopian tube to the uterus. Because it must rely upon its own nucleus for nourishment until it becomes embedded in the wall of the uterus, the supply of nourishment may be insufficient to keep it alive. As a result, it dies even though it may have been fertilized.

Although sterility is popularly attributed to an unfavorable condition in the woman, this is not always true. If the male produces spermatozoa which are slow and sluggish, as happens when the health condition of the male is unfavorable or when he is suffering from the debilitating effects of old age, the sperm may not have the strength to travel up the Fallopian tube, swimming against the pressures of the walls of the tube to force the ovum down and resisting the currents of the liquids in which the ovum is immersed. Should the sperm overcome this handicap, it might not have enough strength left to penetrate the wall of the ovum [15, 57].

PERIODS OF PRENATAL DEVELOPMENT

The normal prenatal period is 10 lunar months or 9 calendar months in length. However, there is great variation in this length, ranging from 180 days, the shortest known time preceding the birth of a live fetus, to

334 days, the legal limit of postmaturity. There are approximately three times as many babies born prematurely as postmaturely [11].

Not only is prenatal development very rapid but it is also orderly and predictable. Hence, it is possible to give a "timetable" of the important developments taking place during this period. The prenatal period is generally divided into three stages or periods, each characterized by its own peculiar type of development. These three periods are: the *period of the ovum*, extending from the moment of conception to the end of the second week; the *period of the embryo*, from the end of the second week to the end of the second month; and the *period of the fetus*, from the end of the second month until birth.

The Period of the Ovum. During the entire two weeks of this period, the zygote, or fertilized ovum, remains practically unchanged in size because it receives little or no nourishment from outside. By the time it reaches the uterus, the size of the zygote, though varying slightly according to how long it has been in the Fallopian tube, is about that of a pinhead. It has been kept alive by the nourishment it received from the nucleus of the ovum. Marked internal changes begin immediately after fertilization, even as the zygote passes down the Fallopian tube into the uterus. The ovum divides and subdivides many times, forming a globular cluster of many cells. Within this cluster, a small cavity forms, causing the cells to separate into outer and inner layers. The *outer layer* later develops into the accessory tissues which protect and nourish the individual during the prenatal period and part of the *inner cluster* develops into the embryo.

While the fertilized ovum is completing its journey down the Fallopian tube, the lining of the uterus is completing its preparation to receive the ovum. This preparation consists of an increase in the blood-vessel and glandular systems of the wall so that it will be a soft, thick, cushion-like structure in which the ovum can be embedded and receive nourishment. This type of preparation occurs during every menstrual cycle and is brought about by the secretion of two hormones, *estrogen*, present in the follicle in which the ovum matures and from which it is released when the follicle ruptures, and *progesterone*, which is produced in the wall of the ovary. Should the preparation be unnecessary, as is true when the ovum has not been fertilized, the tissue in the uterine wall breaks down and is eliminated from the body in the menstrual flow [14, 48].

Implantation. During approximately the first half of the period of the ovum, the zygote is free-roving and unattached and is nourished by the yolk within the ovum. Should this yolk be used up before the zygote becomes implanted in the wall of the uterus, the zygote will die. After the zygote emerges from the Fallopian tube, it usually floats about in the uterus, unattached, for several days. During this time, it must continue to nourish itself from its yolk. Then, when the zygote finds a place in the uterine wall to lodge, it shoots out feelers which push their way through the blood vessels in the wall and thus create a new source of nourishment. *Implantation* usually occurs about 10 days after fertilization. Once this has been accomplished, the zygote becomes a parasite and remains as such throughout the remainder of the prenatal period [48].

Significance of Period. The period of the ovum is important for three reasons: first, the ovum may die before it becomes lodged in the wall of the uterus; second, implantation may not take place; and, third, the ovum may become implanted in the wrong place. If the ovum has too little yolk to keep it alive until it can lodge itself in the uterine wall, or if it remains so long in the tube that the yolk is used up, the zygote will die. An insufficient number of hormones from the mother's thyroid and pituitary glands slows down the pattern of reproduction and is believed, therefore, to be the cause of the zygote's remaining unattached for too long.

When there is a proper balance between the functions of the mother's pituitary gland and the ovaries, the walls of the uterus prepare themselves to receive the zygote. If this preparation is too late, because of glandular imbalance, implantation cannot occur; the zygote disintegrates, and is washed out of the body with the next menstrual flow. And, finally, the zygote may attach itself to a place where it cannot get nourishment and, as a result, it will die. It may become attached to a small fibroid tumor in the uterine wall from which it can get no nourishment. Or, it may not move down into the uterus but attach itself to the wall of the Fallopian tube. This is known as a *tubal pregnancy.* Because normal development cannot take place in the tube, the zygote must be removed surgically.

The Period of the Embryo. The period of the embryo is one of rapid change. From a mass of cells, the embryo develops in the short period of six weeks to a miniature individual. All the essential features of the body, both external and internal, are established at this time. Development follows the *law of developmental direction,* with the major development occurring in the head region first and in the extremities last. Gradually, as the prenatal period progresses, development extends to the lower part of the body so that, at the time of birth, some of the original top-heaviness has been corrected. Figure 7 shows the disproportionately large head at the end of the period of the embryo and the changes in proportion that take place as the prenatal period progresses. After the period of the embryo, the changes that occur are in actual or relative size and in the functioning of the parts of the body already formed, rather than in the appearance of new features.

The outer layer of cells, which separated from the inner shortly after implantation, now develops into the accessory apparatus which will protect and nourish the embryo until the time of birth. These consist of the placenta, umbilical cord, and sac. The *placenta* develops where the zygote embedded itself in the uterine wall at the time of implantation. It is a pie-shaped structure which eventually grows to be about an inch thick and 8 to 10 inches in diameter. The *umbilical cord* is then developed from the placenta and is attached, at the other end, to the abdominal wall of the embryo. A ropelike structure containing blood vessels but no nerves, the umbilical cord eventually becomes the thickness

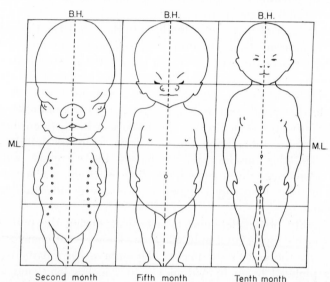

Second month   Fifth month   Tenth month

Fig. 7. Body proportions during the prenatal period. *B.H.,* body height; *M.L.,* midline. (*From C. Murchison, A handbook of child psychology, 2d ed. Worcester, Mass.: Clark Univer. Press, 1933. Used by permission.*)

of a man's finger and measures 10 to 20 inches in length. The third form of accessory apparatus to develop during the period of the embryo is the *amniotic sac,* made up of four membranes and attached to the placenta. It is filled with a watery fluid, the *amniotic fluid,* in which the embryo develops. Its function is to protect the embryo until the time of birth and to keep the temperature of the prenatal environment constant.

The maternal blood flows into the placenta from the arteries in the uterine wall and, in this way, oxygen, food materials, and water are transported from the mother's blood stream, through the umbilical cord, to the embryo. Through the umbilical cord, waste products from the embryo's body are filtered back through the placenta into the mother's blood stream and are removed through her organs of excretion. The embryo develops its own circulatory system but must rely upon the placenta for its nourishment and the elimination of its waste products. There is no direct connection between the maternal and embryonic blood streams, only an indirect connection through the placenta which acts as a filter [11, 48]. Just before birth, the sac in which the embryo has developed ruptures and releases the amniotic fluid which helps to lubricate the passageway for birth. Within a short time after birth, all parts of the accessory apparatus, the sac, cord, and placenta, are expelled from the mother's body as *afterbirth*. Their usefulness ends when the baby leaves its prenatal environment and begins its postnatal development in the environment outside the mother's body.

The inner layer of germ cells divides into the *ectoderm*, the *mesoderm*, and the *endoderm*. The ectoderm produces the epidermis of the skin, hair, nails, parts of the teeth, the skin glands, the sensory cells, and the entire nervous system. At the beginning of the period of the embryo, a neural tube is formed by a groove in the ectoderm. Eventually this develops into the spinal cord and the upper part of the brain. By the fifth week, the principal structures of the brain can be distinguished at the top of the neural tube. From the mesoderm come the dermis, or inner layer of skin, the muscles, and circulatory and excretory organs. The endoderm produces the lining of the digestive tract, trachea, bronchia, Eustachian tube, lungs, liver, pancreas, salivary glands, thyroid gland, and thymus.

The rapidity of development taking place during the period of the embryo can be appreciated only when one knows what changes occur at this time. By the end of the period, the embryo has enlarged from the size of a pinhead to an individual 1½ to 2 inches long, and weighing about two-thirds of an ounce. This increase is estimated to be about 2 million per cent. At no other time in the entire life span is growth or development at proportionally so rapid a rate. The form of the embryo is distinctly human though the proportions differ so markedly from those of an adult that one cannot refer to an embryo as a "miniature adult." The head is enormous and the arms and legs are very small. There are *eyes* with *eyelids* in the form of folds of skin above the eyes, *ears* that are low on the side of the head, a broad *nose*, a large bulging *forehead*, a *mouth* that opens, and a very small lower *jaw* which makes the embryo appear chinless.

The rounded, elongated *trunk* contains a *liver*, one-tenth of the entire body volume, from which bile is excreted; *intestines* which are shoved into the umbilical cord; a *diaphragm* which divides the chest from the abdominal cavity; and *sex organs* which are differentiated enough both externally and internally to make it possible to distinguish the sex of an individual when operatively removed. The *arms* have elbows and the *legs,* knees. The *fingers* and *toes* are webbed at this time. There is a *tail* which reaches its maximum development during this period and then regresses. The majority of the body *muscles* are now formed and those of the arms and legs are capable of functioning. There is *cartilage* in the backbone, ribs, and arm and leg bones. Around the cartilage is hard bone which spreads nearer and nearer the surface as time goes on and replaces the cartilage.

In operatively removed fetuses, an examination of the umbilical cord shows regular twists which, it is believed, have come from *turnings* of the embryo in the uterus. It is also believed, though not definitely proved, that *peristaltic movements* begin before the end of this period. *Spontaneous movements* in the form of wormlike contractions of the arms, legs, and thorax can likewise be observed. All of these are of a random, uncoordinated type.

Significance of Period. By the end of this period, the individual is distinctly human. All the important features, organs, and the glands of the body have started to develop and the embryo represents a miniature human being. However, this period is not without its hazards. Falls, emotional shocks, malnutrition, glandular disturbances, and other not fully determined causes may dislodge the embryo from its place in the uterine wall, thus resulting in a *miscarriage,* or "spontaneous abortion." There are many popular explanations for miscarriages, most of which are now disproved. The majority of these center around the mother's activities, emphasizing the fact that she was too active, she was too excitable, she smoked or drank too much, or that she took too many automobile trips. There is also a popular belief that miscarriage is a "blessing in disguise" because it is nature's way of getting rid of the unfit [54]. This belief has helped to ease the sorrow of many women who otherwise would have suffered from feelings of guilt for the role they played in bringing about the death of their unborn children.

While it is true that a certain percentage of miscarriages come from the elimination of the unfit, most are the result of other causes. Of these, an amount of progesterone insufficient to keep the uterine walls from contracting and thus dislodging the embryo before it is firmly implanted is believed to be the most common and most serious. Other proved causes are insufficiency of the thyroid hormone, insufficiency of vitamin E, pronounced malnutrition or starvation, and serious diseases, such as pneumonia, smallpox, diphtheria, German measles, and diabetes. For reasons as yet unknown, female embryos have a better chance of survival than male. For every 100 females lost through miscarriage, for example, there are 160 males [48]. When miscarriage is due to a defective zygote, it usually occurs early in the prenatal period. If, on the other hand, it is due to some unfavorable condition in the prenatal environment, it gen-

erally comes in the third or fourth month of pregnancy, with a peak in
the tenth or eleventh week [26] (see Figure 8).

Of all the unfavorable environmental conditions, a deficiency of
progesterone is believed to be the most serious. This hormone, released
from the follicle of the ovary in which the ovum matures, and later supplemented by supplies from the placenta, may be insufficient to maintain the state of quiet essential for the developing embryo. When this
happens, the walls of the uterus begin to contract and this may dislodge
the embryo, which is not yet firmly enough anchored to withstand the
pressure. Even though the embryo is healthy, it will be miscarried under
such conditions, die and be discharged from the mother's body. Such a

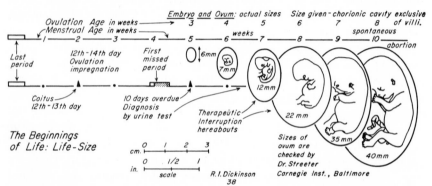

Fig. 8. The usual times for miscarriages. (*From E. L. Potter, Pregnancy. In
M. Fishbein and E. W. Burgess, Successful marriage, rev. ed. Garden City, N.Y.:
Doubleday, 1955. Used by permission.*)

miscarriage is most likely to occur at the time when there would normally
be a menstrual flow, were it not for pregnancy [48].

Furthermore, although *developmental irregularities* may occur at any
time during the prenatal period, they are most likely to occur during the
period of the embryo when the different characteristics of the body are
in the process of formation [12]. If these irregularities are serious, the
individual develops into a *monster* or badly deformed human being.
There is a special time in the timetable of prenatal development for the
development of each organ. If something hinders an organ from developing at the proper time, "it will never be able to express itself fully since
the moment for the rapid growth of some other part will have arrived"
[55]. Developmental irregularities are not likely to occur, however, if
unfavorable factors in the prenatal environment occur before a certain
part of the body has started to develop or after it has formed. After the
first five months of pregnancy, rubella, or German measles, in the mother,
for example, has been found to have no effect on her offspring [37].

There are many traditional beliefs about the causes of developmental irregularities. Some of these emphasize heredity, but most stress the role played by maternal impressions. However, there are two lines of medical evidence to disprove these beliefs about maternal impressions. First, there is evidence that the same types of abnormalities are found in the lower animals as in humans, but the low level of mental development in the animals would make them incapable of maternal impressions. Second, there is no direct nervous connection between the mother and the embryo. There are no nerves in the umbilical cord and, as a result, the mother's thoughts, feelings, and emotions could have no direct influence on the embryo.

It is now known that developmental irregularities are due to either *internal* (inherent in the ovum from the start) or *external* (acting on the embryo from a very early stage) causes. As Corner has suggested, structural abnormalities may be the result "either of a good egg in a bad environment or a bad egg in a good environment" [12]. Little is known about the *internal* causes except that heredity plays a part in the occurrence of certain deformities. *External,* or environmental causes, on the other hand, account for most of the abnormalities. Many abnormalities formerly believed to be hereditary in origin are now being found to be the result of unfavorable environmental conditions during the period when the deformed structure is in the process of development. Cleft palate and harelip, which formerly were believed to be hereditary, have recently been demonstrated to be caused by severe emotional stress on the part of the mother within the eighth and twelfth weeks of pregnancy, the period during which the upper jawbone of the human embryo forms [45].

In lower animals, experiments have demonstrated that changes can be brought about in the very early stages of growth by chemical, thermal, or other agents. A systematic reduction of oxygen at different periods in the pregnancy of mice resulted in deformities of their offspring. When the deprivation of oxygen was on the eighth day of pregnancy, for example, the offspring had an incompletely formed skull, and a harelip resulted from oxygen deprivation occurring on the twelfth day [30].

In humans, when some foreign agent changes the rate of development, the course of growth in the different parts of the organism is altered and abnormalities result. If the mother develops a case of rubella during the first 3 or 4 months of pregnancy, such defects as blindness, deafness, anomalies in the structure of the heart, microcephaly, or mental deficiency may result in her offspring [30, 37]. It is known that irradiation therapy by deep X ray or radium during pregnancy affects the developing embryo and causes deformities. Glandular deficiencies, as in the case of thyroid deficiency which causes *cretinism,* deformities of physical structures, and mental deficiency, also play an important role in producing monsters. However, the *timing* of the disturbance is the crucial factor rather than the disturbance itself [24, 30].

The Period of the Fetus. The development that takes place in the period of the fetus consists mainly of changes in actual or relative size of the parts of the body already established during the preceding period rather than in the appearance of new parts. This period extends from the end of the second lunar month until birth, which normally occurs at the end of the tenth lunar month. While the actual growth and development are greater than during the preceding period, they occur at a relatively slower rate. As is true during the period of the embryo, development during the period of the fetus follows the *law of developmental direction.* In the early part of the period, the body length shows a rapid increase followed by a steady decline in growth rate toward the end of the period, when increase occurs in the length of the limbs. The most rapid growth comes in the early part of the period.

The increase in *body length* at this time is slightly over sevenfold. By the end of the third lunar month, the fetus measures approximately $3\frac{1}{2}$ inches in length and weighs $\frac{3}{4}$ ounce; at five months, 10 inches and 9 to 10 ounces; at eight months, 16 to 18 inches and 4 to 5 pounds; and, at ten months, 20 inches and 7 to $7\frac{1}{2}$ pounds. The *head* is almost one-third of the total body length at the beginning of the period, one-fourth at the sixth month, and slightly less than one-fourth at birth. During this period, the *face* becomes relatively a little broader, and there are many changes in the nose, mouth, and throat. Sockets for the teeth appear at this time. During the early part of this period, the *skin* is wrinkled, owing to the comparative absence of subcutaneous fat. At the end of the period, the skin is very red, owing to the visibility of the vascular system just beneath it. The *hair* on the scalp is short, poorly pigmented, and often scanty. There is usually soft, wooly hair covering most of the body, *lanugo hair,* which is shed shortly after birth [11]. Rapid growth takes place in the *trunk* also. The increase is between seven- and ninefold. Before the third fetal month, the *arms* are longer than the *legs.* Later, the reverse is true. During the entire period of the fetus, both the arm length and the hand length increase eightfold. During the fourth month, the toe and finger patterns are established. They continue to develop so that, by birth, the hands and feet, though proportionally small, are well developed. The nails on the toes and fingers grow gradually during the last part of the period of the fetus [11].

At the end of the third lunar month, the *internal organs* are well developed. In some instances, they begin to function at this time. *Fetal heartbeat,* for example, can be detected through the use of a stethoscope by the fourteenth or sixteenth week. By the end of the fifth lunar month, the different internal organs have assumed positions nearly like those in an adult body. Changes in relative weights of the thymus, thyroid, and adrenal glands occur during this period. At the fourth prenatal month, the adrenals are relatively the largest, the thyroid is immature, and the thymus begins to grow steadily. The greatest decrease in weight in these glands after labor comes in the case of the thymus [17]. Most of the primary ossification centers have appeared before the end of the fourth fetal month [47]. By the third lunar month, short, threadlike prolongations, which later develop into the *axons* and *dendrites* of the *neurons,* appear. Two months later, the complete number of neurons possessed by a mature individual are present, though many are still in an immature state of development. From then on, development consists of extension of the axons and dendrites, acquisition of a covering or myelin sheath, and modification of the synapses [23]. Not all parts of the brain develop at the same time. The regions that control motor activities develop far in advance of the other areas of the brain [11].

The condition of the *sense organs* during the fetal period is difficult to determine except in the case of operatively removed fetuses or in prematurely born infants. There are indications, however, that stimulation of the sense cells in the fetus is impossible because of the constant conditions which exist within the uterus. *Taste* buds, which begin to develop in the third fetal month, are found on the hard palate, the tonsils, and in parts of the esophagus, as well as on the tongue. Because of the constant condition that exists in the uterine environment, there is no adequate stimulation of the taste buds until after birth. *Smell* reactions in prematurely born infants show that the smell mechanism is well developed before birth. But like taste, olfaction cannot begin until the nasal cavity is filled with air [11].

Stimulation of the visual cells in the *eye* does not take place until birth, though the eye itself begins to develop in the second or third week after fertilization. The eyes of the fetus move beneath their fused lids as early as the twelfth week after conception. For six or more months before birth, the eyes move with increasing coordination, even though they are in darkness. This is nature's preparation to meet the demands that will be made upon the eyes when subjected to light. Two months before birth, the retina assumes an adult arrangement. Four months before birth, the fovea forms and establishes itself definitely at the final adult distance from the optic nerve head. The eye more than doubles its weight before birth as contrasted with the brain, which is three and a half times heavier from birth to maturity, and the body, which is twenty-one times heavier. In spite of the increase in weight, the distance between the fovea and the nerve head remains absolute [21].

The infant remains partially deaf, even after birth, until the Eustachian tube of the *ear* is opened and the liquid from the middle ear is drained out. However, the fetus can hear strong sounds produced by doorbells, buzzers, and wooden knockers struck against a dish attached to the mother's abdomen. Fetal reaction to such sounds occurs four or five weeks before birth [4]. *Cutaneous* sensitivity begins in the nose and mouth region, then spreads gradually over the remaining surface of the body. Even in prematurely born infants, little or no response is made to

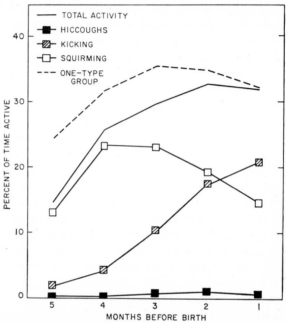

Fig. 9. Types of fetal activity. (*From H. Newberry, The measurement of three types of fetal activity. J. comp. Psychol., 1941, 32, 521–530. Used by permission.*)

pain stimulations, showing that the pain sense is poorly developed during the prenatal period. The *temperature* sense is much the same in premature as in full-term infants. Reactions to stimuli warmer than the body are stronger than to stimuli that are colder. The semicircular canals in the inner ear, responsible for *balance*, begin to function early in the fetal period and attain their adult size by the end of this period [11].

Fetal Activity. The *muscles* are well developed, and *spontaneous movements* of the arms and legs appear by the third lunar month. Fetal activity differs markedly in different fetuses, not only in amount but also in type (see Figure 9). In some instances, the fetus is active as much as 75 per cent of the time; in others, as little as 5 per cent. In some fetuses, constant turning and twisting are noted; in others, the movements are limited to kicks of the legs and thrusts of the arms. Some have hiccups almost every day, others rarely hiccup. There is a significant increase in the amount of fetal movement from the sixth to the ninth lunar month. During the last lunar month before birth, there is increased pressure on the fetal head, thus inhibiting bodily movement, and crowding of the fetal body in the amniotic sac, thus limiting the space for movement [28, 46].

Early fetal activity is greater in the head than in the leg region, showing the operation of the *law of developmental direction*. Toward the end of the period of the fetus, however, the amount of activity in the leg region is similar to that in the head region [28]. Activity is greater at the end of the day than in the morning, suggesting that the mother's fatigue may be a contributing cause [27]. The periods of activity increase in length but decrease in number as the fetus grows older [34].

Two distinct types of fetal activity have been reported: specific *reflexes* and generalized movements, or *mass activity*, involving most of the body. Between the fourth and fifth prenatal months, most of the basic reflexes, such as swallowing and the flexion reflex, are established. Mass activity, in response to external stimuli, occurs as early as the third prenatal month, owing to the immature development of the nerves and muscles. Later, mass activity becomes spontaneous and does not have to be stimulated by external stimuli. As the period of the fetus progresses, mass activity becomes more differentiated, thus allowing different parts of the body to move independently of the rest of the body [11, 20].

Variations in fetal activity have been found to be associated with different conditions in the fetal environment. Maternal activity temporarily decreases fetal activity. The reason for this, it is believed, is that after maternal activity, there is an increased supply of oxygen available for the fetus. When the mother is severely fatigued, more frequent and more violent fetal activity occurs [27]. Fetuses are equally active when the mother is engaged in any activity other than eating, which brings about a temporary decline in fetal activity. Sudden feelings of fear or anger on the mother's part produce immediate and marked increases in the number and violence of fetal movements. Fetuses of mothers undergoing severe emotional stress exhibit many times the amount of activity they previously did [4].

It has been noted that infants who were most active as fetuses show certain motor performances at an earlier age than do those who were less active. Excessive activity of fetuses, on the other hand, may cause infants to be considerably underweight for their body length at birth, because energy-producing foods are used up in activity rather than stored as fat. Infants who were less active as fetuses are covered with more fat tissue at birth, but they have been found to be slower in acquiring skills postnatally. However, they generally have less difficulty in adjusting to their postnatal environment than those who were excessively active during the fetal period [19, 46, 53].

Significance of Period. The period of the fetus is by far the longest of all the prenatal periods. In spite of this fact, it is relatively less important than the two periods that precede it. By the beginning of this period, all the important features of the body of the new individual have been established and it has begun its life as a parasite, depending on the nourishment and protection it will receive from the mother's body. The fetus has reached a state of development by the end of the seventh lunar month which makes survival possible, should birth occur at that time. This is known as the *age of viability.* By the end of the next month, the body is completely formed though smaller in size than the body of a normal, full-term infant, and chances of survival, should birth occur then, are greatly increased.

As with the preceding periods, the period of the fetus is not without hazards. There is always the possibility of a miscarriage in the fourth or fifth month, or of a seriously premature birth. Sometimes, even those infants who weigh less than the borderline size between viability and nonviability—2 pounds 3 ounces—do survive but their chances are less than those of heavier fetuses [11, 26].

Miscarriages and prematurity are not the only hazards of this period. Markedly unfavorable conditions in the prenatal environment will have their effect on the developing fetus, although the conditions may not be pronounced enough to cause developmental irregularities, as is true of the period of the embryo, when different parts of the body are in the formative stage. Only those developments which take place during the period of the fetus, such as the mineralization of the skeleton, will be profoundly influenced. However, unfavorable conditions in the prenatal environment will retard fetal development, as in the case of *cretins,* whose physical and mental development are deformed as a result of thyroid and pituitary deficiencies.

Since growth is most rapid during the period of the fetus, *proteins* are needed for tissue building and repair, *fats* for the formation of fat tissue and fuel for the body, and *carbohydrates* for strength and energy. If the mother suffers from serious *malnutrition* due to poverty, ignorance of proper diet, or war conditions, serious damage may be done to the fetus in the form of general physical weakness, rickets, nervous instability, or mental deficiency [9]. Whether these effects will eventually be compensated for will be determined largely by the conditions that exist in the early postnatal environment [44].

An Rh-factor complication or any diseased condition of the mother which affects her general metabolism, such as *syphilis, gonorrhea, endo-*

crine disorders, tuberculosis, diabetes, or toxins in the blood stream, may
produce physical defects, mental deficiency, prematurity of birth, or
stillbirths [48]. Glandular changes in the mother due to prolonged emotional strain affect the physical and mental development of the fetus.
These "blood-borne" anxieties also carry over into the period of the newborn and affect the infant's adjustment to postnatal life [53, 58]. Little
is known about the effects of alcohol and tobacco, or the use of X ray
during the period of the fetus. Only when the mother shows signs of
nervousness and wakefulness from excessive use is there reason to believe
that they will harm the fetus.

BIBLIOGRAPHY

1. Allen, G.: Comments on the analysis of twin samples. *Acta genet. med. Gemellol.*, 1955, 4, 143–160.
2. Alm, I.: The long-term prognosis for prematurely born children: a follow-up study of 999 premature boys born in wedlock and of 1,002 controls. *Acta paediat., Stockh.*, 1953, 42, Suppl. 94.
3. Bain, R.: Making normal people. *Marriage Fam. Living*, 1954, 16, 27–31.
4. Bernard, J., and L. W. Sontag: Fetal reactivity to tonal stimulation: a prelimi-nary report. *J. genet. Psychol.*, 1947, 70, 205–210.
5. Bernstein, M. E.: Studies in the human sex ratio. II. The proportion of unisexual siblings. *Hum. Biol.*, 1952, 24, 35–43.
6. Bernstein, M. E.: Parental age and sex ratio: *Science*, 1953, 118, 448–449.
7. Bernstein, M. E.: Studies on the human sex ratio. Evidence of genetic variation of the primary sex ratio in man. *J. Hered.*, 1954, 44, 59–64.
8. Blatz, W. E.: *The five sisters*. New York: Morrow, 1938.
9. Burke, B. S., S. S. Stevenson, J. Worcester, and H. G. Stuart: Nutrition studies during pregnancy. V. Relation of maternal nutrition to condition of infant at birth. *J. Nutrit.*, 1949, 38, 453–467.
10. Burlingham, D. T.: *Twins*. New York: International Univer. Press, 1952.
11. Carmichael, L.: The onset and early development of behavior. *In* L. Carmichael, *Manual of child psychology*, 2d ed. New York: Wiley, 1954. Pp. 60–187.
12. Corner, G. W.: *Ourselves unborn*. New Haven: Yale Univer. Press, 1944.
13. Dahlberg, G.: The tendency to twin births. *Acta genet. med. Gemellol.*, 1952, 1, 80–88.
14. Davis, M. E.: Ovulation and fertility. *In* M. Fishbein and R. J. R. Kennedy, *Modern marriage and family living*. New York: Oxford Univer. Press, 1957. Pp. 357–367.
15. Dickinson, R. L.: Anatomy and physiology of the sex organs. *In* M. Fishbein and R. J. R. Kennedy, *Modern marriage and family living*. New York: Oxford Univer. Press, 1957. Pp. 187–203.
16. Dinitz, S., R. R. Dynes, and A. C. Clarke: Preferences for male or female chil-dren: traditional or affectional? *Marriage Fam. Living*, 1954, 16, 128–134.
17. Ekholm, E., and K. Niemineva: On prenatal changes in the relative weights of the human adrenals, the thymus, and the thyroid gland. *Acta paediat., Stockh.*, 1950, 39, 67–86.
18. Fancher, H. L.: The relationship between the occupational status of individuals and the sex ratio of their offspring. *Hum. Biol.*, 1956, 28, 316–322.

19. Fries, M. E.: Psychosomatic relationship between mother and infant. *Psychosom. Med.*, 1944, 6, 159–162.
20. Gesell, A.: Growth potentials of the human infant. *Sci. Mon.*, N.Y., 1949, 68, 252–256.
21. Gesell, A.: The developmental aspect of child vision. *J. Pediat.*, 1949, 15, 310–317.
22. Gesell, A.: The ontogenesis of infant behavior. *In* L. Carmichael, *Manual of child psychology*, 2d ed. New York: Wiley, 1954, Pp. 335–373.
23. Gesell, A. F. L. Ilg, and L. B. Ames: *Youth: the years from ten to sixteen.* New York: Harper, 1956.
24. Gilbert, M. S.: *Biography of the unborn.* Baltimore: Williams and Wilkins, 1939.
25. Gough, H. G.: Identifying psychological femininity. *Educ. psychol. Measmt*, 1952, 12, 427–439.
26. Guttmacher, A. F.: Miscarriages and abortions. *In* M. Fishbein and E. W. Burgess, *Successful marriage,* 2d ed. Garden City, N.Y.: Doubleday, 1955. Pp. 195–206.
27. Harris, D. B., and E. S. Harris: A study of fetal movements in relation to mother's activity. *Hum. Biol.*, 1946, 18, 221–237.
28. Hooker, D.: The development of behavior in the human fetus. *In* W. Dennis, *Readings in child psychology.* New York: Prentice-Hall, 1951. Pp. 1–14.
29. Howard, R. W.: The developmental history of a group of triplets. *J. genet. Psychol.*, 1947, 70, 191–204.
30. Ingalls, T. H.: Congenital deformities not inherited. *The New York Times,* 1950, Dec. 20.
31. Jones, H. E.: The environment and mental development. *In* L. Carmichael, *Manual of child psychology,* 2d ed. New York: Wiley, 1954. Pp. 631–696.
32. Jones, H. E.: Perceived differences among twins. *Eugen. Quart.*, 1955, 1, 98–102.
33. Kallman, F. J., and G. Sander: Twin studies in senescence. *Amer. J. Psychiat.*, 1949, 106, 29–36.
34. Kellogg, W. N.: A method for recording the activity of the human fetus *in utero,* with specimen results. *J. genet. Psychol.*, 1941, 51, 307–326.
35. Kuhlen, R. G., and G. G. Thompson: *Psychological studies of human development.* New York: Appleton-Century-Crofts, 1952.
36. Lilienfeld, A. M., and B. Pasamanick: A study of variations in the frequency of twin births by race and socio-economic status. *Amer. J. hum. Genet.*, 1955, 7, 204–217.
37. Lundström, R.: Rubella during pregnancy: its effects on prenatal mortality, the incidence of congenital abnormalities and immaturity. *Acta paediat., Stockh.*, 1952, 41, 583–594.
38. McCarthy, D.: Language development. *In* L. Carmichael, *Manual of child psychology,* 2d ed. New York: Wiley, 1954. Pp. 492–630.
39. McKeown, T., and C. R. Lowe: The sex ratio of still-births related to cause and duration of gestation. *Hum. Biol.*, 1951, 23, 41–60.
40. Mowrer, E. R.: Some factors in the affectional adjustment of twins. *Amer. sociol. Rev.*, 1954, 19, 468–471.
41. Myers, R. G.: War and post-war experience in regard to the sex ratios at birth in various countries. *Hum. Biol.*, 1949, 21, 257–259.
42. Myers, R. G.: Same sexed families. *J. Hered.*, 1949, 40, 260–270.
43. Neiburgs, H. E., and R. B. Greenblatt: Specific estrogenic and androgenic smears in relation to the fetal sex during pregnancy. *Amer. J. Obstet. Gynaec.*, 1949, 57, 356–363.

44. New York Times Report: Child's I.Q. linked to mother's diet. *The New York Times*, 1955, Mar. 17.
45. New York Times Report: Studies give clue to cleft palate. *The New York Times*, 1956, Sept. 8.
46. Newberry, H.: The measurement of three types of fetal activity. *J. comp. Psychol.*, 1941, 32, 521–530.
47. Noback, C. R., and J. G. Robertson: Sequences of appearance of ossification centers in the human skeleton during the first five prenatal months. *Amer. J. Anat.*, 1951, 89, 1–28.
48. Potter, E. L.: Pregnancy. *In* M. Fishbein and R. J. R. Kennedy, *Modern marriage and family living*. New York: Oxford Univer. Press, 1957. Pp. 378–386.
49. Rapp, G. W., and G. C. Richardson: A saliva test for prenatal sex determination. *Science*, 1952, 115, 265.
50. Scheinfeld, A.: *The new you and heredity*. Philadelphia: Lippincott, 1950.
51. Sears, R. R., J. W. M. Whiting, V. Nowlis, and P. S. Sears: Some child-rearing antecedents of aggression and dependency in young children. *Genet. Psychol. Monogr.*, 1953, 47, 135–234.
52. Sherriffs, A. C., and R. F. Jarrett: Sex differences in attitudes about sex differences. *J. Psychol.*, 1953, 35, 161–168.
53. Sontag, L. W.: Some psychosomatic aspects of childhood. *Nerv. Child*, 1946, 5, 296–304.
54. Spencer, W. P.: Heredity: facts and fallacies. *In* M. Fishbein and R. J. R. Kennedy, *Modern marriage and family living*. New York: Oxford Univer. Press, 1957. Pp. 341–356.
55. Stockard, C. R.: *The physiological basis of personality*. New York: Norton, 1931.
56. Stocks, P.: Recent statistics of multiple births in England and Wales. *Acta genet. med. Gemellol.*, 1952, 1, 8–12.
57. Thoms, H.: New wonders of conception. *Woman's Home Companion*, 1954, Nov., pp. 7–8, 100–103.
58. Wallin, P., and R. P. Riley: Reactions of mothers to pregnancy and adjustment of offspring in infancy. *Amer. J. Orthopsychiat.*, 1950, 20, 616–622.

3

Infancy

Infancy, or the period of the newborn, is the shortest of all the developmental periods in the life span. It begins at birth and ends when the infant is two weeks old. Infancy is generally subdivided into two periods, the *period of the partunate* and the *period of the neonate.* The period of the partunate lasts for the first 15 to 30 minutes of postnatal life, from the time the infant emerges into the world until the umbilical cord has been cut.

The cutting of the cord marks the beginning of the second subdivision of the infancy period, the period of the neonate. At this time, the infant is no longer a parasite but has become, with the cutting of the umbilical cord, a separate, distinct, and independent individual. This period covers the remainder of the infancy period and is characterized by the making of adjustments to a new environment in the world outside the mother's body. According to medical criteria, the adjustment is completed with the fall of the navel; according to psychological criteria, it is completed when the infant has regained the weight lost after birth and begins to show signs of developmental progress in behavior.

Infancy is a period when major adjustments must be made. While these are being made, no developmental progress is apparent. The period is, therefore, a *plateau* in the developmental span. Until the adjustments have been made, the infant will remain on a plateau, or may even regress to a lower stage in his development. The four major adjustments that must be made before the infant can resume his developmental progress are: (1) adjustment to *temperature changes,* from the constant temperature of approximately 100°F in the sac in the mother's uterus to

54

the variable temperature of between 60 and 70° in the hospital or home; (2) adjustment to *breathing*, which involves the inflation of the lungs as a source of oxygen supply in place of the placenta and cord through which the necessary supply of oxygen was received during prenatal life; (3) adjustment to *sucking and swallowing* as a means of getting nourishment in place of the nourishment received from the placenta through the umbilical cord; and (4) adjustment to *elimination* through the organs of excretion rather than through the cord and placenta which served this purpose during prenatal life.

Difficulties in Adjustment. That these four adjustments are difficult for the newborn infant is apparent in the fact that he generally loses weight during the first week of life. Normally, however, he is able to adjust to these changes in the pattern of his life after a week and then begins to regain the lost weight. Some babies, however, find the adjustments too difficult and, as a result, are unable to survive. How difficult the adjustment is may be seen in the high rate of infant mortality. Of the 1.8 babies out of every 1,000 who die during the first year of life, 70 per cent die during the infancy period. Within this period, the most critical time is the day of birth, when 29 per cent of all neonatal deaths occur. The next most critical days are the second and third after birth [18, 55].

There are many factors which influence the success with which the infant makes the necessary adjustments to postnatal life. These include the type and severity of birth, the health of the mother and her emotional states during the prenatal period, and the conditions that exist in the postnatal environment [57]. Girls generally adjust to their postnatal environment better than boys [23], whites better than nonwhites [40], those from the higher socioeconomic groups better than those from the lower [10], and those whose birth weight is greater better than those who are smaller and have been born before full term [23, 55]. Neonatal death rate increases with increasing birth order, another indication of difficulty in adjustment to the postnatal environment. Malnutrition of the mother during pregnancy has been found to be responsible for premature births, stillbirths, and infant mortality during the early days of life. Improvement in maternal nutrition, on the other hand, helps to prevent these hazards and makes postnatal adjustment easier for the infant [45].

EFFECTS OF BIRTH

Contrary to tradition, normal birth is not the great shock to the infant that one would suppose it to be. The skin sensitivities are not well enough developed before birth to enable the infant to experience the pain which would otherwise result from the pressure of the intense muscular contractions necessary to push the fetus down the birth canal.

However, that does not mean that even in the case of normal birth there may not be some aftereffects. As Pratt has pointed out, "The effects of birth on the infant may be inconsequential and transitory or they may greatly affect the course of subsequent development" [47]. These effects may be *direct*, in that some part of the body of the infant is damaged in birth and thus the pattern of his future development will be affected, or they may be *indirect*, in that they affect the attitude of his parents toward him and this, in turn, will be reflected in his emotional, social, and personality development.

Types of Birth. There are three types of birth. The first is the *natural* or spontaneous type in which the position of the fetus in the mother's uterus and the size of the fetus in relation to the mother's reproductive organs make it possible for the fetus to emerge into the world in the normal, head-first position. However, not all births are of this type. Sometimes the infant is too large in relation to the mother's reproductive organs. Or, the position of the fetus may be such that he is born with the buttocks appearing first, followed by the legs and finally the head—a *breech birth*. In a *transverse presentation*, the position of the fetus is crosswise in the mother's uterus, and instruments must be used in delivery unless the position can be changed before the birth process begins. The second type of birth is thus the *instrument birth*, which occurs when the fetus is too large to emerge spontaneously from the mother's body, or when the position of the fetus makes normal birth impossible. When X-ray pictures of the fetus indicate that a complication in birth is possible, the birth may be of the third type, the *caesarean section*, in which the infant emerges into the world through a slit in the mother's abdominal wall instead of through the birth canal [26, 46].

There are more hazards associated with instrument births and with caesarean sections than with spontaneous births. Electroencephalogram records of the brain waves of newborn infants reveal that even the ordinary birth process shows some disturbance in the brain, though this is usually only temporary in nature [26, 57]. The two great "killers" at the time of birth are *injuries to the brain or nervous system* and *anoxia*, or interruption of the oxygen supply to the brain before and during birth. Even those infants who do not die as a result of these adverse conditions may be temporarily or permanently injured by them, although the damage may not be apparent until months or even years after birth [62].

A *difficult birth*, which necessitates the use of instruments to aid delivery, is likely to produce more damage and more severe damage than a spontaneous birth. Small women show a relatively high stillbirth rate as compared with larger women [4], the reason being that the fetus may have to be delivered with the aid of instruments. Even if the position of the fetus is normal, the relative size of the fetus may be too great for its body and head to pass down the mother's birth canal without help. In the case of a transverse presentation, the use of instruments is essential. Even in difficult births where the use of instruments has not been necessary, there is likely to be damage, but when instruments are used, the likelihood of damage is greatly increased. Compression of the brain as the fetal head passes down the birth canal, and hemorrhages in and around the brain may occur. Pressure on the bones may cause a fracture of a bone; there may be temporary or permanent damage to some of the nerve centers; there may be damage to the sense organs, especially the eyes or the ears; or there may be a slight interruption of the oxygen supply to the brain, which results in destruction of some of the brain cells. Motor disabilities, paralysis, cerebral palsy, and mental deficiency are frequently reported as aftermaths of difficult births, especially when instruments have had to be used [6, 47].

A long and difficult birth or birth in the breech position may be accompanied by *oxygen deprivation*. As a result, the fetus may suffocate before its head emerges [6]. Or, the brain cells may be injured or killed by oxygen deprivation, thus resulting in mental deficiency or injury to some part of the body. A total lack of oxygen in the brain cells for 18 seconds will kill them [16]. The fetus delivered by caesarean section frequently has difficulty in establishing respiration and, as a result, may die from oxygen deprivation or suffer injury to the brain cells. In addition, the development of a hyaline membrane in the lungs, shortly after birth, is common among infants born by caesarean section, and this leads to oxygen deprivation which may prove fatal to the infant who apparently was normal and healthy at the time of birth [16].

Effects of Birth. A comparison of the IQs of children in their early teens who were born spontaneously with those who were assisted into the world by instrumental or other operative methods has led to the conclusion that "instrumental delivery has not had a devastating effect upon the mentality of children who survive" [64]. However these children reveal more unfavorable personality characteristics, such as general hyperactivity, restlessness, irritability, distractability, anxiety, speech defects—especially stuttering—and poor concentration, than those who were born spontaneously [9]. Caesarean babies, by contrast, are the quietest, crying less and making better adjustments to their postnatal environment than those who are born either spontaneously or with the aid of instruments [51]. However, because they have more difficulty in establishing respiration, their brains may be temporarily or permanently affected by anoxia.

Thus, it is apparent that the type of birth may have a temporary or permanent effect, of slight or major consequence, on the individual, and this, in turn, will affect the pattern of his future development. Even when the birth per se does not have any appreciable effect on the individual *directly, indirectly,* it is of great importance because of the effect it has on the parents' attitude toward the child during the years of his childhood. The effect is especially marked on the mother. A difficult birth is likely to make the mother overprotective toward the child. Because it was so difficult for her to give birth to him, she does everything within her power to protect him from any possible harm. This overprotectiveness is often intensified if the mother has been warned by her doctor against having any more children. When the baby has been damaged in birth, especially when his life hangs in the balance, the effect on parental attitudes may be so great that it will affect their future relationships with the child and thus affect his emotional, social, and personality development. "Blue babies," born with a congenital malformation of the heart, are usually normal if an operation is performed successfully. However, their social and emotional adjustments are markedly influenced, as they grow older, by the attitudes of their parents toward them, especially their mothers [56].

The mother who gives birth to children easily and with relatively little pain, on the other hand, is far more likely to have a relaxed, unconcerned attitude toward her children than the mother for whom childbirth is difficult. As a result, she will not overprotect her children and will give them an opportunity to develop normally with a minimum of unnecessary restraints. While parental attitude will not influence the level of the child's intelligence, it will have a marked effect on his personality and the development of his native abilities.

TIME OF BIRTH

When a baby is born is unimportant in comparison with *how* he is born, unless, of course, he is born prematurely. In spite of the many traditional beliefs about the significance of the day of the week or the season of the year that a baby is born, there is little scientific evidence to show that these are contributing factors in the mental and physical development of the individual [38]. What variations there are in intelligence, sociability, physique, or personality among those born at different seasons of the year may come mainly from the health factor or from the fact that parents of the higher intellectual levels regulate the time when the baby will be born [31]. As Gordon and Novack have pointed out from the results of their study of intellectual differences among those born at different seasons of the year, "There is nothing in the data reported above that denies a slight IQ advantage for cold-weather conceptions; on the other hand, there is nothing that would warrant long

vacations for the country's obstetricians for the first half of each year"
[25].

Should the infant arrive in the world prematurely, this may affect his
pattern of future development very seriously. An infant is considered
premature if the gestation period has been between 28 and 38 weeks
long, or when the birth weight is 5 pounds 8 ounces or less. Additional
proof of prematurity is found in body measurements of the infant. Should
the head circumference be less than 33 centimeters and the crown-rump
length less than 32 centimeters, the infant is considered to be premature
[17]. Because the length of the gestation period cannot always be
estimated accurately, birth weight and size are more commonly used as
criteria for determining prematurity. The smaller the infant at birth, the
less chance he has for survival. An infant who weighs 3 pounds 5 ounces
or more, for example, has four times as great a chance for survival as
does the infant whose birth weight is less than this [12, 16].

Prematurity is more common among first-born than among later-born
children, and among boys than among girls [12]. It is more frequent in
the lower than in the upper socioeconomic classes, and among nonwhites
than among whites [50]. Small women have a higher percentage of
prematurely born babies than larger women [50]. The larger the number
of multiple births, the greater the chances are of premature birth. There
are, for example, proportionally more cases of prematurity among twins
and triplets than among singletons [47].

Seven out of every one hundred babies born today are premature. In
the past 10 years, there has been an increase in the number of prematurely born babies because medical science has found ways to prevent miscarriages but has not, as yet, solved the problem of keeping the
fetus from arriving in the world ahead of schedule. One-third of all
infant deaths occur in prematurely born infants [16]. The reason for this
high mortality rate is that the prematurely born infant is relatively unfit
for extrauterine life because his prenatal development has not been
completed. As a result, every difficulty the normal, full-term infant faces
in his adjustment to his new environment is much harder for the premature infant to meet, for the latter has arrived in the world before
being ready to meet the problems of adjustment that all newborn infants
must meet.

The special problems of adjustment the prematures must solve come
mainly from the undeveloped state of the brain rather than from undeveloped body organs. The frontal region of the brain has been found
to be better developed than the other areas of the cortex, but this is not
adequate to cope with the problems of adjustment in the extrauterine
environment [30]. Because the skull is too soft, the brain of the premature is often injured by the pressures of birth, or it may be deprived

of the necessary supply of oxygen owing to difficulties in breathing. The premature infant requires nearly three times as much oxygen as a full-term infant because his breathing is characterized by jerks and gasps. He often has difficulty in expanding his lungs, and muscular weakness makes breathing difficult. In prematures who weigh less than 3 pounds, it is not uncommon for a hyaline membrane to develop inside the lungs within the first 36 hours after birth. This blocks the small air spaces and passages, and is responsible for many of the deaths among the prematures [16].

The premature infant is often anemic and requires blood transfusions. Because his sucking and swallowing reflexes are underdeveloped, he will require special feeding with a medicine dropper or tube. As body temperature is not yet properly controlled, the premature infant requires special equipment to duplicate as nearly as possible the constant temperature of intrauterine life. Furthermore, because he is subject to infection, he requires careful medical supervision. In the modern incubators, the intrauterine environment is duplicated as nearly as possible. Because of his immaturity, the premature infant cannot be expected to conform to a schedule of feeding [28]. To ensure optimum mental and physical development, premature infants need supervised care for the first two or three years of their lives [8].

In spite of the medical advances in the care of prematurely born infants, the mortality rate is still high and the chances of permanent physical and mental injury are still great. To prevent brain injuries during birth, doctors relax the muscles of the birth passage and put forceps on the fetus's skull to shield it in the last few minutes of labor. They have devices to clear out the mucus from the lungs and inflate collapsed areas. They can use oxygen to aid the infant's breathing, though this may result in injury to the eyes if the use must be continued over a period of time [16, 65].

But, as there is no known way to hasten the ripening of the brain cells which are essential to survival without artificial aid, emphasis is now being placed on *preventing* prematurity [16]. Good maternal health and medical care during the pregnancy period not only cut down the number of prematurely born infants but also enable more prematures to live [8]. It is hoped that by increasing the amount of *releasin* in the mother's blood during the latter part of pregnancy, premature births can be eliminated. Releasin is a hormone produced by the female reproductive glands. When there is a deficiency of this hormone, uterine contractions begin too soon and bring about premature labor. Thus by increasing the amount of releasin, the cause of prematurity would be eliminated [33].

Effects of Prematurity. The prematurely born infant is at a disadvantage from the start because, according to tradition, it is believed that he will

never be strong like the full-term infant, and that he is likely to mature
into a dullard. Among the ancients, it was customary to take prematurely
born infants, along with other defectives, to a mountain where they were
allowed to perish. Even in modern civilization, where every possible
attempt is made to save the lives of those born ahead of schedule, there
is still the belief that, because the development before birth has been
incomplete, the infant will never grow up to be like other children. Because of these supposed physical and mental handicaps, parents of prematurely born infants have a tendency to be overprotective of their
children throughout the years of their childhood [34].

In light of these widely accepted beliefs, the following statement by
Gesell, based on his research studies of the development of prematurely
born infants, is especially interesting and significant. According to Gesell,
"The healthy premature infant does not acquire any unnatural precocity
from his head start. Neither does he suffer any setback. This should be
a great comfort to his anxious mother. She should be assured that the
healthy premature infant follows the basic sequence of normal mental
growth, making due allowance for his spurious age. . . . The developmental status of the premature infant must always be appraised in terms
of corrected age rather than in those of his spurious chronological age.
Born or unborn, the infant cleaves to the inherent sequences of behavior
maturation. He remains faithful to his fetality, even when birth has made
him an infant" [20]. If, however, the premature infant is not healthy,
or if he suffers some injury at birth, the long-term effects will be serious
in proportion to the unfavorableness of the birth conditions [35].

In *physical development,* gain in weight comes later in prematures
than in full-term infants, and this is especially true of prematures who
are very small at birth. By the preschool age, the differences in height,
weight, and general physical development of prematures and full-term
babies is less than in babyhood, though even at twenty years, the prematurely born individuals are slightly smaller than those born at full
term [3, 15, 24]. During the first year of life, premature infants have
more illnesses than those born at full term and, as they grow older,
they suffer more from malnutrition, dwarfism, obesity, and eye defects.
Otherwise, prematurity has not been found to affect physical growth to
any appreciable extent [15, 29].

In measuring development, if the starting point is taken from conception rather than from birth, prematurely born infants who are healthy
generally develop fast in their early postnatal environment and show
little difference in *developmental status,* as compared with full-term
babies, by the end of the first year of life. This is true of Negro infants
as well as of whites [24]. Unless corrections in age are made for the premature infants, they are found to lag behind full-term infants in sitting,

standing, and walking. Those who were smallest at birth are most retarded [15, 34]. When, on the other hand, corrections are made for age, the prematurely born infant who weighs 4 or 5 pounds at birth is ahead of the full-term infant in his developmental status by the end of the first year of life, but if his birth weight is under 4 pounds, the premature infant generally lags behind the full-term infant by a month or two until he is eighteen months old [3].

In *motor control,* prematurely born infants are somewhat backward. In *postural* and *locomotor* control, not only is their development delayed but they are also frequently awkward, clumsy, and have poor posture. They are either active, or slow and sluggish. Likewise, in control of the *hands,* they are retarded, especially in the use of the index finger for pointing and in the pincer grasp [15]. A comparison of ten-year-olds showed significantly more symptoms of brain injury in the prematures than in those born at full term [61].

Speech also is slower in developing in the prematurely born than in the full-term infant. Babytalk persists longer and more letter substitutions, such as "tix" for "six," are used. Furthermore, more defects, especially stuttering, appear in the speech of the prematures [13, 15]. In *sensory behavior* they are more alert than full-term infants. They are especially sensitive to sounds, noises, moving objects, and colors, though they are more easily distracted by voices, traffic noises, and other babies than are those born at full term [13].

When testing the intelligence of babies, if the amount of prematurity is taken into consideration, there is no significant difference in the IQ scores of prematurely born as compared with full-term infants [25, 29, 54]. The incidence of mental defect in prematures is no different from estimates for the general population, though there is a somewhat higher incidence of serious mental defects among the prematurely born. The smallest prematures contribute more than their share to the ranks of the mental defectives. The lowest IQs are generally found among those who had cerebral hemorrhages postnatally [7, 35].

In their *relationships with other people,* as they grow older, prematurely born children are generally inferior to other children, though they are more advanced in this area of behavior in the early years of life than in the area of motor development. They are likely to be shy and much attached to their mothers. This is primarily the result of the overprotection given by parents, owing to the physical weakness of the premature at birth [54]. In the preschool years, there are more behavior problems, especially feeding problems, among the prematures than among those born at full term [15]. In the late teens, the prematures have been reported to make less satisfactory social adjustments than full-term boys and girls [3, 29, 35].

Prematurely born babies are sometimes "gentle" with moderate affective reactions, but more often they are petulant, shy, irascible, and negativistic [34]. The latter type of *emotional behavior* is likely to result from parental overprotection of the children who were born before term. *Nervous traits*, most investigators agree, are definitely more numerous among children who were born prematurely than among children born at full term. Poor sleep, fatigability, irritability, shyness, temper outbursts, fright, poor concentration, forgetfulness, thumb and finger sucking, dogged determination not to comply with directions, hypersensitivity to sounds, and a tendency to burst into tears at the slightest provocation are some of the behavior disorders commonly found among children born ahead of schedule.

Nervous habits, such as nail biting and chronic masturbation, persist into the late adolescent years more often among those born prematurely than among those born at full term [29]. The explanations for the greater incidence of behavior disorders among the prematures have almost unanimously laid the blame on environmental conditions. Because prematurely born children are overprotected at first and then pushed to catch up to other children of their age, they develop nervous traits. Anxiety, intensified in inverse ratio to the size of the baby at birth, and feelings of guilt, which may underlie and increase the anxiety, affect the mother's attitude, and this, in turn, makes her hover over the baby with great solicitude [48]. Later, as the child grows older, the mother is likely to overurge the child in the hopes of closing the gap between him and the child who was born at full term, thus creating environmental conditions that prolong the child's nervousness.

CHARACTERISTICS OF THE INFANT

The birth of the infant does not necessarily mean that the prenatal period has been the normal length of 280 days. Some infants are born prematurely, some postmaturely. Under such conditions, it is obvious that the same level of physical and mental development will not be present in all infants. The description of the neonate, given below, will refer to the normal, full-term infant.

Physical Development. At birth, the average infant weighs 7½ pounds and measures 19½ inches. *Weight* in relation to *height* is less at birth, on the average, in the more active fetuses than in those less active [57]. Boys, on the whole, are slightly longer and heavier than girls. There are marked individual differences, however, in infants of both sexes. Ranges in weight are from 3 to 16 pounds, and in length from 17 to 21 or 22 inches. Variability in size is dependent not so much upon sex as upon factors in the prenatal environment, especially prenatal feeding. On the average, infants whose mothers had prenatal diets that were rated as "superior" have been found to weigh 2 to 3 pounds more at birth than do infants whose mothers had diets that were rated as "very poor." They are likewise approximately 2 inches longer, on the average, at birth than are those whose prenatal environment was not so favorable. Because of

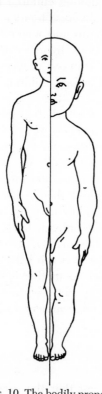

the relationship of maternal diet to infant size at birth, the average size of infants in the poor districts is significantly smaller than in the better districts [22]. First-born infants generally are smaller in length and weigh less than do later-born infants [43]. During the first few days after birth, losses in weight are usual though not universal. A loss of 6 to 7 per cent of the birth weight is common. By the tenth day after birth, most infants regain part of the weight lost immediately after birth. Light infants, as a rule, show smaller postnatal weight losses than do those who are heavier at birth and they also regain the lost weight more quickly. Infants born in the summer and autumn tend to regain their lost weight slightly sooner than do infants born in the winter and spring. Infants who are fed for the first time 6 or more hours after birth lose less weight than those who are fed earlier [53].

Fig. 10. The bodily proportions of the newborn infant and the adult. (*After Stratz. From K. Bühler, Mental development of the child. New York: Harcourt, Brace, 1930. Used by permission.*)

Infantile Features. The *muscles* of the newborn infant are soft, small, and uncontrolled. At the time of birth, less development has taken place in the muscles of the neck and legs than in those of the hands and arms. The *bones*, like the muscles, are soft and flexible because they are composed chiefly of cartilage or gristle [60]. Because of their softness, they can readily be misshapen. The *skin* is soft, deep pink in color, and often blotchy. The *flesh* is firm and elastic. Frequently, soft downy *hair* is found on the head and back, though this soon disappears. *Natal teeth* occur approximately once in every 2,000 births. They are of the primary, or "baby," type and are usually lower central incisors [39].

Physical Proportions. A study of the physical proportions of the newborn will reveal that he is not a miniature adult (see Figure 10). His head is approximately one-fourth of his body length as compared with the adult head which is approximately one-seventh of the total body length. The cranial region, the area over the eyes, is proportionally much larger than the rest of the head while the chin region is proportionally too small. The neck is so short that it is barely visible. The eyes are almost mature in size but because of the weakness of the eye muscles they move in an uncontrolled way in their sockets. In the trunk, the shoulders are narrow, while the abdomen is large and bulging. Proportionally, the arms and legs of the infant are much too short. The hands and feet are miniature.

Physiological Functions. Before birth, respiration, nutrition, and elimination are carried on through interchanges in the membranes of the placenta. With the birth cry, the lungs are inflated and respiration begins. Reflex sucking movements occur when the infant is hungry or when the lips are touched. Breast-fed infants develop stronger sucking reflexes than do infants fed by the bottle. Because nourishment comes in a continuous stream through the cord and placenta before birth, the hunger rhythm does not develop until several weeks after birth. The hunger demands of the newborn are, therefore, irregular not only as to intervals between feedings but also as to amounts. By the age of two or three weeks, a hunger rhythm develops. Then infants can adjust to a feeding schedule [5, 44]. Elimination of waste products begins a few hours after birth. Most *voidings* occur during periods of wakefulness and when the infant is quiet, usually within an hour after feeding. *Defecations* likewise occur when the infant is awake and quiet, shortly after feeding [27].

At birth, the *pulse rate* ranges from 130 to 150 beats a minute but drops to an average of 118 beats a minute several days after birth. This compares with the average adult rate of 70. *Respiration* rate in the infant ranges from 40 to 45 a minute, as compared with the average rate of 18. Neonatal *heartbeat* is more rapid than that of the adult because the infant's heart is small as compared with the arteries. Even in the healthy infant, the *temperature* is higher and more variable than in the adult. The infant's *stomach* empties in 4 to 5 hours, the *small intestines* in 7 to 8 hours, and the *large intestines* in 2 to 14 hours. The *hunger contractions* of the infant are more vigorous than those of the adult [47].

The infant *sleeps* or dozes for approximately 80 per cent of the time as compared with 49 per cent at the age of one year. By the fourth day of life, the amount of time spent in sleep drops to 68 per cent. Neonatal sleep is broken by short waking periods which occur every 2 or 3 hours, with fewer and shorter waking periods during the night than during the day. The infant is wakened by internal stimuli, such as discomfort, pain, and hunger. The only environmental stimuli that disturb him are very loud noises and changes in temperature. External stimuli are least effective immediately after feeding and during the latter periods of violent activity, both of the body and stomach, and of hunger. The infant falls asleep readily and can be awakened easily because he sleeps lightly. The greatest depth of neonatal sleep comes during the first hour. After that, sleep is lighter and can be broken easily [47].

The typical sleep curve for newborn infants shows a state of complete waking at feeding time followed by an intermediate stage when there are occasional stirs of the body and irregular movements, then deep sleep for 5 to 20 minutes, followed by an intermediate stage, and then complete waking. Deep sleep is in the middle of the sleep period and, contrary to

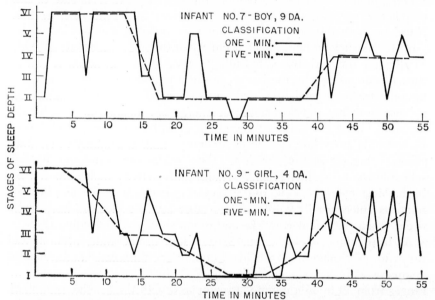

Fig. 11. Typical sleep curves for infants. (*From M. C. Reynard and F. C. Dockeray, The comparison of temporal intervals in judging depth of sleep in newborn infants. J. genet. Psychol., 1939, 55, 103–120. Used by permission.*)

popular opinion, is very short in duration [49]. Typical sleep curves for infants are shown in Figure 11. During this time, it is hard to waken the infant. While variations in infant posture during sleep are great, the characteristic position, when prone, is one similar to that of the fetus during intrauterine life. By the end of the first month of life, this position is generally outgrown, owing to the tonus of the baby's musculature. Throughout the neonatal period, there is a gradual increase in body movements during sleep, as is true also of the waking period [47].

Activities of the Infant. The activities of the infant are generally divided into two categories, *mass activity* and *specific activities*. *Mass activity* includes general movements of the whole body. Owing to the neurological immaturity of the infant, mass activity is highly uncoordinated. It may occur independently of specific external stimuli. Movements limited to one area of the body are relatively infrequent because the immature condition of the nervous system results in a diffusion of energy when a stimulus is applied to one area of the body. When a sensory stimulus is applied to any part of the body, activity occurs throughout the entire body. It is most pronounced, however, in the area that has been stimulated. When the left hand is stimulated, for example, the infant moves not only that arm but the other arm as well. In addition, he is likely to kick his legs, twist his trunk, turn his head from side to side and, if the stimulus has been intense, he will cry. Otherwise, he may sneeze or yawn.

Because activity is diffused, the amount of energy expended is great. It has been estimated that the energy expended by an infant is two or three times greater than that expended by an adult when pound to pound comparisons are made. Likewise, because crying is accompanied by mass activity, a great amount of energy is expended and the infant becomes fatigued quickly. The condition of the infant's body has a marked influence on mass activity. Hunger, pain, and bodily discomfort give rise to great activity, while limited activity follows nursing. Breast-fed babies show slightly greater general body activity than those fed by the bottle [14]. Caesarean babies are the quietest of all babies [19]. Infants, on the other hand, who were most active as fetuses have been found to be the most active during the period of the newborn [57].

In sleep, infants move about 20 per cent of the time, even in the absence of external stimuli. Changes in light stimulate motility. The greatest amount of activity occurs in moderate light and the least, in dim light. All light is disturbing and becomes increasingly so with added intensity. Sounds also produce an increase in mass activity in infants. When clothing and covers are removed, activity increases. These are most disturbing when the physiological factors are unfavorable. The greatest amount of movement is in the trunk and legs, the least in the head [47]. Variations in mass activity at different times of the day are shown in Figure 12.

Specific activities involve certain limited areas of the body. They include *reflexes*, which are definite responses to specific sensory stimuli and which remain unchanged with repetition of the same stimulus, and *general* responses, which use larger groups of muscles than are involved in reflexes and which may be aroused by either external or internal stimuli. Most of the important reflexes of the body, as the pupillary, lip, tongue, sucking, flexion, knee jerk, sneezing, and others, are present at birth. The first reflexes to appear have distinct survival value. The others appear within a few hours or days after birth. With practice, the reflexes

become stronger. Breast-fed infants, for example, develop stronger sucking reflexes than do bottle-fed infants [14].

Several reflexes, as the *Babinski,* the *Moro-embrace,* and the *Darwinian,*
which have no survival value, appear shortly after birth but disappear
during the early months of life. The Babinski, or fanning of the toes
following a gentle stroking of the sole of the infant's foot, is accompanied
by movement of the entire leg in the infant. At the age of four months,
the speed of the withdrawal has diminished, and fewer segments of the

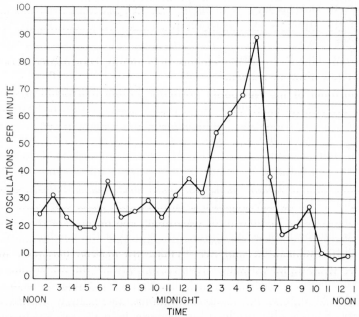

Fig. 12. Variations in mass activity at different times of the day. (*From O. C.
Irwin, The amount and nature of activities of newborn infants under constant external stimulating conditions during the first ten days of life. Genet. Psychol. Monogr.,
1930, 8, 1–92. Used by permission.*)

leg are involved. By the age of 2½ years, the response is limited to
movements of the ankle and toes. A distinct weakening of the Darwinian,
or grasp, reflex occurs by the end of the second month of life. Almost
all newborn infants can suspend body weight, but this ability begins to
decline rapidly after the first postnatal month [42].

When the infant is placed flat on his back and the table or mattress on
which he is lying is struck hard, he throws out his arms in a movement
resembling an embrace. This is the Moro-embrace reflex. At first, there
is a marked response of the whole body, accompanied by crying.
Gradually, the amount of general bodily activity is reduced. By the

eighth month, the Moro reflex consists of a quick, fine body jerk, accompanied by crying [47].

General responses involve larger portions of the body than the reflexes. Like the reflexes, they are present at birth and are direct responses to external or internal stimuli. Some of the most common of these are visual fixation on light, spontaneous eye movements, shedding of tears, feeding responses such as sucking, swallowing, tongue, cheek, and lip movements, sucking of the fingers, yawning, hiccuping, rhythmic mouthing movements, frowning and wrinkling of the brow, turning and lifting the head, turning of the trunk, body jerk, hand and arm movements, prancing and kicking, leg and foot movements. All of these are uncoordinated, undefined, and aimless. However, they are important because they are the basis from which skilled movements of a highly coordinated type will develop as a result of learning.

Vocalization of the Newborn. Normally, *crying* will begin at birth or shortly afterward. There have been cases, however, of prenatal crying. Occasionally, in a long and difficult birth, the fetus will cry even while in the uterus. Prebirth cries are rare and dangerous, for there is always the possibility that the fetus will be choked by the fluid in the uterus [52]. The birth cry is a purely reflex type of activity and results from air being drawn rapidly over the vocal cords, thus causing them to vibrate. The cry of the newborn is uttered with force and loudness and is characterized by regularity of breathing. The purpose of the birth cry is to inflate the lungs, thus making breathing possible, and to supply the blood with sufficient oxygen [41]. There are marked variations in the birth cry from infant to infant. To a certain extent, the cry is influenced by the physical condition of the infant and by the type of birth. Premature infants or those in poor condition cry in a moaning fashion. Prolonged labor, resulting in exhaustion of the infant, is characteristically accompanied by a short, weak cry. A quick, expulsive form of delivery, on the other hand, is accompanied by a sharp, deep cry [41].

Shortly after birth, the cry of infants shows variations in pitch, intensity, and continuity. It is then possible to tell, within limits, what is the matter. When the cry is staccatolike, intermittent, and monotonous in pitch, it means general bodily discomfort or hunger. The cry becomes more incessant if the discomfort is not relieved. When discomfort turns into pain, the cry rises in pitch. Should the pain lead to increasing physical weakness, piercing tones then give way to low moans. Rage is expressed through a long, piercing cry during which the breath is held, the infant's face becomes a purplish-red, and there are gulping sounds. Even after rage subsides, there are intermittent sobs [47].

Cries come from the physiological condition of the infant, generally hunger, pain, discomfort, or fatigue. The cry is in the nature of a reflex and is a response to a definite stimulus. Infants cry more often when hungry and for unknown reasons than for any other causes. Wet diapers are the third most common cause of crying and noise the least common [2] (see Figure 13). Bodily activity of some sort almost always accompanies the infant's crying. The more vigorous the crying, the more widespread the activity. In pain, hunger, or colic, the bodily activity that accompanies crying is a signal that the infant needs attention. It is thus a form of language [41].

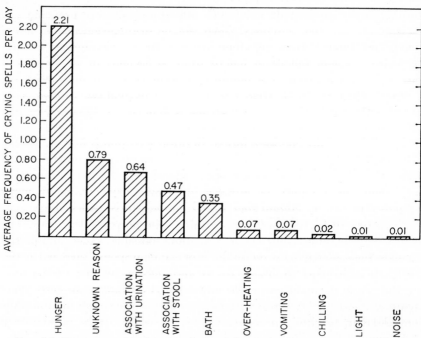

Fig. 13. Frequency distribution of the different causes of crying spells of an average baby on an average day. (*From C. A. Aldrich, C. Sung, and C. Knop, The crying of newly born babies. III. The early home period. J. Pediat., 1945, 27, 428–435. Used by permission.*)

The amount of crying a newborn infant does is an individual matter. Observations of a group of newborn infants have revealed that the least amount of crying is 48.2 minutes per day and the most, 243 minutes per day. The average for the entire group was 117 minutes per day [1]. Crying was reduced 51.4 per cent when the nursing care of the newborn infant was individualized [2]. Infants delivered by caesarean section cry less than those born in normal or instrumental births [19]. When the amount of crying was correlated with labor time, the correlation was found to be 0.17, little better than chance [51].

In addition to crying, the newborn infant occasionally makes *explosive sounds* similar to heavy breathing. They are uttered without meaning or intent and occur purely by chance whenever the vocal muscles contract. They are commonly called "coos," "gurgles," or "grunts." These are gradually strengthened and develop into *babbling*, which later develops into *speech*. *Sneezing* is a reflex type of explosive sound which first occurs within a few hours after birth and occasionally before the birth cry itself. Healthy infants sneeze several times a day, thus cleaning the nose of any foreign matter [41].

Yawning, another type of explosive sound, may be heard as early as 5 minutes after birth. *Whining*, which can be distinguished from crying, occurs during irregular breathing. *Hiccuping* occurs during the first week of life and ranges in length from 35 seconds to 18 minutes 20 seconds, with a mean of 6 minutes 34 seconds. Hiccuping begins and ends abruptly. It varies from barely audible inspirations to loud sharp sounds. Hiccups usually come in groups of loud sounds interspersed with groups of relatively quiet inspirations [47].

Sensitivities of the Newborn Infant. Because sensation is best studied by the introspective method, and because introspection is impossible at the prespeech level of development, the only criterion that can be used to determine the presence or absence of sensory capacity is the motor response to sensory stimuli that would normally arise when these sense organs are stimulated. However, it is often difficult to tell whether a motor response is made to a stimulus or whether the reaction is a part of general mass activity. Furthermore, absence of response does not necessarily mean absence of sensitivity. It may only mean that the stimulus used was too weak to elicit a response and yet a stronger stimulus might harm the delicate sense organs of the infant. What is known, at the present time, about sensory reactions in the newborn is somewhat limited.

Sight. The retina of the eye, which contains the sense cells for vision, has not reached its mature development at birth. The cones in the fovea are short and poorly defined, though the number of cones per unit area is the same as in the adult eye. This would suggest that the infant at birth is totally or partially color-blind. Within a day or two after birth, the pupillary reflex is well established, as is true of the protective responses of turning the head, closing the eyelids, and crying. The ability to follow moving objects and then move the eye backward, *optic nystagmus*, appears several hours after birth. During the first week of life, most infants respond to light by signs of discomfort. Infants seven to nine days old respond in a slightly dissimilar way to colors of the same physical energy [47].

Early ocular fixations, in infants born 8 weeks prematurely, are channelized in the direction of the position of the head. The eyes move saccadically in momentary afterpursuit, though the infant does not give true regard to a dangling object moved slowly across the field of vision. Visual competence at birth exceeds that of the premature. Maturation is more important than experience in this area. On the first day of life, incipient fixation of a near, approaching object can be observed. In the first week, there is sustained fixation of near objects and, by the end of the first month, there is fixation of more distant objects. The infant "takes hold of the physical world ocularly long before he grasps it 'manually'" [21].

Hearing. At birth, hearing is at the lowest stage of development of all the sensitivities. Many infants are totally deaf at birth and for several days thereafter owing to the stoppage of the middle ear with amniotic fluid. Even loud noises near the ear produce little if any reaction. The average newborn gives no evidence of hearing ordinary sounds during the first two days of life, though most make some response to such sounds during the third to seventh day [47].

Smell. The sense of smell is well developed at birth. This high sensitivity is shown by squirming, crying, and suckling movements, even when the infant is asleep. The infant will refuse to take the breast when it has been rubbed with such an odor as petroleum [47].

Taste. Taste, like smell, is well developed at birth. Reactions to sweet are primarily positive; to salt, sour, and bitter, negative. Wide individual differences in taste thresholds are found, however, among newborn infants [47].

Skin Sensitivities. The skin sensitivities of touch, pressure, temperature, and pain are present at birth. Some parts of the body are, however, more sensitive to *touch* than others, especially the lips. The skin on the trunk, thighs, and forearms is, on the other hand, less sensitive. *Cold* stimuli produce prompter and more pronounced reactions than do *heat* stimuli. Sensitivity to *temperature* stimuli is shown by differential sucking reactions to changes of temperature in milk. While marked individual differences exist, the thresholds for the same infants remain constant [47].

For the first day or two of life, sensitivity to *pain* is weak. Highest sensitivity is found on the lips, eyelashes, soles of the feet, mucous membrane of the nose, and the skin of the forehead. As compared with an adult, the body, legs, underarms, and hands are relatively insensitive. Pain responses appear earlier in the anterior end of the body and develop more rapidly than those in the posterior end. Sleep increases the threshold of pain sensitivity [47].

Organic Sensitivities. Hunger contractions are fully developed at birth and appear shortly after birth. They differ from those of an adult only in that they occur at more frequent intervals. They occur every 10 or 15 minutes and end in a complete tetanus or rigid contraction of the muscles. Stomach contractions appear even before the stomach contains food [47].

State of Consciousness. Because of the relatively undeveloped state of the most important sense organs, the eyes and the ears, one could not logically expect the newborn infant to be keenly aware of what goes on in the environment surrounding him. His awareness would more likely be "one great, blooming, buzzing confusion" [32]. And, because the mind of the newborn infant is different from that of the older child, and because his experiences are linked to those of intrauterine life, the newborn infant experiences the world differently, just as "an unmusical person hears a symphony differently from one who is musical" [36].

Emotions of the Neonate. In view of the incoordination that characterizes the activities of the newborn infant, it would be illogical to expect that emotional states at birth would be so well defined that they could be readily identified as specific emotions. Instead of specific patterns, the newborn's reactions can be divided into two groups, the pleasant or positive responses and the unpleasant or negative responses. *Unpleasant responses* can be elicited by changing the infant's position abruptly, by sudden loud noises, by hampering the infant's movements, and by a wet diaper or a cold object applied to the skin. The infant cries in response to these disagreeable stimuli. *Pleasurable responses,* on the other hand, can be elicited by patting, rocking, warmth, snug holding, and sucking [5]. These are not as clear-cut and definite as the unpleasant responses and resemble more a state of quiescence than an emotional state [58]. The outstanding characteristic of the infant's emotional make-up is the complete absence of gradations of responses showing different degrees of intensity. Whatever the stimulus, the resultant emotion is intense in character and sudden in appearance. Observations of prematurely born infants show that emotional reactivity is present several months before birth. It is not known whether the fetus makes any emotional responses. The probability is that they lie dormant until birth as is true of the respiratory mechanism. As Bakwin has stressed, "The ability to respond emotionally is present in the newborn as part of the developmental process and does not have to be learned. Maturing emotions require gratification if optimum health is to be attained" [5].

Beginning of Personality. The foundations of personality, as of other physical and mental traits, come from the maturing of hereditary traits. These traits begin to develop on the delivery table and although they will be influenced by learning, by direct social contacts, and by conditioning, inheritance will play a major role in their development. There are definite indications of personality at birth. Personality differences are apparent in infants as shown by their responses to food, by crying, and motor activities. From these variations, the personality is built. Observations of babies during the first two years of life have revealed a constancy of traits that indicates that the nucleus of personality was present at birth [59].

Studies of the *prenatal environment* have suggested that a disturbed prenatal environment, resulting from the mother's emotional or metabolic processes, may cause a modification of the newborn infant's behavior pattern. These disturbances are especially important during the latter part of intrauterine life and may cause a state of hyperactivity and irritability in the newborn infant [45, 57]. Sontag has commented on the effects of the prenatal environment on personality thus:

> As a newborn infant, his muscular activity level is high, as is the level of certain other of his physiological functions. He is the infant who is prone to have an exaggerated bowel activity and a higher fluctuation of heart rate. Such disturbances of somatic function may include cardiospasm. Infants who do not tolerate their feedings, regurgitating them or passing them as undigested curds, often have a history of such disturbing prenatal environment [57].

Excessive fatigue of the mother, exposure to loud and prolonged noise and vibration, etc., in the fetal environment, may reduce the adaptability of the infant to his new environment at birth, rendering him less able to utilize food successfully. It may also make him nervous, irritable, and given to crying. As a result, the infant will seem less "desirable" in the eyes of his parents, thus affecting their attitude toward him from the very start of his life [57].

There is little evidence that the *birth trauma*, or psychological shock to the infant that comes when he is separated from the mother at birth, has any lasting effects on his personality [47, 51]. There is evidence, however, that infants who are separated from their mothers after birth do not make as good an adjustment to their postnatal life as do infants who are with their mothers [58]. There is also evidence that the *mother's attitude* toward the infant, which is reflected in her behavior, influences the personality of the infant. If, for example, the mother is not happy about having a baby or if the baby is not of the desired sex, this will be sensed, if not understood, by the infant [37, 63]. Furthermore, the mother's reaction to her new baby is often confused and unstable, shifting from day to day or even from hour to hour, if she suspects something is wrong with the infant [11]. This is reflected in her behavior and is an important determinant in the developing personality pattern of the infant.

BIBLIOGRAPHY

1. Aldrich, C. A., C. Sung, and C. Knop: The crying of newly born babies. *J. Pediat.* 1945, 26, 313–326; 27, 89–95, 428–435.

2. Aldrich, C. A., M. A. Norval, C. Knop, and P. Venegas: The crying of newly born babies. VI. A follow-up study after additional nursing care had been provided. *J. Pediat.*, 1946, 28, 665–670.

3. Alm, I.: The long-term prognosis for prematurely born children. *Acta paediat., Stockh.*, 1953, 42, 591–594.

4. Baird, D., and E. M. Scott: Intelligence and child-bearing. *Eugen. Rev.*, 1953, 45, 139–154.

5. Bakwin, H.: The emotional status at birth. *Amer. J. Dis. Child.*, 1947, 74, 373–376.

6. Benda, C. E.: Psychopathology of childhood. *In* L. Carmichael, *Manual of child psychology*, 2d ed. New York: Wiley, 1954. Pp. 1115–1161.

7. Beskow, B.: Mental disturbances in premature children at school age. *Acta paediat., Stockh.*, 1949, 37, 125–149.

8. Blegen, S. D.: The premature child. *Acta paediat., Stockh.*, 1953, 42, Suppl. 88.

9. Boland, J. L.: Type of birth as related to stuttering. *J. Speech Hearing Disorders*, 1951, 16, 40–43.

10. Burke, B. S., S. S. Stevenson, J. Worcester, and H. G. Stuart: Nutrition studies during pregnancy. V. Relation of maternal nutrition to condition of infant at birth. *J. Nutrit.*, 1949, 38, 453–467.

11. Carithers, H. A.: Mother-pediatrician relationship in the neonatal period. *J. Pediat.*, 1951, 38, 654–660.

12. Crump, E. B., C. Wilson-Webb, and M. P. Pointer: Prematurity in the Negro infant. *Amer. J. Dis. Child.*, 1952, 83, 463–474.

13. Davis, D. C.: Comparative studies of the growth and development of premature and full-term children with special reference to oral communication. *Speech Monogr.*, 1952, 19, 114–115.

14. Davis, H. V., R. R. Sears, H. C. Miller, and A. J. Brodbeck: Effects of cup, bottle, and breast feeding on oral activities of newborn infants. *Pediatrics*, 1948, 3, 549–558.

15. Drillien, C. M.: Studies in prematurity. V. Development and progress of the prematurely born child in the pre-school period. *Arch. Dis. Childh.*, 1948, 23, 69–83.

16. Eichenlaub, J. E.: The premature. *Today's Hlth*, 1956, Dec., pp. 38–39, 46.

17. Ellis, R. W. B.: Assessment of prematurity by birth weight, crown-rump length, and head circumference. *Arch. Dis. Childh.*, 1951, 26, 411–422.

18. Federal Security Agency Report: *Estimated number of deaths and death rate for specified causes, United States, 1950*. Washington, D.C.: National Office of Vital Statistics, 1950.

19. Fries, M. E.: Mental hygiene in pregnancy, delivery, and the puerperium. *Ment. Hyg., N.Y.*, 1941, 25, 221–236.

20. Gesell, A.: Behavior aspects of the care of the premature infant. *J. Pediat.*, 1946, 29, 210–212.

21. Gesell, A.: The developmental aspect of child vision. *J. Pediat.*, 1949, 35, 310–317.

22. Gibson, J. R., and T. McKeown: Observations on all births (23,970) in Birmingham, 1947. III. Survival. *Brit. J. soc. Med.*, 1951, 5, 177–183.

23. Gibson, J. R., and T. McKeown: Observations on all births (23,970) in Birmingham, 1947. VI. Birth weight, duration of gestation, and survival related to sex. *Brit. J. soc. Med.*, 1952, 6, 150–152, 183–187.

24. Glaser, K., A. H. Parmelee, and E. B. Plattner: Growth patterns of prematurely born infants. *Pediatrics* (*Springfield*), 1950, 5, 130–144.

25. Gordon, H. C., and B. J. Novack: I.Q. and month of birth. *Science*, 1950, 112, 62–63.

26. Greenhill, J. P.: The birth of the baby. *In* M. Fishbein and R. J. R. Kennedy, *Modern marriage and family living*. New York: Oxford Univer. Press, 1957. Pp. 387–400.

27. Halverson, H. M.: Genital and sphincter behavior of the male infant. *J. genet. Psychol.*, 1940, 56, 95–136.

28. Hardy, J. B., and E. O. Goldstein: The feeding of premature infants. *J. Pediat.*, 1951, 38, 154–157.

29. Howard, P. J., and C. H. Morrell: Premature infants in later life: study of intelligence and personality of 22 premature infants at ages 8 to 19 years. *Pediatrics*, 1952, 9, 577–584.

30. Hughes, J. H., B. C. Davis, and M. L. Brennan: Electroencephalography of the newborn infant. VI. Studies on premature infants. *Pediatrics (Springfield)*, 1951, 7, 707.

31. Huntington, E.: Season of birth and fame. *J. genet. Psychol.*, 1944, 64, 323–328.

32. James, W.: *The principles of psychology*. New York: Holt, 1890.

33. Kaempffert, W.: Discovery is expected to save the lives of many thousand unborn infants. *The New York Times*, 1956, July 15.

34. Knehr, C. A., and A. Sobel: Mental ability of prematurely born children at early school age. *J. Psychol.*, 1949, 27, 355–361.

35. Knobloch, H., R. Rider, P. Harper, and B. Pasamanick: Neuropsychiatric sequelae of prematurity: a longitudinal study. *J. Amer. med. Ass.*, 1956, 161, 581–585.

36. Koffka, K.: *The growth of the mind*. New York: Harcourt, 1925.

37. Levy, D. M., and A. Hess: Problems in determining maternal attitudes toward newborn infants. *Psychiatry*, 1952, 15, 273–286.

38. Lewinski, R. J.: Variations in mental ability according to month, season, and period of birth. *J. genet. Psychol.*, 1954, 85, 281–288.

39. Massler, M., and B. S. Savara: Natal and neonatal teeth. *J. Pediat.*, 1950, 36, 349–359.

40. Mayer, A. J., and R. V. Marks: Differentials in infant mortality by race, economic level, and cause of death for Detroit: 1940 to 1950. *Hum. Biol.*, 1954, 26, 145–155.

41. McCarthy, D.: Language development. *In* L. Carmichael, *Manual of child psychology*, 2d ed., New York: Wiley, 1954. Pp. 492–630.

42. McGraw, M. B.: Development of the plantar response in healthy infants. *Amer. J. Dis. Child.*, 1941, 61, 1215–1221.

43. Meredith, H. V.: Birth order and body size. II. Neonatal and childhood materials. *Amer. J. phys. Anthrop.*, 1950, 8, 195–225.

44. Olmstead, R. W., and E. B. Jackson: Self-demand feeding in the first week of life. *Pediatrics*, 1950, 6, 396–401.

45. Peckos, P. S.: Nutrition during growth and development. *Child Develpm.*, 1957, 28, 273–285.

46. Potter, E. L.: Pregnancy. *In* M. Fishbein and R. J. R. Kennedy, *Modern marriage and family living*. New York: Oxford Univer. Press, 1957. Pp. 378–386.

47. Pratt, K. C.: The neonate. *In* L. Carmichael, *Manual of child psychology*, 2d ed. New York: Wiley, 1954. Pp. 215–291.

48. Prugh, D. G.: Emotional problems of the premature infant's parents. *Nurs. Outlook*, 1953, 1, 461–464.

49. Reynard, M. C., and F. C. Dockeray: The comparison of the temporal intervals

in judging depth of sleep in newborn infants. *J. genet. Psychol.*, 1939, 55, 108–126.

50. Rider, R. V., M. Taback, and H. Knobloch: Associations between premature birth and sociometric status. *Amer. J. publ. Hlth*, 1955, 45, 1022–1028.

51. Ruja, H.: The relation between neonate crying and the length of labor. *J. genet. Psychol.*, 1948, 73, 53–55.

52. Russell, P. M.: Vagitus uterinus; cry in utero. *Lancet*, 1957, Pt. 1, 137–138.

53. Salber, E. J., and E. S. Bradshaw: The effect of birth weight and time of first feed on the weight of Bantu babies in the first 10 days of life. *Hum. Biol.*, 1954, 26, 156–171.

54. Schacter, M., and S. Cotte: A study of the mental development of premature infants, *Pediatrics*, 1951, 8, 955.

55. Schlesinger, E. R., and N. C. Allaway: The combined effect of birth weight and length of gestation on neonatal mortality among single premature births. *Pediatrics*, 1955, 15, 698–704.

56. Solomon, W. W.: Postoperative adjustment of "blue babies." *Smith Coll. Stud. soc. Wk*, 1949, 19, 139–140.

57. Sontag, L. W.: Some psychosomatic aspects of childhood. *Nerv. Child*, 1946, 5, 296–304.

58. Spitz, R. A.: The role of ecological factors in emotional development in infancy. *Child Develpm.*, 1949, 20, 145–155.

59. Stagner, R.: *Psychology of personality*, 2d ed. New York: McGraw-Hill, 1948.

60. Tompkins, W. T., and D. G. Wiehl: Epiphyseal maturation in the newborn as related to maternal nutritional status. *Amer. J. Obstet. Gynaec.*, 1954, 68, 1366–1376.

61. Uddenberg, G.: Diagnostic studies in prematures. *Acta psychiat., Kbh.*, 1955, Suppl. 104.

62. Usdin, G. L., and M. L. Weil: Effect of apnea neonatorium on intellectual development. *Pediatrics*, 1952, 9, 387–394.

63. Wallin, P., and R. P. Riley: Reactions of mothers to pregnancy and adjustment of offspring in infancy. *Amer. J. Orthopsychiat.*, 1950, 20, 616–622.

64. Wile, I. S., and R. Davis: The relation of birth to behavior. *Amer. J. Orthopsychiat.*, 1941, 11, 320–334.

65. Yankauer, A., H. Jacobziner, and D. M. Schneider: The rise and fall of retrolental fibroplasia in New York State. *New York J. Med.*, 1956, 56, 1474–1477.

4

Babyhood

Babyhood extends from the end of the period of infancy, 2 weeks after birth, until the end of the second year of life. By that time, the average baby is relatively independent of adult aid and can do many things for himself which formerly had to be done for him. While many babies attain relative independence before their second birthdays, the average baby is two years old before he reaches this stage in his development. Decrease in helplessness and an accompanying increase in independence come from the rapid development of body control which enables the baby to sit, stand, walk, and manipulate objects at will. Independence also increases with the baby's improvement in the ability to communicate his needs and wishes to others in forms which they can understand.

The years of babyhood are the true foundation years of life because at this time the foundations of many behavior patterns, many attitudes toward others and toward the self, and many patterns of emotional expression are being established [31]. While these foundations are not so firmly established at the end of babyhood that they cannot be changed should they prove to be inefficient or socially unacceptable, they are nevertheless firmly enough established that changing them means relearning, with its accompaniment of emotional tension and confusion. Because subsequent development will be shaped by these foundations, babyhood may be regarded as a "critical" age in the development of the individual.

Babyhood is also a "dangerous" age. While illnesses in babyhood are less often fatal today than they were in the past, because of improved medical care in the prenatal and early postnatal months and the use of the new "wonder drugs" to minimize the severity of diseases, the mortality rate in the babyhood years is still high. Two-thirds of all deaths in the first year of life come in the first month [28, 50]. With each passing month, the chances that illness will prove to be fatal decrease. During the second year of life, however, accidents may prove to be fatal or will produce some injury that will permanently affect the course of the individual's life. The strong desire to explore his environment is not held in check by knowledge of possible harm and, as a result, the baby has many accidents, some of which are minor while others are serious.

And finally, babyhood is an "appealing" age. The helplessness and dependency of the small baby appeals to adults as well as to older children. Furthermore, the baby is easy to manage when he is helpless and this likewise adds to his appeal to adults. Gradually, as his helplessness is replaced by ability to do things for himself, the baby is less easily managed and more resistant to adult help. Unfortunately, far too often parents cannot or do not adjust their concept of the baby's abilities quickly enough to keep pace with his development. As a result, the baby is frustrated in his attempts to do the things he can and wants to do. This makes him resistant and negativistic in his attitudes toward adults, qualities which make him less appealing than he was when he was helpless and, as a result, easily managed.

PHYSICAL DEVELOPMENT

Babyhood is one of the two periods of rapid growth during the life span; the other comes at puberty. During the first six months of life, growth continues at the rapid rate characteristic of the prenatal period and then begins to slow down. In the second year, growth is at a rapidly decelerating rate [42]. Expressed in percentages, increase in weight during the first year of life is 200 per cent, and in the second, 25 to 30 per cent. Increase in height is 50 per cent in the first year as contrasted with 20 per cent in the second year [39]. Baby clothes reflect this universal and predictable pattern of growth. Infant sizes, far too large for the newborn unless adjustments are made, are outgrown before the baby is six months old. A second set of clothing is needed for the last six months of the first year while a third set, even larger in size, is adequate to meet the baby's needs from his first to his second birthday.

The pattern of physical growth in babyhood is much the same for boys and girls. During the first year, the increase in weight is proportionally greater than the increase in height; in the second year, the reverse is true [39]. There are variations in the growth curves for individual babies according to the season of the year. The period from October to December is one of maximum, and from April to June, one of minimum weight gain. Maximum gain in height comes from April to June and minimum, from October to December [62]. Measurements of height and weight of Negro babies throughout the first year of life have shown that those who came from middle-class families were significantly superior to those from poorer Negro families and that there was no difference in these measurements between Negro and white babies when the groups came from comparable economic levels. Differences, however, begin to appear in the second year because, typically, the Negro child is of a more slender build than the white child [59].

Variations in weight are more pronounced than variations in height. Some babies weigh only 3 to 4 pounds at birth while others weigh as much as 10 to 12 pounds. There is relatively little difference in birth height even when the differences in weight are pronounced. Variations continue throughout the babyhood years, with variations in weight always greater than variations in height. Variations in weight are partly dependent upon body build and partly on the baby's eating habits. Because weight is more susceptible to environmental influences than is height, it is understandable that the former variations would be greater than the latter [75].

Weight. The newborn infant weighs, on the average, 7½ pounds, boys being slightly heavier than girls. After the initial loss in weight immediately after birth, weight increases begin. By the end of the second or third week of life, weight loss following birth should have been regained. By the time the baby is four months old, birth weight is normally doubled. This means that the average baby of that age weighs 14 to 15 pounds. At eight months, weight varies from 16 to 19 pounds and, at one year, the birth weight should be trebled, or approximately 21 pounds. By his second birthday, the typical American baby weighs 25 pounds. The slowing down of weight gain increases during the final quarter of the first year and throughout the entire second year, owing to the greater expenditure of energy in creeping, sitting, and walking.

Weight increases in babyhood come mainly from an increase in fat tissue. Toward the end of fetal life, fat tissue begins to increase except in very active fetuses. Throughout the first six months of life, fat nearly doubles in thickness because of the high fat content of the milk, which plays such an important role in the young baby's diet. Some babies continue to gain weight from fat increases throughout the entire babyhood period, but for most babies, the pace of fat increases slows down. At the age of one month, fat babies have been found to be significantly longer than thin ones but this is not true after that. This temporary difference is due to a holdover from the superior size and developmental advancement at birth. Nor is there any evidence that fat babies are consistently healthier, stronger, or faster-growing than thinner babies [23].

Height. Increases in height come at a proportionally slower rate than weight increases during the first year and at a more rapid rate during the second year [39]. At birth, the length varies from 19 to 20 inches, with boys, on the average, slightly longer than girls. By the time the baby is four months old, he measures between 23 and 24 inches in length. At eight months, the average height is 26 to 28 inches; at one year, 28 to 30 inches; and at two years, approximately 32 to 34 inches [59]. As is true of weight, variations in height among babies depend upon such factors as sex, parentage, and racial stock.

Physical Proportions. During the first half year of postnatal life, changes in body proportions are slight. From then on, changes begin to appear, with head growth slower than trunk and limb growth [75]. The marked top-heaviness, characteristically present at birth, gradually decreases as the trunk and legs lengthen. The baby appears to be more thickset during the first year as a result of the proportionally greater increase in girth and transverse diameters than in length. Before babyhood is over, however, he appears to be more slender and less chunky in build [39].

Gradually, the head appears less enormous than it did at birth, owing to the development of the lower part of the face—especially the jaw, the appearance of teeth which makes the mouth seem in better proportion to the rest of the face, and the appearance of a short but actually noticeable neck. The upper part of the head, the cranial region, seems to be in better proportion to the rest of the head as babyhood progresses because the development of hair on the top of the head breaks the large expanse so apparent when the baby's head is bald. Even the nose begins to take on some shape as the cartilage framework develops.

The arms and hands increase in length between 60 and 75 per cent during babyhood, and the legs, approximately 40 per cent. The legs are thus growing at a slower rate than the arms. Furthermore, for the first few months of life, the legs are flexed so that the soles of the feet point toward each other, making the legs look even shorter than they are. There is rapid growth in both hands and feet during babyhood, not only in size but in muscular development as well [16]. Babies tend to have proportionally longer left arms, forearms and hands, and wider left palms than children five to six years of age [75]. Figure 14 shows body proportions at different ages.

Bones. As is true of growth in size, babyhood is a period of rapid growth in the bones. Bone development follows the same general trend as growth in size, which means that development is most rapid during the first year of life and is followed by a period of relatively slow development during the second year [29]. The number of bones in the body increases at this time, with bone tissue gradually replacing cartilage or membrane in certain areas. During babyhood, the bones begin to ossify as well as to increase in size and number. *Ossification* begins in the early part of the first year of life but is not completed until puberty.

The soft spongy tissue of the bones of the newborn gradually hardens, but at different rates in different parts of the body. By the age of eighteen months, for example, the *fontanels,* or soft spots on the skull, are closed in approximately 50 per cent of all babies and, at two years, in approximately all babies [75]. Ossification is dependent upon proper nutrition and the secretion of a hormone from the thyroid glands. Should either or both of these be deficient, ossification will be retarded and the

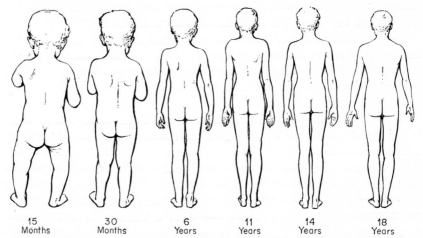

15	30	6	11	14	18
Months	Months	Years	Years	Years	Years

Fig. 14. Changes in body proportions with growth. The same boy at 15 months, 30 months, 6 years, 11 years, 14 years, and 18 years. (*From N. Bayley, Individual patterns of development. Child Develpm., 1956, 27, 45–74. Used by permission.*)

baby will develop bowed legs and other skeletal deformities which will remain for the rest of his life [44]. Because the bones are soft during babyhood, the body is pliable. This explains why a baby can get into strange positions, such as sucking his toes when lying on his back. It is at this time also that bones can readily be misshapen if too much pressure is placed on them for too long a time or if the baby is permitted to sleep on a mattress that sags.

Teeth. Of the 20 "baby," or temporary, teeth, approximately 16 have erupted before babyhood is over. The first tooth to make its appearance cuts through the gum generally between the ages of six and eight months, though some babies get their first teeth when they are only two or three months old and some not until their first birthdays have passed. The lower central incisors come in first, followed by the upper incisors. By the age of one year, the average baby has four to six teeth, and by the second year, 16 teeth. The time of eruption of the teeth is variable and depends upon such factors as hereditary tendencies, health, nutrition, and sex. The sequence of eruption is more important than the age of eruption, because when there are irregularities in the sequence, it is likely to throw the jaws out of position and cause poor alignment of the teeth [75].

The first teeth to cut through, the "biting" teeth, are thin and sharp. As a result, the eruptions are less painful than in the case of the molars, or "chewing" teeth, in the back of the jaw. As these cut through during the second year, teething gives rise to more physical upsets, more discomfort and, in turn, more fretfulness and irritability than during the first year of life when the eruption of teeth is less painful.

Nervous System. Rapid growth in the nervous system characterizes the first three to four years of postnatal life. This growth consists primarily of the development of immature cells present at birth rather than of the formation of new cells. Brain growth is shown in the increase of cranial size, made possible by the loosely connected bones of the skull. It has been estimated that one-fourth of the adult brain weight is attained at birth, one-half by the age of nine months, and three-fourths by the end of the second year.

Sense-organ Development. The sense organs develop rapidly during babyhood and are capable of functioning on a satisfactory level during the early months of life. With the development of coordination of the eye muscles by the third month, the baby is capable of *seeing* things clearly and distinctly. However, because the eye muscles remain weak for many months, eye incoordination is frequent, especially at times when the baby is fatigued, hungry, or has been crying. It is believed, though not conclusively proved, that at about the same age, three months, the cones of the retina are developed well enough to permit him to see all colors. *Hearing* is acute in babies, as may be seen in their early response to the sound of the human voice. At two months of age, babies exhibit a greater acuity to the voice than to such sounds as whistling, knocking, handclapping, and the noise of a spoon. Shortly after the baby is two months old, he responds equally well to noises of all kinds.

Smell and *taste*, which are well developed at birth, continue to be acute throughout babyhood. Because of their acuity, foods that are bland in taste to adults are pleasing to the baby, while foods that appeal to an adult are so strong in taste to a baby that he rejects them. Because of the thin texture of babies' skin and the fact that there are as many sense organs for *touch, pressure, pain,* and *temperature* in the skin surface of a baby as there will be when he reaches maturity, a baby is highly responsive to all skin stimuli. He feels heat, cold, and pain acutely and he responds more vigorously to light touch and tickling stimuli than he will when he is older [16, 75].

Babyhood Illnesses. For the first two to four months of life, nature provides an immunity to disease which safeguards the health of the young baby. If the mother's diet during the prenatal period is good, the incidence of illness in babies during the first six months of life is less than when the mother's diet is poor, and the number of deaths resulting from illness is greatly reduced. After the first half year of life, the immunity built up during the prenatal period gradually wears off.

For the remaining months of babyhood, illnesses are frequent and sometimes fatal. The frequency of deaths resulting from illness increases as the baby approaches his first birthday. More babies die from whooping cough during the first year of life than from all the other common infectious diseases combined. The disease kills more girls than boys at this time. Respiratory and gastrointestinal diseases are the next most frequent causes of death during the first year of life. The number of fatal illnesses decreases during the second year of life [50].

With modern medical discoveries, however, fewer deaths occur from these illnesses than formerly, especially in cities where better medical attention is available than in small towns and rural districts. In addition to the more serious diseases, minor illnesses such as colds and digestive upsets are common. With prompt diagnosis of these and proper medical care, they can be checked before any serious harm occurs. When, however, they are neglected, as is frequently true in the case of common colds, they can and often do develop with lightning rapidity into more serious disturbances, especially ear infections. *Accidents* are frequent during the second year of life. Many of these are only minor in seriousness and leave no harmful effects; others are serious or even fatal. Boys, as a rule, have more accidents than girls in babyhood as well as when they are older [28].

PHYSIOLOGICAL FUNCTIONS

Babyhood is the time when the fundamental physiological patterns of eating, sleeping, and elimination should be established. While the habit formation will not be completed when babyhood ends, a good foundation should have been established by that time. Otherwise, the problem of developing good physiological habits will become increasingly difficult as each month passes.

Sleep Patterns. During the third week of life, the baby sleeps on an average of 15 hours, and this remains constant until the fourteenth week when the amount declines gradually to an average of 14 hours in the twenty-sixth week. The mean duration of night sleep increases from 8½ hours at 3 weeks to 10 hours at 12 weeks and then remains constant during the rest of the first year of life. During the first three months, the decline in day sleep is balanced by an increase in night sleep. Throughout the first year, wakefulness-sleep cycles of approximately 1 hour in length occur in both day and night sleep, with deep sleep lasting only about 23 minutes [38]. The baby stirs abruptly and wakens to be fed after deep sleep or returns to sleep for another cycle of motility which accompanies partial sleep. He is relatively quiet during periods of deep sleep [7]. Heat seems to have no effect on his sleep patterns during the first year of life [19].

As the baby's stomach enlarges by the end of the first year, the sleep periods become longer. During the second year, the baby sleeps generally from 6 P.M. to 5 or 6 A.M., with a morning nap of 1 hour and an afternoon nap of 2 hours. By his second birthday, the night sleep and afternoon nap remain about the same length, but the morning nap is generally discontinued [16]. Because the baby cannot, at first, move his body from the position in which it has been placed, he becomes tired and fretful if allowed to remain too long in one position. He must therefore be turned from time to time to avoid misshapen bones and to relieve fatigue. When he can roll, between the ages of four and six months, the baby is able not only to turn his body but also to discover a position he prefers. Motility in sleep decreases with age [7].

Eating Patterns. While sucking and swallowing reflexes are present at birth, even in prematurely born infants, they are far from well developed. The newborn infant frequently sucks in air when he is swallowing, thus causing him to choke or to develop colic pains. From birth until four or five months of age, all eating is in the infantile form of sucking and swallowing. Food, as a result, must be in a liquid form. Chewing generally appears in the developmental pattern a month later than biting. But, like biting, it is in an infantile form and requires much practice before it becomes serviceable. At first, the baby chews in "rabbit style," using only his front teeth and, if the portion he has bitten off is too large for him to cope with successfully, he either holds it in his mouth without chewing or he spits it out. Given a reasonable opportunity for practice, however, and food in a semisolid form to encourage biting and chewing, the baby will have mastered the foundational eating skills by his first birthday.

The use of the bottle and of foods in liquid form during the second half of the first year of life will encourage the continuation of infantile sucking until it becomes such a well-established habit that the baby will have difficulty in progressing to the more mature forms of eating which require biting, chewing, and swallowing of semisolids. To avoid the prolongation of infantile feeding, a cup should be substituted when the baby is six months old so that he will have to drink instead of sucking. In early weaning, thumb sucking frequently becomes a substitute for sucking the nipple [16]. When the baby is given long sucking periods, he engages in more nonnutritive sucking, such as thumb sucking, has more crying, more restlessness, and more sleep difficulties than when the sucking periods are shorter. This suggests that the baby becomes tense when a long time is needed to suck his food and this affects his later behavior [15].

Food dislikes, which begin to creep into the baby's eating during the second year of life, frequently trace their origin to the prolongation of infantile eating patterns. After becoming accustomed to food in liquid form, it is difficult for the baby to adjust to it in a semisolid form. Furthermore, like all habit breaking, there is emotional resistance to giving up infantile habits after they have become firmly established. This, in turn, adds to the baby's revolt against his food, even though he may like its taste.

Because every baby has his own rhythm of feeding, just as he has his own rhythm of sleep, it is essential that mothers take into consideration the individual baby's hunger rhythm instead of forcing upon the baby an artificial feeding schedule. When an artificial schedule is forced on the baby, it causes a sense of frustration in the baby, leads to rejection of the food, and predisposes the baby to other emotional upsets. In the matter of quantity of food as well as in the time of eating, babies should have more liberty to satisfy their wants than they are generally given [56].

Patterns of Elimination. There is a popular belief that babies who are bright can be "trained" sooner than those who are less bright. The unfortunate effect of this belief is an attempt on the part of many parents to force their babies to learn habits of elimination before they are ready. In establishing habits of bowel and bladder control, timing is far more important than technique. These habits cannot be established until a state of readiness in the development of muscles and nerves is present. Bowel control begins, on the average, at six months and bladder control, between the ages of fifteen and sixteen months. In the case of the former, habits of control are established by the end of babyhood though temporary lapses may be expected when the baby is tired, ill, or emotionally excited. Bladder control, on the other hand, is in a rudimentary state at the close of babyhood. Dryness during the daytime can be expected for a major part of the time except when deviations from the scheduled routine of the day, illness, fatigue, or emotional tension interfere. There are, however, marked individual differences in babies, as there are at all stages of development [73]. Dryness at night cannot be achieved in the average child until several years later.

MUSCLE CONTROL

To be independent, the baby must gain control over his muscles. This is essential if he is to do what he wants to do, when he wants to do it. Muscle control is one of the major areas of development during the baby-hood years and, unless environmental obstacles interfere, the baby should emerge from babyhood as a relatively independent individual.

Fig. 15. Developmental phases in the assumption of an erect posture. (*From M. B. McGraw, Growth: a study of Johnny and Jimmy. New York: Appleton-Cen-tury-Crofts, 1935. Used by permission.*)

Development of control over the muscles follows a definite and pre-dictable pattern governed by the *law of developmental direction*. Accord-ing to this law, muscle control sweeps over the body from head to feet, with the muscles in the head region coming under voluntary control first and those in the leg region last. The pattern of motor control is illustrated in Figure 15. At first, the baby's body is in constant motion similar to the mass activity of the newborn infant. During periods of heat, there is greater body motility and greater extension of the limbs than when the temperature is more moderate [19].

Maturation and learning work together in the development of muscle control. Through maturation of the muscles, bones, and nerve structures, and through a change in body proportions, the baby is ready to use his body in a coordinated manner. He must, however, be given an opportunity to learn how to do this. Until this state of readiness is present, teaching will be of little or no value. It may even be harmful because it frequently fosters fear or resentment on the baby's part, both of which will militate against his learning the skill. The approximate ages at which muscle control appears in the different areas of the body and the usual patterns of development are as follows:

Head Region. Control of eye movements comes early in life. *Optic nystagmus,* or the response of the eyes to a succession of moving objects, comes within the first 12 hours after birth, and *ocular pursuit movements,* within the third and fourth weeks. *Horizontal eye movements* develop between the second and third months of life, *vertical eye movements* between the third and fourth months, and *circular eye movements,* several weeks later. By the end of the fourth month of life, even the most difficult eye movements are normally present [25]. While *reflex smiling,* or smiling in response to some tactual stimulus, appears as early as the first week of life, "social smiling," or smiling in response to a smile of another person, does not appear until between the third and fourth months [26].

The newborn infant, when placed on his stomach, can *hold up his head* during the first twenty minutes of life. When supported in a prone position at the chest and abdomen, the baby can hold his head erect in a horizontal plane at the age of one month, and at two months he can hold his head above the horizontal plane at an angle of 30 degrees. Because holding up the head when lying on the back is more difficult than when in a prone position, this ability does not develop much before the fifth month. By the age of four to six months, most babies can hold up their heads when seated on someone's lap. At this age, the baby's head maintains a mid-position when the body is supine, and he actively rotates his head, turning it freely from side to side. At five months, he turns his head freely when sitting in a chair [16].

Trunk Region. The two important developments that take place in the trunk region are the abilities to turn the body by *rolling* and by *sitting up.* At birth, the infant cannot turn his body from the position in which he has been placed, though he can move it slightly by squirming. By the time he is two months old, however, he is generally able to turn from side to back; from back to side at four months; and at six months, from stomach to stomach. The complete turn is generally made at first with several partial turns with rest periods between each turn. When he rolls, the baby turns his head first, then his shoulders, then the pelvis, and last, by pushing-kicking movements of the legs, he makes a turn of his entire body.

A sixteen-week-old baby can pull himself to a sitting position; at twenty weeks, he can sit with erect back when supported; and at twenty-eight weeks, he will sit momentarily without support when placed in a sitting position. The average baby will sit, unsupported, for 10 or more minutes between the ninth and tenth months. Boys achieve this skill slightly later than girls. In early sitting, the baby often bends forward with arms outstretched, to maintain his balance. His legs are bowed, with the soles of his feet turned toward each other, thus giving him a wide base for balance. Because early sitting is unstable, the baby frequently topples over when he tries to move [26].

In pulling himself to a sitting position, the baby first turns from a dorsal to a ventral position, then squats on all fours, and finally pushes himself upright. Not until the second or third year does the baby cease to turn his whole body axis. By the fourth or fifth year, the adult method of rolling up the body symmetrically with the aid of the arms is used. Sitting down, like sitting up, is difficult for a baby and requires much practice. At first, the baby merely topples over or falls down by giving way in the lower part of the trunk. With practice, aided by demonstration or by trial and error, he gradually learns to bend his knees and slide down instead of keeping his knees stiff. Most babies have learned how to do this by their first birthdays [26].

Arm and Hand Region. The waving, slashing arm movements and the opening and shutting of the hands of the newborn infant gradually give way to coordinated movements. The first coordinated movement is a *defense reaction* when some stimulus is approaching the face. During the first day or two of life, these movements are poorly coordinated. But, by the end of the period of the newborn, a well-coordinated defensive movement can generally be made in one trial. *Thumb opposition,* or the working of the thumb in opposition to the fingers, normally appears in grasping between the third and fourth months, and in picking up objects, between the eighth and tenth months [26]. *Eye-hand coordination,* or the direction of the movements of the hands by the eyes, is developed well enough by the sixth or seventh month of life that random reaching no longer exists and the baby can pick up even little objects when he reaches for them [65]. Most babies, by the time they are a year old, have acquired a fairly mature pattern of reaching [25].

Leg Region. The ability to maintain an upright posture comes only after a long series of preparatory coordinations [25]. Even when the baby is ready to walk, he needs varying amounts of stimulation and assistance from others before he masters this ability [31]. The earliest form of locomotion comes in the slight shifting of the body as a result of vigorous *kicking* of the legs. This occurs by the end of the second week of life. Then comes *rolling* followed by *hitching,* or locomotion in a sitting position in which the body is pushed backward through the combined pushing of the legs and arms. Rolling and hitching characteristically appear by the sixth month. *Crawling,* in which the body is prone on the floor with the head and shoulders raised by supporting the weight of that area on the elbows, reaches its peak between the seventh and ninth months. In crawling, most of the body movement comes from pulling with the arms and swiminglike movements of the legs.

As greater body strength develops, the baby *creeps* by raising his body from the floor and pushing himself forward on his hands and knees. This generally occurs between the tenth and eleventh months. Sometimes the baby raises his knees from the floor, stiffens his legs, and walks on "all fours." As a general rule, *standing with support* overlaps creeping in the developmental sequence. Gradually the baby will let go, first with one hand and then with the other. The average age for standing alone is one year. The average age for pulling himself to a standing position is 10 to 10½ months with girls slightly ahead of boys in this. The typical standing position is with the feet far apart, the toes turned outward, and the head and shoulders held forward to give the body better balance.

With practice in standing, the baby acquires enough self-confidence to take a step. Gradually, with practice and increased self-confidence, he takes more and more steps, thus *walking with support.* This usually occurs while the baby is acquiring the ability to stand alone. At first, he walks in a stiff-legged manner, with legs far apart, toes turned outward, and arms held outright like a tightrope walker, or close to the body. The head is held erect and slightly forward to maintain balance. Because he cannot watch the floor without throwing his body off balance, and because he raises his feet far from the floor and takes uneven steps, the baby has many falls when he is first learning to walk. By fourteen months, two-thirds of the babies walk without support and by the age of eighteen months, the average baby walks like an adult, no longer using the stiff-legged position he formerly used to maintain his balance [25, 26]. After that time, improved coordination in the arms and legs results in a smoother gait and less falling.

There are marked individual differences in the ages at which babies pass through the different preparatory stages leading up to walking and in the ages at which they began to walk. Some babies are walking well by their first birthdays while others have not yet started to walk. However, there is evidence that the age at which the baby starts to walk is compatible with the rate of his total development. Babies who sit early, for example, walk earlier than babies who start to sit later. It is possible to predict with a fair degree of accuracy when a baby will start to walk if one knows what the rate of his development in other motor coordinations is. A fairly accurate rule is to multiply the age of his creeping by one and a half or the age of sitting alone by two to predict when he will start to walk alone [16].

Later Skills. After body control has been obtained, the baby can use his muscular coordination for new activities. On the foundations laid by maturation, he can build *skills*. Learning is essential in the development of skills but it must be correctly timed if it is to produce good results. Training must therefore be correlated with the baby's maturational readiness [31]. Given an opportunity for practice, an incentive to learn, and a good model to copy, the baby will acquire many skills that will be useful to him in his daily activities and which will serve as the foundations for other skills that will be needed as he grows older. None of these skills will, of course, be perfected in the relatively short span of babyhood years. However, the foundations will be laid at this time and improvements will follow at a later date.

Because babyhood is the time when the foundations of many skills are being laid, the matter of learning should not be left to chance nor should the baby learn by trial and error. This is likely to lead to the establishment of behavior patterns which will prove to be so inefficient that they will have to be replaced by other and more efficient patterns later on. This means a relearning task for the child and, like all relearning, it is time-consuming, confusing, frustrating, and delays other learning which should be taking place at that time. The baby who, for example, is permitted to hold his spoon by placing his hand over the handle of the spoon will, in time, discover that this is not the "correct" way to hold his spoon and, furthermore, that it is difficult to avoid spilling food with such a grasp. Time and energy will then have to be spent in learning the "correct" method instead of advancing to more complicated skills in self-feeding.

HAND SKILLS. During babyhood, the hand skills that are learned center mainly around self-feeding, self-dressing, and play. In the latter part of the first year, the baby shows an interest in *self-feeding*. By the time he is eight months old, the baby can hold his bottle after it has been placed in his mouth, and a month later, he can take it out and put it in without help. Around his first birthday, he can use a cup when held with both hands, and later, with practice, he can hold it with one hand. At fifteen months, the baby can grasp a spoon and insert it in a dish. When he carries it to his mouth, he is apt to turn it upside down before it reaches his mouth. By the end of the second year, the baby no longer turns the spoon in his mouth and there is only a moderate amount of spilling. Some babies start to use the fork in addition to the spoon at this age. However, the baby generally spears the food with the prongs of the fork and spills a major part of the food as he carries it to his mouth. Even though the baby can feed himself fairly well with his spoon during the second year, he often prefers finger feeding to spoon feeding [26, 47].

Hand skills in *dressing* develop first in the ability to remove clothing. At the end of the first year, most babies can pull off their socks, shoes, caps, and mittens. By the end of babyhood, they can generally remove all garments unless they are buttoned in the back. From the age of a year and a half, there is an attempt on the baby's part to put on his clothes. Caps and mittens are usually put on first. Putting on clothes is easier than fastening them, and few babies can pull zippers, snap snaps, or put buttons in and out of holes. The period of most rapid improvement in dressing comes after babyhood, between 1½ and 3½ years [36]. In addition to trying to dress themselves, most babies want to *bathe* themselves. This is limited mainly to running the cloth over the face and down the center of the body. They hold a brush and try to *brush their hair,* and they try to *scrub their teeth* with a toothbrush.

In the early months of babyhood, the baby can hold a toy only when it is placed in his mouth. Later he can carry it to his mouth and suck it. *Play skills,* needed to manipulate toys and play with them, do not develop until late in the first year, but mainly in the second year. At twelve months, a baby can hold a pencil or crayon and scribble with them. Before he is two years old, he can open boxes, unscrew lids from bottles or jars, turn the leaves of a book, build a tower with four or five blocks, insert pegs in a peg board, string beads, cut a gash in paper with scissors, and scribble with a pencil or crayon [26]. Some babies attempt to roll and even throw balls but none are able to do so well before they are two years old [16, 27]. They can, however, manipulate most of the simpler toys designed for babies.

HANDEDNESS. During the early months of life, a baby is ambidextrous, with no preference for either hand. By six months of age, however, there is an unequal use of the two hands, both in preferential use and in greater strength. During the first year, there is no evidence of hand preference and babies shift from the use of one to the other hand, depending largely on the position of the object the baby reaches for. If the object is closer to the right hand, the baby will use the right hand; if closer to the left, he will use the left hand. Shifting likewise occurs during the second year but not as frequently as during the first. Thus, during babyhood, the individual is neither dominantly left- nor right-handed, though he shows, especially in the second year, a tendency to use one hand more than the other [25, 33].

LEG SKILLS. After the ability to walk has been achieved, attempts are made to acquire related skills, such as *running, skipping, jumping,* and *climbing.* Because the major part of babyhood is devoted to developing the ability to walk, these related skills are only in a rudimentary state of development by the close of the period. Running, for example, is little more than fast walking with uneven steps. General clumsiness and many falls are characteristic of the baby's first running. Early jumping is an exaggerated stepping with one foot and then the other. Climbing up and down steps is achieved first by crawling and creeping. Later, when the baby can walk alone, he goes up and down stairs in an upright position, holding on to the railing of the stairs, placing one foot on the step, and then drawing the other foot up to it. By the end of babyhood, a few babies can ride a tricycle but most of them cannot. By the end of the second year, there are deliberate swimming movements, especially in the lower extremities, and a tendency to remain in a prone position in the water [26, 27].

Delayed Motor Development. Many babies fall below the norms given above in developing control over their bodies. Because later skills depend upon the development of control of different areas of the body, delayed motor development proves to be serious as a child emerges into childhood and begins to play with other children. The more seriously he lags behind the group in the acquisition of body control, the slower he is likely to be in acquiring the skills other children possess [31]. Furthermore, because the desire to be independent makes its appearance early in the second year, a baby whose motor development lags is frustrated when he tries to do things for himself and fails.

There are many causes of delayed motor development in babyhood, most of which are controllable. The most important of these causes are: lack of opportunity to develop muscle control because of a restrictive environment which discourages practice; parental fears of the baby's being harmed by using his muscles too soon; restrictive clothing; lack of incentive to develop muscle control because he is pampered and things are done for him; body size and proportions which make movements of the body difficult; low-grade intelligence which delays motor development in proportion to its deviation from the average; fear engendered by previous accidents or constant parental warnings; and poor health caused by disease and malnutrition. The motor development of babies from the lower socioeconomic groups is generally superior to that of babies from the higher groups. This may be explained by the more permissive child-training methods used by parents of the lower socioeconomic groups and the tendency for parents of the upper groups to "push" the baby [78]. Institutionalized babies, deprived of opportunities for developing skills through practice, have been found to be retarded in their motor development as compared with babies from environments that offer opportunities for practice. Even though the baby remains in a relatively restricted environment until he is 4½ to 6 years old, there is little evidence of retardation in his motor development at that age, suggesting that the effects of lack of opportunity for practice are temporary rather than permanent, as is commonly believed. There is no evidence that emotional shock, lack of mothering, or other emotion-arousing conditions are responsible for the motor retardation of the baby during the first year of life; evidence points mainly to lack of opportunity for practice [20].

SPEECH DEVELOPMENT

Because learning to talk is a long and laborious task, many babies try to make known their needs by using substitutes for speech, especially crying and gestures. When these substitutes prove to be effective, the baby's speech development is delayed and he continues to use infantile methods of communication even after he is capable of using words.

Prespeech Forms. There are three prespeech forms which normally appear in the developmental pattern. They are crying, babbling, and gestures. *Crying* is the most frequently used of the three prespeech forms during the early months of life though, from the long-range point of view, babbling is the most important because, from it, real speech eventually develops.

CRYING. The cries of the newborn baby gradually become differentiated so that, by the third or fourth week of life, it is possible to tell from the tone and intensity of the cry and from the bodily movements accompanying it, what it signifies. Pain, for example, is expressed in shrill loud cries, interrupted by groaning and whimpering. Hunger cries are loud and interrupted by sucking movements. Cries from colic are accompanied by a peculiar, high-pitched scream, with alternate and forceful flexion and extension of the legs [70]. The cries of a young baby are differentiated more by intensity than by meaning. Stress of excitement causes greater tension of the muscles, thus flattening the sound and making it more shrill [43].

Hunger and overheating are the most common *causes* of crying during the early weeks of life, and noise, light, clothing, and vomiting are the least common causes [2]. As a baby grows older, pain, especially from digestion, strong sensory stimuli, strong disturbances during sleep, failure of an intended reaction such as inability to move because of too tight covers, loss or removal of a toy, removal of contact with others, and fear of strange places are also common causes of crying. Before he is three months old, the baby has learned that crying is a sure method of gaining attention. At four months, he will cry when an adult stops playing with him and, at five months, he will increase his crying if an adult enters the room and pays no attention to him) [43].

Almost all crying is accompanied by behavior patterns which differ from the patterns of noncrying. In crying, for example, there is vigorous limb activity, strong flexor tendencies, and disorganization of postures prevailing when crying started. Noncrying behavior patterns, on the

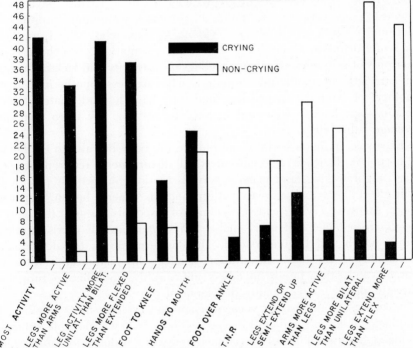

FIG. 16. Differences between bodily activity in crying and noncrying. (*From L. B. Ames, Motor correlates of infant crying. J. genet. Psychol., 1941, 59, 239–247. Used by permission.*)

other hand, are characterized by greater arm than leg activity, the holding of set postures, and limb extension [4]. Behavior patterns in crying and noncrying are shown in Figure 16. As the baby grows older, less and less activity accompanies his crying. By the end of babyhood, no more activity occurs with crying than with other emotional outbursts. Throughout babyhood, however, crying is accompanied by reddening of the skin and irregular breathing. At first, no tears are shed, but after the first month of life, crying is accompanied by the shedding of tears) [70].

Normally, the baby cries less and less as he grows older. However, there are marked individual differences in the amount of crying at all ages. By the age of six weeks, babies whose needs have been met promptly cry very little as compared with babies whose needs have not been met promptly or have been met inconsistently [70]. The baby whose parents do not respond promptly to his cries is *conditioned* to cry and this soon develops into a generalized response which the baby uses even in mild states of want to prevent distress. The baby is thus learning to cry instead of learning to use noncrying methods of communication [55]. Babies who cry excessively without a physical cause have been found to come from nervous family backgrounds where much apprehension and neurotic instability are evident. Mothers who suffer from feelings of frustration about vocational or other ambitions, who have poor concepts of self, who experience feelings of insecurity and lack of facility in carrying out mothering activities, who are less "mothering" than mothers of babies who cry less, and who have less adequate marital relationships have been found to have babies who cry more than the average baby [40].

Excessive crying is harmful not only to the baby but also to the home atmosphere. It leads to gastrointestinal disturbances, regurgitation of food, night waking, and general nervous tension. Should this persist, it will affect the baby's growth pattern and his general health. Furthermore, excessive crying leads to feelings of insecurity because the baby's needs are not met and he is unable to communicate his needs in other forms which will be understood. This, in turn, affects the developing personality of the baby. In addition, it affects his relationships with his parents and other family members unfavorably, and this, in turn, indirectly affects his personality development [55, 70].

BABBLING. As the baby's vocal mechanism develops, he is capable of producing a larger number of explosive sounds than was possible at birth. Some of these sounds will be retained and will develop into *babbling* or *lalling.* In time, some will form the basis of real speech. The number of sounds produced in babbling gradually increases and, with practice, the baby can, by the time he is six months old, combine certain vowel and consonant sounds such as "ma-ma," "da-da," or "na-na." Babbling begins during the second or third month of life, reaches its peak by the eighth month, and then gradually gives way to real speech. Because it is not used as a form of communication but as a type of playful activity, its real value from the point of view of speech development is the exercise it gives the vocal mechanism as a preliminary control which will make possible imitation of words spoken by others [40, 43, 45].

GESTURES. The baby uses gestures as a substitute for speech while adults and older children use them as supplements to speech, to give emphasis to words. Even after he is able to say a few words, the baby will continue to use gestures, combining them with the words he knows, to make his first sentence. Outstretched arms and smiling, for example, readily communicate the idea that the baby wants to be picked up, while pushing away his plate, especially when accompanied by the word "no," quickly tells you that the baby does not want to eat the food placed before him [43, 45, 55].

Comprehension. At every age, a child comprehends the meanings of what others say more readily than he can put into words his own thoughts and feelings. This is true of babyhood also [45]. The facial expression, tone of voice, and gestures of the speaker help him to understand the meaning of what is being said. This would be impossible if he had to rely entirely upon interpreting the sounds he heard [41]. Pleasure, anger, and fear can be comprehended as early as the third month of life. Until the baby is eighteen months old, words must be reinforced with gestures, such as pointing to an object, if he is to understand the meaning. By the age of two years, according to the Terman-Merrill Scale of Intelligence Tests, the average baby should comprehend well enough to respond correctly to two out of six simple commands, as, "Give me the kitty" or "Put the spoon in the cup," when the objects are placed on the table before him [74].

Vocabulary Building. To speak, the baby must learn words associated with objects and activities. His early vocabulary consists primarily of nouns related to persons and objects in his environment, and of verbs which designate action, such as "give" and "hold." Shortly before babyhood is over, a few adjectives and adverbs creep into his vocabulary. Adjectives describing his reactions to people and things, such as "nice" and "naughty," appear first. Prepositions, conjunctions, and pronouns generally are not used until early in childhood. Not only does the baby learn new words as he grows older, but he learns new meanings for old words [77].

The size of a baby's vocabulary at different ages can be judged by considering only those words whose meaning the baby knows. Other words may be spoken in "parrot fashion" and, even though correctly pronounced, are not a part of the baby's vocabulary because they cannot be used to communicate meaning. It has been estimated, from studies of large numbers of babies, that at eighteen months of age, the mean numbers of different words used by babies is 10, and at twenty-four months, 29.1. At this age, girls definitely surpass boys in the size of vocabulary used. However, because the size of the baby's vocabulary depends upon so many factors, especially intelligence, incentive, and opportunity to learn new words, there are marked individual differences. It has been reported that the vocabulary range for two-year-olds is from 6 to 126 words [45].

Use of Sentences. The first sentences used by a baby are generally one-word sentences consisting of a noun or verb accompanied by a gesture. "Doll," accompanied by pointing to a doll, expresses the meaning "Give me the doll." One-word sentences appear in a baby's speech between the ages of twelve and eighteen months. Gradually, more words creep into the sentences, but the use of gestures is not abandoned until well into childhood. Early word combinations appear between the ages of 17.5 months and 2 years. These early word combinations contain one or more nouns, a verb, and occasionally adjectives and adverbs. Typical early word combinations are "Cup all gone" and "Shut that door" [16, 26, 45].

Pronunciation. Because speech is learned by imitation, it is essential that a baby have a good model if he is to learn to pronounce his words correctly. But a good model alone is not enough. The model must be presented slowly and distinctly so the baby can hear every sound. He should be encouraged to say the word over and over again, following a repetition of the model, until he learns to say that word correctly. In most cases, mispronunciation of words is the result of crude perceptions rather than of inability to pronounce the elemental sounds. Between the ages of twelve and eighteen months, much of the baby's speech is incomprehensible because his pronunciation is so poor. When he cannot make himself understood, the baby becomes so frustrated that he reverts to the only form of communication he has found to be satisfactory, crying) [55]. After eighteen months, there are gradual but marked improvements in pronunciation [45].

Mispronunciations are generally called "babytalk." Babytalk takes different forms, the most common of which are: the omission of one or more syllables, usually in the middle of a word, as "buttfly" for "butterfly"; substitution of letters, syllables, or even words for the word heard, as "tolly" for "dolly" or "choo-choo" for "train"; and interchanges of letters or syllables in the longer and less frequently used words, as "tautmobile" for "automobile." Consonants and consonant blends are more difficult for babies to pronounce than vowels and diphthongs. The most difficult consonants are *z, w, s, d,* and *g,* and the difficult blends are *st, str, sk, dr,* and *fl. O* is the most difficult vowel for babies to pronounce correctly. The baby more often omits the final consonant than the initial consonant in his pronunciation of a word [66].

Because parents and relatives frequently regard babytalk as "cute," they permit it to continue or even encourage its use by talking babytalk themselves when they speak to the baby. As a result, an incorrect auditory image is developed. This serves as a model for future pronunciations of that word. Continued mispronunciation of a word results in the formation of a word habit which may be difficult to break and to replace with a habit of correct pronunciation when the baby emerges into childhood and discovers that his playmates cannot understand him or ridicule him because he "talks like a baby."

Delayed Speech. Delayed speech, like delayed motor control, is serious in babyhood because, at this age, the foundations are being laid for the tools of communication which will be needed as the baby's social horizons broaden. In early childhood, with the awakening of interest in people outside the home, the child whose speech lags markedly behind that of other children finds himself in the role of an outsider. If he cannot make himself understood by them, he cannot become one of the group [26, 31].

There are many causes of delayed speech in babyhood, the most important of which are low-grade intelligence, poor social environment, lack of incentive to talk, an inadequate or defective model, prolonged illness, deafness, and multiple births. Any one or several of these causes can readily delay the baby's speech by several months, affecting not only the age at which he first begins to talk, but also the size of his vocabulary and his ability to combine words into sentences [16, 45].

EMOTIONS

From the simple, almost completely undifferentiated forms in which they appear at birth, emotions develop, through maturation and learning, into different emotional states which can be aroused by a wide variety of stimuli. With age, emotional responses become less diffuse, less random, and more differentiated. They likewise become more specialized and directed toward the situation in which they occur. From the general emotional excitement which appears at birth, fear, anger, disgust, distress, delight, elation, and affection gradually develop [12, 64]. Genetic studies of a large number of babies have shown a pattern sequence in emotional development similar in its major aspects for all. In this pattern, different emotional responses appear at particular times and, with increasing age, there is a change in the form the response takes [17, 34] (see Figure 17).

Crying and screaming, for example, appear in the first few minutes after birth. By the age of four to eight months, calling is added to crying; between sixteen and twenty months, saying "no" is added, and between twenty and twenty-four months, asking accompanies "no." Similarly, running away when frightened does not appear until the twelve- to sixteen-month period, and hiding the face does not appear until the age of sixteen to twenty months. Emotions in babyhood are characterized by behavior responses proportionately great for the stimuli that gave rise to them, especially in the case of anger and fear. They are brief in duration, though intense while they last. They appear frequently, but are transitory and give way to other emotions when the baby's attention is distracted [34].

Anger. (Anger is the most common emotion in babyhood) because there are many anger-provoking stimuli in the baby's environment and because babies quickly learn that anger is an easy way to get attention or satisfy their desires. In babyhood, anger is often aroused in response to interference with the movements the baby wishes to make, such as putting on his clothes when he wants to play with a toy; thwarting of some wish, such as not being picked up when he cries for attention; and not being able to do what he sets out to do, such as getting a box from a shelf that is too high for him to reach. A few of the most common situations that give rise to anger at the close of babyhood are having to sit on the toilet chair, having property taken away, having the face washed, being left alone in the room or having the adult leave the room [34]. The baby's inability to make himself understood through his early attempts at speech is also a constant source of irritation to him [45].

FIG. 17. Schematic presentation of a genetic theory of emotional changes. (*Modified from K. M. Banham, Senescence and the emotions: a genetic theory. J. genet. Psychol., 1951, 78, 175–183. Used by permission.*)

No two babies, of course, experience anger for the same reasons, but the general pattern is the same for all. Thwarting of some wish or interfering with what they are trying to do will invariably lead to an angry outburst. Anger responses in babies show fewer variations than they do in older children. Typically, in an angry outburst the energy is not directed toward any serviceable end. It is expended in screaming, kicking the legs, and waving the arms in a random fashion. To add to this repertoire of actions, many babies hold their breath, jump up and down, throw themselves on the floor, and hit or kick anything within reach [16, 34]. Too much frustration in babyhood may result in the development of aggressive response which will be directed toward others, even though they have in no way acted as a source of frustration for the baby's wishes.

Fear. Unlike anger, fear-provoking stimuli are relatively infrequent in the environment of a baby. Babies are protected as much as possible from the common dangers of life, such as automobiles, falls from high places, loud noises, strange people and places, and animals that come upon them suddenly with a bark or a roar. And, because of their limited intelligence, they are incapable of seeing the threat in such situations as a loss of financial security through the death of the father or the danger to their health when a polio epidemic strikes their community. They do, however, learn to fear certain things in spite of their restricted environment. Through association with the native fear of loud noises or of falling, through imitation of those who are afraid, or through memories of an unpleasant experience, they build up fears of people and things in their environment [34].

How many or how severe these babyhood fears are will vary greatly from individual to individual. In general, the things most feared at this age are animals; dark rooms; high places; strange persons, objects, and situations; and loud noises. They also fear persons or things associated with loud noises, pain, and tactual-sensory shock, falling, and sudden displacements. Toward the end of babyhood, fears of animals, of dark places, and of being alone begin to appear [34]. Even though fears are, for the most part, learned as a result of individual experience and vary from individual to individual, there are two characteristics that are common to all fear stimuli. The first is that the stimulus occurs suddenly and unexpectedly, thus giving the baby little opportunity to adjust himself to it. Fear of strangers, for example, which is so common between the ages of nine and twelve months, comes principally from the fact that a stranger approaches the baby suddenly in place of the familiar person he was prepared to see. The second characteristic of fear stimuli is that they embody novelty or strangeness. Even a familiar person dressed in an unfamiliar manner, as when the mother wears a hat and coat in place of her usual housedress, may frighten a young baby. As soon as the novelty disappears, so does the fear [17].

The typical fear response in babyhood consists of an attempt to withdraw from the frightening stimulus accompanied by whimpering, crying, temporary holding of the breath, and a checking of the activity in which the individual is engaged. A frightened baby will turn his head and hide his face before he is capable of running away and hiding. His response is thus one of helplessness and his cry is for help. After he has learned to walk and run, he will hide behind a person or a piece of furniture, often peeking out to see if it is safe to emerge. If his curiosity is aroused, together with his fear, he will vacillate between his desire to see what is going on and his fear of the person or object that aroused his fear.

Curiosity. For the first two or three months of life, until eye coordination is well developed, only strong stimuli directed toward the baby will attract his attention. When, however, the ability to see clearly and distinctly has developed, anything *new* or *unusual* will motivate the baby to explore, unless the newness is so pronounced that it gives rise to fear. As fear wanes, curiosity will replace it. Typically, curiosity in young babies is expressed by tensing the facial muscles, opening the mouth and stretching out the tongue, and wrinkling the forehead. By the middle of the first year, the baby leans toward the object that aroused his curiosity and grasps for it. When he reaches it, he handles, pulls, sucks, shakes, and rattles it. This sensorimotor exploration frequently results in damage to the object and harm to the baby.

Joy. Joy, which in its milder forms is known as pleasure or happiness, is bound up at first with physical well-being. By the second or third month of life, social situations will likewise give rise to smiling and laughing and, several months later, the baby will respond joyfully to tickling. The most common situations causing laughter in the second year of life are being played with, playing with toys, watching other children at play, and making sounds which are more or less musical. The baby's joy is greatly increased when an activity is difficult for him or when there is some obstacle he must overcome to carry out the activity successfully [5, 34].

Joy expresses itself in smiling and laughing. Movements of the arms and legs and slight respiratory changes, as may be seen in the pulsations of the abdomen, accompany laughter at this age. When joy is intense, the baby coos, gurgles, or even shouts with glee, and all the bodily movements are intensified. There are definite age trends in the amount and also in the stimuli that elicit smiling and laughing. At eighteen months, the baby smiles mostly at his own activities. The type that amuses him most is his own gross motor activity or his own social approach to a person. At two years, smiles in relation to another person occur less frequently, but now these smiles are accompanied by verbalizations. Smiles in relation to his own activity come next in frequency [5].

Affection. Affectionate responses to people develop in a patterned fashion. Affectionate behavior appears in an outgoing striving and approach. The baby fixes his gaze on a person's face, kicks, holds out and waves his arms, smiles, and tries to raise his body. Because these movements are so uncoordinated at first, he cannot reach the loved one. He can, however, usually reach the loved one by the age of six months. During the second half of the first year, affectionate behavior is directed toward familiar persons, though strangers may win the baby's affection quickly. Affection is conditioned or built up as a result of pleasant experiences with a particular person, especially one who takes care of his bodily needs, plays with him, or is responsible for giving him pleasure [34]. The baby's affections develop primarily in relation to people and only secondarily in relation to things [11].

During the second year, the baby includes himself and his toys in his affection. These are the "love objects" which substitute for human objects of affection [11]. It is unusual for a baby to respond in an affectionate manner to other babies, though he may show the same affection for an older child or an adolescent who acts as a baby sitter as he does for an adult. When there is a family pet that the baby can play with without fear, he develops an affection for that pet.

Babies express their affection in outgoing, expansive ways. Preoccupation with self and withdrawn and withholding behavior are secondary reactions, coming when a baby is rebuffed, smothered with unwanted ministrations, ignored, or neglected. This is often found in two-year-olds, who then seek other companionship. When parents are oversolicitous and overdemonstrative, they do not encourage the baby to express his affection [11]. Instead, they encourage him to focus his affection on himself. The typical expression of affection in babyhood consists of hugging, patting, or kissing the loved object or person. Kissing is a less frequent response than hugging, patting, or even stroking. How demonstrative the baby is will depend largely upon the amount of affection he has received from others.

SOCIAL DEVELOPMENT

Early social experiences play a dominant role in determining the child's attitudes toward social relationships and the pattern of his behavior in his relationships with others. And, because the baby's life is centered around the home, the foundations for later social behavior and attitudes are "home-grown." These are not determined by any one specific aspect of the home but rather by the total character of the home environment [22]. How important a role the home plays in the socialization of the individual has been emphasized thus by Bain: "When the child enters school, he begins to reap the rewards or suffer the ills which flow from the first six years of life" [8]. Studies of social adjustments of older children have revealed that their social behavior remains consistent as they grow older, thus emphasizing the importance of good foundations [58].

Because the first social relationships of a child are in the home, the family group plays an important role in determining what his attitude and behavior in social situations will be. The family group should contribute a readiness to belong and a feeling that he is an accepted part of any subsequent groups that he may enter. When accepted at home, the feeling of belonging will carry over to other groups. The ability to understand and appreciate people will come from contacts with relatives and neighbors. For the most part, the baby's relationships are favorable with

the members of his family during the first year of life when his helplessness makes him appealing. By the second year, his desire for independence and his resistance to adult authority make him less appealing
and, as a result, attitudes of family members toward him change. The importance of this is discussed in this chapter under "Family Relationships."

Early Patterns. At birth, the infant is nongregarious. So long as his
physical needs are attended to, it makes no difference to him who
ministers to his needs. And, because of the immature state of development of his eye muscles, he cannot see well enough to be able to distinguish one person from another, or to tell what is a person and what is
an inanimate object. At this time, he can be soothed as well by caresses
from a hot-water bottle or from a soft pillow as by caresses from his
mother. He will, however, turn when he hears a human voice at the age
of two months [16].

Between the second and third months of life, his ability to see has
improved to the point where he can distinguish people. He has now discovered that it is people rather than things who supply his needs. At
this age, he shows contentment when with people and is discontented
and "fussy" when left alone. This is the beginning of "social behavior."
Typically, the first social responses are to *adults.* The baby, by the third
month, shows the beginnings of interest in people. This interest is seen
in the baby's crying when a person leaves him, showing displeasure
when a person is not looking at him, and watching people's facial expressions.

By the fourth or fifth month, the baby makes anticipatory adjustments
to being picked up, smiles in response to the person who speaks to him
and, a month later, reacts differently to scolding and smiling and to
angry and unfriendly voices. To attract the attention of other babies or
children, he bounces up and down, kicks, and laughs or blows. At this
age, the baby differentiates between "friends" and "strangers" by smiling
at the former and by sobering or showing fear to the latter [26, 63].

When the baby is eight or nine months old, he attempts to imitate the
speech, simple activities, and gestures of others. At the age of one year,
he can refrain from doing things in response to the warning, "No, no,"
and he shows, by crying and drawing away, a definite dislike or even
fear of strangers. This shy behavior is especially pronounced between
the sixty-sixth and eighty-sixth weeks of life. In the middle of the second
year, *negativism,* in the form of stubborn resistance to requests and demands of adults, normally appears. Girls, as a rule, show more negativism than do boys. Negativism at this age shows itself in physical resistance, in silence, in physical withdrawal, or "tenseness" which is the
opposite of "cuddliness" [13]. By the end of babyhood, however, the
young child can and does cooperate with adults in a number of simple

routine activities. He is, thus, in a state of "equilibrium" which makes him more social in his behavior [26].

Social reactions to *other babies* or *children* lag behind social reactions to adults in the developmental pattern. The first indication that a baby perceives another comes between the fourth and sixth months of life. A month or two later, the baby smiles at other babies and shows an interest in their crying. Between the ninth and thirteenth months, however, interest in other babies increases and is shown in attempts to explore their clothes and hair, to imitate their behavior and vocalization, to cooperate in the use of toys, and in fighting when a toy is taken away by another baby. From the thirteenth to eighteenth month, the baby's interest shifts from play materials to his playmate, resulting in a decrease in fighting for toys and an increase in a cooperative use of them. During the last 6 months of babyhood, the baby is definitely interested in play with others and uses play materials to establish social relationships with them [16].

PLAY

Play, or any activity that is engaged in for the enjoyment it gives, begins in a simple form in babyhood. It consists primarily of random movements and of stimulation of the sense organs. The free, spontaneous play of babies is characterized by lack of rules and regulations and is more often solitary than social. At first, the baby derives enjoyment from stimulating his sense organs and from playing with his limbs. By the time he is three months old, control of his hands is developed well enough to enable him to play with toys. At this age, he also derives enjoyment from turning from back to side, kicking, bouncing, wiggling, reaching for his toes, and watching his fingers move.

Between the fifth and eighth months, play is less random and consists of play with the toes, bouncing, squirming, head shaking, pulling himself to a standing position, and cooperative motor games, such as pat-a-cake. In the last quarter of the first year of life, the baby's play consists mainly of kicking, bouncing, leaning over the arm of a chair, rolling, playing with his toes, crawling for a toy, pulling himself to a sitting position, standing, climbing, moving furniture, and babbling.

During the baby's second year, play becomes more organized and toys are used for many of the different playful activities. Characteristically, the fifteen-month-old baby's play consists of endless exercise of walking activities, throwing and picking up objects and then throwing them again, and of putting them in and taking them out of receptacles. Owing to his poor muscle coordinations, the baby is often destructive in play with his toys or in his exploratory manipulation of objects in his environment. He does not, for example, mean to break a necklace he grabs for, nor does he mean to pull the tail off of a favorite stuffed animal. At eighteen months, the baby pulls toys, carries or hugs a doll or stuffed animal, imitates many adult activities, such as reading a newspaper or sweeping, and actively gets into everything. At this age, his play is solitary and his role when other children are present is that of an onlooker.

In the last half of the second year, the baby feels, pats, and pounds his toys, he is interested in dolls and stuffed animals, he strings wooden beads, he puts them in and takes them out of holes in the top of boxes, transports blocks in wagons rather than building with them, scribbles with crayons, and imitates activities of persons in his environment. When he is with other children, he does not play with them but his play is parallel with theirs. There is little social give-and-take but much grabbing and snatching of another child's toys [26].

Games and Amusements. Before a baby is a year old, he plays simple little "mother games" with adults or older children. Finger play, peek-a-boo, pat-a-cake, pigs to market, mirror play, and hide-and-seek behind a handkerchief, a piece of cloth, or furniture are the traditional "mother games" that almost every American baby learns. A baby likes to be amused by being sung to, by listening to music, or by having someone tell him a story. He enjoys having someone point out pictures in a book or even looking at the pictures himself. While he understands little of what he hears, he enjoys the rhythmic sounds of nursery rhymes and lullabies. He also is fascinated by hearing stories about himself, familiar persons, animals, or household objects.

BEGINNINGS OF UNDERSTANDING

Because a baby begins life with no understanding of what he observes in his environment, he must acquire, through maturation and learning, a meaning of what he observes. What meanings he acquires will depend partly on the level of his intelligence and partly on his previous experiences. And, as meanings are acquired, he will interpret new experiences in terms of memories of previous experiences. The association of ideas with objects and situations results in the development of *concepts.*

The baby's *behavior* shows that, at an early age, concepts develop rapidly. For example, his recognition of familiar persons and objects in his environment is shown through his pleasurable responses just as recognition of strange persons and objects is accompanied by fear. Likewise, his responses to his toys, the sight of his outdoor clothes, or the family pet all give indications of his understanding of what they mean. At first, he responds to the total situation rather to any one part of it. As a result, when objects and situations have elements in common they are responded to as if they were the same [76].

The baby's earliest perceptions come through the use of sensory exploration. He looks at, listens to, touches, smells, and tastes anything he can get into his hands. Later, as muscle coordination develops, he is able to acquire more meanings through handling whatever is within his reach. He discovers smoothness, roughness, softness, warmth, and other qualities which would not be apparent if he were limited to the use of sense organs alone. Then, as he reaches the end of babyhood, he begins to put together words into sentences. These are generally in the form of questions, beginning with "who," "what," or "why" [57].

As early as the first year of life, the baby's behavior indicates that he is interpreting new experiences in terms of old. By the time he is two years old, he is capable of making simple generalizations based on similar experiences in which he has observed relationships [48]. The baby's limited knowledge and experience result in his inability to distinguish between living and inanimate objects. As a result, he believes that all objects are animate and have the same qualities as human beings [76].

Space concepts are poor at first. When the baby reaches for an object, he more often reaches in the wrong direction than in the right. Finally, by trial and error, he reaches the object. He rarely reaches for an object more than 20 inches away when he is a year old. This would indicate that he has some estimate of distance. Likewise, concepts of weight are very inaccurate at first. The baby perceives a small object as light in weight and a large object as heavy. As a result of this error in perception, he frequently drops the things he is examining because he has not made the necessary muscular adjustment to hold the object that proves to be heavier than he had anticipated [26].

Concepts of time are also very inaccurate. A baby has no idea of the length of time needed for a specific job, such as feeding himself or putting on his clothes. Furthermore, he has no concept of time duration and, if it were not for a fairly rigid daily schedule, he would not know morning from afternoon. By the time he is two years old, the average baby knows and uses time words, such as "today" [67]. Concepts of self appear earlier than concepts of other people. Through watching and handling the different parts of his body and by looking into a mirror, the baby discovers meanings about his body. However, he does not distinguish between himself and the environment as early as he distinguishes other people from the environment. The ability to distinguish between himself and other people, as shown in shyness in the presence of others, comes in the latter part of the first year. The genitals become a focal point of interest early in life because of their association with the excretory functions. Also, they can be stimulated by patting and touching [6].

Social concepts, or the understanding of the thoughts, feelings, and emotional reactions of others, are likewise in the formative stage of development in babyhood. During the first half year of life, the baby can distinguish persons by the tone of their voices and by their facial expressions. He can distinguish angry, frightened, and friendly voices. At one month, he can differentiate the human voice from other sounds; at three months, he smiles when people come near him, though he smiles at an angry person in the same way as he does at one who looks friendly. He can distinguish between familiar and unfamiliar persons at five months of age, and he responds to an angry face with crying, though it is not until he is eight months old that he responds to the emotional behavior of others in such a way as to indicate an understanding of their facial expressions [63]. There is little evidence, even by the end of babyhood, that the baby understands the underlying meaning of what he observes in others [26].

The earliest indication of *aesthetic perception* is to be found in color preferences. While babies at three months of age look at colors twice as long as at gray, there is no significant difference in their response to different colors. But, from the ages of six to twenty-four months, babies respond differently to different colors, with the order of preference as follows: red, yellow, blue, and green [16]. *Music appreciation* is shown in the baby's liking for music, especially that with a tune such as one finds in lullabies. Many an emotional outburst can be quieted by singing to the baby.

A baby perceives vocal play or babbling as *comic* at four months of age and he enjoys tormenting people who dress him or feed him. He also likes to blow bubbles in water given him to drink and at six months old, he derives enjoyment from dropping things that have been handed to him. At nine months, watching things fall, such as a splash made by milk falling from his mouth onto the floor, is perceived as comic. When he is a year old, he likes to make funny faces and, several months later, hiding from people and laughing when they cannot find him is a source of much amusement. The two-year-old is amused by trying to squeeze through a narrow place or by carrying out different kinds of stunts [47].

MORAL ATTITUDES AND BEHAVIOR

The baby has no conscience and no scale of values. He is, therefore, neither moral nor immoral but *nonmoral* in the sense that his behavior is not guided by moral standards [31]. Eventually he will learn, from his parents and later from his teachers and playmates, the moral codes of the group and the necessity for conforming to these codes. This will be done partly by imitating the behavior of those with whom he comes in contact and partly from the teachings of his parents and others in authority. Learning to behave in a socially approved manner is a long, slow process extending through childhood and into adolescence. However, the foundations are laid in babyhood and on these foundations, the child builds a moral code which guides his behavior as he grows older) [35].

The baby's behavior is guided by impulse. He judges right and wrong in relation to the pleasure or pain of the act rather than in terms of the good or harm to the group. Because of his limited intelligence, he cannot judge behavior in terms of how it affects others but only in terms of its effect on him. An act, therefore, is perceived by him as wrong only when it has some ill effect on him. He has no sense of guilt because he lacks definite standards of right and wrong. He does not, for example, feel guilty when he takes things belonging to others because he has no standards of property rights.

Discipline. The whole purpose of discipline is to teach the individual what is right and what is wrong and to see that he acts in accordance with this knowledge. As Geisel has stressed, "The infant comes among us as a little savage, and the first fifteen years of his life are in a very real sense the disciplinary years, for his growing up is really a process of learning to do right things at the right time, in the right place, and meaningfully" [24]. Throughout the babyhood years, the baby must learn to make correct specific responses to specific situations in the home and in the neighborhood. It is important at all ages, but especially during the early years of life when moral habits are being established, that discipline be consistent. Acts that are wrong should be wrong at all times, regardless of who is in charge. Otherwise, it will be confusing to the baby and he will not know what is expected of him.

With strict discipline, involving emphasis on punishment for wrongdoing, even a young baby can be forced into a pattern of behavior that makes him less troublesome to his parents during the second year of life when his exploratory behavior and his refusal to comply with parental wishes make him less easy to handle than he was during the first year. However, as Dubois has pointed out, "Parents must think in terms not only of the immediate behavior at two, six, or sixteen years . . . but also of the ultimate results of discipline at twenty, forty, and sixty, when parental control is no longer in force" [21]. Before the baby is punished for wrongdoing, he must *learn* what is wrong. This he cannot do overnight. Therefore, during babyhood, the emphasis should be on the educational aspect of discipline, teaching the baby what is right and what is wrong, and on rewarding him with approval and affection when he does what is right, rather than on punishment, which should be reserved for *intentional wrongdoing.* If parent-child relationships are to remain favorable and if the baby is to develop a healthy personality pattern, punishment should be kept to a minimum and should be reserved for emergencies when the baby's persistence in doing something he has been told not to do might lead to physical or psychological harm [30].

FAMILY RELATIONSHIPS

The individual's attitudes and behavior throughout life are markedly influenced by his early experiences. And, because the baby's early environment is primarily limited to the home, family relationships play a dominant role in determining what sort of individual he will grow up to be. His parents, brothers and sisters, grandparents, and other relatives who come in more or less constant contact with him during these early formative years of life set the pattern for his attitudes toward people, things, and life in general. While this pattern will unquestionably be changed and modified as he grows older and as his environment broadens, the core of the pattern is likely to remain with little or no modification. During the first year of life, the baby's behavior is influenced more by maternal handling than by any other environmental factor; during the second year, the birth of a sibling may lead to great emotional maladjustment [37].

The importance of the parent-child relationship in the early part of life can best be illustrated by cases where babies have been separated from their mothers and are institutionalized. When deprived of an opportunity to love and be loved, babies are retarded in their normal physical and mental development, as well as in speech and socialization, and the pattern of their personality is often seriously affected. The baby deprived of normal opportunities to express love becomes quiet, listless, and unresponsive to the smiles of others; he shows extreme forms of temper as if seeking attention; and he gives the general appearance of unhappiness [9]. If the separation from the mother lasts no longer than 3 months, the reestablishment of emotional interchange with the mother will rapidly restore the developmental level of the baby. When, on the other hand, emotional interchange with the mother is lacking for 5 or more months, the baby's development has been found to continue to decline in comparison with the development of other babies of the same age [54].

When a baby is deprived of close contact with the mother, as is true of institutionalized babies, the substitution of one person to care for the baby in place of several brings about changes in the baby's behavior. Not only does the baby with a "mother substitute" learn to discriminate and show recognition of this mother substitute but he also shows an improvement in the pattern of his development as compared with babies deprived of this type of social contact. In sitting, standing, and vocalization, babies with mother substitutes have been found to develop faster than babies cared for by several people. Figure 18 shows the comparison of vocalization for an experimental group of babies who had mother substitutes and for a control group which did not have the care of one person. Not only did the provision for a mother substitute make the babies more responsive to the person who acted in this role but they also became socially more responsive to strangers instead of showing fear as the babies of the control group did. This shows not only the importance of close personal contact with one person during the early months of life,

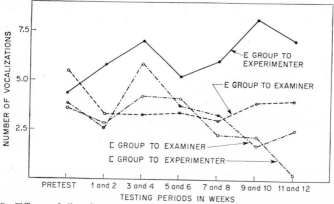

Fig. 18. Effect of "mothering" on vocalization during babyhood. (*From H. L. Rheingold, The modification of social responsiveness in institutional babies. Monogr. Soc. Res. Child Develpm., 1956, 21, No. 2. Used by permission.*)

but it also shows that the social behavior of babies can be modified by environmental influences [53].

The seriousness of unfavorable parent-child relationships during the early years of life has been stressed thus by Ribble: "Poor relationship with the parents leads to reactions in the infant which tend to become the basis of adult personality disorders" [54]. However, this tendency may be offset by favorable experiences later in life. Even though the individual suffered, as an infant, from emotional deprivation or some other unfavorable factor in his relationship with his parents, later gratifications may compensate for this and the result will be a healthy personality. On the other hand, satisfying experiences in babyhood will not necessarily be adequate to compensate for unfavorable factors in the parent-child relationship or for economic deprivation as the child grows older. Although it is true that the foundations of attitudes, behavior patterns, and the personality structure are laid in babyhood, events of childhood and the later years are of great importance in reinforcing or even changing the character structure tentatively formed in the early years of life [51].

Child-training Methods. No one practice or method in doing things makes for good or bad adjustment on the child's part. It is the *attitude* of the parent toward the child that determines how well or how poorly he will adjust at home and outside the home [72]. There are marked variations in the child-training methods used by different social classes

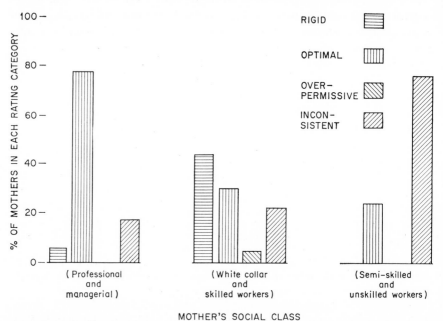

FIG. 19. Relationship between mother's social class membership and her predominant type of child-care practice. (*From E. H. Klatskin, E. B. Jackson, and L. C. Wilkin, The influence of degree of flexibility in maternal child care practices on early child behavior. Amer. J. Orthopsychiat., 1956, 26, 79–93. Used by permission.*)

and by different parents within the same social class [37] (see Figure 19). Parents generally use child-training methods similar to those used by their parents. When, however, parents have been brought up in homes where different methods were used, there is likely to be a conflict as to which is the better method to use, or parents will make certain modifications in their methods. The mother's perception of her role as mother and the type of personality she has will markedly influence her interpretation of the methods she uses [14].

During babyhood, most of the emphasis in child training is on eating, sleeping, and toileting. In training the baby in these areas, the methods used may be *authoritarian* or *democratic.* In the former, the parent is strict and uses punishment to enforce compliance; in the latter, the parent is more permissive, more understanding of the baby's needs and capacities, more lenient, and less punitive. Parents who are better educated are more likely to be more permissive in their child-training methods than are those whose education has been limited [63]. Parents from the middle socioeconomic group are more exacting in their training, they begin training earlier, and they expect greater compliance on the baby's part than do parents from the upper and lower classes [37]. The method of training the parents use and their attitude toward the baby's reactions to the training will have a marked influence on their relationships with the baby.

Changes in Parent-Child Relationships. The relationship between the baby and his parents is not static but changes as the baby changes from a helpless, dependent individual to a relatively independent one. With this change in relationship comes a variation in parental attitudes from acceptance to rejection, and then back to acceptance. Whether the parental attitude will be one of acceptance or rejection will depend to a large extent upon the changing characteristics of the baby [18]. As the baby grows older and becomes more independent, there is a decrease in warmth and increase in restrictiveness on the part of the parents [10]. Only in exceptional cases where there is parental rejection does the young baby experience anything but a warm and loving relationship with his parents and other members of the family. Should he be the first-born, this loving relationship will be accompanied by more attention and companionship from his parents than would be true of a second or later-born baby.

Because early babyhood is a period of extreme helplessness, it is common for parents to develop the habit of caring for and protecting the baby so completely that the baby's motivation to learn to do things for himself tends to be stifled. The first-born child of the family is more likely to be the victim of parental overprotectiveness and to develop habits of dependency than is the later-born child, except when the later-born child is physically or mentally weak. Because of these parental attitudes of overprotectiveness, the first-born child develops into an overly dependent child more often than do his siblings who have not been subjected to such treatment [60].

Overdependency of the child may be instigated by the parent, usually the mother, who is overprotective. Or, it may be instigated by the baby and willingly or unwillingly acceded to by the mother. In babyhood, there are two critical periods when overdependency may begin. The first comes at the end of the first year of life when the baby tests the mother to see if he can depend on her. At this age, the baby is still very helpless and his needs must be met since lack of attention to these needs will be harmful to his developing personality. But many mothers go beyond the baby's needs and do not encourage independence when it is possible. The second critical period comes at the end of the second year when there are social demands on the individual to change his old ways of doing things. This causes the baby to cling, if possible, to his status of infantile dependency instead of trying to develop independence [69].

When the baby's motivation to be independent of parental help is very strong, it expresses itself in a conflict between parent and child. This conflict usually begins during the latter part of the second year of life and is characterized by frequent and violent temper outbursts. Furthermore, because parental overprotectiveness retards the normal pattern of learning skills, a baby is likely to become angry at himself and at anyone near him if he cannot do what he sets out to do. This is likely to lead to a changed relationship between parent and child.

A baby needs the continuous care of one person for the first nine to twelve months of his life to give him a feeling of security. The mother is the only person who can be relied upon for this. Being deprived of the mother's care at this time is one of the most serious factors in his physical, intellectual, and emotional development [46]. As Ribble has stressed, the baby's "deepest need by far is the understanding care of one consistent individual, his mother." Professional nurses, relatives, or friends of the family will not give the baby the continuous care he needs. When babies are deprived of this, they are found to have, as they grow older, "diffusely impulsive patterned behavior that is unorganized and remains unorganized. . . . The behavior remains infantile" [54].

Because the mother is the baby's most frequent companion in his play activities and because the mother takes care of his bodily needs, the beginning of a preference for the mother is generally apparent toward the close of babyhood. A father who spends a reasonable amount of time with his baby, who shares with the mother some of the routine duties connected with baby care, and who gives his undivided attention to playing with the baby when he is with him will win as much of the baby's affection as does the mother.

For a child who is still in the period of babyhood, the birth of another child in the family is not as disturbing as it would be later on. While it is true that he will miss the constant attention that he has been accustomed to receive from his parents, his social development has not yet reached the point where he wants constant attention from others. While trying out his newly acquired skills and exploring his environment, he is satisfied to be alone with only an occasional glance of approval or commendation from an adult. His limited intelligence does not enable him to associate the change in his relationship with his parents with the newcomer in the home and, consequently, he is not jealous.

PERSONALITY

Personality does not consist of a sum of traits but an integration and organization of traits into a pattern. The "core" or "center of gravity" of this pattern is made up of attitudes and habits that are fixed early in life but are subject to change and modification as the individual grows older and his life experiences broaden and change [48]. The attitudes and habits which constitute the core of the personality pattern are centered around the individual and thus constitute his concept of himself as an individual. This concept is based on a "mirror image" of himself; that is, his feelings about himself reflect his interpretation of the way important people in his life, his parents and siblings when he is young and his teachers and peers as he grows older, feel about him and how they treat him [16].

At birth, the potential qualities for personality development are present, and from these the pattern of personality will develop. There are three factors inherent in the individual's personality development— *heredity, early experiences* within the family, and *events of later life,* which influence the form of the pattern already set in the early years of life [3]. As Rainwater has pointed out, "Personality is formed from the interaction of significant figures (first the mother, later the father and siblings, later extrafamilial figures) in his environment with the child. The child brings to this interaction a certain biological constitution, certain needs and drives, and certain intellectual capacities which determine his reactions to the way in which he is acted upon by these significant figures" [52]. Because no two individuals have the same physical or mental endowments or the same environmental experiences, no two personality patterns will develop along the same lines or become identical.

Critical Period. Babyhood is a "critical period" in the development of personality because at this time the foundations are laid, and upon these foundations will be built the adult personality structure. Although adults may remember little of what happened in the early years of their lives, these experiences have been of vital importance in the shaping of their personalities and have left lasting impressions upon them [32]. Because the baby's environment is limited almost exclusively to the home and because his parents, but especially his mother, are his most constant companions, there is no question about the fact that the individual's personality is markedly influenced by the parent-child relationship in babyhood. As new channels of self-expression open up with the development of motor control, the baby will become rebellious and antagonistic if the parents oppose him. Should he be fortunate enough to have an environment which fosters the development of his personality, he will develop into a cooperative and responsive individual [1].

How greatly environmental obstructions affect the personality development of the baby has been suggested by studies of institutionalized babies, reported in the section on "Family Relationships." While it is not certain whether the damage is permanent or temporary if the baby remains in an institution for only the first three or four years of life, there is evidence that if he remains longer, the personality distortion will be severe and long-lasting [9]. Almost as serious as emotional deprivation is the baby's constant contact with a mother who shows periodic mood swings. Follow-up studies of such babies at later stages of development have suggested that such contacts in babyhood may be the forerunner of psychopathy in older children [64]. There is evidence that functions which are most actively developing at the time when some unfavorable environmental condition occurs are most subject to damage. For example, when the baby is developing independence, being overprotected is especially harmful. Thus, "mothering" per se is not harmful, but the wrong type of mother-child relationship is at the basis of personality distortions [71].

Personality Foundations. Genetic studies of the persistence of personality traits over a period of years have revealed that patterns established early in life remain almost unchanged as the child grows older. While it is true that certain traits of the personality pattern change, the "core" consisting of the self concept remains fundamentally the same. Only when radical steps are taken, or when there is a marked change in the environmental factors responsible for shaping this core, will a change be made in the concept of self established during the early years of life. This emphasizes the importance of early experiences in the shaping of the personality pattern.

As Breckenridge and Vincent have emphasized, "Some personalities are far more flexible than others, and change radically under radical changes in environment; others have a 'granite-like' quality which withstands the impact even of the most radical changes of environment" [16]. The personality traits that have been found to be the most persistent are those associated with physical development, intelligence, and temperament; those that are least persistent are the traits associated with social experiences, such as attitudes, values, and introversion or extroversion. The most variable traits are those which involve social relations [48].

Because change in personality is largely dependent upon changes in environment and because the home environment of the individual is least likely to change during the early years of life, the foundations of personality laid in early life are likely to persist in a relatively unchanged form as the baby grows older. When changes do occur, they may be *quantitative,* in that there is a strengthening or weakening of a trait already present, or they may be *qualitative,* in that a socially undesirable trait is replaced by a socially more desirable one. For the most part, personality changes consist mainly of building up traits already present instead of establishing new and different ones [16, 48].

While the core of personality is in the process of becoming established, as is true of babyhood and early childhood, undesirable personality traits can be changed without disturbing the whole personality balance. As time goes on, the core of habits and attitudes, especially those that are closely related to the individual's concept of self, becomes less and less flexible. Then a change in personality traits may upset the personality balance. For that reason, it is vitally important that the attitudes and habits that compose the core of personality be of the sort that will be just as serviceable in adulthood as they will be while the child is young. A child who is aggressive at two is likely to be consistently aggressive as he grows older. Similarly, a child who is shy is likely to seek the type of environment that will encourage the development of this trait, avoiding the types of environment that would make him feel ill at ease or self-conscious. As a result, his shyness will likely become stronger rather than weaker with age.

A number of studies of the same groups of children from babyhood into late childhood or adolescence have revealed the "prophetic character" of the first year's behavior traits. Not only have these studies revealed persistence in the dominant pattern of personality as it is established in the first years of life, but they have also suggested that it is possible to formulate a prognosis of the baby's future personality early in the first year of life. Marked consistency in the personality traits of "Shirley's Babies," for example, was noted during the first years of their lives. Fifteen and a half years later, there was definite evidence that personality similarities had persisted and some of the individuals could readily be identified because of the uniqueness of their personality patterns [49]. A study of six individuals 50 years after their mother had recorded judgments about them in her diary shows a persistence in 70 per cent of those traits. In general, the favorable traits became more favorable and the less favorable improved through the influence of social pressures as the individuals grew older [61]. Because all experimental evidence to date indicates that personality traits established in babyhood are likely to remain relatively unchanged throughout life, unless remedial measures are used to bring about changes, it is apparent that babyhood is justly called a "critical age" in the development of personality.

BIBLIOGRAPHY

1. Aldrich, C. A.: The pediatrician looks at personality. *Amer. J. Orthopsychiat.*, 1947, 17, 571–574.
2. Aldrich, C. A., C. Sung, and C. Knop: The crying of newly born babies. *J. Pediat.*, 1945, 26, 313–326; 27, 89–96, 428–435.

3. Alexander, F.: The dynamics of personality development. *Soc. Casewk*, 1951, 32, 139–143.

4. Ames, L. B.: Motor correlates of infant crying. *J. genet. Psychol.*, 1941, 59, 239–247.

5. Ames, L. B.: Development of interpersonal smiling responses in the preschool years. *J. genet. Psychol.*, 1949, 74, 273–291.

6. Ames, L. B.: The sense of self of nursery school children as manifested by their verbal behavior. *J. genet. Psychol.*, 1952, 81, 193–232.

7. Aserinsky, E., and N. Kleitman: A motility cycle in sleeping infants as manifested by ocular and gross bodily activity. *J. appl. Physiol.*, 1955, 8, 11–18.

8. Bain, R.: Making normal people. *Marriage Fam. Living*, 1954, 16, 27–31.

9. Bakwin, H.: Emotional deprivation in infants. *J. Pediat.*, 1949, 35, 512–521.

10. Baldwin, A. L.: Changes in parent behavior during childhood. *Amer. Psychologist*, 1947, 2, 425–426.

11. Banham, K. M.: The development of differential behavior in infancy. *J. genet. Psychol.*, 1950, 76, 283–289.

12. Banham, K. M.: Senescence and emotions: a genetic theory. *J. genet. Psychol.*, 1951, 78, 175–183.

13. Banham, K. M.: Obstinate children are adaptable. *Ment. Hyg., N.Y.*, 1952, 36, 84–89.

14. Behers, M. L.: Child rearing and the character structure of the mother. *Child Develpm.*, 1954, 25, 225–238.

15. Blau, T. H., and L. R. Blau: The sucking reflex: the effects of long feeding vs. short feeding on the behavior of the human infant. *J. abnorm. soc. Psychol.*, 1955, 51, 123–125.

16. Breckenridge, M. E., and E. L. Vincent: *Child development*, 3d ed. Philadelphia: Saunders, 1955.

17. Bousfield, W. A., and W. D. Orbison: Ontogenesis of emotional behavior. *Psychol. Rev.*, 1952, 59, 1–7.

18. Coleman, W. R., E. Kris, and S. Provence: The study of variations of early parental attitudes. *Psychoanal. Stud. Child*, 1954, 8, 20–47.

19. Cooke, R. E.: The behavioral response of infants to heat stress. *Yale J. biol. Med.*, 1952, 24, 334–340.

20. Dennis, W., and P. Najarian: Infant development under environmental handicap. *Psychol. Monogr.*, 1957, 71, No. 7.

21. DuBois, F. S.: The security of discipline. *Ment. Hyg., N.Y.*, 1952, 36, 353–371.

22. Freeman, H. E., and M. Showel: The role of the family in the socialization process. *J. soc. Psychol.*, 1953, 39, 97–101.

23. Garn, S. M.: Fat thickness and growth progress during infancy. *Hum. Biol.*, 1956, 28, 232–250.

24. Geisel, G. B.: Discipline viewed as a developmental need of the child. *Nerv. Child*, 1951, 9, 115–121.

25. Gesell, A.: The ontogenesis of infant behavior. *In* L. Carmichael, *Manual of child psychology*, 2d ed. New York: Wiley, 1954. Pp. 335–373.

26. Gesell, A., and F. L. Ilg: *Child development*. New York: Harper, 1949.

27. Gutteridge, M. V.: A study of motor achievements of young children. *Arch. Psychol., N.Y.*, 1939, No. 244.

28. Hanlon, C. R., J. B. Butchart, and P. R. Kempf: Injuries in childhood. *J. Pediat.*, 1949, 34, 688–698.

29. Harding, V. S. V.: A method of evaluating osseous development from birth to 14 years. *Child Develpm.*, 1952, 23, 247–271.

30. Havighurst, R. J.: The function of successful discipline. *Understanding the Child*, 1952, 21, 35–38.

31. Havighurst, R. J.: *Human development and education.* New York: Longmans, 1953.

32. Hay-Shaw, C.: Maintenance of mental health. *Ment. Hlth, Lond.*, 1949, 9, 3–6.

33. Hildreth, G.: The development and training of hand dominance. *J. genet. Psychol.*, 1949, 75, 197–220; 1950, 76, 39–100.

34. Jersild, A. T.: Emotional development. *In* L. Carmichael, *Manual of child psychology*, 2d ed. New York: Wiley, 1954. Pp. 833–917.

35. Jones, V.: Character development in children—an objective approach. *In* L. Carmichael, *Manual of child psychology*, 2d ed. New York: Wiley, 1954. Pp. 781–832.

36. Key, C. B., M. R. White, W. P. Honzig, A. B. Heimey, and D. Erwin: The process of learning to dress among nursery school children. *Genet. Psychol. Monogr.*, 1936, 18, 67–163.

37. Klatskin, E. H., E. B. Jackson, and L. C. Wilkin: The influence of degree of flexibility in maternal child care practices on early child behavior. *Amer. J. Orthopsychiat.*, 1956, 26, 79–93.

38. Kleitman, N., and T. G. Englemann: Sleep characteristics of infants. *J. appl. Physiol.*, 1953, 6, 269–282.

39. Krogman, W. M.: The physical growth of the child. *In* M. Fishbein and R. J. R. Kennedy, *Modern marriage and family living.* New York: Oxford Univer. Press, 1957. Pp. 417–425.

40. Lakin, M.: Personality factors in mothers of excessively crying (colicky) infants. *Monogr. Soc. Res. Child Develpm.*, 1957, 22, No. 1.

41. Lewis, M. M.: *Infant speech: a study of the beginnings of language*, 2d ed. New York: Humanities Press, 1951.

42. Lombard, O. M.: Breadth of bone and muscle by age and sex in childhood. *Child Develpm.*, 1950, 21, 229–239.

43. Lynip, A. W.: The use of magnetic devices in the collection and analysis of the preverbal utterances of an infant. *Genet. Psychol. Monogr.*, 1951, 44, 221–262.

44. Margolese, M. S.: Mental disorders in childhood due to endocrine disorders. *Nerv. Child*, 1948, 7, 55–77.

45. McCarthy, D.: Language development. *In* L. Carmichael, *Manual of child psychology*, 2d ed. New York: Wiley, 1954, Pp. 492–630.

46. Mead, M.: Some theoretical considerations on the problem of mother-child separation. *Amer. J. Orthopsychiat.*, 1954, 24, 471–483.

47. Merry, F. K., and R. V. Merry: *The first two decades of life*, 2d ed., New York: Harper, 1958.

48. Munn, N. L. *The evolution and growth of human behavior.* New York: Houghton Mifflin, 1955.

49. Neilon, P.: Shirley's babies after fifteen years: a personality study. *J. genet. Psychol.*, 1948, 73, 175–186.

50. Norval, M. A., and R. L. J. Kennedy: Illnesses within the first year of life. *J. Pediat.*, 1949, 35, 43–48.

51. O'Connor, N.: The evidence for the permanently disturbing effects of mother-child separation. *Acta Psychol.*, 1956, 12, 174–197.

52. Rainwater, L.: A study of personality differences between middle and lower class adolescents: the Szondi Test in culture-personality research. *Genet. Psychol. Monogr.*, 1956, 54, 3–86.

53. Rheingold, H. L.: The modification of social responsiveness in institutional babies. *Monogr. Soc. Res. Child Develpm.*, 1956, 21, No. 2.

54. Ribble, M. A.: *The rights of infants.* New York: Columbia Univer. Press, 1943.

55. Rosenzweig, S.: Babies are taught to cry: an hypothesis. *Ment. Hyg., N.Y.,* 1954, 38, 81–84.

56. Rowan-Legg, C. E.: Self-demand feeding in infants. *Canad. med. Ass. J.,* 1949, 60, 388–391.

57. Russell, D. H.: The development of thinking processes. *Rev. educ. Res.,* 1953, 23, 137–145.

58. Ryan, M. E.: Social adjustment of kindergarten children ten years later. *Smith Coll. Stud. soc. Wk,* 1949, 19, 138–139.

59. Scott, R. B., et al.: Growth and development of Negro infants. III. Growth during the first year of life as observed in private pediatric practice. *J. Pediat.,* 1950, 37, 885–893.

60. Sears, R. R.: Ordinal position in the family as a psychological variable. *Amer. J. Sociol.,* 1950, 15, 397–401.

61. Smith, M. E.: A comparison of certain personality traits as rated in the same individuals in childhood and fifty years later. *Child Develpm.,* 1952, 29, 159–180.

62. Sontag, L. W.: Some psychosomatic aspects of childhood. *Nerv. Child,* 1946, 5, 296–304.

63. Spitz, R. A.: The smiling response: a contribution to the ontogenesis of social relations. *Genet. Psychol. Monogr.,* 1946, 34, 57–125.

64. Spitz, R. A.: The role of ecological factors in emotional development in infancy. *Child Develpm.,* 1949, 20, 145–155.

65. Spitz, R. A.: Purposive grasping. *Personality,* 1951, 1, 144–148.

66. Spriesterbach, D. C., and J. F. Curtis: Misarticulation and discrimination of speech sounds. *Quart. J. Speech,* 1951, 37, 483–491.

67. Springer, D. V.: Development in young children of an understanding of time and the clock. *J. genet. Psychol.,* 1952, 80, 83–96.

68. Staples, R., and G. W. Smith: Attitudes of grandmothers and mothers toward child-rearing practices. *Child Develpm.,* 1954, 25, 91–97.

69. Stendler, C. B.: Critical periods in socialization and over-dependency. *Child Develpm.,* 1952, 23, 3–12.

70. Stewart, A. H., et al.: Excessive infant crying (colic) in relation to parent behavior. *Amer. J. Psychiat.,* 1954, 110, 687–694.

71. Stone, L. J.: A critique of studies of infant isolation. *Child Develpm.,* 1954, 25, 9–20.

72. Stout, I. W., and G. Langdon: A study of the home life of well-adjusted children. *J. educ. Sociol.,* 1950, 23, 442–460.

73. Sweet, C.: Enuresis: a psychologic problem of childhood. *J. Amer. med. Ass.,* 1946, 32, 279–281.

74. Terman, L. M., and M. A. Merrill: *Measuring intelligence.* Boston: Houghton Mifflin, 1937.

75. Thompson, H.: Physical growth. *In* L. Carmichael, *Manual of child psychology,* 2d ed. New York: Wiley, 1954. Pp. 292–334.

76. Vinacke, W. E.: Concept formation in children of school age. *Education,* 1954, 74, 527–534.

77. Werner, H., and E. Kaplan: The acquisition of word meanings: a developmental study. *Monogr. Soc. Res. Child Develpm.,* 1950, 51, No. 1.

78. Williams, J. R., and R. B. Scott: Growth and development of Negro infants. II. Motor development and its relationship to child rearing practices in two groups of Negro infants. *Child Develpm.,* 1953, 24, 103–121.

》 5 《

Early Childhood

Early childhood extends from two to six years of age. At the one end, it is marked by the conclusion of babyhood, (the age when helplessness decreases and is gradually replaced by growing independence,) and at the other end, by the entrance into school. Because six years of age is the beginning of the compulsory school period in our culture, it serves as a convenient dividing line between early and late childhood. Early childhood is called the "preschool age" by educators because it is the period preceding the entrance into school. A growing number of children, it is true, are going to nursery schools and kindergartens, but these are *preschools*, not school proper. To the psychologist, early childhood is the "pregang age," the time when the child is learning the foundations of social behavior which will prepare him for the more highly organized social life he will be required to adjust to when he enters first grade in school.

Early childhood is the period in the life span when the major development is that of control over the environment. Having acquired a workable control of his own body during the first two years of life, the child is now ready to explore his environment. No longer is he satisfied to be a spectator. He wants to know what his environment is, how it works, how it feels, and how he can be a part of it. This includes people as well as inanimate objects.

Dawn of Problem Behavior. While parents are interested in their children at every age, the home interest in the young child is less sentimental and more practical than it was during babyhood. Most of the problems that parents face with babies center around their physical care. With the dawn of childhood, the child presents many behavior problems for his parents to cope with. He is developing a distinctive personality and is demanding an independence which, in most cases, he is incapable of handling successfully. A young child is often an obstinate, stubborn, disobedient, negativistic, antagonistic individual. He has frequent temper tantrums, he is bothered by nightmares at night and irrational fears during the day, and he suffers from jealousies. All in all, life for the parents and the young child is frequently far from happy. And yet, a "good" child who conforms so completely to adult standards and expectations that he gives his parents little concern is headed for trouble.

PHYSICAL DEVELOPMENT

Growth during early childhood proceeds at a slow rate as compared with the rapid rate of growth in babyhood. A comparison of the percentage of growth in height and weight at this time will show how slow it is. The 50 per cent increase in height which occurred during the first year of life drops to 8 per cent between the ages of three to four years and still lower, to 5 per cent, between five and six years. The 200 per cent increase in weight during the first year of life, which dropped to between 25 and 30 per cent during the second year, drops still further to 12 per cent in the period between three and six years [64]. Early childhood is a time of relatively even growth, though there are seasonal variations, with July to mid-December the most favorable season for increases in weight and April to mid-August the most favorable for height increases [107].

The average increase in *height* is 3 inches annually. By the age of six years, the average child measures 46.5 inches, with a range from 44.5 to 48.5 inches. While marked individual differences occur, there are no real sex differences in height during this period [64]. Children of superior intelligence tend to be taller during the preschool period than those of average intelligence [107]. It is now possible to predict with a fair degree of accuracy the adult height of a young child by X rays of the bones of his wrist and hand [13]. Furthermore, because the young child's height is influenced by hereditary tendencies, his parents' height must be taken into consideration in predicting his adult height [12].

Weight, like height, develops at a slow rate during this period, with an average increase of 3 to 5 pounds annually. At the age of six years, the child should be approximately seven times his birth weight. The average girl weighs 48.5 pounds, with a range from 40.5 to 56.5 pounds, and the average boy, 49 pounds, with a range from 43 to 55 pounds [64]. Variations in weight during this period, as the ranges suggest, are greater than variations in height. Family influences are partially responsible for weight variations as the child's body build, which influences his weight, tends to resemble that of his parents [12]. In addition, this is the age when bad family eating habits and parental insistence on the child's eating more than he may want or need are likely to result in a tendency to over-weight [108].

Body Proportions. During early childhood, body proportions change and the "baby look" disappears. Changes in proportions follow the *law of developmental direction* (see Figure 14, page 82). At 5½ years, for example, the proportions have changed to such a point that, from then until maturity, there will be an increase of over 50 per cent in the arm span as compared with only a 7 per cent increase in head circumference. The surface area of the *head* is 13 per cent of the total body surface area as contrasted with 21 per cent at birth [107]. The cranial region in rela-tion to the face has a ratio of 1 to 5 at five years as compared with a ratio of 1 to 8 at birth. At six years, the circumference of the head is 90 per cent of its adult size and its weight is 90 per cent of the adult weight. There is an appreciable increase in both the length and width of the head between the second and fifth years, after which the increase tapers off. The young child's head is broader in relation to length than is the adult's head. After five years of age, the annual increase is greater in length than in width, thus making the head gradually conform to adult proportions. Short and narrow heads show a somewhat greater increase in size during early childhood than do long and broad heads [107].

Throughout early childhood, the *facial features* remain small. The nose is particularly small and rather flat on the surface of the face. The mouth is likewise proportionately too small because of the small baby teeth. However, there is a more pronounced chin, owing to the development of the lower jaw, and the neck elongates. The soft downy hair of the baby is gradually replaced by hair of a coarser texture which is frequently un-manageable at this age. The hair of the young child begins to show some of the characteristics of "terminal hair" and its pigmentation becomes slightly darker.

Up to the age of six years, the *trunk* is twice as long and wide as it was at birth. By the third year, the protruding abdomen of the baby flattens out and the shoulders become broader. The *arms* and *legs* like-wise lengthen and the *hands* and *feet* grow bigger. When the child is right-handed, the right arm is proportionally longer than in adults. There are marked variations in the size and shape of feet during early child-hood, though boys, at every age, have slightly larger feet than girls. The arches of the feet are well developed by the time the child is five years old. Heavy children tend to have flatter arches than do light children of the same age [107].

The *bones* gradually harden throughout early childhood so that the chances of their becoming misshapen, as a result of pressure or of poor posture, grow less and less each year. The *muscles* likewise grow larger and stronger, thus making it possible for the young child to do more and to fatigue less quickly than he did when he was younger. By the end of early childhood, there are generally one or two permanent *teeth*. Girls usually shed their temporary teeth earlier than boys do and they get their permanent teeth sooner than boys. The higher the intelligence of the child, the earlier is he likely to shed his temporary teeth and get his permanent teeth [107].

Physiological Habits. During early childhood, the physiological habits whose foundations were laid in babyhood become well established. The young child eats the same food as the rest of the family and he no longer has to have specially prepared food. At this time, his *appetite* is no longer as ravenous as it was in the early part of babyhood, partly because his growth rate has slowed down and he no longer needs as much food as he formerly did and partly because he has now developed marked food likes and dislikes. These likes and dislikes frequently develop because the foods prepared to suit adult tastes are too highly seasoned for the young child whose sense of taste is keener than that of adults, owing to the fact that he has taste buds in his cheeks as well as on his tongue. This is the age when "eating problems" reach their peak because of family pressures on the child to eat and the child's stubborn resistance to these adult proddings.

Sleep patterns, well established in babyhood, are often disrupted by the young child's revolt against daytime naps and against going to bed on time at night. In his attempt to stall off the inevitable, the young child is likely to work himself up into a state of emotional tension. This militates against relaxation, which is essential to falling asleep. In spite of daily variations in the amount of sleep, depending on such factors as amount of exercise during the day and type of activity, three-year-olds sleep approximately 12 out of the 24 hours. Each successive year during childhood, the average daily amount of sleep is approximately one-half hour less than in the previous year [30].

Boys generally sleep about 1 hour less than girls of the same age. However, girls go to sleep slightly more quickly than boys and sleep more soundly. Approximately an hour is required for the young child to fall asleep. The sleep posture of the young child changes on the average of once every 25 minutes, with the right side the favored position. During the early part of sleep, movements of the body are less frequent than in the latter part. When a young child has acquired good sleep habits, the presence of other children in the sleep environment does not interfere with the child's sleep. Going to bed late does not guarantee that the child will sleep late the next morning to compensate for loss of sleep on the preceding day. Parental attitudes concerning sleep are very important.

They are often responsible for bringing on sleep problems in the young child [30].

By the time the child is three to four years old, *bladder control* at night should be achieved. Many young children, however, have occasional night accidents after that age, especially if they are tired or excited during the day. This is true also of daytime accidents. By the time the child is ready to enter school, bladder control should be so complete that even fatigue and emotional tension will not interfere with it. Some young children continue to experience enuresis, or bed wetting, beyond the time that bladder control is normally achieved. In a few cases, this is the result of low-grade intelligence. In most instances, however, the cause is

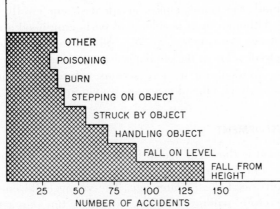

Fig. 20. Types of nonfatal home accidents during the early childhood years. (*From J. M. Dennis and A. D. Kaiser, Are home accidents in children preventable? Pediatrics, 1954, 13, 568–575. Used by permission.*)

traceable to nervous tension exaggerated by feelings of inadequacy on the child's part which have been fostered by parental scoldings or punishments for wetting his bed "like a baby." Ignorance of the age at which a young child can be expected to control his bladder causes parents to scold and punish the child when he wets himself, thus leading to a psychosomatic problem [104].

Diseases. Young children are highly susceptible to disease. Stomach and digestive disturbances, colds, earaches, and, in families where there are older children, measles, mumps, chicken pox, and other children's diseases are common [11]. While many diseases in early childhood are physiological in origin, others are psychosomatic and result from tensions between parent and child. When parents react to a child's illness as a family calamity, show feelings of guilt, or blame the child for the inconvenience his illness causes, the child's attitude will be poor. If, on the other hand, the parent's attitude is more wholesome and family life is carried on in a normal fashion, the child's attitude will be more favorable.) He will learn that illness means necessary withdrawal but he does not learn to use illness as an escape from reality. The common psychosomatic disorders that have been found to stem from parent-child tensions are: anorexia nervosa, ulcerative colitis, enuresis, allergic reactions, asthma, and diabetes) [75].

(In addition to illness, most young children experience cuts, bruises, infections, burns, broken bones, strained muscles, or similar minor disturbances resulting from *accidents*.\Boys have more accidents than girls, and younger children more than older children.\ The ages of two and three years are the most vulnerable, and five and six the next most vulnerable.)Unlike the older child, who has more accidents on the street or in the playground, the young child's accidents occur mostly within the home [29, 54]. (Although most accidents of early childhood are not fatal, many of them leave permanent scars of a physical or psychological sort.) They also help to develop in the child a sense of caution which frequently prevents future accidents of a more serious nature. Common types of accidents in the early childhood years are shown in Figure 20.

MOTOR DEVELOPMENT

(Early childhood is the ideal age to learn skills which are not only useful at that time but which will serve as the foundation for more highly coordinated skills needed at a later age.)The young child enjoys repetition and is, therefore, willing to repeat, time after time, an activity until he has acquired the ability to do it well.) He is adventuresome and, hence, is not held back by fear of hurting himself or of the ridicule of his associates as so often happens when a child is older. And, because his body is still very pliable, with few conflicting skills to interfere with the acquisition of new ones, he learns quickly and easily.

In the acquisition of skills, practice must be directed if it is to be effective. If it is left to chance and the child learns by trial and error, he will expend too much time and effort and the end results will be disappointing, thus lessening his motivation to practice further. With directed practice, by contrast, learning takes place more rapidly and the end results are more satisfying to the child. Figure 21 shows the effects of training on the acquisition of skill in distance throwing. In the early stages of skill development, the child's movements are clumsy, awkward, and uncoordinated. Gradually, waste motion is eliminated and the movements become graceful, coordinated, and rhythmic. Furthermore, there is an increase in speed and accuracy with the result that the child can perform an act in a shorter time, with less effort, and with less concentrated attention on what he is doing [32]. (The child's level of aspiration in trying and learning skills depends partly on his curiosity and partly on his past experience. If he fails, he sets his goals lower; after success, he increases his aspiration [87]. Because children are often frustrated in their efforts to learn skills, having set their aspirations too high, they need encouragement to continue to practice until the skill has been learned [53].

The acquisition of skills is of great personal advantage to a child. The more he can do for himself, the less he will have to depend upon others. At a time when the child craves independence and revolts against adult

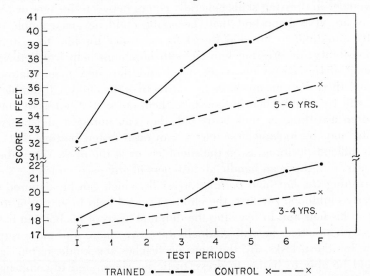

FIG. 21. Effects of training in distance throws among preschool boys. (*From L. Dusenberry, A study of the effects of training in ball throwing by children ages three to seven. Res. Quart. Amer. phys. Educ. Ass. 1952, 23, 9–14. Used by permission.*)

restraints on his activities, it is very important that he be given an opportunity to learn to do many things for himself. Furthermore, skills are an asset to the young child in his early attempts to make social contacts with other children. Because his early social contacts will develop largely through play, the more play skills he has the more successfully he can make contacts with his contemporaries.

Hand Skills. Self-feeding and dressing skills, begun in babyhood, are perfected in early childhood. By the time he is three years old, the child can feed himself with a fork and can spread butter or jam with a knife. Using the knife for cutting is too difficult until the child is a year or two older. Because eating skills at this age are still in the formative stage, the child must concentrate on what he is doing. Should his attention be diverted, he is likely to spill his food or to stop feeding himself until his attention returns to eating. Dawdling usually reaches a peak between the third and fourth years, the time when the young child's ability to feed himself has not yet developed to the point where he can eat and listen to others or watch what they are doing. As his feeding skills improve, the child can eat while listening or watching and, as a result, he will dawdle less.

This is true also of dressing. The young child cannot look at or listen to anything else while he is putting on or fastening his clothes. He must give his undivided attention to the job at hand. Because the greatest improvement in dressing skills generally comes between the ages of 1½ and 3½ years, it is important that the young child be given ample opportunity and time to develop the skills necessary for him to assume the responsibility for dressing himself with minimum help from others. Beginning at the age of two years, most children enjoy manipulating buttons. If these buttons are large and attractive, the child will fumble them and will try to put them in and take them out of the holes. By the time children are three or four years old, they can unfasten and fasten garments, and, by looking in a mirror, can even fasten buttons that are in such difficult positions as on the shoulders or at the neck. When they are six years old, they can handle all fasteners in any position [57].

Brushing the hair and *bathing* are skills which can be acquired easily in early childhood. At first, the child will need help in getting a straight part in his hair and in reaching the different areas of his body in bathing. But, with practice, he will gradually take over more and more responsibility for these tasks. By the time he reaches the kindergarten age, he should be able to bathe, to dress, to tie his shoes, and to comb his hair with no assistance. Girls, when they wear elaborate party clothes or have hair styles too intricate for them to manage, must depend upon outside help for a longer time [53].

Because ball games are one of the favorite play activities of children's groups, the sooner a child learns to *throw and catch a ball,* the better will be his chances of becoming a member of the neighborhood group. Between the ages of five and six years, most children can become proficient in throwing and catching balls [43]. A three-year-old can drive nails into wood with a hammer and a six-year-old can use his carpentry skill to make simple objects like boats and wagons. Nursery school and kindergarten children can use scissors in following the outlines of pictures, and they can mold with clay, make cookies, or sew. By using *crayons, pencils, and paints,* young children are able to color outlined pictures, draw or paint pictures of their own, and make a recognizable man. Between the ages of five and six years, children can make recognizable letters, though their writing is slow, laborious, and poor at this age [6].

While preference for one hand appears in babyhood, a definite hand

preference is not established at that age. Between the ages of 2½ and
3½ years, there is a marked shift to bilaterality. Then, from the ages of
4 to 6 years, unilateral preference predominates. Because bilaterality does
not appear again, except for a brief period around the age of 7 years, it
is important that young children who show a tendency to use the left
hand more frequently than the right be encouraged to try to use the
right hand whenever possible. Since hand skills are being established at
this age, it will be easier for the child to acquire these skills with his right
hand at the very start, if he is eventually to become right-handed. As Hildreth has pointed out: "Handedness should be trained, not left to chance,
since manual dexterity can affect an individual's educational and vocational success" [51].

Leg Skills. Once the skill of walking has been established, the young
child turns his attention to learning other skilled movements requiring
the use of his legs. He learns to hop, skip, gallop, and jump by the age of
five or six years [43]. At this time, not only can he run with very few
falls but he can play games at the same time. Climbing skills are likewise
well established in early childhood, though many urban children soon
exhaust the possibility of climbing in their restricted environments.
Should the environment offer opportunities for climbing, the five- or six-
year-old is capable of climbing well and of doing stunts such as racing,
competing, and climbing in dramatic projects [43]. At three years, a
child can ascend and descend ladders [53].

Few children acquire the ability to *swim* before they are four years
old, primarily because they lack the opportunity to learn or to get the
amount of practice necessary to acquire such a complicated skill. Between the ages of three and four years, *tricycling* can be learned. "Stunting," such as riding backward or turning the corner sharply, then enters
into the skill. Other skills acquired by young children include *jumping
rope, balancing* on rails or on the top of a wall, *roller skating, ice skating,*
if the skates have double runners, and *dancing* [43].

Delayed Motor Development. Early childhood is a critical age for acquiring muscular skills. The child who is hampered by overprotective
parents who are afraid he will injure himself, by fear engendered by accidents or warnings to "be careful," by environmental obstacles, or by
lack of opportunity to practice until the skills have been formed, becomes
awkward as compared with other children of his age. When he tries to
do what other children do, he cannot keep up with them. As a result, he
is left out of their play. This limits further his opportunity for learning
and makes him increasingly more backward in his social contacts. Each
year, as he grows older, play with other children should be an increasingly important part of his daily life. But unless special training at home
or at school is given to him to enable him to catch up to the skills al-

ready acquired by other children of his age, he will find himself in the role of a social isolate.

SPEECH DEVELOPMENT

The foundations of speech are laid in babyhood. On these foundations will be built the speech skills which, by the time early childhood is over, will be so well established that the child's future speech will be greatly influenced by them. For this reason, early childhood is a critical period in the developmental pattern of the speech of the individual. The ability to *comprehend meaning* of what others say develops rapidly at this time. The young child can understand most of what is said to him either through comprehension of the words used or of the gestures and facial expressions that accompany these words [72]. By the time he enters school, the child should have a large enough comprehension vocabulary to understand instructions given to him by unfamiliar people, and to understand the meaning of stories read to him. Listening to the radio and watching television are proving to be helpful in the development of the comprehension vocabularies of today's children [21, 72].

Throughout the preschool years, the child's *vocabulary* increases rapidly owing partly to direct teaching of words and partly to his curiosity about word meanings, which leads him to ask people what these words mean. Verbs, adjectives, pronouns, conjunctions, and prepositions increase in frequency of use at this age. Descriptive adjective phrases increase markedly from the ages of $2\frac{1}{2}$ to $4\frac{1}{2}$ years. Pronouns and verbs are more widely used than nouns at this time. Nouns and interjections decrease in frequency of usage with age, and articles, conjunctions, prepositions, and infinitives increase. Not only does the young child learn many new words, but he also learns new meanings for old words [72]. The size of the young child's vocabulary at different ages will depend not on intelligence alone but also on opportunities and motivation to learn. Girls, as a general rule, have larger vocabularies at every age than boys [47].

In addition to building up a vocabulary that will be of general usage, young children learn many *words of a specific kind*. The child learns to use such words as "Thank you," "Please," or "I'm sorry"; he acquires a vocabulary of color words so that, at the age of five years, he can name without error the colors, red, blue, yellow, and green. He learns the meanings of numbers so that by the age of five years he can count 3 objects from 12 placed before him and, a year later, he knows how to count 3, 9, 5, 10, or 7 out of 12 objects. All coins are classed as "money" or "pennies" by very young children. However, by the time children are five or six years old, they can distinguish and name pennies, nickels, dimes, and even quarters. The preschool child knows and uses such time words as "morning," "afternoon," "night," "winter," and "summer" [105]. Many young children pick up *slang* or even *swear words* from their older brothers and sisters, their parents, or their playmates. They use these words in a parrotlike fashion without any comprehension of their true meaning [21].

Sentence usage follows a fairly definite and predictable pattern in early childhood. Short sentences of three or four words are used as early as two years of age and commonly at three years. These sentences have an excess of nouns but lack verbs, prepositions, and conjunctions. Many of the child's early sentences are incomplete. From the age of three years on, however, complete sentences of six to eight words frequently appear in a young child's speech. All parts of speech are then used. By the time he is six years old, the child should have command of practically every form of sentence structure. Young children tend to increase the length of their sentences by combining two or more simple sentences with the conjunction "and." Bright children and those from the higher socioeconomic groups usually use longer, more complex, and better-constructed sentences than children of the same age who come from less favorable environments or who are not so bright [21, 72].

Up to the age of three or four years, *grammatical errors* are common. The major difficulties are in the correct usage of pronouns, verbs, and verb tenses. It is also very common for young children to be confused about when to use single and plural nouns. Typical errors in verb usage relate to the confusion in the use of "can" and "may," "lay" and "lie." In the case of nouns, it is difficult for them to understand why one does not say "foots" instead of "feet" or "mans" instead of "men." They commonly use the single form of verbs with a plural subject. Because the young child is learning to form sentences, it is most important that grammatical mistakes be corrected when they occur. Otherwise, the child will develop the habit of thinking incorrectly. Through hearing correct speech and through school instruction, many of the grammatical mistakes of early childhood will be corrected. While most young children improve their speech by making fewer grammatical mistakes from three years of age on, they do so at a slower rate than they increase their vocabularies [47].

Speech Defects. Some young children pronounce their words clearly and distinctly; some do not. It is not unusual for infantile *pronunciations* to persist until the child is three or even four years old. The more the child is with other children, however, the more comprehensible his speech becomes. By the fifth or sixth year, most infantile forms of pronunciation are gone. *Lisping*, or letter-sound substitution, as *th* for *z* or *as* and *w* for *r*, is one of the most common speech errors of early childhood. During the transitional stage from first to second teeth, there is likely to be a gap in the front of the jaws where the second teeth will eventually cut through. At this time, there is often a slight lisp which, unless corrected as the new teeth develop, will become established into a habit [21, 72].

Stuttering, or the repetition of sounds, syllables, or even words, is caused mainly by nervous and emotional tension.) Generally, stuttering begins at a very early age, when the child is just learning to talk. Between the ages of two and four years, hesitating, repetitious speech is more or less characteristic of all children. At this time, they are mastering the art of self-feeding and self-dressing, they are learning to talk in sentences, and are trying to be independent of adult domination. Stuttering also occurs frequently between the fifth and sixth years. Both of these periods represent important breaks in the child's life. During the years from two to four, the child is breaking away from babyhood, and from five to six, he is breaking away from the home environment and establishing himself in the broader social environment of the school and neighborhood.) Stuttering in a minor form is part of the early speech pattern of all children. As children reach the end of early childhood, there is normally a decrease in the amount of stuttering. (The defect is nearly twice as common among boys as among girls)[72, 74].

Content of Speech. What young children talk about varies from child to child as does their need for speech. (At first, speech generally accompanies motor activity and takes the form of thinking out loud.) When a little boy is playing with his train, for example, he will say, "Now I'll put the train on the tracks." (Early speech is a monologue in the form of a running commentary on the child's activity rather than a conversation.) As children grow older, there is an increase in the quantity of their speech. They talk more, though boys, as a rule, talk less than girls. There is also an increase in remarks about people and objects, though girls tend to talk more about people than boys do. In their play with other children, children show more tendency to evoke a response from their hearers than to verbalize for the sake of doing so. (There is a clear tendency for children to talk more to other people and less to themselves as they grow older [5].)

(Although only about 2 per cent of the statements of young children are critical, most of them are unfavorable.) The purpose of these unfavorable criticisms is to gain the assistance of someone in a situation beyond the child's control. (Thus the criticism takes the form of tattling, or it is directed at interference with themselves or their possessions and takes the form of a complaint [21]. As the size of the group becomes larger, the language of the child becomes more sociable and less egocentric. He is also slightly less critical, asks fewer questions, and gives more commands. (Small social groupings are most favorable for the speech of young children.) At the kindergarten age, children talk mostly to other children of their own sex [5].

(The most frequent *topic of conversation* among young children relates to themselves and their activities.) When a second person is the subject of a remark, the remark is generally a command for that person to do something [21]. Topics such as likes and dislikes among people, clothes, where one lives, and matters of everyday routine predominate in the young child's conversation. Nearly one-third of his conversations relate to family, mother, father, brothers and sisters, and similar topics.) Boasting is common at all ages. The young child boasts about material possessions such as his toys, his clothes, or the family car [5].

Variations in Speech. There are marked variations in the speech development of young children. These variations depend not so much upon ability to learn to speak as upon *opportunities for learning.* In large families, for example, the young child has fewer contacts with his parents than does the child from the smaller family, and this retards his speech development [72]. Similarly, the child whose parents use a foreign language in the home is confronted with the problem of *bilingualism* and must use a different language when he tries to communicate with outsiders. This adds confusion to his learning and is likely to retard his speech development in both languages [93]. As Thompson has stressed, "There can be no doubt that the child reared in a bilingual environment is handicapped in his language growth" [106]. The better the *socioeconomic status* of the child's family, the better will be the models of speech he has to imitate and the more encouragement will he receive to learn words and combine them into correct sentences) [47, 72].

EMOTIONAL DEVELOPMENT

(Early childhood is a period of heightened emotionality, characterized by temper tantrums, intense fears, and unreasonable outbursts of jealousy.) At this time, the emotions become more differentiated than they were in babyhood and the pattern of expression can be more readily interpreted. (Part of the intense emotionality of children at this age may be traced to fatigue from strenuous and prolonged play, from their rebellion against taking naps, and from eating too little for their needs— the result of their rebellion against eating at meals, a common problem at this age.) Most young children feel that they are capable of doing more than their parents will permit them to do and revolt against the restrictions placed upon them.) In addition, they become angry when they find they are incapable of doing what they think they can do easily and successfully.) When, for example, they cannot make a toy work or a button slip through a hole, they feel frustrated and fly into a fit of rage. As the child's social environment broadens and he enters Sunday school, nursery school or kindergarten, and plays with children in the neighborhood, there is the nervous tension that accompanies any adjustment. The younger and less experienced the child, the greater the tension is likely to be.

Variations in Emotionality. There are marked variations in emotionality among different children during early childhood and in the same child from time to time. These variations come partly from differences in the *health condition* of the child and partly from differences in the *environment*. They are also influenced by the *patterns of emotional behavior* established during the babyhood years. The child who, as a baby, was kept in a quiet environment, free from noise and excitement, and whose needs were met promptly and consistently, is less likely to suffer from intense emotional outbursts as he grows older than is the child who, as a baby, lived in an environment filled with noise and excitement, or learned that he had to become very angry before anyone would bother to come to him. The young child who has been accustomed to having the undivided attention of the mother may bitterly resent her preoccupation with the new baby and show it by frequent and intense outbursts of anger and jealousy. His change from a happy, calm child to a tense and irascible one comes mainly from the change in his environment.

The *sex* and *ordinal position* of the child within the family has been found to have a marked influence on his emotionality. The first-born child has more status to defend than has the second-born and he is handicapped in his struggle with his sibling by parental restrictions. Second-born children, encouraged by their parents to defend themselves, are less hesitant to express their anger and attack directly. There is more emotional stress for the child if his sibling is of the other sex or if there is a large age difference so that he and the sibling cannot receive similar attention from the parent at the same time [60]. Regardless of his sex or ordinal position, the child whose parents expect him to measure up to standards they set will experience more emotional tension than will the child whose parents are more permissive [55].

Common Emotions. The most common emotions experienced at this stage of development are anger, fear, jealousy, affection, curiosity, and joy. Each has a well-developed pattern of expression in early childhood and each is aroused by stimuli which are commonly experienced by most young children.

ANGER. Anger is the most common emotion in early childhood, partly because there are so many anger-provoking situations in a young child's life and partly because a young child quickly discovers that the use of anger is a quick and easy way to get what he wants, whether it be attention or the fulfillment of some desire. The situations that most frequently give rise to anger in young children consist of conflicts over playthings, conflicts over toilet and dressing, interruptions of interesting activities, thwarting of wishes, vigorous attacks from another child, another child's taking a desired object, or another child's calling names) [55].

The social environment of the home plays an important role in the frequency and intensity of the young child's anger. More frequent temper tantrums among young children, for example, have been found to occur in homes where there are many guests and where there are more than two adults. (Similarly, the child with siblings has more temper outbursts than the only child) [42]. Furthermore, the type of discipline and the child-training methods used by parents influence the frequency and intensity of the child's angry outbursts. When parents, for example, try to transform and pattern the child's natural responses into socially acceptable forms, as in the case of eating behavior, he is likely to respond with anger. Constant provoking of such emotional reactions may result in the development of chronic affective responses [36].

When a young child becomes angry, he expresses his anger in intense outbursts, or "temper tantrums." Tantrums are characterized by crying, screaming, stamping, kicking, jumping up and down, striking, throwing one's self on the floor, holding the breath, stiffening the body, or making it limp. By the age of four years, anger responses are directed more toward a given end than they are when the child is younger. Then there are more attempts to retaliate by hurting the feelings or injuring the body of the offender. Temper tantrums reach their peak of severity between the ages of three and four years. As early childhood draws to a close, temper tantrums become shorter in duration and give way to sulking, brooding, and whining. Most tantrums last from 1 to 3 minutes. While some children have acquired control over their anger by the end of early childhood, most have not and, as a result, express their anger in outbursts of varying degrees of severity [16]. Up to the age of three years, there are no apparent sex differences in the number and severity of temper tantrums. After that age, boys have more frequent and more intense tantrums than do girls [42] (see Figure 22).

FEAR. The young child is afraid of more things than is the baby or the older child. The development of his intelligence makes it possible for him to recognize potential dangers in situations which formerly were not recognized as such. Fear of snakes, for example, does not appear much before the age of 3½ years but, by the age of 4 years, definite fear appears. In a physical-threat situation, such as walking a plank, young children are frightened first by the novelty of the situation, but their fear decreases as the novelty wears off [48]. At first, fear is general rather than specific. It is more like a state of panic than fear proper. As children become older, fear responses become increasingly more specific. The (typical *fear responses* of young children include running away and hiding, avoiding situations that frighten them, and making such verbal responses as, "Take it away," "I don't want to go," or "I can't do it.")Crying and whimpering usually accompany these responses [53].

(Conditioning, or learning by association, imitation, and memories of unpleasant experiences, play important roles in the development of fear among young children.)Fear of certain specific events, such as fright at the sound of applause on the radio and fear of elevators, may lead to fears of similar or associated events, such as fear of all radios and fear of being shut up in a small space. Stories and pictures with frightening elements, radio and television programs, or movies may be the basis of many fears of young children, especially when the situations presented have elements in common with experiences in the child's life.) Many fears develop from imitating a person who is frightened. It is quite common for preschool children to show fears similar to those of their mothers. And, finally, many fears develop as an

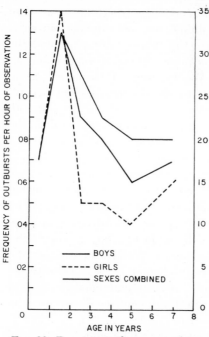

Fig. 22. Decrease in frequency of temper outbursts with age. (*Based on material from F. L. Goodenough, Anger in young children. Minneapolis: Univer. of Minnesota Press, 1931. From K. C. Garrison, Growth and development. New York: Longmans, Green, 1952. Used by permission.*)

aftermath of some unpleasant experience, such as fear of doctors or of dentists [55].

(The number and severity of fears decrease as children grow older (see Figure 23). This is partly the result of the child's realization that there is nothing to be afraid of in the situation he formerly feared, partly to social pressures which have made him conceal his fear to avoid being ridiculed, partly from social imitation, and partly from adult guidance in acquiring a liking for or a negative attitude toward things he formerly feared. Fear of unfamiliar persons, environments, and experiences disappears as the child becomes better acquainted with them [55].

JEALOUSY. (Jealousy is an angry resentment directed toward people.)It is always called forth by social situations, especially those involving individuals whom the child loves.) Among young children, jealousy is invariably aroused when parents or those who have taken care of the child seemingly shift their interest and attention to someone else, especially a new arrival in the family.(Most often jealousy begins between the ages of two and five years, with the birth of a younger sibling.) Telling the child ahead of time of the anticipated arrival of the sibling does not

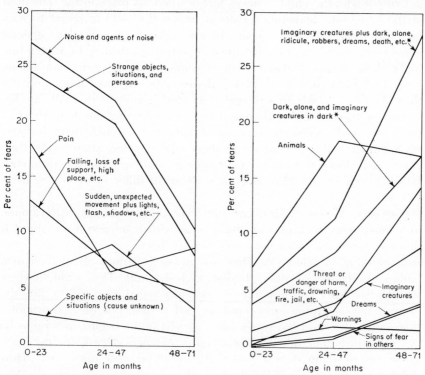

FIG. 23. Relative frequency of various fear situations among young children. (*From A. T. Jersild, Emotional development. In L. Carmichael, Manual of child psychology, 2d ed. New York: Wiley, 1954. Pp. 833–917. Used by permission.*)

necessarily avoid jealousy nor does it determine the attitude of the child toward the sibling.

(The young child may also be jealous of an older sibling who is granted more privileges than he, a situation which he frequently interprets as parental favoritism. Or he may be jealous of a sibling who, because of poor health, must be given more attention than he.) The child is far less likely to be jealous of children outside the home than of his siblings because his contacts with outsiders are limited and occur at times when the mother or some loved adult is not likely to be present. Young children are, however, often jealous of their fathers. They develop a proprietary attitude toward the mother because of her constant association with them, and they resent her affection for their father. The peak of jealousy comes between two and three years, and then begins to lessen as the child's interests broaden) [55, 110].

In early childhood, jealousy expresses itself in much the same way as anger does except that it is usually directed against another person, the individual who the child believes has usurped his place in the affections of the loved one. Sometimes jealousy causes the child to revert to such infantile forms of behavior as thumb sucking, bed wetting, general naughtiness, or bidding for attention by refusing to eat or by pretending to be ill or afraid. Jealousy is more common among girls than among boys. First-born children display jealousy more often and more violently than do their later-born siblings. It is more common in small families of two or three children than in larger ones. Oversolicitous mothers or those whose discipline is inconsistent have more trouble with jealousy among their children than do mothers who pay less attention to their children. Jealousy is more frequent among children whose age difference falls between 18 and 42 months than when the difference is less or more [19, 55].

CURIOSITY. Young children are into everything. Nothing in the house, in a store, or in the homes of others escapes their interest if the object is different from what they have seen before. They even explore other persons' clothing by feeling it. They are intensely curious about their own bodies, the bodies of other children and of adults. They want to know why bodies differ and how they work. Since social pressures in the form of warnings and punishment put an end to some of the sensorimotor exploration the child has previously engaged in, he begins, as soon as he can put words together into meaningful sentences, to ask endless questions, such as, "How does it work?" "Where did it come from?" and "How did it get there?"

The "questioning age" begins between the second and third years and reaches its peak at the sixth year of the child's life. When his questions are answered, the child's curiosity is satisfied because he has been able to obtain information not possible through his own exploration. When, however, he does not receive satisfactory answers or if his questions are unanswered, his curiosity is likely to be dampened and, as a result, his information is limited as compared with that of other children of his age and level of intelligence.

JOY. To young children, there are many sources of joy and many things to laugh about. However, there is a definite age trend in the amount of smiling and laughter and also in the stimuli that elicit these responses. The young child responds to more different stimuli than does the baby, and he is more influenced by situations in which other children are present. Physical well-being, incongruous situations, sudden or unexpected noises, slight calamities, or a play on words never fail to bring forth a laugh. The child is pleased by new discoveries, especially when obstacles have been placed in the way of these discoveries or when his achievements surpass those of other children. Teasing others, playing pranks on children or adults, and putting animals or other children in a predicament lead to feelings of superiority which make him happy. He can understand incongruities and slapstick comedy better than other forms of humor and thus finds them amusing in real-life situations, in the comics, in the movies, or on the television screen [21]. The *joy response* consists of smiling, laughing—often uproariously, clapping the hands, jumping up and down, or hugging the object or person who elicited this emotion. The manner in which the child will express his joy will depend not only on the intensity of the emotion but also on the social pressures on him to control it [4].

AFFECTION. Like the baby, the young child learns to love those who give him pleasure and satisfaction. Not only human beings but animals and inanimate objects call forth expressions of affection on the part of the young child. Frequently the child expresses affection for a pet or for a favorite toy in much the same way as he expresses affection for the members of his family. Affectionate behavior in the young child indicates warm regard, friendliness, sympathy, or helplessness. It may be expressed physically or verbally, though verbal expressions are more frequent than physical. Girls tend to be more affectionate than boys, and both choose children and adults of their own sex for their affectionate responses more than they do members of the opposite sex [111]. Around the fourth year, the child's emotional dependence on the family gives way to emotional dependence on other children [48]. The child who does not receive affection from others, whether it be from family members or from outsiders, is likely to become "self-bound" and this interferes with his emotional exchange with others [1].

Young children express their affection in much the same uncontrolled manner as they express other emotions. They hug, kiss, and pat the loved person or object. They want to be with the loved one constantly, they cry or whimper when the loved one leaves them, and they want to do what the loved one is doing, even though their assistance may be more of a hindrance than a help. The child feels much the same way about favorite pets and toys as he does about beloved persons. He wants to have the pet or toy with him constantly, even when he goes to bed, and he is frequently merciless in his fondling of it. As the young child's need for affection shifts from family members to outsiders, there are changes in the expression of affection from seeking reassurance and affection from others to seeking attention and approval [48]. The most spontaneous expressions of affection generally occur among children of the lower economic groups [55].

SOCIAL DEVELOPMENT

In the home, the baby first learns to love and to be loved. The success of these early social experiences determines, to a large extent, the success of his later relationships with persons outside the home. As the social world of the young child expands, early parental attachments are gradually outgrown and are replaced by relationships with individuals outside the family circle. Early social experiences outside the home are often emotionally disturbing to the child, especially if he is younger than the other children with whom he associates and, as a result, is teased and bullied by them [48]. His success in adjusting to outside social contacts will be influenced largely by the type of social experiences he has had at home. Children brought up democratically, for example, make better social adjustments outside the home than do those from an authoritarian home environment [19]. Likewise, the child's position in the family, whether first-born, last-born, or only child, and the type of relationship he has had with his siblings will affect his social adjustments outside the home [19].

Early childhood is the "pregang" stage of social development. At this time the child should acquire the preliminary training and experience needed to become a member of a "gang" in late childhood. Should geographic isolation, parental restrictions, or unfavorable attitude on the part of the child cut him off from contact with other children of his age, the child will be deprived of experiences necessary to make satisfactory social adjustments, not only then but as he grows older. The *kind* of social contacts the young child has is more important than the number. If he enjoys his contacts with others, even if they are only occasional, his attitude toward future social contacts will be more favorable than if he has many social contacts of a less favorable kind. Furthermore, the advantage he takes of the opportunities offered him for social contacts will be greatly influenced by how pleasurable his past social contacts have been [21].

While babies are content with the companionship of adults, young children are not. Between the ages of two and three years, the child begins to grow restless when his companions are limited to adults. At this time, he shows a decided interest in watching other children and he attempts to make social contacts with them. "Parallel play," in which the child plays independently beside children rather than with them, is the earliest form of social activity with his contemporaries. Following this comes "associative play," in which the child plays with other children in similar, if not identical, activities, and "cooperative play," in which he is a part of a group. Frequently children play the role of an onlooker in which they watch other children at play, talk to other children, but do not actually enter into the play of the group. By the time the child is four years old, he shows the rudiments of team play, is conscious of the opinions of others, and tries to gain attention by "showing-off"[38].

Social Behavior. Certain forms of social behavior are carry-overs of behavior established during babyhood or are developed as a result of the child's contacts with other children. The most important forms of social behavior necessary for successful social adjustment appear and begin to develop at this time. In the early years of childhood, they are not developed well enough to enable the child to get along successfully with others at all times. However, this is a crucial stage in their development because, at this time, the basic social attitudes—attitudes toward certain people, certain groups, and social life as an experience that is pleasant or unpleasant—and the patterns of his social behavior are established[37]. Children under three years of age show a low level of social interaction because they are not ready for this and lack social experience. After three, there is a marked increase in social interaction. The quality, as well as the amount, of social behavior the child develops—whether, for example, he shows dominance, leadership, dependent submissiveness, conformity, or compliance with the wishes of others—depends largely on the environment and the child's relationship to it[101]. Follow-up studies of children as they grow older have revealed that social attitudes and behavior established during the preschool years persist with little modification and change [86].

The most important forms of social behavior to appear at this age are negativism, imitation, rivalry, aggression, quarreling, cooperation, ascendancy, selfishness, sympathy, and desire for social approval. Many of these appear to be unsocial or antisocial rather than social, but each is important to the socialization of the child and each plays an important role in the transition from an unsocial, egocentric individual to a social one.

NEGATIVISM, or resistance to adult authority, begins in babyhood as a result of the aggressive use of discipline in the home or of an intolerant attitude toward childish behavior. At the age of two or three years, negativism is a normal phase of ego development. It is an exaggerated reaction to the need for relinquishing the earlier grandiose concept of self. Resistance to parental authority generally reaches its peak between the third and fourth years, after which it is directed more toward other children or strange adults. The negativistic child, who is difficult to manage and to live with, usually becomes cooperative when he has established himself as an individual and has learned to gain satisfaction from complying with the wishes of others. Well-adjusted children show negativism, but it is less frequent and less severe than that of poorly adjusted children [76].

The form negativism takes varies from age to age and from child to child. The usual forms consist of verbal responses, motor responses, and silence. As children grow older, they often pretend not to hear or understand a request, they dawdle over routine activities, or completely neglect them. Well-adjusted children usually express their negativism in direct forms while those who are poorly adjusted express negativistic feelings in diffuse and generalized ways [76]. Between the ages of four and six years, a decline in physical resistance and an increase in verbal forms usually occur.

IMITATION. The earliest forms of imitation use parents as models. With the beginnings of interest in other children, the child imitates their speech, actions, and emotions. He is, in this way, trying to identify himself with the group.

RIVALRY. The desire to excel or outdo others is apparent as early as the fourth year of life. The young child's bragging about his possessions is a form of rivalry. It is usually displayed in the presence of another, generally an adult for whose attention the child is competing. The young child is more anxious for adult than for peer attention and uses any means he can to win it [40]. Rivalry is very common in the home, especially where sibling jealousy exists. It is more often found in families where the children are of both sexes or where the mother shows a preference for one child [19].

AGGRESSION. Aggression is a common reaction to frustration. The young child who shows marked aggressiveness is one who is highly frustrated and who has been punished a great deal for his aggressiveness [87]. Aggressiveness is especially strong in children who want power and dominance or who are identified with an aggressive adult [65, 80]. Boys are, as a rule, more aggressive than girls [111] (see Figure 24). Popular children express their aggression within the context of their play and have a definite, single recipient of their aggression, while unpopular children tend to attack anyone they are with, whether or not that person has done anything to deserve it [31]. Aggression varies according to the time of day, the setting of the play situation, and the degree of familiarity with the other children. The better the child knows the other children, the more aggressive he is likely to be. Children tend to be more aggressive when there is an adult around whose attention they want to attract [91]. Although all children show some aggression, both boys and girls initiate more social contacts by affectional than by aggressive behavior. Aggressiveness in children increases from two to four years, and then declines [111].

The form of aggression changes with age from crying and direct attack on another child to verbal attacks, leaving the situation, and appeal to adults [7]. By the time the child is four or five years old, he expresses aggression verbally more often than by direct, physical attack [111]. The younger the child, the more attacking he does and the more he cries. As he grows older, his verbal attacks generally take the form of name calling or blaming others [34]. He also attacks indirectly by tattling to an adult about what the other child has done. Children who are popular

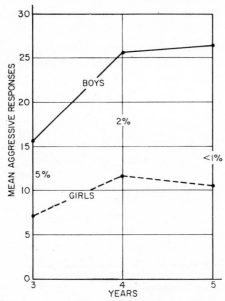

FIG. 24. Sex differences in aggression during the preschool years. (*From P. S. Sears, Doll play aggression in normal young children: influence of sex, age, sibling status, father's absence. Psychol. Monogr., 1951, 65, No. 6. Used by permission.*)

with other children use their verbal attacks less to attract the adult's attention to themselves than do children who are unpopular. The less popular the child, the more he tries to attract attention to himself by his aggressive attacks, whether they be physical or verbal [31].

QUARRELING. Much of the quarreling of young children comes from lack of experience in cooperative play. When the child quarrels, he takes away toys that the other child is playing with, he is destructive of the other child's work, and he generally screams, cries, kicks, hits, and bites. The outbursts, though intense, are usually short in duration. After they are over, they are forgotten and the friendly relationship that prevailed before the quarrel is resumed. Quarreling generally starts in a conflict over property, such as toys. The younger the child, the fewer opportunities there are for quarrels because contacts with other children are generally briefer than they are as the child grows older, and their quarrels are shorter in duration. The age of three years is generally the peak of quarreling. After that, improved social adjustments bring about a decrease in the frequency and intensity of quarrels. Boys are more quarrelsome than girls, especially when paired with other boys [90]. Children of the lower socioeconomic levels quarrel more than do those of the higher [73]. The more social contacts a child has with other children, the more quarreling he is likely to do. However, quarrels have a socializing value in that they teach the child what others will and will not tolerate.

COOPERATION. Because very young children are self-centered and quarrelsome, there is little cooperation in their play with other children.

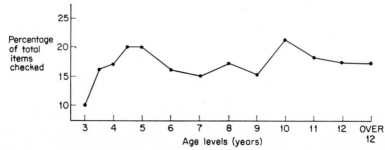

FIG. 25. Increase in social interaction, in terms of ascendence-submission, with opportunities for social contacts. (*From L. H. Stott and R. S. Ball, Consistency and change in ascendance-submission in the social interaction of children. Child Develpm., 1957, 28, 259–272. Used by permission.*)

Even with adults they cooperate little because the adult has a tendency to give in to the child and to allow him to have his own way. By the end of the third year, however, cooperative play and group activities are more frequent and longer in duration. With practice, the child learns to cooperate with other children and to play in an increasingly harmonious manner. The stronger the ties of friendship between young children, the more cooperative is their play [17].

ASCENDENT BEHAVIOR. Almost all young children show a strong tendency to be "bossy." The child attempts to secure materials that he wants from other children and to direct and influence the behavior of his playmates. From three years of age on, ascendency increases with the increase in opportunities for social contacts. This reaches its peak around the fifth year. While ascendent behavior is increasing, there is a marked decrease in isolate behavior, but submissive behavior changes little (see Figure 25). Whether ascendent behavior will take the form of bossiness, leadership, or undifferentiated ascendence will depend partly on the child's environment [101]. Girls are significantly more dominating than boys in their play with other children during the preschool years [78].

SELFISHNESS. Selfishness reaches its peak between the fourth and sixth years. It is not surprising that after being the center of attention during the early part of his life, the young child is egocentric and wants everything his way. Only after he learns from playing with other children that being selfish is a handicap to him does he try to submerge his self-interests into those of the group [53]. Then he begins to be more generous with his possessions and is willing to share them with his playmates. Generosity, however, is still in a very undeveloped form in the early childhood period [109].

SYMPATHY. Sympathy requires an understanding of the feelings and emotions of others. Children at the age of two or three years do not respond sympathetically to the black-and-blue wounds, swelling, bumps, and minor flesh distortions of others, to stories of a distressing nature, such as Red Riding Hood being eaten up by the wolf, to pictures of accidents, to being crippled, or to funerals. Occasionally a three-year-old will respond sympathetically to persons whose distress is made apparent by the use of bandages colored with iodine and by scars and scratches; to physical dilemmas, such as a fall from a bicycle; and to a child attacked by another child. The child shows his sympathy by attempting to help others, by trying to remove the cause of distress, by protecting those in distress, by warning and telling others about the individual in distress, and by suggesting solutions. Occasionally, however, unsympathetic responses such as laughing at a person in distress occur [109].

SOCIAL APPROVAL. Like the baby, the young child is anxious to have the approval of others. At first, the approval of adults is more important to him than the approval of other children. The young child seeks the attention of adults by glances, questions, comments, and urgent responses for overt notice. Boys seek the attention of women more than of men [39] (see Figure 26). As interest in being with the group increases, the desire for approval from his companions becomes more important to the child than approval from adults. This may lead the child to be naughty and disturbing. Socially unacceptable behavior is frequently motivated by the child's preference for approval from his companions to that from adults.

Companions. The young child's companions are limited in number and variety. For the most part, they consist of the adults in the family, siblings, and children in the immediate neighborhood. Only if the child attends Sunday school, nursery school, or kindergarten does the circle of his companions enlarge. The young child's relationships at home play an important role in his adjustment to children outside the home. Only children or those with siblings widely separated in age or of a different sex are likely to be withdrawn when they are with other children. (When the siblings are of the same sex, the child has more difficulty in associating with peers of the opposite sex.) The child who is younger than the playmates available for him to play with strives to keep up with them and is dominated by them.) If he is older than his playmates and his siblings, he generally is "bossy" and becomes their leader. (This early play experience with siblings and companions outside the home has a marked influence on how successfully the child makes the transition to school)

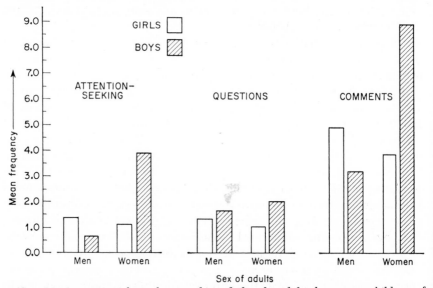

Fig. 26. Attention-seeking from male and female adults by young children of both sexes. (*From J. L. Gewirtz, Three determinants of attention-seeking in young children. Monogr. Soc. Res. Child Develpm., 1954, 19, No. 2. Used by permission.*)

[17, 62]. By the age of four years, children show a decided preference for companions of their own sex, and there is an increase in the tendency to choose companions of their own race as they grow older) [27, 97].

Young children show far less stability in their friendships than do older children. Because their companions are, in reality, playmates rather than true friends, children are likely to lose interest in their companions when their own play interests change. In a study of kindergarten children, it was found that, during a 10-week period, boys changed their friends more often than girls and the most frequent changes came between the fourth and sixth weeks. Boys changed from girl to boy playmates to avoid being considered "sissies" by the other children, and they shifted from one boy to another when they found that a boy they played with was a "toughie." Girls likewise shifted from boy to girl friends, showing the beginning of sex preferences which are so strong in friendships developed during the late childhood years [95].

Imaginary playmates are common among young children, especially when parent-child relationships are unfavorable or when the child has few opportunities for real playmates. It is a natural developmental phenomenon in many children and is especially characteristic of the age period from 2½ to 4½ years [94]. This is the time when the craving for friendship with other children begins to appear. The child who is unable, for one reason or another, to satisfy this craving frequently compensates with imaginary companions. This, however, is not a satisfactory solution to the lonely-child problem. Having learned to play with an imaginary companion, the child does not get the training in social cooperation essential to satisfactory adjustment to real children. He is likely to acquire the habit of dominating his playmates, which is possible with an imaginary playmate but frequently is not possible with a real child. When he discovers that the technique that worked so successfully with his imaginary playmate does not work with real children, the child is likely to become a maladjusted member of the group [94].

Leadership. In early childhood, the leader is characteristically superior in size, intelligence, and usually in age to the other members of the group. Superior age and intelligence make it possible for him to offer suggestions for play which the other children, because of their habitual reliance upon adult suggestions, are willing to follow. The big child has the advantage over smaller children in that children tend to respect size as a result of their constant contact with adults and their habits of obedience to adult requests.

Most leaders in early childhood are tyrannical bosses who show little consideration for the wishes of others, who use brute force and threats to control the behavior of others, and who become sullen and angry when others rebel. When tyranny becomes too great, the leader loses status and is replaced by another. In addition to "bossy" leaders, or the bully type, leaders in early childhood are sometimes "diplomats" who lead others by indirect and artful suggestions or by bargains. Girls, at this age, frequently assume the role of leadership in groups containing boys. Physical attractiveness, socioeconomic status, religion, and nationality are unimportant qualities of a leader in the early childhood years [99].

Social Acceptability. When the child begins to play with other children, his acceptance or rejection by them soon becomes apparent. Whether he is popular or not is not necessarily determined by his activity in the group. Sometimes the aggressively bossy child, who pushes himself into everything, is thoroughly disliked by other children. The outstanding trait that makes for popularity among young children is the acceptance

of a situation, such as willingness to do what others do, offering no resistance, complying with requests, and accepting gracefully what
happens. The popular child is conscientious in his conformity to the
group ways. Girls, at this age, are more popular than boys with members of both sexes. Bright children are generally more popular than the
less bright [112]. The child who is less dependent on adults and who
participates more in social activities is more popular than the dependent
child. However, as children learn to function in a group, they become
less dependent on adults. There is no marked sex difference in dependency on adults or in social participation, but girls, as a rule, are
more popular than boys [71].

The unpopular child at the preschool age, on the other hand, is one
who attacks vigorously, who strikes frequently, or pushes and pulls.
Personal affronts and lack of respect for the property rights of others do
not win friends for him. Added to the aggressive behavior of unpopular
children are frequent attempts to escape responsibility, such as clinging
to an adult or running away; dawdling; refusals to comply to the requests of others; and failure to conform to the routine. Furthermore,
the unpopular child usually has objectionable personality traits. The
child who is rejected by others often tries to force himself into the group
and this increases his unpopularity. The child who is handicapped, as is
true of children with hearing problems, often fights to become a member
of a group and its leader. However, if challenged by the group, he will
usually withdraw and play alone [92]. Being rejected by others tends
to make a child "self-bound," and this sets up barriers that interfere with
possible acceptance as the child grows older.

PLAY

Early childhood is often referred to as "the toy age," because at this
time, toys play a very important role in the types of play the child enjoys. At this age, the child imagines that toys have life qualities, that
they are capable of talking, acting, and feeling as he does. Interest in toy
play is strong up to seven years of age, then lags, suggesting a loss of
interest in such play. The length of time that the child will play with toys
and the enjoyment he will derive from such play will depend partly upon
the toy and partly on whether he is playing alone or in a group situation.
When the right toy is used for the right age and the right level of
development, the child will persevere longer in his play, even when the
activity is difficult for him [77, 112].

The way children play in early childhood and the types of play material they prefer are influenced by *intelligence* and *sex*. Children of high
intelligence, for example, show a preference for dramatic play and

creative activities, and for books which inform rather than merely amuse) [70]. Even in the preschool years, children become aware of the fact that certain types of play and certain toys are considered appropriate for girls while others are appropriate for boys. This influences the type of play equipment they use and the way they play with it. Boys, throughout early childhood, show a wider range of play interests than girls [25, 52]. The amount of play equipment children have and the amount of space they have to play in, both of which are influenced by the *socioeconomic status* of the family, will also influence the patterns of their play)[103].

Dramatization. (Dramatization begins to enter into the child's play between the second and third years. Dolls, soldiers, and stuffed animals become living creatures; and wagons, dollhouses, and coaches, all of which are reproductions in miniature of the same equipment used for daily living, make it possible for the child to dramatize scenes from real life in his play.) Dramatic play follows a definite pattern in which personification, such as talking to dolls or stuffed animals, predominates before the age of three years. Following this is make-believe use of materials, such as drinking from an empty cup, and then, among those who are four years of age and older, there are make-believe situations involving companions and the use of materials, such as playing house, or dramatizing scenes from movies, television shows, or books that have been read to them.) In dramatic play, the child often pretends he is someone he loves or would like to resemble)[82]. Very bright children engage more in dramatic play than do those of lower intellectual levels [3].

Construction. (The young child spends much of his play time making things with sand, mud, clay, blocks, beads, paints, crayons, scissors, and paste. He uses blocks, for example, to build bridges, tunnels, or houses [77]. Most of his constructions are in imitation of what he sees in daily life) [46]. (The young child's *drawings* and *paintings* are symbolic, not direct copies of objects.) He draws or paints things as he remembers them, and he is more interested in color than in form, proportions, or perspective. He puts in details that interest him, such as the buttons on a man's coat, and these are usually proportionally too large. Most of his drawings are of people, usually adults, houses, trees, trains, animals, and flowers [14].

Games. (Around the fourth or fifth year, the child becomes interested in playing games with the children in the neighborhood. These "neighborhood games," such as tag, hide-and-seek, cat-and-mouse, cops-and-robbers, advancing statues, and going to Jerusalem, are of the *undefined-group* type in which any number of children can take part.) The children copy one another and follow orders from the leader, who is generally the child who has organized the game.) Games at this age are simple, involve few rules, and often are invented on the spot. Games that test skill, such as jumping rope, playing jacks, and bouncing balls, are likewise popular toward the end of early childhood. These are played individually rather than in a group and involve little competition.

Reading. (Long before the child can read, he likes to look at pictures in his storybooks and to have someone read to him.) Simple fairy and nature stories have great appeal at this age because of the young child's inability to distinguish animate from inanimate objects. The classic fairy tales, such as "Little Red Riding Hood" and "Cinderella," the more modern, fanciful stories, such as "Little Black Sambo," the Mother Goose jingles, and stories about animals and everyday people doing everyday things all appeal to young children. (They prefer stories that "could happen," however, to those that "actually happened," and enjoy stories that are sprinkled with a *bit* of unreality more than those that are factual and real.) On the other hand, children dislike stories that are too unrealistic, because these are too far removed from their experiences to be comprehended [24]. Young children like to look at the pictures in the *comics* and to have the comics read to them. At this age, they show no definite preferences in comics, as older children do. Any comic that lacks a terror element appeals to them [96].

Movies, Radio, and Television. Most young children attend movies very infrequently and then largely the Saturday-afternoon performances meant specifically for children. Because these shows are planned mainly for older children, they are likely to include so much noise and shooting that the young child will become frightened, close his eyes, and cry, or he will become restless because he does not understand the picture. Radio listening and television watching, on the other hand, appeal far more to him because there are programs designed specifically for preschool children, and these can be enjoyed in the security of the home, not away from home with a large crowd of strangers. (For the most part, the programs he likes parallel what he likes in reading—stories about people and animals with a bit of unreality) [67]. The young child who has few opportunities to play with other children, or who does not find play with other children enjoyable, spends proportionally too much of his play time before the television screen. The harmful effects of too much radio listening or television watching are apparent in the frequent nightmares and nervous tensions of the young child [113].

DEVELOPMENT OF UNDERSTANDING

(Concept formation advances rapidly during the years of early childhood.) New experiences lead to new meanings which are associated with meanings established in babyhood. The child now begins to notice details which formerly escaped his attention. As a result, he is not so apt to confuse objects, situations, or people that have elements in common, as he formerly did. His concepts become more specific and meaningful to him, though he still perceives wholes rather than parts of the objects. His feelings and emotions influence what he sees. His concepts are often erroneous, however, and this is especially true of social concepts. Because of his limited social experience, the child understandably misinterprets what others say or do [85].

To motor manipulation the young child adds questioning in his quest for meanings. The "questioning age" begins around the third year and reaches its peak when the child enters school. Questioning is used not only to gain new information but to check upon and supplement information gained through experimentation. Boys ask questions at a faster rate than do girls, and they ask more questions involving causal explanations. Questions beginning with "what" and "where" are most common from two to four years, and those beginning with "why" and "how" and "when" are most frequent after four. The young child also derives new meanings from stories read to him, from the pictures in the comics, and from radio and television programs [38].

Concepts of Life. Young children, because of their limited knowledge and experience, believe that all objects have the same life qualities as humans. "Living" is more often applied to inanimate objects than "having life." *Animism*, or the tendency to ascribe living qualities to inanimate objects, is responsible for many of the faulty concepts of young children. When asked, "What makes the engine go?" even young children recognize that a person is involved in the movement of the engine [85]. Young children regard *death* as a change of abode or departure. They are unable to comprehend the fact that death is a final process because they look upon everything, including the dead and lifeless, as having living qualities [79].

Space Perception. The ability, established in babyhood, to distinguish short *distances* is improved upon at this age. From his play with tricycles, carts, blocks, and other toys, the child becomes familiar with common cues which help him to perceive short distances if they are studied in relation to his body. Longer distances, because they are unrelated to his body, are still very difficult to judge accurately. By the age of four years, perception of short distances is similar to that of an adult. The child's ability to perceive differences in form increases gradually from two to six years. Perception of *relative size* also develops at this age. At the age of three years, young children can select the largest and smallest objects from a group of objects of varying sizes. By the age of five years, they can select middle-sized objects. When the difference in size is very small, perception of relative differences becomes increasingly inaccurate. The concept of roundness is well established between the ages of three and six years [85].

Concepts of Weight. Until the child learns that different materials have different weights, he is apt to estimate weight exclusively in terms of size. A ball of cotton, for example, would be judged heavier than a rubber ball of smaller size. As a result, the young child breaks many objects because he does not make the necessary muscular adjustment to handle them safely. With experience, he learns that he must judge the material the object is made of as well as its size. By the age of five years, the child is able to tell the difference between 3- and 15-gram weights when they are the same size [105].

Number Concepts. Numbers mean little to young children. While they may use numbers in a parrotlike fashion, their concepts of numbers from 1 to 10 are vague and meaningless in most instances. Children who go to nursery school or kindergarten frequently learn the meanings of numbers from 1 to 5 but have only vague concepts about numbers above that [69].

Time Concepts. Young children have no idea of the length of time nor do they have means by which to judge it. They cannot tell time by a clock much before five or six years of age. They have not yet learned how to estimate time in terms of their own activities. Because they do not have a crowded schedule, they are apt to dally over different activities, thus adding to their difficulty in estimating time with any degree of accuracy. By associating specific activities with different times of the day, with the days of the week, and with the seasons of the year, the child can make more accurate estimates. By the time they are four or five years old, most children know what day of the week it is. Only if the month, season, or year are told them at home or in kindergarten are they likely to know these periods before age six [85, 98].

Concepts of Self. The concept of self, which starts in babyhood when the baby begins exploring the different parts of his body and looking into a mirror, develops very rapidly during early childhood because of the child's interest in himself [5]. By the time he is three years old, he should know whether he is a boy or a girl, what his full name is, and where his nose, eyes, mouth, and hair are. At this age, children generally know also the different parts of their bodies, such as their hands, feet, toes, legs, arms, and "tummies," and what articles of clothing belong to the different parts of the body. The six-year-old can distinguish the right from the left side of his body [105]. When he begins to play with other children, he compares himself with them and, as a result, is likely to be self-conscious and shy if he feels that he does not compare favorably [21].

The child's concept of himself as a member of a *racial* group develops earlier among Negro children than among white children. Negro children in nursery school have a more definite concept of their difference from the group and their similarity to another group than do white children of the same age. By the time the child is five years old, he uses ethnic terms to describe himself, as "colored," "Jewish," or "American." The child's awareness of sex differences and of sex-appropriate behavior appears as early as the second year of life when he begins to ask questions about physical sex differences. By the time he is four years old, he identifies his own sex and that of others correctly, using clothing, hair style, and genitals as clues [63].

By the time he is five years old, the young child has a clear concept of appropriate sex roles, as he shows in the patterns of his play and in his general behavior. Children with older siblings learn appropriate sex roles earlier than do those who have younger siblings or are only children. Should the older sibling be of the opposite sex, the girl is likely to become a "tomboy" and the boy, a "sissy" because each imitates the patterns of behavior of the older sibling [33, 60]. Boys of nursery-school age are more clearly aware of appropriate sex-role behavior than are girls, and they do not try to look or act like girls. This is not as true of girls. Fathers are more concerned with sex-appropriate behavior than mothers are and they put pressure on their sons to behave in a masculine way. As a result, boys are more conscious of sex-appropriate behavior and define their sex roles more sharply than do girls [41]. Both boys and girls of nursery school age are aware of sex differences, but they often have a preference for the sex role of their own sex or of the opposite sex. By 5½ years, boys show a predominantly masculine-role preference while girls at that age are about equally divided, with some preferring the masculine and others, the feminine role [23]. Children from the working and executive classes have clearer sex-role concepts than do those from the middle economic groups [83].

Social Concepts. Social perception, or the ability to understand the thoughts and emotions of others from observing their facial expressions and behavior, is essential to satisfactory social adjustments. Young children, as a result of their constant contact with parents, brothers, sisters, and playmates, learn to "size up" these individuals with a fair degree of accuracy. Because of their limited contact with strangers, young children frequently size them up incorrectly. Much of the tactlessness of young children can be traced to poor social perception. Awareness of *racial* differences occurs in the preschool age. By the age of three years, for example, it has been found that Negro children have learned and accepted the majority stereotype of Negroes [81]. At this age, children can identify *sex* differences in other children but not in adults until slightly later [56]. Within the family, they have specific concepts of the role played by the mother and the father [45].

Aesthetic Concepts. The young child's perception of beauty depends largely on his ability to understand the meaning of what he sees or hears. He likes pictures of familiar people and animals doing familiar things [18]. He prefers people of his own sex to those of the opposite sex and he considers people of his own racial background more beautiful than those of other races [97]. The younger the child, the more he likes colors which are bright and gaudy. Pastel shades are usually perceived as ugly by young children. Liking for music of certain types is strong among young children. They prefer songs and music with a definite "tune" or rhythm. With repetition of the child's favorite music, the more beautiful he believes it to be. As is true of pictures, the child's ability to understand music plays an important role in his perception of its beauty.

Comic Perception. Up to the age of three years, the child laughs in response to some pleasurable experience, such as tickling. From then until he is six years old, strange and unusual things, provided they are not so exaggerated as to be frightening, are perceived as funny. Among the things most often perceived as funny by nursery school children are motions and noises made by the child himself or by others, socially unacceptable situations, grimaces made by the child himself or by others, inferiority in others, word play, and imitative laughter. The funny antics of domestic animals and the misfortunes of others are likewise sources of humor at this age. The ability to perceive the comic correlates very highly with intelligence at this age as is true of all other ages [5].

MORAL DEVELOPMENT

Training in conforming to the social codes of the group, begun in the second year of life, must continue throughout childhood. The young child's intellectual development has not yet reached the point where he can learn or apply abstract principles of right and wrong. He must learn moral behavior in specific situations. And, because his retention is still poor, the learning is a slow process. Being told not to do something one day may not readily be remembered the next day or the day after that. This learning is complicated when several different persons, at different times, require that he do different things in the same situation. He cannot understand why an act is wrong today when the same act, yesterday, passed unnoticed.

The young child is expected to transform his naturally impulsive behavior into orderly, patterned conduct, respecting the rights and property of others. He is expected to "learn to say 'No' and 'Don't' to himself and to refrain from prohibited acts" [35]. He is expected to "learn to regulate his personal desires and compulsions so that, when a situational conflict arises, he does what he ought to do rather than what he wants to do" [49] (see Figure 27). When their children are as young as three to four years of age, parents emphasize the importance of self-control in aggression and in destroying or taking property of others. Middle-class parents have been found to be demanding about property, and lower-class parents are strict about the young child's use of tabooed language. Middle-class parents, in general, are stricter in their demands that the

Fig. 27. Young children are expected to conform to parent-approved patterns of behavior and are punished when they fall below these standards. (*Card 6 of the male series of the punishment situation index dealing with the lack of neatness in personal habits. From P. K. Morgan and E. L. Gaier, The direction of aggression in the mother-child punishment situation. Child Develpm., 1956, 27, 447–457. Used by permission.*)

child conform to socially approved standards of behavior than are parents from the lower or upper classes [28].

Moral Concepts. The young child's moral concepts are subjective in nature. He judges acts as right or wrong in terms of the consequences of his own acts. The foundation of moral conduct and the basic moral attitudes of the group to which the child belongs should become well established during early childhood. Because of his mental immaturity, the child cannot understand the whys and wherefores of behavior. He merely learns how to act without knowing why he does so. As early childhood comes to an end, habits of obedience should be established, provided the child has had consistent discipline.

Even though he does not understand why certain acts are good and others bad, the child knows that some acts are labeled "good" and some, "bad." From this information, he lays the foundation for moral concepts that will guide his behavior as he grows older. Even though he may try to evade rules by going to different persons for permission to do something labeled "naughty" by a parent, and even though he may try to test the authority of the person in charge of him, the young child does not question the rules, suggest alternative acts, or bargain with the person in authority as the older child does. Nor does he feel guilty when

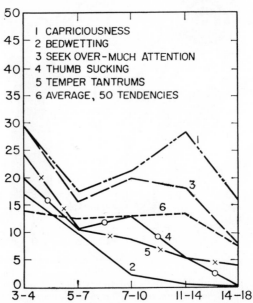

Fig. 28. Most frequent misdemeanors of three- and four-year olds. (*From A. Long, Parents' reports of undesirable behavior in children. Child Develpm.,* 1941, 12, 43–62. *Used by permission.*)

caught doing something that is wrong. He may, however, become frightened at the prospect of punishment or he may rationalize to explain why he did what he did.

Misdemeanors. Young children learn that naughtiness, or willful disobedience of a minor sort, will generally give them more attention than good behavior. If, therefore, they feel that they are being ignored, they are frequently naughty in the hope of getting the attention they crave. Even the temporary discomfort of punishment does not outweigh the satisfaction derived from having adult attention focused on them. The most common misdemeanors of early childhood are capriciousness, bed wetting, seeking attention, thumb sucking, temper tantrums, and dawdling. The frequency of different types of misdemeanor in early childhood is shown in Figure 28. Most of these are associated with immaturity and appear less and less frequently as the child grows older. More girls than boys are hostile and suspicious at this age, and more girls than boys are willful [66]. Among kindergarten children, the most common behavior problems reported by teachers consist of enuresis, shyness, timidity, nervous behavior, and fear [102]. Early childhood is a time when periods of "disequilibrium" occur frequently, when the child is difficult to manage, and when misbehavior is common [53].

Discipline. The educational aspect of discipline, which consists of training the child to conform to the mores of the group, should be the outstanding part of discipline during early childhood, just as it is in babyhood. As new social horizons open up, when the child first plays with other children or enters nursery school, he must learn how to act in a socially approved manner in these new groups. Most parents put little emphasis on the educational aspect of discipline and concentrate on punishments. Unfavorable disciplinary techniques commonly used consist of spanking, isolating the child in his room, sending him to bed, making him sit on a chair, withdrawing a privilege, threatening to leave or cease to love the child, invidious comparisons with siblings, ridicule, sarcasm, nagging, and harping on a misdemeanor. Rewards in the form of candy, toys, being taken somewhere, or given a special treat are used, somewhat sparingly, by parents of young children [9, 28].

The effect of discipline on the child's personality is more important than the effect on his behavior. The more physical punishment is used, the more likely the child is to become sullen, obstinate, and negativistic in his attitude and behavior. Very strict discipline in the early years of life, when the major emphasis is on punishment, frequently leads to unhappiness, maladjustments, or delinquency as the child grows older. It is generally assumed that punishment will prevent the reoccurrence of undesirable behavior. However, after being punished, young children rarely report that they feel penitent or have resolved to avoid the disapproved behavior in the future. This would suggest that punishment does not achieve its goal among young children [9].

EARLY CHILDHOOD INTERESTS

With growth in intelligence comes an awakening of new interests. The young child's interests broaden and intensify as his environment expands and as he comes in contact with more and more people outside the home environment. At this age, his interests center chiefly on himself and all that pertains to his own possessions. The first-born child is likely to have a wider range of interests than later-born children because he has more

contacts with adults. Second- and later-born siblings imitate the interests
of an older sibling of the same sex. If the older sibling is of the opposite
sex, there is less imitation and, as a result, the younger child has fewer
interests [61].

Religion. Religious beliefs are, for the most part, meaningless to a
young child. His intelligence has not yet developed to a point where he
can understand abstractions, nor does he understand many of the words
used in his religious training. He may absorb words and phrases so that
he can repeat them in a parrotlike fashion but they have little real
meaning for him. However, the young child is curious about religion.
Many of the questions asked by young children relate to religious
matters. Because so many of the mysteries centered around birth, death,
growth, and the elements are explained to him in religious terms, his
curiosity about religious matters is great. He tries to satisfy this curiosity
by asking innumerable questions and he accepts what is told him without questioning or doubting the answers given.

The young child's religious concepts are realistic. He interprets what
he hears in terms of what he knows. To him, God is a man who wears
clothes different from the clothes of the persons he knows, and who has
a flowing beard and hair. Angels are men and women with white wings,
while heaven is a place where every human wish is gratified. This is the
"fairy-tale stage" of religious beliefs [44]. That is why religious stories
have such strong appeal to young children. The young child's attitude
toward religion is a compound of awe and reverence. The pageantry
and solemnity of the church service are awe-inspiring. His interest in
religion is egocentric. To him, prayer is a way of gaining childish desires.
This is in keeping with his personality make-up. He visualizes God as a
person who can and will do things for him just as his parents do when
he asks them [68].

The Human Body. The young child is curious about his own body and
the bodies of other children. From the age of $3\frac{1}{2}$ years on, children
show a greater interest in their own bodies than was shown earlier. This
interest takes the form of comments and questions about various parts
of the body, of examining these parts and calling attention to them, and
occasionally, of exhibitionism. The areas that attract a child's attention
especially are the navel, eyes, hair, breasts, and anus. Children are
also curious about elimination, though their attitude towards it is matter-
of-fact and unconcerned [38]. They recognize anatomical differences
between boys and girls but only as incidental characteristics. The cues
they use to distinguish between the sexes are differences in clothes, hair
styles, or names [25].

Sex. Curiosity about sex matters begins to appear in early childhood.
Children at this age are definitely curious about the origin of babies and

ask frequent questions about this matter. This curiosity is intensified if there is a new baby in the family or neighborhood, or if a pet animal has offspring. God is frequently referred to as the source of babies, and many children believe they come from a hospital or a store, or that the stork brings them. The most common questions asked by young children relate to the origin of babies, physical sex differences, sex organs and their functions, and the coming of another baby [25]. The child's attitude toward sex and his sexual behavior are influenced by social pressures between the ages of three and four years. The ease or embarrassment with which he discusses the genitals, excretory functions, or the origin of babies suggests that he has already been influenced by social attitudes [58].

Appearance. The young child has little interest in his appearance but he does have a strong interest in his clothes. At an early age, he discovers that clothing attracts attention to himself. Adults make favorable comments about his clothes, and his playmates not only admire him but often envy him because of them. Children as young as three years of age not only notice one another's clothes, but they refer to the newness, the color, or any feature that is different in the clothing of other children. New clothes have a special appeal for a young child, and he likes others to notice them. If they fail to do so, he calls their attention to his clothes with such comments as, "See my new hat" or "I have new shoes." The first clothes of a particular type, especially when they are like the clothes of older children, such as the first black shoes or the first long trousers, are worn with intense pride. To the young child, they are insignia of growing up. When he can manipulate them himself, without any help, this is an added source of satisfaction to him [84].

FAMILY RELATIONSHIPS

The young child's environment is limited to the family circle except for short periods of time when he is with neighborhood children or in nursery school. As is true of the baby, the young child's attitudes toward people, things, and life in general are patterned by his home life. Although no one method of child training is responsible for making the child well or poorly adjusted, the child who is brought up in a democratic home generally makes better adjustments to outsiders than does the child from an authoritarian home [2, 50, 89]. Parents who are well adjusted pass on to their children, through *personality transmission,* attitudes and behavior patterns that will contribute to the success of the child's adjustments. Young children, in their relationships with others, show much the same patterns of behavior as those they have observed in their own family relationships [15].

At this age, the child begins to be aware of his status in the family. If he is the first-born, he is likely to feel insecure after the arrival of one or two other children in the family. Not only is more expected of him than before, but he feels that the newcomer is usurping his place in the affections of his parents. Should the child be a second- or a later-born child, he may find himself playing the role of the family pet, with attention from older brothers and sisters as well as from his parents. More likely,

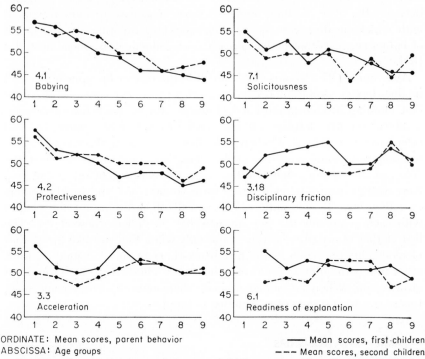

ORDINATE: Mean scores, parent behavior
ABSCISSA: Age groups

—— Mean scores, first children
– – – Mean scores, second children

Fig. 29. Changes in parental behavior as children grow older. (*From J. K. Lasko, Parent behavior toward first and second children. Genet. Psychol. Monogr.,* 1954, 49, 97–137. *Used by permission.*)

however, he will discover that his older siblings resent his presence and show it by treating him as if he were a nuisance. Very early, the child learns to play a certain role in his family, depending on his sex, his ordinal position in the family, and the age differential between him and his siblings [20]. Second-born children, especially those with an older male sibling, try to keep up the pace set by this older sibling and compete with him for the mother's attention [59]. The only child uses his parents as his models and, as a result, is often more mature for his age than are children with siblings [19].

Changes in parental attitudes toward the child come in early childhood. No longer is he the helpless infant who is soft and cuddly as he was when he was a baby. Now he is a rebellious, self-assertive, mischievous individual who is constantly into everything, demanding attention, and refusing to do what he is asked to do unless it strikes his fancy. Parents have definite concepts of what they think a "good" child should be and what they believe to be appropriate behavior for boys and girls [50]. Because young children rarely come up to parental expectations, parents show less warmth and affection and are more disciplinary in their relationships with the child than they were when he was younger [9]. Figure 29 shows changes in parental behavior toward first- and second-born children as the children grow older.

Preference for Parent. Because the mother spends more time with the young child than the father does and because mothers as a rule have a better understanding of the troublesome behavior of young children than fathers do, young children generally prefer the mother to the father. While children of both sexes show a greater preference for their mothers than for their fathers, more girls than boys at this age place their fathers first in their affection. The explanation for this may be that fathers are more tolerant of their daughters than of their sons. Both boys and girls show a definite preference for the father when the mother punishes them and vice versa. They prefer the mother for such activities as bathing them or reading to them, and the father for playing with them [7]. The father who is away from the child for any length of time often expects more of the child than does the father who is with the child continuously. As a result, he becomes critical of the child and his behavior, thus alienating the child, who then turns to the mother for affection [100].

PERSONALITY

The pattern of the child's personality, the foundations of which were laid in babyhood, begins to take form in early childhood. Personality development comes through the continuous altering of the child's awareness of the world, his perception of people and situations, and his relationship to them. The child learns to think and feel about himself as he is defined by others. His image of himself thus develops from the way his parents and others treat him and how he thinks they feel about him. The core of a healthy personality is an image of the self which the child can accept favorably [36].

The parents, siblings, and relatives constitute, for the most part, the social world of the child. How they feel about him and how they treat him are therefore important factors in the shaping of his concept of himself [22]. Because the mother plays a more important role in the young child's life than any other person, her attitudes toward the child and her treatment of him play major roles in his personality development [26]. The child with siblings soon learns to accept a certain role in the family constellation, whether it be the role of the "responsible" child or that of the "spoiled" child, and this will influence his concept of self [20].

By the time the child enters school, the pattern of his personality can be readily distinguished. Some children are leaders and some are followers; some are despotic while others are meek; some are sociable while others are solitary; some like to show off and be the center of attention while others prefer to shun the limelight. Sex differences in personality patterns are apparent at this time. Boys are active, expressive of anger, quarrelsome, insistent on their rights, alibi-building, exhibition-istic, and uncooperative while girls are inclined to be obedient, affectionate, responsible, and tenacious of purpose. How closely the child will conform to the personality pattern characteristic of his sex will be determined by whether his siblings, especially an older sibling whom he uses as a model, are of his sex or not [60]. It is likewise of great importance that the child's first contacts with other children be of a pleasant sort. Otherwise, he will develop unfavorable attitudes about himself. He is likely also to shun social relationships in the future and to build up compensations of an unsocial sort.

Persistence of Personality Traits. Genetic studies of the same children over a period of time have shown that the pattern of personality remains persistently uniform. Because of this fact, it is possible to predict with a high degree of accuracy what a child's future personality is likely to be from the pattern established in the early childhood years. In spite of the persistence of personality traits, it is possible, at this early age, to eliminate habits and attitudes which predispose a child to act in a socially unacceptable manner. In young children, the core of personality, or the "center of gravity," which is made up of habits and attitudes relating to the child himself and his relationship to other people, can be changed because it is not yet well established. Changing it will not disturb the total personality balance as it is likely to do when the child is older [21].

For this reason, it is of crucial importance to see that the environment of a young child is such that undesirable attitudes will not be established. Should any appear, such as the feeling of being unwanted, unloved, or inferior to others, this is the time to nip them in the bud. Among young children, certain aspects of personality do change, partly as a result of advancing maturity, partly from experience, partly from the social and cultural environment in which he lives, and partly from factors within himself, such as emotional pressures, or identification with people. A difficult child may, for example, become more tractable just as a happy, contented child may develop into a sullen one as he grows older. Whether the changes that take place are for the better or for the worse will be determined largely by the child's environment and whether his environment meets his needs. The way the child's dependence needs are met, for example, will shape his personality [48]. Training in the development of self-confidence and in cooperative behavior will result in personality changes, provided this training is given early, before undesirable personality traits have been permitted to become so well developed that changing them is difficult if not impossible.

BIBLIOGRAPHY

1. Alexander, T.: Certain characteristics of the self as related to affection. *Child Develpm.*, 1951, 22, 285–290.
2. Alper, T. G., H. T. Blane, and B. T. Abrams: Reactions of middle and lower class children to finger paints as a function of class difference in child-training practices. *J. abnorm. soc. Psychol.*, 1955, 51, 439–448.
3. Amen, E. W., and N. Renison: A study of the relationship between play patterns and anxiety in young children. *Genet. Psychol. Monogr.*, 1954, 50, 3–41.
4. Ames, L. B.: Development of interpersonal smiling responses in the preschool years. *J. genet. Psychol.*, 1949, 74, 273–291.
5. Ames, L. B.: The sense of self of nursery school children as manifested by their verbal behavior. *J. genet. Psychol.*, 1952, 81, 193–232.
6. Ames, L. B., and F. L. Ilg: Developmental trends in writing behavior. *J. genet. Psychol.*, 1951, 79, 28–46.
7. Ammons, C. H., and R. B. Ammons: Aggression in doll-play: interviews of two- to six-year-old white males. *J. genet. Psychol.*, 1953, 82, 205–213.
8. Ausubel, D. P.: Negativism as a phase of ego development. *Amer. J. Orthopsychiat.*, 1950, 20, 796–805.
9. Bakwin, H., and R. M. Bakwin: Discipline in children. *J. Pediat.*, 1951, 39, 623–634.
10. Banham, K. M.: Obstinate children are adaptable. *Ment. Hyg., N.Y.*, 1952, 36, 84–89.
11. Bayer, L. M., and M. M. Snyder: Illness experience of a group of normal children. *Child Develpm.*, 1950, 21, 93–120.
12. Bayley, N.: Some increasing parent-child similarities during the growth of children. *J. educ. Psychol.*, 1954, 45, 1–21.
13. Bayley, N., and S. R. Pinnau: Tables for predicting adult height from skeletal age: revised for use with the Greulich-Pyle Hand Standards. *J. Pediat.*, 1952, 40, 423–441.
14. Bell, J. E.: Perceptual development and the drawings of children. *Amer. J. Orthopsychiat.*, 1952, 22, 386–393.
15. Block, J.: Personality characteristics associated with fathers' attitudes toward child-rearing. *Child Develpm.*, 1955, 26, 41–48.
16. Block, J., and B. Martin: Predicting the behavior of children under frustration. *J. abnorm. soc. Psychol.*, 1955, 51, 281–285.
17. Boll, E. S.: The role of preschool playmates—a situational approach. *Child Develpm.*, 1957, 28, 327–342.

18. Bon, I. R., and D. C. Lopez: Preferences in colors and illustrations of elementary school children in Puerto Rico. *J. educ. Psychol.*, 1953, 44, 490–496.

19. Bossard, J. H. S.: *Parent and child.* Philadelphia: Univer. Pennsylvania Press, 1953.

20. Bossard, J. H. S., and E. S. Boll: Personality roles in the large family. *Child Develpm.*, 1955, 26, 71–78.

21. Breckenridge, M. E., and E. L. Vincent: *Child development*, 3d ed. Philadelphia: Saunders, 1955.

22. Brodbeck, A. J., and H. V. Perlmutter: Self-dislike as a determinant of marked ingroup-outgroup preferences. *J. Psychol.*, 1954, 38, 271–280.

23. Brown, D. G.: Masculinity-femininity development in children. *J. consult. Psychol.*, 1957, 21, 197–202.

24. Cappa, D.: Types of story books enjoyed by kindergarten children. *J. educ. Res.*, 1956, 49, 555–557.

25. Conn, J. H.: Children's awareness of sex differences. II. Play attitudes and game preferences. *J. child Psychiat.*, 1951, 2, 82–99.

26. Crandall, V. J., and A. Preston: Patterns and levels of maternal behavior. *Child Develpm.*, 1955, 26, 267–277.

27. Dahlke, H. O.: Determinants of sociometric relations among children in the elementary school. *Sociometry*, 1953, 16, 327–338.

28. Dameron, L. E.: Mother-child interaction in the development of self-restraint. *J. genet. Psychol.*, 1955, 86, 289–308.

29. Dennis, J. M., and A. D. Kaiser: Are home accidents in children preventable? *Pediatrics*, 1954, 13, 568–575.

30. Despert, J. L.: Sleep in preschool children: a preliminary study. *Nerv. Child*, 1949, 8, 8–27.

31. Dunnington, M. J.: Behavioral differences of sociometric status groups in a nursery school. *Child Develpm.*, 1957, 28, 103–111.

32. Dusenberry, L.: A study of the effects of training in ball throwing by children ages three to seven. *Res. Quart. Amer. phys. Educ. Ass.*, 1952, 23, 9–14.

33. Fauls, L. B., and W. D. Smith: Sex-role learning of five-year-olds. *J. genet. Psychol.*, 1956, 89, 105–117.

34. Ferguson, R. G.: Some developmental factors in childhood aggression. *J. educ. Res.*, 1954, 48, 15–27.

35. Frank, L. K.: The concept of maturity. *Child Develpm.*, 1950, 21, 21–24.

36. Frank, L. K.: Play in personality development. *Amer. J. Orthopsychiat.*, 1955, 25, 576–590.

37. Freeman, H. E., and M. Showell: The role of the family in the socialization process. *J. soc. Psychol.*, 1953, 37, 97–101.

38. Gesell, A., and F. L. Ilg: *Child development.* New York: Harper, 1949.

39. Gewirtz, J. L.: Three determinants of attention-seeking in young children. *Monogr. Soc. Res. Child Develpm.*, 1954, 19, No. 2.

40. Gewirtz, J. L.: A factor analysis of some attention-seeking behaviors of young children. *Child Develpm.*, 1956, 27, 17–36.

41. Goodenough, E. W.: Interest in persons as an aspect of sex differences in the early years. *Genet. Psychol. Monogr.*, 1957, 55, 287–323.

42. Goodenough, F. L.: *Anger in young children.* Minneapolis: Univer. Minnesota Press, 1931.

43. Gutteridge, M. V.: A study of motor achievements of young children. *Arch. Psychol., N.Y.*, 1939, No. 244.

44. Harms, E.: The development of religious experience in children. *Amer. J. Sociol.*, 1944, 50, 112–122.
45. Hartley, E. L., and D. C. Krugman: Note on children's social role perception. *J. Psychol.*, 1948, 26, 399–405.
46. Hartley, R. E., L. K. Frank, and R. M. Goldensen: *Understanding children's play.* New York: Columbia Univer. Press, 1952.
47. Havighurst, R. J.: *Human development and education.* New York: Longmans, 1953.
48. Heathers, G.: Acquiring dependence and independence: a theoretical orientation. *J. genet. Psychol.*, 1955, 87, 277–291.
49. Hemming, J.: The development of children's moral values. *Brit. J. educ. Psychol.*, 1957, 27, 77–88.
50. Highberger, R.: Maternal behavior and attitudes related to behavior of the preschool child. *J. Home Econ.*, 1956, 48, 260–264.
51. Hildreth, G.: The development and training of hand dominance. *J. genet. Psychol.*, 1950, 76, 39–144.
52. Honzik, M. P.: Sex differences in the occurrence of materials in the play constructions of preadolescents. *Child Develpm.*, 1951, 22, 15–35.
53. Ilg, F. L., J. Learned, A. Lockwood, and L. B. Ames: The three-and-a-half-year-old. *J. genet. Psychol.*, 1949, 75, 21–31.
54. Jacobziner, H.: Accidents—a major child health problem. *J. Pediat.*, 1955, 46, 419–436.
55. Jersild, A. T.: Emotional development. *In* L. Carmichael, *Manual of child psychology*, 2d ed. New York: Wiley, 1954. Pp. 833–917.
56. Katcher, A., and M. M. Levin: Children's conception of body size. *Child Develpm.*, 1955, 26, 103–110.
57. Key, C. B., M. R. White, W. P. Honzik, A. B. Heiney, and D. Erwin: The process of learning to dress among nursery school children. *Genet. Psychol. Monogr.*, 1936, 18, 67–163.
58. Kinsey, A. C., W. B. Pomeroy, C. E. Martin, and P. H. Gebhard: *Sexual behavior in the human female.* Philadelphia: Saunders, 1953.
59. Koch, H. L.: The relation of "primary mental ability" in five- and six-year-olds to sex of child and characteristics of his siblings. *Child Develpm.*, 1954, 25, 209–223.
60. Koch, H. L.: Sissiness and tomboyishness in relation to sibling characteristics. *J. genet. Psychol.*, 1956, 88, 231–244.
61. Koch, H. L.: Children's work attitudes and sibling characteristics. *Child Develpm.*, 1956, 27, 289–310.
62. Koch, H. L.: The relation in young children between characteristics of their playmates and certain attributes of their siblings. *Child Develpm.*, 1957, 28, 175–202.
63. Knopf, I. J., and T. W. Richards: The child's differentiation in sex as reflected in drawings of the human figure. *J. genet. Psychol.*, 1952, 81, 99–112.
64. Krogman, W. M.: The physical growth of the child. *In* M. Fishbein and R. J. R. Kennedy, *Modern marriage and family living.* New York: Oxford Univer. Press, 1957. Pp. 417–425.
65. Levin, H., and R. R. Sears: Identification with parents as a determinant of doll play aggression. *Child Develpm.*, 1956, 27, 135–153.
66. Long, A.: Parents' reports of undesirable behavior in children. *Child Develpm.*, 1941, 12, 43–62.

67. Lyness, P. L.: Patterns in the mass communications tastes of the young audience. *J. educ. Psychol.*, 1951, 42, 449–467.

68. Manwell, E. M., and S. L. Fahs: *Consider the children—how they grow*, rev. ed. Boston: Beacon Press, 1951.

69. Martin, W. E.: Qualitative expressions in young children. *Genet. Psychol. Monogr.*, 1951, 44, 147–219.

70. Maybury, M. W.: Selection of materials by nursery school children of superior mental intelligence. *J. educ. Res.*, 1952, 46, 17–31.

71. McCandless, B. R., and H. R. Marshall: Sex differences in social acceptance and participation of preschool children. *Child Develpm.*, 1957, 28, 421–425.

72. McCarthy, D.: Language development. *In* L. Carmichael, *Manual of child psychology*, 2d ed. New York: Wiley, 1954. Pp. 492–630.

73. McKee, J. P., and F. B. Leader: The relationship of socioeconomic status and aggression to the competitive behavior of preschool children. *Child Develpm.*, 1955, 26, 135–142.

74. Missildine, W. H., and P. J. Glasner: Stuttering: a reorientation. *J. Pediat.*, 1947, 31, 300–305.

75. Mohr, G. J.: Psychosomatic problems in childhood. *Child Develpm.*, 1948, 19, 137–142.

76. Moustakas, C. E.: The frequency and intensity of negative attitudes expressed in play therapy: a comparison of well-adjusted and disturbed young children. *J. genet. Psychol.*, 1955, 86, 309–325.

77. Moyer, K. E., and B. von H. Gilmer: Experimental study of children's preferences and use of blocks in play. *J. genet. Psychol.*, 1956, 89, 3–10.

78. Mummery, D. V.: A comparative study of the ascendant behavior of Northern and Southern nursery school children. *Child Develpm.*, 1950, 21, 183–196.

79. Nagy, M. H.: The child's theories concerning death. *J. genet. Psychol.*, 1948, 73, 3–27.

80. Otis, N. B., and B. R. McCandless: Responses to repeated frustration of young children differentiated according to need area. *J. abnorm. soc. Psychol.*, 1955, 50, 349–353.

81. Pasamanick, B., and H. Knobloch: Early language behavior in Negro children and the testing of intelligence. *J. abnorm. soc. Psychol.*, 1955, 50, 401–402.

82. Peller, L. E.: Models of children's play. *Ment. Hyg., N.Y.*, 1952, 36, 66–83.

83. Rabban, M.: Sex-role identification in young children in two diverse social groups. *Genet. Psychol. Monogr.*, 1950, 42, 81–158.

84. Read, K. H.: Clothes help build personality. *J. Home Econ.*, 1950, 42, 348–350.

85. Russell, D. H.: The development of thinking processes. *Rev. educ. Res.*, 1953, 23, 137–145.

86. Ryan, M. E.: Social adjustment of kindergarten children ten years later. *Smith Coll. Stud. soc. Wk*, 1949, 19, 138–139.

87. Sears, P. S., and H. Levin: Levels of aspiration in preschool children. *Child Develpm.*, 1957, 28, 317–326.

88. Sears, R. R.: Effects of frustration and anxiety on fantasy aggression. *Amer. J. Orthopsychiat.*, 1951, 21, 498–505.

89. Sears, R. R., E. E. Maccoby, and H. Levin: *Patterns of child rearing*. Evanston, Ill.: Row, Peterson, 1957.

90. Sears, R. R., J. W. M. Whiting, V. Nowlis, and P. S. Sears: Some child-rearing antecedents of aggression and dependency in young children. *Genet. Psychol. Monogr.*, 1953, 47, 135–234.

91. Siegel, A. E.: Aggressive behavior of young children in the absence of an adult. *Child Develpm.*, 1957, 28, 371–378.

92. Simmons, J. S.: Social integration of preschool children having hearing problems. *Sociol. soc. Res.*, 1955, 40, 99–101.

93. Soffietti, J. P.: Bilingualism and biculturalism. *J. educ. Psychol.*, 1955, 46, 222–227.

94. Sperling, O. E.: An imaginary companion representing a pre-stage of the super-ego. *Psychoanal. Stud. Child*, 1954, 9, 252–258.

95. Speroff, B. J.: The stability of sociometric choice among kindergarten children. *Sociometry*, 1955, 10, 129–131.

96. Spiegelman, M., C. Terwilliger, and F. Fearing: The content of the comic strip: a study of a mass medium of communication. *J. soc. Psychol.*, 1952, 35, 37–57.

97. Springer, D. V.: Awareness of racial differences in preschool children in Hawaii. *Genet. Psychol. Monogr.*, 1950, 41, 215–270.

98. Springer, D. V.: Development in young children of an understanding of time and the clock. *J. genet. Psychol.*, 1952, 80, 83–96.

99. Stogdill, R. M.: Personal factors associated with leadership: a survey of the literature. *J. Psychol.*, 1948, 25, 35–71.

100. Stolz, L. M., et al.: *Father relationships with war-born children.* Stanford, Calif.: Stanford Univer. Press, 1954.

101. Stott, L. H., and R. S. Ball: Consistency and change in ascendance-submission in the social interaction of children. *Child Develpm.*, 1957, 28, 259–272.

102. Stouffer, G. A. W., and J. Owens: Behavior problems identified by today's teachers and compared with those reported by E. K. Wickman. *J. educ. Res.*, 1955, 48, 321–331.

103. Sullenger, T. E., L. H. Parke, and W. K. Wallin: The leisure time activities of elementary school children. *J. educ. Res.*, 1953, 46, 551–554.

104. Sweet, C.: Enuresis: a psychologic problem of childhood. *J. Amer. med. Ass.*, 1946, 132, 279–281.

105. Terman, L. M., and M. A. Merrill: *Measuring intelligence.* Boston: Houghton Mifflin, 1937.

106. Thompson, G. G.: *Child psychology.* Boston: Houghton Mifflin, 1952.

107. Thompson, H.: Physical growth. *In* L. Carmichael, *Manual of child psychology*, 2d ed. New York: Wiley, 1954. Pp. 292–334.

108. Tolstrup, K.: On psychologenic obesity in children. *Acta paediat., Stockh.*, 1953, 42, 299–304.

109. Ugurel-Semin, R.: Moral behavior and moral judgments of children. *J. abnorm. soc. Psychol.*, 1952, 47, 463–474.

110. Vollmer, H.: Jealousy in children. *Amer. J. Orthopsychiat.*, 1946, 16, 660–671.

111. Walters, J., D. Pearce, and L. Dahms: Affectional and aggressive behavior of preschool children. *Child Develpm.*, 1957, 28, 15–26.

112. Wilson, L. A.: The influence of a child purpose on the perseverance of young children. *J. exp. Educ.*, 1955, 23, 353–358.

113. Witty, P. A.: Comics, television, and our children. *Today's Hlth*, 1955, Feb., pp. 18–21.

» 6 «

Late Childhood

Late childhood extends from the age of six years to the onset of puberty, between eleven and twelve years. It is marked, at the beginning, by the child's entrance into school, a milestone in his life which is responsible for many of the changes that take place in his attitudes and behavior during this period. Late childhood has been called by various names, each describing one outstanding characteristic of the developmental level present at this time. According to educators, this is the "elementary school age." Parents regard it as the "smart," or "Big Injun," age, when the child thinks he knows everything and does not hesitate to inform others of his superior knowledge. They also regard it as the "dirty age" because the child glories in being dirty, slovenly, and careless in his appearance.

To the psychologist, this is the "gang age" because, at this time, the major concern of every normal boy or girl is to be accepted by his contemporaries and to be regarded as a member of a "gang." H. L. Hollingworth has suggested this stage is the "moron hurdle" over which the individual must pass and make satisfactory adjustments to adult life. The impulsiveness and lack of foresight, so characteristic of the moron, are equally characteristic of the older child. He cannot see beyond his nose and he acts on the impulse of the moment, regardless of the consequences.

PHYSICAL DEVELOPMENT

Late childhood is a period of slow and relatively uniform growth. At the onset of puberty, the average girl of eleven years has a *height* of 58 inches and the average boy of the same age, a height of 57.5 inches. Because boys begin their puberty growth spurt approximately a year later than girls, they are slightly shorter, on the average, than are girls of the same age. Throughout late childhood, growth in height is at a slow, even rate of approximately 3 inches annually [62]. (X rays of the bones of the wrist and hand give a more accurate prediction of adult height at this period than in early childhood.)With each passing year, the child's height shows a general tendency to increase in correlation with his parents' height, and this adds to the accuracy of the prediction [10].

Weight increases are likewise slow and fairly uniform at this age. At the onset of puberty, the average girl of eleven years weighs 88.5 pounds and the average boy of the same age weighs 85.5 pounds. At twelve

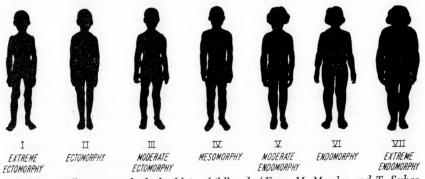

| I | II | III | IV | V | VI | VII |
| EXTREME ECTOMORPHY | ECTOMORPHY | MODERATE ECTOMORPHY | MESOMORPHY | MODERATE ENDOMORPHY | ENDOMORPHY | EXTREME ENDOMORPHY |

Fig. 30. Differences in body build in childhood. (*From M. Massler and T. Suher, Calculation of "normal" weight in children. Child Develpm., 1951, 22, 75–94. Used by permission.*)

years of age, the average girl weighs 100.5 pounds and the average boy, 96 pounds [62]. Children of today weigh more than they did 10 years ago, but there has not been a comparable increase in height. (More girls are overweight than boys, especially in the latter part of late childhood) [37]. During this period, fat tissue is responsible for 21 to 29 per cent of the total body weight [69]. The child's weight is markedly influenced by his body build. (The *ectomorph*, who has a long, slender body, for example, can be expected to weigh less than a *mesomorph*, who has a heavy, hard, and rectangularly outlined body) [71]. Differences in body build among children are illustrated in Figure 30. Weight for children of the same age is likewise influenced by their intellectual level, the socioeconomic status of the family, and their birth weight [99].

This is the age when children who make poor social adjustments frequently turn to overeating as a compensation for lack of social acceptance. This is especially true of children from small families or those who have been the "babies of the family" [40]. Habits of overeating, resulting from parental pressures in the earlier years, likewise contribute to overweight [18]. As a result of his being overweight, the child loses out in active play, thus missing the opportunity to acquire the social skills so essential to social success.

Body proportions change during the late childhood years (see Figure 14, page 82). Although the head is still proportionally too large for the rest of the body, the disproportions decrease slightly at this time. At the age of twelve years, for example, the surface area of the head is approximately 10 per cent of the total body surface as compared with 13 per cent at five years. With the gradual eruption of permanent teeth throughout this period, the mouth changes and the lower part of the face increases in size, thus eliminating some of the facial disproportion that existed in the earlier years of life [32]. Changes in occlusion (fitting together of the upper and lower teeth) occur during the transition from baby to permanent teeth and this has a marked effect on the shape of the lower part of the child's face. When the two jaws do not fit together, resulting in malocclusion, the shape of the lower part of the face is seriously affected [99]. During late childhood, the forehead flattens, the lips fill out, and the nose becomes larger and acquires more shape, owing to the development of the cartilage framework. These changes help to eliminate the "babyish" look of the young child (see Figure 31).

As childhood progresses, the trunk elongates and becomes slimmer. The chest broadens and flattens, the neck becomes longer, thus permitting the shoulders to drop, and the pelvis increases in size. By the age of eight years, the arms and legs are nearly 50 per cent longer than they were at two years and are very thin with no marked development in the musculature. This is responsible for the spindly, all-arms, all-legs look of the older child. The hands and feet grow very slowly in late childhood, though boys' hands and feet are generally larger than those of girls [99].

This is a homely age. Very pretty babies and young children go through this homely stage just as do those who are not so attractive. In the case of the former, however, they generally emerge from this homeliness and blossom into attractive boys and girls. There are a number of reasons for the unattractiveness of the older child's appearance, most important of which are the transition from baby teeth to permanent teeth; stringy, unmanageable hair which results from the transition from the fine-textured hair of the young child to the coarser-textured hair of the adolescent; spindly arms and legs which give the child a young-colt appearance; and poor grooming which comes from the child's lack of interest in his appearance and his revolt against cleanliness, which he associates with "sissies."

Illnesses. During the early part of this period, most children are subjected to different children's *diseases,* as measles, mumps, chicken pox, and whooping cough. Aside from these diseases, late childhood is normally a very healthy age. There may be an occasional stomach upset caused by indiscreet eating, or a cold resulting from the child's refusal to protect himself adequately from rain or snow. These, however, are only transitory and rarely have any serious effect on the child's physical well-being [9]. Poor health conditions, as evidenced in underweight, poor

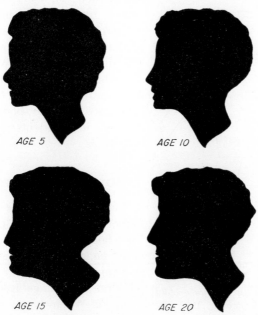

AGE 5   AGE 10

AGE 15   AGE 20

Fig. 31. Changes in facial proportions with age. Profiles of the same girl at four different ages. (*From L. Cole, Psychology of adolescence, 4th ed. New York: Rinehart, 1954. Used by permission.*)

posture, rounded shoulders, bowlegs, and carious teeth, are more common than good health in children of the lower-income classes [99].

Children suffer from every possible type of *physical defect.* Some of these are present at birth; others are acquired at different times throughout childhood as a result of illness, accident, or neglect of the child's physical well-being. The most common defects include dental caries, visual and auditory impairments, orthopedic disabilities, and diseased tonsils and adenoids [19]. Late childhood is the age when *imaginary illness* is not uncommon. The child has learned, from earlier experiences, that when he is ill he is not expected to carry on his usual activities, he receives more attention than usual, and the home discipline is markedly relaxed. When distressing or intolerable conditions exist in the child's life, he may use a trifling illness as a means of gaining outside help.

(Accidents in childhood are responsible for more deaths than are ill-nesses.) The older child has, as a rule, fewer accidents than the younger child. It has been found, for example, that approximately two-thirds of all accidents to children occur before they are nine years old. Most accidents to the older child occur outside the home and boys have more accidents than do girls. Some children seem to be more accident-prone than others. They are, as a rule, over-active, restless, adventuresome, im-pulsive, and less popular than are the children who have fewer accidents. Children with the fewest accidents have been found to be timid, submis-sive, and well controlled [41, 54, 63]. The areas of the body most often injured in accidents are shown in Figure 32.

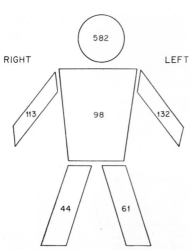

FIG. 32. Parts of the body most often injured in nonfatal accidents during childhood. (*From H. Jacob-ziner, Accidents—a major child health problem. J. Pediat.,* 1955, 46, 419–436. *Used by permission.*)

MOTOR DEVELOPMENT

Because motor skills play such an important role in the child's success in school and in his play with other children, the child whose motor de-velopment lags behind that of other children of his age is greatly handi-capped. When he is awkward and lacks skills other children have, he is likely to withdraw from the group and develop unhealthy attitudes toward himself and social life. The child who lags behind his contemporaries may have had too little opportunity to learn skills when he was younger, or an obese condition may be the cause of his backwardness in this area of development. Obese children, who lack skills, usually have difficulties in making social adjustments and seek such solitary forms of entertainment as reading, movies, listening to the radio, or watching television.

(Given an opportunity, most children take keen delight in motor activity of all sorts.) They are healthy, full of energy, and anxious to be on the go constantly. They are willing to practice endlessly to achieve success and they show great pride in their accomplishments, especially if these are recognized favorably by their friends. With practice comes increase in speed and accuracy. Waste movements are gradually eliminated and the child's performance requires minimum attention on his part. This adds to his self-confidence and, as a result, he becomes more daring, often "stunting" to attract the attention of his friends [19].

Types of Skill. The skills the child learns will depend partly upon his environment, partly upon his opportunities for learning, and partly upon what is in vogue among his classmates. Marked sex differences, for example, exist not only in play skills at this age but also in the level of perfection of these skills. Girls, as a rule, surpass boys in skills involving finer muscles, such as painting, sewing, weaving, and hammering while boys are superior to girls in skills involving the grosser muscles, such as basketball throw, socker kick for distance, and standing and running broad jump for distance [19].

The *self-help skills* connected with eating, dressing, and bathing should be well enough developed by six years of age so that the child will need only occasional help. The results may not be up to adult standards at first, but with practice, these skills will be perfected to the point where the child can perform them with as much speed and excellence as an adult. At *school,* the child develops the skills needed in writing, painting, drawing, dancing, singing, and making things with tools. *Social-help skills,* learned in relation to tasks in the home, such as dusting, sweeping, washing and drying dishes, making beds, or cooking, not only give the child pleasure but add to his feeling of self-importance. *Play skills,* such as throwing and catching balls, riding bicycles, skating, swimming, and constructing things from wood, clay, or other materials, are learned in connection with the child's play. Children who have superior skills make better adjustments to school and in their social relationships outside of school than children whose skills are inferior to those of their agemates [48].

Handedness. The child's skill will be influenced to a marked extent by whether he is right- or left-handed, or ambidextrous. By the time he reaches his sixth birthday, the child has usually established hand dominance in the sense that he uses one hand predominantly and shifts from the use of one to the other very infrequently. If he has learned to use his right hand, his adjustments will be easier than if he has learned to use the left hand, not only because most tools, instruments, and materials are made for right-handed people, but also because models of teaching are planned for the right-handed. The child who is left-handed will be confused and frustrated when he tries to use materials designed for right-handed people or when he attempts to learn new skills by imitating models meant for the right-handed [7].

The child who has not established hand dominance by the time he enters school and, instead, uses one hand for some skills and the other hand for other skills will not only find it confusing to shift from one hand to the other but is likely to have less well-developed skills than if he had learned the majority of them with one hand [53]. Unfortunately, by the time the child reaches late adolescence, it is too late to attempt to establish hand dominance or to change from the use of the left to the right hand. By that time, skills are well enough learned so that changing them is likely to be confusing to the child and he will resist the change, which he finds both difficult and frustrating. The result is often nervous tension which expresses itself in speech disorders, reading disabilities, and nervous mannerisms [7, 53].

SPEECH DEVELOPMENT

As the child's social horizons broaden, he discovers that speech is an important tool for group belonging. This realization gives him a strong motivation to learn to speak better. He also learns that the simpler forms of communication, such as crying and gestures, are socially unacceptable and this gives him an added incentive to improve his speech. Furthermore, the school places emphasis on vocabulary building and sentence structure. As he learns to read, he adds to his vocabulary and becomes familiar with correct sentence structures.

In spite of the fact that all children are given similar opportunities for improving their speech in school, there are marked variations in the speech of children within the same grade. Children of intellectual superiority show linguistic superiority in size of vocabulary, length and correctness of sentence structure, and maturity of the content of their speech. The same is true of children with upper socioeconomic status. At every age, children from the upper socioeconomic groups have superior linguistic skills to those of the lower groups. Not only do parents of the upper groups feel that speech is important and that they should therefore help their children to learn to speak correctly, but they also provide a better model for their children to imitate.

Variations occur between the sexes as well as within the sex groups. Boys, at every age, are inferior to girls in size of vocabulary, in correctness of sentence structure, and in ability to express their meanings adequately. They also have more speech defects than girls [73]. The child from a bilingual home is not ready, linguistically, for school and, as a result, is handicapped in his school adjustments. This is apparent in his poor academic and social adjustments throughout the elementary school years, even when his intellectual ability is adequate for him to do academic work of a high caliber [29, 73].

Vocabulary. As is true of every age, the child's *comprehension* vocabulary exceeds his use vocabulary. He knows the meaning of many words in a vague way and can understand them when they are used in combination with other words, but he does not know them well enough to hazard using them himself. (Throughout late childhood, the child's *general* vocabulary grows by leaps and bounds.) From his studies in school, his reading, his listening to other people, the radio, or television, the child builds up a vocabulary which he uses in his speech and writing. (It has been estimated that the average first grader knows between 20,000 and 24,000 words, or 5 to 6 per cent of the words in a standard dictionary. By the sixth grade, he knows approximately 50,000 words.) The number of words a child knows well enough to use in his speech and writing determines, in a large measure, his success in school [73].

(Words with *special* meanings and limited use are also learned at this age.) The older child, who has had little opportunity to acquire an adequate vocabulary in early childhood, learns after he goes to school the words which are in common usage in his school environment. By the end of the first grade, if not before, his *etiquette* vocabulary should be as large as that of the adults of his environment. (Girls, as a general rule, have larger *color* vocabularies than boys because of the girls' greater interest in colors.) From the study of arithmetic and his out-of-school contacts with money, the older child learns the names and meanings of *numbers* and different denominations of *money*. While the true significance of words relating to large numbers may not be fully appreciated, the child knows in a vague way what they mean. His *time* vocabulary likewise increases and is generally as large as that of the adults with whom he comes in contact.

(*Slang* and *swear words* become important parts of the older child's vocabulary.) No longer does he use such words in a parrotlike fashion as the younger child does. Now, such words are used to express thoughts and feelings for which he has no other adequate means of expression. These words he learns from older brothers and sisters or high school students in the neighborhood. He thus identifies himself with older children and this gives him a feeling of self-importance. Girls, as a rule, use less slang and less obnoxious forms of slang than do boys. (To the typical boy, the rougher the language, the better he likes it and the more he feels that it distinguishes him from girls.) Boys take keen delight in using slang and swearing at times when they will attract attention. Late childhood is a "slang age," and few children escape using the slang that is in vogue at the time [19].

(A new form of language makes its appearance in late childhood. This is *secret language*, which is used in the child's communication with his intimate friends.) Secret language may take the form of distortions of the child's own speech or it may be imitations of the secret language used by older children. *Written forms* consist of codes formed by symbols or crude drawings to express words or complete thoughts. The common *verbal forms* are generally known as "pig Latin" or "pidgin English." *Kinetic language* usually consists of the use of gestures and the formation of words by the means of the fingers, as in the language of the deaf and dumb. Girls use secret language more frequently than do boys and they spend more time developing new symbols and word signs than do boys. From ten years of age until early adolescence is the peak of the secret-language age, though most children start to use secret language in some form from the time they enter the third grade.

Pronunciation. Except in cases where a child has a speech defect of one sort or another, errors in pronunciation are uncommon at this age. A new word may be incorrectly pronounced the first time it is used but, after hearing a correct pronunciation of it once or twice, the child is generally able to pronounce it correctly. The older child does, however, have a tendency to talk at the top of his lungs and to shout as if he thought everyone were deaf. This is not only disagreeable for those who must listen to his shouting, but it also has a tendency to coarsen the tonal quality of his voice. Boys are especially given to shouting because they think a quiet, pleasant, modulated voice is a sign of a "sissy."

Sentences. The six-year-old child should have command of nearly every kind of sentence structure. From then until he is nine or ten years old, the length of his sentences will increase. These long sentences, so characteristic of children, are generally rambling and loosely knit. Gradually, after the age of nine years, the child begins to use shorter and more compact sentences [73]. When conversing with other children, the child uses many phrases instead of complete sentences. Because sentence construction is difficult for a child, *grammatical errors* are very common even at this age. The number and seriousness of these errors will vary, however, according to the correctness or incorrectness of the speech the child hears at home or among his playmates. There is a high correlation between the grammatical errors made by the child and those made by his parents [80].

Speech disorders are far less likely to begin in late childhood than in early childhood. However, stuttering, stammering, and slurring, which may have started several years earlier, will likely grow worse as time goes on unless remedial measures are taken to correct them. Because these disorders all trace their origins to nervous tension, they are likely to grow worse rather than better after the child enters school, owing to the child's embarrassment when other children laugh at his "funny speech." Children who stutter show more, and more serious, symptoms of maladjustment than do nonstutterers [74]. Children from middle-class families more often develop into stutterers than do those from lower-class families. There are more stutterers among children who come from less crowded than from more crowded homes [76]. Except when there is some physical cause, such as a space between the two upper front teeth or malocclusion of the jaws, few children lisp by the time they reach the school age [73].

Content of Speech. The older child's speech is less egocentric than is that of the preschool child. Just when he will shift from *egocentric* to *socialized* speech will depend not so much upon his age as upon whether his personality is egocentric or social, the number of social contacts he has had and the satisfaction he has derived from them, and the size of the group to which he is speaking. The larger the group, the more socialized the speech. When the child is with his contemporaries, his speech is generally less egocentric than when he is with adults [19]. Favorite topics of conversation, when children are with their contemporaries, consist of talk about their own experiences, home, family, games, sports, movies, their gang activities, sex and sex organs, and accidents. The child feels freer to discuss these topics and to express his opinions when no adults are present [35].

When the older child talks about himself, it is usually in the form of *boasting.* Unlike the younger child, he boasts less about material possessions than about his skill and strength in games. Boasting, as a rule, is very common between the ages of nine and twelve years, especially among boys. The older child also likes to *criticize* and to *make fun* of other people. Sometimes he criticizes people openly, sometimes behind their backs. When criticizing adults, the child generally puts his criticism in the form of a suggestion or complaint, as "Why don't you do so and so?" or "You won't let me do what my friends do." Criticism of other children frequently takes the form of name calling, teasing, or insults. Questions, answers, commands, and directions are other common categories of the older child's speech [19].

EMOTIONAL DEVELOPMENT

The older child soon discovers that violent expressions of emotions, especially of the unpleasant emotions, are socially unacceptable to his contemporaries. They regard temper outbursts as "babyish"; withdrawal reactions in fear as indicative of a " 'fraid cat"; and hurting another in jealousy as poor sportsmanship. Hence a child acquires a strong motivation to learn to control the outward expressions of his emotions. Changes in emotional behavior are shown in Figure 33. At home, however, there is not the same strong motivation to control his emotions. As a result, the child frequently expresses his emotions as forcibly as he did when he was younger. Under such circumstances, it is not surprising that parents criticize or punish him for "not acting his age."

Characteristically, emotional expressions in late childhood are pleasant. The child giggles or laughs uproariously, squirms, twitches, or even rolls on the floor, and in general shows a release of pent-up animal spirits. Even though these emotional expressions are immature as compared with adult standards, they indicate that the child is happy and making good adjustments. Not all emotionality at this age, however, is of a pleasant sort. Numerous outbursts of temper occur and the child suffers from anxiety and feelings of frustration. Girls often dissolve into tears or have

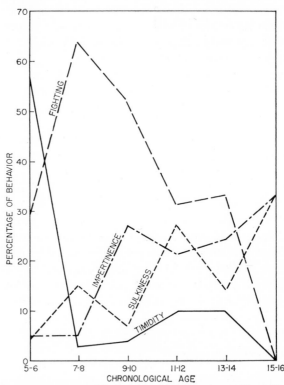

Fig. 33. Changes in emotional behavior as children grow older. (*From K. C. Garrison, Growth and development. New York: Longmans, Green, 1952. Used by permission.*)

temper outbursts reminiscent of their preschool days; boys are more likely to express their annoyances or anxieties by being sullen and sulky. The child who feels out of place in school—because he is either too bright or too dull for his classmates—whose home environment is restrictive and whose parents expect more of him than he is capable of doing, or whose aspirations are unrealistic and doomed to failure is likely to experience more unpleasant than pleasant emotions. This will lead to poorer adjustments in the home and outside and will increase the child's unfavorable emotionality [55].

Common Emotions. Most of the common emotions found in late child-hood are the same as those found in early childhood. They differ from those of early childhood, however, in two respects: first, in the type of situation that gives rise to the emotions, and second, in the form of ex-pression. These changes are the result of broadened experience and learn-ing rather than maturation. As the child's intelligence increases and his experiences broaden, he interprets situations differently than when he was younger. As a result, he responds to them differently. Furthermore, his broader experiences, resulting from his contact with more people out-side the home, enable him to discover how different people feel about different emotional expressions. In his desire to win social approval, he tries to learn to conform to socially approved patterns of emotional ex-pression and to curb forms of expression he discovers are socially dis-approved of. The common emotional patterns of late childhood are:

FEAR. Fear is less common among older children than among younger. Many objects, situations, animals, and people which terrify young chil-dren are accepted calmly by older children [42]. Fears of fire, darkness, illness, disease, doctors, dentists, operations, being hit by a car, and be-ing bitten by a dog are most common at this age. Girls show more fears of different things than do boys. While fears aroused by concrete and tangible stimuli decrease with age, there is a marked increase in the frequency of fears of imaginary, fanciful, supernatural, or remote dangers; of the dark and imaginary creatures associated with the dark; and of matters associated with corpses and death. Older children are also afraid of being "different," of being ridiculed or teased, and of being a failure in what they undertake. Because the older child is aware of the social disapproval of his friends when he shows his fear, he tries to avoid any situation that might be frightening, thus saving himself from the humilia-tion of being seen in a state of fear. *Shyness,* a form of fear in social situations, is generally expressed by such nervous mannerisms as holding the head on one side, pulling at the nose, ears, or clothing, or shifting from one foot to another [55].

Worries, or fears caused by imaginary stimuli, begin to make their ap-pearance at this age. Family or school problems, problems related to per-sonal and social adjustments, or to health are the most common worries of older children. School worries, such as failing a test, being late for school, or being left behind in school, are more common than out-of-school worries. Girls worry more than boys, especially about school and safety. The child's friends have a marked influence on the number and severity of his worries. When, for example, the group discusses schoolwork, each child is likely to begin to worry about passing or being promoted if one of the children says that he has had a warning from the teacher. Social pressures thus intensify the worries of each individual child [83].

Generalized *anxiety*, "a painful uneasiness of mind concerning impending or anticipated ill," is more common than any one, specific worry. The child is often unaware of the cause of his anxiety and does not realize that it comes from feelings of insecurity, rather than from some external situation [20]. Anxiety is greater in children who are unpopular than in those who are well accepted by their peers. As a rule, anxiety is greater among girls than among boys and it increases as the child grows older and more pressures are placed on him. The anxious child is handicapped in learning, especially when the learning task is difficult, as in reading and arithmetic; he makes more errors than the less anxious child; and his poor achievement tends to increase the insecurity which is at the basis of his anxiety [72] (see Figure 34).

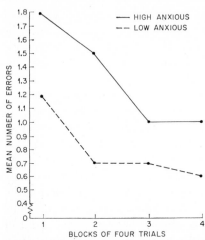

FIG. 34. Error curves for anxious and nonanxious children in the performance of a complex learning task. (*From D. S. Palermo, A. Castaneda, and B. R. Mc-Candless, The relationship of anxiety in children to performance in a complex learning task. Child Develpm., 1956, 27, 333–337. Used by permission.*)

ANGER. There are more anger-provoking situations in late childhood than in early childhood because the older child has a stronger desire for independence than he had when he was younger. He is therefore more frequently frustrated in his efforts to achieve this independence than is the more docile, younger child. The older child also becomes angry when an activity in progress is interrupted, when he is constantly criticized, when unfavorable comparisons with older children are made, and when he is "lectured." It also annoys him to be blamed or punished for something he did not do, to see someone else cheat or do unfair things, or to be accused of lying. And, finally, he becomes angry more often than the young child does from his own ineptitude. He frequently sets levels of aspiration beyond his capacity and, when his achievements fall short of these goals, it makes him angry. Anger is one of the strongest of the emotions during this period [42].

Instead of flying off the handle in a temper tantrum as a young child does, the older child expresses his anger in sulkiness, negativism, refusal to speak, quarrelsomeness, fussiness, and being generally disagreeable to everyone about everything. The tendency to quarrel, especially with siblings, reaches its peak between the ages of ten and twelve years and then decreases. When an older child expresses his anger in a manner characteristic of younger children, he generally wins the disapproval of other children and finds himself no longer acceptble to the group. Social pressures are thus primarily responsible for changing the form in which anger expresses itself among older children [11]. Furthermore, the child's strenuous play, which helps to release some of the pent-up emotional energy, and his increase in skills which overcome some of his ineptitude are partially responsible for changing the form of anger expressions [55].

The older child experiences more *frustrations,* or feelings of helplessness when a drive is blocked, than do younger children. Sometimes the blocks come from his social environment, from parents or teachers who will not permit him to do what he wants to do, and sometimes from his own unrealistic aspirations, which he discovers he is incapable of reaching. Some children react in an aggressive way by striking out at the offending object or person, while other children react in a passive way, withdrawing from the block. In free, unrestricted social situations in which adult authority and discipline are absent, aggressive reactions are more frequent and also more violent [108].

JEALOUSY. Sibling jealousy does not die out when the child enters school. Sometimes, in fact, it is intensified because the child feels that, during his absence from home, the younger child has the whole of his mother's attention while he is among unfriendly strangers. The school child may, if he has experienced jealousy at home, transfer his jealousy to his classmates, especially toward those who are popular or who excel in studies or sports. Instead of the bodily attacks on the child who seems to hold the center of adult attention, as is characteristic of young children, the older child shows his jealousy directly through quarreling, telling tales, ridiculing, teasing, bullying, making disparaging comments, or instigating quarrels. He may express his jealously indirectly by ignoring the child of whom he is jealous, by sarcastic comments, by engaging in daydreams of the "martyr" type, or by lying and cheating [55]. As childhood progresses, indirect expressions of jealousy are more common than direct expressions [42].

CURIOSITY. Curiosity is not so strong in the older child as in the younger. This may be explained partially by the fact that there is less for the older child to explore because he is already familiar with the commonplace things in his daily life and partly because he has learned from experience that curiosity can get him into trouble and that it is best to check it. The older child is, however, curious about new things that appear in his environment and about those things which, when he was younger, he was not permitted to explore, such as matches, old trunks in the attic, or the working of the stove. As his environment widens to include areas in the community beyond his immediate neighborhood, his curiosity leads him to explore these new and unfamiliar things.

The older child satisfies his curiosity in much the same ways as he did when he was younger. He examines things that mystify him and he frequently takes them apart to see how they work. In addition to direct explorations, the older child asks innumerable questions to supplement what he has been able to learn for himself. But, unlike the younger child, he does not have to limit his questions to his parents. He can seek information from teachers, relatives, any adults he comes in contact with, or even from older children. And, finally, the older child can draw upon the resources of his school or community library for information. By the time he reaches the third grade, he reads well enough to get meaning out of what he has read. From then on, reading as a source of information becomes increasingly important to him.

AFFECTION. Affection is expressed very slightly by older children. Boys feel that they are "too old" to be kissed or hugged and they are likely to be embarrassed when anyone, even a member of the family, demonstrates any affection for them, especially if the demonstrations are in public. They even resent being called by names of endearment. While girls are not so restrained as boys in this respect, they too dislike being "fussed over" by anyone. And, because both boys and girls dislike people to show affection for them, they are very undemonstrative in their relations with others. They are far more likely to show affection for a pet animal than they are for a person. Their affection for people, however, is shown indirectly by their desire to be constantly with those whom they love, to do things to help them, or to assist them in any way they possibly can. This is especially apparent in the child's reactions to his friends. He wants to be with them constantly. When he is away from them, he tries to keep in close touch with them, by telephone conversations, or by letter writing. The older child usually has "favorites" among his siblings and parents and, for them, he has greater affection than for the family members who are not his favorites [17]. When he does show affection, it generally comes in "bursts" at unexpected times [42].

JOY. As children grow older, much the same things arouse pleasant emotions as when they were younger. They never fail to smile or laugh at incongruous situations, violations of conventions, absurdities, slight calamities, sudden or unexpected noises, or anything that seems out of place in the situation in which they are. Their laughter is intensified when they are feeling physically fit. As comprehension of words increases, the child gets more pleasure from play on words and from jokes than he did when he was younger. He is now able to laugh at his own predicament, though he may do so mainly to convince others that he is a "good sport." Anything that gives him a feeling of superiority, such as practical jokes, eating forbidden foods, taking a puff of a cigarette or a taste of liquor, gives him keen pleasure [19].

Expressions of joy are much more controlled in older than in younger children. While the young child may show his pleasure by clapping his hands, jumping up and down in glee, or even rolling on the floor, the older child rarely behaves in this way because he learns that his contemporaries consider such behavior "infantile." He does, however, show his glee in loud, raucous laughter. Frequently boys slap their companions on the back or head when they are particularly happy, and girls may throw their arms around a friend, hug, and kiss her as expressions of their joy.

SOCIAL DEVELOPMENT

Interest in peer activities, an increasingly strong desire to be an accepted member of the gang, and discontentment when away from it have given the name "the gang age"* to the closing years of childhood. At this time, social development is taking place rapidly and the child quickly passes from the self-centered, selfish individual, whose social contacts are characterized by constant disagreements and fights, to the point where he is a cooperative, well-adjusted member of a social group composed of his peers. Learning to live in a social world is hard for the child, especially if he has not had a good preliminary training for it at home during the early years of his life. His success in making adjustments to the social life of his school and neighborhood will have a marked influence on his childhood happiness [23].

No longer is the child satisfied to play at home alone or to do things with members of his family. Even one or two friends are not enough for him. He wants to be with the "gang" because only then will there be a sufficient number of individuals to play the games he now enjoys and to give the excitement to his play which solitary play or play with another child lacks. From the time the child enters school until the physical changes at puberty begin to develop, the desire to be with and to be accepted by the gang becomes increasingly strong. This is just as true of girls as of boys. The greater home restrictions placed upon the girl's behavior and the increasingly heavy burden of home duties frequently keep the girl from taking as active a part in the "gang" life that boys of the same age enjoy. Figure 59, page 284, shows the increase in time spent outside the home as children grow older.

* "Gang," as used in the following discussion, refers to a specific type of social grouping characteristic of the late childhood years. The childhood gang is not made up of hoodlums whose primary interest is in mischief making, but rather of boys or girls of the same age whose primary interest is in having a good time together.

Gangs. Typically, the childhood gang is composed of individuals of the same sex. At first, there may be only three or four members but, with a growing interest in sports, the gang becomes larger so that there will be enough players to make a team. Boys' gangs, as a rule, are larger than girls' gangs. The size of the gang, however, is influenced by the number of children available and the activities the gang members want to engage in [42]. In areas where there few or no facilities for team play, gangs are likely to turn their energies into mischief-making channels. However, all boys' gangs, at some time or other, engage in some activities not considered desirable by adults, such as annoying people, stealing fruit, smoking, or holding "smut" sessions. Girls' gangs, by contrast, less frequently engage in socially unacceptable behavior, though they occasionally smoke or engage in scandel mongering. Most of their time is spent in talking about rival gangs, their parents, siblings, and teachers, in raising money for charity, in playing games or making things, or in acting out plays. While gang activities vary from community to community and among the different social classes within a community, there is a marked similarity in their interest in games and sports, going to the movies or athletic contests, exploring the community, or just sitting around to talk and eat. Boys, more often than girls, try to test the barriers imposed by adults and, as a result, may become noisy, troublesome, and rowdy [27].

The gang generally has some central meeting place where each member is sure to find some of his gangmates when they are not in school. This meeting place may be a street corner, a garage, the cellar of a home, a barn, a vacant lot, a deserted house, or the corner drugstore. Boys, as a rule, have their meeting place as far away as possible from parental supervision and interference. Girls, on the other hand, are likely to have their gang headquarters in the home of one of the gang members where there is a minimum of interference from the family, where they can talk without fear of being overheard, and where they have both space and freedom to do as they please. Just about the time the child begins to undergo the puberty changes, between eleven and twelve years, he loses interest in gang activities and drops out of the gang [27].

INFLUENCE OF GANG. Because it is of vital importance to the child to be an accepted member of a gang, he becomes very susceptible to the suggestions of the members. Insecure in his status and afraid that he will be rejected by the gang unless he conforms wholeheartedly to the standards set by its members, the child bends over backward to be like his gangmates in dress, opinions, and behavior. When a conflict arises between parental standards and those of the group, the child is likely to conform to the latter rather than to the former. While conforming to the gang's standards, the child is also learning to think of himself as an individual and to develop a self-concept based on knowledge of how his gangmates rate him [66].

From his contacts with the gang, the child learns to compete with others, to cooperate and work as a member of a team, to accept responsibilities and to see them through, to take the part of others when they are mistreated or neglected, and to be a good sport in adversity as well as in success. This training in socialization, which can be derived through no other medium than day-in, day-out contact with his peers, is of far more value to the child, not only in childhood but throughout the remaining years of his life, than the temporary disturbance to parent-child relationships which this training is likely to engender.

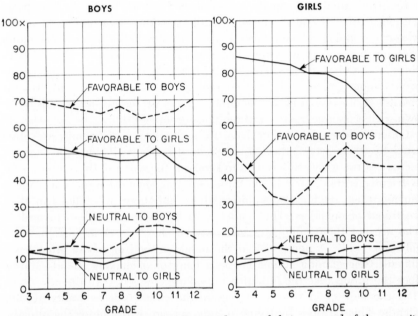

FIG. 35. Attitudes of boys and girls toward peers of their own and of the opposite sex at different ages. (*From D. B. Harris and S. C. Tseng, Children's attitudes toward peers and parents as revealed by sentence completions. Child Develpm.*, 1957, 28, 401–411. *Used by permission.*)

Friends. Both boys and girls at this age definitely prefer the companionship of individuals of their own sex. Boys, on the whole, have a more favorable attitude toward girls as childhood comes to an end than girls have toward boys. Antipathy for members of the opposite sex reaches a high point just before puberty, at which time the girls regard boys as boisterous, are impatient with their noisiness and lack of manners, and are generally antagonistic toward them. Girls' attitudes toward boys are more emotionally toned than are boys' attitudes toward girls. Boys, by contrast, are more objective and neutral than antagonistic in their attitudes toward girls [47]. Figure 35 shows attitudes of boys and girls toward peers of their own sex and of the opposite sex. There is reason to believe that the unfavorable attitude of girls toward boys at this age stems partly from girls' resentment at the greater freedom boys are permitted to enjoy and partly from the fact that, as girls reach puberty, the greater social maturity that accompanies their early sexual maturity makes the typical behavior of boys of their own age seem "immature."

There are many factors influencing the older child's choice of friends. As a rule, he chooses those he perceives as similar to himself and those who meet his inner needs. Propinquity in the school or neighborhood is important because, unlike the adolescent or adult, the child is limited to a relatively small area in the selection of his friends. There is a strong tendency for children to choose friends from their own grades in school whose chronological and mental ages are similar to theirs. Personality traits are an important determining factor in the choice of friends, with cheerfulness, friendliness, cooperativeness, kindness, honesty, generosity, even temperedness, and good sportsmanship ranking high [15, 31]. As childhood draws to a close, the child shows a preference for friends of his own socioeconomic, racial, and religious groups [48].

Older children, once they have formed a group of friends, are often cruel to others whom they do not regard as their friends. Much of the secrecy of the gangs is designed to keep out the children they do not want as friends. Instead of ignoring these children, they often make a point of hurting their feelings by taunting them and they are callous in their treatment of outsiders. This tendency to be cruel and callous toward all who are not their gangmates generally reaches a peak around the eleventh year [42]. A new child in the neighborhood or school often has a difficult time gaining acceptance in a gang or of making friends. Rarely does the group take the initiative in making contacts with the new child. It is the new child who must initiate the contacts if he wants to have friends. This he does by trying to talk or play with one of the already-formed groups, by observing and imitating their play, and by trying to attract their attention to himself. At first, he is usually ignored or rebuffed. If he is willing to try again and again, he may succeed in getting one member of the group interested in him and, through this contact, he may eventually win a place in the gang. A child who is a newcomer is often unsuccessful in winning a place for himself in the gangs of his class and, as a result, has few friends and few opportunities for social contacts [81].

Even though gangs are tightly knit social units, shrouded in secrecy to keep out newcomers or others they do not want as members, there is a great deal of fighting going on within the ranks. Often children in a gang are not on "speaking terms" with their friends. Many of these quarrels are made up and the friendships reestablished; others are not [42]. As a result, children's friendships are rarely static. The child shifts

from best friend to enemy, or from casual acquaintance to close friendship, quickly and often for little reason. Quarreling, bossiness, disloyalty
or underhandedness, conceit, and incompatibility are the reasons most
often given by children for changing friends. However, as children grow
older, they show better social insight in the choice of their friends than
they did when their choice was based mainly on similarity of play
interests and, as a result, their friendships become more stable. Children
who are popular have been found to change their friends almost as often

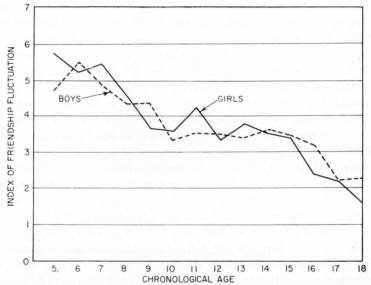

FIG. 36. Decrease in friendship fluctuations with increasing age. (*From J. E.
Horrocks and M. E. Buker, A study of the friendship fluctuations of preadolescents.
J. genet. Psychol., 1951, 78, 131–144. Used by permission.*)

as unpopular children [15]. Friendship fluctuations at different ages are
shown in Figure 36.

Social Acceptability. The older child is well aware of what his classmates think of him and whether they like him or not. If he is popular, he
will have friends and belong to a gang; if he is unpopular, he will not be
accepted by any gang and will have few or no friends. Some children,
especially those who are very bright or who have some special ability
that makes them interested in things that have little interest for their
contemporaries, find little in common with their contemporaries and, as
a result, are *voluntary isolates,* as contrasted with the *involuntary isolate,*
who craves friends but is rejected by others.

Comparisons of popular with unpopular children have revealed that those who are popular conform more to classroom requirements and expectations, smile more frequently, engage in some form of cooperative, voluntary group activity, make more voluntary contributions to the group, are less likely to be alone during play, are less aggressive, and are primarily "group centered" rather than self-centered. While they invariably have certain traits that are social liabilities, popular children have enough positive traits that are social assets to counterbalance these. They are, on the whole, well-adjusted individuals [44].

Children who are socially unacceptable to their peers are usually either of the quiet, withdrawn, reserved type or of the aggressive, "problem" type that antagonizes other children [16]. Bright children are better liked than those of average or below-average intelligence. The child who is overage for his class in school has little chance for social acceptance among his classmates. Overage children are not only ignored in class and play activities but are actively disliked by their classmates [77]. The unfortunate thing about lack of social acceptance at this age is that it cuts the child off from social contacts at the very age when such contacts are of vital importance for the child in learning to make satisfactory adjustments to other children.

Leaders. While an aggressive, dominating child may force himself into the role of leader, these tactics will not work when the child becomes older. The leader of a gang represents the gang's ideal. In the case of boys, the boy must be a good athlete, a good sport, and an all-round superior individual. Because boys and girls of this age develop an attitude of hero worship toward someone who possesses qualities they admire, the leader who can hold the respect of the gang and thus assure his popularity must be superior in most respects to the rest of the group, especially in intelligence, dependability, appearance, poise, diplomacy, democratic ideals, self-confidence, emotional stability, athletic ability, and awareness of the wishes of others [12]. And this superiority must express itself. The quiet, introverted individual is likely to be overlooked and not selected as the leader, regardless of how many superior qualities he may possess. In all leaders, extroversion is more marked than introversion. The larger the group, the more leadership skill the leader must have if he is retain his position of leadership. The more experience in leadership the child has when he is younger, the better will be his chances of being selected as a leader when the group becomes larger [45, 48].

PLAY

Late childhood is frequently called the "play age." This name is likely to be misleading because it suggests that more time than ever before is devoted to play. Consideration of the subject will quickly show that this would be impossible. The school child has far less time available for play than he had before he entered school. The name, "the play age," comes from the fact that there is, during this period, an overlapping of play activities characteristic of the younger years and those of adolescence. The older child clings to some of his favorite toys of the preschool years until he is eight or nine years old while, at the same time, he begins to show an active interest in the organized games and sports of the high-school or college student.

For the first time in the child's life, *socioeconomic* differences are beginning to be apparent in his play. Children of different social-class backgrounds engage in leisure activities that are both quantitatively and qualitatively different. Among older children, the favored activities of those of the lowest economic group consist of going to the movies, radio, and church. By contrast, in the upper middle-class group, radio, church, movies, and family activities rank in first place. Children of the middle-class group participate more in organized recreational groups, such as the Scouts and YMCA, while those who come from the lower economic groups engage in activities mostly in centers or clubs for "underprivileged children" [68]. The older child's play is also markedly influenced by his *sex*, with boys engaging in more games and sports of a strenuous sort than girls, additionally important are the child's *intellectual* level, the type of *neighborhood* in which he lives, and the play opportunities it offers. For most children, play becomes less active as childhood progresses, and amusements in the form of movies, radio, television, and reading gain in popularity [97].

Favorite Play Activities. The older child enjoys a wide range of play activities, some of which are more popular early in his school career, and others, with advancing age. Among the most popular are:

Constructive Play. Making things just for the fun of making them and with little forethought of the eventual use that may be made of the products is a popular form of play among older children. *Construction* with wood and tools appeals to boys, while girls prefer finer types of construction, such as sewing, drawing, painting, clay modeling, and jewelry making [42]. *Drawing, painting,* and *clay modeling,* which young children engage in frequently, gradually decrease in popularity as childhood advances. This is not so much because the child loses interest in these activities but rather because of the self-consciousness that comes when he realizes that his productions fall below those of other children or when he is criticized by his classmates and teachers [13]. *Singing* is another type of creative play the older child enjoys. He likes songs of easily perceived tonal values and slow cadence because they are "singable" and can be enjoyed by all, regardless of musical ability.

Collecting. Collecting as a form of play increases in popularity as childhood progresses. The peak age for boys generally comes at ten years and a year later for girls. The older child is more selective in his collections than when he was younger. No longer does he make collections of anything or everything that attracts his attention. Instead, he limits his collections to a few special items and tries to get a wide variety of each item. There is a marked similarity in what different children of a given age collect, varying from neighborhood to neighborhood and influenced by the fad of the moment.

Games and Sports. Early in the school life of a child, his games are the simple, undifferentiated type characteristic of early childhood. Tag, hide-and-seek, cops-and-robbers, and similar neighborhood games are still played. However, he is now anxious to play the games of older children and he begins to practice basketball, football, baseball, hockey, or whatever sport is in vogue at his school. By the time the child is ten or eleven years old, his games are largely competitive in spirit. No longer is he satisfied with the loosely organized neighborhood games alone. He wants to be a member of a team where each player has his own role. His interest is now concentrated on skill and excellence, rather than merely having fun.

When the child first becomes a member of a team, he is likely to continue to play an individualistic game, trying to outdo the other team members. This is a carry-over of the role he played in the neighborhood games. Gradually, he learns to subordinate personal interests, to cooperate with his teammates, and to be satisfied with the distinction of being a member of a team, even though he receives no recognition as an individual. Because it takes time for a child to shift from an individual to a cooperative member of a group, the transition is generally not achieved until the closing years of late childhood. Games and sports have great value as socializing agents for the child. From them, he learns to cooperate, to get along with others, to play the role of follower as well as leader, and to evaluate himself and his abilities realistically by comparing himself with his teammates. As Dubois has pointed out, "When young people do not participate in sports, . . . they frequently are headed for trouble because they have not had the opportunity to learn to win humbly, to lose gracefully, and to endure physical discomfort to attain a goal" [36].

Amusements. The active life of an older child might, at first glance, preclude all amusements. Such, however, is not the case. There are times during the day, and more often in the evening, over week ends, and on holidays, when it is impossible for the child to be with his friends. During these periods of isolation, he spends what time he has free from schoolwork and from home responsibilities in amusing himself, not by playing solitary games but by reading, listening to the radio, watching television, or, whenever he has an opportunity, by going to the movies. In all these activities, he would prefer to have some of his friends with him but, if this is impossible, he can content himself alone for a short period of time.

READING. The older child is too much of a realist to be able to enjoy the make-believe element of a fairy tale. While he continues to be interested in fairy tales for a year or two after entering school, his reading time is devoted mostly to books of adventure. He derives keen satisfaction from imagining himself in the role of the hero of these stories and of doing things which his prosaic life denies him. Books about heroes and heroines, history, school life, or present-day national figures, such as athletic heroes, movie actors and actresses, appeal to his interest in hero worshiping. In addition, boys enjoy reading books and stories about popular science, while girls read about nature. In late childhood, marked sex differences in reading interests develop, as well as differences resulting from the intellectual level of the child [19].

In addition to reading books, older children show an interest in reading *magazines* and *newspapers*. Regardless of intellectual level, almost all American children today enjoy reading the *comics*. The first interest the child has in the newspaper is in the section devoted to the comics [42]. The appeal of the comics is chiefly emotional and is achieved by their being "skewed toward reality," with real people in unreal situations or vice versa. While some comics have a humorous element, most are adventure stories in which the characters are engaged in dangerous adventures or noble deeds. Animal characters appear more in the comics that appeal to younger children while humans play the important roles in the comics older children prefer [94]. The popularity of different themes in comics is shown in Figure 37.

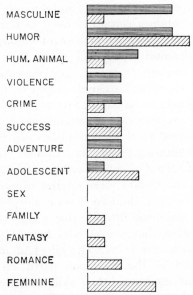

FIG. 37. Popularity of different themes of comics for boys and girls. (Girls' values are cross-hatched.) (*From R. F. Butterworth and G. G. Thompson, Factors related to age-grade trends and sex differences in children's preferences for comic books. J. genet. Psychol., 1951, 78, 71–96. Used by permission.*)

There are many reasons why comics appeal to children. Not only are they amusing, exciting, easy to read, and cheap, but they may also stimulate the child's fantasy life. They may present an escape from everyday reality, help the child to forget unpleasant experiences, and give him something to look forward to. Boys are attracted to those comics whose contents, action, and stories are predominantly masculine and written from a masculine standpoint, whose stories feature a good deal of crime and violence, or whose main theme centers around sports and athletics. Girls, on the other hand, show a preference for comic books that feature feminine characters and pursuits that are typically adolescent, and which contain a certain element of romance and dating [24]. While there is a great deal of criticism of children's reading of the comics, no one has demonstrated conclusively that they are detrimental. Unless properly selected, however, they introduce children to things they would not otherwise be closely exposed to, such as crime and sex, and they are likely to be harmful to the development of reading skills [105, 106].

MOVIES. Movie attendance becomes an increasingly popular amusement as childhood progresses and is one of the favorite activities of children's gangs [42]. Comics and cartoons are their favorite movies up to the age of nine or ten. After that, they prefer adventure. Boys, on the whole, show more interest in movies of the adventure type than do girls. Because children become deeply absorbed in what they see and have a noncritical attitude that makes them accept in an unquestioning fashion what they see, movies have a marked influence on their attitude and behavior [106]. The effect of movies, however, depends partly on the age of the child and partly on his intelligence. Younger children are affected more than older children, and those with lower IQs, more than those with higher IQs. The criticism that children become more aggressive after seeing films of the cowboy or villain type has not been found to be valid; in fact, there is a decrease in aggression after seeing such films, especially among the more aggressive children [1].

RADIO AND TELEVISION. Unless there is a television set in the home, the school child will spend between one and three hours a day listening to the radio. Because television combines the features that appeal to the child in both the movies and radio, children prefer television to radio until they reach adolescence. Children of the younger ages and those of the lower socioeconomic groups, whose opportunities for other forms of play are often limited, spend more time watching television than do older children, who prefer to be with their gang, or than children from the higher socioeconomic groups, who have opportunities for a wider range of play activities.

Program preferences for radio and television follow much the same lines as preferences for reading and movies. Figure 38 shows the radio

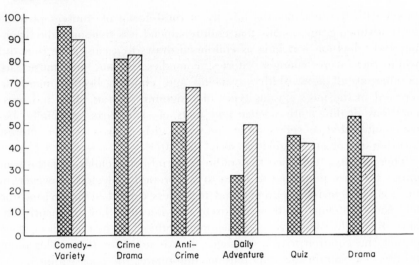

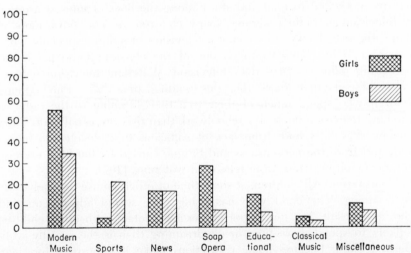

FIG. 38. Radio program preferences of boys and girls in late childhood. (*From E. A. Ricciuti, Children and radio: a study of listeners and non-listeners to various types of radio programs in terms of selected ability, attitudes, and behavior measures. Genet. Psychol. Monogr., 1951, 44, 69–143. Used by permission.*)

program preferences of boys and girls in late childhood. However, the child must listen to or watch what is available at the time he is free; he cannot always satisfy his preference. Children become more critical of the programs on radio and television by the time they are ten years old and this critical attitude increases as they grow older [42]. This, combined with the fact that the novelty of these forms of amusement wane with advancing age, means that children spend less time on radio listening and television watching as childhood draws to a close than they did when they were younger. Stories, comedies, humor, and music are popular at all ages. With advancing age, children become more interested in the more serious types of programs, such as plays and presentations dealing with science and feats of skill. Boys, especially, become interested in sports programs while girls show a greater interest in programs of an imaginative sort [106, 107].

There is little evidence that radio is harmful for children if the programs they are permitted to listen to are properly selected. However, in the case of television, parents tend to be less careful in supervising the television watching of their children, and because they frequently believe that television has an educational value for their children, they permit the children to watch longer than is good for them. This often results in eyestrain, nervous tension, nightmares, or poor eating habits due to fatigue and emotional excitement, and it may cause them to have distorted values about the seriousness of crime. While some children may be motivated to read and study along the lines of interest aroused by television or radio programs, many children are not. Boys, more so than girls, read books after seeing a television program, especially when the program has been based on one of the classics. Radio has a less motivating influence than does television. Watching television reduces the child's playtime more than his reading time [25]. Furthermore, children who spend much of their free time listening to the radio or watching television do poorer schoolwork than they are capable of. Their schoolwork suffers both from lack of sufficient time devoted to homework and from the nervousness and fatigue caused by too little exercise and too much eyestrain from television watching [107].

DAYDREAMING. All children, at some time or other, amuse themselves by daydreaming. The child who has made poor school adjustments and who, as a result, has few opportunities for contact with other children is likely to spend more time in daydreaming than is the socially well-adjusted child. Because home restrictions make it impossible for them to spend as much time with their playmates as boys do, girls generally daydream more than boys. Typically, the daydream of this age is of the "conquering-hero" type. The dreamer sees himself as he would like to be in real life. While the background and setting of childish daydreams vary from one child to another, the dreamer is invariably the hero or the heroine of the dream. Daydreaming gives the child an opportunity for self-glorification which may prove to be so pleasant to him that he substitutes daydreaming for real social contacts, thus increasing his poor social adjustments [19, 48].

DEVELOPMENT OF UNDERSTANDING

As the child's world expands with his entrance into school, so do his interests. And with the broadening of interests comes an understanding of people and things which formerly held little or no meaning for him. Not only is his understanding of his environment increased by the formal teaching he receives in the classroom but it is also broadened by exchanging ideas with his playmates and by his ability to read. In the rapid building of new concepts at this age, and in the absence of an adequate fund of information to act as a critical check on the formation of these concepts, *errors* are frequent. Children, for example, often overestimate or underestimate time, they develop misconceptions about themselves if the group underestimates or overestimates their abilities, they develop a crude and often cruel sense of humor, and they are likely to judge the total personality of others in terms of one or two traits rather than in terms of the personality pattern as a whole. As time goes on and their experiences increase, they become more critical in their estimates, with the result that errors in perception are gradually reduced.

Space no longer is a vague, meaningless thing for an older child. From the use of weights and rulers he comes to learn the meaning of ounces, pounds, inches, feet, yards, and even miles. Schoolwork in arithmetic helps him to formulate more definite ideas of space and distance than he could develop through his own personal experiences. Similarly, *numbers* take on new meanings for him as he begins to use money and as he works with arithmetic problems [84]. The study of history and of geography, with special emphasis on the manners, customs, and modes of living of people in other lands and in different periods of history, broadens his concepts of *time*. Even more important, the rigid schedule of the school day, with the ringing of a bell at the end of a given period of time, enables him to estimate time more accurately in terms of what he can accomplish in a stated period [42, 102].

From his broadened experiences and from his studies in school, the older child develops more realistic concepts of *living*. No longer does he attribute living qualities to all inanimate objects as he did when he was younger. Some children, at this age, find it difficult to distinguish between "living" and "has-life" qualities in such objects as a tree, the moon, or a river [61]. The child is likewise more realistic about *death* and recognizes its finality. He accepts the fact that everyone dies but he has little personal interest in death. Furthermore, he is not concerned about the hereafter or what happens to people or animals after they die. In general, this lack of concern stems from his general lack of interest in religion as a personal matter at this age [42].

A child's concept of *self* is clarified when he sees himself through the eyes of teachers and classmates, rather than through the prejudices that often color the parents' concepts of the child, and when, through his own eyes, the child compares his abilities with those of his peers. He is aware of sex differences and of appropriate *sex roles* which become a part of his self-concept. Girls are more embarrassed and self-conscious about being girls than boys are about being boys [42]. From seven years of age on, boys show a strong masculine-role preference, with few preferring the feminine role. Girls, on the other hand, have a much stronger preference for the masculine than for the feminine role. Because they have been allowed and often encouraged to dress and act like boys when they were younger, and because they prefer the freedom and privileges they identify with the masculine role, they prefer it to the feminine role until ten or eleven years when, as they approach puberty, there is an increased preference for things that are feminine [22]. Regardless of preferences, both boys and girls in late childhood know what the social group with which they are identified expects of members of their sexes, and they are aware, from the way their classmates treat them, of how well they conform to these standards. Shortly after he enters school, the child becomes aware of his *racial-group* membership and the social attitude toward this group. Toward the end of childhood, he adds to his self-concept the meaning of social-class status, as defined in terms of parental occupation [96, 102].

Social appraisals, or the ability to size up the personality, abilities, and disabilities of others, likewise develop rapidly at this age as a child spends more and more time with other children. In the absence of adult supervision, children are likely to comment with brutal frankness on qualities of the playmates they dislike. This is a great help to a child who is learning to make his own appraisals of others because he can see, through the eyes of others, characteristics that are socially acceptable and those that are not. The child becomes aware of group differences at an early age. As a result of home and environmental influences, the child recognizes racial, religious, and socioeconomic differences among the children with whom he plays or with whom he is associated in school. And he accepts the adults' attitudes toward these groups, thus giving rise to group consciousness and the beginnings of social prejudice. Prejudice against a member of a minority group is usually not based on the personal experience of the child but is the reflection of the cultural patterns and stereotypes of the child's environment [38].

The child's social concepts include prejudices against members of the opposite sex as well as against those of minority groups. When adults encourage children to differentiate between their boy and girl companions and expect them to behave differently toward members of the two sexes, the child learns to view the two sexes differently and to regard one as superior to the other [28]. Social concepts of appropriate behavior and personality characteristics of members of the two sexes vary from one social class to another, and the child learns the stereotype accepted by the social class with which he is identified [48].

From his contacts with people outside the home, but especially from his classmates, the child learns to appraise the *beautiful* and the *comic*. No longer are things beautiful or ugly just because he likes or dislikes them. Beauty and ugliness of color, of nature, or of the human face and form are conditioned by group standards, rather than by individual reactions [6]. Similarly, from his group contacts, he discovers that certain things are considered funny while others are not. He learns to laugh when the group laughs and to lift an eyebrow in scorn when others do the same. Seeing others in a predicament; making faces; drawing caricatures of teachers and others in authority; playing practical jokes, especially on adults or disliked children; referring to sex and religion; and defying authority, even if this leads to punishment—all make the group laugh. Each individual child thereupon thinks these are funny situations and laughs too [48]. Even at ten years of age, the child is "not very skilled at high-class humor." He enjoys "corny jokes," sex, and smutty stories, and at eleven, he still enjoys some slapstick [42].

MORAL ATTITUDES AND BEHAVIOR

As the child's horizon broadens and his contacts with other people increase, he discovers that what was considered right or wrong at home is not always viewed thus by those outside the home. As a result, new standards of morality are gradually built up and these frequently conflict with parental standards. The child's moral code is now determined to a large extent by the moral code of the group to which he belongs. Furthermore, his concepts no longer are narrow and specific as they were when he was younger. He gradually generalizes his concepts so that they refer to any situation rather than to a specific situation. For example, he learns that stealing is wrong regardless of whether it means stealing money, material possessions, or the work of others. From the ages of nine to twelve years, children have higher ideals of honesty than they previously had. Similarly, the child now regards lying as wrong, whether the lie is told to a parent, a teacher, or a classmate, with or without fingers crossed. As a child reaches the end of childhood, his moral code gradually approaches that of adults [57].

Unlike the younger child, who is not concerned unless his misbehavior is detected and punished, the older child has a deep personal concern. He does not want to fall short of the standards of his peers and, as a result, is more interested in self-protection than in truth. When he does not come up to the mark, he finds a scapegoat, such as a parent or sibling, and blames them for his shortcomings. At this age, boys cheat and girls steal, especially in stores [42]. If caught, the child is more likely to feel ashamed than guilty because few children have acquired, much before adolescence, a sense of obligation to control their behavior in the absence of punishment. *Moral shame* is thus a powerful agent in the development of moral behavior [4]. Likewise, the child no longer accepts in an unquestioning way punishments meted out by adults for behavior of which they disapprove. Now the child has a strong sense of fairness and justice, and he does not hesitate to complain if he feels that he has been unfairly punished. Many children feel that the mother does not often take the blame herself for incidents that occur but rather tends to blame the children and this they resent [75]. The older child is critical of the shortcomings of others, whether adults or his peers, and he condemns them severely for smoking, drinking, cheating, lying, or doing anything that falls below his standards or those of the group with which he is identified [42, 48].

Only when the group as a whole approves and condones behavior that is in direct contradiction to adult standards will the child accept it uncritically. Older children, especially boys, frequently delight in doing things that they know are wrong because of the sense of personal importance they derive. Misbehavior in the school and neighborhood by gangs of older boys or girls is usually motivated by this desire. On the whole, their misbehavior is annoying to adults and is an attempt to throw off the restrictions of adult authority rather than anything else [57]. However, all children misbehave at home and at school at some time or other, even when not with their gangmates. The most common forms of misbehavior in the school have been reported to be stealing, cheating, lying, using vulgar and obscene language, destruction of school materials, truancy, annoying other children by teasing and bullying, reading comics during school hours, chewing gum, irresponsibility, disorderliness, and boisterousness. Boys are greater offenders than girls [95]. Children whose misbehavior is repeated and is of a serious nature generally come from poor home backgrounds and are unaccepted by their peers [36, 48].

Discipline. Discipline becomes a serious problem with older children. Continuing to use the disciplinary techniques that proved to be effective when the child was younger is likely to lead to strong resentments on the part of the older child. Praise and occasional rewards for good behavior, depriving the child of some pleasure he has anticipated or of some privilege he has been accustomed to, and sending him off to his room alone "to think it over" are generally far more effective than corporal punishment, which the older child strongly resents. Lower-class parents continue to use corporal punishment on the older child, often in a severe form, while middle-class parents are more likely to try to stimulate feelings of guilt and shame in the child or to threaten him with the loss of parental love. As a result, the lower-class child concentrates on avoiding punishment by lying and being sneaky whereas the middle-class child tries to conform to parental wishes [85].

Throughout the closing years of childhood, teaching the child what is right and wrong is just as important as it was during the early years of childhood. But the teaching should take a new form. Emphasis should be placed on explanations of why certain forms of behavior are acceptable while others are not and on helping the child to broaden the specific moral concepts formed when he was younger into more generalized, abstract concepts of right and wrong. Unfortunately, too little emphasis is placed on the educational aspect of discipline at this age, on the faulty assumption that the child should "know by now the difference between right and wrong." Rewards, in the form of praise or an occasional special treat for meeting a difficult situation successfully, are infrequently used. They have a strong educational value, however, in that they tell the child that what he has done is right; furthermore, they offer him a strong motivation to repeat such behavior [36].

Every child needs discipline. Discipline gives him a feeling of security because he knows where his boundaries, limits, and freedoms are; it helps him to live according to certain standards in order that he will have less feeling of guilt; it gives him an opportunity for praise and love when he does the right thing and an ego-bolstering sense of confidence. Thus, discipline is a developmental need of the child. The child's attitude toward discipline depends upon his age and his environmental influences. When children are young, they like to feel that parents know best. By late childhood, they rebel against their parents and parental standards when they learn that there are different standards and that different disciplinary methods are used among their friends. The great emphasis on gang standards may lead to open rebellion in the home. Too strict discipline is likely to lead the child to misbehavior to prove to himself and his friends that he is independent; too lenient discipline is confusing to the child and creates a feeling of insecurity [36, 57]. Most children, as they reach the end of childhood, feel that home control of their behavior is nonthreatening and not unduly restrictive, thus eliminating some of the earlier friction with parents based on feelings of resentment toward discipline [49].

SOME CHILDHOOD INTERESTS

What the older child is interested in depends, as it does in the earlier years of childhood, upon the opportunities he has to develop interests. A child brought up in a totally unreligious family may or may not become interested in religion, depending on whether or not he has an opportunity to learn about religion at school or from his discussions with his friends. Similarly, a child whose gang shows a marked contempt for anything but the simplest and plainest clothes will have little or no interest in clothes. In the development of interests, interpersonal relationships are more important than specific teaching. The child who, for example, dislikes his teacher may learn to dislike the subject she teaches and school in general. "Likes" and "dislikes" thus play an important role in the development of interests [101].

Although each child will develop certain interests that are individual in nature, every child in a particular culture develops other interests that are almost universally found among the children of that culture. These include interests in:

Religion. While the novelty of Sunday school attendance has worn off, in part at least, by the time the child reaches first grade, he still enjoys going to Sunday school. This offers him an opportunity to be with his friends on a day when otherwise he might not be permitted to play with them or when family plans would limit his companionship to adults. He is, of course, interested in what he learns in Sunday school, but as each year passes, he is likely to develop an attitude of skepticism toward some of the teaching [42]. And he does not hesitate to show this skepticism by asking his Sunday school teacher or his parents to explain certain incomprehensible parts of what he learns, nor does he refrain from arguing and trying to prove that they are not right.

Religious teaching in the early years of his life has, however, left its imprint on the older child's mind. He has many vague concepts which gradually become clearer and more accurate as he grows older and he can comprehend abstract theories better. Most children have a fairly clear concept of God, but the concept varies from child to child depending upon the teaching he has had and his experiences with his own father. Similarly, his concepts of sin and forgiveness will be influenced by his religious teaching and the way he has been treated when he misbehaved. As the older child discovers from experience that many of his prayers were not answered, he prays mainly from habit or because it is expected of him, not voluntarily. Prayer thus degenerates into a ritual with little or no meaning for him [88].

The Human Body. After having explored the outer areas and orifices of his own body when he was younger, the older child is now anxious to know what goes on inside his body. Being unable to observe bodily functions directly, he tries to satisfy his curiosity by asking innumerable questions and by reading stories or books that describe the body and how it works. Most children, until they are seven years old, think of the brain as being round in shape and composed of bone, blood, and skin, indicating a confusion between the brain and skull. By the time they are eight years old, they attribute thinking and other intellectual activities to the brain. Nerves are thought of as threadlike structures covering the head, with the major function of feeling. Like the brain, they are thought of as made up of bone, blood, and flesh. The lungs are thought of as round bags, made up of bone, skin, blood, and flesh, located in the nose or throat, where breathing takes place. It is not until children are nine years old that they realize that breathing is a process of taking in and expelling air.

Digestion is thought of as taking place in the mouth and stomach, with the stomach, composed of bone, skin, flesh, and blood, located in the upper part of the trunk. The older child has little understanding of the relationship of eating to digestion and elimination. Instead, he believes that the stomach is for storing or eating food [78]. To an older child, all diseases come from germs which he thinks of as worms or flies. These germs, the child believes, enter the body through the mouth, nose, or skin and can leave the body through the mouth, nose, skin, or anus by coughing, sneezing, or anal evacuation [79]. The older child is aware of sex differences in appearance and recognizes that male bodies differ from female bodies.

Appearance. So long as the child is not so homely that he will be ridiculed by other children, his appearance is of little concern to him. He is not bothered by his height or weight, unless they deviate so markedly from the height and weight of his classmates that he feels conspicuous, nor do such physical defects as freckles, crooked teeth, or stringy hair bother him. Because there are no standards of sex-appropriate appearance for children, he has no concern in that area either. In general, he accepts his appearance as it is and does not worry about how he might improve it. By the fifth or sixth grade, girls begin to be more interested in their appearance than they were when they were younger, and tidiness then begins to be important to them. Boys of the same age, on the other hand, prefer an unkempt appearance because they believe it is more "masculine" [42]. The older girl discovers that to be popular she must make a good appearance, but for boys, a good appearance is likely to cause them to be labeled "sissies" [100].

The older child is keenly interested in clothes as a badge of conformity to the group. New clothes, clothing of a style usually associated with older children, and clothing in his favorite colors still appeal to the child of school age as they did when he was a preschooler. As a general rule, colors of garments are the only real source of appeal to children up to the age of nine years, and it is because of the garment's color that the child selects it. Beginning around the eighth or ninth year, slavish conventionality in the style of clothing of the group makes its appearance. At this age, the child is not only becoming self-conscious but he is anxious to be acceptable to the group in appearance as well as in behavior. Both boys and girls at this age want to be noticed as little as possible and, to make themselves inconspicuous, they hide behind a cloak of conventional garments. So long as his clothes are durable, easy to manipulate, admired or approved by the group, comfortable and, above all, in conformity with the style of the group pattern, that is all that matters to the older child. It is of little concern to him if his clothes are becoming or not, or if they suit the occasion for which he wants to wear them. Above all, he does not want his clothes to attract attention to himself [42].

The older child's clothes do much to increase his self-confidence and to add to his feeling of "belonging." What his friends think about his clothes is quickly sensed by the child, and this influences not only his attitude toward his clothes but his attitude toward himself. The importance of clothes to the older child has been expressed thus by Read: "Children do like clothes and find real satisfaction in them. Bright colors or gay materials, the feel of different textures in clothing, the comfortable, familiar garment as well as the new one—these are all things that bring pleasure to the child. Clothes make a contribution to the process of growing up when they are right from his standpoint. They can help to make the man" [86].

Sex. There is a heightened interest in sex at this age as compared with the casual interest in the subject displayed by younger children. Not only is the older child keenly aware of and interested in genital differences, but he also wants to know in more detail about the relations between sexes, the birth process, how development takes place within the mother's body, and the relation of the father to reproduction. The older child's curiosity is not purely intellectual but has a strong emotional drive. As the child becomes older, his curiosity is less outspoken and more disguised than it was when he was younger because of the unfavorable attitude of many parents toward the child's questions or their avoidance of the subject. As a result of unfavorable parental attitudes, many children get their information from their friends, from suggestive pictures in the comics, from "dirty" stories and jokes, or from books. Girls, more than boys, get their first information from their parents, usually the mothers. By the time the child is ten years old, he has a large fund of information or misinformation about sex [3].

In addition to asking questions about sex, children derive some of their information from *sex exploration*, either of their own bodies or through the mutual exploration of the bodies of children of their own or the opposite sex. Sex exploration takes many forms, the most common of which are peeping, direct observation of the reproductive anatomy, matching masculine prowess in the toilet, manual exploration, exhibitionism, oral contacts, masturbation, and attempts at intercourse. This is generally accompanied by provocative giggling, obscene language, and secrets. Homosexual play is more common than heterosexual play, and masturbation is more common among boys than among girls. Children from the lower classes are not taught that it is wrong to express their sexual impulses through masturbation and exploratory activities with other children, while children of the middle class learn at an early age that such activities are considered "wrong" if not actually "wicked" [85].

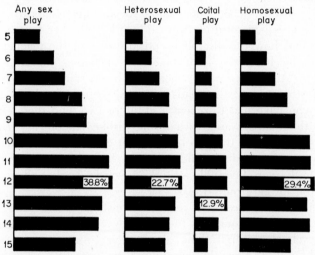

FIG. 39. Types of sex play engaged in by boys of different ages. (*From A. C. Kinsey, W. B. Pomeroy, and C. E. Martin, Sexual behavior in the human male. Philadelphia: Saunders, 1948. Used by permission.*)

The child's friends are usually his companions for sexual play, though his initial experience in homosexual and heterosexual play is usually with an older child or an adult. When the child's curiosity is satisfied, or when he is made to feel guilty for such play, sexual exploration gradually diminishes. With the onset of adolescence, most of the sex play has ended [60]. Figure 39 shows different types of sex play engaged in by boys of different ages.

School. The young child looks forward eagerly to the time when he will be old enough to go to school. To him, this means "growing up" as well as an opportunity to learn to read and write. For the first year or two, most children like school; they enjoy their studies, and they like their teachers. However, before the end of the second year, a change in attitude becomes apparent and in place of enthusiasm and interest come boredom, antagonism toward school, and a critical attitude toward the teacher. While he may still like some of the nonacademic aspects of school, such as recess or play with his friends, and some of the non-academic studies, such as singing and shop work, he is likely to be bored with his classes and resent the restrictions placed on his freedom [56]. Many older children, especially boys, like to "tease" the teacher and stir up trouble [42].

Children's interest in school varies from a strong absorption in their studies to an equally strong dislike which makes them rebel against going to school. There are many factors influencing their attitudes, the most important of which have been found to be: attitudes of parents and friends toward school; the child's social adjustments to school; his academic success; his attitude toward "work," whether favorable or un-favorable; and how the discipline and attitudes of the teacher compare with those he has been accustomed to at home. Children who are younger than their classmates when they begin school often make poor social adjustments and this leads to a dislike for school [59]. Overage children, who have had to repeat a grade or two, find themselves social misfits in their classes and, as a result, dislike school [77]. In general, girls like school better than do boys, bright children more than dull, and younger more than older. Children of the higher socioeconomic groups have generally more favorable attitudes toward school at all ages than do those of the lower groups [39].

Vocational Ambitions. As a result of constant questionings, from the time they were very young, as to what they want to be when they grow up, most school children think about their future careers. Their first vocational aims are generally very unrealistic, with little or no considera-tion of their abilities for the careers they select. As a rule, their first ambitions are to follow in the footsteps of a parent, a relative, or some-one outside the family whom they love and admire. Their ambition is to go into a line of work that appeals to them as glamorous or exciting, or has high prestige [42]. While few children decide definitely about their future vocations until junior or senior high school, or even until they are in college, they are likely to establish favorable or unfavorable attitudes toward different vocations during their childhood days. These attitudes, once established, can and often do have a lasting influence on their vocational selections and vocational adjustments as they grow older [51].

FAMILY RELATIONSHIPS

In spite of the broadened environment of the older child, the *parents,* but especially the mother, still exert a marked influence on his develop-ing personality. Whether this influence will be good or bad will depend, to a large extent, upon the type of relationship that exists between the child and his parents. This relationship, in turn, will be markedly influenced by the type of personality the parent has and his attitude toward the child and toward his role as a parent. Well-adjusted parents provide a better home environment and have better relationships with their children than do poorly adjusted parents [89]. Parents who have high and often unrealistic ambitions for their children, which is often found among middle-class parents, are likely to make their children feel insecure and unaccepted when they fail to live up to parental expectations. Mothers who have given up a successful career for motherhood often expect the same high standards of performance from their children that they have been accustomed to expect in their careers. By the time the child enters school, most parents expect the child to assume responsibilities for the care of his possessions, for help around the home, and for routine activities, such as going to bed on time. Whether the child will live up to these expectations or not will depend partly on the personality of the child and partly on his previous training in assuming responsibilities [103].

Parental attitudes toward their parental responsibilities and *methods of child-training* are likewise important factors in determining parents' relationships with their children. Parents who cling to the traditional concept of the parental role, which includes exercising considerable restraint over the child to guarantee that he will be successful and avoiding too much love and affection for fear of "spoiling the child," produce an unfavorable home climate for good parent-child relationships [2]. Children of indulgent parents, especially indulgent mothers, have difficulties in making social adjustments because they expect similar treatment from people outside the home. Children of dominating parents, on the other hand, are likely to be shy, anxious, fearful, and submissive, or rebellious and antagonistic toward anyone in authority. Differences in child-training methods according to the social-class status of the parents are shown in Figure 19, page 112.

The child who is overprotected at home will develop into a dependent individual who feels insecure and unable to cope with the independence other children handle successfully. When the home is broken by death or divorce, or when one parent is away from home for long periods of time, the remaining parent may be overprotective or may reject the child, thus establishing an unhealthy relationship which is reflected in the child's poor social adjustments outside the home [17]. When the missing parent is replaced by a stepparent, the older child, who is less dependent than he was when he was younger and who remembers his former parent, is likely to resent the stepparent bitterly and cause friction in the home [93].

For the first time in the child's life, the *socioeconomic status* of his family becomes important. As he goes to the homes of friends and has an opportunity to compare his home with the homes of his friends, he is satisfied if he has as much as, if not more than, they in the way of material possessions. But he is dissatisfied and unhappy if his home falls below the standard of the homes of his friends. Because of the close relationship between the family socioeconomic status and the father's *occupation,* the latter comes to be an important factor in the child's relationships with his parents. For the older child, parental occupation has a cultural significance that gives him prestige or denies it. How his peers feel about it will be reflected in the child's attitude toward the occupation and also toward his father [17, 82]. The child's feelings about the mother's working outside the home depends partly upon how much this interferes with his life and how his peers feel about it. Some children accept the mother's working without question while others bitterly resent it [17].

The role the child learns to play in the family and the type of relationships he has with his *siblings* will form the basis of his relationships with his peers outside the home and will influence the pattern of his behavior. It is popularly believed that a child is lucky if he is one of several children in the family but the only child is regarded with pity. Behind this belief is the conviction that a child with siblings learns to conform to other children and to become a social being in a manner which is impossible for the only child. Furthermore, siblings supply ever-ready playmates for the child, an advantage which the only child lacks. Studies of only children have not revealed their inferiority in social adjustments. In social acceptability, only children rate higher than children from a family of several siblings. Furthermore, because of his constant association with adults at home, the only child usually is more mature for his age than is the non-only child, a trait that contributes to good social adjustments and often is responsible for leadership. While it is true that only children are sometimes the victims of overprotectiveness, they are spared the psychological damage that comes with sibling rivalry and jealousy [17].

The child from a large family soon learns to play a certain role in the family constellation, whether it be the role of the "dependable one," the "spoiled one," or the "capable one." The role he plays will be influenced largely by the order of birth. The first-born, for example, is generally expected to play the role of parent substitute in the care of the younger children while the status of the middle child is often undetermined, thus creating a problem situation for him which he meets by trying to rival the oldest or the youngest children [64]. The youngest child never has to meet the problem of competition with a younger sibling, though he may often feel neglected and resented by his older siblings. Thus, it is apparent that the child's relationships with his siblings will not only affect his concept of self but will establish patterns of behavior which are carried into his relationships with his peers.

Family Frictions. As the childhood years progress, family relationships generally worsen. The sweet, docile, helplessly dependent younger child grows into a gawky, careless, homely, independent individual who tries hard to throw off the yoke of parental domination. The older child's changed attitude toward his parents and the changes in his behavior are usually accompanied by a changed attitude on the part of parents toward the child. Parents of nine-year-olds, for example, have been found to be less warm, less indulgent, less affectionate, more restrictive in their controls, more punitive for misbehavior, and less intellectually stimulating to the older child than they are to children of three years or younger [8]. Part of this change may come from parental absorption in the care of younger children in the family, but the older child's rebellion against their authority is fundamentally at the basis of the change. Furthermore, if the behavior and attitudes of the child's friends do not come up to parental standards, parents criticize the child's friends and try to curb his contacts with them. This further broadens the gap between parent and child and leads to increased friction. By the end of childhood, most children protest against parental rules and advice and they argue with their parents about these matters [42]. Changes in parent-child relationships with advancing age are shown in Figure 29, page 160.

In addition to the friction which he has with his parents, the child of this late-childhood period is in more or less constant conflict with his *siblings.* The antagonism between the sexes that develops outside the home is carried into the home and leads to conflicts between brothers and sisters who, during early childhood, usually had a more harmonious relationship than exists between siblings of the same sexes. Older brothers and sisters, especially if they are adolescents, criticize and find fault with the child's "rowdy" behavior, his crude manners, and his continual shouting. He, in turn, likes to bully and tease, to make fun of, or even to fight with younger siblings. In spite of this treatment of his younger siblings, the child generally gets along better with them than he does with his older siblings [42]. As a result of these sibling conflicts, there is almost continuous turmoil in the home. If parents attempt to put a stop to this, they are accused of "playing favorites," thus adding to the child's resentments toward his parents and putting further strain on the parent-child relationship [17, 64].

There are, of course, times of peace and harmony in the home. Older children, if gradually given an opportunity to assume responsibilities, are great helpers in carrying the family burden. And there are times when they show real affection for and interest in their siblings, even to the point of helping in the care of the younger and following the advice and pattern of behavior set by the older siblings. But these favorable relationships are outweighed in number and frequency by the less favorable. Deterioration of relationships within the family spreads to *relatives.* While the younger child frequently shows great affection for grandparents, uncles, aunts, and cousins, the older child is likely to regard them as "too old," "too bossy," or "bores." He resents their authority even

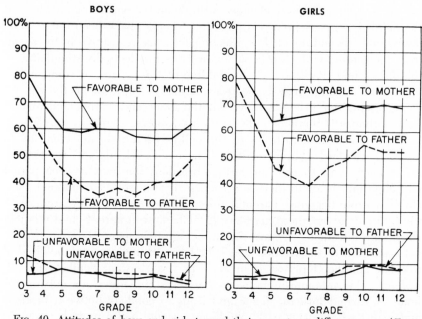

Fig. 40. Attitudes of boys and girls toward their parents at different ages. (*From D. B. Harris and S. C. Tseng, Children's attitudes toward peers and parents as revealed by sentence completions. Child Develpm., 1957, 28, 401–411. Used by permission.*)

more than he resents parental authority and he puts up a protest whenever he is expected to be a part of a family gathering, either in his home or in the home of a relative [17].

Parental Preferences. In spite of the child's attempt to break away from parental domination, he is still dependent upon his parents to help him in emergencies or in new situations where he feels inadequate to cope with the situation alone. Because his mother is likely to be more constantly present than his father, he becomes accustomed to turning to her for aid. Furthermore, because mothers, as a rule, have a more tolerant and understanding attitude toward the troublesome behavior of older children than do fathers, a stronger bond grows up between mother and child than between father and child. The older child feels that the mother is more willing to talk over his plans and problems, to explain reasons for punishment, and is generally "easier to get along with" than the father. As a result, most older children, as is true of younger children, prefer their mothers to their fathers. The child's dependence on the mother is well illustrated by the fact that most older children prefer to have their mothers stay at home rather than take out-of-the-home employment. While both boys and girls prefer the mother to the father, they have a favorable attitude toward both parents until they reach the third to fifth grades, when there is a marked drop in their attitudes toward their parents, especially toward the father [50]. This is illustrated in Figure 40.

While younger children accept their parents uncritically, the older child becomes increasingly *critical* of his parents' behavior, appearance, attitudes, and manners. Boys are more critical and less satisfied with their parents and home conditions than are girls. While they feel closer to the mother than to the father, they still are critical of her, as they are of the father [50]. Both boys and girls resent having their parents, especially their fathers, scold them, lose their tempers, be cross, come home late, use poor English, be careless about their appearance, or have poor manners. They approve, on the other hand, of parents who are companionable, loving, affectionate, understanding, good-natured, sympathetic, interested in them and their affairs, and concerned about doing all they can to make the home a cheerful place [17, 19]. From their contacts with other children and their parents, from reading, and from stereotypes of parents presented in movies or television, the child forms a concept of the *ideal parent*. He then compares his parents with these ideals. If his parents fall short of these ideals in any way, as they invariably do, he becomes critical of their shortcomings and this critical attitude soon becomes general, spreading to everything parents do or say [98].

PERSONALITY

As the child's social horizons broaden with his entrance into school, new factors of importance begin to influence the development of his personality. His whole concept of himself must frequently be revised. Having seen himself almost exclusively through the eyes of his parents for the first part of his life, it is not surprising if his concept of himself is biased. Now he sees himself as his teachers, his classmates, and his neighbors see him. Even his parents react differently toward him now and this helps to shatter the foundations upon which his concept of himself was based. Because the child's attitude toward himself is affected by the attitudes of significant people—his parents, teachers, siblings, and peers—toward him, his self-concept is made up of "reflected appraisals." If these appraisals are favorable, the child will have a favorable self-concept; otherwise, he will tend to devalue himself. In many cases, the child's *beliefs* of how people appraise him are not in harmony with their real appraisals, but he bases his self-concept on what he believes their appraisals are [58].

The older child begins to think of himself as an individual, distinct and different from other people. He has not, as yet, clear-cut and definite ideas of his abilities and disabilities, nor is he sure of how people will accept him. Because of this feeling of insecurity, he tries to follow the accepted pattern of the group to which he belongs and molds himself into this pattern as closely as he can. The type of self-concept the child develops determines whether he will be steered to or from delinquency as he grows older, regardless of neighborhood pressures. This explains why some adolescents succumb and others do not. As children, they have developed self-concepts that either insulate them against or make them prone to delinquency [87]. However, social pressures do play an important role in influencing the child's self-concept. This is shown by the fact that relatively few children, when they first enter school, have any real desire to change themselves, while a large percentage of older children do. This is especially true of girls who, after discovering the more favored position of boys in our culture, say they would like to be boys if they could [26, 56].

As childhood draws to a close and the child begins his hero worship of characters in history and in fiction, on the stage or on the screen, or in the world of sports or national affairs, he forms a concept of the *ideal self*, the kind of person he would like to be. At first, this ideal is patterned along the lines set by parents, teachers, and others from his immediate environment. Later, as his horizons broaden, people he does not know but has heard or read about form the nucleus of this ideal self. From these many sources, the older child builds up a composite picture of an ideal self which he uses as a model. Few children have the capacities to achieve the ideal they set for themselves and thus feel inadequate when they fall below this ideal [48].

Admired Traits. As the child spends more and more time with other children, he becomes increasingly aware of the fact that there are certain personality traits other children admire and others they dislike. The pressure of social opinion thus plays an important role in shaping the older child's personality. He tries to mold his personality into the pattern approved by the group in hopes of gaining the social recognition and acceptance he craves. Because the two sexes are widely separated at this age, it is not surprising to find that each sex has its own standard of an acceptable personality pattern for its members. This results in the establishment of certain habits of behavior specifically associated with the sex of the child [26]. According to these standards, the *typical boy* is wiggly, quarrelsome, aggressive, bossy, and a show-off, while the *typical girl* is quiet, popular, full of fun, a good sport, not aggressive, or bossy, or quarrelsome, but tidy, feminine in interests, and a "little lady" [100]. Figure 41 shows the admired traits for members of both sexes in childhood.

Children's ideals of acceptable personality traits change, however, with age. In general, the older the child, the more aggressive he must be if he is to be admired and accepted. There are also social-class differences in admired personality traits. The boy is expected to be more aggressive than the girl in all cultural groups, but this is especially so in the case of boys of the lower socioeconomic groups [52]. Socioeconomic differences are also found in the degree of responsibility developed by children, with those of the higher groups admiring responsibility more than those of the lower groups [46]. The child who is popular and accepted by his peers possesses the traits that are admired by his peers according to their socioeconomic group.

Persistence of Personality Pattern. With each passing year, the child's personality becomes less and less flexible, and more and more fixed in a set pattern. The shy, retiring, self-effacing individual continues to be such even when he discovers that this does not contribute to his acceptance by the group. The child whose aggressiveness stemmed from parental rejection continues to be aggressive, even though his aggressiveness may take on new and more subtle forms as he grows older. Early in the school life of the child, symptoms of personality trouble begin to appear and these are likely to become progressively worse unless remedial aid is given. The common forms of personality patterns symptomatic of future trouble are those that are characterized by habitual withdrawal, excessive excitability, excessive resentment against authority, chronic depression, chronic anxiety, or emotional "deadening" [19]. If, however, the child is helped to gain insight about himself and others, he will make better adjustments, and as a result, positive personality changes will occur. Without this help, however, the personality traits that lead to poor personal and social adjustment are likely to continue and to become stronger with age [92].

Personality Factors. While many of the factors that helped to shape the personality pattern of the younger child continue to be operative in the latter years of childhood, new factors enter in and play increasingly important roles. The child's *physique* becomes one of the dominating personality factors in late childhood. A pilot study of the relationship

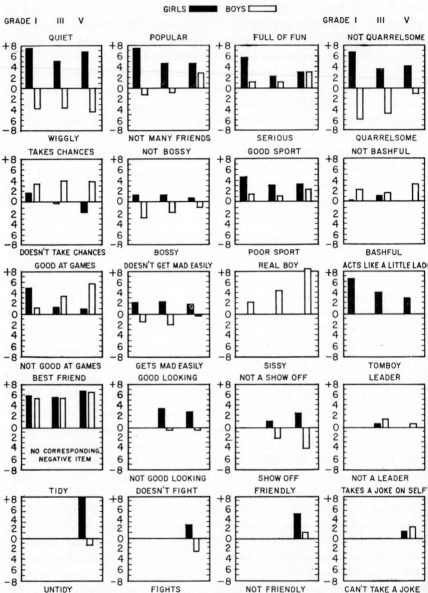

FIG. 41. Standards of acceptable personality patterns for members of the two sexes in late childhood. (*From R. D. Tuddenham, Studies in reputation. I. Sex and grade differences in school children's evaluation of their peers. II. The diagnosis of social adjustment. Psychol. Monogr., 1952, 66, No. 1. Used by permission.*)

between personality and body build has suggested that differences in personality pattern are partly the result of differences in body build. The *ectomorph,* who has a tall, slender build, is more withdrawn, less able to respond to his environment, and less socially adaptable than the child with an endomorphic build. As a result, he puts his drive into academic achievement and becomes a good student. The *endomorph,* who has a short, stocky, fat build is socially well adjusted and able to cope with new situations in his environment. The *mesomorph,* with his muscular build, holds a middle-of-the-road position between the ectomorph and endomorph [30]. The child's concept of self is affected by his body size and build, his level of physical maturity in comparison with his classmates, and his general appearance. The child who is large for his age, for example, or is larger than the children he associates with is often expected by parents and teachers to behave in a more mature manner than they would expect if his size were more in keeping with his age. Then, when he fails to live up to their expectations, he develops feelings of inadequacy. Or the child who differs from his peers by being markedly overweight is likely to develop feelings of inadequacy, especially if his classmates ridicule him and give him a nickname that indicates their disapproval [18].

The *general health* of the child is important when it cuts him off from the play of other children, thus making him feel inferior. Children who suffer from a physical defect, such as blindness, deafness, or lameness, may try hard to conform to the demands of their social environment, but they can do so only at the expense of anxiety and inner tension. Handicaps make the child more vulnerable to feelings of threat and cause greater emotional instability, thus affecting the personality pattern [104].

While the young child accepts in an unquestioning manner the *name* and *nickname* given to him at home, the older child realizes the importance of these. If the name is accepted without ridicule or criticism by his friends, well and good. Should the group, however, comment unfavorably about it, this affects the child unfavorably just as if they commented unfavorably about his appearance. Children of minority groups find that their names often lead to prejudice and, as a result, they often try to change their names or use a nickname that will conceal their minority-group status [21]. Because most nicknames serve as a form of ridicule of some physical or personality trait that is outstanding in the child, the child is likely to build up resentments against those who use it or to feel inferior if the nickname is widely used. Nicknames such as "Fatty," "Skinny," or "Slumpy" imply physical differences and show how other children feel about these differences. As children grow older, they learn to distinguish between nicknames that imply ridicule and those that imply acceptance and affection. How they interpret their nicknames will determine the effect the nickname will have on their personality patterns [33].

The *socially approved pattern* of the culture to which the child belongs begins to be felt in the shaping of his personality at this time. Each individual child is gradually molded into this pattern by his parents, his teachers, and by other adults with whom he comes in contact. Any attempt to deviate from this pattern is thus apt to lead to criticism. From his peers, he learns what is the socially approved pattern for members of his sex in his cultural group [82]. Because there are pressures and prejudices against those who belong to *minority groups,* the child begins to sense these prejudices soon after he enters school. This gradually builds up a feeling of inferiority which, in time, is expressed in poor social adjustments, antisocial behavior, and in the child's whole outlook on life [43].

In our culture, social prestige is associated with a favorable *socioeconomic status* of the family. The child whose family does not measure up favorably becomes increasingly aware of this as the years pass. He compares his toys, his clothes, his home, his parents' status in the community, and his father's occupation with those of his friends to his personal disadvantage and dissatisfaction. There is a close relationship between the social status of the child's family and his personality adjustment [91]. Whether the child's home is in a *rural* or *urban* area will influence the type of personality pattern he develops. Children from rural districts have been found to be superior to those of urban districts in self- and social adjustments and receive better ratings from their teachers and peers [70].

When the child enters school, the *school environment* begins to exert a marked influence on the development of his personality. His teachers influence the molding of his personality. Well-adjusted teachers do much to bring about good adjustment in their pupils; poorly adjusted teachers may have the opposite influence on their pupils. Teachers who are happy in their work and like children can do much to help every child's personality development. While the basic personality pattern is set in the home, the school situation will affect it either favorably or unfavorably. Poor grades, lack of promotion, and discipline that makes the child feel inadequate can play havoc with the developing personality of the child [34]. Similarly, the acceptance or lack of acceptance by his classmates will influence his personality through the effect on his self-concept. "Stars" and isolates are especially affected, others less so [48, 90].

Intelligence that deviates from the norm of the group invariably exerts a detrimental influence on the child's personality. The child who is duller than the rest of the group quickly senses his intellectual inferiority and the attitude of the group toward him. This builds up a feeling of personal inadequacy which is expressed in every area of his behavior. By contrast, the very bright child not only feels superior to the group and out of step with their interests, but he generally develops an intolerance toward those not so bright as he. The dull child becomes shy, introverted, and apathetic [67]. Bright children, as a rule, set *levels of aspiration* within their capacities while dull children usually have unrealistic aspirations. Even though the bright child may fail to reach his goal, he will react realistically to the failure and will not permit it to affect detrimentally his self-concept, as usually happens with the less bright child who reacts to failure so unfavorably that it leads to feelings of inadequacy [48]. The socioeconomic status of the family and the child-training methods used have marked influences on the type of aspirations the child sets and his success or failure in reaching them [65]. While the *home environment* becomes increasingly less important as the child grows older, *family relationships* continue to exert a marked influence. How the child feels about his parents, how satisfactory or unsatisfactory his relationship with them is, their attitudes toward him, the pattern of home life, and his relationships with his siblings—all play their role in determining what sort of individual he will become. The child's ordinal position, whether the oldest, youngest, or the middle child, has been found to be an important factor in shaping his personality [17]. Only children, in contrast to those with siblings, sometimes show more dependent behavior and less self-confidence than do children with siblings [26].

So far as the child's self-concept is concerned, his perception of his parents' and siblings' attitude toward him is more important than the attitudes themselves [5]. The importance of the home environment in shaping the child's personality pattern is emphasized by the differences in personality patterns of children brought up in institutions as compared with those brought up in a home with parents and siblings. The former are less well adjusted and less happy than the latter [14]. When the home environment is made to suit the needs of the child, and when a mutual give-and-take exists, a healthy, well-balanced personality development results.

BIBLIOGRAPHY

1. Albert, R. S.: The role of mass media and the effect of aggressive film content upon children's aggressive responses and identification choices. *Genet. Psychol. Monogr.*, 1957, 55, 221–285.
2. Aldons, J., and L. Kell: Child-rearing values of mothers in relation to their children's perceptions of their mother's control: an exploratory study. *Marriage Fam. Living*, 1956, 18, 72–74.

3. Angelino, H., and E. V. Mech: Some "first" sources of sex information as reported by sixty-seven college women. *J. Psychol.*, 1955, 39, 321–324.
4. Ausubel, D. P.: Relationships between shame and guilt in the socialization process. *Psychol. Rev.*, 1955, 62, 378–390.
5. Ausubel, D. P., E. E. Balthazar, I. Rosenthal, L. S. Blackman, S. H. Schpoont, and J. Welkowitz: Perceived parent attitudes as determinants of children's ego structures. *Child Develpm.*, 1954, 25, 173–183.
6. Ausubel, D. P., F. Dewitt, B. Golden, and S. H. Schpoont: Prestige suggestion in children's art preferences. *J. genet. Psychol.*, 1956, 89, 85–93.
7. Bakwin, H.: Lateral dominance. *J. Pediat.*, 1950, 36, 385–391.
8. Baldwin, A. L.: Differences in parent behavior toward three- and nine-year-old children. *J. Pers.*, 1945, 15, 143–165.
9. Bayer, L. M., and M. M. Snyder: Illness experiences of a group of normal children. *Child Develpm.*, 1950, 21, 93–120.
10. Bayley, N., and S. R. Pinnau: Tables for predicting adult height from skeletal age: revised for use with the Greulich-Pyle Hand Standards. *J. Pediat.*, 1952, 40, 423–441.
11. Beller, S.: Angry girls—behavior control by girls in latency. *Smith Coll. Stud. soc. Wk*, 1953, 23, 205–226.
12. Bell, G. B., and H. E. Hall: The relationship between leadership and latency. *J. abnorm. soc. Psychol.*, 1954, 49, 156–157.
13. Bell, J. E.: Perceptual development and the drawings of children. *Amer. J. Orthopsychiat.*, 1952, 22, 386–393.
14. Bodman, F., M. MacKinley, and K. Sykes: The social adaptation of institution children. *Lancet*, 1950, 258, 173–176.
15. Bonney, M. E.: Choosing between the sexes on a sociometric measurement. *J. soc. Psychol.*, 1954, 39, 99–114.
16. Bonney, M. E.: Social behavior differences between second grade children of high and low sociometric status. *J. educ. Res.*, 1955, 48, 481–495.
17. Bossard, J. H. S.: *Parent and child.* Philadelphia: Univer. Pennsylvania Press, 1953.
18. Bram, I.: Psychic factors in obesity. *Arch. Pediat.*, 1950, 67, 543–552.
19. Breckenridge, M. E., and E. L. Vincent: *Child development*, 3d ed. Philadelphia: Saunders, 1955.
20. Broida, D. C., and G. G. Thompson: The relationship between certain Rorschach "insecurity" hypotheses and children's reactions to psychological stress. *J. Pers.*, 1954, 23, 167–181.
21. Broom, L., H. P. Beem, and V. Harris: Characteristics of 1,107 petitions for change of name. *Amer. sociol. Rev.*, 1955, 20, 33–39.
22. Brown, D. G.: Masculinity-femininity development in children. *J. consult. Psychol.*, 1957, 21, 197–202.
23. Bühler, C.: School as a phase of human life. *Education*, 1952, 73, 219–222.
24. Butterworth, R. F., and G. G. Thompson: Factors related to age-grade trends and sex differences in children's preferences for comic books. *J. genet. Psychol.*, 1951, 78, 71–96.
25. Carsley, J. D.: The interests of children (aged 10–11) in books. *Brit. J. educ. Psychol.*, 1957, 27, 13–23.
26. Cattell, R. B., and R. W. Coan: Personality factors in middle childhood as revealed by parents' ratings. *Child Develpm.*, 1957, 28, 439–458.
27. Crane, A. R.: Pre-adolescent gangs: a socio-psychological interpretation. *J. genet. Psychol.*, 1955, 86, 275–279.

28. Crow, A.: Parental attitudes toward boy-girl relations. *J. educ. Sociol.*, 1955, 29, 126–133.
29. Darcy, N. T.: A review of the literature on the effects of bilingualism upon the measurement of intelligence. *J. genet. Psychol.*, 1953, 82, 21–57.
30. Davidson, W. A., R. G. McInnes, and R. W. Parnell: The distribution of personality characteristics in seven-year-old children: a combined psychological, psychiatric, and sonatotype study. *Brit. J. educ. Psychol.*, 1957, 27, 48–61.
31. Davitz, J. R.: Social perception and sociometric choice of children. *J. abnorm. soc. Psychol.*, 1955, 50, 173–176.
32. Demisch, A., and P. Wartmann: Calcification of the mandibular third molar and its relation to skeletal and chronological age in children. *Child Develpm.*, 1956, 27, 459–473.
33. Dexter, E. S.: Three items related to personality: popularity, nicknames, and homesickness. *J. soc. Psychol.*, 1949, 30, 155–158.
34. Dombrose, L. A.: Do teachers cause neurotic conflicts in children? *Ment. Hyg.*, N.Y., 1955, 39, 99–110.
35. Dreger, R. M.: Spontaneous conversation and story-telling of children in a naturalistic setting. *J. Psychol.*, 1955, 40, 163–180.
36. DuBois, F. S.: The security of discipline. *Ment. Hyg.*, N.Y., 1952, 36, 353–372.
37. Eppright, E. S., and V. D. Sidwell: Physical measurements of Iowa school children. *J. Nutrit.*, 1954, 54, 543–556.
38. Fishman, J. A.: Negative stereotypes concerning Americans among American-born children receiving various types of minority-group education. *Genet. Psychol. Monogr.*, 1955, 51, 107–182.
39. Fitt, A. B.: An experimental study of children's attitudes toward school in Auckland, N.Z. *Brit. J. educ. Psychol.*, 1956, 26, 25–30.
40. Fry, P. C.: A comparative study of "obese" children selected on the basis of fat pads. *J. clin. Nutrit.*, 1953, 1, 453–468.
41. Fuller, E. M., and H. B. Baune: Injury-proneness and adjustment in a second grade. *Sociometry*, 1951, 14, 210–225.
42. Gesell, A., F. L. Ilg, and L. B. Ames: *Youth: the years from ten to sixteen*. New York: Harper, 1956.
43. Goff, R. M.: Some educational implications of the influence of rejection on aspiration levels of minority group children. *J. exp. Educ.*, 1954, 23, 179–183.
44. Gronlund, N. E.: Generality of sociometric status over criteria in measurement of social acceptability. *Elem. Sch. J.*, 1955, 55, 173–176.
45. Hare, A. P.: A study of interaction and consensus in different sized groups. *Amer. sociol. Rev.*, 1952, 17, 261–267.
46. Harris, D. B., A. M. Rose, K. E. Clark, and F. Valasek: Personality differences between responsible and less responsible children. *J. genet. Psychol.*, 1955, 87, 103–106.
47. Harris, D. B., and S. C. Tseng: Children's attitudes toward peers and parents as revealed by sentence completions. *Child Develpm.*, 1957, 28, 401–411.
48. Havighurst, R. J.: *Human development and education*. New York: Longmans, 1953.
49. Hawkes, G. R., L. G. Burchinal, and B. Gardner: Measurement of pre-adolescents' views of family control of behavior. *Child Develpm.*, 1957, 28, 388–392.
50. Hawkes, G. R., L. G. Burchinal, and B. Gardner: Pre-adolescents' views of some of their relationships with their parents. *Child Develpm.*, 1957, 28, 393–399.
51. Heisler, F.: An elementary-school background for vocational guidance. *Elem. Sch. J.*, 1955, 55, 513–516.

52. Hess, R. D., and G. Handel: Patterns of aggression in parents and their children. *J. genet. Psychol.*, 1956, 89, 199–212.
53. Hildreth, G.: Development and training of hand dominance. *J. genet. Psychol.*, 1950, 76, 39–144.
54. Jacobziner, H.: Accidents—a major child health problem. *J. Pediat.*, 1955, 46, 419–436.
55. Jersild, A. T.: Emotional development. In L. Carmichael, *Manual of child psychology*, 2d ed. New York: Wiley, 1954. Pp. 833–917.
56. Jersild, A. T., and R. J. Tasch: *Children's interests and what they suggest for education.* New York: Teachers Coll., Columbia Univer., Bureau of Publications, 1949.
57. Jones, V.: Character development in children—an objective approach. In L. Carmichael, *Manual of child psychology*, 2d ed. New York: Wiley, 1954. Pp. 781–832.
58. Jourard, S. M., and R. M. Remy: Perceived parental attitude, the self and security. *J. consult. Psychol.*, 1955, 19, 364–366.
59. King, E. B.: Effect of age on entrance into grade 1 upon achievement in elementary school. *Elem. Sch. J.*, 1955, 55, 331–336.
60. Kinsey, A. C., W. B. Pomeroy, C. E. Martin, and P. H. Gebhard: *Sexual behavior in the human female.* Philadelphia: Saunders, 1953.
61. Klingberg, G.: The distinction between living and not living among 7–10-year-old children, with some remarks concerning the so-called animism controversy. *J. genet. Psychol.*, 1957, 90, 227–238.
62. Krogman, W. M.: The physical growth of the child. In M. Fishbein and R. J. R. Kennedy, *Modern marriage and family living.* New York: Oxford Univer. Press, 1957. Pp. 417–425.
63. Langford, W. S., et al.: Pilot study of childhood accidents: preliminary report. *Pediatrics*, 1953, 11, 405–415.
64. Lasko, J. K.: Parent behavior toward first and second children. *Genet. Psychol. Monogr.*, 1954, 49, 97–137.
65. Leshan, L. L.: Time orientation and social class. *J. abnorm. soc. Psychol.*, 1952, 47, 589–596.
66. Lewis, E.: The function of group play during middle childhood in developing the ego complex. *Brit. J. med. Psychol.*, 1954, 27, 15–29.
67. Lightfoot, G. F.: Personality characteristics of bright and dull children. *Teach. Coll. Contr. Educ.*, 1951, No. 969.
68. MacDonald, M., C. McGuire, and R. J. Havighurst: Leisure activities and the socio-economic status of children. *Amer. J. Sociol.*, 1949, 54, 505–519.
69. Macy, I. G., and H. J. Kelly: Body composition in childhood. *Hum. Biol.*, 1956, 28, 289–308.
70. Mangus, A. R.: Personality adjustments of rural and urban children. *Amer. sociol. Rev.*, 1948, 13, 566–575.
71. Massler, M., and T. Suher: Calculation of "normal" weight in children. *Child Develpm.*, 1951, 22, 75–94.
72. McCandless, B. R., A. Castaneda, and D. S. Palermo: Anxiety in children. *Child Develpm.*, 1956, 27, 317–326, 327–332, 333–337, 379–382, 385–391.
73. McCarthy, D.: Language development. In L. Carmichael, *Manual of child psychology*, 2d ed. New York: Wiley, 1954, Pp. 492–630.
74. Moncur, J. P.: Symptoms of maladjustment differentiating young stutterers from non-stutterers. *Child Develpm.*, 1955, 26, 91–96.

75. Morgan, P. K., and E. L. Gaier: The direction of aggression in the mother-child punishment situation. *Child Develpm.*, 1956, 27, 447–457.
76. Morgenstern, J. J.: Socio-economic factors in stuttering. *J. Speech Hearing Disorders*, 1956, 21, 25–33.
77. Morrison, I. E., and I. F. Perry: Acceptance of overage children by their classmates. *Elem. Sch. J.*, 1956, 56, 217–220.
78. Nagy, M. H.: Children's conceptions of some bodily functions. *J. genet. Psychol.*, 1953, 83, 199–216.
79. Nagy, M. H.: The representation of "germs" by children. *J. genet. Psychol.*, 1953, 83, 227–240.
80. Noel, D. I.: A comparative study of the relationship between the quality of the child's language usage and the quality and types of language used in the home. *J. educ. Res.*, 1953, 47, 161–167.
81. Phillips, E. L., S. Shenker, and P. Revitz: The assimilation of the new child into the group. *Psychiatry*, 1951, 14, 319–325.
82. Podolsky, E.: The father's occupation and the child's emotions. *Understanding the Child*, 1954, 23, 22–25.
83. Pratt, K. C.: A study of the "fears" of rural children. *J. genet. Psychol.*, 1945, 67, 179–194.
84. Pratt, K. C., W. E. Hartmann, and J. C. Mead: Interdeterminate number concepts. III. Representation by children through selection of appropriate aggregations. *J. genet. Psychol.*, 1954, 87, 39–63.
85. Rainwater, L.: A study of personality differences between middle and lower class adolescents: the Szondi Test in culture-personality research. *Genet. Psychol. Monogr.*, 1956, 54, 3–86.
86. Read, K. H.: Clothes help build personality. *J. Home Econ.*, 1950, 42, 348–350.
87. Reckless, W. C., S. Dinitz, and B. Kay: The self component in potential delinquency and potential non-delinquency. *Amer. sociol. Rev.*, 1957, 22, 566–570.
88. Remmers, H. H., M. S. Myers, and E. M. Bennett: Purdue survey. *Purdue Opin. Panel*, 1951, 10, No. 3.
89. Rexford, E. N., and S. T. van Amerognen: The influence of unsolved maternal oral conflicts upon impulsive acting out in young children. *Amer. J. Orthopsychiat.*, 1957, 27, 75–87.
90. Satterlee, R. L.: Sociometric analysis and personality adjustment. *Calif. J. educ. Res.*, 1955, 6, 181–184.
91. Sewell, W. H., and A. O. Haller: Social status and the personality adjustment of the child. *Sociometry*, 1956, 19, 114–125.
92. Slobetz, F., and A. Lund: Some effects of a personal developmental program at the fifth grade level. *J. educ. Res.*, 1955, 49, 373–378.
93. Smith, W. C.: Remarriage and the stepchild. *In* M. Fishbein and R. J. R. Kennedy, *Modern marriage and family living*. New York: Oxford Univer. Press, 1957. Pp. 457–475.
94. Spiegelman, M., C. Terwilliger, and F. Fearing: The content of the comic strips: a study of a mass medium of communication. *J. soc. Psychol.*, 1952, 35, 37–57.
95. Stouffer, G. A. W., and J. Owens: Behavior problems identified by today's teachers and compared with those reported by E. K. Wickman. *J. educ. Res.*, 1955, 48, 321–331.
96. Strauss, A. L.: The learning of roles and of concepts as twin processes. *J. genet. Psychol.*, 1956, 88, 211–217.

97. Sullenger, T. E., L. H. Parke, and W. K. Wallin: The leisure time activities of elementary school children: *J. educ. Res.*, 1953, 46, 551–554.

98. Tasch, R. J.: The role of the father in the family. *J. exp. Educ.*, 1952, 20, 319–361.

99. Thompson, H.: Physical growth. *In* L. Carmichael, *Manual of child psychology*, 2d ed. New York: Wiley, 1954. Pp. 292–334.

100. Tuddenham, R. D.: Studies in reputation. I. Sex and grade differences in school children's evaluation of their peers. II. The diagnosis of social adjustment. *Psychol. Monogr.*, 1952, 66, No. 1.

101. Tyler, L. E.: The development of vocational interests: I. The organization of likes and dislikes in ten-year-old children. *J. genet. Psychol.*, 1955, 86, 33–34.

102. Vinacke, W. E.: Concept formation in children of school age. *Education*, 1954, 74, 527–534.

103. Waters, J., F. I. Stromberg, and G. Lonian: Perceptions concerning development of responsibility in young children. *Elem. Sch. J.*, 1957, 57, 209–216.

104. Wenar, C.: The effects of a motor handicap on personality. III. The effects on certain fantasies and adjustive techniques. *Child Develpm.*, 1956, 27, 9–15.

105. Wertham, F.: The curse of the comic books. *Relig. Educ.*, 1954, 49, 394–406.

106. Witty, P. A.: Children's interest in comics, radio, motion pictures, and TV. *Educ. Admin. Superv.*, 1952, 38, 138–147.

107. Witty, P. A.: Comics, television, and our children. *Today's Hlth*, 1955, Feb., pp. 18–21.

108. Zuk, G. H.: The influence of social context on impulse and control tendencies in preadolescents. *Genet. Psychol. Monogr.*, 1956, 54, 117–166.

» 7 «

Puberty

Puberty is a period in the developmental span when the individual changes from an asexual to a sexual being. The name for this period comes from the Latin word *pubertas* meaning "age of manhood." The period overlaps the end of childhood and extends into the early part of adolescence. The beginning of the puberty period is sometimes called *preadolescence* while the latter part is known as *early adolescence*. Because it is customary to draw the line between childhood and adolescence at the time when the child reaches sexual maturity and to regard him as a child until he has reached this stage of his development, the period of puberty must be regarded as an *overlapping* period, a time when the child is no longer characteristically a child because of the changes in his body and his behavior, nor is he yet an adolescent.

Rapid Changes. Puberty is a period of rapid physical and psychological changes. It marks the transition from a childish body, a childish outlook on life, and childish forms of behavior to a mature body and to changed attitudes and behavior. These rapid changes, however, lead to confusion, feelings of insecurity, and, in many cases, unfavorable behavior. It is a time of "predictabilities and unpredictabilities" [30]. Puberty is sometimes called the *negative phase*, "phase" suggesting a period of short duration in the total life span, and "negative" suggesting that the child takes an "anti-" attitude toward life or that he is negating some of the good qualities he had previously developed. In the case of girls, the worst of the negative phase is over with the *menarche*, or first menstrual period.

Early Recognition of Puberty. As far back as the time of Aristotle, it was recognized that when boys are about fourteen years old, they begin to "engender seed." When this occurs, there are changes in their physical structure such as the appearance of hair on the body and a marked change in the tonal quality of their voices. Aristotle also noted that when girls experience their first menstrual flow, their breasts develop and their voices change. Of even greater significance was his emphasis on behavioral changes. He stressed the fact that at this time girls are irritable, passionate, ardent, and in need of constant surveillance because of their developing sexual impulses.

Among primitive peoples, recognition of the changes that accompany puberty are fairly universal. Different rites are observed by different tribes to show their recognition of the fact that the child is emerging from childhood into maturity and is, therefore, reaching the stage when he or she should have the rights, privileges, and responsibilities that accompany maturity. Among some tribes, the rites of puberty are public and are accompanied by singing, dancing, and tests of strength, power, and skill. In other primitive groups, the rites are familial, rather than public. The rituals connected with the attainment of sexual maturity serve to arouse in the pubescent child new attitudes toward himself and his status in the tribe and to channel into socially acceptable forms of behavior the new feelings that come with physical changes [34].

We, as is true of other civilized peoples today, expect distinctly different forms of behavior from the boy or girl who is sexually mature than from the younger child. These social expectations influence the individual's attitudes toward himself and, in turn, they affect the quality of his behavior. While few civilized peoples recognize formally the transition from childhood to adolescence as primitive peoples do in their puberty rites, social expectations serve much the same role in that they inform the pubescent child of what society now expects of him, and the force of social approval or disapproval motivates the child to follow these social expectations. However, there is a strong tendency among civilized peoples to treat the individual in accordance with his *physical age* rather than his *chronological age*. This is hard on both early and late maturers. In the case of the former, there is a tendency to expect too much, because of his mature body, and in the case of the latter, there is a tendency to treat him as a child even when he is mentally capable of behaving in a more mature manner [34].

AGE OF PUBERTY

It is difficult or even impossible to give a definite age for puberty because sexual maturing varies so widely in different individuals. The widely accepted practice today is to subdivide the puberty period into three stages, as follows:

1. The *prepubescent,* or immature, stage when the secondary sex characteristics are beginning to develop but the reproductive function is not yet developed.

2. The *pubescent,* or mature, stage when the secondary sex characteristics continue to develop but are not yet complete and when sex cells are produced in the sex organs.

3. The *postpubescent,* or mature, stage when the secondary sex characteristics are well developed and when the sex organs are functioning in a mature manner.

Approximately 50 per cent of all girls mature between 12.5 and 14.5 years, with an average at 13 years for girls of the middle and upper socioeconomic groups and 13.5 for girls of the lower groups. Since boys mature, on the average, approximately one year later than girls, the average age for sexual maturing of boys falls between 14 and 16.5 years, with 50 per cent of all boys maturing between 14 and 15.5 years. There is evidence that boys and girls reach puberty earlier now than they did fifty years ago [39]. Between the ages of twelve and fourteen years, differences between the sexes are especially marked, with many more mature girls than mature boys. This difference is reflected in the larger and more mature bodies of the girls and in their more aggressive, more sex-conscious, and more mature behavior [5].

Variations. Variations in age of sexual maturing are due to variations in the functioning of the endocrine glands, which are responsible for bringing about the changes that occur at this time. These, in turn, are influenced by the hereditary factor as well as the intelligence and general health condition of the individual. Studies of variations in age of sexual maturing have revealed that children from the Temperate Zones mature earlier than those from the Arctic or Tropical Zones, and those from urban environments earlier than those from rural areas [26, 33]. A predominately protein diet has been found to lead to early maturing among girls while a diet in which carbohydrates predominate leads to late maturing. In addition to good food, good social conditions favor early maturing [27]. Figure 42 illustrates variations in age of puberty for boys.

The body build of the child has been found to influence the age of sexual maturing. The child who matures early is likely to be large for his age and have a broad build with a feminine-type body (broad hips and short legs); those who mature late are smaller than the average child in late childhood and often have a slender build with a masculine-type body (broad shoulders and long legs) [27]. Obese children have been found to reach puberty about one year earlier than the average [51]. The influence of body build on age of maturing is illustrated in Figure 43. In the case of the late maturer, growth is usually irregular and asymmetrical, with growth of the body dimensions and of the internal organs lagging behind growth in stature. In the early maturer, growth is more regular and there is less organic imbalance [6, 49]. Age of maturing

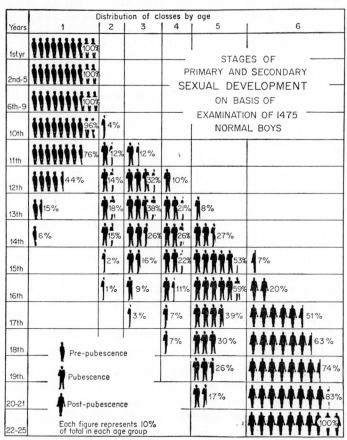

Fig. 42. Age distribution of the various stages of primary and secondary sexual development. (*From W. A. Schonfeld, Primary and secondary sexual characteristics. Amer. J. Dis. Child.*, 1943, 65, 535–549. *Used by permission.*)

affects the development of the different body tissues, with early maturers being larger in total breadth of calf and in the breadth of fat, muscle, and bone within the calf than late maturers [40].

The child who is precocious in his sexual maturing has a shorter childhood with its freedom from responsibilities but he has a longer adolescence, thus giving him more time to make the social and emotional adjustments needed for a successful adult life. By contrast, the child whose sexual maturity is delayed has a longer period of childhood during which he is not expected to assume the responsibilities of maturity. But he is handicapped by a shorter period of adolescence when adjustments to adult life are normally made [20, 47].

Time Needed for Maturing. Children do not turn into men and women overnight. The total time needed for maturing is approximately 3 years for girls and 2 to 4 years for boys. Boys show less uniformity in this

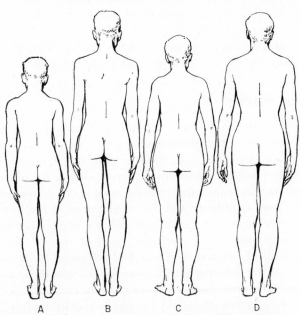

A   B   C   D

Fig. 43. Influence of age of maturing on body build. Comparison of two boys who differ in skeletal maturity. Boys *A* and *C* are both thirteen years old, and boys *B* and *D* are boys *A* and *C* at seventeen years of age. Note the differences in body build for the retarded and accelerated boys at the two ages. (*From N. Bayley, Individual patterns of development. Child Develpm., 1956, 27, 45–74. Used by permission.*)

process than do girls. Approximately 1 to 2 years are required for the preliminary changes from an asexual to a sexual state, the prepubescent stage, and 1 to 2 years for the changes to be completed after the individual's sex organs have become mature. The period of puberty changes lasts from 2 to 4 years. With but few exceptions, this stage has been found to last nearly twice as long as the prepuberty and postpuberty stages in boys. The child who is slow in starting to mature usually matures more rapidly than the average child once he gets started, and often even more rapidly than those whose puberty started earlier than the average [20]. Puberty usually lasts longer for those who begin earlier than the average than for those who begin later than the average [39].

As is'true of age of maturing, there are marked differences in speed of maturing among different children. The fast maturer has greater spurts of rapid growth, his periods of acceleration and stopping come abruptly, and he attains adult proportions very quickly. There is an early development of the sex organs and the secondary sex characteristics, and the osseous development comes earlier than the average. The slow maturer, by contrast, has less intense periods of acceleration, his growth being more even and gradual, and his growth continues for a longer time. The sex organs and secondary sex characteristics are later than the average in developing, and the osseous development is also later [6, 49].

CAUSES OF PUBERTY

Until recently, the exact cause or causes of puberty changes were a mystery. It was known that puberty changes occur at a fairly regular and predictable time, that the ages differ slightly for boys and girls, and that the changes follow a prescribed pattern similar for all members of the same sex. It was known that, among boys, there is some relationship between the onset of puberty and the development of the testes because, when boys were castrated, pubic hair did not appear nor was there a change in voice pitch. Not, however, until studies of the *endocrine glands,* or glands of internal secretion, had advanced to the point where the functions of the different glands were known was there any scientific information on the underlying cause of puberty changes.

About 5 years before the child becomes sexually mature, there is a small excretion of the sex hormones in both boys and girls. This is increased as time passes and eventually leads to the maturing of the structure and function of the sex organs. About a year and a half before the menarche, girls show a cyclic excretion of the female sex hormone, estrogen [37]. It has been established that there is a close relationship between the *pituitary gland,* located at the base of the brain, and the *gonads,* or sex glands. In this relationship, it is the pituitary that stimulates the gonads to increased activity. When this occurs, the hormones, or chemical secretions from the gonads, bring about the physical and mental changes characteristic of puberty.

Function of Pituitary Gland. The pituitary gland produces two hormones, both closely related to puberty changes. The first is the *growth hormone* which is influential in determining the size of the individual, and the second is the *gonadotropic,* or gonad-stimulating, hormone which acts on the gonads and stimulates them to increased activity. Just before puberty, there is a gradual increase in the amount of gonadotropic hormone from the pituitary gland and an increased sensitivity of the gonads to this hormone. Puberty is thus initiated by these two conditions. After the puberty changes have been completed, the interaction between the gonadotropic hormone and the gonads continues throughout the reproductive life of the individual, gradually decreasing as menopause in women and the climacteric in men occur, thus terminating the reproductive cycle.

Function of the Gonads. The gonads are the sex glands of the reproductive system. The male gonads are the *testes* (singular, testis), and the female, the *ovaries.* While the gonads are present at birth, they are in an immature state of development and function until puberty, when their growth and activity are stimulated by the gonadotropic hormone from the pituitary gland. That explains why children are almost neutral as regards sex in their physical development, in attitudes, and in behavior. With the growth and development of the gonads at puberty, marked physical, psychological, and behavioral changes appear. Not only do the sex organs increase in size and become functionally active, but the *secondary sex characteristics,* or physical traits not directly related to reproduction but which distinguish the male from the female body, develop.

Interaction of Pituitary and Gonads. In both boys and girls, the hormones from the gonads, which have been stimulated by the hormones from the pituitary, act in turn on the pituitary and cause a gradual reduction in the amount of the growth hormone which, as was previously pointed out, is produced by the anterior lobe of the pituitary gland. Eventually, the gonadal hormones stop the activity of the growth hormone completely and thus stop the process of physical growth. If body size is to be normal or near normal, there must be not only reciprocal activity on the part of the gonads and pituitary but also proper timing in this reciprocal activity. When an individual is below average in size at maturity, it means that there has not been enough of the growth hormone in late childhood and early puberty. If, however, the gonadal hormones are not released in adequate amounts soon enough, the individual's growth, particularly the growth of the limbs, continues for too long and he becomes larger than the average adult [25].

Abnormal Functioning. Abnormalities in the functioning of the gonads have been studied in both animal and human subjects. When there is an inadequate supply of gonadal hormones because of subnormal development of the gonads or an insufficient supply of gonadotropic hormone from the pituitary gland, or when there is injury to or destruction of the gonads from a disease such as mumps in boys, removal of the gonads by castration in boys, or the removal of certain areas of the reproductive apparatus in girls, puberty is delayed and normal development of the sex organs and secondary sex characteristics is prevented. As a result, individuals remain childish in appearance or take on the characteristics of the opposite sex, depending on when these interruptions occur in the developmental cycle. When puberty is markedly delayed, the secondary sex characteristics eventually develop, but boys become somewhat effeminate in appearance and girls become somewhat masculine in appearance and behavior and have uteri that are small and undeveloped. Markedly delayed puberty is generally accompanied by obesity in both boys and girls, though this may disappear after puberty sets in [43].

Hyperactivity of the gonads or an excessive supply of gonadal hormones, on the other hand, brings about a precocious development of puberty. This condition is known as "puberty precox" and is caused by an imbalance in the functioning of the pituitary gland and the gonads resulting from an excessive amount of gonadotropic hormone at an earlier age than usual. There are medical records of young children who are mature in their sexual development and yet as small in stature as other children of their own age. These children, it appears, do not pass through a normal puberty, nor do they acquire the secondary sex characteristics in as well-developed forms as those who mature at the usual age, even though their sex glands produce mature reproductive cells. Evidence does not indicate that inheritance is responsible for puberty precox, but rather that it is caused by the early activation of the pituitary gland [24].

CRITERIA OF PUBERTY

Because of the practical difficulty in applying a large number of criteria to determine the onset of puberty and the stage of development reached in puberty, attempts have been made to use one criterion. Of those that have been used, some are easy to apply, others are difficult. The accuracy of this method, however, is open to speculation. Of the single criteria that have been used to date, the following are the most important.

The *menarche,* or the first menstruation, is a commonly used criterion of sexual maturity among girls. But menstruation means neither the beginning nor the end of the physical changes occurring at puberty. When the menarche occurs, the sex organs and secondary sex characteristics have all started to develop, but none of them are complete at this stage. All continue to develop for varying lengths of time after the menarche. More correctly, the menarche may be considered a mid-point in puberty.

Among boys, a popularly used criterion of puberty is *nocturnal emissions.* During sleep, the penis sometimes becomes erect, and semen, or fluid with sperm cells, spurts out. This is a normal way for the male reproductive organ to rid itself of excessive amounts of semen. Studies of large groups of boys have revealed that not all boys experience this phenomenon and not all recognize it as such. Furthermore, nocturnal emissions, like the menarche, occur after some puberty development has taken place and cannot, therefore, be used as an accurate criterion of the onset of puberty.

Chemical analysis of the first urine passed by boys in the morning to determine whether or not semen is present has proved to be an effective technique, although it is difficult to use. Urine has also been analyzed to determine the amount of *creatine* and *gonadotropic hormone* (*androgen*) present. Creatine is normally found in immature boys. If, therefore, the urine is free from creatine, the boy is sexually mature. Androgen is normally not found in the urine of boys under 12½ years of age. After 12½ years, some test positive and after 16, all do, unless there is a marked retardation in their sexual development. Analysis of the girl's urine to see if the female gonadotropic hormone, *estrogen*, is present is used to determine whether she is sexually mature. Normally, the amounts of estrogen are greatly increased after the girl is eleven years old [26]. The practical difficulty of obtaining specimens of the early-morning urine of boys and girls limits the use of this method.

X rays of the *bone development* of boys and girls show that as growth begins to spurt, at the close of childhood, genital growth always occurs at a certain point in the bone development of the individual. If X rays are taken of the different parts of the body, but especially of the hands and knees, during the preadolescent growth spurt, it is possible to tell just when puberty begins and at what rate it is progressing. From X rays of the hand and wrist, it is possible to predict the age of the menarche in girls. When this method is used in children, predictions of early or late sexual maturing can be made [18, 19]. To date, this has proved to be the most dependable method of determining sexual maturity, though it, like the chemical analysis of early-morning urine, has certain practical difficulties that make its widespread use unfeasible.

PHYSICAL CHANGES AT PUBERTY

There are four important physical changes occurring at puberty: *rapid physical growth;* changes in *body proportions;* the development of the *primary sex characteristics,* or the sex organs proper; and the development of the *secondary sex characteristics,* or the physical features which distinguish the male from the female. Of these, only the primary sex characteristics play a direct role in reproduction; the others are only indirectly related to reproduction.

1. Rapid Physical Growth. Puberty is one of the two times during the life span of the individual when rapid physical growth occurs. The first comes during the prenatal period and the first half of the first postnatal year. Growth then slows down and, from about two years of age until puberty, it continues at a relatively steady and slow rate. The second period of rapid growth is generally referred to as the "adolescent growth spurt." In reality, it is a preadolescent rather than an adolescent spurt because it precedes slightly or comes simultaneously with the physical changes of puberty. This growth spurt lasts for a year or two before the

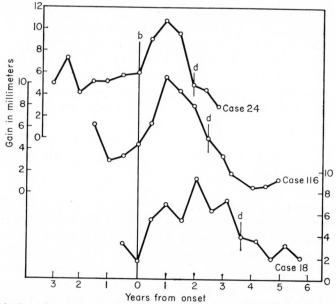

Fig. 44. Growth curves of height for three boys, illustrating variations in the duration of the pubertal growth spurt. (*From H. R. Stolz and L. M. Stolz, Somatic development of adolescent boys. New York: Macmillan, 1951. Used by permission.*)

boy or girl becomes sexually mature and for 6 months to a year afterward. This means that the entire period of rapid growth lasts for about 3 years.

Because girls mature sexually sooner than boys, the growth spurt for girls begins between 8.5 and 11.5 years, with a peak coming, on the average, at 12.5 years. From then on, the rate of growth slows down until it gradually comes to a standstill between 15 and 16 years. The pattern of rapid growth for boys is similar to that for girls except that their growth spurt starts later and continues for a longer time. For boys, the growth spurt starts between 10.5 and 14.5 years, reaches a peak between 14.5 and 15.5 years, and is then followed by a gradual decline until 19 or 20 years, when growth is completed. Increases in height, weight, and strength come at approximately the same time [47]. Variations in the growth spurt for boys are shown in Figure 44.

Rapid physical growth at puberty is the result of maturation, not of environmental forces such as food or exercise, as is often believed. The pituitary gland which sets the gonads, or sex glands, into action also releases a "growth hormone" from the anterior lobe. This is responsible for the rapid growth taking place at this time. Without adequate amounts of this hormone, *dwarfism* occurs; too much of it produces *giantism*. The timing of the release of the growth hormone is more important than its quantity. The gonadotropic hormone, also released by the pituitary, not only stimulates the development of the gonads but it also acts on the growth hormone and causes a gradual reduction either in its quantity or in its effectiveness. This results in a slowing down of growth.

Height. The spurt in stature generally precedes that in weight. The period of most rapid increase in height comes in the early part of puberty. Among girls, the years from ten to fourteen are ones of very rapid increase in height. The average annual gain in the year preceding the menarche is 3 inches, though a 5- to 6-inch gain is not unusual. Two years preceding the menarche, the average increase is 2.5 inches, making a total increase of 5.5 inches in the two years preceding the menarche. After the menarche, the rate of growth slows down [18]. The average height for American girls of today is 63 inches at thirteen years, the time when the average girl becomes sexually mature: at fourteen years, the average girl measures 64 inches, and at fifteen years, 65 inches. From then until eighteen years, there is an increase of only 1 inch, thus making the average girl 66 inches tall. After that, there is little or no gain in height [28].

For boys, the onset of the period of rapid growth in height comes, on the average, at 12.8 years and ends, on the average at 15.3 years, with a peak in the velocity of their growth at 14 years. The greatest increase in height comes in the year following the onset of puberty. The average American boy of today measures 62 inches at thirteen years; at fourteen years, he measures 65 inches, and at sixteen years, 67.5 inches. After that, the rate of his growth slows down so that at eighteen years, the average boy measures 69.5 inches [28]. Boys attain their mature height a year or two later than girls, generally between twenty and twenty-two years.

Age of maturing affects the growth spurt in height. Boys who begin their spurt early complete it early; those who begin late are late in ending. There is a slight tendency for early developers to have a longer duration than late developers [47]. Late-maturing girls continue to grow after the mature height of early-maturing girls has been completed, with the result that they are generally taller at maturity than are the girls who started to mature earlier. Because growth in height is nearly complete at the time of the menarche, late-maturing girls have a longer time in which to grow. In boys, the advent of puberty accelerates growth in height with the result that the early-maturing boys are likely to be taller for a time than are those who mature later [5].

Because of the marked individual differences in rate of growth and age of maturing, predicting *adult stature* is difficult until after the puberty growth spurt. While adult stature is affected by many factors, such as hereditary endowment, racial stock, health conditions, especially during periods when growth is normally rapid, and general environmental conditions, age of maturing seems to play an important role in determining what the ultimate height of the individual will be. The early-maturing child will, as an adult, generally be shorter than would have been anticipated from his height as a child, while the child who matures late will probably be taller as an adult than would have been predicted from his childhood height [5, 30]. Children who are slow in the speed of maturing generally grow taller than those whose maturing is at a more rapid rate [5].

Weight. Increase in weight during puberty comes not from increase in fat alone but from increase in bone and muscle tissue. During puberty, the *bones* not only grow longer but they change in shape, proportions, and internal structure. The cartilage and fibrous tissue that made up the bones in childhood are now replaced by a harder tissue created by the conversion of the cartilage into bone. This is brought about by the thyroid hormone. By seventeen years, the girl's bones are mature or nearly mature in size and ossification. For boys, the skeletal development is completed approximately two years later [31]. In childhood, the *muscles* make up approximately one-fourth of the total body weight, while at sixteen years, they make up about 45 per cent of the weight. The most pronounced increase in muscle tissue comes between twelve and fifteen years for girls and between fifteen and sixteen years for boys [47]. Thus, even though the weight of the pubescent boy or girl increases rapidly, they often look lanky and scrawny.

The pattern of development of weight differs for boys and girls and is influenced by the age and tempo of maturing (see Figure 45). For girls, the greatest gain in weight is just before and just after the menarche. For the average girl maturing at thirteen years, weight increases from 88.5 pounds at the onset of puberty at eleven years to 126.5 pounds at fifteen years, when her growth spurt is almost complete. Only slight increases in weight will occur after that. For boys, the maximum gain in weight comes later, because they mature later. The average

weight for boys at twelve years, when they begin their growth spurt, is
96 pounds, at sixteen years, it has increased to 142 pounds. As is true
of girls, the increase after that will be relatively small. Between ten and
fifteen years, girls are generally heavier than boys of the same age, but
after fifteen years, the reverse is true. There are, however, greater variations in weight increases than in height increases between the sexes and
within the sexes [28, 47].

There are *sex differences* in the distribution of fat during puberty. In
the neck, thorax, abdomen, the front and the back, relative skinfold

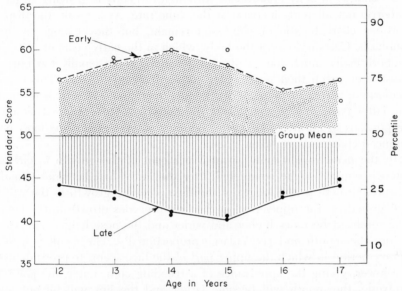

Fig. 45. Weight comparisons of boys who matured early and late. (*From M. C.
Jones, The later careers of boys who were early- and late-maturers. Child Develpm.,
1957, 28, 113–128. Used by permission.*)

thickness increases more in boys than in girls. Boys also show greater
gains in the lumbar region. For girls, relative fat thickness decreases
during puberty in the neck, abdomen, the total front, and the front of
the thorax, but it increases in the back of the thorax and the total back
[45]. Children who mature early are heavier at the same chronological
ages than children who mature late or at the average age. By fifteen or
sixteen years, however, the differences in weight between the early and
late maturers begin to disappear [7].

It is not uncommon for both boys and girls to have a *puberty fat
period*. Between ten and twelve years, at or near the onset of the growth
spurt, there is a tendency for boys and girls to have marked increases in
fat over the abdomen, around the nipples, in the hips and thighs, and

in the cheeks, neck, and jaw. This fat usually disappears after pubertal maturing and rapid growth in height are well started, though it may remain for two or more years during the early part of the puberty period. Part of the fat comes from hormone dislocation which accompanies puberty and part from appetite increases which accompany rapid growth and which are satisfied by indiscreet eating. As balance in hormonal functioning is regained and as the pubescent learns to cut down on his caloric intake, fat will disappear. Approximately 50 per cent of all boys and girls experience a puberty fat period [5, 17, 50].

2. Change in Body Proportions. Although the body is growing larger at puberty, not all parts increase at the same rate. As a result, the disproportions characteristic of childhood remain, but they change in their emphasis. Certain areas of the body, which in the early years of life were proportionally much too small, now become proportionally too big because they reach their mature size sooner than other areas. This is particularly apparent in the case of the nose, feet, and hands. It is not until the latter part of adolescence that the body will have attained its adult proportions in all areas. However, before puberty is over, the most pronounced changes have taken place.

In the *head* region, only about 5 per cent of the growth in circumference remains to be completed after the individual becomes sexually mature. Growth in the length of the face precedes growth in the width, and growth in the upper part of the face precedes growth in the lower. The forehead becomes higher and wider and the nose longer and wider before the mouth and jaw enlarge proportionally. The result is a temporary period in which the upper part of the face seems to protrude over the lower, giving the appearance of a receding chin. Later, the jaw will protrude, the mouth will become larger and the lips will fill out (see Figure 31, page 171). With this growth in facial contour, the boy's face becomes somewhat rugged and angular while the girl's face is more oval.

The thin, long *trunk* of the older child begins to broaden at the hips and shoulders and a waistline develops. This appears high at first because the legs grow proportionally more than the trunk. As the trunk lengthens, the waistline drops, thus giving the body adult proportions. Whether the hips or shoulders will be broader is influenced by the age of maturing. Boys who mature early usually have broader hips than boys who mature later, and girls who mature later have slightly broader hips than early-maturing girls. The typical masculine figure with slender hips and broad shoulders is characteristic of late-maturing boys. Late-maturing girls have broader shoulders than early-maturing girls. Typically, boys' shoulders are broader than their hips while the reverse is true for girls [5, 47].

Just before puberty, the *legs* are disproportionally long in relation to the trunk and continue to be so until approximately fifteen years. In late-maturing children, the leg growth continues for a longer time than in early maturers, with the result that the late maturer is a long-legged individual at maturity while the early maturer is short-legged. There is a tendency for the legs of the early maturer to be stocky while those of the late maturer are generally slender. Much the same pattern of growth is found in the *arms*, whose growth precedes the rapid spurt of growth in the trunk, thus giving the impression of disproportionally long arms. As is true of leg growth, the growth of the arms is affected by the age of maturing. Early maturers have a tendency to have shorter arms than late

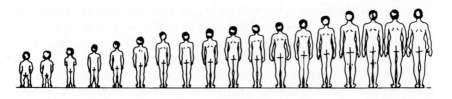

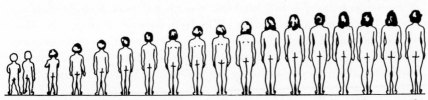

Fig. 46. Changes in body proportions for one boy and one girl from fifteen months to eighteen years. (*From N. Bayley, Individual patterns of development. Child Develpm.*, 1956, 27, 45–74. *Used by permission.*)

maturers just as the early maturer is shorter-legged than the late maturer. Not until the growth of the arms and legs is nearly complete do they seem to be in right proportion to the *hands* and *feet*, both of which reach their mature size early in puberty. The spurt in growth of the foot precedes that of the long bones and of stature by 6 to 18 months. Growth of the foot is completed 3 years after the maximum rate is reached while stature continues to increase for an average of 4.5 years [2]. Changes in body proportions for boys and girls from babyhood to maturity are shown in Figure 46. Figure 14, page 82, also shows changes in body proportions at different ages.

3. Primary Sex Characteristics. The sex organs during childhood are small and functionally immature. The individual is, as a result, incapable of producing offspring. During puberty, the sex organs increase in size and become mature in functioning. The male gonads or *testes*, which are located in the *scrotum*, or sac, outside the body, are only approximately 10 per cent of their mature size at the age of fourteen years. Then there is rapid growth for a year or two, after which growth slows down and the testes reach their mature size when the boy is twenty or twenty-one years old. The testes have a dual function: they produce the spermatozoa or sex cells and one or more of the hormones that control the physical and psychological adjustments needed for reproduction. The testes are functionally mature by approximately the middle of puberty, when *nocturnal emissions* appear.

Shortly after the rapid growth of the testes begins, the growth of the *penis* is markedly accelerated. The spurt in penis growth comes within 4 months of the spurt in growth in height and ends slightly before the end of the growth in height. The growth is first in length and is then followed by a gradual increase in circumference. The penis attains its mature length sooner than its mature girth [42, 47].

At an average age of between fourteen and fifteen years, when the male reproductive organs are mature in function, *nocturnal emissions* generally occur. This is nature's way of eliminating excessive amounts of semen. Nocturnal emissions generally occur when there are dreams of sex excitement, from a full bladder, constipated bowels, tight pajamas, or from being too warmly covered. The frequency of nocturnal emissions will be influenced by the frequency of the stimulating circumstances, though an average of four a week is common. Many boys are unaware of what is taking place until they see the telltale spot on the bedclothes or pajamas [25].

Because the female reproductive apparatus is mostly inside the body, its growth is barely perceptible, except for the enlargement of the abdomen. As the bony framework of the girl's body enlarges, the space within which the reproductive organs are lodged also enlarges, with the result that the abdomen flattens out. The female gonads or *ovaries* go through a growth spurt at puberty. When girls are twelve years old, their ovaries are approximately 40 per cent of their mature weight. From then until sixteen or seventeen years, there is an acceleration in growth but they do not reach their mature weight and size until the girl is twenty or twenty-one years old, though they are functionally mature in approximately the middle of the puberty period. The primary function of the ovaries is to produce *ova* (singular, *ovum*) or germ cells necessary for reproduction. In addition, they produce *theelin* and *progestin*, regulatory hormones which initiate and bring to a completion the period of pregnancy, the *follicular* hormone, and the *corpus luteum*. The female sex hormones are responsible for bringing about the development in structure and function of the female reproductive organs with their characteristic menstrual cycles and the secondary sex characteristics of the female body, especially the breasts with their mammary glands, which secrete nourishment when reproduction has taken place [26, 41].

The first real indication a girl has that her reproductive mechanism is becoming mature is the *menarche,* or first menstrual flow. This is the beginning of a series of periodic discharges of blood, mucus, and broken-down cell tissue from the uterus that will occur with varying degrees of regularity every 28 days until *menopause,* or change of life, in the late forties or early fifties. The menarche is generally followed by a period of menstrual irregularity during which menstruation comes at irregular and unpredictable times and its duration varies markedly. This period, which lasts for six months to a year, or even longer, is known as the *stage of adolescent sterility* during which time *ovulation,* or the ripening and release of a ripe ovum from a follicle in the ovary, does not occur and the individual is, therefore, sterile. Even after several menstrual periods, it is questionable whether the girl's sex mechanism is mature enough to make conception possible [4]. Menstruation starts before the girl's ovaries are capable of producing ripe eggs, and egg production begins before the uterus is mature enough to support the bearing of a child. There is evidence that the lag between the menarche and the capacity to conceive, the stage of adolescent sterility, is shorter in the case of girls who are late maturers than is true of the early maturers [13].

Frequently, headaches, backaches, cramps, and abdominal pain, accompanied by fainting, vomiting, skin irritations, and even swelling of the legs and ankles, occur in the early menstrual periods. As a result, the girl feels tired, depressed, and irritable at the time of her periods. As menstruation establishes itself as a regular function, its irregularity decreases, as do the physical and psychological disturbances which accompany its early appearances.

4. Secondary Sex Characteristics. As puberty progresses, boys and girls become increasingly dissimilar in appearance. This change is caused by the gradual development of the *secondary sex characteristics.* Whether the secondary sex characteristics develop at the same time as the primary sex characteristics, or whether their development precedes that of the primary sex characteristics by a slight margin of time has not yet been definitely proved. It is believed, however, that the secondary sex characteristics precede the primary in the normal pattern of development and hence are more nearly at their mature state of development when puberty comes to a close than are the primary sex characteristics.

Figure 47 shows a "timetable" for the maturation of some of the secondary sex characteristics of boys and girls. While most boys and girls follow a fairly predictable pattern, there are marked variations within each sex group in the ages at which different characteristics appear. In precocious sex development, the pattern of development of the secondary sex characteristics remains the same in boys and girls as when development comes at the average age, though the characteristics appear earlier than average. Similarly, in retarded maturing, the timetable remains constant, though each characteristic appears at a later time than in the boy or girl who matures at approximately the average age. The following paragraphs will discuss the secondary sex characteristics that have re-

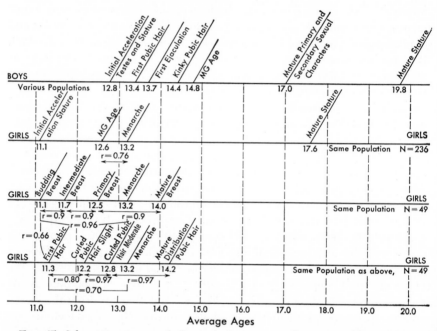

FIG. 47. Schematic picture of the typical sequence of events in the process of sexual maturation of boys and girls. (*From F. K. Shuttleworth, The adolescent period: a graphic atlas. Monogr. Soc. Res. Child Develpm., 1949, 14, No. 1. Used by permission.*)

ceived most attention in scientific investigations, the characteristic forms these changes take, and the average ages at which they occur.

In Boys. Pubic hair first appears about 1 year after the testes and penis have started to increase in size. Prepubsecent or lightly pigmented, straight hair first appears between the thirteenth and fourteenth years, with a median at 13.6 years. At a median age of 14 to 14.5 years, pubescent hair which is more luxuriant in growth and slightly pigmented appears. Six months to a year later, the characteristically kinky twist and greater pigmentation are present. For the average American boy, pubic hair is well developed around the age of 15 years. There is a definite tendency for the rate of gain in pubic-hair development to be greater during the first half of the puberty period than during the second half, though marked individual differences occur [47].

Axillary and *facial hair* begin to appear when pubic hair has almost completed its growth. Like pubic hair, axillary and facial hairs are lightly pigmented, fine in texture, and few in numbers at first. Few boys have enough facial hair to necessitate shaving before they are sixteen or seventeen years old. In addition, most boys develop relatively heavy growths of hair on their arms, legs, shoulders, and chests. Far less universal among boys is the change of the hairline at puberty from a bowlike curve to a curve with two wedge-shaped indentations over each lateral frontal region [41].

The delicate, soft, transparent *skin* of the child gradually becomes coarser and thicker at puberty, owing to an increase in the subcutaneous tissue. The transparency of the child's skin then gives way to a sallow coloring. The pores become larger, thus giving the skin a coarser look. The *sebaceous*, or oil-producing, glands become larger and more active at puberty. These are associated with hair follicles which, for a time, are disproportionally small. This causes a temporary maladjustment in the glands' functioning which leads to *acne*. The *apocrine* sweat glands, located in the armpits, begin to enlarge shortly before puberty and start to function even before axillary hair appears. The result is axillary perspiration, with its characteristic odor, which increases in quantity as puberty progresses.

Growth of the *muscles* is closely related to the functional status of the testes. Soon after growth and maturation of the testes has begun, the muscles of the trunk and limbs increase markedly in size [18]. It is this increase that is responsible for giving the lanky arms and legs of the boy some shape, and for producing the broad shoulders, characteristic of the masculine build. With growth in the muscles comes increase in strength. There is a close relationship between gains in muscular strength and gains in muscular weight. The peak of strength increase occurs at that time during the growth spurt when there is the greatest gain in height and weight [47].

Voice changes generally come after some pubic hair has appeared. The median age for the first indication of the deepening of the voice is 13.4 years, though the breaking and conspicuous loss of control do not appear until the boy is between 16 and 18 years of age. Following this, there is a year or two before the change is completed and the youth has acquired control of his voice. Huskiness usually occurs in the early stages of voice change and few boys escape this. "Breaking" of the voice, on the other hand, varies in intensity and frequency with the speed of maturing. After the voice changes have been completed, late in adolescence, there is a drop of at least an octave in pitch, an increase in volume, and a pleasanter total quality [8].

Breast knots, or slight knobs around the male mammary glands, appear between the ages of twelve and fourteen years. They last for only a few weeks, then decrease rapidly in number and size. At about the same time, the male mammary glands enlarge in one or both breasts. Like the breast knots, this is only a temporary condition and disappears within a short

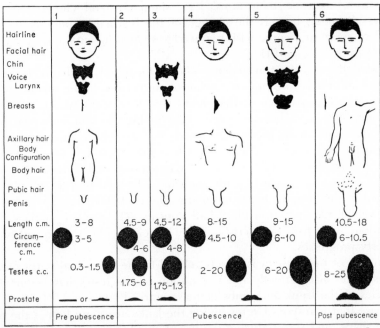

FIG. 48. Stages of sexual development and maturation. (From W. A. Schonfeld, Primary and secondary sexual characteristics. Amer. J. Dis. Child., 1943, 65, 535–549. Used by permission.)

time, after which the breasts become flat, as in childhood [47]. Figure 48 shows the characteristic pattern of development of the important secondary sex characteristics of boys.

In Girls. The pattern of development of the secondary sex characteristics in girls is regular and predictable, as in boys. The first of the female characteristics to develop are the hips which increase in width and roundness, caused partly by the enlargement of the pelvic bone and partly by the development of subcutaneous fat. At about the same time, the breasts begin to develop (see Figure 49). The slightly elevated nipple of the child begins to elevate further as is true also of the surrounding areola. The bud stage of breast development generally occurs between the tenth and eleventh years of girls who mature at the average age. Following this comes the *primary breast stage*, during which there is an increase in the amount of fat underlying and immediately surrounding the nipple and areola, causing the areola to be raised above the level of the chest wall in a conical shape. This development takes place before the menarche. Following the menarche, the breasts complete their development in the *mature breast stage*, when the breasts become larger and rounder with the development of the mammary glands. At this time,

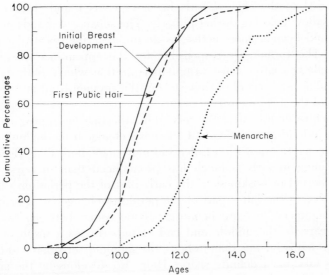

FIG. 49. Breast development in relation to first pubic hair and the menarche. (*From E. L. Reynolds, Individual differences in physical changes associated with adolescence in girls. Amer. J. Dis. Child., 1948, 75, 329–350. Used by permission.*)

the areola is incorporated in the breast itself so that only the nipple protrudes. It takes nearly three years after breast development starts before the nipple protrudes above the rest of the breast structure [49].

Pubic hair does not appear in any considerable quantity until hip and breast development are well under way, though a few unpigmented hairs appear at the beginning of pubertal changes. This scanty development remains relatively unchanged for a number of months when suddenly the hair becomes more pigmented, changes from straight to kinky, and becomes much more luxuriant in quantity. The first pubic hairs are generally found on the outer lips of the vulva and then gradually spread in a horizontal line across the vulva. After the pubic hair is fairly well developed, *axillary hair* begins to appear in the armpits. Axillary hair usually, but not always, appears after the menarche. The first axillary hairs are fine, straight, and only slightly pigmented. It takes about a year before there are approximately as many axillary hairs as found in adults and these become coarser, have a slight kink, and are more pigmented than the early axillary hairs.

At the time the axillary hairs begin to appear, there is an appearance of a slight *down* on the upper lip, following which is the appearance of down on the upper part of the cheeks and then on the sides and lower border of the chin. This down does not become as heavy in texture, as pigmented, or as luxuriant as the hair on the boy's face. As is true of the boy's skin, the *skin* of girls becomes coarser and thicker, with a slightly sallow coloring during puberty. The *sebaceous* glands in the skin enlarge and become more active, as do the *apocrine* sweat glands in the armpits. The former are responsible for the appearance of adolescent acne, while the latter cause armpit perspiration which, with its characteristic odor, is especially heavy during the premenstrual and menstrual portions of the girl's menstrual cycle.

Just before or just after the menarche, the time of appearance differing from individual to individual, there is a change from the high-pitched, childish *voice* to one with a fuller and more melodious tone. Because the voice change in girls is much less pronounced than in boys, there is rarely a period of huskiness in the early part of the period or a breaking of the voice in the latter part of the period of change [8]. For girls, the most pronounced increase in *muscle* tissue comes between twelve and fifteen years, in the middle and end of puberty. As a result of this increase, which is far less than in boys, the shoulders broaden and the arms and legs take on a definite shape. Hair also develops on the arms and legs late in the puberty period [26, 41].

EFFECTS ON BEHAVIOR

Rapid growth and bodily changes are likely to be accompanied by fatigue, listlessness, and other unfavorable symptoms. At puberty, this condition is frequently exaggerated by the increase in duties and responsibilities placed upon the individual just at the time when he is least able to shoulder them successfully. Because he is now larger in stature, his parents assume that he can carry more of the burdens of the home than he did when he was younger. In much the same spirit, the school piles work on shoulders not yet broad enough or strong enough to carry them. Fatigue invariably predisposes the individual to nervousness, irritability, and general emotionality.

Digestive disturbances are frequent and appetite is finicky. The prepubescent child is upset by glandular changes and changes in the size and position of the internal organs. These changes interfere with the normal functions of digestion. Anemia is frequent at this period not because of marked changes in blood chemistry but because of the erratic eating habits of the individual. This, in turn, increases the already present tendency to be tired and listless. Headaches, backaches, and a general feeling of wretchedness which accompany the menarche and subsequent menstrual periods are not limited to girls, nor do they occur only at the time of menstruation. Both boys and girls suffer intermittently from them, the frequency and severity depending to a large extent upon how rapidly the pubescent changes are occurring and upon how healthy the individuals were when puberty began.

Children of poor environments, where nutritional diets are poor and good habits of sleep have not usually been formed in childhood, are more likely to be affected unfavorably by pubertal changes than are children whose childhood health has been favorable, provided the rate of maturing is the same for both. While puberty may be regarded as a "sickly age" when the individual is not up to par, there are relatively few diseases characteristic of this age. Nor does the person suffer from any definite illness which necessitates his being out of school or missing the social life of his companions. If he were actually ill, he would be treated with more sympathy and understanding than he usually is; less would be expected of him; and, of special significance to his social adjustments, much of his unsocial behavior would be understood and tolerated, as it rarely is.

Changes in attitudes and behavior appear as the physical changes of puberty take place and are undoubtedly due to maturation rather than to learning. They are the result of the increase in gonad secretions just as are the physical changes that are taking place. How great or how trivial the psychological effects of puberty will be will depend partly upon the speed of maturing, with its impact on the general physical well-being of the individual, and partly upon the individual's foreknowledge and consequent psychological preparation for the changes. In the absence of preparation, or when the preparation has consisted mainly of inaccurate information which has given rise to unhealthy attitudes, the general effect on behavior is more unfavorable, even when the rate of maturing is slow, than when the preparation has been adequate and wholesome and the speed of development fast.

While all children show some of the characteristic behavior forms of puberty, these forms are more marked before the individual becomes sexually mature, or during the period known as the *negative phase* [15]. Girls, as a general rule, are more seriously affected by puberty than are boys, partly because girls mature, on the average, more rapidly than boys and partly because there are more social restrictions on their behavior just at the time when they are trying to free themselves from these restrictions. There are, however, such marked individual differences from child to child that it is impossible to predict just how puberty will affect any given child, boy or girl [21].

Both boys and girls are keenly aware of their bodies and the changes that are taking place in them. One of the primary developmental tasks both now and during adolescence is the acceptance of the changing body as a symbol of the changing self. The psychological effects of puberty are also complicated by the social expectancy of parents, teachers, and other adults. A boy or a girl of a given chronological age is expected to act according to standards for that age. The twelve-year-old, for example, is expected to have different interests and to act differently from a four-teen-year-old. When the developmental pattern approximates the group mean, such adjustments will be relatively easy. When, however, there is a marked discrepancy between social expectancy and a child's matura-tional readiness, there are likely to be problems for him and for society [47].

Among the many effects of puberty on attitude and behavior, the following have been found to be the most common. All of these, in one way or another, lead to difficult social adjustments for the individual or present problems for his parents and teachers to cope with, thus justify-ing the name "negative phase."

Desire for Isolation. As early as babyhood, there is a craving for the companionship of others. This desire reaches its peak in the "gang age" of late childhood. Then, in a relatively short time, sometimes within a week or even over a week end, the child loses interest in his playmates, withdraws from the group, and spends his time alone in his room with his door shut. This withdrawal from the group is frequently accompanied by quarreling with former friends and the consequent breaking off of many childhood friendships [15, 17]. There is also a sudden and marked withdrawal from family activities, usually between twelve and thirteen years [17].

Disinclination to Work. The child who formerly was constantly on the go and never seemed to tire from work or play, now seems constantly tired. As a result, he does as little work as he can. Home responsibilities are allowed to slide and school studies are neglected. As a result, many an "A" student slips into the just-barely-passing group and the previously poor student turns into a failure. Unquestionably this disinclination to work is not willful laziness but a direct outgrowth of the rapid physical growth and development which sap his energy. The more sudden the physical changes at puberty, the more sudden will be the changes in the child's schoolwork and his achievements in school [10]. When the child shirks his responsibilities or does them carelessly and slowly, he is blamed for being lazy and slipshod. This, in turn, builds up antagonisms and resentments which result in even less desire on the child's part to do what is expected of him [14].

Incoordinations. The onset of puberty, with its rapid and uneven growth, is accompanied by a temporary retardation in certain types of coordination, balance, and agility. From 12.5 to 14 years in boys, there is a lag or even a recession in measurements by the Brace Test of motor ability. The tests that show the characteristic pubescent lag, such as the beam-walking test, all include the factor of dynamic balance. After rapid physical growth slows down and after the boy or girl has adjusted to changes in body proportions, incoordinations begin to show a marked decrease [11].

Boredom. The pubescent child is bored with the play he formerly enjoyed, with his schoolwork, with social activities, and with life in general [17]. And he does not hesitate to show this boredom by refusing to engage in activities he formerly enjoyed or by criticizing them as "stupid" and "babyish." In neither case does he win the sympathy or approval of his friends and playmates. When reproved for this attitude, he sinks into a state of sullen gloom and develops an "I don't care" or a "no one loves me" attitude.

Restlessness. As invariably occurs when a person is bored, the pubescent child is restless. Things which formerly absorbed his interest and held his attention no longer do so. Because his interests are changing, as his body changes, he has not yet discovered new interests that can absorb his attention as his childhood interests did. He, therefore, goes from one thing to another, never completely satisfied with one and always on the search for something that he can enjoy as he previously enjoyed his childhood experiences.

Restlessness has a physical basis too. Rapid and uneven growth give rise to tensions which find their outlet in restlessness. The pubescent child finds it difficult to sit or stand in one position for any length of time and, therefore, is constantly squirming or twitching. And, finally, some of his restlessness is rooted in his heightened emotionality. It is an outward expression of internal tension caused by emotions which do not always get complete expression in overt acts. The more the pubescent child tries to keep his emotions under control, thus inhibiting their expressions, the more tense and, in turn, the more restless he will be [15, 17].

Social Antagonism. The pubescent child is antagonistic in his attitude toward his family, his friends, and society in general. He goes around with a chip on his shoulder and a snarl on his face. Not only does he seem to resent the happiness of others, but he seems to go out of his way to spoil their fun by being as disagreeable, as uncooperative, and as antagonistic toward their wishes as he can be. At home, he is jealous and critical of his siblings, calling them names, picking fights for no reason at all, and intentionally antagonizing them. The mother is generally the butt of his severest criticisms and he will often make a point of doing something he knows she does not want him to do. He will argue endlessly, just to stir up trouble, and he will do all he can to stir up trouble among his siblings. He behaves outside the home in much the same manner, picking fights with his friends and quarreling over the most trivial matters, calling them names and trying to hurt their feelings.

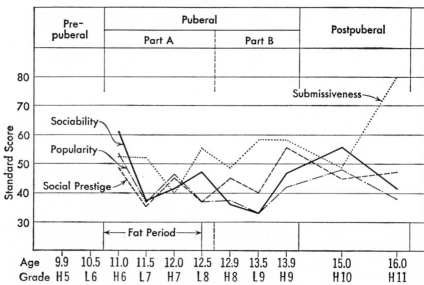

Fig. 50. Ratings on social behavior of a boy during different periods of sexual maturing. (*From H. R. Stolz and L. M. Stolz, Somatic development of adolescent boys. New York: Macmillan, 1951. Used by permission.*)

This often results in the breakup of former friendships [15, 17]. Figure 50 shows the ratings on social behavior at puberty, emphasizing how unfavorably the pubescent child's behavior is regarded by others. As puberty progresses, the child becomes more mature in his social behavior, showing a friendlier, more cooperative, and more tolerant attitude toward others [9, 46].

Resistance to Authority. Throughout childhood, there is a growing resistance to authority and an accompanying demand for greater independence. At puberty, the pace of this growth is speeded up. Conflicts of boys and girls with their parents generally reach a peak at around thirteen years. There are more conflicts with the mother than with the father because of the closer association in the home with the mother than with the father. As mothers become less restrictive, there is a decrease in conflicts [29]. The pubescent child tries to resist all authority and, when he discovers that his attempts at resistance are blocked, he becomes sullen and resentful, or he tries to alibi himself out of a situation he knows will lead to punishment for disobedience. Most of the *misdemeanors*, or misbehavior of a minor sort, so common at this age come from the pubescent's attempts to resist authority.

Typically, the pubescent child does nothing so wrong that he can be classed as a juvenile delinquent. But he is troublesome and frequently he seems to be so intentionally with the hope of irritating people by "getting under their skin." Whispering, inattentiveness, carelessness, tattling, resentfulness, suspiciousness, tardiness, insubordination, rudeness, impatience with restrictions, self-assertiveness, and avoidance of members of the opposite sex are the most frequently reported misdemeanors at this age [48]. These misdemeanors, which reach their peak of intensity and frequency when boys and girls become pubescent, decline as pubescent development continues and as the individual's sexual development is completed (see Figure 51).

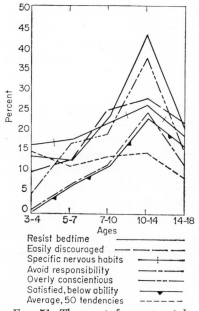

Fig. 51. The most frequent misdemeanors during puberty for children ranging in age from eleven to fourteen years. (*From A. Long, Parents' reports of undesirable behavior in children. Child Develpm., 1941, 12, 43–62. Used by permission.*)

Sex Antagonism. The antagonism between the sexes which normally develops during the latter part of childhood reaches its peak at puberty (see Figure 35, page 185). Open hostility between the sexes is common at this age, with girls, as a rule, showing a stronger aversion toward boys than boys toward girls. This antagonism is intensified by the girls' resentment of the physical disturbances maturing imposes upon them, especially menstruation, as contrasted with the less severe burden sexual maturing places upon boys. No longer do boys and girls show their antagonism toward one another simply by withdrawing from each other as they did during childhood. Now there is open hostility between the two sexes, expressed in constant criticisms and disparaging comments. Both boys and girls seem to go out of their way to hurt members of the opposite sex by biting comments and bitter sarcasm. These are not limited to their contemporaries but are aimed at any and all members of the opposite sex, regardless of their age, their kinship to the pubescent child, or how pleasant their former relationship has been. The mother becomes the target of criticism for the sons, and the father, for the daughters [15]. Girls are generally greater offenders in this respect than boys [17].

Heightened Emotionality. The tension and confusion resulting from changed attitudes and interests, the disturbances caused by physical and glandular changes, and the general tendency to feel below par physically most of the time result in heightened emotionality at this age. Moodiness, sulkiness, and a tendency to burst into tears at the slightest provocation are characteristic emotional states of the pubescent child. Little pleases them, anything or everything said about them or to them is likely to be taken as a criticism, feelings are constantly being hurt and prides offended. Typically, the pubescent child reacts with irritation or strongly rebellious feelings to the most innocent and friendly remarks which he interprets to be critical or antagonistic [15, 17]. He is touchy and irritable, especially with his siblings, and engages in much verbal fighting with them. He regards his younger siblings as "pests" or "spoiled brats" and is jealous of his older siblings [14, 21].

Puberty is a time of *worries* or imaginary fears. Girls, between the ages of eleven and thirteen years, have been found to worry about problems of personal and social adequacy, such as how they can "fit in," how they appear to others, and how they are growing up. Boys experience similar worries a year or two later because of their later maturing. While both sexes worry, boys worry more about personal and social adequacy and girls more about their families, their homes, and their schoolwork. There is a significant rise in the number and intensity of worries up until the time the child becomes sexually mature, after which there is a decline in worrying [32].

There is such a marked and noticeable change from the general good humor that characterized the latter period of childhood that this pubescent moodiness is frequently commented upon by the adults in the child's presence [17]. This only adds to the chip he already carries on his shoulder and increases his belief that no one loves him and the whole world is against him. Semihysterical states of crying are common among girls at this age, while boys are more likely to experience their resentment toward the world in melancholy silence, in sulkiness, or in temper outbursts that are reminiscent of the preschool years. As the child becomes mature physically, he becomes more mature emotionally (see Figure 33, page 178). As a result, he is less tense and more relaxed, making him an easier and pleasanter person to live and work with [10, 14].

Lack of Self-confidence. The child who was formerly self-assured to the point where he felt that he could stand his ground in any and every circumstance and who boasted openly about his achievements now passes through a stage where his self-confidence crumbles literally over-night. No longer does he feel that he can succeed in whatever he under-takes as he formerly did. Instead, he doubts his own abilities to such an extent that he hesitates to tackle many of the tasks that he formerly carried out easily and with great success. This lack of self-confidence, intensified by worries about his personal and social adequacy, is some-times hidden behind a cloak of cocksureness or rebellion. His refusal to do things expected of him often stems from fear that he cannot do them, or he may boast of his abilities and then give alibis when he does not carry through his boasts [10, 15].

Lack of self-confidence comes partly from lowered physical resistance which makes every molehill look like a mountain, partly from constant social pressures on the child to do more than he formerly did and to "act his age," and partly from the criticisms of his elders and of his con-temporaries about the way he does things or the fact that he does not do them. Many girls and boys emerge from puberty with so little self-confidence left that regaining it during the adolescent years is one of the major problems they must face. As a general rule, those children who seemed most capable and most confident of their abilities in late childhood are hit hardest in this area by puberty, primarily because more is expected of them than of children who were formerly timid and unsure of themselves.

Preoccupation with Sex. The growth and maturing of the sex organs with the new sensations that accompany these changes and the develop-ment of the secondary sex characteristics all focus the pubescent child's attention on sex matters. Now, because of the physical changes taking place in their own bodies, the sex interests of pubescent boys and girls become subjective and personal in nature. This leads to a growing aware-ness of sex and sex differences [15, 17]. Interest is not in pregnancy or childbirth but in sex life itself and how it affects the child personally [52]. Interest in sex frequently becomes so strong during puberty that it occupies much of the time and thought of the pubescent child and is the subject of many of his daydreams.

Attentive study of the different areas of his body, exploration of the genitals to see what new sensations can be produced by manipulation of different types, careful observation of the forms and shapes of the bodies of other members of his own sex, not only of his contemporaries but of adults as well, to see how they compare with his body, reading books in hopes of gaining information he craves but has not yet found, looking up words in the dictionary in the hope of throwing light on explanations of sex given in medical or technical books, and studying lewd drawings and off-color jokes for clues to further knowledge about this all too secret subject are some of the many ways in which pubescent girls and boys reveal their preoccupation with sex matters. Studies have revealed that masturbation usually reaches its peak between thirteen and fourteen years in boys and a year or two earlier in girls (see Figure 39, page 203). This means that its peak coincides with the time of greatest changes in the sex organs, when new sensations are appearing [52]. After boys and girls become sexually mature, there is normally a decline in masturbation, especially among those who are making good heterosexual adjustments [26].

Excessive Modesty. The pubescent child is very self-conscious about the changes that are taking place in his body, and he makes every possible effort to hide them. Unlike the child who shows little if any modesty even in the presence of strangers, both boys and girls at puberty are likely to be terror stricken at the thought of having to undress even partially when they have a medical examination. They turn their backs to their classmates when changing clothes in the gymnasium dressing rooms, and they become angry if any member of the family enters the room while they are undressing or bathing. This excessive modesty, which develops quite suddenly at puberty, is a direct outgrowth of the rapid physical changes which are taking place in the child's body. He is self-conscious about these changes and tries to hide them in fear that others will observe them and, perhaps, comment unfavorably upon them, even though he may be secretly pleased by these signs of growing up [17].

Daydreaming. Daydreaming is one of the favorite pastimes of the pubescent child. Time which formerly was spent in active play with other children, in schoolwork or home responsibilities, is now spent in reverie. Typically, the pubescent child's daydream is of the "suffering-hero" type in which the dreamer sees himself in his daydream in the role of a martyr, misunderstood and mistreated by parents, teachers, friends, and society in general. Then, when his dream reaches a point where things are almost unbearable, the dreamer suddenly finds the tables turned. No longer is he a martyr but a hero.

Daydreaming of this type is a source of great emotional satisfaction to the individual who indulges in it. He enjoys his role even when he is suffering great agonies because he knows full well that, in the end, things will turn out in his favor. However pleasurable such daydreams may be, they tend to intensify an already-present belief on the child's part that "nobody loves me." The more frequently the child revels in such daydreams, the more out of step he is with reality and the poorer his social adjustments will be.

SOURCES OF CONCERN

One of the developmental tasks of growing up is the acceptance of the newly developed body and the recognition that nature produces foundations, limited in size and shape, which the individual can then change to fit his ideals. Many children enter puberty with childhood ideals of what they will look like when they are grown up. Because these ideals rarely take into consideration the foundations laid by heredity, they must be markedly revised. Furthermore, most children enter puberty with little foreknowledge of the time needed to mature or the pattern that maturing takes. The result is that they are deeply concerned as they watch their bodies change, often so slowly that they wonder if they will ever grow up.

The reticence and antagonism toward adults, so characteristic of this age, keep children from turning to adults for help in meeting their concerns. Some pubescent children discuss their concerns with their friends but many are not on intimate enough terms with their former friends to want to reveal their worries. In addition, the lack of self-confidence in pubescent children and the compensatory bragging so common at this age make them hesitant to let anyone know that they are concerned. As a result, most pubescents keep their worries about their changing bodies and changing feelings to themselves, brood over them, and eventually turn molehills into mountains.

The pubescent's concern is intensified by parental concern, especially when parents verbalize this concern in the presence of the child [44]. One of the biggest contributions parents and teachers can make to the child's successful growing up is to prepare him ahead of time for what to expect and when to expect it [3]. Unfortunately, far too many parents are ignorant of correct facts, as are many teachers. They, like the pubescent child, compare the state of development of one child with that of another child of the same age, not realizing that every child follows his own pattern of development at his own rate. As a result, should the child deviate from other children of the same age, parents begin to wonder if he is completely normal, thus adding to the child's concerns instead of minimizing them.

While it is a rare pubescent who never worries about his changing body, different pubescents worry about different aspects of their bodies. Usually, they find one physical characteristic which they feel is homely, disproportionate, or sexually inappropriate and magnify its seriousness out of reasonable proportion [16, 47]. Girls, as a rule, are more concerned about different physical characteristics than are boys. In general, the sources of concern can be divided into two categories, concern about whether certain physical characteristics are *normal* and concern about whether they are *sexually appropriate*.

Concern about Normalcy. Because boys and girls are very conscious of every change that takes place in their bodies, and because they have an ideal of what they want their bodies to be, based partly on adult standards and partly on their childhood aspirations, they become concerned when they see how far short their bodies fall from their ideal and begin to wonder if they are "normal" [14, 15]. Both boys and girls are concerned about the changes in their *sex organs*. Among boys, there is the fear that the rapidly growing penis will show through their clothing and there is worry because it seems so thin in comparison with the penis of the adult man. Because the girl's genitalia grow more internally than externally, she has less cause for concern on that score than has the pubescent boy. However, the unexplained protrusion of her abdomen, which normally accompanies early genital growth, does disturb her.

The *menarche* in girls may be a traumatic experience, even if they have had some forewarning of what to expect. If the menarche is accompanied by vomiting, pain, headaches, and backaches, all of which are common accompaniments of the menarche, the traumatic effect is heightened. It is not unusual for girls to wonder if they will "bleed to death" or to believe that something serious is the matter with them. What the girl's attitude will be depends largely upon her information and the attitude of her informer. Without wholesome preparation for this experience, the traumatic effect is heightened to a pitch where it is apt to leave an indelible impression on the girl's mind [1, 3, 26]. It will influence her attitude to the female role, parenthood, and even breast feeding of her baby [38].

Subsequent menstrual periods are likely to be disturbing to a girl not only because of the discomforts they bring but also because the girl resents the restrictions this condition imposes upon her activities. Furthermore, she is afraid of any telltale signs that will reveal the fact that she is menstruating. As a general rule, girls become more introverted in their attitudes during the menstrual period, and this tendency is increased with increases in pain and discomfort. The cultural attitudes of the group with which the girl is identified have marked influences on her attitude toward menstruation. If the group regards it as a normal function, the girl will be less concerned, even when her menstrual periods are accompanied by pain or discomfort, than when the group regards it as "being sick" or the "curse," neither of which suggests that it is a normal function of the female body [1].

The boy's first *nocturnal emission* is much the same traumatic experience for him as the menarche is for the girl. In absence of fore-knowledge of this experience, he is likely to believe that something is seriously wrong with him. Furthermore, he is disturbed and embarrassed by the stains left on his pajamas or on the sheets of his bed. Each subsequent nocturnal emission is likely to be a source of embarrassment to him. If, however, he does not experience nocturnal emission, he frequently has tension and discomfort in his penis which may lead to *masturbation,* to relieve the tension. This, in turn, is likely to lead to shame, embarrassment, or feelings of guilt, depending upon what attitudes toward masturbation were engendered when he was a child. Many boys, and girls too, have accepted the traditional beliefs that masturbation is "wrong," that it may lead to insanity, mental deficiency, or acne, and that people can tell from these telltale signs that the individual has masturbated. The acceptance of these "old wives' tales" heightens the concern the pubescent child experiences when he engages in masturbation to relieve the tensions caused by changes in his developing sex organs [25, 26].

Body disproportions, which are an inevitable accompaniment of growth, cause concern bordering on alarm for the pubescent child. The too big hands and feet are especially disturbing to a girl because she has been brought up on the tradition that "ladies have small hands and feet." She shows how great this concern is to her by wearing shoes too small for her feet, by wearing high heels before the arches of her feet are developed enough to wear such heels with comfort, and by holding her hands in her pockets or behind her back so that no one can see them. The temporarily too large nose sends both boys and girls into states of depression every time they look into the mirror. Long and lanky arms and legs, too small shoulders, and a tendency for the chin to recede until growth in the lower part of the face catches up with growth in the upper part, are likewise very disturbing. Not realizing that such disproportions are temporary and are caused by differences in rates of growth for different parts of the body, the pubescent child is convinced that he will never look like a "normal" person [16].

When uneven growth is accompanied by *awkwardness,* as so often happens in the early stages of puberty, and when it is especially pronounced because of rapid maturing, the pubescent child is disturbed and embarrassed. Having acquired skills in childhood which made him master of his body, it is not surprising if he wonders what is wrong with him when he bumps into furniture, trips over rugs and his own feet, or drops things he formerly was able to hold without any difficulty. If his awkwardness is met with ridicule, this increases his embarrassment; similarly, reproof adds to his feeling of inadequacy and his concern about his normalcy [12].

Few pubescent children, or even their parents, are aware of the pattern of development of the *secondary sex characteristics*. The slow and irregular development of hair on the body and face, of skin changes which frequently give rise to acne, of the muscles and voice changes, and of the hips and breasts are the focal points of concern. Girls are sure their breasts are going to be abnormal because of their early conical shape and they are worried that their hips will be too large for the rest of their bodies. They are disturbed by the appearance of down on their faces and wonder if it will develop into a beard or mustache. The secondary sex characteristics which disturb boys most are facial hair which comes in so slowly in comparison with body hair that they worry about ever having enough to shave, the huskiness and cracking in the early voice changes, and the slow development of their muscles, which retards the development of the strength associated with normal males [3, 16].

Of all the sources of concern that lead the pubescent child to wonder if he is normal, perhaps differences in *age of maturing* and in *rate of maturing* are the most serious. Children and young adolescents keenly want to be like their friends and classmates in every respect and, in fact, interpret being different as being inferior. Deviations from the norm of the group in appearance are therefore even more serious to the child than deviations in other areas because these physical deviations are constantly visible to the group.

A slight deviation from the average age of sexual maturing among members of a group is not a great handicap to any child. But when maturing is markedly accelerated or delayed, the effects on both boys and girls are more serious. Those who mature earlier than their classmates feel like misfits among their former friends partly because they are too big and too grown-up in appearance for them and partly because, with the characteristic interests that accompany pubertal development, they have little in common with them. Children, on the other hand, who are slow in maturing, feel embarrassed because of their small, undeveloped bodies; they feel out of things when they cannot bring themselves to be interested in the things which are so absorbing to their more mature classmates; and, if their maturing is markedly delayed, they worry for fear that they will remain little boys or girls for the rest of their lives [3].

To compensate for slow maturing, many boys and girls withdraw from the groups to which they formerly belonged and develop solitary interests. This, however, is rarely satisfying to them, especially if they have enjoyed an active social life with other children throughout their childhood years and have had a circle of friends to which they belonged. Now they feel lost without their friends and yet, because they have little in common with them, it is not surprising that they find themselves in the role of social misfits. Other children whose sexual maturing is delayed may compensate by trying to dress, act, and feel like their more sexually mature friends. This, likewise, is frequently not a satisfying form of compensation because the individual's behavior often gives his friends the impression that he is "just a kid who is trying to put on airs and pretend that he is older than he is" [23, 31].

Studies have shown how marked an influence the age of maturing has on the behavior of the individual and on his concept of self. Because the physically accelerated are accepted and treated by adults and peers as more mature, they have little need to strive for status. As a result, they make good social adjustments and often become the leaders of their groups. Because late maturers are treated by adults and peers as children, they must strive for status. This leads to many forms of immature behavior, such as showing off, to try to counteract the impression that they are "kids." Furthermore, they develop negative self-concepts and feelings of inadequacy, of being rejected and discriminated against. This results in an attitude of hostility and rebellion against the family, a tendency to be quarrelsome, argumentative and demanding of attention, and a desire to escape from the family and defy all adult authority. Early maturers, by contrast, have more favorable self-concepts. This makes them warmer, friendlier, more emotionally stable, physically better coordinated, and more sure of themselves. As a result, they are better poised, more forceful and assertive, and better adjusted, both personally and socially [22, 34, 36]. Figure 52 shows the difference in early and late maturers in personality adjustments.

The age of sexual maturing affects the two sexes slightly differently. On the whole, early-maturing girls are faced with more serious adjustment problems than are boys or late-maturing girls. The reason for this is that the early-maturing girl is not only out of step in her interests and behavior with members of her own sex but also with members of the opposite sex who normally mature a year or two later than girls do. Furthermore, society is more critical of the behavior of girls than of boys. The girl whose sexual development is precocious frequently gets the reputation of being "fast" not only among her contemporaries but also among the parents of her contemporaries. And yet, her behavior is generally normal for her level of development even though precocious for her chronological age. In addition to the social disadvantage of precocious sexual development, the girl who becomes sexually mature before she has had enough experience or has developed enough emotional maturity to cope with the mature experiences she will be faced with is likely to become sexually delinquent [31].

Early maturing is a greater advantage to a boy than it is to a girl partly because the increased strength which accompanies the boy's sexual maturing makes him more proficient in sports and places him in demand for dates and parties among the girls. Figure 53 shows differences in strength for early- and late-maturing boys. Because of his superior strength, the early-maturing boy has little reason to wonder if he is normal. The late maturer, by contrast, wonders if there is something wrong with him and this concern is increased by the concern of his parents. Because he is not interested in the social life of his peers, in girls, parties,

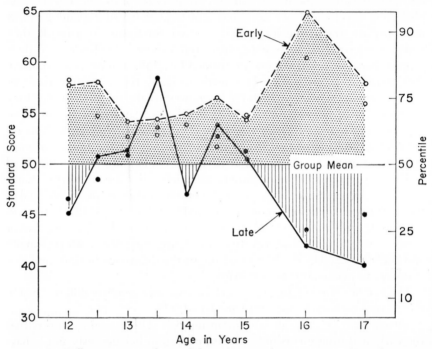

Fig. 52. Differences in early- and late-maturing boys in personality adjustment as shown in self-acceptance (being relaxed, unaffected, and matter-of-fact). (*From M. C. Jones, The later careers of boys who were early- and late-maturers. Child Develpm., 1957, 28, 113–128. Used by permission.*)

clothes, and grooming, he feels left out of things. At home, he resents the lack of independence his parents give him as compared with what his more mature contemporaries enjoy and this further increases his feeling of being out of step with his former friends. The marked feelings of inadequacy resulting from such problems make him try to compensate by attention-seeking behavior, or he may try to excel in academic work where physical strength and body size are unimportant [31, 36].

Studies of the long-term effects of age of maturing have revealed that the influence of early and late maturing is not limited to puberty but carries through the adolescent years and into maturity. Personality patterns established in puberty as a result of the influence of age of maturing on the individual's self-concept continue to influence the personal and social adjustments of the individual as he grows older. The early maturer, who has the advantage of being able to develop more mature feelings and behavior and to reinforce them by the social learning process, continues to feel and act in a more mature manner as he grows older. Through repetition, the late maturer reinforces his immature feelings and behavior patterns and these then develop into habits which are carried into the adult years [34]. However, as Mussen and Jones have

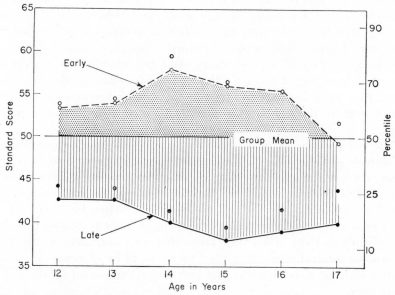

Fig. 53. Strength comparisons of boys who were early- and late-maturers. (*From M. C. Jones, The later careers of boys who were early- and late-maturers. Child Develpm., 1957, 28, 113–128. Used by permission.*)

emphasized, the impact of the age of maturing upon the individual will depend on the early foundations and the treatment the individual receives from his parents, teachers, and peers during puberty and through the adolescent years. It need not be inevitable that late maturers be adversely affected [36].

Even when boys and girls mature at approximately the average age for their sex, they are concerned about their attitudes toward the opposite sex and the attitudes of the opposite sex toward them. Because girls mature a year or more ahead of boys, they become interested in boys, in dates, and in dressing up to attract the attention of boys sooner than boys become interested in girls. Many girls, not understanding why boys are not interested in them, wonder if they are normal when they are unable to attract the attention and win the favor of boys. Boys, in turn, wonder if they are normal when they have no interest in girls or dates, especially as they observe older or sexually mature boys setting a pattern of behavior they would like to imitate.

Concern about Sex Appropriateness. As has been stressed earlier, children become well aware of what society considers appropriate in appearance and behavior long before childhood comes to a close. From their attendance at movies, from watching television, reading comics and books, and from their observations of the body builds and behavior of adults they admire, the pubescent child has a clear concept of *masculinity* and *femininity* in appearance and behavior. It is not surprising, therefore, that with these ideals as sources of comparison for their own bodies, children are concerned when they observe discrepancies between their ideals and reality. And, because they are usually unaware of how long it takes for their bodies to complete their development, they judge according to the present state of development and then worry because their bodies fall short of their ideals of sex appropriateness.

The sudden *increase in size,* due to the pubertal growth spurt, is likely to disturb girls because they are afraid they will become so large that boys will not want to date them or that they will be wallflowers at a dance. This concern would be markedly lessened if girls realized that rapid growth continues for only a short time. When boys see girls of their own ages literally towering over them, it is not surprising that they are disturbed. Even when they know that girls normally outstrip boys in size for several years, it is hard for them to be objective about the matter and not worry for fear that they will remain small for the rest of their lives.

For both boys and girls, excessive *fat* which frequently comes in the early part of puberty, is a source of great concern. In our culture, fat is considered unattractive and, therefore, it disturbs the individual who does not conform to social expectations. Girls who have a prototype of female beauty based on moving-picture heroines, glamour girls in society, and cover girls on magazines are very distressed when they look at their own bodies. For a boy, fat is considered sexually inappropriate, especially when there is an accumulation of fat on the thighs, around the waist, and in the mammary region. While this generally disappears as puberty progresses, it may affect personality development unfavorably for many years after the somatic stigma has passed [47].

There is a widespread belief that small genitalia mean lack of normal sexual development. When the boy's *penis* is developing, he is greatly concerned by its thinness. And, because growth in circumference follows growth in length, the boy feels that he has a sexually inappropriate sex-organ development. How concerned he is about this is seen in the fact that many boys add artificial padding to their supporters to create the impression that their penises are sexually appropriate. The girl's developing *breasts* and broadening *hips* disturb her in much the same way as the boy is disturbed by his developing penis. Until the breasts become curved and filled out by the development of the mammary glands and subcutaneous tissue, the girl worries about her unfeminine breasts. Broad *hips* are regarded as sexually inappropriate for both sexes, but especially so for boys. Therefore, boys and girls during the early stages of puberty, especially if they experience a period of fatness, feel that they are doomed to resemble an asexual person. The same is true of fat over the *abdomen*, which is common among boys in the early part of puberty. During the early stages of their sex-organ development girls also experience a period when their abdomens protrude. Excessive fat is considered unattractive in our present culture, but fat in the wrong places is considered sexually inappropriate.

The *secondary sex characteristics* that are late in developing are likely to be the sources of greatest concern. For the most part, these are the ones that differentiate the two sexes most clearly. In the case of boys, *hair* on the face, large *muscles* in the shoulder and arm regions, and *voice changes* come late in the puberty period. As the boy watches hair develop in other areas of his body but not on his face, he naturally wonders if he will continue to have the smooth-faced look of a girl or whether he will look masculine. *Breast knots*, which develop early in puberty and then gradually disappear, usually before the boy's first nocturnal emission, add to his concern about his sex appropriateness.

The girl is more concerned about the hair that appears on her body and face and about skin eruptions than is the boy. Typically, a feminine woman is supposed te have a beautiful complexion. As puberty progresses, *acne* usually gets worse rather than better and *hair* is darker and more profuse than in the early stages of puberty. Facial hair frequently alarms the girl because she is afraid she may have to shave like a boy. Girls, like boys, become *voice-conscious* at puberty. Like the boy who is afraid he will never have a truly masculine voice with its deep pitch, the girl is concerned about whether she will go through life with the high-pitched voice of a child instead of the lower-pitched, more melodious voice of the adult woman.

BIBLIOGRAPHY

1. Abel, T. M., and N. F. Joffee: Cultural backgrounds of female puberty. *Amer. J. Psychother.*, 1950, 4, 90–113.
2. Anderson, M., M. Blais, and W. T. Green: Growth of the normal foot during childhood and adolescence. *Amer. J. phys. Anthrop.*, 1956, 14, 287–308.

3. Angelino, H., and E. V. Mech: "Fears and worries" concerning physical changes: a preliminary survey of 32 females. *J. Psychol.*, 1955, 39, 195–198.

4. Ashley-Montagu, M. F.: The existence of a sterile phase in female adolescence. *Complex*, 1950, 1, 27–39.

5. Bayley, N.: Growth curves of height and weight by age for boys and girls scaled according to physical maturity. *J. Pediat.*, 1956, 48, 187–194.

6. Bayley, N.: Individual patterns of development. *Child Develpm.*, 1956, 27, 45–74.

7. Bryan, A. A., and B. C. Greenberg: Methodology in the study of the physical measurements of school children. II. Sexual maturation-determination of immaturity points. *Hum. Biol.*, 1952, 24, 117–144.

8. Curry, E. T.: Hoarseness and voice change in male adolescents. *J. Speech Hearing Disorders*, 1949, 14, 23–25.

9. Dale, R. J.: A method for measuring developmental tasks: scales for selected tasks at the beginning of adolescence. *Child Develpm.*, 1955, 26, 111–122.

10. Davidson, H. L., and L. S. Gottlieb: The emotional maturity of pre- and post-menarcheal girls. *J. genet. Psychol.*, 1955, 86, 261–266.

11. Espenschade, A., R. R. Dable, and R. Schoendube: Dynamic balance in adolescent boys. *Res. Quart. Amer. phys. Educ. Ass.*, 1953, 24, 270–275.

12. Fleege, U. H.: *Self-revelation of the adolescent boy.* Milwaukee: Bruce, 1945.

13. Ford, C. S., and F. A. Beach: *Patterns of sexual behavior.* New York: Harper, 1951.

14. Frank, L. K.: Personality development in adolescent girls. *Monogr. Soc. Res. Child Develpm.*, 1951, 16, No. 53.

15. Frank, L. K., and M. Frank: *Your adolescent, at home and in school.* New York: Viking, 1956.

16. Frazier, A., and L. K. Lisonbee: Adolescent concerns with physique. *Sch. Rev.*, 1950, 58, 397–405.

17. Gesell, A., F. L. Ilg, and L. B. Ames: *Youth: the years from ten to sixteen.* New York: Harper, 1956.

18. Gruelich, W. W.: The rationale of assessing the developmental status of children from roentgenograms of the hand and wrist. *Child Develpm.*, 1950, 21, 33–44.

19. Harding, V. V.: A method of evaluating osseous development from birth to 14 years. *Child Develpm.*, 1952, 23, 181–184, 247–271.

20. Jensen, K.: Physical growth and physiological aspects of development. *Rev. educ. Res.*, 1950, 20, 390–410.

21. Jersild, A. T.: *The psychology of adolescence.* New York: Macmillan, 1957.

22. Jones, M. C.: The later careers of boys who were early- or late-maturers. *Child Develpm.*, 1957, 28, 113–128.

23. Jones, M. C., and N. Bayley: Physical maturing among boys as related to behavior. *J. educ. Psychol.*, 1950, 41, 129–148.

24. Jungck, E. C., N. H. Brown, and N. Carmona: Constitutional precocious puberty in the male. *Amer. J. Dis. Child.*, 1956, 91, 138–143.

25. Kinsey, A. C., W. B. Pomeroy, and C. E. Martin: *Sexual behavior in the human male.* Philadelphia: Saunders, 1948.

26. Kinsey, A. C., W. B. Pomeroy, C. E. Martin, and P. H. Gebhard: *Sexual behavior in the human female.* Philadelphia: Saunders, 1953.

27. Kralj-Čerček, L.: The influence of food, body build, and social origin on the age at menarche. *Hum. Biol.*, 1956, 28, 393–406.

28. Krogman, W. M.: The physical growth of the child. *In* M. Fishbein and R. J. R.

Kennedy, *Modern marriage and family living.* New York: Oxford Univer. Press, 1957. Pp. 417–425.

29. Liccione, J. V.: The changing family relationships of adolescent girls. *J. abnorm. soc. Psychol.,* 1955, 51, 421–426.

30. Maresh, M. M.: Linear growth of long bones of extremities from infancy through adolescence. *Amer. J. Dis. Child.,* 1955, 89, 725–742.

31. Margolese, M. S.: Mental disorders in childhood due to endocrine disorders. *Nerv. Child.,* 1948, 7, 55–77.

32. McNally, E.: The worries of the younger pupils in Scottish secondary schools. *Brit. J. educ. Psychol.,* 1951, 21, 235–237.

33. Mills, C. A.: Temperature influence over human growth and development. *Hum. Biol.,* 1950, 22, 71–74.

34. More, D. M.: Developmental concordance and discordance during puberty and early adolescence. *Monogr. Soc. Res. Child Develpm.,* 1953, 18, 1–128.

35. Morgan, C. T., and E. Stellar: *Physiological psychology,* 2d ed. New York: McGraw-Hill, 1950.

36. Mussen, P. H., and M. C. Jones: Self-conceptions, motivations, and interpersonal attitudes of late- and early-maturing boys. *Child Develpm.,* 1957, 28, 243–256.

37. Nathanson, I. T., L. Towne, and J. C. Aub: Urinary sex hormone studies. *Monogr. Soc. Res. Child Develpm.,* 1943, 8, 70–81.

38. Newton, N.: *Maternal emotions.* New York: Harper, 1955.

39. Provis, H. S., and R. W. B. Ellis: An anthropometric study of Edinburgh school children. *Arch. Dis. Childh.,* 1955, 30, 328–337.

40. Reynolds, E. L.: Sexual maturation and the growth of fat, muscle, and bone in girls. *Child Develpm.,* 1946, 17, 121–144.

41. Reynolds, E. L., and J. V. Wines: Individual differences in physical changes associated with adolescence in girls. *Amer. J. Dis. Child.,* 1948, 75, 329–350.

42. Reynolds, E. L., and J. V. Wines: Physical changes associated with adolescence in boys. *Amer. J. Dis. Child.,* 1951, 82, 529–547.

43. Richardson, J. S.: The endocrines in adolescence. *Practitioner,* 1949, 162, 280–286.

44. Schonfeld, W. A.: Deficient development of masculinity. *Amer. J. Dis. Child.,* 1950, 79, 17–29.

45. Skerlj, B.: Further evidence of age changes in body form based on material of D. A. W. Edwards, *Hum. Biol.,* 1954, 26, 330–336.

46. Smith, W. D., and D. Lebo: Some changing aspects of the self-concept of pubescent males. *J. genet. Psychol.,* 1956, 88, 61–75.

47. Stolz, H. R., and L. M. Stolz: *Somatic development of adolescent boys.* New York: Macmillan, 1951.

48. Stouffer, G. A. W., and J. Owens: Behavior problems identified by today's teachers and compared with those reported by E. K. Wickman. *J. educ. Res.,* 1955, 48, 321–331.

49. Stuart, H. C.: Physical growth during adolescence. *Amer. J. Dis. Child.,* 1947, 74, 495–502.

50. Wolff, E., and L. M. Bayer: Psychosomatic disorders of childhood and adolescence. *Amer. J. Orthopsychiat.,* 1952, 22, 510–521.

51. Wolff, O. H.: Obesity in childhood: a study of the birth weight, the height, and the onset of puberty. *Quart. J. Med.,* 1955, 24, 109–123.

52. Wolman, B.: Sexual development in Israeli adolescents. *Amer. J. Psychother.,* 1951, 5, 531–559.

Early Adolescence

Adolescence is a period of transition when the child is neither a child nor an adult. As Ausubel has pointed out, "Adolescence in our culture can be described as a time of transition in the bio-social status of the individual. It is a period during which marked changes occur in duties, responsibilities, privileges, and relationships with others. . . . Under such conditions, changed attitudes toward self, parents, peers, and others become inevitable" [5]. The adolescent's status in our modern society is vague and confused. At one time, he is treated as a child and then, when he acts like a child, he is reproved and told to "act his age." When he attempts to act like an adult, he is often accused of being "too big for his breeches."

The term "adolescence" comes from the Latin word *adolescere*, which means "to grow" or "to grow to maturity." Among primitive peoples and in earlier civilizations, puberty and adolescence coincided. The child was considered an adult when his body had completed its development and when he was capable of reproduction. As the term "adolescence" is used today, it has a broader meaning and includes mental, emotional, and social as well as physical maturity. Legally, in American society, maturity is reached when the individual is twenty-one years old. Adolescence is a period of *preparation for adulthood*, a time when childish behavior and attitudes are replaced by attitudes and behavior of an adult type.

From the beginning of civilization, it has been recognized that adolescence is a period of change. At first, the changes were thought to be primarily physiological in character, with major emphasis on sexual development. In time, it became apparent that there were also changes

262

in interests and attitudes which led to changed behavior. This, in turn, led to the belief that as the child matured sexually, he would leave behind all the undesirable physical and mental traits of childhood. At the turn of this century, G. Stanley Hall reported that adolescence was a period of extremes in behavior, marked by emotional "storm and stress." This was attributed to the physical and glandular changes taking place at this time.

Studies of adolescents in recent years have revealed that it is during the early part of adolescence, when physical changes are taking place very rapidly, that changes in attitudes and behavior are most rapid. As physical changes slow down, so also do changes in attitudes and behavior. Furthermore, it has become apparent that heightened emotionality is far from universal and that it occurs even after the physical changes have slowed down, thus suggesting social rather than physical causes. Normally, however, the "storm and stress" Hall emphasized are much greater in the early part of the adolescent period than in the latter part, when the individual is reaching adulthood.

Length of Period. Until recently, adolescence was regarded as a period in the life span which begins when the individual becomes sexually mature and ends when he reaches legal maturity, at twenty-one years of age in our culture. Recent studies of the changes in behavior throughout adolescence have revealed not only that these changes are more rapid in the early than in the latter part of adolescence, but also that the behavior and attitudes of the individual in the early part of the period are markedly different from those in the latter part of the period. As a result, it has become a widespread practice to divide adolescence into two periods, *early* and *late* adolescence.

Early adolescence begins when the individual becomes sexually mature. This varies markedly from individual to individual and between the sexes. For the average girl of today, early adolescence begins at thirteen years and, for boys, approximately a year later. The dividing line between early and late adolescence is placed around seventeen years, the age when the average American boy or girl of today enters the senior year of high school. He then is recognized by his parents to be nearly grown-up, on the verge of entering the adult world of work or ready to go away to college or some professional training school. His status in the school likewise makes him feel responsibilities he never before was expected to assume and, as a result of this new and formally recognized status, both at school and at home, he has an incentive to behave in a more mature manner.

Because boys mature, on the average, later than girls, they have a shorter period of early adolescence and, as a result, they frequently seem more immature for their age than do girls. However, as they are accorded, along with girls, a more mature status in the home and school, they usually "settle down" quickly and show, as girls do, a maturity of behavior which is in marked contrast with that of the younger adolescent. It is this change in patterns of behavior, so characteristic of the last year of high school, which is taken as a dividing line between the early and the late part of the adolescent period. Roughly, then, early adolescence extends from thirteen to sixteen or seventeen years, from the end of junior high school to the end of the senior year of senior high school.

Early adolescence is the period in the life span which is usually referred to as the age of "storm and stress." There is no question about the fact that this is a period of many frictions with parents, teachers, and friends; that the young adolescent experiences more emotionality than he did when he was younger; and that he is a difficult person to live or work with. This period is also referred to as the "teens," sometimes even the "terrible teens." While many people use the term "teens" or "teenage" to refer to that part of late adolescence which falls within the span of the teen years, more correctly the latter teens should be called "youth" to distinguish that period from the early part of adolescence. The differences in behavior and attitudes in early and late adolescence make this distinction justifiable.

Young adolescents realize that they are subjected, as a group, to condemnation, criticism, and general devaluation by adults. They are aware of the stereotype of a "teenager" as a sloppy, irresponsible, unreliable individual who is inclined toward destructiveness and antisocial behavior. This stereotype has been strengthened by the widespread publicity given, through the different mass media, to juvenile gangs, juvenile delinquency, petting, necking, and the sexual irregularities of some adolescents today. Furthermore, the traditional belief that adolescence is a period of "storm and stress," a time when the individual is difficult to live with and to manage, adds to this unfavorable stereotype of the young adolescent. The belief on the adolescent's part that adults have a poor opinion of him makes the transition to adulthood difficult for him, leads to much friction with his parents, and places a barrier between the adolescent and his parents which prevents him from turning to them for help in meeting his problems. As Hess and Goldblatt have pointed out, "With the possible exception of old age, no other phase of individual development is so clearly marked by negative connotations and lack of positive sanctions" [45].

Characteristics of Period. There are several outstanding characteristics of the early adolescent years that distinguish it from childhood and from the closing years of adolescence. Some of these are unquestionably the result of maturation and accompany the rapid and pronounced physical changes that have taken place. Others, on the other hand, are the result

of cultural influences and are more characteristic of American youth
than of the youth of other cultures. Of these characteristics, the most
outstanding are: *Characteristics of Period* ————— →/Instability

1. *The Young Adolescent Is Unstable.* At this age, instability is ex-²/ Has many problems
treme. From tears to laughter, from self-confidence to self-depreciation,
from selfishness to altruism, and from enthusiasm to indifference—all are
common reactions of young adolescents. One minute the young adolescent is up in the clouds and the next he is in the depths of despair. This
instability is very apparent in his social relationships. There are marked
fluctuations in his friendships, especially with members of the opposite
sex, and in the qualities he likes or dislikes among others. Instability in
aspirations, notably in vocational aspirations, is so common that planning for the future is very difficult. In general, the young adolescent is
an unpredictable person, even to himself.

This instability is largely the result of feelings of insecurity. The
physiological and psychological changes which accompany sexual
maturity come so quickly that the individual is unsure of himself, of his
capacities, and of his interests. The greater demands placed on him by
home and school add to his feelings of insecurity and intensify his instability. Added to this is the fact that he is often treated in an am-
biguous manner by both parents and teachers. One minute he is told
he is too young to drive a car and the next he is given a responsibility
usually assumed by an adult. He thus finds himself in a new and overlapping situation where his role is not structured [45]. As Luchins has
pointed out, the young adolescent must "learn to dance in harmony with
many different tunes while still attempting to maintain some degree of
harmony with himself" [62].

Then, too, some of the young adolescent's instability stems from the
gaps that exist between his aspirations and his attainments. Very often,
as in the case of his vocational aspirations, the adolescent's goals are
beyond his reach, and when he discovers that he is unable to attain the
goals he has set for himself, he is frustrated and unhappy. Much of his
emotional tension, which is a reaction to frustration, is the result of a
childhood stereotype of the "adult." Now that he sees himself as an adult,
physically, he expects to be able to play the role of an adult in every
area of his life, only to discover that he is ready, neither physically nor
psychologically, to do so. Furthermore, he expects to be treated as an
adult by others and is resentful when the status of adult is denied him
[62].

2. *The Young Adolescent Has Many Problems.* Every age has its problems. But, for the young adolescent, problems seem more numerous and
more insurmountable than at other ages. In childhood, parents or
teachers helped him with his problems. Now he feels that his problems

are his own and that his parents and teachers are "too old" to understand and to help him. Many of the problems that confront a young adolescent relate to areas of life, such as heterosexual relationships, in which he has had no previous experience and, as a result, he often feels at a loss to know how to meet them. As Landis has pointed out, "In our day of a self-sufficient teen-age society and unchaperoned paired relationships, teen-agers are called upon to make more decisions before they are 20 years of age than their great grandparents made in a lifetime" [59].

Studies of the problems of young adolescents have revealed that the problems are numerous and, for the most part, center around physical appearance and health, social relationships in the home and with outsiders, relationships with members of the opposite sex, schoolwork, plans for the future—including education, choice of vocation, and selection of a life mate—sex and moral behavior, religion, and finances [30, 100]. Financial problems are more serious to boys, while girls are more concerned about parent-child relationships and problems of a social nature, such as making friends and knowing the correct thing to do. On the whole, girls have more problems that disturb them than have boys during early adolescence [36]. Typical problems of boys and girls in early adolescence are shown in Figure 54.

The number and seriousness of problems at this age vary from individual to individual within the sex groups. Adolescents who do not understand themselves or their problems, or who feel that their parents do not understand them, have greater problems than do the adolescents who have more insight into their problems. If childhood discipline has been too authoritarian, the adolescent is unprepared to make decisions and face responsibilities for his choice. This makes his problems seem greater than they do to the adolescent from a more democratic home who is better prepared to meet his problems. Furthermore, the adolescent from a democratic home feels freer to turn to his parents for help than does the adolescent from an authoritarian home, and this helps him to solve his problems more quickly and more satisfactorily. All problems the adolescent must face are increased when the home situation is unsatisfactory, or when the home is broken by death or divorce. This is especially true of financial, personal, and family-relationship problems. In general, bright adolescents have fewer problems and concerns than adolescents of average intelligence, suggesting that bright children make better adjustments to adolescence than do those of average intelligence [36, 101].

Problems decrease in seriousness for the adolescent when he feels free to discuss them with parents or teachers. However, many adolescents are unwilling to discuss their problems with their parents or outsiders, fearing that their problems will not be understood, or that in discussing them they will reveal their inability to meet their own problems and thus be blamed, criticized, or rejected, and fearing also that they will lose their independence if they seek help from others) [45]. The type and seriousness of the problem determine the adolescent's readiness to seek help. The more serious the problem, the less willing is the adolescent to seek help in solving it [47]. Until the adolescent has solved his problems to his satisfaction, he will be preoccupied with himself and his problems.

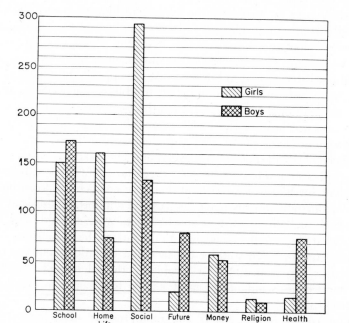

Fig. 54. Typical problems of boys and girls during early adolescence. (*From O. Y. Lewis, Problems of adolescents. Calif. J. sec. Educ.,* 1949, 24, 215–221. *Used by permission.*)

Furthermore, he will suffer from feelings of inadequacy and inferiority which, in many cases, he will try to hide by a cocky self-assurance. This attitude will, in turn, be interpreted by his parents to mean that he displays a better opinion of himself than is justified or than he actually has [34, 45].

How well the adolescent is able to solve his problems is crucial to his subsequent life career in business, in the home, and in social life. If he is able to deal with these problems without too much inner turmoil, he will develop self-confidence and feelings of adequacy; if not, he will develop feelings of frustration and inadequacy which may leave permanent psychological scars [50, 72]. As Frank has pointed out, in discussing the problems adolescents must face and solve, "The schools should not try to prepare them for future living by specific instruction and training for tasks they will meet later, but help them to meet their present adolescent problems. . . . Here, as in all other ages, the best preparation for tomorrow is to live adequately today, to deal with today's requirements so as to be able to go forward without too much 'unfinished business'" [34].

In addition to the problems the adolescent himself faces, adults whose responsibility it is to guide and supervise the lives of these young people find early adolescence a "problem age" for them. One of the most troublesome aspects of this age is the obstinacy of the young adolescent. He will not listen to reason but does just the opposite of what he is asked to do, or he just "moons" around. This troublesome age comes at a time in the life span of the individual when there are strong conflicts between his desires and those of the social group. He wants to be acceptable to his growing circle of friends and acquaintances but he discovers that the same behavior will not please everyone. There is an increase in the number of social interests he has, there are new responsibilities and obligations for him to assume, and there are conflicts between his desire for independence and his need for parental support. These lead to conflicts which make him resistant and obstinate when he finds that he cannot do what the group expects him to do and, at the same time, do what he wants to do [9]. In spite of the fact that the adolescent wants to be regarded as a person, not as a "problem," the adolescent is difficult to understand if he is judged by adult standards rather than by adolescent standards [35].

3. *The Young Adolescent Is Unhappy.* Instead of being one of the happiest and most constructive periods in life, adolescence is too frequently spoiled by adults who make the period more full of conflict than necessary. They fear the adolescent will not grow up to be sufficiently obedient, cooperative, or grateful, or that he will go astray sexually. While there are times of happiness, these are often overshadowed by periods of extreme unhappiness and discontent. The young adolescent is concerned about his appearance, especially when it does not come up to his expectations. He is greatly concerned about the awkwardness and clumsiness that develop at this age. Not understanding the normal pattern of growth, he is likely to feel that his growth is complete and that there is no further hope for improvement. The social and economic status of his family is likely to make the young adolescent unhappy. Unless his family measures up to the families of his friends in social status or income, and unless he finds himself in a position of

acceptance on the part of his contemporaries, he will be unhappy, often to the point where he develops an antagonistic attitude toward his family and threatens to leave home.

(The discontent that the adolescent feels about his appearance is often accentuated by disappointment when his mental capacity or personality does not come up to his expectations) He would like to be at the top of his class in school, he would like to have abilities that would win recognition for him, and, above all, he would like to be popular.(Feelings of inadequacy and insecurity are the outstanding unpleasant memories of adolescence as reported by adults. School failures, loss of friends, quarrels with parents and friends, breakup of friendships with members of the opposite sex, death of relatives or friends, feelings of inferiority, and lack of popularity are recalled as the outstanding sources of concern to the adolescent) Because they are remembered over a period of time, it is unquestionably true that they were sources of great unhappiness when they occurred. While there is undoubtedly more unhappiness in early adolescence than in childhood, these periods of unhappiness are only transitory and are counteracted by periods of happiness. The better adjusted the young adolescent, the happier he will be [10].

PHYSICAL DEVELOPMENT

(The rapid physical growth, characteristic of puberty, begins to slow down when the individual reaches early adolescence.) However, growth is far from complete when puberty ends and it is not entirely complete at the end of early adolescence. However, there is a slackening of the pace of growth and there is more marked internal than external development. This cannot be so readily observed or identified as growth in height and weight or the development of the secondary sex characteristics.

Because girls, as a whole, mature sooner than boys and because growth in *height* and *weight* generally spurt at that time and then slow down as puberty comes to a close, the girl reaches her mature height at the close of early adolescence if she has matured at the average age. Slow-maturing girls, on the other hand, do not reach their mature size until early in the late adolescent period. The average American girl of today at sixteen years is 65.5 inches tall, within one-half inch of the height of the average American woman. Boys of the same age are 69 inches tall, likewise within one-half inch of the average height of American men of today [56]. For the first time, boys' height exceeds girls' height (see Figure 55). Much the same pattern is followed in weight increases, though there are more marked individual differences in weight among members of each sex. The average girl of sixteen years of age weighs

131 pounds, as compared with the adult average of 135 pounds, while the average sixteen-year-old boy weighs 142 pounds as contrasted with the average adult weight of 152 pounds for men [56].

The *body proportions* of a young adolescent are not those of an adult (see Figures 14 and 31, pages 82 and 171). Gradually, disproportions, so characteristic of the growth years, right themselves and reach one by one their mature level of development. Whether adult proportions will be attained before the end of early adolescence will depend mainly on age

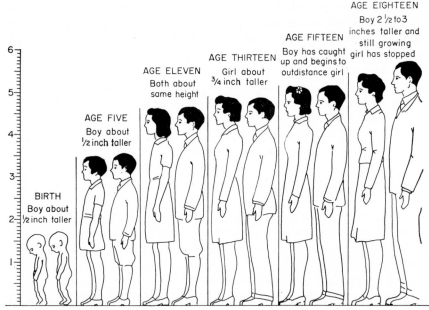

FIG. 55. By early adolescence, boys begin to outdistance girls in height and weight. (*From A. Scheinfeld, Women and men. New York: Harcourt, Brace, 1943. Used by permission.*)

and rate of sexual maturing. The *sex organs*, while not completely mature in size and functioning, have reached a stage of maturity that makes procreation possible. Most of the *secondary sex characteristics* are at a mature level of development, especially among those whose puberty development occurred at the average or before-average age. By the end of early adolescence, boys and girls resemble men and women in size and general appearance more than they resemble children. What few changes occur in late adolescence will have a barely perceptible influence on general appearance.

Internal growth, though not readily apparent, is marked during early adolescence and is closely correlated with growth of height and weight

[69]. There is a change in the relative size of the organs of the *digestive* system. The stomach becomes longer and less tubular than it was in childhood, thus increasing its capacity. The intestines grow in length and circumference, and the muscles in the stomach and intestinal walls become stronger and thicker, resulting in stronger peristaltic motions. The liver increases in weight and the esophagus becomes larger. The rapid growth of the body which started at puberty necessitates an increase in food intake at this time. In caloric content, the young adolescent's daily food intake equals that of an adult who does hard manual labor. Not only are large amounts of food consumed at every meal but the young adolescent is likely to eat more or less continuously between meals. Heavy emphasis is placed on sweets and starches in the young adolescent's diet.

In the *circulatory* system there is an increase in the size of the heart and in the length and thickness of the walls of the blood vessels. Growth in the size of the heart is relatively greater, however, than growth in the diameter of the veins or arteries. As a result, a large heart must pump blood through small arteries. Until this condition is corrected, during late adolescence, too strenuous exercise may cause an enlargement of the heart or a valvular disease. Tension in the arteries, resulting from disproportions in the size of the heart and of the arteries, causes much of the restlessness that is characteristic of the young adolescent.

The greatest increase in weight and volume of the lungs comes at puberty. Lung increase keeps pace with the increase in width and depth of the chest which is taking place at that time. After puberty has been completed, there is little increase in lung size. In adolescence, as a result of the increased size of the lungs, breathing is slower than it was in childhood though the volume of inhaled and exhaled air is greater. Up to the age of fourteen years, there is not much difference between the two sexes in lung capacity. After that, boys surpass girls to a marked degree.

Because of the increased activity of the gonads at puberty, there is a temporary imbalance of the whole *endocrine system* during early adolescence. The glands, which during childhood were dominant, now take a less prominent position in the endocrine system, and those which were formerly less prominent now become dominant. The adrenal glands, attached to the kidneys, lose weight during the first year of life and do not regain their birth size until the middle of adolescence. Among girls, the thyroid glands, located in the throat, enlarge at the time of the menarche and this produces irregularities in the basal metabolic rate of girls. In both boys and girls, there is a temporary rise in the basal metabolic rate early in adolescence and then this sinks again. The sex glands develop rapidly at that time and become functionally active. They do not, however, reach their mature size until late in adolescence or early in adulthood [70].

Health Conditions. After the puberty changes are, for the most part, complete, the adolescent's health begins to improve. The ailments he experienced at puberty, none of which was severe enough to invalid him, gradually clear up and the young adolescent feels better with each successive month. True, he frequently experiences digestive upsets, caused by indiscreet eating, and colds, caused by carelessness or lack of proper precautions. But, for the most part, these are mild and of short duration. Few adolescents, however, are free from minor ailments. Defective teeth, eye troubles, stomach upsets, headaches, earaches, and asthma are a few of the common disorders the young adolescent experiences occasionally or chronically. Many of these disorders are carry-overs of conditions that existed in childhood and have become progressively worse with time. Carious teeth, for example, frequently become worse in adolescence because of neglect or crowding the diet with starches and sweets. Eyestrain becomes a more serious problem for the young adolescent than it was for the child because of the heavier burden of schoolwork [37]. Typically, the adolescent has little interest in his health. Only those who have poor health or some physical defect are enough interested in their health to take ordinary precautions [1].

MOTOR CAPACITIES

Development of muscular power follows growth in muscle size. This, however, will not alone guarantee muscular skills. The individual needs training, opportunities for practice, absence of environmental obstacles, and a strong motivation to develop skills. At no time is motor development that is below the level of his contemporaries more serious to the individual than it is during adolescence. Unless his muscular skills are on a par with those of his friends, the young adolescent finds himself so out of step in this area of his development with his contemporaries that he cannot take part in the games and sports they enjoy. This has serious impact on his social adjustments and on his concept of himself. Boys with high athletic achievement have been found to be superior in personal and social adjustment, as well as in schoolwork, to boys of low athletic achievement. Because of the prestige value of athletics to boys, those who are superior in athletics are likely to be more popular than those whose athletic ability is mediocre [12]. The effects of physical strength on the social adjustments of young adolescent boys is illustrated in Figure 56.

Adolescent Awkwardness. Not all young adolescents are awkward but few escape awkwardness in some degree. Adolescents whose sexual maturation has proceeded at a slow rate or those who have attained a high level of proficiency during the childhood years are likely to experience less awkwardness than are those who have matured rapidly or whose motor proficiency has lagged behind the level attained by their contemporaries. Some young adolescents are awkward in all of their movements; some are awkward in movements of the legs primarily; some are awkward mostly in the use of their hands. General awkwardness in

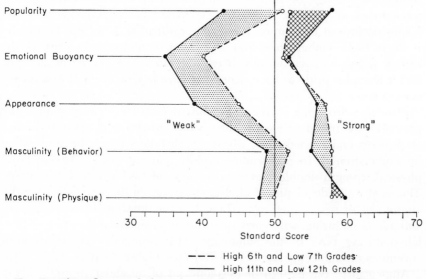

FIG. 56. The influence of physical strength on social adjustment. Profiles of strong and weak boys at two ages. (*From H. E. Jones, Physical ability as a factor in social adjustment. J. educ. Res., 1946, 40, 287–301. Used by permission.*)

early adolescence is less universally found than specific awkwardness in limited areas of the body.

Adolescent awkwardness comes from the pattern of muscle growth that characteristically occurs at puberty and early adolescence. During childhood, the muscles grow slowly and relatively uniformly. This enables the child to develop control of his body as changes occur in the muscular development. As a result, he should have good muscular coordination. The situation is changed in early adolescence. Not only do the muscles and bones grow rapidly but they bear a new ratio to one another. The muscles are elongated and pulled into new patterns. As a result, the motor achievements acquired in childhood are upset and this brings about a state of awkwardness and clumsiness. This condition will persist until new controls and new achievements are attained [37].

Boys and girls are subject to adolescent awkwardness, though in boys awkwardness is likely to be more pronounced than in girls. Unless their growth spurt has been unusually rapid, girls are less awkward than boys because a boy's framework is typically larger than that of a girl. Furthermore, because boys have less fat than girls, they look more gawky and awkward than girls at this age, a fact that contributes to their feelings of inadequacy. This, in turn, contributes to the awkwardness of their movements. The most pronounced awkwardness in boys occurs with the sudden beginnings of growth at puberty and becomes less and less pronounced as puberty progresses. It may take several years for the young adolescent to acquire muscular coordination. Until this occurs, he is likely to be embarrassed and self-conscious, not only because of the clumsy things he does but also because he thinks of himself as an adult and it hurts his pride to have people criticize him or laugh at him for his clumsiness.

Muscular Strength. Increase in muscular strength accompanies the growth of the muscles. Because the greatest growth of the muscles comes at puberty and immediately afterward, that likewise is the time when muscular strength increases most rapidly and noticeably. Among boys, physical strength doubles between the ages of twelve and sixteen years. The most rapid development of strength comes in the year following the attainment of sexual maturity. There is a relationship between strength and age of maturing, with early-maturing boys significantly stronger than late-maturing boys of the same age. This superiority continues until seventeen or eighteen years of age [50] (see Figure 53, page 257).

Among girls, the pattern of development of muscular strength differs markedly from that of boys. Early-maturing girls show a rapid increase in strength up to the age of twelve years, after which there is a slow rate of increase. Late-maturing girls are relatively retarded in strength development, though in time, their level of strength reaches that of girls who mature earlier. In both early- and late-maturing girls, the greatest increase in strength comes near the time of the menarche. At all ages after puberty, boys surpass girls in strength, and this superiority increases with age. The reason for this difference is that the muscles of girls do not develop as much as do those of boys during adolescence. Girls generally attain their maximum strength at about seventeen years of age while boys do not attain their maximum strength until they are twenty-one or twenty-two years old [51].

The pubescent child often experiences *muscular fatigue* which makes him listless and encourages him to avoid all exercise whenever possible. However, as adolescence progresses, fatigue decreases. Boys show muscular fatigue slightly less than do girls. Tall adolescents, owing to their tendency to stoop in hopes of making themselves look less tall and conspicuous, suffer from fatigue more than do adolescents who feel that their height is about right. This is especially true of girls.

Skills. Because motor skills, whether in sports or in social activities such as dancing, play such an important role in the social acceptance of the young adolescent, there is a strong motivation to develop skills and a willingness to practice until the skills have been learned. Furthermore, the adolescent has the advantage of having someone to teach him skills, whether it be an athletic coach, a dance teacher, a parent, or another adolescent who has already mastered the skill the adolescent wants to learn. This helps to eliminate trial-and-error learning or imitation of inferior models—methods used by many children in acquiring skills. This guidance in learning, combined with a strong motivation to learn, not only helps the adolescent learn skills quickly but develops his skills so that they compare favorably with those of adults.

Growth in ability to perform motor acts reaches its maximum at the age of fourteen years for girls and at seventeen for boys. Tests to measure agility, control, strength, and static balance show the greatest increase in ability for boys after fourteen years of age. For girls, improvement comes up to fourteen and then lags, owing more to changes in interests than to lack of capacity. Speed of voluntary movement increases continually from the beginning of early adolescence to the end of the period, but at a progressively slower rate of increase. A thirteen-year-old, for example, has six-sevenths as much speed as a seventeen-year-old [29, 51].

ADOLESCENT EMOTIONS

Traditionally, adolescence is a period of "storm and stress," of heightened emotional tension that comes from the physical and glandular changes taking place at this time. While it is true that growth does continue through the early years of adolescence, it is at a progressively slower rate with each successive year. What growth is taking place is primarily a completion of the pattern already set at puberty. It is necessary, therefore, to look for other explanations of the emotional tension so characteristic of this age. And the explanations are to be found in social conditions that surround the adolescent of today. The pressures and expectations of the social group on individuals who, throughout the years of childhood, have had little if any preparation to meet the changed conditions that will face them at adolescence, are chiefly to blame for adolescent emotionality.

Not all adolescents, by any means, are subject to storm and stress of an exaggerated sort. True, most of them do experience emotional instability from time to time. This is logical because the adolescent **is** making adjustments to new patterns of behavior and to new social expectations. And, as is true of adjustments to new experiences at any age, there is bound to be some emotional tension connected with these adjustments. Prolonged and continuous emotional tension, on the other hand, is symptomatic of poor adjustments. The age at which the child matures has been found to influence the intensity of his emotions and the form they take in early adolescence. Late maturers, for example, have been found to rate higher in animation and eagerness than do early maturers [51].

While adolescent emotions are often intense, uncontrolled in expression, and irrational, there is generally an improvement in emotional behavior with each year. Fourteen-year-olds, for example, are often irritable; they get excited easily and "explode" emotionally instead of controlling their feelings. A year later, there is definite evidence of an attempt on the adolescent's part to cover up his feelings, and this then leads to moodiness. The sixteen-year-old, by contrast, doesn't "believe in worrying," and takes a calmer approach to problems than he did when he was younger. At this age, there is evidence of a strong desire to control his emotions [37]. As a result, there is little evidence of the traditional "storm and stress" as early adolescence draws to a close.

Common Emotional Patterns. The emotional patterns of the adolescent years are much the same as those of childhood. They differ from childish emotions, however, in the type of stimuli that give rise to these emotions and in the form of expression they take. The following are the most important emotional patterns of the early adolescent years:

ANGER. Adolescent anger differs from that of childhood not in the number of anger experiences at the two age levels but rather in the stimuli that give rise to anger, in the duration of anger, and in the type of response made. Anger situations in adolescence are, for the most part, social. This is in marked contrast to those of childhood. Then the child becomes angry when some activity he is engaging in is interrupted or when he is kept from doing something that he wants to do. The adolescent, by contrast, is made angry when he is teased, ridiculed, criticized, or "lectured," when he feels that he or his friends are unfairly treated or punished by parents and teachers, when privileges he considers fair are refused, when he is "treated like a child," when people impose upon him, or when people are bossy and sarcastic. In addition, he becomes angry when things do not go right, when he is unable to accomplish what he sets out to do, when he is interrupted at times when he is busy and preoccupied, or when his private property is encroached upon by parents or siblings.

The young adolescent experiences many *frustrations* or feelings of helplessness when he is blocked in doing what he wants to do, and this makes him angry. In his desire to achieve independence, he finds himself constantly blocked by parents, teachers, or others in authority. Then, too, there are many *annoyances,* or things that irritate him. Sometimes they are due to the way people act, sometimes they come from things that he dislikes, and sometimes from his own behavior. If annoyances are too frequent, they are likely to affect the adolescent in much the same way as anger stimuli do.

While many young adolescents do fly off the handle in a temper tantrum not unlike that of a child in its intensity, the more common form of angry *response* is sulkiness or being generally disagreeable. The sulky individual refuses to talk or to do what he is expected to do. Any overt response he may make is generally in the form of talking. He calls people names; he makes extravagant statements about "hating" them, himself, and life in general; and he often swears at or tongue-lashes the person who has made him angry. Instead of trying to get his revenge by hitting and kicking, as a child does, the adolescent frequently substitutes belittling or ridiculing the person he would like to fight with. Frequently young adolescents throw things, stamp their feet, hit, kick, and, in the case of girls, cry when they are angry. Gradually, however, the adolescent comes to realize that such overt expressions are regarded as signs of immaturity and he learns to control them.

In addition to verbal fighting, the young adolescent often leaves the room, slamming the door behind him, and then locks himself in his room, refusing to speak to anyone or come out until his anger subsides. By fifteen years, however, most adolescents abandon this form of response as infantile and merely show their feelings when angry by "stony glances," glaring at the person who has angered them, or muttering under their breath. Control over anger responses is so well developed by the latter part of early adolescence that only occasionally do sixteen-year-olds "blow up," shout, slam doors, or cry when they are angry [37]. How the adolescent will react when angry, however, depends not so much upon age alone but also upon the social class with which he is identified. Those of the lower socioeconomic groups, or those who belong to a minority group, are likely to be more aggressive when angry than are those from higher socioeconomic groups. This is especially true of boys [67]. It is not unusual for adolescents who have acquired control over their angry responses to show hostility toward a parent, usually the mother, and treat her as the scapegoat for their pent-up anger. They plan revenge but this is rarely more than a fantasy [61]. Figure 33, page 178, shows changes in the anger responses with age, indicating a decrease in fighting and increase in verbal responses and sulkiness.

FEAR. By the time the child has reached adolescence, he has learned from experience that many of the things he formerly feared are not dangerous or harmful. As a result, his former fears vanish. However, in place of fears of childhood come new fears related to his more mature experiences, such as fears of being alone in the dark, being out alone at night, or being in social situations, especially when large numbers are present or when he is with strangers, and fears of school and school subjects. In general, shifts in things feared come when there are shifts in values and experiences. Because social situations are more important to an adolescent than to a child, he has more fears related to that area of his life. Similarly, with the broadening of his social horizons come new experiences and, like the child, the adolescent is likely to fear things that are new and different. Fears usually reach their peak of frequency and intensity around twelve years of age and then decline throughout early adolescence. By sixteen years of age, many adolescents claim that they have "no fears" [18, 37].

Like the young child who is afraid of people and new or strange social situations, the young adolescent is very shy in the presence of all but his most intimate friends. He wants to make a good impression on strangers, on adults, and on members of the opposite sex but he lacks confidence in his ability to do so. The resulting fear makes him shy and ill at ease, an almost universal characteristic of young adolescents. This differs markedly from the fears of situations which older children have and which make them cautious. Figure 33, page 178, shows the increase in timidity in early adolescence.

The typical fear response in adolescence is rigidity of the body, accompanied by paling, trembling, and perspiring. Unlike the child who runs away and hides when he is frightened, the adolescent infrequently responds in this way because he knows it would be a socially unacceptable form of behavior which would label him as a " 'fraid cat" and would win for him the scorn of his contemporaries. However, the adolescent does run away before the situation that might give rise to fear occurs. In other words, he *avoids* such situations. He then finds some justifiable excuse for his behavior and thus rationalizes his avoidance of a situation that he is afraid to face directly.

WORRY. Worry is a form of fear that comes from imaginary rather than real causes. As the number and intensity of fears decline with each passing year, the young adolescent substitutes worries about things, people, and situations which are primarily a product of his imagination. He works himself up into a state of fear about what *might* happen, though he may have little reason for believing that their occurrence is possible or even probable. As is true of fear, worries are concentrated mainly in areas of the adolescent's experiences that are important to him, especially social experiences and schoolwork [37]. Worries about examinations, about making a speech before a group, or about taking part in some athletic contest come from the adolescent's imagined fears that he will not make a good impression or that he will not measure up to his own or other people's anticipations. These worries are generally as intense if not more so than fears which come from real situations. And they can have an effect on the physical and psychological well-being of the individual as devastating as real fear has.

Among young adolescents, schoolwork is the most common source of worry. Those whose schoolwork is not satisfactory worry more about it than do those whose work is satisfactory. Tests and examinations in school are the chief source of worry connected with schoolwork. Young adolescent girls worry also about their appearance, about lack of understanding between themselves and their parents, about boy-and-girl relationships, difficulties in making friends, suitable places for recreation, vocational choice, religion, health problems, clothes, money, and such personal problems as personality weakness and lack of emotional control. Boys worry more than girls about ability and money. Some young adolescents worry because they feel they are not worrying enough or because their friends worry more than they do [37].

There are differences in the worries of adolescents of different socioeconomic groups. These differences are in quality, or things worried about, rather than in quantity. In the case of school worries, for example, boys from the lower socioeconomic groups worry more about the teacher and stage fright when called on to recite in class while boys from the upper classes concentrate their worries on getting into college, especially the college of their choice (see Figure 57). In their worries about social relations, girls of the lower classes are more concerned about their reputations, popularity, dates, and marriage while girls of the upper class are least concerned about their reputations and more concerned about popularity, dates, and their boy friends. Girls have twice as many worries about social relations as do boys (see Figure 58). Girls of the lower-class groups are more concerned about their clothes and appearance than are girls of the upper groups, and far more so than are boys [3].

JEALOUSY. While jealousy is commonly thought of as an infantile emotion, it appears in an intense and well-camouflaged form during early adolescence. As is true of the jealous child, the jealous adolescent feels insecure in his relationship with loved individuals. The young adolescent is interested in members of the opposite sex en masse and craves popularity with them. Those who attain this desired goal arouse jealous reactions in those who are overlooked or scorned by members of the opposite sex. When interest in one member of the opposite sex appears, as it frequently does at the close of early adolescence, the individual who loses the loved one to another is as intensely jealous as the child whose position as center of attention in the family is suddenly usurped by the new arrival. Young adolescents are also jealous of peers who have more privileges and more independence, or who are more successful in schoolwork or athletics than they [37].

When children are jealous, they either attack the individual who

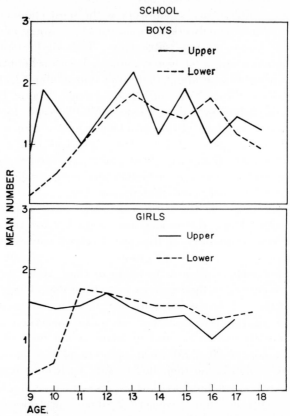

FIG. 57. School worries of young adolescents from high and low socioeconomic groups. (*From H. Angelino, J. Dollins, and E. V. Mech, Trends in the "fears and worries" of school children as related to socio-economic status and age. J. genet. Psychol., 1956, 89, 263–276. Used by permission.*)

they believe has usurped their place in the parent's affection or they revert to infantile behavior in order to win the attention they feel they have lost. The adolescent, instead of making bodily attacks upon those of whom he is jealous, makes verbal attacks. These attacks are generally in such a subtle form that it is often difficult to recognize them as such. The most common forms of verbal attack consist of sarcastic comments, ridiculing the individual, preferably in the presence of his parents or friends, and making derogatory comments about the person behind his back when he cannot defend himself. Regression to infantile forms of behavior is far less common among adolescents than among children. Girls sometimes, however, do whine and cry when their feelings are hurt or when they feel that they have been neglected. Emotionally immature

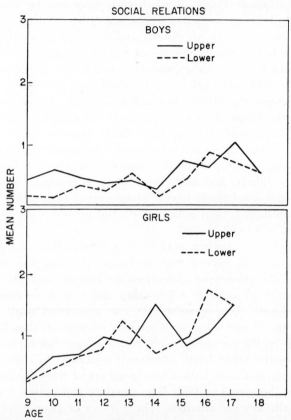

Fig. 58. Worries about social relations among boys and girls in early adolescence. (*From H. Angelino, J. Dollins, and E. V. Mech, Trends in the "fears and worries" of school children as related to socio-economic status and age. J. genet. Psychol., 1956, 89, 263–276. Used by permission.*)

boys rarely engage in this infantile type of behavior though they may make bodily attacks upon the individual who has aroused their jealousy, just as they did when they were children.

ENVY. Envy, like jealousy, is directed against an individual. It differs from jealousy in that the emotion is not stimulated by the individual of whom the adolescent is jealous but rather by the material possessions of this individual. It is a form of *covetousness* which is rarely found in any marked degree among children because children lack the ability to appreciate the true value of material objects. So long as a child has material possessions similar in outward appearance to those of his friends, any inferiority there may be in their quality does not disturb him. To an adolescent, however, quality as well as quantity is important. He not only wants as many things as his friends have but he also wants his possessions to be as good as theirs. The size of his home, the make of the family car, the quality of his clothes, and the number and type of vacation trips his family can afford are important to him.

As is true of jealousy, the typical envy reaction is verbal in form. The envious adolescent may criticize and make fun of possessions superior to his in an unconscious attempt to convince himself—as the fox did in the fable about the grapes he could not reach and therefore called "sour"— that they are not worth having. More likely, however, envy will express itself in complaining about the inferiority of the quality of his possessions, in exaggerating to his parents the number and superior quality of the possessions of others, and in saying that he is going to "get a job and have the things his friends have." These verbal expressions, which are more common in girls than in boys, are a bid for sympathy and attention on their part.

AFFECTION. While children may have as strong affectional associations for pets and favorite toys as they do for people, this does not occur in adolescence. The adolescent's affections are concentrated on people with whom he has a pleasurable relationship and who have made him feel secure and loved. As a general rule, the affectional relationship with members of the family is less strong among adolescents than it is in childhood, owing to the strained family relationships that typically exist at this time. On the other hand, affectional relationships with people outside the home, generally with a few members of their own sex, with an adult who is the object of their hero worship, and with a few members of the opposite sex are common. The number of people for whom the adolescent has a strong affection is small, as compared with that of the child. As a result, his emotional reaction toward these few individuals is typically stronger than it is for the large group the child is fond of.

Adolescent affection is an absorbing type of emotion that drives the adolescent to seek constantly the companionship of the individual or individuals for whom his affection is strongest. When he is away from them, he tries to keep in constant touch by telephone calls and letters. In addition, the adolescent tries to do everything he can to make the loved one happy, whether it be helping him with his schoolwork, planning forms of entertainment he will enjoy, or giving him presents. As early adolescence is a self-conscious, shy age, there is little demonstration of affection in kissing, hugging, and hand holding, as is true of the early childhood years. He does, however, reveal his affection by watching and listening to the loved one with rapt attention and by smiling constantly when in the presence of the loved one.

JOY. Joy, which in its milder forms is known as "happiness" or "delight," is a general, rather than a specific, emotional state. It comes from the adolescent's good adjustments to his work and to the social situations with which he is identified, from his ability to perceive the comic in a situation, from a release of pent-up emotional energy following worry, fear, anger, or jealousy, and from feelings of superiority which result from successful achievements on the adolescent's part [18]. The characteristic joy response is stereotyped in form and differs little from one individual to another. The entire body, as well as the face, is relaxed. There is a tendency to smile and, if the situation warrants it, smiling is followed by laughter. Each individual has his own characteristic form of laugh, though boys in general have laughs that are lower in tonal quality than girls have. Giggling frequently accompanies the joy emotion in girls, while boys are more likely to laugh so uproariously that their whole bodies shake. Uproarious laughter among girls is considered "unladylike" and, for that reason, girls seek more socially acceptable forms of expression.

CURIOSITY. By the time the individual has reached adolescence, his natural curiosity has been suppressed by environmental restraints. Furthermore, there is not much, by this time, that he has not already explored. As a result, there are fewer things to stimulate his curiosity than there were when he was younger. There are, however, new things entering the young adolescent's life and these are a source of curiosity to him. Members of the opposite sex present new experiences and the whole matter of sex and the relationships between the two sexes stimulate his curiosity. New areas of knowledge are opened up through his studies in junior and senior high school and the broader social relationships in the community likewise arouse his desire to learn more about them.

Then, too, there is the ever-present interest in the constant changes that are taking place in the adolescent's own body. Naturally these changes arouse curiosity, especially if preparatory information about these changes has been lacking or is only slight. The new physical sensations that accompany the maturation of the sex organs are sources of curiosity to the young adolescent, especially in the case of boys. While direct exploration of the things that arouse his curiosity occurs in adolescence as it does in childhood, the major response in curiosity consists of talking with anyone and everyone, asking questions, and making comments. From this, the adolescent not only learns new facts but he also acquires points of view which he might not otherwise have if his exploration were limited to questioning.

SOCIAL BEHAVIOR

Although the social development of the adolescent starts in babyhood and continues throughout the years of childhood, with a temporary set-back during the period of puberty, the most difficult of all social adjustments for the individual to make come during adolescence. These adjustments are related to members of the opposite sex, in a relationship that never existed before in the individual's life, and to adults outside the family and school environments. A good foundation of social adjustments,

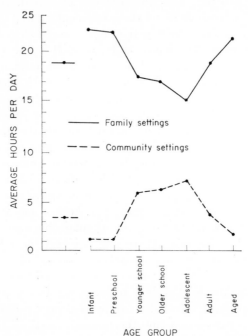

FIG. 59. Average hours per day spent in family and community settings at different ages. (*From H. F. Wright, Psychological development in Midwest. Child Develpm.,* 1956, 27, 265–286. *Used by permission.*)

established during the early years of life, will go a long way toward helping the young adolescent to adjust successfully to the new social demands placed upon him. A poor foundation of social adjustments, on the other hand, will add seriously to the difficulties every adolescent normally experiences at this time. Many young adolescents are so incapable of meeting these new demands successfully that they abandon the attempt and regress to earlier forms of social relationships or they develop compensatory forms of behavior to replace the normal social behavior of their contemporaries.

Influence of the Social Group. The individual at every age is a product of his social environment. As childhood advances and the child's social horizons broaden, the social group outside the home plays an increasingly important role in determining what sort of individual he will be (see Figure 59). In early adolescence, this influence is intensified by the adolescent's desire to be socially acceptable and the consequent effect of striving on his part to conform in every way to patterns approved by the group. Being like his friends in looks, actions, and thoughts not only helps to guarantee acceptance but it also eliminates the feeling of inferiority which comes when he is different. It is a form of "protective coloration." When they discover that good grades make them "different," some young adolescents strive to be "one of the crowd" by ceasing to distinguish themselves with good grades. They may even go out of their way to get into trouble, hoping for a public reprimand that will abolish the impression that they are "good students" [31].

A new factor enters into the young adolescent's social life which never before existed. No longer is he identified with just one group outside the home, the "gang," as he was in childhood. The broadening of his interests and experiences means that he is identified with several groups, often of distinctly different types of individuals with different interests and different points of view. From social contacts on a broader scale, young adolescents learn how to organize their own activities, select their own leaders, create on a small scale a society of adults, and, thereby, how to behave like adults. With members of the opposite sex, they learn adult social skills, such as dancing, carrying on conversations, and behaving in the socially approved manner [41].

How much or how little influence these different groups will have on the adolescent will depend to a large extent upon his degree of intimacy with each group. That, in turn, will be dependent upon the degree of success he achieves in his social adjustments with each group and his acceptance by the members of the different groups. In addition, within each group there are degrees of intimacy in his relationship with the different members of that group. These have been subdivided into three categories, according to the degree of intimacy that exists between the individual and other members of the group. In the *primary interactions* there is the closest intimacy. The number of persons with whom the individual has such relationships is small and these are regarded as his intimate friends. *Secondary interactions* are less intimate relationships, while the *tertiary interactions* are purely casual relationships. In the case of the primary and, to a lesser degree, the secondary relationships, the influence of members of the group on the adolescent is pronounced. Tertiary relationships have little influence on the adolescent's behavior [17].

Changes in Social Behavior. Changes in social attitudes and behavior are not entirely the product of group influences. With sexual maturing come changes which are so universally found among boys and girls of different environmental backgrounds that they cannot be attributed to environmental factors but rather to maturational factors. After pubescence has been completed, the young adolescent boy characteristically shows positive social attitudes as contrasted with the negative attitudes normally found at the time of puberty. These positive social attitudes include impatience with restrictions, sympathy for the weak, gregariousness, interest in social causes, desire to reform others, and loyalty to a person but not to a school. Much the same changes occur in girls except that loyalty to a person is replaced by loyalty to a clique [37, 51].

The most pronounced shifts in social interests and activities come between the ages of twelve and fourteen years. Of these shifts, the most significant are from variety and instability of interests to fewer and deeper interests; from talkative, noisy, and daring to more dignified, controlled behavior; from an identification with the herd to identification with a small select group; from family status being an unimportant factor in influencing relationships with contemporaries to an increasing influence of the family socioeconomic status in the selection of friends of both sexes; from informal to formal social activities; and from occasional dating to dates and "steadies."

Of all the changes that take place in social attitudes and behavior, the most pronounced is in the area of heterosexual relationships. From disliking members of the opposite sex to preferring their companionship to that of members of their own sex is a radical shift in a short period of time. The adolescent's behavior in social situations with members of his own sex differs from that with members of the opposite sex, as is illustrated in Figure 60. Social activities, whether with members of the same sex or with the opposite sex, reach their peak during the high school age. For that reason, at no time in life is social acceptance, or lack of it, so important as during the early years of adolescence.

Social Groupings. The "gangs" of childhood days gradually break up at puberty and in early adolescence as the individual's interests shift from the strenuous play activities of childhood to the less strenuous and more formal social activities of adolescence. In their place come new social groupings. Like the child, the adolescent feels the need for companionship with his contemporaries and from this he derives feelings of security which he lacks when his companionship is limited to adults. The tendency in early adolescence is to be more selective and to cultivate fewer friendships than the child had. The social groupings of boys are, as a rule, larger and more loosely knit whereas those of girls are smaller and more sharply defined [37].

Degrees of intimacy, or *social distance,* between friends appear for the first time during the early years of adolescence. No longer does the individual feel much the same way about all of his friends as he did when he was younger. Some he prefers to others and some are so congenial that he prefers their companionship to that of other friends. Social distance depends partly upon the degree of intimacy that exists between two individuals and partly upon the degree of emotional warmth. Frequency of contact is responsible, in part, for the degree of intimacy that exists

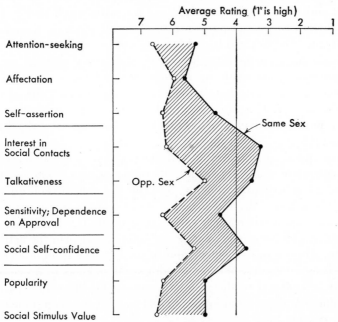

Fig. 60. Social ratings of a twelfth-grade boy, showing differences in behavior in the company of the two sexes. (*From F. B. Newman and H. E. Jones, The adolescent in social groups. Stanford, Calif.: Stanford Univer. Press, 1946. Used by permission.*)

[17]. The most common social groupings in early adolescence are *chums, cliques,* and *crowds.*

CHUMS. The adolescent's closest friends and best friends are his "chums," or, as boys prefer to call them, his "pals." How many chums the adolescent will have varies from one individual to another, and from one time to another in the same individual. As a rule, shortly after puberty, a girl will select one other girl as her confidante. Much the same pattern is followed by boys. As time goes on, the number of chums may and frequently does increase but it never is as large as the number of less intimate friends. And because of the satisfaction the adolescent derives from such social relationships, more time is spent with chums than with other friends. Chums are generally of the same sex and have interests and abilities of a similar sort. Their relationship is so close and so satisfying that it is natural that chums would have a marked influence on each other. While they may disagree at times and may even quarrel bitterly, the bond of friendship between them is so strong that the quarrels are soon patched up and forgotten [37, 46].

CLIQUES. Cliques are small exclusive social groupings. They are made up of three or four intimate friends who have much in common in both interests and abilities. Frequently, they are made up of several pairs of chums, though this is not necessarily true in all cases. As the adolescent years advance and boy-girl friendships become more frequent, cliques are often made up of a girl and her chum and a boy and his pal. Early cliques, however, are made up of individuals of the same sex. Cliques, like chums, are far more lasting social groupings than are the friendships of childhood days. They are held together by strong ties of affection and common interests which are frequently lacking in the friendships of childhood [76].

Cliques spend as much of their time together as possible. Their activities consist of going to movies, attending athletic contests, studying together, going to parties, talking, and telephoning to each other when parted. The secret clubs and societies of high school are an outgrowth of cliques. In schools where such clubs are permitted, it is the cliques that take over, decide who may or may not belong, and plan the activities of the clubs. They want no supervision or interference from adults and resent such as intrusions. When the adolescent belongs to a clique, he is expected to conform to the standards set up by the clique even when these standards differ from home standards. This results in much friction with his parents [46].

CROWDS. The largest of the social groupings of adolescence is the *crowd*. It is composed of individuals with common interests and common abilities. And, because the crowd is larger than other social groupings of adolescence, there is social distance among its members. Typically, it starts with a clique as its foundation. Then new members are added, either single individuals, chums, or other cliques. Naturally, under such conditions, not all members are equally congenial and, as a result, social distance or degrees of intimacy are bound to be found. As is true of cliques, crowds at first are made up of members of one sex. Later, with the development of interest in members of the opposite sex, the crowd becomes heterogeneous in its membership, with an equal number of members of both sexes. *Crowd activities* are predominantly social in character. The major interests center around talking, playing games, dancing, and eating. While these may seem unexciting and even meaningless, as judged by adult standards, they fulfill the strong need every adolescent has for companionship with his contemporaries.

There are *advantages and disadvantages* in crowd life. On the positive side, being a member of a crowd gives the adolescent a feeling of security; it offers him invaluable experience in getting along successfully with people, provides pleasant leisure-time activities and an opportunity to develop such social skills as talking and dancing, which will prove to be useful not only throughout the adolescent years but also for the years of maturity, and it gives him an opportunity to meet and know members of the opposite sex in socially approved situations. On the minus side, crowd life may prove to be so absorbing to an adolescent that he neglects his duties and responsibilities at home, at school, and in the community; it is likely to encourage an intolerant, snobbish attitude toward contemporaries who do not belong to that crowd or any other crowd; and it makes a difficult if not intolerable situation for adolescents who do not belong to a crowd and who, as a result, miss the fun that crowd members enjoy.

ORGANIZED GROUPS. Unfortunately not all adolescent boys and girls belong to crowds nor have they close friends. To meet the needs of such adolescents, schools, churches, and community organizations have, in recent years, established *youth groups,* open to any adolescent in a certain age range who may wish to join. These groups provide opportunities for social life for those who might otherwise be deprived of it and they plan activities that will be interesting to the group, whether they be sports, parties, handcrafts, or activities of an altruistic nature. Such groups are especially popular for those who come from the poorer areas of the community and who, without an adult leader, would be unable to organize their own activities and would, therefore, spend their time in aggressive "horseplay" [64].

GANGS. Although most boys and girls "outgrow" gang life when they reach adolescence, there are some boys and girls who are poorly adjusted to school and who have few friends among their classmates. They spend their time hanging around street corners with others who lack social acceptance among the cliques of their class and thus satisfy their need for the companionship of their contemporaries. Sometimes these gangs are made up of members of the two sexes but, for the most part, they are limited to one sex, as is true of the gangs of childhood. While not all adolescent gangs are made up of individuals who become juvenile delinquents, the majority of adolescent gangs spend their time in antisocial behavior, seeking revenge on those who have not accepted them or on society in general. Should the leader be revengeful in his attitude, he can stir up the other gang members to violence and thus satisfy his personal desire for revenge [106].

Adolescent Friendships. The young adolescent soon learns that friendships are not established just because individuals happen to be in the same class in school. Now there is a strong element of selection not apparent in the earlier years. To be accepted as a friend, he must conform to the socially approved pattern of his contemporaries and he must have personality traits that they like. There must also be conformity to the individual's value system, which is markedly influenced by the values of the group with which the adolescent is identified. What the group admires in childhood will not be the same as what it admires in adolescence. As a result of this change in values, the adolescent's childhood friends will not necessarily be his friends in adolescence [104]. Figure 61 shows the change with age in traits admired in others.

The problem of friendship selection is complicated in the latter part of early adolescence by the newly awakened interest in members of the opposite sex. So long as his friends were limited to members of his own sex, the individual knew what was acceptable to them and what was not. Now, however, a new element enters into the problem. He must be acceptable to members of the opposite sex if he is to establish friendships with them and, because of inexperience in this area of his behavior, he is unfamiliar with what they consider acceptable. As early adolescence draws to a close, there is a preference for friends of the opposite sex to friends of the same sex, though both boys and girls have a few intimate friends of their own sex with whom they associate constantly [37].

In the selection of friends, the adolescent is not guided by adult advice as he was when he was younger. He wants to select his own friends and resents adult interference in this matter. As a result of his inexperience, especially in the choice of friends of the opposite sex, he frequently chooses individuals who, at first, seem congenial but who, as time goes on, do not measure up to his standards. As a result, a quarrel ensues and the friendship is broken, often permanently. There is a tendency, as adolescence progresses, for friendships to become more stable than they were in the earlier years [48] (see Figure 36, page 187). This would suggest that the adolescent, through experience, is learning to evaluate his contemporaries better and to be more selective in his choice of friends than he was when he was younger.

The young adolescent likes to have a large number of friends of different degrees of intimacy. This, he feels, is an indication of his popularity. As he grows older, however, he narrows down the number and regards the "right" kind of friends as more important than a large number. What is looked upon as the "right" kind differs from one year to another and within different groups. Childhood friends, selected because they were good play companions, are not necessarily the "right" kind of friends for the young adolescent. Now play of the childhood type has

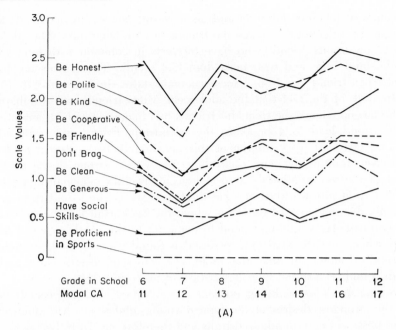

Grade in School 6 7 8 9 10 11 12
Modal CA 11 12 13 14 15 16 17

(A)

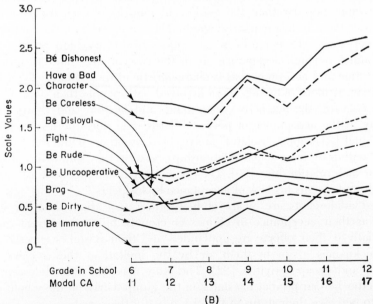

Grade in School 6 7 8 9 10 11 12
Modal CA 11 12 13 14 15 16 17

(B)

Fig. 61. Age trends in basic values as reflected in the extent to which various behaviors are considered praiseworthy (A) or blameworthy (B) by girls. (*Based on material of G. G. Thompson, Age trends in social values during the adolescent years. Amer. Psychologist, 1948, 4, 250. From S. L. Pressey and R. G. Kuhlen, Psychological development through the life span. New York: Harper, 1957. Used by permission.*)

given way to other interests and, as a result, new types of friends are frequently selected to replace the friends of childhood days. The adolescent now wants friends who have interests in common with him, who understand him, and who make him feel secure. These goals are best met when friends are from a socioeconomic status similar to his [46, 76].

In spite of the fact that the adolescent wants friends and is unhappy if he has no friends, he treats his friends in a manner which, at any other age, would lead to a break in the friendship. Friendships, especially among girls, are very intense at this age and there is a great deal of criticism, faultfinding, and quarreling. There is a strong desire on the part of the young adolescent to change his friend's personality and behavior to fit into his ideal of what the friend should be [37]. Criticism is usually directed toward those for whom the adolescent has the strongest attachment. He wants his friend to come up to the ideal he has of him and when an individual on a pedestal is found to have faults, criticism naturally follows. In time, the adolescent comes to accept reality as he finds it and, as a result, he is less critical of his friends [86].

Social Acceptance. Being popular or "accepted" by his peers is one of the strongest desires of the typical young adolescent. An adolescent who possesses certain admired traits and therefore has "prestige" is likely to be more popular than the adolescent who lacks such traits or who possesses them in less marked degrees. There are variations in the degree of acceptance different adolescents enjoy, from very high prestige accompanied by high acceptance, as in the case of the "star," to little or no prestige and acceptance, as is characteristic of the "isolate." Typically, the "star" is more outgoing, more involved with people than with things, more colorful, daring, active, easygoing, and flexible, and shows more leeway in the acceptance of peer standards than does the less accepted individual [54]. Some "isolates" are rejected by others while some voluntarily withdraw from social relationships because they find little satisfaction in such relationships [66]. The involuntary isolate, by contrast, wants friends and resents his lack of acceptance by his peers.

Most adolescents are aware of how others feel about them by such clues as their acceptance in cliques or crowds, how others treat them, especially if their efforts are applauded and their mistakes excused, by the nicknames given to them, or by the invitations they receive for parties and group activities [22]. The more accepted the adolescent is, the better he can predict his status in the group. Girls, on the whole, are able to perceive their status in the group better than are boys (see Figure 62). Those who overestimate their acceptance are less well adjusted than those who underestimate their acceptance because the former set their aspirations too high and are then disappointed when they fail to get the acceptance they had anticipated [6, 68]. The ability to perceive one's own status develops more slowly than the ability to perceive the status of others, with the most marked increase coming in the early part of adolescence.

Having been popular in childhood does not guarantee popularity in adolescence. The young adolescent expects his friends to possess certain traits that are not important to a child. Similarly, traits which may have made him popular in childhood, such as being noisy, daring, and even rude to his elders, will have just the opposite effect in adolescence. The

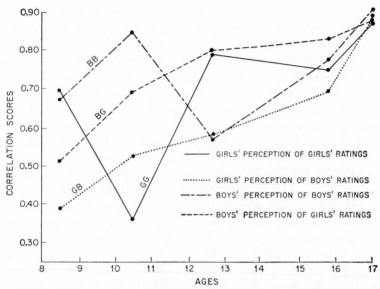

FIG. 62. Sex differences in perception of sociometric status. (*From D. P. Ausubel, H. M. Schiff, and E. B. Glasser, A preliminary study of developmental trends in socioempathy: accuracy of perception of own and others' sociometric status. Child Develpm., 1952, 23, 111–128. Used by permission.*)

socially acceptable adolescent is active, socially aggressive, and extroverted. When he is with others, he cooperates and helps willingly, he is courteous and considerate of others, he assumes leadership in a group, he is truthful and "aboveboard" in his conduct, he controls his temper in annoying situations, he is unselfish with his belongings, he displays resourcefulness and initiative, he is willing and carries out accepted responsibilities, he observes rules and regulations, and he contributes well-considered suggestions to the thinking of the group. In addition, he makes a good appearance, comes from a family with average or above average socioeconomic status, and possesses enough social insight to be able to adjust quickly and successfully to different people and social situations [46, 89].

Home relationships have a marked influence on the degree of popularity the young adolescent enjoys with his peers. Popular adolescents have been found to have warm and friendly feelings toward their families, to participate in activities with their families, and to have been permitted to participate in activities outside the home [105]. School success may bring girls high respect with members of their own sex but they are less popular with their own sex and with boys than are girls whose school success is lower. High or low marks, on the other hand, have no effect on the popularity of boys [54].

Traits that make young adolescents unpopular include showing off, bullying and antagonizing others, feeling misunderstood or "picked on," carrying grudges, being resentful, using escape mechanisms such as alibis, domineering and bossing others, and being highly nervous, timid and withdrawing, or stubborn, sullen, and sulky. Manners also begin to be important at this age. An adolescent whose manners fall below the norms of his contemporaries is likely to be regarded as a "boor" by them. The unpopular adolescent often has unfavorable relationships with his family, thus developing unfavorable attitudes which influence his relationships with people outside the home [33]. Or, the unpopularity may stem from the fact that he lives too far away from the group to be able to participate in group activities [13]. Rural students in urban high schools are a minority group and are not accepted by urban students unless they accept urban values and patterns of behavior [77]. Should the adolescent belong to a minority religious or racial group, it is likely to militate against his acceptance by adolescents of the majority group [63]. The unpopular adolescent often comes from a lower socioeconomic group than the majority of his classmates, does poor schoolwork, and lacks the knowledge of social skills which adolescents of higher socioeconomic status have acquired [53].

Acceptance or lack of it plays an important role in the adolescent's attitudes and behavior. The popular adolescent feels secure and happy, and this, in turn, gives him the necessary self-confidence to try to develop the characteristics that will add still further to his popularity. He is optimistic about his future and confident of his chances for success [87]. Because he feels that he is wanted, he is a more active participant in group activities and more willing to conform to the standards of the group than is the adolescent who feels unwanted [39]. The adolescent who is unpopular is often unhappy and resentful toward those who have refused to accept him. This frequently produces a lasting effect on his personality. The unpopular adolescent may develop substitute satisfactions, such as friendships with older or younger individuals, daydreaming, or an absorbing hobby. Because none of these is as satisfying as friendships with contemporaries, the unpopular adolescent is likely to develop personality traits which will detrimentally affect his future social adjustments [81].

Leaders. Popularity alone will not guarantee leadership though it is unusual to have a leader who is disliked by a majority of the group. To be a leader an adolescent must have qualities which are superior to and admired by the members of the group of which he is a leader. And, because the interests and activities of adolescents are more varied than they are during childhood, the qualities that make for leadership in one group may not make for leadership in others. In general, however, leaders are more active than nonleaders in social activities. They participate more and their participation is of a more aggressive sort. Whether or not they will be selected as leaders will be markedly influenced by the interest and ability they show in the activity with which the group is concerned. To be an athletic leader, for example, requires a high level of skill in sports while the leader of a dramatic club must show some ability in acting.

There are certain *qualities* that adolescents expect their leaders to possess. The clothes-conscious young adolescent expects his leader to make a good *appearance.* He must be nice-looking, well-groomed, and wear stylish, becoming clothes. The characteristic leader of young adolescents will also be slightly above average in *intelligence,* above average in *academic achievement,* and above average in his *level of maturity,* owing to his age, to early maturing, or to training. Leaders, as a rule, come from families of higher *socioeconomic status* than do nonleaders. This not only gives them prestige in the eyes of their peers but it also makes possible better dressing and grooming, the possession of social know-how, and opportunities for entertaining [98].

Personality, however, seems to be the outstanding quality that determines whether the adolescent will or will not be a leader. Dependability, loyalty, extroversion, a wide range of interests, self-confidence, speed of decision, liveliness, good sportsmanship, sociability, sense of humor, poise, originality, efficiency, persistence, adaptability, tact, and cooperativeness—these are a few of the qualities an adolescent leader possesses [98]. Because a leader, characteristically, is a more active participant in social life than a nonleader, he develops *social insight* and *self-insight.* He can judge himself realistically and can size up the interests and wishes of the group he leads. The leader is not "self-bound" in the sense that he is concerned with his personal interests and problems; instead, he directs his energies outward and concerns himself with the interests and problems of the group [20]. By fourteen or fifteen years, girls choose boys for leaders of school activities in preference to girls whereas boys feel that a boy should be a leader rather than a girl. As a result, leaders in activities where the two sexes are involved are more often boys than girls [26].

INTERESTS

New interests develop during the adolescent years as a result of the physical and social changes that take place at this time. What interests the adolescent has depend upon his sex, his intelligence, the environment in which he lives, opportunities for learning, what his contemporaries are interested in, his own innate abilities, the interests of his family, and many other factors. Adolescent interests may, however, be roughly divided into three categories: *social* interests, *personal* interests, and *recreational* interests. All young adolescents possess these interests to a greater or less extent, and they all have certain specific interests that fall within these categories.

Social Interests. Social interests are those that relate to social situations and people, such as parties and conversations. After a period of little interest in any form of social activity, during puberty, the young adolescent becomes markedly interested in all forms of group activities, as well as activities with one or more intimate friends. These interests do not, however, develop overnight. Rather, they grow gradually, the rate depending to a large extent upon the satisfaction the adolescent derives from such activities and the opportunities he has to engage in them.

Interest in *parties,* which was strong during the early years of childhood and then lagged as childhood progressed, is revived in early adolescence with the awakening of interest in members of the opposite sex. During the junior high school age, interest in parties with members of the opposite sex first begins to manifest itself because young adolescents like to be with members of the opposite sex and to play games or dance with them. At this age, girls are more interested in parties than are boys. They even go so far as to try to train the boys to dance and to be their party escorts. Left to their own devices, boys would not become interested in parties until a year or two later than girls because of their later sexual maturing. Even in the high school groups, more girls than boys attend the school parties [46, 51].

Drinking, at parties or on dates, is becoming increasingly popular among high school students. Boys usually begin to drink with their clique members, often to celebrate some athletic victory. By the junior year in high school, however, they drink at parties and on dates. Girls, for the most part, start to drink at parties or on dates, rarely with their clique members. Some adolescents begin to drink at home, if this is part of the pattern of family life, but most begin outside the home, as part of the pattern of social life. Frequently, drinks are served at parties in the homes by the junior year in high school. When drinking is done outside the home, it is usually at a roadhouse or out-of-town tavern [46].

While most young adolescents are tongue-tied when they are with adults, they talk endlessly when they are with their friends. In fact, *conversations* are one of their favorite forms of social activities. Just getting together in a group and talking about the things that interest them or disturb them gives them a feeling of security that goes a long way toward helping them to puzzle out problems that have been a source of concern. Even after seeing his friends at school, the adolescent is hardly in the house before he calls up one of his intimate friends on the telephone and continues his conversation with that friend until his family puts a stop to it.

The favorite topics of conversation among young adolescents differ for the two sexes. Girls talk mostly about parties, dates, jokes, books, movies, movie stars, ball games, and teachers, while the favorite topics of conversation among boys include ball games, dates, movies, and politics. A shift of interest in conversational topics has been observed among high school boys as they progress from freshman to senior year. The younger boys talk mostly about sports, girls, school, teachers, and studies, while the older boys concentrate mostly on conversation about girls, sports, social activities, dates, and sex [26].

The young adolescent is sincerely interested in *other people*, especially those who he feels have been misunderstood, mistreated, or oppressed. This interest is shown by active participation in school and community affairs which are planned to help the less fortunate and by championing the causes of these people in arguments and discussions. The young adolescent also begins to show an interest in *government* and *politics*, and even in *world affairs* but, for the most part, this interest is expressed mainly by reading and discussions.

Interest in others becomes so strong among many adolescent boys and girls that they bend their efforts to *reforming* their families, their friends, and even their schools and communities. The young adolescent is very free in offering suggestions, whether solicited or not, and in attempting to force his ideas and suggestions on others, regardless of their attitudes and feelings about the matter. Criticisms of parents and attempts to reform them are characteristic of almost all young adolescents, but especially of girls. The junior and senior high schools likewise come in for a large share of the adolescent's criticisms and attempts at reform. Most of the criticisms are of a destructive rather than of a constructive sort, and suggestions offered for reforms are more often impractical than practical [26, 37].

Personal Interests. Interest in themselves is the strongest interest young adolescents have. This comes partly from the rapid bodily changes which took place during puberty and which continue, at a decreasing rate, throughout early adolescence, and partly from the realization that social acceptance is markedly influenced by the general appearance of the individual. Much of the unpredictable behavior of the young adolescent stems from his attempts to try out different clothes, hair styles, manners, and attitudes in an effort to assert himself as a person with all the rights and privileges of an adult which he feels belong to him. This results in what, to an adult, may be regarded as "faddism" because of the constant shifting and changing so characteristic of this age [26].

With the awakening of interest in members of the opposite sex, interest in *appearance*, in *dress*, and in *personal adornment* increases. This is true especially of girls because they realize how important appearance is to popularity with members of the opposite sex. Interest in appearance covers not only clothes and personal adornment but every aspect of appearance. Hair, body size, facial features, skin, and nails are all focal points of interest to the young adolescent. Any feature that does not come up to standard is likely to be the source of great concern to the young adolescent. Both boys and girls discover, even before childhood is over, that *clothes* go a long way toward covering up undesirable physical features and toward enhancing good features. They make use of this knowledge during early adolescence when personal appearance becomes important to them.

High school girls regard right clothes as necessary to happiness. Wrong clothes can lead to uneasiness in social situations and a good appearance can be an aid in building self-confidence. They select clothes that appeal to boys rather than to girls when their interest in boys appears. Becomingness of color and style is more important to girls than is usefulness. Because the adolescent's happiness and self-confidence depend upon his contemporaries' attitudes toward his clothes, he is anxious to conform to what the group approves of in the matter of dress. While boys claim not to be interested in clothes, grooming, or appearance, their behavior indicates that their interest is greater than they will admit. Like girls, they recognize the fact that appearance plays an important role in social acceptance and, as a result, they try to make as attractive an appearance as possible, especially when they become interested in members of the opposite sex, in parties, and in dates [88, 91].

A strong desire for *independence*, which made its appearance in a milder form in the closing years of childhood, develops in early adolescence. It is as if an overwhelming urge were released among these young adolescents to assert their independence, to explore new and thrilling kinds of relationships with one another, and to proclaim their rights of self-expression as individuals. Lower-class families are more permissive and give more independence to adolescents than do those of the middle and upper classes who supervise the adolescent's behavior more carefully [83]. Resistance to adult authority is most pronounced in early adolescence when the individual is trying to establish himself socially.

This leads to many clashes with parents and other adults in authority. Because girls are expected to conform more to parental wishes than are boys, they rebel more than boys against home restraints [26]. Much of the *radicalism* of young adolescents can be traced to their attempts to think and act independently [43].

To achieve independence, money is essential. This leads to a heightened interest in *money*, not only from the point of view of the size of their allowances and the freedom with which they can spend their money but also from the point of view of how they can earn money to

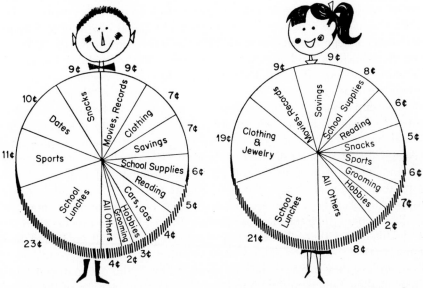

Fig. 63. How young adolescent boys and girls spend their money. (*Based on data compiled by Eugene Gilbert for Life Magazine, May 13, 1957. Used by permission.*)

supplement their allowances [27]. There is a marked increase in the number of adolescents working part time from freshman to senior year in high school in order to increase the amount of money they have to spend [27, 37]. As they grow older, interest in possessions, such as clothes, cars, watches, and sports equipment, intensifies their interest in money and motivates them to increase their allowances by part-time work. For boys, money is even more important than for girls if they are to participate in school activities and the social life of their peers [1, 27]. How the typical adolescent of today spends his allowance is illustrated in Figure 63.

As boys and girls reach the high school age, they begin to think seriously about their *careers*. Whether or not they can plan ahead depends partly on the economic stability of the family, partly on whether they belong to a social class group where planning ahead is encouraged, and partly on their sex [75]. On the whole, adolescents from middle-class families are encouraged to plan ahead more than are those from the lower classes who, as a rule, are "present-oriented." Girls plan ahead less than boys because the time of marriage is unpredictable and this encourages them to live more from day to day than is true of boys, whose vocational plans will not be interrupted if they marry [16, 37]. Boys, for the most part, are more seriously concerned about the problem of vocational choice than are girls because, to them, it will be a life career while for most girls, a job is just a stopgap until they marry [81].

The unrealistic vocational aspirations of childhood give way to a more realistic concept of what certain lines of work require in the way of ability, education, and training, and of what the individual's capacities actually are [32, 79]. Adolescents of different socioeconomic groups recognize that they are likely to follow the pattern of their fathers in their occupational selection unless circumstances make it possible for them to attain a higher education and thus move into a higher vocational bracket. Boys and girls of minority groups are realistic enough to recognize that they are limited in their vocational selection as compared with members of majority groups [28, 93]. The relationship of vocational aspiration to social class is shown in Figure 64. While many adolescents aspire to jobs above the occupational level of their families, they are realistic about their chances of getting them [107]. However, there is little likelihood that children of professional fathers will go into skilled labor or that the sons of skilled laborers will go into the upper-rank positions unless they are very bright. Most follow in the occupational footsteps of their fathers and go into lines of work characteristic of the socioeconomic class to which their family belongs [80].

Because of the unrealistic attitude toward vocations that most young adolescents carry over from childhood, it is not surprising that they are changeable in their vocational selections, at least for a few years. This instability gradually decreases as adolescents grow older. Girls, as a rule, are more stable in their vocational choices than are boys [65]. Boys, typically, want jobs that have glamor and excitement, regardless of the ability required or the chances that such jobs will be available for them. They also want jobs with high prestige, even if these jobs pay less than those with lower prestige. Many boys from low-status families hope to achieve higher social status through high-status occupations [80]. Girls, as a rule, show a preference for occupations with greater security and less demand on their time. In their vocational choices, they stress, for the most part, service to others, such as teaching or nursing.

Typically, the young adolescent complains about *school* in general and about restrictions, homework, required courses, and the way the school is run. He is critical of his teachers and finds fault with the way they teach. In spite of this, most adolescents get along well academically and socially and "like" school [37]. For many adolescents, school is a way of improving their status in life. Through their schoolwork and social contacts, they are able to move upward and, for this goal, they are willing to work hard, read, and take part in the extracurricular activities connected with school. They are even willing to give up some of their dating and postpone marriage longer than non-college-going students [11].

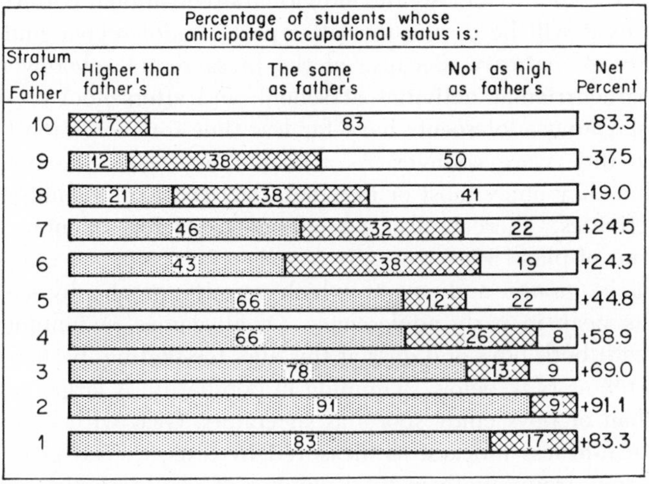

Stratum of Father	Percentage of students whose anticipated occupational status is:			
	Higher than father's	The same as father's	Not as high as father's	Net Percent
10	17	83		-83.3
9	12	38	50	-37.5
8	21	38	41	-19.0
7	46	32	22	+24.5
6	43	38	19	+24.3
5	66	12	22	+44.8
4	66	26	8	+58.9
3	78	13	9	+69.0
2	91	9		+91.1
1	83	17		+83.3

10 = high
1 = low

Fig. 64. Vocational aspirations of seniors in high school in relation to social class status. (*From L. T. Empey, Social class and occupational aspiration: a comparison of absolute and relative measurement. Amer. sociol. Rev., 1956, 21, 703–709. Used by permission.*)

Their interest in studies is influenced by how well they do in them and by their attitude toward their teachers. Boys, especially, prefer school subjects which they believe have "practical" value, such as science and mathematics. Most adolescents approach studies which have the reputation of being "hard" or "impractical" with an unfavorable attitude and, as a result, do poorly in them [102]. The *drop-out problem* is one of the serious ones in high school. Many adolescents who leave school before graduating do so more for social than academic reasons. When they are not accepted in the cliques or have few friends, their attitude toward school is unfavorable and this affects the quality of their work. As a result, they become discouraged and believe they will solve their problem by withdrawal [24].

Recreational Interests. While both boys and girls show a change in the recreations they enjoy in adolescence as compared with childhood, the change is more marked for girls than for boys. In general, there is a breaking away from recreations that require much expenditure of energy and a liking for recreations of the amusement type, where the player is a passive spectator. In early adolescence, just as is true of the early part of late childhood, there is a carry-over of some of the play activities of the early years and the introduction of new and more mature forms of recreation. Gradually, the childish forms of play drop out so that, when early adolescence comes to a close, the individual's recreational pattern is much the same as it will be during the latter part of adolescence and into the early years of maturity. Because of the pressures of schoolwork, home duties, extracurricular activities at school, and afterschool or week-end jobs, most young adolescents have far less time for recreation than they had when they were younger. As a result, they select the types of activities that they enjoy most or in which they excel. This limits the number of activities. There is also a tendency to prefer sedentary to more active forms of play [84].

Interest in *games* and *sports* which require great physical energy reaches its peak in early adolescence. Of all games, swimming is most popular with both boys and girls at this age. Ice-skating, basketball, football, and tennis rank below swimming in popularity. A larger percentage of girls than of boys enjoy sports as spectators. Girls with high strength and physical-fitness indexes, as measured by tests, exceed girls in corresponding low groups both in total number of play activities engaged in and in total time devoted to play activities. Boys, on the other hand, prefer to be active participants in such sports as football, basketball, and swimming. They prefer organized sports to the neighborhood games of childhood. Games of intellect and gambling come into popularity at this age, especially among boys [46].

Reading, just for fun, becomes less popular in early adolescence than it was at the close of childhood. The young adolescent has less time than the child to read for the fun of it because of school and home pressures. Boys, at this age, prefer science and invention, and girls show a preference for romantic stories. They also specialize in the type of subject matter that appeals to them, and they read magazine stories more often than books. Like the child, the young adolescent enjoys reading the comics, either in newspapers or in comic books. Tabloids have an especially strong appeal to the slow reader at this age [37]. Changes with age in interest in different types of mass communication are shown in Figure 65.

Movies that appeal to young adolescents, as is true of reading, must have a romantic as well as an adventure theme. They also like comedies.

Educational pictures, as is true of sex and society themes, have little appeal. Girls, on the whole, prefer pictures with a love theme; the preference of boys is for pictures with an adventure, mystery, or comedy theme. What the adolescent sees, however, depends largely upon what is available in the local theaters. In selecting a movie, the most potent factor influencing the choice is the featured actor or actress. Girls prefer actresses, while boys prefer actors and their choices of movies are motivated by these preferences [37]. Throughout the years of early adolescence, going to the movies is one of the favorite recreations of both

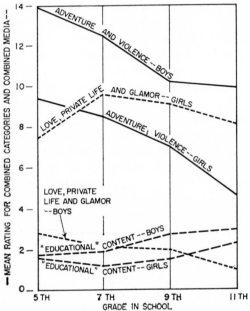

FIG. 65. Changes of interest with age in different types of mass communication. (*From P. I. Lyness, Patterns in the mass communications tastes of the young audience. J. educ. Psychol., 1951, 42, 449–467. Used by permission.*)

boys and girls. Movies are a form of escape mechanism which serve a useful purpose when life becomes too complicated for the young adolescent to meet successfully. Whether the adolescent goes to the movies alone or with his favorite friends, the experience is enjoyable.

Because of the great interest in movies, it is not surprising that they have a profound influence on both boys and girls at this age. Girls, especially, are influenced by the feminine stereotypes they see on the screen, and they try to imitate their clothing, their hair styles, their speech, and their actions. Reading about their favorite actresses in the different movie magazines is one favorite source of reading pleasure.

Much of the criticism and faultfinding with their parents and homes can be traced to the fact that the adolescents do not feel that their parents and homes come up to the standards set by the screen [84].

Listening to the *radio* and watching *television* have, in recent years, become universal favorites among adolescents in America. Since most American homes, including those of mediocre or even poor economic status, have either radio or television sets or both, the adolescent can get his amusement at home without the cost of going to the movies. One to three hours a day, or even more, is spent by the majority of adolescents on this form of amusement. Many young adolescents listen to the radio while they study, claiming that it helps them to concentrate better. There is an increase in preference for programs of dance and popular music as adolescence progresses. Humorous sketches and plays also have great appeal. Among boys especially, mystery, crime, and detective programs are popular. Both boys and girls like programs of the quiz type and those which feature amateurs. There is a drop in interest in television watching around thirteen years of age partly because the type of program has less appeal and partly because it is not possible, as with radio, to watch television and study at the same time. Listening to phonograph records becomes a fad in early adolescence [37, 84].

Much of the adolescent's time that might be spent more profitably on his homework or other duties is spent in *daydreaming*. As is true of the pubescent child, daydreaming is a source of great satisfaction to the individual because, in his daydream, he can be the sort of person he would like to be in real life. But, unlike the suffering-hero daydream of puberty, the characteristic daydream of early adolescence is that of the conquering hero in which the dreamer sees himself as the hero he would like to be in the type of setting that appeals most to him, whether it be on the football field, in the classroom, or on the dance floor. The theme and the setting of the adolescent daydream are often influenced by the movies that the adolescent has seen. While daydreaming is, unquestionably, a waste of time that might be spent more profitably in other activities and while it often leads to an unrealistic concept of self on the part of the dreamer, it also serves as an outlet for pressures that might not otherwise be met satisfactorily by the adolescent. In this respect, daydreaming serves much the same purpose as movies do in the lives of young adolescents [85].

RELIGIOUS INTERESTS

Typically, adolescence is a period of *religious awakening*, when childish religious beliefs are examined critically, evaluated, and then revised to meet the new needs of the individual. Because all of this takes time, the major part of adolescence is devoted to the problem of religious revision. At first, the young adolescent faces his childish beliefs in a critical way, often dogmatically rejecting all or most of them. This, as a rule, begins around the thirteenth year [37]. The adolescent who has grown up in a family where religion plays a dominant role in the family life is likely to be more concerned about religion than is one whose family pays little attention to religion. Blows of fate, such as the death of a relative or near friend, and severe personal hardships also help to focus the adolescent's attention on religion. Religious discussions with his friends or teachers bring religion to the foreground and motivate a critical examination of it on the part of the adolescent. He is often confused by different opinions and this leads him to question his own beliefs [85].

Most young adolescents meet religious beliefs of childhood with a hypercritical attitude. They have a tendency to reject all or at least a majority of their former beliefs because they now find a few of them difficult to accept. They question those beliefs which do not stand the test of scientific scrutiny, and they refuse to accept on faith any teachings as they did when they were children. The more dogmatically religion was taught to them when they were children, the more skeptical they are likely to be when they are adolescent.

Typically, *religious doubt* follows a predictable pattern. The adolescent first becomes skeptical of religious *forms*, such as prayer and duties toward God. Later, doubts are more likely to center around religious *contents*, such as knowledge and belief, and the nature of God and of man. Sin, what becomes of people after they die, failure to go to church, and disliking church are a few of the problems concerning religion that trouble young adolescents. As adolescence progresses, these problems give rise to new ones with their accompanying doubts. Girls, as a rule, are less subject to religious doubt than are boys [81]. Doubting is invariably accompanied by emotional tension. The more pronounced the doubting and the more closely it is related to subjects where doubt is frowned upon, the stronger will be the emotional accompaniment. In general, the more dogmatic the religious teaching of childhood has been, the greater will be the emotional accompaniment of doubting [46, 58].

Absence of religious doubt is a bad sign. It means either that the individual has an intellectual level too low to question beliefs that proved to be satisfactory to him when his intellectual development was on a lower level or it means that his religious teaching has been so dogmatic and so threatening that he is afraid to doubt for fear of possible evil consequences. As a result, he continues to accept the beliefs of his childhood with a logic-tight mind and a tendency to inhibit any questions that might arise in regard to them. This eliminates any possibility of revision of his beliefs which is essential if they are to prove to be satisfactory to him as he reaches maturity. Before their high school days are over, most adolescents have revised their childish concepts of God, of heaven and hell, of sin, of life after death, of miracles, and of the meaning of prayer [85, 95].

Church attendance and other *religious observances* play a far more important role in the life of the young adolescent than most adults believe. The typical high school student of today has a favorable attitude toward church. While the adolescent may revolt against going to Sunday school unless the teaching is of a liberal sort that fits his more mature needs, and while he may object to accompanying the family to church, this does not mean that he has rejected religion. Rather, it suggests that the matter of selection should be left to him so that he can find the Sunday school or the church that will meet his needs best. Girls, as a rule, attend both Sunday school and church more than boys do [46, 85]. Youth organizations within the church have a strong appeal to the young adolescent. While these organizations are usually more social than religious in function, they do serve as a tie between the young person and the church at a time when the tie could easily be broken as a result of the doubts experienced by the adolescent. Church attendance may fall off at this time as may active participation in church activities, but, generally, this is caused by a lack of activity on the part of the group, a lack of friendliness within the group, or by the fact that the meetings are "dead" [37, 58].

MORAL ATTITUDES AND BEHAVIOR

Adolescence puts a strong strain on the moral standards and behavior of the individual. When firm foundations of morality have been established during the years of childhood, they will stand up under the strain. At adolescence, the individual must make decisions for himself and must learn to guide his own behavior according to standards he has learned when he was a child. No longer can he expect the guidance of adults nor can he rely upon them to tell him what to do or what not to do. It is assumed that he knows what is right and what is wrong. Only in new areas of behavior, as in his relationships with members of the opposite sex, do adults feel that there is any real need for further moral training. Furthermore, the young adolescent discovers that there is a "double standard," with certain things considered wrong for girls but not so for boys. As this was not true during childhood days, it means that the young adolescent must reevaluate the moral concepts he learned when he was younger.

As a result of his taking moral matters into his own hands, the young adolescent frequently sets higher moral standards for himself and for others than can be attained at all times. When his behavior falls short of his standards, the young adolescent feels guilty and suffers from a troubled conscience. This leads to disillusionment and anger, directed partly toward himself because of his shortcomings and partly toward others whom he blames for his shortcomings. The young adolescent, however, is usually more willing to accept the blame than is the child [37]. If feelings of guilt occur too frequently or are too severe, the adolescent's feeling of personal adequacy is damaged and he attempts to escape, either into the daydream world or by threats to take his own life, or he develops an "I don't care" attitude. There is no question about the fact that some of the unhappiness of early adolescence stems from a guilty conscience for real or imagined shortcomings.

Perfectionism is not limited to the young adolescent's own behavior. The moral standards by which he judges others are just as high as those by which he judges his own behavior. He has a strong sense of fairness and is intolerant of those whose behavior falls below his standards [37]. This leads to friction and quarreling, which strain relationships that were once strongly cemented by admiration and affection. An intolerant attitude toward the shortcomings of others is as characteristic of the young adolescent as is his intolerant attitude toward his own shortcomings [42].

Moral Concepts. No longer is the individual willing to accept in an unquestioning manner the concepts of right and wrong of either his parents or his contemporaries, as he did when he was a child. He now builds up a moral code of his own, based upon the moral concepts established during childhood days but changed and modified to meet his more mature level of development. Inconsistencies in moral concepts, which he soon discovers from his discussions with other people and from his observations of their behavior, prove to be confusing to the young adolescent. In spite of this confusion, most young adolescents are able to work out a code of moral standards which differs from that of their childhood days and which will serve them well not only now but after they reach maturity. Things which, in childhood, they thought of as "wrong," such as smoking, flirting, divorce, or playing cards, are now accepted in a more tolerant way [82].

Changes from childhood to adolescence in attitudes toward lying show the influence of individual thinking on the part of the adolescent. While older children almost unanimously condemn lying on moral grounds, adolescents admit that "social lies," or lies to avoid hurting other people's feelings, are justified. As social sensitivity increases with age, so does tolerance toward lies of this sort [42]. Much the same sort of confusion is apparent in the attitude of junior high school students toward stealing. Their judgments of whether an act is or is not "stealing" have been found to depend somewhat on whether the property is private or corporate, stealing private property being considered worse than taking corporate property [79]. There is likewise a more tolerant attitude toward cheating in school, with a number of young adolescents feeling that it is justified because so many adolescents cheat and there is so much pressure on the student to maintain a high status in his work [71].

Moral Behavior. Adolescents are, for the most part, consistent in following their moral beliefs with actions of an equally high sort. The tendency to do things behind others' backs, to lie, or to take things if there is a good chance they will not be caught is far less frequent at this age than when the individual was younger. It becomes a matter of honor to try to live up to what he believes is right. There are, of course, exceptions to this general rule. Often a young adolescent does the wrong thing because he does not know how to deal with a problem in a better way. Coming home late from a date, for example, raises the problem of disobeying parents or being considered "tied to parental apron strings" by his friends. There are, on the other hand, times when the young adolescent willfully misbehaves, partly to assert his independence from adult authority and to convince his peers that he is a "good sport." Common misdemeanors, which reach their peak of frequency and severity around fourteen years of age, include annoying the teacher, bullying younger children, unpreparedness, destructiveness of school property, and truancy from school. Home misdemeanors consist of going out without telling parents, staying out beyond the set time, rudeness, and sex misdemeanors. As adolescents grow older, their behavior conforms more to social standards [99] (see Figure 51, page 247).

Some adolescents commit unsocial acts of a more serious nature. When these acts are markedly at variance with the accepted codes of conduct, the individual is known as a *juvenile delinquent.* While statistics on the number of adolescents who fall into the juvenile-delinquent category vary from community to community, there is evidence that the number of adolescents throughout the country who are arrested as juvenile delinquents has been increasing almost steadily since World War II. Boys contribute more heavily to this number than do girls and the percentage in urban areas is far greater than in rural areas [73].

Studies of juvenile delinquency have revealed that antisocial behavior is not an overnight development. Rather, those who later become juvenile delinquents begin to get into trouble as early as their kindergarten days. In general, their misbehavior is similar to that of nondelinquents only it is of a more serious and persistent sort. Most adolescents, for example, engage in minor pilfering or occasional truancy at some time or other but the juvenile delinquent steals consistently or spends more time away from school than in school. By twelve or thirteen years, misdemeanors that are too serious to be recognized as normal distinguish the delinquent from the nondelinquent [8].

Chapter II ~ *TEST SENTENCE COMPLETION*

There is little evidence that the juvenile delinquent behaves in an anti-social way because of ignorance of what society expects. Rather, he is motivated by feelings of resentment, hostility, defiance, or suspiciousness. He feels that society has rejected him and he, in turn, owes society nothing. Frequently, the juvenile delinquent is associated with an *adolescent gang* whose main source of pleasure comes from antisocial behavior. To

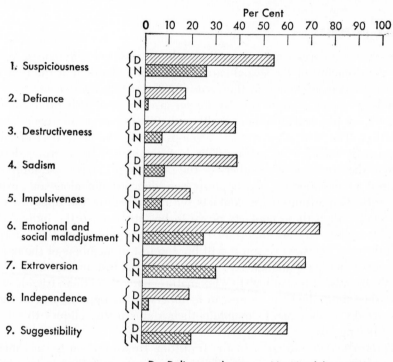

D = Delinquent boys   N = Nondelinquent boys

Fig. 66. Personality traits of delinquent and nondelinquent boys. (*Based on data of S. Glueck and E. T. Glueck, Unravelling juvenile delinquency. New York: Commonwealth Fund, 1950. From L. Cole, Psychology of adolescence, 4th ed. New York: Rinehart, 1954. Used by permission.*)

retain his status in the gang, the adolescent frequently engages in behavior of a type which he would not engage in if he were not influenced by group pressures. Such gangs are generally composed of adolescents who lack social acceptance in school, who come from poor neighborhoods, or from families where they have suffered rejection or been subjected to authoritarian discipline with emphasis on corporal punishment, and from families where poverty exists. Adolescents who come from homes disorganized by death, divorce, or desertion of the father are especially prone to delinquency. This is more true of girls and of younger boys than of older boys, and it explains the higher rate of delinquency among Negroes than among whites [103]. As a result of unfavorable environmental influences, the juvenile delinquent develops a personality pattern which leads to poor social adjustments [8, 38]. Figure 66 shows the differences in personality patterns of delinquent and nondelinquent boys.

SEX INTERESTS

Early sex interests are centered mostly on physical differences. With the development of the sexual capacities of the individual at the time of puberty comes a change in the form of interest that adolescents take in members of the opposite sex. No longer are boys and girls primarily interested in physical differences, although this interest never completely vanishes. The new interest that develops during the early part of adolescence is romantic in nature. This is accompanied by a strong desire to win the approval of members of the opposite sex. *Heterosexuality,* or interest in members of the opposite sex, depends not alone on sexual maturity. Opportunities for contacts with members of the opposite sex, especially when these contacts prove to be satisfying to the individuals involved, also play an important role in determining when this interest will develop and how strong it will be. Interest in members of the opposite sex is markedly influenced by patterns of interest among the adolescent's friends. Boys and girls who mature later than their friends find that they must show an interest in members of the opposite sex, as their friends do, if they are to maintain their status in the cliques to which they belong [50].

Pattern of Sex Interests. In the transition from aversion toward members of the opposite sex, characteristic of puberty, to falling in love with members of the opposite sex, it is quite usual for both boys and girls to center their affections first on a member of their own sex, older than they, who has qualities they admire, and then, later, on a member of the opposite sex who is distinctly older than they. When the attachment is for a person whom the adolescent knows and has personal contacts with, it is usually called a "crush"; when the attachment is for a person not known personally but admired from afar, it is generally referred to as "hero worshiping." However, this distinction is not always made and the latter attachment is also called a "crush."

The object of the adolescent's crush is a person who embodies the qualities the adolescent admires. This person becomes the focal point of the adolescent's admiration and love. Whether it be a teacher, a camp counselor, a sports star, an actor or actress, a crooner, or even an older relative or friend of the family, there is a strong desire on the adolescent's part to imitate this individual. If the object of affection is a person known to the adolescent, there is added to the desire to imitate a strong desire to be with the loved person, to do everything possible to win the favor and attention of that person, and to be constantly thinking and talking about the loved one. Crushes and hero worshiping generally reach their peak around fourteen years of age, after which there is a rapid decline in interest in these love objects [37]. There is no evidence that crushes are a barrier to later heterosexual adjustments [55].

Just before early adolescence draws to a close, interest in members of the opposite sex of approximately the same chronological age replaces interest in older individuals. At first, girls like any boy who will pay any attention to them. They do not discriminate. Much the same is true of boys. Girls in general rather than any girl in particular have a strong appeal for them. By the time a girl is fourteen years old, she normally shows a definite interest in boys of her own age. Boys of fourteen, by contrast, are still shy and hesitant in the presence of girls, though they secretly have a stronger interest in them than they show by their be-havior. This difference is due primarily to differences in age of sexual maturing. Boys, at this time, retain much of their surface antagonism toward girls.

Early love between the sexes is often referred to as *puppy love* by amused adults. Because of the newness of the love situation, and because of the feelings of insecurity that invariably accompany a new and diffi-cult situation, young adolescents frequently try to cover up their em-barrassment by pretending to be at ease and sophisticated. Wisecracking, or mental fencing, teasing, roughhousing, and pulling each other around are backhanded ways of showing mutual interest and are most frequently resorted to when other people are present. It is a bold, aggressive form of behavior as contrasted with the shy, tongue-tied behavior that accom-panies crushes or hero worshiping. Because girls mature earlier than boys, girls are more aggressive than boys in these early sex relationships.

Interest in members of the opposite sex is always accompanied by a desire to attract their attention. This may take different forms, such as affected mannerisms and speech, extremes in dress and hair styles, ap-parent indifference and rudeness to the individuals they want to attract, and participation in petting [26, 55]. Figure 67 shows changes in re-lations between the sexes (see also Figure 35, page 185).

In spite of the desire to be noticed by members of the opposite sex, young adolescent boys and girls are extremely shy and self-conscious when this desire is realized. This shyness is heightened when they are with a group of other boys and girls though it is present when they are alone with just one member of the opposite sex. Shyness and self-consciousness may be revealed in quiet, tongue-tied behavior but, among most adolescents, an attempt is made to cover up their shyness and this leads to noisy, boisterous laughing, aggressive reactions toward the opposite sex, and a tendency to talk too much about nothing. Early in the high school age, and often in junior high school, there is a pairing off

AGES 10 to 12
Antagonism shown
between sex groups

AGES 13 to 14
Girls become inter-
ested in boys, try to
attract their attention,
boys aloof

AGES 14 to 16
Boy group also shows
interest in girls;
some individuals
begin to pair off

AGES 16 to 17; ON
"Going out in couples"
becomes general

FIG. 67. Changes in boy-girl relationships from puberty to early adolescence. (*From "The seven stages in boy-girl relationships," in A. Scheinfeld, Women and men. New York: Harcourt, Brace, 1943. Used by permission.*)

among the boys and girls. This is the beginning of *dating*, which comes for girls between thirteen and fourteen years and, among boys, a year or so later. By the end of early adolescence, most boys and girls not only date with regularity but many of them *go steady*. Early dating is frequently in twosomes or threesomes. The young adolescent who feels unsure of himself finds it easier to cope with the situation in a small group than when alone. This early dating is *clique dating* in that girls of a clique arrange to do things with their friends and their dates. Even when boys and girls go steady, much of their dating in early adolescence is with clique members.

Dating activities consist mainly of attending school dances and athletic events, going to the movies, driving to places to dance, eat, and drink, engaging in some form of sport, such as tennis, bowling, or swimming, and watching television. Boys expect some petting on dates. When girls refuse to engage in petting, they are likely to find themselves dateless. This becomes a serious problem for the young adolescent girl of today. Most of the social activities of the school and of the cliques are organized in such a way that girls are not expected to attend unless accompanied by their "dates." Boys, on the other hand, are welcomed if they come alone or with a group of their friends because this guarantees extra boys for the activities. In communities where early dating and early going steady are the accepted practices, a girl must conform if she is to rate socially not only with members of the opposite sex but with her clique mates as well [21, 46]. As a result of early dating and going steady, there is an increase in marriages and premarital pregnancies among high school students. Girls more often marry boys who are out of school than those who are still in school. Boys, on the other hand, marry less frequently at this early age and, when they do, it is usually a girl in their class at school [57].

Curiosity about Sex. Curiosity about sex matters, which became very pronounced at puberty with the development of physical changes characteristic of that age, begins to wane during early adolescence, provided the individual has been able to get the information he wishes to satisfy his curiosity. There is still, however, a lively interest in sex though this is not likely to preoccupy the time and interest of young adolescents as much as it did earlier, during the puberty period. When girls or boys get together with members of their own sex, they are likely to talk about sex. The more intimate the group, the more intimate the subject of sex becomes. No longer do they seek information about the fundamental facts of sex. This knowledge they already have. Instead, they discuss such matters as what is real love, how can one tell if love is real or not, what is the sex relationship in marriage, problems related to menstruation, and sexual feelings and attractions [26, 55].

Experimentation with sex, to satisfy curiosity, begins during early adolescence or even during the puberty period. Manual manipulation, accompanied by a direct observation of the female reproductive anatomy, exhibitionistic sex play, attempts at intercourse, and oral contacts are common at this age. Petting, in the form of kissing, manual exploration, and manipulation by the boy of the girl's breasts and reproductive organs, has been reported by boys of the early adolescent years. Petting that is offensive to girls, especially when it is accompanied by attempted inter-course, occurs most often when younger adolescent girls date older boys, when the girl comes from a lower-class family, or when there has been steady and voluntary participation in erotic activity by the girl. Girls with older brothers are less frequently subjected to offensive petting than other girls because their brothers warn them and this serves to im-plant caution in the girls [52].

Kissing games are popular during early adolescence because they satisfy the individual's curiosity and, at the same time, give him sexual satisfaction. The liking for kissing increases markedly as early adolescence progresses [82] (see Figure 68). Masturbation as a form of sexual experimentation is common among both boys and girls during the early years of ado-lescence. While masturbation is often engaged in by children, it comes to a peak in frequency and in degree of satisfaction obtained during this period, and its practice is reported to range from an oc-casional indulgence to indulgence several times a day [55]. Because of the social taboos associated with masturbation, most boys and girls have strong feelings of guilt during and after indulgence. These feel-ings, however, are generally not strong enough to prevent the in-dulgence. The frequencies of different forms of sexual experimentation are shown in Figure 39, page 203.

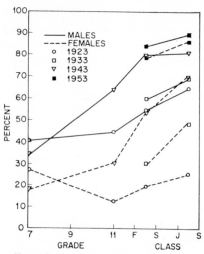

Fig. 68. Increase in liking "kissing" as adolescence progresses. (From S. L. Pressey and A. W. Jones, 1923–1953 and 20–60 age changes in moral codes, anxieties, and interests, as shown by the "X-O Tests." J. Psychol., 1955, 39, 485–502. Used by permission.)

FAMILY RELATIONSHIPS

The relationships of the young adolescent with the members of his family deteriorate as adolescence progresses. The fault lies on both sides. Parents far too often refuse to modify their concept of their child's abilities as he grows older, and, as a result, they treat him in much the same manner as they did when he was younger. In spite of this, they expect him to "act his age," especially when it comes to assuming respon-sibilities. Another source of conflict comes from the use of standards of behavior that were in vogue when the parents were adolescents. The adolescents who are most seriously affected are those whose parents grew up in another country where mores differed from those of the community in which the adolescent is growing up. Conflict is less when adolescents perceive that their parents' interests are similar to theirs and when they believe parents understand them and their needs [15, 19].

The blame for the friction between parents and adolescent children is not all on the parents' side. No one is more irresponsible, more difficult to live with, more unpredictable, or more exasperating than a young adolescent, with the possible exception of a preadolescent. Parents' patience is sorely tried during this transitional period of their children's lives and they cannot be blamed if they sometimes lose patience completely with their children. Constant criticism of parents, siblings, and the home, objections to duties and to the restraints their parents feel necessary, and failure to assume responsibilities in keeping with their age are difficult behavior patterns for parents to accept without criticism or punishment. These sources of irritation generally reach their peak between fourteen and fifteen years, after which there is an improvement in parent-child and sibling relationships [37, 60] (see Figure 69).

While the sources of friction between the adolescent and his parents are myriad, three very common sources of friction are almost universally found. The first stems from the methods of discipline used by parents and the adolescents' resentments against what they consider to be "childish" forms of punishment and unreasonable restraints on their behavior. The second common source of friction arises from the hypercritical attitude of the adolescent toward his parents, his siblings, and his home life. Parents who have made great sacrifices of time, energy, and money to give the adolescent the best home they can and as many advantages as they can afford, naturally resent this seeming lack of appreciation on the part of their children. The most common source of friction centers around the "latchkey" problems stemming from the new social life of the adolescent. These conflicts arise in connection with the people the adolescent associates with, especially members of the opposite sex, the places they go, what they do, when they return home, and what they wear. Conflicts about clothes are especially common in the case of mothers and daughters. From the ninth grade on, these conflicts increase and center around the problems of appropriateness of clothes, type of clothes, and amount of money spent for clothes. There is no class difference in number and severity of conflicts; mothers and daughters of all social classes engage in such conflicts [2].

Because the young adolescent has more contacts with the mother than the father, it is not surprising that there are more mother-adolescent than father-adolescent conflicts [23]. Usually conflicts with the mother reach their peak around fifteen years of age and then decrease; at seventeen years there is a rise in number of conflicts daughters have with their fathers. Conflicts of adolescent boys with their parents generally reach their peak around thirteen years of age and then begin to decline. The explanation for sex differences in conflicts is that adolescent girls are more restricted in their behavior than are boys [81]. After fifteen years of age, girls are less restricted by their mothers than they were earlier

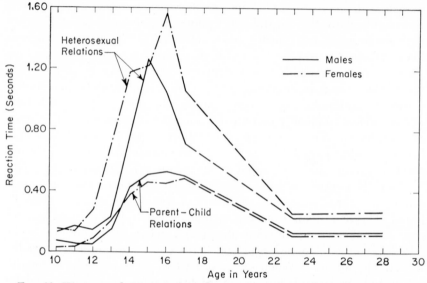

FIG. 69. Waxing and waning of conflicts with parents and members of the opposite sex as age progresses. (*Based on material of M. Powell, Age and sex differences in degree of conflict within certain areas of psychological adjustment. Psychol. Monogr., 1955, 69, No. 2. From S. L. Pressey and R. G. Kuhlen, Psychological development through the life span. New York: Harper, 1957. Used by permission.*)

and this leads to a decrease in mother-daughter friction [60]. As their daughters' early adolescence draws to a close, fathers become more concerned about the boys their daughters date than they were earlier, and this concern is largely responsible for the rise in father-daughter conflicts [23]. Changes in boys' and girls' attitudes toward their parents are shown in Figure 40, page 208.

Deterioration in family relationships during the early years of adolescence is not limited to the parent-child relationship. Relationships with their siblings suffer just as seriously as do those of parents and adolescents. The young adolescent treats his younger brothers and sisters with scorn and constantly finds fault with whatever they say or do. He is jealous of his older brothers and sisters because they enjoy privileges denied him and he resents the criticisms of these older brothers and sisters aimed at his immature behavior [37]. Relatives, especially those of the older generation, no longer are in favor with the young adolescent. He finds family gatherings "boring" and he does not hesitate to show how he feels. He deeply resents any criticism on the part of his relatives concerning his behavior and he objects to their giving him advice of any sort [2].

PERSONALITY

By early adolescence, both boys and girls are well aware of their good and bad traits and they appraise these in terms of similar traits in their friends. They are also well aware of the role personality plays in social relationships and this gives them a strong motivation to "improve their personalities" in the hopes of increasing their social acceptance. To do this, the adolescent must not only have a realistic self-concept but he must be willing to accept this concept [49]. The adolescent who accepts himself in the sense that he "likes" himself and feels that others find likeable qualities in him is better adjusted and makes better social adjustments than does the individual who is self-derogatory and whose attitude toward himself vacillates with the attitude of others toward him [94]. The age of maturing affects the individual's self-concept because it influences the way he is treated by adults and peers and the extent of his concern about his normalcy. The effects of early and late maturing are therefore apparent throughout early adolescence. Boys who are late maturers develop patterns of behavior which stem from their striving for status, while boys who are early maturers show more mature patterns of behavior, a reflection of self-acceptance [50, 72] (see Figure 52, page 256).

New factors enter into the individual's life at this time. These will leave their mark on his personality. What effect they will have, however, will be determined to a large extent by the foundation already established. An adolescent who finds himself in the role of a social outcast will be affected differently by this experience depending on what concept of himself he established when he was younger. If he had a fairly well established inferiority complex when adolescence began, his status in the adolescent group will intensify his feelings of inferiority. If, however, his concept of himself was that of an important person, his present role may modify this concept or it may leave it unaffected while he builds up rationalizations to explain to himself and others why he is not socially acceptable to his peers.

The changes that take place in personality patterns are due, partially at least, to the influence of social pressures. There are certain socially approved and socially disapproved personality traits for both boys and girls. In his desire to be socially accepted and to win the approval not only of his contemporaries but of the social group as a whole, the young adolescent strives to develop personality traits that will win for him approval and acceptance [49]. The young adolescent boy who is admired by his contemporaries must be a leader in games, daring, fearless, and personally acceptable. The approved pattern for girls includes such personality traits as good sportsmanship, activity, ability to organize games and parties, and being glamorous and fascinating. Broad-mindedness, cooperativeness, and reliability are personality traits both boys and girls expect their contemporaries to have [96].

Personality Factors. The factors influencing personality are much the same for the adolescent as for the child. The difference, however, is in emphasis. Some factors which were of relatively little importance during childhood now prove to be of great importance, while those of dominance in childhood may lose some of their strength in adolescence.

The adolescent becomes increasingly aware of likenesses and differences in *personal appearance.* Being different in appearance makes the adolescent feel inferior, even if this difference adds to his physical attractiveness. What his peers consider a "good" body build is used as the standard by which the adolescent judges his appearance. Even though he may deviate from this standard only temporarily, it is likely to leave its mark on the adolescent's self-concept. The influence of the "puberty fat period" has been found to persist through early adolescence, even after that temporary fat period had passed (see Figure 50, page 246). Any physical defect the adolescent may have becomes a source of embarrassment to him. This adds new problems to the adjustment problems every adolescent must face [74].

To the high school student, *clothes* are important not only because they improve the individual's appearance but also because they help the adolescent to identify himself with his peers. Clothes are selected to bring out the individual's good qualities, to cover up his defects, and to make him conform to what is in fashion among his friends. That clothes are important to the adolescent's concept of self has been emphasized by the effects of clothes on adolescent behavior. The adolescent who makes a poor appearance withdraws from activities with other young people and develops a negativistic attitude. He is worried about what others think of him and this makes him self-conscious. The well-dressed adolescent, by contrast, feels more at ease, less self-conscious, and this in turn makes him friendlier and more sociable [88].

The adolescent's *name* now becomes a source of concern to him. Names that are a handicap to an adolescent include those which are associated with stereotypes that are frowned on by society; those that are displeasing when combined with certain surnames; those that have been made unpleasant by certain associations, either personal or social; and those which lend themselves to nicknames that carry unpleasant connotations. The adolescent will dislike any name that makes him shy, embarrassed, or sensitive [4]. *Nicknames* that make the individual feel inferior are also disliked. This is especially true of family nicknames which make the adolescent feel that his family still regards him as "mama's little boy" [44].

In spite of the fact that adolescents spend less time with their parents than they did when they were younger and in spite of the strained relationship that frequently exists at this time, the *family* leaves its mark on the adolescent's personality. An unhappy family life produces marked emotional instability in the young adolescent. Parents who always welcome the children's friends to the home, who share joys and sorrows with their children, and who have enjoyable times with them are more likely to have well-adjusted sons and daughters than are parents whose relationship with their children is less favorable. Adolescents from broken homes, on the other hand, show many personality maladjustments [40]. Because adolescents identify themselves with the parent of their own sex, they acquire, through imitation of that parent, socially approved patterns of attitude and behavior. How marked an influence parents will have will therefore be influenced by the type of relationship the adolescent has with the parent of his own sex [78].

The social group of the adolescent's *peers* has a marked influence on his personality not only because the adolescent's concept of self is a reflection of his peers' concept of him but also because social pressures from the group influence the development of personality traits approved by the group. The more solidly a group is formed and the more secure the status of the adolescent within the group, the greater will be its influence on his personality [90]. Those adolescents who do not belong to any social group, or who are rejected because of minority group status or for some other reason, are unfavorably influenced by their peers because of the adverse effect of this isolation or rejection on their self-concepts. Because the social group is influenced by *cultural* standards, it expects each member to conform to these standards to be acceptable. Thus, the adolescent's personality is influenced by cultural standards more through the peer group than through the family, as is true of the child [40].

Perhaps no one factor plays as important a role in influencing the adolescent's self-concept and, thus, his personality, as *level of aspiration*. Typically, young adolescents set goals beyond their reach partly because they are unrealistic and therefore unable to assess their capacities accurately, and partly because they are subject to parental pressures to get ahead. When they fall below the goals they set for themselves, they are unhappy and dissatisfied. They feel inadequate and this makes them strive to live up to the goals by exerting pressure to do more; this, in turn, leads to anxiety or to the assumption of a defensive stand in which others are blamed for the adolescents' failures. Girls tend to overestimate their abilities and have more unrealistic aspirations than do boys. This is especially true when the girl has a crush on someone who is her ideal and whom she tries to imitate [7, 25, 40].

Personality Maladjustments. The problem child is likely to turn into a maladjusted individual during adolescence unless remedial steps are taken to overcome the problem behavior. Clinical studies have revealed that relatively few forms of maladjustment appear for the first time during adolescence unless there has been some marked physical or glandular change in the individual, or unless he has experienced some sort of severe trauma. More maladjusted adolescents have a case history of problem behavior dating back to the early years of childhood.

Adolescence, but especially the early part of the period, is inevitably a time of stress and maladjustment. This contrasts with the relative stability and tranquillity of the latter part of childhood. At this time, the individual is trying, by trial and error, to adjust himself to the new and strange role of the adult and to an environment suited more to adults than to children. Whether he will learn the adult roles and thus pass through this period successfully or fall a victim to mental disease and maladjustment in the form of regressive behavior will depend primarily upon the foundations laid in childhood and upon the degree of patience, understanding, and kindly guidance he receives from his parents [49]. Because school success, both academic and social, is so important to an adolescent, failure in either or both areas is often at the root of the maladjustments [35]. Adolescents from the upper and upper middle classes, especially those who are gifted, are generally better adjusted than those from the lower classes, or those who are less bright [14, 92].

Personality maladjustments reveal themselves through "danger signals" of greater or lesser severity during the early years of adolescence. The most common danger signals that are symptomatic of underlying trouble are irresponsibility which leads the adolescent to neglect his work or other duties in a desire to win social approval and to have a good time; aggressiveness of an exaggerated form which shows itself in a cocksureness in everything the adolescent says or does; feelings of insecurity at home or outside the home which cause the individual to conform to the group in a slavishly conventional manner; homesickness when away from the familiar surroundings of the family; feelings of martyrdom, not only at home but also when the adolescent is with his contemporaries; excessive daydreaming to compensate for lack of satisfaction from daily life; regression to earlier levels of behavior in an attempt to win favor and recognition; and rationalization, usually in the form of projection of the blame on others, to explain his shortcomings [49].

The poorly adjusted adolescent is an unhappy individual. He finds himself playing the role of a social isolate, he misses out on the good times his contemporaries are enjoying, and he finds little compensation for these losses in his relationships with the members of his family. While most young adolescents experience unhappiness in some degree, the poorly adjusted individuals not only experience unhappiness in more pronounced forms but they experience it more often. As a result of their unhappiness, they try to develop compensations which will take the place of the normal pleasures they miss and which they see their contemporaries enjoying. This results in more severe maladjustments and eliminates what hope they might otherwise have of becoming acceptable members of a group of their contemporaries. The personality defects which, throughout childhood, seemed too trivial to parents and teachers to be of concern and were thus neglected now exert their influence on the lives of the adolescents in such a manner as to exaggerate the unhappiness which otherwise might have been mild and transitory.

BIBLIOGRAPHY

1. Amatora, Sister M.: Free expression of adolescents' interests. *Genet. Psychol. Monogr.*, 1957, 55, 173–219.
2. Angelino, H., L. A. Barnes, and C. L. Shedd: Attitudes of mothers and adolescent daughters concerning clothing and grooming. *J. Home Econ.*, 1956, 48, 779–782.
3. Angelino, H., J. Dollins, and E. V. Mech: Trends in the "fears and worries" of school children as related to socioeconomic status and age. *J. genet. Psychol.*, 1956, 89, 263–276.
4. Arthaud, R. L., A. N. Hohneck, C. H. Ramsey, and K. C. Pratt: The relation of family name preferences to their frequency in the culture. *J. soc. Psychol.*, 1948, 28, 19–37.
5. Ausubel, D. P.: *Theory and problems of adolescent development.* New York: Grune and Stratton, 1954.
6. Ausubel, D. P., and H. M. Schiff: Some intrapersonal and interpersonal determinants of individual differences in socioempathic ability among adolescents. *J. soc. Psychol.*, 1955, 41, 39–56.
7. Ausubel, D. P., H. M. Schiff, and M. P. Zeleny: "Real-life" measures of level of academic and vocational aspirations in adolescents: relation to laboratory measures and to adjustment. *Child Develpm.*, 1953, 24, 115–168.
8. Bakwin, H.: Juvenile delinquency: *J. Pediat:* 1953, 42, 387–391; 1954, 44, 338–342.
9. Banham, K. M.: Obstinate children are adaptable. *Ment. Hyg., N.Y.:* 1952, 36, 84–89.

10. Barschak, E.: A study of happiness and unhappiness in the childhood and adolescence of girls in different cultures. *J. Psychol.*, 1951, 32, 173–215.
11. Beilin, H.: The pattern of postponability and its relation to social class mobility. *J. soc. Psychol.*, 1956, 44, 33–48.
12. Biddulph, L. G.: Athletic behavior and the personal and social adjustment of high school boys. *Res. Quart. Amer. phys. Educ. Ass.*, 1954, 25, 1–7.
13. Bonney, M. E.: A sociometric study of the peer acceptance of rural students in three consolidated high schools. *Educ. Adm. Supervis.*, 1951, 11, 234–240.
14. Bonsall, M. R., and B. Stefflre: The temperament of gifted children. *Calif. J. educ. Res.*, 1955, 6, 162–165.
15. Briggs, V., and L. R. Schulz: Parental response to concepts of parent-adolescent relationships. *Child Develpm.*, 1955, 26, 279–284.
16. Brim, O. G., and R. Forer: A note on the relation of values and social structure to life planning. *Sociometry*, 1956, 19, 54–60.
17. Brown, F. J.: *Educational sociology*, 2d ed. New York: Prentice-Hall, 1954.
18. Brown, M. L.: These high school fears and satisfactions. *Understanding the Child*, 1954, 23, 74–76, 88.
19. Cava, E. L., and H. L. Raush: Identification and the adolescent boy's perception of his father. *J. abnorm. soc. Psychol.*, 1952, 47, 855–856.
20. Chowdhry, K., and T. M. Newcomb: The relative abilities of leaders and non-leaders to estimate opinions of their own groups. *J. abnorm. soc. Psychol.*, 1952, 47, 51–57.
21. Christensen, H. T.: Dating behavior as evaluated by high-school students. *Amer. J. Sociol.*, 1952, 57, 580–586.
22. Christiansen, J. R., and T. R. Black: Group participation and personality adjustment. *Rur. Sociol.*, 1954, 19, 183–185.
23. Connor, R., T. B. Johannis, and J. Walters: Parent-adolescent relationships. *J. Home Econ.*, 1954, 46, 183–191.
24. Cook, E. S.: An analysis of factors related to withdrawal from high school prior to graduation. *J. educ. Res.*, 1956, 50, 191–196.
25. Crane, A. R.: Stereotypes of the adult held by early adolescents. *J. educ. Res.* 1956, 50, 227–230.
26. Crow, A.: Parental attitudes toward boy-girl relations. *J. educ. Sociol.*, 1955, 29, 126–133.
27. Dunsing, M.: Spending money of adolescents. *J. Home Econ.*, 1956, 48, 405–408.
28. Empey, L. T.: Social class and occupational aspiration: a comparison of absolute and relative measurement. *Amer. sociol. Rev.*, 1956, 21, 703–709.
29. Espenschade, A., R. R. Dable, and R. Schoendube: Dynamic balance in adolescent boys. *Res. Quart. Amer. phys. Educ. Ass.*, 1953, 24, 270–275.
30. Evans, H. M., and S. M. Cory: The problem-centered group and personal-social problems of young people. *Teach. Coll. Rec.*, 1950, 51, 438–459.
31. Ewald, M. O.: The emotionally disturbed child in the classroom. *Education,* 1954, 76, 69–72.
32. Ewens, W. P.: Experience patterns as related to vocational preferences. *Educ. psychol. Measmt*, 1956, 16, 223–231.
33. Feinberg, M. R.: Relation of background experience to social acceptance. *J. abnorm. soc. Psychol.*, 1953, 48, 206–214.
34. Frank, L. K.: Personality development in adolescent girls. *Monogr. Soc. Res. Child Develpm.*, 1951, 16, No. 53.
35. Gallagher, J. R.: Various aspects of adolescence. *J. Pediat.*, 1951, 39, 532–543.

36. Garrison, K. C., and B. V. Cunningham: Personal problems of ninth grade pupils. *Sch. Rev.*, 1952, 60, 30–33.
37. Gesell, A., F. L. Ilg, and L. B. Ames: *Youth: the years from ten to sixteen.* New York: Harper, 1956.
38. Glueck, S., and E. T. Glueck: *Unravelling juvenile delinquency.* New York: Commonwealth Fund, 1950.
39. Gough, H. G.: Predicting social participation. *J. soc. Psychol.*, 1952, 35, 227–233.
40. Havighurst, R. J.: Social class and personality structure. *Sociol. soc. Res.*, 1952, 36, 355–363.
41. Havighurst, R. J.: *Human development and education.* New York: Longmans, 1953.
42. Havighurst, R. J., and H. Taba: *Adolescent character and personality.* New York: Wiley, 1949.
43. Helfant, K.: Parents' attitudes vs. adolescent hostility in the determination of adolescent socio-political attitudes. *Psychol. Monogr.*, 1952, 66, No. 13.
44. Helper, M. M.: Learning theory and the self-concept. *J. abnorm. soc. Psychol.*, 1955, 51, 184–194.
45. Hess, R. D., and I. Goldblatt: The status of adolescents in American society: a problem in social identity. *Child Develpm.*, 1957, 28, 459–468.
46. Hollingshead, A. de B.: *Elmtown's youth.* New York: Wiley, 1949.
47. Holman, M.: Adolescent attitudes toward seeking help with personal problems. *Smith Coll. Stud. soc. Wk*, 1955, 25, 1–31.
48. Horrocks, J. E., and M. E. Buker: A study of the friendship fluctuations of preadolescents. *J. genet. Psychol.*, 1951, 78, 131–141.
49. Jersild, A. T.: *The psychology of adolescence.* New York: Macmillan, 1957.
50. Jones, M. C.: The later careers of boys who were early- or late-maturers. *Child Develpm.*, 1957, 28, 113–128.
51. Jones, M. C., and N. Bayley: Physical maturing among boys as related to behavior. *J. educ. Psychol.*, 1950, 41, 129–148.
52. Kanin, E. J.: Male aggression in dating-courtship relations. *Amer. J. Sociol.*, 1957, 63, 197–204.
53. Keislar, E. R.: A distinction between social acceptance and prestige among adolescents. *Child Develpm.*, 1953, 24, 275–283.
54. Keislar, E. R.: Peer group ratings of high school pupils with high and low school marks. *J. exp. Educ.*, 1955, 23, 375–378.
55. Kinsey, A. C., W. B. Pomeroy, C. E. Martin, and P. H. Gebhard: *Sexual behavior in the human female.* Philadelphia: Saunders, 1953.
56. Krogman, W. M.: The physical growth of the child. *In* M. Fishbein and R. J. R. Kennedy, *Modern marriage and family living.* New York: Oxford Univer. Press, 1957. Pp. 417–425.
57. Landis, J. T., and K. C. Kidd: Attitudes and polices concerning marriages among high school students. *Marriage Fam. Living*, 1956, 18, 128–136.
58. Landis, P. H.: *Adolescence and youth: the process of maturing,* 2d ed. New York: McGraw-Hill, 1952.
59. Landis, P. H.: The ordering and forbidding technique and teen-age adjustments. *Sch. and Soc.*, 1954, 80, 105–106.
60. Liccione, J. V.: The changing family relationships of adolescent girls. *J. abnorm. soc. Psychol.*, 1955, 51, 421–426.
61. Lowrey, L. G.: Adolescent frustrations and evasions. *In* P. H. Hoch and J.

Zubin, *Psychopathology of childhood.* New York: Grune and Stratton, 1955. Pp. 267–284.

62. Luchins, A. S.: On the theories and problems of adolescence. *J. genet. Psychol.,* 1954, 85, 47–63.

63. Lundberg, G. A., and L. Dickson: Interethnic relations in a high school population. *Amer. J. Sociol.,* 1952, 48, 1–10.

64. Maas, H. S.: The role of member in clubs of lower-class and middle-class adolescents. *Child Develpm.,* 1954, 25, 241–251.

65. Mallinson, G. G., and W. M. Crumrine: An investigation of the stability of interests of high-school students. *J. educ. Res.,* 1952, 45, 369–383.

66. Marks, J. B.: Interests, leadership, and sociometric status among adolescents. *Sociometry,* 1954, 17, 340–349.

67. McCary, J. L.: Ethnic and cultural reactions to frustration. *J. Pers.,* 1950, 18, 321–336.

68. McGuire, C.: Family and age-mates in personality formation. *Marriage Fam. Living,* 1953, 15, 17–23.

69. McKee, J. P., and D. H. Eichorn: The relation between metabolism and height and weight during adolescence. *Child Develpm.,* 1955, 26, 205–212.

70. Morgan, C. T., and E. Stellar: *Physiological psychology,* 2d ed., New York: McGraw-Hill, 1950.

71. Mueller, K. H.: Can cheating be killed? *Personnel Guid. J.,* 1953, 31, 465–468.

72. Mussen, P. H., and M. C. Jones: Self-conceptions, motivations, and interpersonal attitudes of late- and early-maturing boys. *Child Develpm.,* 1957, 28, 243–256.

73. New York Times Report: Delinquency rise worries U.S. aide. *The New York Times,* 1957, July 14.

74. Norris, H. J., and W. M. Cruickshank: Adjustment of physically handicapped adolescent youth. *Exceptional Child,* 1955, 21, 282–288.

75. Norton, J. L.: Pattern of vocational interest development and actual job choice. *J. genet. Psychol.,* 1953, 82, 235–262, 263–278.

76. Oppenheim, A. N.: Social status and clique formation among grammar school boys. *Brit. J. Sociol.,* 1955, 6, 228–245.

77. Orzack, L. H.: Preference and prejudice patterns among rural and urban school males. *Rur. Sociol.,* 1956, 21, 29–33.

78. Payne, D. E., and P. H. Mussen: Parent-child relations and father identification among adolescent boys. *J. abnorm. soc. Psychol.,* 1956, 52, 358–362.

79. Payne, R.: Development of occupational and migration expectations and choices among urban, small town, and rural adolescent boys. *Rur. Sociol.,* 1956, 21, 117–125.

80. Philblad, C. T., and C. L. Gregory: The role of test intelligence and occupational background as factors in occupational choice. *Sociometry,* 1956, 19, 192–199.

81. Powell, M.: Age and sex differences in degree of conflict within certain areas of psychological adjustment. *Psychol. Monogr.,* 1955, 69, No. 2.

82. Pressey, S. L., and A. W. Jones: 1923–1953 and 20–60 age changes in moral codes, anxieties, and interests, as shown by the "X-O Tests." *J. Psychol.,* 1955, 39, 485–502.

83. Psathas, G.: Ethnicity, social class, and adolescent independence from parental control. *Amer. sociol. Rev.,* 1957, 22, 415–423.

84. Recreation Survey: Recreational interests and needs of high school youth. *Recreation,* 1954, 47, 43–46.

85. Remmers, H. H., M. S. Myers, and E. M. Bennett: Purdue survey. *Purdue Opin. Panel*, 1951, 10, No. 3.
86. Resnick, J.: Toward understanding adolescent behavior. *Peab. J. Educ.*, 1953, 30, 205–208.
87. Rose, A. M.: Reference groups of high school youth. *Child Develpm.*, 1956, 27, 351–363.
88. Ryan, M. S.: *Psychological effects of clothing*. Ithaca, N.Y.: Cornell Univer. Agricultural Experiment Station, 1953, Bulls. 882, 898, 900.
89. Schiff, H.: Judgmental response sets in the perception of sociometric status. *Sociometry*, 1954, 17, 207–227.
90. Seidler, M. B., and M. J. Rivitz: A Jewish peer group. *Amer. J. Sociol.*, 1955, 61, 11–15.
91. Silverman, S. S.: Clothing and appearance: their psychological implications for teen-age girls. *Teach. Coll. Contr. Educ.*, 1945, No. 912.
92. Sims, V. M.: Relations between social-class identification and personality adjustment of a group of high school and college students. *J. soc. Psychol.*, 1954, 40, 323–327.
93. Singer, S. L., and B. Stefflre: A note on racial differences in job values and desires. *J. soc. Psychol.*, 1956, 43, 333–337.
94. Spivack, S. S.: A study of a method of appraising self-acceptance and self-rejection. *J. genet. Psychol.*, 1956, 88, 183–202.
95. Stacey, L. L., and M. L. Reichen: Attitudes toward death and future life among normal and subnormal adolescent girls. *Exceptional Child*, 1954, 20, 259–262.
96. Steiner, I. D.: Some social class values associated with objectively and subjectively defined social class membership. *Soc. Forces*, 1953, 31, 327–332.
97. Stephenson, R. M.: Mobility orientation and stratification of 1,000 ninth graders. *Amer. sociol. Rev.*, 1957, 22, 204–212.
98. Stogdill, R. M.: Personal factors associated with leadership: a survey of the literature. *J. Psychol.*, 1948, 25, 35–71.
99. Stouffer, G. A. W., and J. Owens: Behavior problems identified by today's teachers and compared with those reported by E. K. Wickman. *J. educ. Res.*, 1955, 48, 321–331.
100. Strang, R.: Adolescents' views on one aspect of their development. *J. educ. Psychol.*, 1955, 46, 423–432.
101. Strang, R.: Gifted adolescents' views on growing up. *Exceptional Child*, 1956, 23, 10–15, 20.
102. Strang, R.: Students' perceptions of factors affecting their studying. *Ment. Hyg.*, N.Y., 1957, 41, 97–102.
103. Toby, J.: The differential impact of family disorganization. *Amer. sociol. Rev.*, 1957, 22, 505–512.
104. Tryon, C. M.: Evaluation of adolescent personality by adolescents. *Monogr. Soc. Res. Child Develpm.*, 1939, 4, No. 4.
105. Warnath, C. F.: The relation of family cohesiveness and adolescent independence to social effectiveness. *Marriage Fam. Living*, 1955, 19, 346–348.
106. Wolman, B.: Spontaneous groups of children and adolescents in Israel. *J. soc. Psychol.*, 1951, 34, 171–182.
107. Youmans, E. G.: Occupational expectations of twelfth grade Michigan boys. *J. exp. Educ.*, 1956, 24, 259–271.

» 9 «

Late Adolescence

Late adolescence, like early adolescence, is a transitional period in the individual's life. The adjustments to a mature status and to mature levels of behavior, begun during early adolescence, are gradually completed at this time. The developmental tasks of adolescence (see pages 14 to 15) which serve as a basis for adult adjustments should normally be completed before the individual reaches legal maturity to enable him to assume his status in adult society. Most adolescents make greater strides in achieving this goal during late adolescence than during early adolescence partly because they have already laid the foundations for mature behavior during early adolescence, partly because they have a more clearly defined status now than they had earlier and, as a result, know what is expected of them, and partly because they have a stronger motivation to prepare themselves for the independence which legal maturity will bring them than they had earlier when this time of independence seemed so remote.

Late adolescence, which is part of the adolescent period, is recognized as beginning around seventeen years of age, the time when the average American boy or girl attains the status of a senior in high school. As was emphasized in the preceding chapter, the attainment of a recognized status both at school and in the home serves as a motivation to the adolescent to acquire more mature behavior patterns and, at the same time, gives him a more definite pattern of expected behavior as a goal to strive for. Whether or not he reaches this goal before he becomes twenty-one years of age has no influence on his attainment of adult status. He is automatically an *adult*, with all the legal rights, privileges, and respon-

326

sibilities of an adult, when he reaches that age. This contrasts markedly with primitive cultures which withhold the status of adulthood, regardless of chronological age, until the adolescent has demonstrated, at the *puberty rites,* that he has mastered the developmental tasks of youth sufficiently well to be prepared to assume successfully the status of adulthood.

To distinguish the older adolescent from the younger, several *names* are commonly applied to boys and girls in late adolescence. They are often referred to as "youth," or as "young men" and "young women." The emphasis on the labels "men" and "women" indicates that society recognizes a maturity of behavior not found in the same individuals during the early years of adolescence. But, because they are not legally mature, older adolescents cannot correctly be labeled "men" and "women" and for that reason, the term "young" is applied to distinguish them from adults. Although the older adolescent is a teenager until he reaches twenty years of age, the label "teenager" is rarely applied to the older adolescent because, in our modern culture, this term has come to be so closely associated with the characteristic patterns of behavior of the young adolescent that it would not only give an incorrect picture of the level of development of the older adolescent but it would be deeply resented by the older adolescent who associates this label with behavior patterns characteristic of his younger years.

Characteristics of Late Adolescence. The instability of early adolescence is gradually replaced by greater *stability* as adolescence progresses. One can count on the older adolescent more than on the younger and the older adolescent can count on himself. This change is especially apparent in the greater stability of interests, whether in clothes, recreation, or choice of a life career; in his friendships with members of his own sex as well as with members of the opposite sex; in his emotional behavior, especially in the decrease in moodiness; and in his attitudes, which are not easily swayed by propaganda or the opinions of others, as they were during early adolescence [74] (see Figure 69, page 316).

Because of his greater stability, the older adolescent makes better adjustments to life. How early in adolescence and how successfully he will replace his earlier instability with stability will depend largely upon the environment in which he has grown up. Should he remain in the family home, and should his parents tend to overprotect him, he is likely to remain immature in this area of his development. On the other hand, opportunities to live away from parental overprotectiveness, in camps, boarding schools, colleges, or in the armed services, will give the adolescent an opportunity to make his own decisions, free from parental pressures, and this will result in greater stability on his part. Furthermore, people other than his immediate family will not accept instability in the older adolescent with as much tolerance as parents will and this gives the adolescent a motivation to become more stable. The adolescent who has grown up in a large family, where more is expected of him and where there is likely to be less parental overprotectiveness, is generally a more stable individual in adolescence than is the individual from a smaller family [15].

Many of the *problems* that arose in the early years of adolescence and which were not satisfactorily solved at that time persist into late adolescence. In addition, new problems relating to new demands on the older adolescent arise. Unless the earlier problems have been solved to the adolescent's satisfaction before the new ones occur, he is likely to feel hopelessly weighed down by them and at a loss to know where or to whom to turn for help. If, however, the adolescent learned, when he was younger, how to meet smaller problems, he is then better able to deal satisfactorily wtih the larger problems that confront him in the closing years of adolescence. He is able to attack new problems in an objective manner, make his decision without relying unduly upon parents, teachers, or friends, and then he is willing to stand by the decision he has made unless there is evidence to show that it was wrong. An intellectually immature person of the same age, by contrast, will rely upon others for help in making his decisions; he will be influenced by prejudices and superstitious beliefs and will either want to change his decision if he discovers it meets with criticism from others or he will be rigid in his adherence to a decision even when there is evidence that it is wrong [46, 74].

The problems of the older adolescent are, in general, much the same as those faced by the younger adolescent. How he meets these problems and how mature his attack on them is are the factors that distinguish the younger from the older adolescent. And, of the many problems the older adolescent must face, the severity of each will be influenced by the adolescent's pattern of living, whether he is still a student or at work, and whether he is living with his family or away from home. In general, his problems relate to personal attractiveness, social and family adjustment, career and life work, money, academic success, and sex relationships. Young men generally find problems relating to money and sex most serious while for young women, the most serious problems are those in the areas of personal attractiveness, social and family relationships [89, 100].

Many older adolescents, as is true of younger adolescents, feel that they are misunderstood by their families, teachers, friends, and employers. This intensifies their problems and results in a psychological isolation from possible sources of help in meeting their problems. When, however, they discover that others have problems similar to theirs, their attitudes change and they attack their problems more aggressively. In general, the older adolescent learns how to solve the problems he encounters with increasing success with each passing year and, as a result, he is better adjusted, happier, and easier to live with than the young adolescent whose inability to cope successfully with his problems makes him moody, irritable, and obstinate. He is far less of a problem for his family and for others with whom he is associated than is the young adolescent [7].

How *happy* or unhappy the older adolescent is will be greatly influenced by the degree of adjustment he makes in the home and in his social contacts. This, in turn, will be influenced by the success with which he solves the problems he encounters. Late adolescence, in general, is a happier period of life than early adolescence partly because the older adolescent is granted a status more in keeping with his level of development. He is given more independence and consequently suffers from fewer frustrations; he is more realistic about his capacities and sets goals more within his reach; and he has built up a degree of self-confidence based on knowledge of past successes which counteracts some of the feelings of inadequacy that plague the young adolescent.

Because few adults separate early from late adolescence, there is a tendency, when asked to think back over their lives and rate different periods in terms of happiness, to think only of the unhappiness they experienced during their high school days. As a result, retrospective reports place adolescence in the general category of "unhappy ages" [93]. However, questioning of college students reveals that they feel the latter years of adolescence are happier than the earlier years because there is better adjustment with their families and friends, and their relationships with members of the opposite sex are more satisfactory than they were in the early days of dating when the newness of the experience made them unsure of their ability to cope with the situation adequately [55]. When the wants of an individual are met and satisfied, the individual will be happy. The stronger the want, the more essential it is to meet it satisfactorily if the individual is to be happy.

PHYSICAL GROWTH

The growth spurt that started at puberty and continued at a diminishing rate during early adolescence gradually halts during late adolescence. What increase there is in height and weight at this age is barely perceptible. This enables the older adolescent to integrate the functions of the different muscular patterns and, as a result, the awkwardness that was characteristic of the preceding period gradually rights itself. How *tall* or short, how *heavy* or light the adolescent will be when his growth is completed depends upon such factors as hereditary endowment, prenatal and postnatal feeding and health, racial stock, general environmental conditions, opportunities for exercise during the growth years, and climatic conditions. Age of maturing likewise influences the ultimate size of the individual, with late maturers tending to be somewhat shorter than early maturers [9].

The average American woman of today is 66 inches tall and weighs 135 pounds; the average American man is 69.5 inches and weighs 152 pounds. Both height and weight are at their mature levels around eighteen years for girls and a year or so later for boys [54] (see Figure 55, page 270). Individual differences in weight are far greater, both between the sexes and within the two sex groups, than are differences in height. There is no evidence to show that age of maturing has any permanent effect on weight, though early maturers are, on the average, heavier than late maturers until the growth spurt has been completed [9]. What increases in weight there are in late adolescence are generally distributed in areas of the body where previously there was little or no fat. As a result, the scrawny look of the young adolescent gradually gives way to the rounded curves of the older adolescent.

The *disproportions* of the young adolescent, which were the cause of such great concern to him, gradually right themselves in late adolescence as the individual's body takes on the form of the adult. Gradually the features which lagged behind in their growth catch up with the more rapidly developing features and, as a result, they now are in correct proportion as measured by adult standards (see Figures 14 and 46, pages 82 and 235). The too-large *nose*, for example, now begins to be in correct proportion as the lower *jaw*, the last part of the face to attain its mature size, grows larger and the *lips* become fuller (see Figure 31, page 171). As the *chest* broadens and the *trunk* elongates, the waistline drops and the scrawny look of the young adolescent's body disappears. By late adolescence, the *breasts* and *hips* of a girl are fully developed so that her body now has the pleasing curves of the mature woman. Late maturers tend to have slightly broader *shoulders* than those who mature early. The *legs* of early-maturing boys and girls have a tendency to be stocky; those of late-maturing individuals tend to be more slender. Much the same pattern is found in the shape of the *arms*. The shape of the upper arm follows the growth of the muscles, which reach their mature size shortly after late adolescence begins [9]. Figure 70 shows the effects of age of maturing on body proportions when growth is completed.

Measurements of different *bones* indicate that the skeleton stops growing at an average age of eighteen years. *Tissues* other than bones continue to develop after the bones have reached their mature size. The third molars or "wisdom teeth," for example, frequently do not erupt until late in adolescence or early in the twenties. Although the *secondary sex characteristics* are normally mature in size and functioning late in adolescence, the *sex organs* may not be mature for a year or two later. Changes in skin texture and coloring, which proved to be a source of great concern to young adolescents, are nearly complete when late adolescence begins. *Acne* and other *skin disturbances* gradually disappear and the skin now is free from blemishes except in cases of indiscreet eating or at the time of the menstrual period in girls. The excessive oiliness of the young adolescent's skin, resulting from the temporarily increased activity of the sebaceous, or oil-producing glands, subsides and the skin and hair of the older adolescent are less oily than they were several years before. By late adolescence, the *hair* on the face, the body, and the head has reached mature growth.

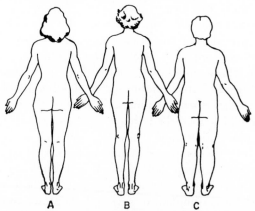

FIG. 70. Three girls, at eighteen years, who matured differently. *A* was accelerated; *B* was retarded; *C*'s growth was irregular. (*From N. Bayley, Individual patterns of development. Child Develpm., 1956, 27, 45–74. Used by permission.*)

The changes in the structure and functioning of the *internal organs*, begun during early adolescence, continue through late adolescence until a mature level of development has been reached. The *heart*, which at the age of twelve years is seven times as heavy as it was at birth, grows rapidly so that, at the age of seventeen or eighteen years, it is twelve times as heavy as it was at birth. By contrast, the increase in the *veins* and *arteries* is only 15 per cent. At the end of adolescence, the ratio of the size of the heart to the arteries is 290 to 61, as compared with a ratio of 25 to 20 at birth. Throughout childhood, there is little difference between the sexes in *blood pressure*. With puberty, there is an increase in blood pressure for both boys and girls, with boys having a higher blood pressure than girls.

At the age of seventeen years, the lung capacity of girls has almost reached its mature level; for boys, the mature level is not reached for several years after that. Because of this, the difference in *lung capacity* for the two sexes becomes increasingly greater from the beginning of adolescence to the time when the mature level of development has been reached. In boys, the greater increase in the size, capacity, and power of the lungs is made possible by the broadening and elongating of the bones of the chest. The rapid growth in the *digestive system* that took place during early adolescence slows down during late adolescence. With this slowing down and the slowing down of growth in height and weight comes a decrease in appetite. Added to this is a strong motivation to curtail food intake so as to keep the figure from becoming too fat. This motivation is especially strong among older adolescent girls who are more or less constantly "on a diet." How successfully they will be able to keep to their diets will depend largely upon how well adjusted they are both emotionally and socially [86].

Good health and *resistance to disease* are the rule rather than the exception to the rule during late adolescence. Adolescents who have had a healthy childhood are more likely to be healthy in late adolescence than are those whose childhood was marked by a series of illnesses. Similarly, good health habits established in childhood will go a long way toward guaranteeing a healthy adolescence. Even the menstrual discomforts and pain which disturbed the young adolescent girl are far less serious for the older adolescent. Those who are well adjusted make extra efforts to overcome the temporary handicap menstruation may cause and, as a result, are able to keep their physical and intellectual achievements up to standard when they have a goal to reach. Those who are poorly adjusted, by contrast, complain of severe discomforts and intensify their feelings of inadequacy to cope with the problems of their menstrual periods [75].

Like the younger adolescent, the older adolescent frequently uses illness as a form of escape from unpleasant duties or responsibilities. Because he worries about different situations he feels inadequate to meet successfully, he often makes himself sick by bringing on headaches, digestive disturbances, or sleeplessness. Real upsets are frequently exaggerated to the point that the adolescent believes he is too sick to face the situation that confronts him. *Imaginary* illness is more frequent among girls than among boys and is more often brought on by social situations in which members of the opposite sex are involved than by school or college work [82].

MOTOR SKILLS

The awkwardness which is so common during the early years of adolescence is generally a thing of the past when late adolescence begins.

The older adolescent has gained control of his enlarged body and has learned how to use it as successfully as he did when he was younger. Furthermore, the increase in physical strength that accompanies the growth of the muscular system motivates him to make use of his newly acquired strength. In boys, where muscular strength surpasses that of girls, pride in achievement motivates them to acquire skills of a complicated sort which they were incapable of acquiring when they were younger.

Marked sex differences in physical strength appear in late adolescence. This is the result not of exercise but of the maturation of boys' muscles to a degree that far surpasses that of girls. Boys, as a rule, do not realize that their muscular superiority comes from natural development and are likely to feel superior to girls because of their excellence in this area of their development. Girls, on the other hand, withdraw from situations where their muscular inferiority would be obvious, such as athletic contests or games where speed is an essential factor.

For boys, competitive athletic skills are among the chief sources of social esteem. This accounts for the strong interest most older adolescent boys have in competitive sports, either as active participants or passive spectators, and for the fact that girls, during the later adolescent period, show a declining interest in sports as participants but an increasing interest as spectators. Because of the social esteem associated with muscular strength, physical strength plays an important role in the social adjustments of boys in the late years of adolescence. Since physical strength is not so important a factor of prestige among girls as it is among boys, girls concentrate their efforts on developing skills where strength is not important. They take delight in dancing in the most intricate manner or in diving and other sports where muscular coordination is far more important than strength. When they do compete in athletics, it is with girls whose abilities are more on a par with theirs than are the abilities of boys.

EMOTIONS IN LATE ADOLESCENCE

The heightened emotionality, so characteristic of the early years of adolescence, gradually subsides, provided environmental adjustments are made to meet the new capacities and demands of an older adolescent. However, there is likely to be a period of emotional tension toward the end of adolescence which comes from new problems that normally present themselves at that age and to the rebellion against adult restrictions, especially on the part of girls. At this time, problems related to their romances are very real. So long as the romance is moving along smoothly, the adolescent is happy. But when things begin to go wrong, the adolescent sinks into states of despondency. Then, too, there are worries about his future which become very serious when he faces the end of his schooling. Nervous tension in college students, for example, is shown in nervous habits, especially of the oral and facial types [103].

Emotional Patterns. The older adolescent experiences much the same emotions as the child and the young adolescent, but there are differences in the frequency with which different emotions are aroused, the intensity of these emotions, the typical responses made, and the types of stimuli that give rise to them.

ANGER. Of all the emotions, anger is aroused in late adolescence more often than any other emotion. *Thwarting of self-assertion,* or restraints on the adolescent's desire to do something he wants to do, and *interruption of habitual activities* are the two most common causes of anger at this age. Illustrations of situations that thwart self-assertion are unjust accusations, insulting or sarcastic comments, and unwelcome advice. When such habitual activities as studying or sleeping are interrupted, they give rise to anger. People more often cause anger among adolescents than do things. Failure to accomplish what one sets out to do, to come up to one's own expectations, likewise gives rise to anger. Girls respond more often and more violently to social situations than do boys while boys are more often angered by things. The number of anger experiences the older adolescent has depends more on his environment than on his age. The more thwarting there is, the more often will he become angry [3, 50].

The older adolescent has generally learned to keep his angry responses under control to the point where he no longer kicks, hits, and throws things. He does, however, try to get his revenge in other ways, the most common of which is tongue-lashing. Name calling, sarcastic comments, swearing, and ridiculing others are his way of hitting back. In addition, he may substitute for the violent reactions of the earlier years such activities as pacing the floor, going for a walk, throwing things within his reach, becoming sulky and refusing to speak, or by mannerisms which he knows irritate people, such as whistling under his breath or tapping on the table [36]. The duration of an angry outburst in late adolescence is longer than in early adolescence because of the older adolescent's attempts to keep his anger under control instead of reacting with violent outbursts as he did when he was younger [50].

FEAR AND WORRY. The older adolescent fears fewer things but worries more than he did when he was younger. By the time adolescence comes to a close, the individual should be relatively free of fears that come from the external environment. There should also be a waning of fears of people and social situations as the individual's social experiences increase and as he has opportunities to meet people of all types. Fears of his own ineptitudes, or fears arising from imaginary situations may, on the other hand, increase as adolescence progresses [3].

Like the younger adolescent, the older adolescent does not run away from a frightening situation, no matter how great his fear may be. He stands his ground, even though he may become tongue-tied and shake so that all can see him. If he anticipates an unpleasant situation or one that may prove to be frightening to him, such as having to speak before a group or meet members of the opposite sex who are strangers to him, he is likely to shun the situation, offering some plausible excuse for his absence. He becomes quite adept at this as he grows older and plans his activities in such a way that he can truthfully say, "I have another engagement," when something comes up that he does not want to do or that he is hesitant about facing.

Worries, or imaginary fears, are far more common and more intense than are fears of real situations at this age. Few adolescents escape worrying at some time or other, especially when they hear their friends say they are worried about this or that. Many of the worries of the older adolescent are similar to those of the younger adolescent, especially if he is still in school or college where money, academic work, and popularity are all problems confronting him as they did when he was younger [50]. With the trend toward earlier marriage and changed patterns of courtship, worries about being popular with members of the opposite sex, looks, marriage, money, friends, family, and being unfairly treated are especially common. In general, most of these worries stem, either directly or indirectly, from feelings of inadequacy. The number of worries the older adolescent has will be influenced by many factors, especially his socioeconomic status, family conditions, past successes or failures, and the number and severity of worries of the people with whom he is most intimately and most frequently associated [70]. Changes in worries with age are shown in Figure 71.

JEALOUSY. Toward the middle or end of adolescence, interest in members of the opposite sex in general changes to an interest in one individual of the opposite sex. With this shift of interest comes a proprietary interest in that individual accompanied by a feeling of uncertainty about that individual's feelings. Under such conditions, jealousy is inevitable. Like the child who is unsure of his mother's love after the arrival of a new member of the family, the adolescent is never sure of what the loved one is doing when out of sight. Both boys and girls experience jealousy in their heterosexual relationships at this age [50]. In the case of girls, however, the jealousy is likely to be more intense than in the case of boys because it is they who must play the passive role and not take aggressive steps to hold onto what they want as boys do.

Any suspicion of a waning of interest on the part of the loved one or an unexplained lateness for a date or a last-minute canceling of a date will give rise to suspicions on the girl's part that invariably include the possibility of another girl for whom the boy has developed a romantic attachment. When jealousy is aroused, it usually expresses itself in verbal fighting rather than in bodily attack as is true of children. The use of sarcasm when speaking to the person who has aroused the jealousy, "sticking a knife in the back" by talking against that person when he is

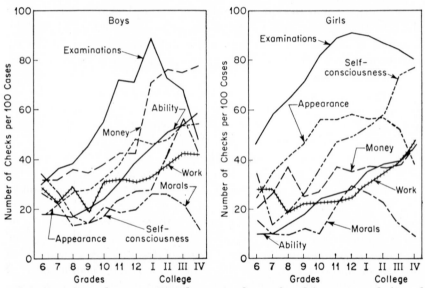

Fig. 71. Age trends in worries and anxieties during the adolescent period. (*Based on unpublished data of S. L. Pressey. From S. L. Pressey and R. G. Kuhlen, Psychological development through the life span. New York: Harper, 1957. Used by permission.*)

not there to defend himself, or using veiled suggestions about his character or moral standards are typically adolescent forms of hitting back at those against whom the individual's jealousy has been directed.

ENVY. The older adolescent is fully aware of the prestige value of expensive clothes, a car, and a large home. He realizes that those who are popular are in a favored socioeconomic position where they can have material possessions which many of their friends do not have. Furthermore, those who hold leadership positions are more likely to be from the favored than from the less favored socioeconomic groups. And, finally, in heterosexual relationships, boys and girls who have plenty of this world's goods have an obvious advantage over those who are less favored. It is not surprising, then, that material possessions have strong appeal for the older adolescent.

When an adolescent is envious of the possessions of others, he rarely keeps this fact to himself. Instead, he complains about his own bad fortune, he labels those who have what he would like to have as "lucky," and he makes others uncomfortable by his self-pity. Other adolescents take jobs to earn the necessary money to get these things or they find an easy approach to the problem through stealing. Back of much juvenile delinquency is envy of others more fortunate than the delinquent.

HAPPINESS. There are, in general, four types of situations that give rise to pleasant emotional reactions at this age. The first consists of *good adjustments* to the situation in which the individual finds himself. When the adolescent "fits," he is happy [50]. When, on the other hand, he feels that he is a misfit, he is unhappy and discontented. The ability to *perceive the comic* element in a situation is the second cause of happiness in adolescence. What an adolescent perceives as comic, however, varies according to his intellectual level, how he feels at the moment, what his previous experiences have been, and many other factors. The one thing that older adolescents rarely perceive as comic is a situation in which they are personally involved and in which the source of ridicule concerns them. While he thoroughly enjoys laughing at others, the older adolescent finds it quite a different story when the joke is on him. His inability to enjoy subjective humor stems from the fact that he is insecure in his feelings and is sensitive to the opinions of others.

Like the younger adolescent, the older adolescent may experience joy in situations in which he feels *superior* and in situations which offer an *outlet* for *pent-up emotional energy*, especially that of an unpleasant nature such as anger, fear, or jealousy. There is far less of the uncontrolled giggling and crying among older adolescents than among younger and, as good social adjustments are gradually being made, the older adolescent derives less intense satisfaction from feeling superior to his contemporaries than he did when he was younger.

AFFECTION. Because the older adolescent's affection is concentrated on one individual at a time, it is more intense than at any previous time in his life. There is a marked trend toward concentration of affection on one individual of the opposite sex, together with an idealization of that individual, which adds to the intensity of the emotional reaction. Not all older adolescents, however, concentrate their affection on one individual or on members of the opposite sex. Many have deep affection for a small circle of friends of the same sex, some concentrate their affection on a member of the same sex as a form of hero worship, while still others have a deeper affection for a parent than for anyone else. If, however, the adolescent is well adjusted, he generally falls in love with a member of the opposite sex before the adolescent years come to a close [50].

Emotional Maturity. The older adolescent recognizes the importance of learning to control his emotional reactions while, at the same time, not allowing them to be so controlled that they make him nervous, irritable, and edgy. The individual has achieved maturity in this area of his development if, by the end of adolescence, he does not "blow up" emotionally when others are present but waits for a convenient time and place to let off emotional steam in a socially acceptable manner. He assesses a situation critically before responding to it emotionally instead of reacting to it on its surface value, as the child or immature person does. This, in turn, results in his ignoring many stimuli which, when he was younger, he would have reacted to emotionally. And, finally, the emotionally mature person is stable in his emotional responses and does not swing from one emotional reaction or mood to another, as he did when he was younger [50, 52].

SOCIAL BEHAVIOR

In late adolescence, there is a narrowing down of the circle of intimate friends or chums and a broadening of the group. This means that the older adolescent has fewer intimate friends than he had when he was younger, more friends of a less intimate type, and more acquaintances. Another outstanding difference that becomes apparent at this age is the shifting of interest in friends of the same sex to friends of the opposite sex. While the older adolescent still maintains his friendships with members of his own sex, there is a growing preference for friends of the opposite sex. This change occurs slightly earlier in girls than in boys because of the more precocious sexual development of the girl. Improvements in different forms of social behavior are shown in the ratings given in Figure 50, page 246.

The slavish conventionality of the younger adolescent, which came from feelings of insecurity in the new social situations he was meeting for the first time, gradually gives way to *self-assertiveness* [50]. Instead of trying to submerge his individuality so that he is just one of a group cut from the same pattern, there is now a desire to be recognized as an individual and to win the approval of the group. While early attempts at self-assertiveness are often crude, through experimentation the older adolescent learns what is socially approved and what is not. He then uses more subtle ways of attracting attention, such as wearing the latest and most becoming styles of clothes instead of clothes of bright and conspicuous colors, expressing somewhat radical points of view in place of the crude boasting of personal possessions and achievements, or telling amusing stories in place of off-color jokes.

As a result of broader opportunities for social participation, the older adolescent's *social insight* improves. He is now able to judge members of the opposite sex as well as members of his own sex better than he could when he was younger and, as a result, he makes better adjustments in social situations and quarrels less than he did when he was younger [5] (see Figure 62, page 293). How well he adjusts to others is influenced by the level of his social insight, which in turn influences the degree of his *social participation* [34]. The greater the social participation, the greater the adolescent's *social competency*, as seen in his ability to dance, carry on conversations, play the sports and games that are popular with individuals of his age, and know the socially correct way to behave in different social situations. The older adolescent who has been an active participant in social affairs during the early years of adolescence is generally competent in these areas and, as a result, he has self-confidence which is expressed in poise and ease in social situations [16].

Social discrimination, or what is popularly known as "snobbishness," generally reaches its peak during the years of late adolescence. There is a strong tendency on the part of both boys and girls to discriminate against those whom they consider their social inferiors, either because of race, color, religion, or socioeconomic status. The adolescent is intentionally rude to people whom he considers his inferiors. He makes a point of talking against such individuals, behind their backs, and takes delight in seeing to it that they are excluded from parties and other social gatherings. This intolerance normally begins to wane as adolescence comes to a close, unless group pressures are strong and group opinion unfavorable [44]. The older adolescent, especially if he has been away from home in school, college, the armed services, or at work, modifies his attitude toward people against whom he was formerly prejudiced as his insight increases and his understanding of why they behave as they do grows through personal contacts [99].

Social Groupings. The older adolescent, like the younger, has friends of different levels of social distance. His most intimate friends, his "chums," are limited in number and these are the ones with whom he spends most of his time. *Cliques,* made up of chums and their friends of the opposite sex, play a role of major importance in the social life of the older adolescent as dating replaces social activities with members of the same sex [50]. The clique becomes a unit of the larger and less closely knit social group, the *crowd,* which is usually composed of several cliques of similar interests and socioeconomic status that have banded together for the purpose of organizing parties and other social functions.

The older adolescent who goes to college has opportunities for joining groups of his contemporaries which are not always available to the individual who leaves school at the completion of high school and goes to work. In work, the individual's contacts are with people of all ages, most of whom have friends and families of their own outside of their jobs. Unless the noncollege older adolescent has friends from his school days who live and work near enough to make frequent contacts possible, he may find himself limited to a few friends connected with his work and out of touch with any group large enough to form a crowd [43]. Much the same is true of the older adolescent who goes to a professional training school which offers few opportunities for social life and where the major emphasis is placed on work. Except for the older adolescents whose environment in college is similar to that of high school, social groupings are less well defined and, in that respect, are similar to those of the adult years. The older adolescent has little interest in "youth groups" with planned activities and a leader. After seventeen years of age, few adolescents belong to such groups [73].

Friends. In late adolescence, the number of friends is less important than having the right kind of friends. The older adolescent thus limits the number of his friends but increases the circle of his acquaintances. He spends less and less time with members of his own sex and increasingly more time with members of the opposite sex. As a result of this new trend, the social distance between members of the same sex broadens while that between members of the two sexes narrows. By the end of adolescence, both boys and girls are spending more time with, and showing a greater interest in, friends of the opposite sex than friends of their own sex. Because of the strong interest in members of the opposite sex, the older adolescent selects *friends of his own sex* who are not only congenial to him but who will be acceptable to the members of the crowd with which he is identified. These friends must conform to his ideal and must have interests and values similar to his [92]. Admired traits differ with various socioeconomic and racial groups. Negro adolescents, for example, value assertiveness and submissiveness more than do whites, who consider both undesirable, while whites put more value on joviality than do Negroes [81].

The older adolescent generally has friends who live in different parts of the community than he or even in different communities. His most intimate friends, however, are those who live close enough to him so that he can see them often and can do things with them without too much effort. The general *prejudice* the younger adolescent has toward individuals of certain races, creeds, or colors is usually replaced, in late adolescence, with specific prejudices against certain individuals within these groups [60]. An adolescent might have a friendly relationship with another adolescent of a different religious, racial, or social status and yet not include him in the circle of his intimate friends or try to bring him into the crowd to which he belongs. Church groups have a tendency to prefer their own members as friends [12]. To girls, the socioeconomic status of their friends' families is more important than it is to boys [43].

By late adolescence, both boys and girls have definite standards of what they expect *friends of the opposite sex* to be. While it is true that they revise these standards as time goes on and as they learn from experience that certain qualities they believed very important at first, such as good looks, are less important than qualities they attached only minor importance to, such as ambition and ability, there is at all times a standard approved by the group which the adolescent accepts and uses in the selection of his friends. Standards for friends of the opposite sex change from the high school to the college age. While, at both ages, boys have a great admiration for girls who have a sense of humor, they admire quietness when they are younger but dislike it greatly when they are older. Much the same is true for daring. The older the adolescent, the more he admires a daring girl. The young adolescent girl admires a boy who is quiet and inactive but, later on, she shows a dislike for such traits. At all ages, she likes boys to be masculine, tidy, and to have a sense of humor [45, 50].

Leaders. The older adolescent, like the younger, looks upon his leader as the individual who represents him in the eyes of society. Because of this, he wants his leader to be such that others will admire and respect him. For that reason, appearance is an important quality of leadership, regardless of what social grouping the individual leads. Furthermore, he must have ability above that of the rest of the group so that the members of the group can look up to and respect him. Because there are so many different kinds of groups in late adolescence—athletic, social, intellectual, religious, and class or community groups—the leader of one group will not necessarily have the ability to be a leader of another group. Leadership is now a function of the situation, as it is in adult life. A popular person is not necessarily a leader, but leaders are always popular among the members of the groups they lead [45].

Leaders in late adolescence, as is true in the earlier years of the individual's life, make a better appearance than do nonleaders. While *physique* in and of itself is not responsible for leadership, it gives prestige to the individual and, at the same time, contributes favorably to his concept of himself. On the average, the leader has superior *health*. Because of this, he has more energy and is more eager to do things, both of which contribute to the quality of initiative. Now, more than ever before, a leader must be well dressed and well groomed. Even though he is physically attractive, this is not enough. A good appearance depends as much on *clothes* and on *grooming* as on good physical characteristics. When a group is made up of members of both sexes, a pleasing appearance, aided by stylish, becoming clothes, is an essential characteristic of a leader. Superiority of leaders over nonleaders is apparent in *intelligence, academic achievements,* and in *level* of *maturity* [22].

The *prestige* that comes from *family background* and superior *socioeconomic status,* or from membership in a select group such as a college fraternity or sorority, contributes to the individual's chances of being selected as a leader. Because of their more favored socioeconomic status, such individuals have had opportunities to acquire *social skills* and *know-how,* thus increasing their self-confidence, which, in turn, encourages them to be more active *participants* in social life. Furthermore, from their social contacts, they develop the ability to size up social situations quickly and accurately with the result that their *social insight* is generally superior to that of nonleaders. Perhaps the most important single factor that contributes to leadership is *personality.* Leaders have been found to be more responsible, extroverted, energetic, resourceful, and more able to take initiative than nonleaders. They are emotionally stable, well-adjusted, happy individuals with few neurotic tendencies. In the case of girls, leaders have a tendency to be slightly more masculine than feminine in their interests [8, 22].

While leaders come and go in childhood, this is not true of adolescence. The individual who is a leader in his freshman year in college is more likely to be a leader throughout his entire college career than is the individual who has held no leadership positions in high school or college. The training and experience derived from being a leader, plus the prestige which puts him in a focal point of attention when leaders are to be selected, give an individual an advantage over those whose experience in leadership has been limited. However, *persistence of leadership* depends partly upon the stability of the group and partly upon the adaptability of the leader. The prestige of being a leader is, to a large extent, lost unless the group remains stable. Furthermore, a leader who tends to be autocratic is likely to be rigid and inflexible, thus militating against adaptability. However, as most leaders are active participants in a wide variety of social activities, they develop social insight which shows them the importance of adjusting to the wishes of the group if they wish to maintain a leadership status [104].

Social Acceptability. The older adolescent, like the younger, is happy and well adjusted only if he achieves a reasonable degree of social acceptance. Being unpopular with either sex or with both cuts him off from the social life of his contemporaries and leaves him with no opportunities for the type of recreation that his contemporaries engage in. The older adolescent, even more so than the younger, is well aware of how others feel about him. But, unlike the younger adolescent, he is more realistic in his attitude toward possible future improvement in his social acceptability. If he has not been able, for one reason or another, to increase his social acceptance during his high school years, he has little hope of being able to do so later. As a result, either he accepts the situation as it is, even though begrudgingly, or he withdraws from situations where his lack of social acceptance is a constant source of emotional disturbance to him. For this reason, many able high school students leave school when they reach the end of the compulsory age and do not go on to college, and many college students who do not make a fraternity or sorority, or who fail to win acceptance among their classmates, withdraw and go to work, or they devote themselves to their studies in the hopes of increasing their social acceptance through their academic prestige.

Because the older adolescent who goes to college, to a professional training school, or to work after he completes high school is more likely to be associated with a group of people who are strangers to him than at any time since he started school, *first impressions* play an important role in determining his later acceptance. If he creates the impression of being a cold, aloof, or unattractive person, this is likely to lead to poor acceptance, which will militate against the group's opportunity to know him better and to discover if this first impression is correct. First impressions are influenced by the individual's appearance, his behavior, the people he is with, his socioeconomic status as determined by his clothes and manners, the resemblance to people already known to the observer, and many other factors. Once an impression has been formed, it affects the individual's behavior toward that person. If favorable, it will contribute to his acceptance; if unfavorable, it may result in rejection or being ignored [33].

How well accepted the older adolescent will be is determined not only by the impression he makes on others but also upon the size and nature of the group. When the group is small, the criteria used by the members of the group in judging the acceptability of a potential member are more personal than when the group is larger. If the goals of the group are mainly social, more emphasis will be placed on the socioeconomic status and social know-how of the individual than when the goals are less social and the individual's interests and contributions to the group are primary factors in determining his acceptance.

Studies of socially accepted older adolescents have revealed that they do not fall into a "type" nor are they free from socially or even ethically disapproved traits. They may and often do have some socially undesirable traits but these are compensated for by desirable ones. However, some traits are more likely to be found in socially accepted individuals, such as sincerity, objective interest in others, consideration for others, self-respect and self-confidence, active participation in approved group activities, and generally well-adjusted personality patterns. The poorly accepted, by contrast, may have the same traits but in a less well developed form. They are likely to be poorly adjusted, showing ego-centered attitudes and behavior, attention-demanding behavior, vulgar and disparaging attitudes toward the opposite sex, excessive drinking or sex behavior, and adroitness in escaping responsibility for anti-social acts. They also lack self-confidence, self-respect, and ability to perceive their own status and that of others [13, 39].

Social Maturity. As adolescence draws to a close and the individual will soon be given the status of an adult, he will be socially mature enough to handle this status successfully, provided the socialization

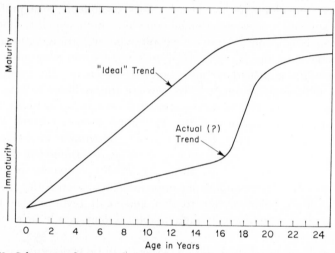

FIG. 72. Schematic diagram showing how self-reliance and emancipation from parents might best develop and how development probably takes place in the American culture under conditions of parental resistance to independence. (*From S. L. Pressey and R. G. Kuhlen, Psychological development through the life span. New York: Harper, 1957. Used by permission.*)

process that has been going on since early childhood has prepared him for this status. The socially mature individual has "a sense of his proper place and role as a member of a group" [68]. He is willing and able to orient himself "in the various activities and customs of the group, to make a proportionate contribution to the work to be done, to take a suitable part in the social exchange, to assume a reasonable amount of responsibility, and to adjust himself to the inevitable limitations and restrictions of community life without waste of energy or loss of satisfaction" [57]. He can be original and yet conform to the broad pattern of the cultural environment.

The adolescent who achieves social maturity and is ready to adjust to adult life has emancipated himself from the home in the sense that he can make his own decisions, support himself and family, and be happy when away from the familiar scenes of childhood. Many college students fail to attain "emotional emancipation" from their parents [56]. It is not usually until they finish their education and become financially independent that they are able to achieve "emotional emancipation." The socially mature individual treats the members of his family as friends and, in this role, he shows affection, loyalty, consideration, and respect for all family members. As a citizen, the socially mature person accepts his obligations and performs them faithfully. He makes good adjustments to all types of people without prejudice based on their religion, race, or skin color. He accepts his friends as they are and does not criticize or try to change them as a socially immature person does; he is loyal to them and feels a sense of responsibility toward them when they need his help. While social life may add greatly to his happiness, the mature person is self-sufficient enough that he can be happy when circumstances make it impossible for him to be with his family, friends, or acquaintances [35, 57, 68]. Figure 72 shows the "ideal" trend and the "actual" trend in achieving independence.

INTERESTS IN LATE ADOLESCENCE

Environment and sex are the two major factors that determine what the older adolescent's interests will be. Boys and girls from small towns or rural districts have interests which are in keeping with their environment; those from large cities develop interests as a result of the different opportunities the city environment offers. Late adolescence is the age when the full impact of socially approved patterns of behavior for the two sexes are felt. Girls are supposed to behave in keeping with their sex and boys with theirs. As a result of the socially approved standards, it is not surprising that, at this age, girls have interests that are very different from those of boys.

As adolescence progresses, many of the interests that were carried over from the childhood years wane and are replaced by interests of a mature sort. Because of the greater responsibilities of the older adolescent and the consequent decrease in time to spend as he may wish, the older adolescent is forced to limit the range of his interests. This is especially true in the area of recreational interests. Furthermore, with experience he acquires a more mature sense of values than he had when he was younger and this is reflected in a shift of emphasis on different interests. Interests that were of major importance to him in early adolescence, such as interest in clothes and appearance, are of less importance as he grows older, while interest in a life career, which in early adolescence was secondary to interests related to his life at the moment, now becomes one of the dominant interests of his life. Experience also helps the older adolescent to evaluate his interests more critically and, as a result, he knows which are important to him. As a result of this critical evaluation, he stabilizes his interests [85].

Types of Interests. The range of interests of older adolescents may be subdivided, arbitrarily, into the three major categories used in the description of interests among younger adolescents, as presented in the preceding chapter. These subdivisions include *social, personal,* and *recreational* interests.

Social Interests. Parties of all types, especially those that include members of the opposite sex, rank first among the social interests at this age. The boys who, during early adolescence, showed little interest in parties and dances and who had to be persuaded by the girls to attend now show as keen an interest in parties as girls do. But, if the party is to be to the liking of the boy, it must be informal. Furthermore, if the party is to appeal to the older adolescent boy, it must offer an opportunity for *drinking*. This is true of college as well as of noncollege adolescents [84].

Talking to anyone and everyone is a favorite activity of an older adolescent. No longer does he limit his talking to his intimate friends as he did several years earlier. Now he talks to anyone who will listen and frequently he does not care whether they are paying attention to him or not. Talking is a form of thinking out loud for him, and he derives keen satisfaction from verbalizing his thoughts, thus clarifying them. It serves as practice in acquiring ease and confidence in a social skill which is essential to good social adjustments. For many older adolescents, talking is a form of catharsis, a method of blowing off emotional steam and getting rid of gripes. For all adolescents, talking to others of their own age helps them to get new points of view and this results in a more liberal attitude toward many subjects and problems on which they formerly held rigid attitudes. This is especially true when talking takes the form of arguments [27].

Studies of what older adolescents talk about when they get together with members of their own sex have revealed that the favorite topics of conversation for boys are dates, sports, clothes, and drinking; for girls, they are dates, clothes, food, and dancing. Nothing of great seriousness is discussed when older adolescents meet with their contemporaries. Rather, their conversations are a form of indoor sport. Sex and smutty stories likewise are popular topics when adolescents are with intimate friends. The older adolescent's conversational topics are very similar to those of the young adult [97].

The older adolescent, especially when the major part of his time is spent in college or in some other educational institution, becomes keenly interested in *government* and *national and world affairs*. He reads and talks about these matters far more than he did when he was younger and he forms definite opinions which are often radical and unrealistic. Because of his relative ignorance in this area, the individual is often swayed by persuasive speakers and writers who are likely to hold radical points of view. This results in a more liberal attitude than that he acquired from his parents and his early home and school environment [64].

Personal Interests. The older adolescent has three major personal interests: *appearance, independence,* and his *life career.* These are so dominant that they absorb much of his time and thought. When their personal problems are solved or partially solved, and when they make a place for themselves in the social group, older adolescents become more stable and predictable. As a result, they settle down and make better adjustments to life.

The older adolescent's interest in *appearance* is heightened by the realization that appearance plays a role of great importance in social adjustments. Popularity with members of his own sex as well as with members of the opposite sex is determined by whether the individual fits into the group ideal in appearance as well as in behavior. To girls, this is even more important than to boys because of the nonaggressive role they are expected to play [76]. To make a good appearance, an adolescent girl is willing to sacrifice many of the luxuries and even necessities of life in order to have the clothes and beauty aids that will make her as attractive as possible.

Because other girls are critical of her clothes, the older adolescent feels self-conscious, uneasy, and uncomfortable if they are not in style. Furthermore, to be admired or even envied by members of her own sex, and to attract and hold the attention of members of the opposite sex, the girl must make as attractive an appearance as possible. Clothes play an important role in accomplishing this [23]. Interest in appearance is strong among older boys too. They recognize the importance of making a good appearance and they soon discover that when they make a good appearance, it helps to increase their poise and self-confidence in social situations [69]. As physical development nears its completion, the older boy is more attractive looking and makes a generally better appearance than he did when he was in the transitional stage from the childish to the mature body and face. This improvement is illustrated in the ratings shown in Figure 73.

Because of their great value as aids in improving the individual's appearance, and because of their help in camouflaging physical traits that fall below accepted standards, the adolescent is more interested in *clothes* than in any other aspect of his appearance. While conspicuous clothing that draws favorable attention to the individual is more often worn by the older adolescent than by the younger, there is a gradual trend toward the use of extremes in style and cut rather than in colors, as is true when the adolescent first uses clothes for their attention value. Too much jewelry, too bright colors, and too extreme styles, the adolescent learns, are regarded as being in bad taste and win for him attention of an unfavorable sort [67, 76].

The older adolescent shows better *taste* in clothes than does the younger. Colors are selected not only because they are in style or because the wearer likes them but mainly because of their becomingness. Adolescents learn that distinctiveness can be achieved better by line and color

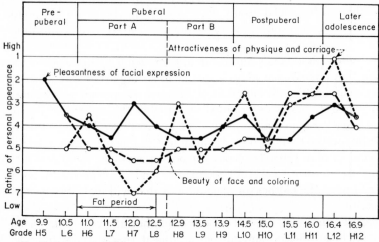

Fig. 73. Ratings on different items of personal appearance at different stages of sexual development. Note the low ratings on face and physique during the early adolescent fat period and the higher ratings as the boy became more mature. (*From H. R. Stolz and L. M. Stolz, Somatic development of adolescent boys. New York: Macmillan, 1951. Used by permission.*)

than by ornamentation. Appropriateness to the occasion is now an important factor in the selection of clothes, as is becomingness to the wearer. Girls, who are not as self-conscious in late adolescence as they were when they were younger, put emphasis on clothes that reveal their feminine curves, just as older boys like to show their broad shoulders and masculine physique to the best advantage. Being in style, however, is so important to an adolescent that becomingness must often be sacrificed. Furthermore, this means a constant replacement of garments as styles change and, as is true of the younger adolescent, the older adolescent finds that clothes become an important item in his budget, often necessitating sacrifice of other wants or needs [76].

The desire for *independence*, which has been growing gradually throughout the years of childhood, reaches its peak of intensity in late adolescence. If adult authority is relaxed gradually so that the adolescent can see himself reaching his goal, there is far less friction between the adolescent and his parents or others in authority than when he sees no improvement in his status. Adolescents who are in the throes of establishing themselves and are meeting obstacles at every turn are the most antagonistic to adult authority, especially to their parents. Because middle-class parents are highly protective of their children, especially their daughters, middle-class youth find growing up especially difficult and they often feel guilty when they try to achieve independence because of parental emphasis on the sacrifices made for them and the loyalty they owe their families [40].

Typically, the older adolescent expects too much independence too quickly. This desire is often exaggerated when the adolescent discovers that his friends have more independence than he. If his parents are unwilling to give him the independence he wants, the adolescent is rebellious and unhappy. This often leads to his running away from home, giving up his schooling, or even marrying to establish the independence his parents have denied him. Too strict home training during this period builds up a dislike for parents, a combative attitude on the adolescent's part, social maladjustments, and a tendency to do things behind parental backs [30].

Money, every adolescent sooner or later discovers, is the key to independence. So long as parents pay the adolescent's bills and give him an allowance for spending money, they can control his behavior. When, on the other hand, he has money he has earned, he can enjoy independence. Interest in money, therefore, becomes an important element in interest in independence. This interest centers mainly on how to earn the most money possible, regardless of the type of work done. Few older adolescents show any more interest in saving or investing money than they did when they were younger nor are they interested in problems related to the management of family finances. To them, money is a means to an end and that end is independence. To achieve this end, they often are willing to sacrifice the possibility of future advancement by giving up their education to enable them to work or by taking jobs that are well paid, regardless of future advancement. Many of the dropouts in college come from a desire to earn money and from the poor academic work which results when the student spends too much time on part-time jobs [53].

The interest in a *life career* that began to be dominant in early adolescence often becomes a source of great concern to an older adolescent when he is confused about what he would like to do or what he is capable of doing. The more he hears or talks about different lines of work, the less sure he is of what he would like to do. Then, too, there is interest in and concern about how he can get a job of the type he would like

[69]. With the realization of how much it costs to live and the earnings a young person can expect, the older adolescent approaches the choice of his career with a practical and realistic attitude which he did not have formerly. The older adolescent is still in the "exploratory stage" during which he tries out, through part-time or full-time jobs, work he thinks he would like to do and gains more information about such work [87].

Interest in a life career is very different for the two sexes. To boys, the choice is for a lifetime; for girls, however, the choice is for a short time before marriage and emphasis is placed on the type of work that can be combined with marriage, should it be necessary to work. Most girls, after graduating from high school or college, are interested in working for a

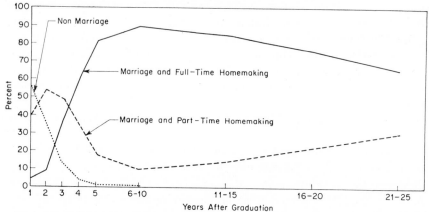

Fig. 74. Role preferences of college women for their adult years. (*From H. T. Christensen and M. M. Swihart, Postgraduation role preferences of senior women in college. Marriage Fam. Living, 1956, 18, 52–57. Used by permission.*)

year or two before marriage, a year or more after marriage until their first babies arrive, and then becoming full-time homemakers until their children are grown, after which they want a part-time job to fill the empty time left by the ending of the duties of child care [20]. Preferences of girls in the area of work, marriage, and a combination of both are shown in Figure 74. Because adolescent boys are well aware of the role they are expected to play as adult men whose responsibility it is to support a family, they often overstrain in their occupational ambitions, choosing an occupation without adequate consideration of their abilities or interests. Desire for work with high prestige now replaces desire for glamour, which was so strong in early adolescence [66].

The difficulties in selecting a life career begin to disappear as adolescence progresses. While it is true that changes in choice will be made, even into the adult years, there is a greater stability in vocational interests in late adolescence than in early adolescence. Choices made then are less likely to change than choices made earlier. This does not mean that there will be no changes but rather that the changes will be less frequent. They will also be based on a realistic assessment of individual abilities and will be influenced by job or college experiences that reveal to the individual an aspect of the work for which he is not fitted or for which he has no interest [26, 87]. In considering work that requires specialized training, the adolescent gives serious consideration to all aspects of it before making a final decision because he realizes that later changes will be difficult to make.

While most older adolescents work part or full time through necessity or to increase their independence, few are satisfied with their work or the work experience. *Job satisfaction* is more unusual than usual during the adolescent years. There are many reasons for this. The unrealistic attitudes toward work have emphasized the glamorous sides of a job and ignored the real situation as it exists, thus disillusioning the adolescent after the first thrill of earning money has worn off. Most adolescents are immature in their desire for play and recreation, and for help and special privileges, which they have been accustomed to in school. In the adult work world, they are expected to behave like other adults, adjusting themselves to adult levels of expectation. The long hours, the few vacations, and the monotony of the work itself lead to dissatisfaction which is expressed in changing from job to job in the hopes of finding one that will measure up to the adolescent's expectations, or in attempting to compensate with social activities in the free time away from work [91]. The more education the adolescent has, the more choice he will have in job selection and the more likely he will be to find satisfaction in his work [48].

Recreational Interests. As adolescence progresses, the range of interests in different forms of recreation diminishes. Instead, more time is spent on the few forms of recreation the adolescent derives enjoyment from, and less time in all is spent on recreation than at earlier periods of the individual's life. With the pressures from studies, work, home responsibilities, and occasional community obligations, the amount of leisure time the older adolescent has to spend as he pleases is limited. As a result, he selects those forms of recreation that give him greatest pleasure, either because he excels in them and this adds to his social prestige or because they offer opportunities for social contacts, especially with members of the opposite sex. The narrowing down of recreational interests comes gradually, as adolescence progresses, and is usually more pronounced in girls than in boys [88] (see Figure 75).

There is a gradual decline of interest in strenuous physical exercise and in *organized games*. Unless the adolescent has enough ability to excel and to play on a team, he prefers to be a spectator rather than an active participant. Whenever possible, the older adolescent thinks up excuses to avoid strenuous activities and prefers to devote his time to recreations that require less effort on his part. This is particularly true of girls. Only when games permit playing with members of the opposite sex, such as tennis, bowling, or skating, does the average older adolescent engage in them voluntarily. Girls are not interested in the competitive angle of sports though they may enjoy sports as a form of recreation or as an aid

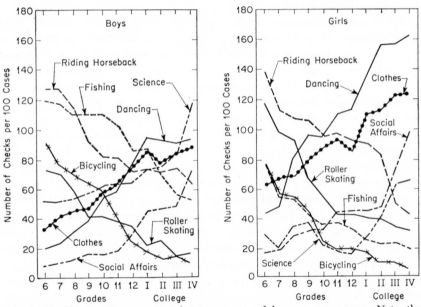

Fig. 75. Changes in recreational interests as adolescence progresses. Note the greater narrowing down of boys' than of girls' interests. (*Based on unpublished data of S. L. Pressey. From S. L. Pressey and R. G. Kuhlen, Psychological development through the life span. New York: Harper, 1957. Used by permission.*)

to their appearance [10]. *Games of intellect,* especially when they offer a chance for gambling, assume a position of importance in the recreational life of the older adolescent. Boys as well as girls like to play cards though, to boys, the interest is heightened if a small stake is involved. Playing cards is a popular amusement for parties in which members of one or both sexes are involved.

When time permits, the older adolescent has a *hobby.* This is likely to be useful rather than merely a means of filling in idle time, as is true of younger children's hobbies. Many girls make clothes as a hobby, and boys collect information on sports events or some other subject that is absorbing to them at the time. The hobby may take the form of drawing which is generally of the caricature type at this age [47] or of playing the piano or singing, just for the adolescents' own amusement or for the entertainment of their friends. Collecting and repeatedly playing records of the popular music of the day is one of the favorite hobbies of the older adolescent, just as it is of the high school student.

Dancing is a form of recreation that few older adolescents can afford to shun if they want to be popular or to be invited to join in the activities of their contemporaries. While many older boys and girls, especially the former, have no real interest in dancing, an increasingly large number learn to dance and attend dances as the adolescent years progress. From early to late adolescence, there is a gradual decrease in the number of individuals who do not dance. Although the young adolescent is more interested in the activity of dancing than he is in his partner, the reverse is true in the latter part of adolescence. Dancing is one of the most popular activities for dates [43].

The older adolescent reads for pleasure, if his work or social life permits. At this age, when his leisure time is limited, he would rather spend it with his contemporaries than spend it alone *reading*. When he does read, it is more likely to be fiction than nonfiction, and short stories rather than books. Romance, adventure, strong characterization, fantasy, and social awareness are prominent in books and stories popular with the older adolescent. When reading newspapers, adolescents now read the serious parts as well as the comics and sport sections. The magazines they prefer are the popular ones of light fiction, rather than the serious type. Even those adolescents who are no longer students seem to retain the reading habits established in school for a time after they leave school. However, the amount that they read and what they read depends upon the level of their intelligence, the time available for reading, their cultural and socioeconomic background, and many other factors [1].

The older adolescent, like the younger, enjoys listening to the *radio* for the major part of the time he is at home. As a matter of fact, he actually does not listen to it but it seems to give him pleasure to have it turned on while he is dressing, reading, or studying. In that way, it acts as a form of companionship in the absence of human companionship. Girls, as a whole, prefer romantic stories, popular and classical music, and quiz programs; boys prefer adventure, mystery, popular music, and quiz programs. The effect of radio listening on the older adolescent is more intellectual than emotional. His point of view and his attitudes toward important problems are markedly influenced by what he hears over the air. *Television* has less appeal for the older adolescent than has radio partly because it is impossible to study or work while watching television and partly because the programs available at the time the older adolescent is free to watch have less appeal to him than to a younger or to an adult audience [102].

As a general rule, the older adolescent attends *movies* less than the younger adolescent. This does not necessarily mean a waning of interest in movies but rather a greater interest in other forms of recreation. As interest in members of the opposite sex grows, there is a stronger desire to engage in recreational activities in which members of the opposite sex can take part and which give opportunities for conversation [43, 102]. The types of pictures the older adolescent prefers are those that follow the pattern of his reading and radio-listening interests. Romance stands in first place of preference for girls, and adventure and mystery are more popular with boys. But, as movie attendance during late adolescence is more often with members of the opposite sex than with friends of the same sex or members of the family, it is the girl who usually decides what movie will be seen. The leading character of the movie is responsible for its selection more often than any other factor [102].

RELIGIOUS ATTITUDES AND BEHAVIOR

The older adolescent still has plenty of problems to solve before he arrives at a satisfactory religious belief. The intensity of religious doubt, with its accompanying feelings of guilt, gradually subsides as adolescence draws to a close and the individual can then face his problems more objectively and solve them with less emotional bias [69]. Adolescents who go away to college or work away from home come in contact with people with different religious beliefs to a greater extent than do those who remain at home and whose circle of friends is likely to be limited to those of similar religious backgrounds. Many of the half-thought-out beliefs of the younger adolescent are clarified when the individual has opportunities to discuss them with others and when his courses of study present facts that contradict many of his earlier beliefs. However, many doubts are not entirely cleared up even though they may seem less serious to the individual as he grows older [2].

The older adolescent emerges from a period of doubting with new religious beliefs and a greater tolerance for the religious beliefs and practices of others than he formerly had. The beliefs that undergo the greatest change at this time are the specific beliefs about the appearance and behavior of God, angels, and the devil, about miracles, and about life after death. Because most religious beliefs are "family bound," they are less likely to be changed, even with changes in world conditions, than are other beliefs and attitudes [6]. Some adolescents who are unable to reconcile their religious beliefs with their broader knowledge change their religious faith to one that meets their needs better or they reject all

religion and become agnostics or atheists. This, however, is more exceptional than usual. Most older adolescents feel the need of religion in their
lives, especially when they have had religious training in their childhood
[2]. Even among college students, there is evidence that there is a greater
interest in religion than is popularly believed and that the college student of today has more favorable attitudes toward religion than was true
in the past [70]. Most are religiously "moderate," avoiding one extreme
or another in their religious attitudes [17] (see Figure 76).

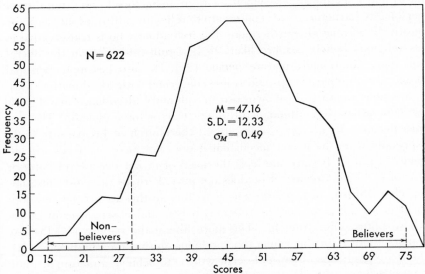

FIG. 76. The older adolescent is religiously "moderate" as shown by distribution
of scores on a religious inventory. (From D. G. Brown and W. L. Lowe, Religious
beliefs and personality characteristics of college students. J. soc. Psychol., 1951,
33, 103–129. Used by permission.)

In spite of the changes in religious beliefs that occur during the latter
years of adolescence, relatively few older adolescents change their religious affiliation. If the two parents have different faiths, the tendency is
for the adolescent to adhere to the mother's faith, as he did when he was
a child. When shifts do occur, they are usually to more "liberal faiths"
or out of religion completely [2]. On the other hand, changes in religious beliefs are likely to be accompanied by a decline in church attendance and in participation in the different organizations connected with
the church. How often adolescents attend church will be influenced also
by their previous attendance habits. Boys, on the average, show a greater
decrease in attendance in late adolescence than do girls [29]. There is
usually a change in attitude toward prayer and a decrease in frequency

of praying in late adolescence. The older adolescent regards prayer as a source of help in times of trouble rather than a means of getting material possessions or making up for some wrong he has done [98].

Religious Maturity. While maturity in the area of religious beliefs and observances is not essential to a successful adjustment to life, it is important because it contributes to the individual's happiness. No adult with childish religious beliefs can be contented with these beliefs, no matter how satisfactory they were to him when he was a child. As a result, he revises his beliefs, often accepting some beliefs from different faiths and rejecting others which seem unsatisfactory to him. Rigidity of personality structure and conservative religious attitudes are usually positively correlated. Furthermore, the individual who is conservative in his religious beliefs is more likely to be "guilt-ridden" than the liberal and more emotionally mature person [25]. He also has more personal conflicts with other groups and is less concerned with social matters [58].

Religious maturity is shown also in voluntary attendance at religious services rather than attendance through fear or force of habit. The mature person will not necessarily attend the church of his parents' faith, especially when he is convinced that it does not meet his needs. He engages in prayer because he feels the need of it, not because of habit or fear of evil consequences if he does not pray. Perhaps the most outstanding characteristic of a person who is mature in this area of his development is *tolerance* toward the religious beliefs and observances of others whose faiths differ from his. The more liberal the parents and the less conflict there is in the home about religion during the childhood years, the more likely the older adolescent will be to achieve a mature attitude toward religion as he grows up [90].

MORAL CONCEPTS AND BEHAVIOR

Pronounced changes in attitudes toward right and wrong come in late adolescence. Up to sixteen years, boys and girls find it difficult to apply the moral concepts they have learned to the increasing range of conflicting situations that arise with their broadening social experiences. As they grow older and their experiences broaden in college or at work, they have more definite concepts of right and wrong, they are better able to cope with new and conflicting situations, and they act in accordance with their moral concepts without pressure from outside. In addition, they are capable of generalizing moral concepts which have been learned in relation to specific acts. These concepts can then be applied to similar acts and will thus form the basis of a workable code that can be used in any situation that might arise [41].

Changes in moral attitudes include a tolerance toward certain acts which were formerly condemned, such as smoking, immodesty, flirting, and extravagance. College seniors, for example, have been found to be more liberal than eighth- or twelfth-grade students in high school, and this is especially true of girls who have been away from the home influence for the first time during the late adolescent years. The greatest change in attitudes comes in relation to the somewhat "borderline acts," such as smoking or playing cards (see Figure 77). While there is an in-

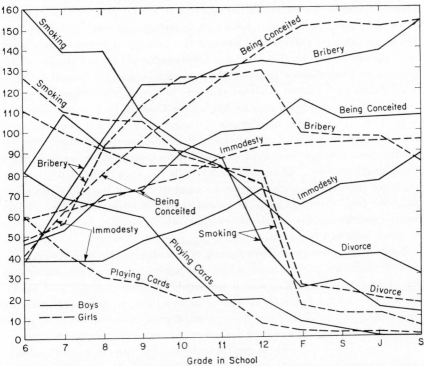

Fig. 77. Changes in moral values as adolescence progresses. (*Based on unpublished data of S. L. Pressey. From S. L. Pressey and R. G. Kuhlen, Psychological development through the life span. New York: Harper, 1957. Used by permission.*)

crease in tolerance toward certain acts, there is an increase in intolerance toward others. The older adolescent, for example, considers bribery and being conceited more serious than does the younger adolescent. Thus, the change is more of a shift in emphasis than an establishment of new codes of behavior [70].

At this age, the influence of "double standards," or separate codes of behavior for the two sexes, becomes even more marked than in early adolescence. Especially in the area of sex behavior, the girl discovers that certain acts are classed as "wrong" for her while, in the case of boys, the same acts are condoned. Even though there is a trend toward breaking down these "double standards," especially since World War II, girls are still more harshly judged for some acts than are boys [41, 70].

Moral Behavior. It is assumed by parents and teachers that the older adolescent knows what to do and how to do it. Any deviation from the socially approved code of behavior is regarded as intentional on the adolescent's part, a defiance of the rules or laws which deserves punishment. The adolescent, on the other hand, is often motivated to do things which he knows are wrong either because of group pressures or in order to satisfy some immediate need which is strong and compelling, such as the desire for recognition which leads the individual to cheat in a sport or academic work, or the need for satisfying a strong sex desire which leads to masturbation or premarital intercourse.

When the adolescent realizes that his behavior has fallen below society's codes or the standards he has set for himself, he becomes angry at himself or at someone he regards as responsible for his shortcomings. This leads to feelings of guilt which, if experienced too often, will develop into a marked feeling of personal inadequacy. When punished for his wrongdoing, he will usually react with resentment toward the punisher not because he feels that he does not deserve it but more often because he feels the form of punishment is too infantile, that it is unfairly harsh considering the misdeed, or that others equally involved in the misdeed have not been punished [83].

Back of most *juvenile delinquency* is resentment, built up over a period of years, for punishments which the adolescent considers unfair and for treatment from others which has made him feel inferior and inadequate. The adolescent who is unable or unwilling to get satisfaction by conforming to social dictates derives satisfaction from hurting the social group as a revenge for real or imagined wrongs inflicted by that group. While most boys and girls begin their delinquent careers in early adolescence, the peak of arrests comes during the nineteenth year. A large percentage of these delinquents have been in trouble before and are expressing their resentments further by repeated misdeeds which they justify to themselves by believing that society has mistreated them [32].

Moral Maturity. The moral concepts of the older adolescent closely approximate those of the adult. He knows what society expects and even though he may disagree with some of the moral concepts, he follows them because he realizes that no one can be a law unto himself. In this adult moral code, there is stability. Things that are right in one environment are right in all environments. The morally mature individual acts in accordance with this code not because he is afraid of being caught and punished but because he believes it is the right thing to do. In late adolescence, there is a lessening of that early adolescent intolerance toward one's own and others' shortcomings. The morally mature person tries to understand and sympathize with those who fall short of society's expectations. When he falls short of society's codes, he has sufficient self-critical ability to recognize it and to feel guilty. In the case of the morally mature individual, guilt thus proves to be a strong motivating force to conform to society's mores [4].

SEX INTERESTS AND BEHAVIOR

The infatuations of the hero-worshiping, crush, and puppy-love stages of early adolescence give way to romantic attachments as dating becomes the accepted pattern of social behavior for the older adolescent. These romantic attachments are often so intense and so absorbing that the individuals involved have little time or thought for anything else. As a result, the older adolescent loses interest in group activities and prefers to be alone with the loved one. Any activity in which members of the opposite sex cannot participate, such as team sports, loses its appeal when dating becomes the favorite form of recreation.

Dating is of different types and different degrees of seriousness. In early adolescence, and sometimes into the beginning of late adolescence, dating is of the *competitive* or mobile type, which involves many partners and does not involve an "understanding." It is purely a pleasurable experience, with a minimum of emotional involvement, between individuals who are congenial friends. It is generally known as "playing the field" and, as such, it is a technique for finding a congenial member of the opposite sex who may, in time, become a life mate. Competitive dating ends generally with a minimum of emotional upset and is terminated more often by the boy than the girl. How much time will be devoted to such dating, how long it will persist, and how early it will begin will be influenced by patterns of behavior in the community, whether or not the adolescent belongs to a clique, whether the adolescent wants to marry early, and many other factors. Figure 78 shows that interest in love, courtship, and marriage reaches its peak as adolescence progresses [79].

Selection of "Dates." The fact that the selection of a dating partner is a male prerogative in our culture puts the burden of responsibility on girls to make themselves attractive so that they will be assured of selection. In the past, materialistic factors played an important role in dating. The girl who had clothes, a home, car, and money superior to other girls "rated" higher with the boys and was assured of dates. Today, young men put emphasis on a pleasant, cheerful personality, neatness, consideration for others, dependability, and good looks, with little attention to clothes, money, or social prestige. Girls prefer boys who have good manners, are neat, attractive, and appropriately dressed, who dance well and can carry on a conversation. Having a car, money, or social prestige are of less importance. In general, qualities needed for good human relationships and for a good life mate are at the basis of date selection [11] (see Figure 79). With the modern trend toward breaking down prejudice, racial, religious, and socioeconomic-status differences play a less important role in date selection than formerly. Boys from upper socioeconomic or majority groups, more often than girls from these groups, cross class, color,

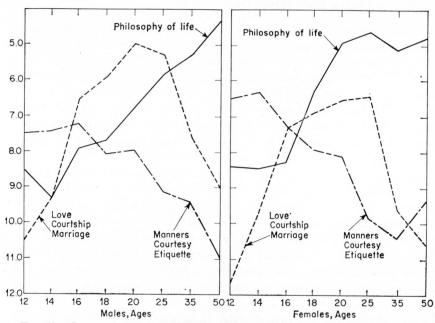

Fig. 78. Changes in interest with age in three life areas, especially those relating to courtship and marriage. (*Based on unpublished data of P. M. Symonds, From F. K. Shuttleworth, The adolescent period: a graphic atlas. Monogr. Soc. Res. Child Develpm., 1949, 14, No. 1. Used by permission.*)

and religious lines in selecting dates [28]. In selecting "dates," adolescents generally show a preference for individuals whose characteristics are similar to theirs rather than opposite [80].

"*Going Steady.*" The continuous dating of one individual instead of many generally starts after a year or two of dating. By the senior year in high school, "going steady" is six times as common as playing the field or competitive dating. The most popular adolescents go steady and this gives them prestige in the eyes of their peers because it shows that they are able to attract and hold the friendship of a member of the opposite sex long enough to achieve group recognition and sanction of this relationship. Going steady is of two types, *non-commitment* and *commitment*.

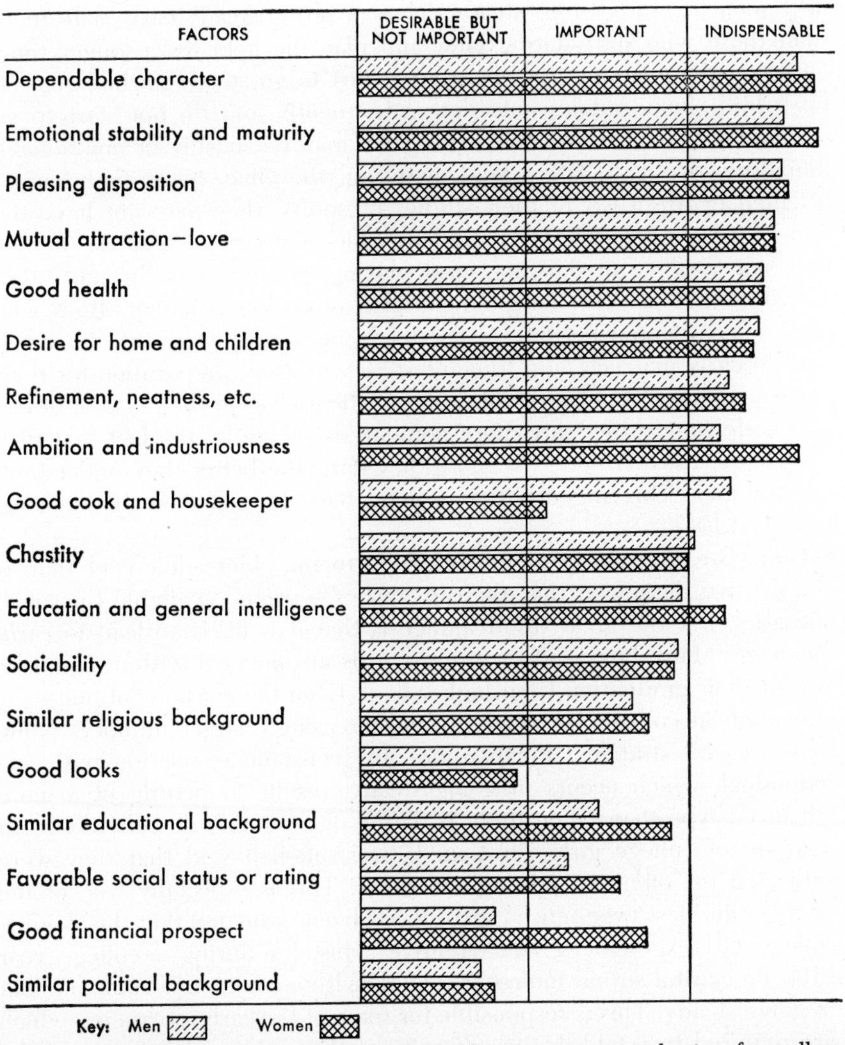

FACTORS	DESIRABLE BUT NOT IMPORTANT	IMPORTANT	INDISPENSABLE
Dependable character			
Emotional stability and maturity			
Pleasing disposition			
Mutual attraction—love			
Good health			
Desire for home and children			
Refinement, neatness, etc.			
Ambition and industriousness			
Good cook and housekeeper			
Chastity			
Education and general intelligence			
Sociability			
Similar religious background			
Good looks			
Similar educational background			
Favorable social status or rating			
Good financial prospect			
Similar political background			

Key: Men ▨   Women ▩

FIG. 79. Relative importance of different factors in mate selection for college students. (*From R. Hill, Campus values in mate selection. J. Home Econ.*, 1945, 37, 554–558. *Used by permission.*)

In the former, there are no plans for future marriage and it is, therefore, a dalliance relationship, dominated by a quest for thrills and a pretense of love and devotion. The commitment type of going steady is marriage oriented, in which there is an "understanding" that eventually the couple will marry. This is likely to be a more stable kind of relationship than the former type [42, 79].

The amount of dating the older adolescent does depends largely on how soon he starts to go steady. Those who go steady early date more than those who start dating later and play the field for a longer time. Girls, on the average, date more and start to go steady earlier than do boys [59]. Some adolescents date infrequently and do not start to go steady until they reach adulthood. They may be socially or emotionally immature, owing to late sexual maturing; they may be strongly career oriented or absorbed in their studies or sports; they may not have the money for clothes and entertainment which dating necessitates; or they may not approve of dancing, card playing, petting, necking, and other activities that are the accepted patterns of dating behavior. Boys who are career oriented hesitate to go steady because they are afraid it will lead to early marriage and thus interfere with their preparation for their chosen careers [21]. Those who can put themselves in the place of others and understand others are more popular, as shown by the fact that they date more. Furthermore, the more they date, the better they understand one another. This suggests that a good basis for marriage is being established [94].

Going steady may be more satisfying to the older adolescent than is competitive dating, in that there is always someone available for social activities, but the great disadvantage is that it is likely to lead to *early marriage*. Many boys and even more girls are married within a year or two of their graduation from high school. Even those who continue their education in college are marrying in increasingly larger numbers while they are still students. Furthermore, the constant association with one individual, which occurs in going steady, results in petting of a more advanced type than when there is dating of a number of individuals. In a group of college girls questioned, over one-half said that they were subjected to "offensive petting" on dates. This is especially true of the younger and less experienced girls. It has been estimated that the average college girl experiences 4.2 "offensive" episodes during a college year [51]. Premarital sexual intercourse is likewise a common accompaniment of going steady. This is responsible for some of the early marriages, which are required to establish the paternity of the child, and it is one of the factors responsible for the high divorce rate among those who marry during the adolescent years [63].

Sex Roles. In spite of the fact that most girls, as they approach the end of adolescence, maintain that their preference for their adult role is that of wife and mother, they often find it difficult to accept their appropriate sex role [20]. Not only is there ambiguity as to what the appropriate sex role is for the woman of today, with concepts varying from one social class to another, but the girl discovers, early in her teens, that boys consider the female role subordinate to that of the male [96]. In the case of boys, on the other hand, sex-appropriate behavior is more clearly defined and the adherence to the approved pattern brings boys greater social acceptance than is true of girls [37]. As a result, the older adolescent girl of today is faced with the dilemma of what role to accept, the traditionally feminine role or the modern feminine role, where she more closely approximates the masculine pattern of behavior than the traditionally feminine pattern [95].

How successfully older adolescents will adjust to members of the opposite sex, how well accepted they will be by members of the same sex, how successfully they will adjust to dating, marriage, or work with members of the opposite sex, and how adequate or inadequate they will feel will be influenced by the degree to which they accept the sex roles approved by the social group with which they are identified. The *psychosexually mature* individual will accept his or her sex role and will try to fulfill this role successfully with minimum resentment toward being a member of that sex. Because the masculine role is more clearly defined, because boys are trained from earliest childhood to be "regular boys" while girls are permitted to behave like boys until they reach adolescence and then are expected to follow the approved feminine pattern, and because the role of men in our culture is more highly approved and respected than the role of women, it is easier for boys to accept the traditionally masculine role than it is for girls to accept the traditionally feminine role. As a result, boys in late adolescence achieve psychosexual maturity more readily and on a wider scale than do girls [61].

FAMILY RELATIONSHIPS

As the adolescent years progress, parents generally come to the realization that their sons and daughters are no longer children and, as a result, they give them more privileges while, at the same time, expecting more in the way of work and assumption of responsibilities. When this parental adjustment to the changed status of the son or daughter is made, the tension that marked the parent-child relationship in early adolescence generally relaxes and the home becomes a pleasanter place in which to live [69]. The more parents are willing to treat their older adolescent children as peers, the better the relationship between them. There are, however, many families in which this change does not occur. As a result, the resentment on the part of the adolescent grows stronger and stronger as time passes [40].

Even though parent-adolescent relationships tend to improve with each passing year (see Figure 69, page 316), there are many conflicts between the adolescent and his parents. For the most part, friction arises over the way the adolescent treats his parents, his lack of acceptance of responsibilities, his use of money, dating, choice of friends, and dating behavior.

The older adolescent feels that parental attempts to restrict his activities, especially with members of the opposite sex, will handicap him in his heterosexual adjustments and cut him off from friends of his own sex. In general, conflicts with parents are more common among girls than boys, and these conflicts are more often with the mother than with the father [24].

Siblings, who, during early adolescence, were frequently a thorn in the side of the adolescent, are now taken in a calmer and more philosophical manner by the older adolescent. He is capable of understanding the behavior of younger siblings better than he could when he was younger,

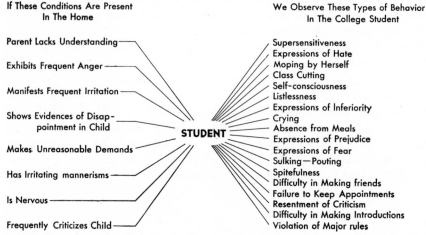

FIG. 80. Relationship between home adjustment and the behavior of college girls. (*From M. D. Woolf, A study of some relationships between home adjustment and the behavior of junior college students. J. soc. Psychol., 1943, 17, 275–286. Used by permission.*)

and after developing a certain degree of poise and self-confidence which he formerly lacked, the older adolescent is not so easily embarrassed or upset by the behavior of his younger siblings. In many instances, the older adolescent develops a parental attitude toward his younger siblings, and this eliminates much of the friction that previously existed in the home. Older siblings are treated more casually, and less envy is shown toward them than was true earlier. Even grandparents and older relatives are accepted by the older adolescent more graciously than they were several years earlier. All in all, family relationships in late adolescence are on a better and sounder basis than at any previous time in the individual's life [14].

The type of relationship the older adolescent has with his parents and siblings will influence his attitudes toward them and his treatment of them [49]. The better the relationship with the parent, the more the adolescent will identify himself with that parent and the more, in turn, he will be influenced by and resemble that parent [38]. Behavior patterns and attitudes of the older adolescent are rooted in the home and community environments and are so well set by late adolescence that they are difficult to change, even when the adolescent's environment changes, as is true when he goes away to college [31]. If the family relationship has been good, not only during adolescence but also during the earlier, formative years, the adolescent will be a well-adjusted individual. Poorly adjusted adolescents, by contrast, generally come from home settings where the family relationship is poor and where the adolescent has had inadequate or the wrong type of training and guidance during the formative years. Figure 80 shows the relationship between home adjustment and the behavior of college girls.

PERSONALITY

The personality pattern, established during childhood years and changed to a greater or lesser extent in early adolescence as a result of the radical physical and emotional changes taking place at that time and as a result of the strong motivation on the individual's part to improve his personality, now stabilizes itself and takes the form it will maintain with few modifications throughout the remaining years of life [50]. This is a "danger period" in personality development because attitudes, habits, and behavior patterns established at this time can be carried over and become a way of life. The adolescent, for example, who does not achieve independence, either because of restrictions that make this impossible or because of feelings of inadequacy which make him unwilling to try to become independent, is likely to remain immature in this area for the rest of his life [101].

The older adolescent is not only aware of the advantages of a pleasing personality as an asset in social acceptance but he is also well aware of what constitutes a pleasing personality. He knows what traits are admired in contemporaries of his own sex as well as in those of the opposite sex. While these admired traits change as adolescence progresses and differ from one social group to another, the adolescent knows what the group with which he is identified admires [62]. Knowing what others admire gives the adolescent a standard by which to assess his own personality pattern and to see how it measures up with those of his contemporaries. From this assessment, he should emerge with a more realistic self-concept than he had when he was younger. However, there is always a tendency on the part of the individual to be biased in the assessment of his qualities. In concepts of the physical self, for example, young men think of themselves as huskier than they are, and young women tend to have self-concepts in which they appear to be more slender than they actually are [78].

The older adolescent is better able to judge how others feel about him than he was when he was younger, and he knows, from the way he is treated, how others feel about him. When he believes that their concept of him is favorable, it affects his concept of himself and makes it possible for him to accept himself as he is, thus laying the foundations for good personal and social adjustments and for happiness. However, to make such adjustments, the self-concept must be stable as well as realistic. A person with a stable self-concept has a higher level of self-esteem, fewer feelings of inadequacy, and shows fewer evidences of compensatory behavior of a defensive sort [18].

The adolescent who believes that others have a poor concept of him, or that their concept of him falls below the level he has tried to achieve, will develop an unfavorable self-concept that will be reflected in personal and social maladjustments. Adolescents who have eccentric names or nicknames they recognize as a form of ridicule become shy, sensitive, and easily embarrassed. They shun social situations and often flunk out of college because their poor personal adjustments affect the quality of their work [77]. Adolescents whose families belong to a minority group are so unfavorably influenced by the discrimination against them that they develop personality patterns characterized by aggression, submissiveness, strong rebellion, or derogation of the in-group, none of which improve their self-concepts or add to their social acceptance [72].

Whether the adolescent has been an early or late maturer influences both the attitudes of adults and contemporaries toward him and their treatment of him. Boys who, for example, are early maturers, are superior in sports to their late-maturing contemporaries and this increases their prestige in the eyes of their contemporaries. Furthermore, their superior size and more mature appearance cause adults to give them some of the independence they crave and to treat them in a different manner than late maturers. The different treatment given to early and late maturers results in different self-concepts and different patterns of social behavior in the two groups. Early maturers, who are treated as near-adults, develop favorable self-concepts and, as a result, make good adjustments. Late maturers, by contrast, are treated more like children than like near-adults and this influences unfavorably their self-concepts, leading to maladjusted behavior. Even in late adolescence, when they catch up to the early maturers in their physical development, the late maturers continue to behave in a maladjusted way, indicating that the unfavorable self-concept acquired from their earlier treatment still persists [65].

Happiness vs. Unhappiness. While late adolescence as well as early adolescence is typically an unhappy age, the relative degree of unhappiness is an indication of the success or failure the adolescent is having in making his adjustments to life. When adjustments are progressing successfully, the adolescent will be less unhappy than when the adjustments are proving to be unsuccessful. The longer the unhappiness lasts and the more intense it is, the stronger the indication of maladjustment on the part of the adolescent.

A well-adjusted individual has goals which are within his capacities and he uses sustained and definitely directed efforts to attain these goals. The maladjusted individual, by contrast, has neither clearly defined goals within his capacities nor plans to attain these goals. In addition, he is unhappy because he cannot attain his goals since they are beyond his capacities.

A comparison of the problems of happy and unhappy adolescents indicates that the problems of these two groups are similar. Those who are unhappy do not have problems that are peculiar to them but rather their unhappiness stems from the fact that they make poorer adjustments to their problems than do happy individuals [40].

The happy adolescent is concerned with facing reality and with affairs outside himself. By contrast, the unhappy adolescent's concern is centered around his own personal problems, his intimate relationships with others, and his personal unhappiness. Because they have not been able to solve the new and difficult problems that adolescence brings into their lives, the unhappy adolescents remain unhappy longer than those who make more successful adjustments and, in many instances, they will carry their unhappiness into the adult years. Only when he is able to satisfy his needs within the system of controls and outlets provided by his culture can the individual be well adjusted and, in turn, happy [19].

BIBLIOGRAPHY

1. Abraham, W.: College students and their reading—a program for action. *Educ. Adm. Supervis.,* 1952, 38, 111–114.
2. Allport, G. W., J. M. Gillespie, and J. Young: The religion of the postwar college student. *J. Psychol.,* 1948, 25, 3–33.
3. Anastasi, A., N. Cohen, and D. Spatz: A study of fear and anger in college students through the controlled diary method. *J. genet. Psychol.,* 1948, 73, 243–249.
4. Ausubel, D. P.: Relationship between shame and guilt in the socialization process. *Psychol. Rev.,* 1955, 62, 378–390.
5. Ausubel, D. P., and H. M. Schiff: Some intrapersonal and interpersonal determinants of individual differences in socioempathic ability among adolescents. *J. soc. Psychol.,* 1955, 41, 39–56.
6. Ayad, J. M., and P. R. Farnsworth: Shifts in the values of opinion items: further data. *J. Psychol.,* 1953, 36, 295–298.

7. Banham, K. M.: Obstinate children are adaptable. *Ment. Hyg., N.Y.*, 1952, 36, 84–89.
8. Bass, B. M., C. R. Wurster, P. A. Doll, and D. J. Clair: Situational and personality factors in leadership among sorority women. *Psychol. Monogr.*, 1953, 67, No. 16.
9. Bayley, N., and S. R. Pinnau: Tables for predicting adult height from skeletal age: revised for use with Greulich-Pyle hand standards. *J. Pediat.*, 1952, 40, 423–441.
10. Bell, M., and C. E. Walters: Attitudes of women at the University of Michigan toward physical education. *Res. Quart. Amer. phys. Educ. Ass.*, 1953, 24, 379–391.
11. Blood, R. O.: Uniformities and diversities in campus dating preferences. *Marriage Fam. Living*, 1956, 18, 37–45.
12. Bonney, M. E.: A study of friendship choices in college in relation to church affiliation, in-church preference, family size, and length of enrollment in college. *J. soc. Psychol.*, 1949, 29, 153–166.
13. Bonney, M. E., R. E. Hoblit, and A. H. Dreyer: A study of some factors related to sociometric status in a man's dormitory. *Sociometry*, 1953, 16, 287–301.
14. Bossard, J. H. S.: *The sociology of child development*, rev. ed. New York: Harper, 1954.
15. Bossard, J. H. S., and W. P. Sanger: The large family system—a research report. *Amer. sociol. Rev.*, 1952, 17, 3–9.
16. Bretsch, H. S.: Social skills and activities of socially accepted and unaccepted adolescents. *J. educ. Psychol.*, 1952, 43, 449–458.
17. Brown, D. G., and W. L. Lowe: Religious beliefs and personality characteristics of college students. *J. soc. Psychol.*, 1951, 33, 103–129.
18. Brownfain, J. J.: Stability of the self-concept as a dimension of personality. *J. abnorm. soc. Psychol.*, 1952, 47, 597–606.
19. Cavan, R. S.: Personal adjustment in old age. *In* A. I. Lansing, *Cowdry's problems of aging*. Baltimore: Williams and Wilkins, 1952. Pp. 1032–1052.
20. Christensen, H. T., and M. M. Swihart: Postgraduation role preferences of senior women in college. *Marriage Fam. Living*, 1956, 18, 52–57.
21. Crist, J. R.: High school dating as a behavior system. *Marriage Fam. Living*, 1953, 15, 23–28.
22. Cobb, K.: Measuring leadership in college women by free association. *J. abnorm. soc. Psychol.*, 1952, 47, 126–128.
23. Cobliner, W. J.: Feminine fashion as an aspect of group psychology: analysis of written replies received by means of a questionnaire. *J. soc. Psychol.*, 1950, 31, 283–289.
24. Connor, R., T. B. Johannis, and J. Walters: Parent-adolescent relationships. *J. Home Econ.*, 1954, 46, 183–191.
25. Dreger, R. M.: Some personality correlates of religious attitudes, as determined by projective techniques. *Psychol. Monogr.*, 1952, 66, No. 3.
26. Dressel, P. L.: Interests—stable or unstable? *J. educ. Res.*, 1954, 48, 95–102.
27. Driver, H. L.: Learning self and social adjustment through small-group discussion. *Ment. Hyg., N.Y.*, 1952, 36, 600–606.
28. Ehrmann, W. W.: Influence of comparative social class of companion upon premarital heterosexual behavior. *Marriage Fam. Living*, 1955, 17, 48–53.
29. Eister, A. W.: Some aspects of institutional behavior with reference to churches. *Amer. sociol. Rev.*, 1952, 17, 64–69.

30. Gardner, G. A.: The mental health of normal adolescents. *Ment. Hyg., N.Y.,* 1947, 31, 529–540.

31. Garrison, K. C.: A comparative study of the attitudes of college students toward certain domestic and world problems. *J. soc. Psychol.,* 1951, 34, 47–54.

32. Glueck, S., and E. T. Glueck: *Unravelling juvenile delinquency.* New York: Commonwealth Fund, 1950.

33. Gough, H. G.: On making a good impression. *J. educ. Res.,* 1952, 46, 33–42.

34. Gough, H. G.: Predicting social participation. *J. soc. Psychol.,* 1952, 35, 227–233.

35. Gough, H. G., H. McClosky, and P. E. Meehl: A personality scale for social responsibility. *J. abnorm. soc. Psychol.,* 1952, 47, 73–80.

36. Grace, H. A., and G. L. Grace: Hostility, communication, and international tensions. III. The hostility factors. *J. educ. Psychol.,* 1951, 42, 293–300.

37. Gray, S. W.: Masculinity-femininity in relation to anxiety and social acceptance. *Child Develpm.,* 1957, 28, 203–214.

38. Gray, S. W., and R. Klaus: The assessment of parental identification. *Genet. Psychol. Monogr.,* 1956, 54, 87–114.

39. Gronlund, N. E.: Sociometric status and sociometric perception. *Sociometry,* 1955, 18, 122–128.

40. Havighurst, R. J.: *Human development and education.* New York: Longmans, 1953.

41. Havighurst, R. J., and H. Taba: *Adolescent character and personality.* New York: Wiley, 1949.

42. Herman, R. D.: The "going steady" complex: a reexamination. *Marriage Fam. Living,* 1955, 17, 36–40.

43. Hollingshead, A. de B.: *Elmtown's youth.* New York: Wiley, 1949.

44. Hood, W. R., and M. Sherif: An appraisal of personality-oriented approaches to prejudice. *Sociol. soc. Res.,* 1955, 40, 79–85.

45. Horrocks, J. E., and B. A. Wear: An analysis of interpersonal choice relationships of college students. *J. soc. Psychol.,* 1953, 38, 87–98.

46. Hunter, E. C.: Attitudes of college freshmen, 1934–1949. *J. Psychol.,* 1951, 31, 281–296.

47. Hurlock, E. B.: The spontaneous drawings of adolescents. *J. genet. Psychol.,* 1943, 63, 141–156.

48. Inlow, G. M.: Job satisfaction of liberal arts graduates. *J. appl. Psychol.,* 1951, 35, 175–181.

49. Itkin, W.: Relationships between attitudes toward parents and parents' attitudes toward children. *J. genet. Psychol.,* 1955, 86, 339–352.

50. Jersild, A. T.: *The psychology of adolescence.* New York: Macmillan, 1957.

51. Kirkpatrick, C., and E. Kanin: Male sex aggression on a university campus. *Amer. sociol. Rev.,* 1957, 22, 52–58.

52. Kirkpatrick, M. E.: The mental hygiene of adolescence in the Anglo-American culture. *Ment. Hyg., N.Y.,* 1952, 36, 394–403.

53. Koelsche, C. L.: A study of the student drop-out problem at Indiana University. *J. educ. Res.,* 1955, 49, 357–364.

54. Krogman, W. M.: The physical growth of the child. *In* M. Fishbein and R. J. R. Kennedy, *Modern marriage and family living.* New York: Oxford Univer. Press, 1957. Pp. 417–425.

55. Lindzey, G., and J. A. Urdan: Personality and social choice. *Sociometry,* 1954, 17, 47–63.

56. Lloyd, R. C.: Parent-youth conflicts of college students. *Sociol. soc. Res.*, 1952, 36, 227–230.

57. Long, A.: Social development among adolescents. *J. Home Econ.*, 1949, 41, 201–202.

58. Lowe, W. L.: Religious beliefs and religious delusions. *Amer. J. Psychother.*, 1955, 9, 54–61.

59. Lowrie, S. H.: Factors involved in the frequency of dating. *Marriage Fam. Living*, 1956, 18, 46–51.

60. Lundberg, G. A., and L. Dickson: Selection association among ethnic groups in a high school population. *Amer. sociol. Rev.*, 1952, 17, 23–35.

61. Marmor, J.: Psychological trends in the American family relationships. *Marriage Fam. Living*, 1951, 13, 145–147.

62. McArthur, C.: Personality differences between middle and upper classes. *J. abnorm. soc. Psychol.*, 1955, 50, 247–254.

63. Monahan, T. S.: Does age at marriage matter in divorce? *Soc. Forces*, 1953, 32, 81–87.

64. Mull, H. K., and A. Sheldon: A comparison of students of 1941 and 1951 in a liberal arts college in respect of their understanding of social issues. *J. soc. Psychol.*, 1953, 38, 283–285.

65. Mussen, P. H., and M. C. Jones: Self-conceptions, motivations, and interpersonal attitudes of late- and early-maturing boys. *Child Develpm.*, 1957, 28, 243–256.

66. Norton, J. L.: Pattern of vocational interest development and actual job choice. *J. genet. Psychol.*, 1953, 82, 235–262.

67. Pearson, L. H.: Teen-agers' preferences in clothes. *J. Home Econ.*, 1950, 42, 801–802.

68. Penchef, E. H.: The concept of social age. *Sociol. soc. Res.*, 1950, 34, 177–183.

69. Powell, M.: Age and sex differences in degree of conflict within certain areas of psychological adjustment. *Psychol. Monogr.*, 1955, 69, No. 2.

70. Pressey, S. L., and A. W. Jones: 1923–1953 and 20–60 age changes in moral codes, anxieties, and interests, as shown by the "X-O Tests." *J. Psychol.*, 1955, 39, 485–502.

71. Pressey, S. L., and R. G. Kuhlen: *Psychological development through the life span.* New York: Harper, 1957.

72. Radke-Yarrow, M. J., and B. Lande: Personality correlates of differential reactions to minority group belonging. *J. soc. Psychol.*, 1953, 38, 253–272.

73. Recreation Survey: Recreational interests and needs of high-school youth. *Recreation*, 1954, 47, 43–46.

74. Remmers, H. H., and N. Weltman: Attitude interrelationships of youth, their parents, and their teachers. *J. soc. Psychol.*, 1947, 26, 61–68.

75. Rose, A. A.: Menstrual pain and personal adjustment. *J. Pers.* 1949, 17, 287–300.

76. Ryan, M. S.: *Psychological effects of clothing.* Ithaca, N.Y.: Cornell Univer. Agricultural Experiment Station, 1953, Bulls. 882, 898, 900.

77. Savage, B. M., and F. L. Wells: A note on singularity in given names. *J. soc. Psychol.*, 1948, 27, 271–272.

78. Schneiderman, L.: The estimation of one's own bodily traits. *J. soc. Psychol.*, 1956, 44, 89–100.

79. Smith, E. A.: Dating and courtship at Pioneer College. *Sociol. soc. Res.*, 1955, 40, 92–98.

80. Smith, E., and J. H. G. Monane: Courtship values in a youth sample. *Amer. sociol. Rev.*, 1953, 18, 635–640.

81. Sommer, R., and L. M. Killian: Areas of value difference: Negro-white relations. *J. soc. Psychol.*, 1954, 39, 237–244.

82. Stanton, W. M., and J. A. Rutledge: Measurable traits of personality and incidence of somatic illness among college students. *Res. Quart. Amer. phys. Educ. Ass.*, 1955, 26, 197–204.

83. Strang, R.: What discipline means to adolescents. *Nerv. Child*, 1951, 9, 139–146.

84. Straus, R., and S. D. Bacon: *Drinking in college.* New Haven, Conn.: Yale Univer. Press, 1953.

85. Strong, E. K.: Permanence of interest scores over 22 years. *J. appl. Psychol.*, 1951, 35, 89–91.

86. Summerskill, J., and C. D. Darling: Emotional adjustment and dieting performance. *J. consult. Psychol.*, 1955, 19, 151–153.

87. Super, D. A.: Dimensions and measurement of vocational maturity. *Teach. Coll. Rec.*, 1955, 57, 151–163.

88. Swensen, J., and J. Rhulman: Leasure activities of a university sophomore class. *Educ. psychol. Measmt*, 1952, 12, 452–466.

89. Tate, M. T., and V. A. Musick: Adjustment problems of college students. *Soc. Forces*, 1954, 33, 182–185.

90. Telford, C. W.: A study of religious attitudes. *J. soc. Psychol.*, 1950, 31, 217–230.

91. Tenen, C.: Some problems of discipline among adolescents in factories. *Occup. Psychol., Lond.*, 1947, 21, 75–81.

92. Thompson, W. R., and R. Nishimura: Some determinants of friendship. *J. Pers.*, 1952, 20, 305–313.

93. Tuckman, J., and I. Lorge: The best years of life: a study in ranking. *J. Psychol.*, 1952, 34, 137–149.

94. Vernon, G. V., and R. L. Stewart: Empathy as a process in the dating situation. *Amer. sociol. Rev.*, 1957, 22, 48–52.

95. Wallin, P.: Cultural contradictions and sex roles: a repeat study. *Amer. sociol. Rev.*, 1950, 15, 288–293.

96. Walters, J., and R. H. Ojemann: A study of the components of adolescent attitudes concerning the role of women. *J. soc. Psychol.*, 1952, 35, 101–110.

97. Watson, J., W. Breed, and H. Posman: A study in urban conversations: sample of 1,001 remarks overheard in Manhattan. *J. soc. Psychol.*, 1948, 28, 121–133.

98. Welford, A. T.: Is religious behavior dependent upon affect or frustration? *J. abnorm. soc. Psychol.*, 1947, 42, 310–319.

99. Wieder, G. S.: Group procedures modifying attitudes of prejudice in the college classroom. *J. educ. Psychol.*, 1954, 45, 332–344.

100. Williams, C. D.: College students' family problems. *J. Home Econ.*, 1950, 42, 179–181.

101. Wittenberg, R. M.: *On call for youth.* New York: Association Press, 1955.

102. Witty, P. A.: Children's interest in comics, radio, motion pictures, and TV. *Educ. Adm. Supervis.*, 1952, 38, 138–147.

103. Young, F. M.: A comparison of the nervous habits of preschool and college students. *J. Pers.*, 1949, 17, 303–309.

104. Zeleny, L. D.: Social leadership. *Sociol. soc. Res.*, 1949, 33, 431–436.

» 10 «

Early Adulthood

Adulthood, which is legally achieved in our culture at the age of twenty-one years, extends to the end of life. During this long span of years, certain physical and psychological changes occur at predictable times, and these are used to mark off adulthood into subdivisions, each with its physical and psychological characteristics and each with adjustment problems stemming from these physical and psychological characteristics and from cultural pressures and expectancies. The first of these subdivisions, *early adulthood,* extends from legal maturity to approximately forty years. While there are marked variations in the ages at which men and women lose their reproductive capacities, with the physical and psychological changes that accompany the climacteric in men and the menopause in women, forty years is accepted as the traditional age at which these changes begin for the average individual.

For that reason, the age of forty is generally accepted as the dividing line between early adulthood and *middle age.* At varying ages, during the forties or fifties, most adults lose their reproductive capacity. With this, certain changes occur which mark the beginning of physical and psychological decline. At first, the decline is barely perceptible and is generally limited to physical changes. However, by the age of sixty years, the decline is more apparent for the average person than it was earlier and, for that reason, sixty is taken as a convenient dividing line to mark the end of middle age and the beginning of *old age,* the last of the subdivisions of adulthood, which extends to the time of death. Whether this will be a short or long period will vary from individual to individual. However, with the growing tendency for men and women in our culture to live longer than at any time in the past, there are more

372

aged today than ever before and, for the most part, old age is a longer
period than ever before in the history of civilization.

Adulthood, in our culture, is not designated by any marked biological
boundaries, such as puberty and the climacteric, although primitive
peoples use these biological landmarks to mark off the years of adulthood. With the advance of civilization, there has been a growing tendency to push up the recognized age of adulthood until now, in our culture, it comes 7 or 8 years after the individual has become sexually
mature. Similarly, the climacteric no longer means old age, as it does in
most primitive cultures and as it did in many civilized cultures in the
past. As a result, adulthood is today a long and poorly differentiated
period in the life span. Awareness of the physiological and psychological
changes that occur as adulthood progresses has been reduced to a minimum because modern medical aids and clothing help to keep men and
women of different ages looking, feeling, and acting much as if they
were of the same age. The dividing lines used today are general, not
specific, landmarks and they come at ages when the average man or
woman can be expected to begin to show some changes in appearance,
bodily functions, interests, attitudes, or behavior, and when certain environmental pressures in our culture give rise to adjustment problems
which few men or women escape.

Social Expectancy. It is expected, when the individual is granted the
status of an adult at legal maturity, that he will be ready to assume the
duties and responsibilities of an adult and that his behavior will conform
to the approved pattern of the adult in our culture. No tests are applied
to see whether he is ready for this status, as is true of the puberty rites
of primitive peoples. However, if he does not come up to social expectations, he makes poor adjustments to an environment where the standards
of behavior are set by successful adults. As is true at any age, poor adjustments lead to feelings of inadequacy and these, in turn, to unhappiness. High-level social expectancy, when combined with high-level and
often unrealistic personal aspirations, may lead to feelings of frustration
so severe as to cause a breakdown or an attempt to escape from the situation that seems impossible to cope with [45].

Social expectations for the young adult in our culture are clearly defined and familiar to the young adult even before he reaches legal
maturity. Perhaps at no other age in life does he know as clearly and
distinctly what society expects of him as at maturity, when society grants
him the status of an adult. These social expectations may be expressed
in the *developmental tasks* (see page 15) of early adulthood, which include selecting a mate, learning to live with a marriage partner, starting
a family, rearing children, managing a home, getting started in an occupation, taking on civic responsibility, and finding a congenial social

group [45]. How well he masters these developmental tasks during the years of early adulthood will influence the degree of success he will achieve when he reaches the peak during middle age, whether this peak relate to work, social recognition, or family living, and it will determine how happy he will be then as well as during the latter periods of his adult life. As is true of the earlier years, failure to master successfully a developmental task for a specific period means a poor foundation on which to build the developmental tasks society will expect him to master later. Conversely, his success in mastering the developmental tasks of early adulthood and thus measuring up to social expectations will be greatly influenced by the kind of foundations that were laid in the earlier periods of his life. As Jersild has pointed out, the adolescent "leaves unfinished many tasks that are the business of adolescence but are carried over into adult life. There is something of the uncompleted work of adolescence in every adult. The big issues with which the adolescent strives . . . are not completely settled just because he officially has finished the adolescent years" [53]. The more "unfinished business" he carries into adulthood, the longer and harder his adjustment to adulthood will be.

PERIOD OF ADJUSTMENT

The adult years present many new problems, different in their major aspects from the problems experienced in the earlier years of life. Furthermore, the adult is expected to cope with these problems without the supervision, guidance, and help he had from parents and teachers when he was younger. Even though he may have made some beginning in coping with adult problems in the latter part of adolescence, as happens when boys and girls enter the adult world of work when they finish high school or when they marry and become parents before they reach legal maturity, he can usually count on parental help should the problems be too much for him to deal with alone. After he becomes legally mature, his parents expect him to meet the problems alone or his pride prevents him from going to them for help. Thus, the adult years are problem years for him just as they are for the young adults who have spent their adolescent years in school or college and have been financially dependent on their parents.

The beginning of late adolescence, when the typical American boy or girl of today is finishing his high school education, is the starting point of the *exploratory stage* of youth, when the individual tries out various life careers to decide which will meet his needs and interests best. This stage extends through the early twenties and ends at between twenty-eight and thirty years of age, when the *selective stage* of maturity begins.

During this stage, the individual definitely decides upon specific life goals and channels his energies so as to reach the goals he has set for himself. The remaining years of early adulthood, into the early forties, are devoted to this task [21, 79].

Because the problems that must be met and the adjustments that must be made are different in their major aspects from the problems and adjustments met earlier, the young adult must use a new and different strategy, based on an understanding of the new terrain, if he is to make a success of his new environment and if he is to solve his adjustment problems to his satisfaction. This will necessitate scouting around and trying out different adjustments for a few years while he gets the lay of the land. That is why the exploratory stage, even though it normally begins during the adolescent years, extends into the early years of adulthood. The individual needs time to find the best adjustment techniques. The more scouting around he does at this time, the more likely he is to make adjustments that will be satisfying to him as he grows older. Adjustment to the problems of adulthood that are made too hastily and without adequate time to explore different possibilities are rarely as satisfactory in the long run as slower and more carefully considered adjustments [45].

From the beginning of adulthood until the early or mid-thirties, the average American of today is preoccupied with problems related to adjustments in the different major areas of his life. These adjustments will not all be made at the same time, nor will their final forms be accepted simultaneously (see Figure 81). While adjustment is being made in one area, there is a marked preoccupation with that interest. Then, when the adjustment is satisfactorily made, the individual's attention shifts to another form of adjustment. It is difficult, if not actually impossible, for a young adult to solve two such major problems as the choice of a life career and a life mate simultaneously. He therefore solves one problem and then turns his attention to the other.

By the mid-thirties, the average adult has established a life pattern that will remain, with only minor changes, for the rest of his life. Many adults do not need this long to establish themselves in their life patterns. Shortly after they reach maturity, they have married, established themselves in the type of work they will do for the remaining years of their lives, and have settled in a community where they intend to live permanently. This early solution to their life problems may prove to be satisfactory in the long run and it may not. If the decision has been based on strong drives, interests, and abilities, well and good. If, however, the decision has been made hastily to satisfy parental urgings or their own desires, the chances are that a time will come when they regret their hasty decisions.

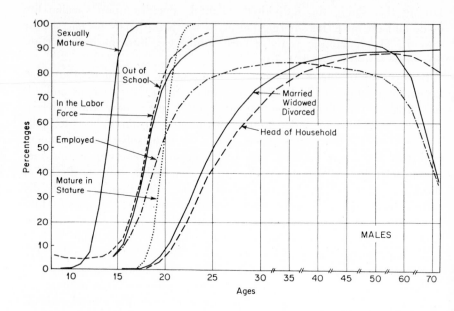

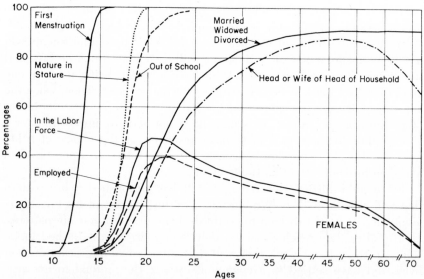

FIG. 81. Pattern of transition to maturity. (*From F. K. Shuttleworth, The adolescent period: a graphic atlas. Monogr. Soc. Res. Child Develpm., 1949, 14, No. 1. Used by permission.*)

Up to the age of thirty years, it is quite common for both men and women to be immature in certain areas of their behavior, at the same time showing marked degrees of maturity in other areas. Gradually with new achievements and new expectations from the social group, much of the immaturity that characterized the behavior in the early part of this period disappears. This results in a more even development on a more mature level than one normally finds in adolescence or in the early years of maturity. There are, however, many individuals who remain immature throughout the major part of their adulthood and who, as a result, can make successful adjustments to life only so long as their environments remain simple and in keeping with their immature level of development. This is well illustrated in the case of the overprotected wife and mother who is taken care of by a doting husband as long as he lives and whose care is later assumed by doting sons and daughters who try to protect their mother from the world just as their father did. Should they not, however, assume the protective role, their mother would quickly find herself incapable of adjusting to an environment that has been planned for adults who have been accustomed to stand on their own feet.

Aids to Adjustment. The young adult is aided in meeting the adjustment problems that adulthood brings by being at the peak of his physical and mental vigor. Before adolescence comes to a close, the *physical growth* of the individual is complete or so nearly complete that what few changes occur thereafter will be barely noticeable. The peak of *physical efficiency* is generally reached in the mid-twenties, after which there is a slow and gradual decline in general physical fitness up to the age of forty or forty-five years, when the rate of decline begins to accelerate. This means that during the period when the most numerous and most difficult adjustment problems must be met and solved, the individual is physically able to do so.

Even the periodic physical disturbances of the female *menstruation* have not been found to have the effects that they are traditionally believed to have. There are variations in physical and psychological states not duplicated in men but, as a general rule, these do not result in disturbances comparable to those of the adolescent girl. Among many women, there is no physical disturbance, though there may be a tendency to greater irritability and nervousness than is experienced at other times. What effects there are are largely subjective and reflect the influence of superstitious beliefs and traditions. Well-adjusted women are able to meet the demands of daily living and do their work as successfully during their menstrual periods as at any other time, though it may require slightly more effort on their part to keep their work up to the normal level [47].

Adjustment in early adulthood is aided by the individual's *motor abilities*. Because of the physical strength and good health normally present in early adulthood, the individual can acquire skills even better than in adolescence, when his body is still developing. Furthermore, he can count on his ability in a given situation and thus possesses a confidence that is generally impossible during adolescence, when uneven and rapid growth throw the muscular patterns temporarily out of balance. In *strength*, the individual is at his peak between the ages of twenty and thirty years, after which there is a slow but steady decline. Maximum *speed* of response, as measured by reaction-time tests, comes between twenty and twenty-five years, after which decline begins at a slow rate. In *learning new motor skills*, the adult in his early twenties is superior to the one who is approaching middle age. The speed of learning these new skills is more affected by age than is the quality of learning [5].

Mental abilities are even more important in adjustments than are motor abilities. Genetic studies of intelligence have revealed that there is a slow but continuous rise in intelligence-test scores up to the mid-twenties, after which the curve begins to flatten out and remains thus until the fifties [10] (see Figure 2, page 10). Analysis of different mental abilities tested by tests of general intelligence has revealed that the important mental abilities needed for learning and for adjustment to new situations, such abilities, for example, as forming comparisons, reasoning by analogy, recall of previously learned information, and creative imagination, reach their peak during the twenties and then begin a slow and gradual decline [38]. Because mental abilities reach their peak of development in the early adult years and remain near their peak until middle age sets in, the young adult is capable of learning as well as a child or an adolescent. It may take him longer to learn than it did when he was younger, but the quality of his learning does not suffer.

It is assumed that, with advancing age, people become less adventuresome and more *conservative*. It is further believed that they become inflexible, rigid, or "set in their ways" to such an extent that they are unwilling to try to adjust to new situations. While there is no question about the fact that mental resistance to change appears with advancing age, it is generally not apparent before middle age. In fact, there is a trend toward more liberal attitudes as people grow older, with those who were radical in their adolescent years becoming slightly more radical and the reactionaries, less reactionary. While women show a shift toward liberalism, they are still more conservative than men [84]. How conservative and inflexible the adult is depends partly on his personality make-up, especially the degree of his self-confidence and security, and partly on the level of his education. The more schooling the individual has had, the more willing he is to adopt a new point of view. In all levels of education, however, the younger the individual, the more ready he is to accept new ideas and new practices.

Handicaps to Adjustment. Adjustments to new situations are never easy and they are made even more difficult when handicaps from the environment or from within the individual himself are present. Unlike primitive and most civilized cultures, child training in the home and education in the schools and colleges in our culture do not prepare young people for the type of life they will be expected to live when they reach adulthood. Our training of the young is characterized by *discontinuities* in the sense that the training given in childhood has little or no relationship to the pattern of life in adulthood. By contrast, in cultures where there is continuity in training, with emphasis on teaching the child what he will need to know to meet the demands of adult life, the transition to adult life is made easy and the adjustments are successful [12]. The American tendency to overprotect the child and to shield him from hardships and disappointments that would interfere with the happy, carefree childhood that parents want their children to have makes adult adjustments to life so difficult that many are incapable of making them successfully [97]. Even in school, the education of the child has little relationship to what he will need in adult life, and this is true also of the education in high school and in the liberal arts colleges. Only when the older student takes a course of study in some professional training school is there any continuity between what he learns in school and what he can use when he goes to work.

Parental overprotectiveness may result in a dependency on the parents that is so marked that the young adult is unable to meet the demands placed on him. While most parents want their children, especially when they reach adolescence, to be emancipated from parental control and become independent, many adolescents feel incapable of adjusting to the strange and complicated demands of the adult world. Parents, even though they want their adolescent sons and daughters to grow up, are afraid of what the world will do to these innocent and inexperienced youth. This usually results in a prolonging of the dependency relationship (see Figure 72, page 344). Becoming independent of parental protectiveness is especially difficult for young people in middle-class socioeconomic families, and girls experience greater difficulties in becoming emancipated than do boys [45]. Few parents who have been overprotective during their children's early life are willing to grant them complete independence in making their own decisions just because they have reached the age of legal maturity. This complicates matters for the individual, making it difficult for him to make decisions that will satisfy himself and his parents. To avoid hurting his parents' feelings or making them feel that he is ungrateful to them for all the sacrifices they have made for him, he frequently makes compromises that are satisfying neither to him nor to them.

Complications of adjustment may stem from the young adult's own *unrealistic concepts* of what he wants and what he is capable of. Too much academic, athletic, or social success in high school or college may give the adolescent such unrealistic concepts of his abilities that he will expect the adult world to be at his feet, just as the adolescent world of his school or college days was. *Parental aspirations* often intensify the adolescent's own aspirations, thus increasing the adjustment problems when the individual reaches adult years. Fathers, more often than mothers, are concerned about behavior that they regard as a prognostication, either directly or indirectly, of traits which will be a handicap to success in adult life, such as lack of initiative, overconformity, insufficient aggressiveness, or excitability. Their concern is more for their sons than for their daughters, especially for the first-born son [1]. This results in setting up standards, often beyond the reach of the young person, and adds to adjustment difficulties not only in adolescence but in adulthood as well. Men under thirty-six years of age report daydreaming much more frequently than those who are older. This suggests that striving for high goals continues throughout the major part of the early adult years [91].

Success of Adjustment. Successful adjustment to adult life can be measured in *achievements* and in *satisfaction*. The person who is able to make good adjustments to adult life will be more successful, in terms of income and social recognition, than is the person whose adjustment is poor. The degree of satisfaction he experiences will be influenced by the success of his adjustments. Knowing how successfully or unsuccessfully he is getting along in the different important areas of his life will affect his happiness. In a culture where success is highly valued, the more successful the individual, the more favorably will society look upon him and, in turn, the more favorably he will see himself. By contrast, the individual who is a failure or near failure cannot be happy knowing how society judges those who fall below social expectations for individuals of his age and socioeconomic groups.

Adulthood is the period of *achievements*. The individual who during the years of preparation lays the groundwork for his future occupation with a minimum of shifting from one vocational aim to another and who receives the necessary training to develop his innate abilities is more likely to achieve success in mature years than is the individual who shifts from one type of work to another. Adults who achieve distinction in adult life have had a preparation for these achievements in many years of relevant activity, combined with a noticeable continuity of purpose and interests. Thus, their accomplishments in adult life are dependent upon earlier sustained training and interests. Extracurricular activities in high school and college and the success with which the individual gets along with others have a closer relationship to financial success and vocational achievements than does scholastic ranking [52].

Studies of achievement have revealed that the peak of achievement in the adult years falls between thirty and thirty-nine years. How early or how late in the adult years the peak will come depends on the area in which the individual attains distinction. In athletic abilities, the peak of performance comes in the mid-twenties, though it varies somewhat for different types of activity. For science, mathematics, music, literary creativity, philosophy, and invention, the peak is usually in the thirties. The maximum production rate for output of the highest quality usually occurs at an earlier age than the maximum rate for less distinguished work by the same individuals. The explanation for this is that the younger adult is less rigid and more motivated to make a name for himself than he is as he approaches middle or old age. Those who are early starters contribute better work and are more prolific than slower starters, suggesting the relationship of successful adjustment to achievement. Further evidence of the relationship of adjustment to achievement is apparent in the finding that individuals who work intensively in their chosen areas instead of shifting about from one line of work to another achieve more and are more successful than their contemporaries who take longer to adjust to the choice of a career [64].

The degree of success the individual has in making satisfactory adjustments to the important problems he faces in adult life will determine the degree of his *happiness*. For in the adult years, as is true of all ages of life, good adjustment and happiness go hand in hand just as poor adjustment and unhappiness are closely associated. The well-adjusted person is pleasantly satisfied with life in its various aspects. He may not achieve great success or fame but he manages to get along with reasonable success and to adapt himself to the problems that arise in his life activities. Happy and unhappy people are very much alike in their problems and interests. The people who are unhappy do not have peculiar interests or problems but they make less satisfactory adjustments to them than do those who achieve happiness.

An assessment of the personal-social adjustments of a group of middle-class mothers has revealed the following characteristics as being indicative of good adjustment on the part of these women to their adult roles of wife and mother: stable value systems; realistic appraisal of themselves; satisfaction with their surroundings; ability to meet emergencies in daily life and a feeling of competence to do so; active participation in social affairs and the possession of many close friends; interests and activities in common with husband; and a warm and affectionate feeling for their children. While mothers of the higher socioeconomic groups are, on the whole, better adjusted than those of the lower groups, there is no evidence that socioeconomic status per se is responsible for good adjustment or that it invariably contributes to greater happiness [29].

Emotional Accompaniment. Adjustments are always difficult and are invariably accompanied by emotional tension. While the individual is trying to get the lay of the new land in which he finds himself, he is likely to be upset emotionally and, like the adolescent who finds himself in a new and different land, the young adult goes through a period of emotional storm and stress. In an attempt to decide what his life career will be, where he wants to live for the remaining years of his life, or with whom he wishes to share his life, the young adult is in a state of indecision during which he tries out first one solution to his problem and then another until he finds a satisfactory one.

In early adulthood, the individual is faced with more adjustment problems than he has ever had to face before, even more than during the early years of adolescence, and he is less well equipped to deal with these adjustment problems than he will be later. While he is attempting to solve these problems, he goes through a period of emotional tension that is far from happy. By the early or mid-thirties, however, he should have solved these problems well enough so that the emotional tension subsides and is replaced with emotional stability and calm [45]. However, if the adult has high aspirations that are not matched with equally high achievements, thus putting him into the "climber" category in which he overstrains in his attempts to live up to the social and occupational levels he is aspiring to reach, he will be in a situation of stress which may eventually lead to an emotional breakdown and will certainly create psychological disorders or psychosomatic problems [37]. The cultural milieu in which the adult finds himself may also contribute to emotional tensions. Even the best-adjusted adult cannot find happiness in a milieu which is totally unsuited to him but into which he has been forced by conditions beyond his control. This will result in constant emotional tension caused by his frustrations and resentments at being forced into a situation foreign to his interests and abilities.

Emotional tension is often expressed in *worries.* Like the adolescent, the young adult has few fears but many worries. What he worries about, however, will depend on what adjustment problems he is facing at the time and how much success or failure he is experiencing in meeting these problems. Money worries, for example, reach their peak at around age thirty, the time when economic problems in business and home life reach their peak. Worries about personal appearance, sexual morality, and making a good impression when meeting people, all of which are directly or indirectly related to courtship and finding a life mate, are most common during the early twenties. After thirty, worries center around health, making a success in business, and job security; as middle age approaches, marital difficulties and family-relationship problems come to the fore. Even though there are individual variations in worries at different ages, there is a predictable pattern since these are closely related to, and in fact, are the outcome of, the adjustment problems more or less universally found among the young adults of our culture [58].

Effects on Personality. The success with which the individual adjusts to the problems of adult life is bound to have some effect on his *concept of self.* The more successfully he adjusts, the more favorable his self-concept will be and the more self-confidence, assurance, and poise he will have. Feelings of inadequacy, on the other hand, are the usual accompaniment of failures in adjustment. However, most adults make reasonably good adjustments to the demands of adult life, even though to do so it may take some longer than others and it may mean a revision downward of the levels of aspiration they carried into the adult years from their unrealistic adolescent aspirations. Consequently, unless there is a marked change in the concept of self, either favorable or unfavorable, there is little reason to expect that there will be any marked change in the personality pattern of the young adult. As a rule, the self-concept remains stable throughout the adult years, with a tendency to become stronger and more fixed with age [20].

Studies of groups of the same individuals over a period of years, from childhood or adolescence into adult years and even to old age, have revealed how consistent the personality pattern is over a period of time. Retesting of a group of engaged couples twenty years later revealed that the absolute changes in the scores on personality tests were very small and similar in direction and magnitude for men and women. Changes that did occur were relatively specific rather than reflections of an over-all tendency to change. While changes in personality during the adult years may be significant, they are not so large or so sudden as to threaten the continuity of the self-concept or to impair the day-to-day inter-personal relationships of the individual. When changes occur suddenly and are radical, they are suggestive of an abnormal condition [57]. Figure 82 shows the self-ratings on a number of personality variables after a period of 20 years. Thorndike emphasized the fact that personality patterns in the early adult years change little from those of youth when he said, "A person's nature at 12 is prophetic of his nature in adult years. . . . The child to whom approval is more cherished than mastery is likely to become a man who seeks applause rather than power, and similarly throughout" [103].

Because the personality pattern of the individual is so well established by adolescence that, under normal conditions, it changes relatively little during early adulthood, it becomes apparent that the personality pattern of the individual influences the type of adjustments he makes to adult life rather than that the type of adjustments he makes influences his personality. While there unquestionably is a cause-effect relationship

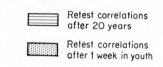

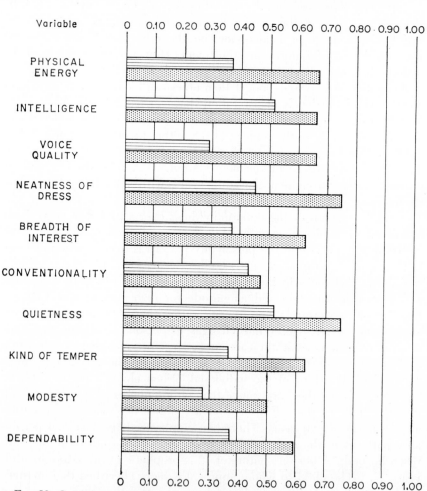

Fig. 82. Consistency in self-ratings of different personality variables over a period of 20 years. (*From E. L. Kelly, Consistency of the adult personality. Amer. Psychologist,* 1955, 10, 659–681. *Used by permission.*)

working both ways, it seems evident, from the results of studies of personality consistency over a period of years, that the cause-effect relationship is stronger in the direction of the personality's influence on adjustments rather than the effect of adjustments on personality. There is substantial evidence that adults who make good adjustments have integrated personality patterns in which the core is a stable, realistic concept of self, whereas those who make poor adjustments have poorly integrated personality patterns with unstable, unrealistic self-concepts [77].

Studies of age of sexual maturing have revealed that the age at which a boy or girl matures, in relation to the same-sex group with which he or she is identified, influences the individual's concept of self so markedly that it has a profound influence on the type of adjustment made during the adolescent years (see pages 254–258). Physically accelerated boys are not only accepted and treated as more mature by adults and peers but they have the prestige advantage that comes from superior strength in sports. By contrast, late maturers, who are treated as children, must strive for status and this makes them seem even more immature. The early maturers make good adjustments, are popular with their peers, and usually become the leaders in extracurricular activities. By contrast, the late maturers, in their attempts to adjust to a situation in which they are at a disadvantage because of their immature appearance, develop certain personality traits that militate against good adjustment, such as touchiness, aggressiveness, rebelliousness, and impulsiveness. Sixteen years later, these same individuals have been found to display personality patterns similar to those they displayed in adolescence, and the effects on their personal and social adjustments are similar to the effects during adolescence. Just as in adolescence, those who matured early have made better adjustments, even in their vocational careers, than the late maturers [54].

ADJUSTMENT PROBLEMS

While adulthood brings many different adjustments for every individual, there are certain adjustments that are almost universal in our culture. Some of these are more difficult for men to make while others are more characteristically difficult for women. Some adjustments must be made early in the adult years; others are the outcome of adjustments made earlier and, as a result, they come later. Even when the individual has a number of adjustments to make at approximately the same time, he generally concentrates on the one or ones that are most important to success in the life pattern he has selected and delays tackling the other areas of adjustment, with their problems, until he has reached a satisfactory solution to the important ones.

Of the many areas in which the young adult must make adjustments, the following are the most common and, in most cases, the most important.

Interests. The individual carries over into the adult years many of the interests he acquired in adolescence or even in childhood. However, as the pattern of life of the young adult takes on new forms, there must be a reassessment of old interests to see if they fit into this new pattern and if they can give the satisfaction to the individual that they gave when he was younger and when the pattern of his life was different. From the practical angle, the young adult must assess his old interests in terms of the time they require, the money and companionship they entail, and the physical strength and energy needed to carry them out satisfactorily. In the early years of adulthood, many of the interests are the same as those of the closing years of adolescence. However, with each passing year, there are changes that must be made and, like all change, this requires adjustment on the part of the individual. The more satisfying an interest is, the more difficult it is to adjust to giving it up or relegating it to a position in which it has little effect on the individual's life.

As patterns of living change, new values are acquired and these influence the interests of the individual. In the adult years, the pattern of women's lives differs markedly from that of men's, much more so than during their school and college days, so it is not surprising that their interests become different [95] (see Figure 83). Because the life pattern for married adults differs markedly from that of unmarried adults of the same age levels, it would be logical to suppose that there would also be differences in the interests of individuals, depending on their marital status. With age, likes and dislikes tend to become stronger, and since these preferences influence the interests of the individual, there is a tendency for interests to become more stable as the individual grows older. In the adult years, age differences in interests are less pronounced than interests due to sex, occupational level, or socioeconomic status [62].

Interests at every age are affected by many factors, the most important of which are opportunities for acquiring them, the life activities of the individual, the people he is associated with, his intelligence and educational status, general health conditions, and early childhood experiences. Interests are often an outcome of frustration and are closely related to level of aspiration. It is not unusual for the individual to be interested in something beyond his reach, or in something he cannot have because of his race, color, or socioeconomic status. Negroes, for example, indicate that they would like to engage in many activities denied them, not only in the area of occupations but in recreations as well [99].

Changes with Age. It is popularly believed that there are marked changes in interest with age. This is not borne out by evidence from experimental studies. The tendency is not to change interests with age so much as to narrow down slightly the range of interests as age advances with the result that, as middle age approaches, there are fewer interests than there were during the years of early maturity. As changes in duties and responsibilities occur, there is normally a shift of emphasis on already-existing interests rather than the establishment of new interests [89]. New interests may be established as the individual grows older

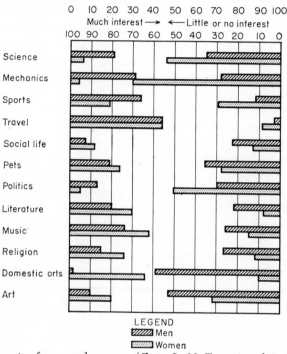

FIG. 83. Interests of men and women. (*From L. M. Terman and C. C. Miles, Sex and personality. New York: McGraw-Hill,* 1936. *Used by permission.*)

but, unless there are changes in his environment, opportunities to develop new interests, and a strong motivation to do so, the chances are that new interests will develop only infrequently as time goes by.

Changes in interests do not all come at the same time. Approximately one-half of all changes come between the ages of twenty-five and thirty-five years; 20 per cent between the ages of thirty-five and forty-five years; and the remaining 30 per cent, between forty-five and fifty-five years. There is little or no change in interests between the ages of fifty-five and sixty-five years. These shifts in interest are probably the result of cultural and environmental rather than actual age changes. The period of most rapid shift in interests comes in adolescence, when there is the most marked change in the physical and psychological make-up of the individual. As Strong has pointed out, at "twenty-five years the adult is largely what he is going to be and even at twenty years he has acquired pretty much the interests he will have throughout life" [99].

Though the number of interests changes little as age advances, the shifts in emphasis on different interests are marked. Interest in active recreations, such as sports and dancing, declines with age and in its place comes an interest in more cultural and sedentary use of leisure time, such as reading and card games. Interest in sex changes differently for the two sexes. For men, this interest increases up to the ages of thirty-five or forty years and then decreases at a slow rate. For women, by contrast, the interest begins to decline in the thirties but at a much more rapid rate than for men.

Interest in manners and courtesy, which ranks high in adolescence, decreases as time goes on. Likewise, interest in money, which to the adolescent and young adult is not only a strong interest but also a serious problem, loses its hold on the individual's attention as he reaches middle age and is in an financial position to supply most of his needs and wants. By contrast, interest in a philosophy of life, which during the adolescent years is not very strong, increases in importance as the individual grows older (see Figure 78, page 360).

Because interests change less in adult years than is generally supposed, it becomes apparent that the larger the range of interests built up during the early years of life, the better able the adult will be to adjust to the changes in interests which must be made as the pattern of his life changes. Furthermore, because new interests, totally unrelated to previously learned interests, are less and less likely to be acquired as the individual grows older, a larger range of interests carried over from earlier years gives him a backlog to fall back on when it is necessary to make changes in already-existing interests. This becomes especially important in the latter periods of life, middle and old age, when necessity forces the individual to relinquish many of his earlier interests. Without adequate reserve to fill in the gaps, the older person finds himself devoid of the interests that make life pleasant and facilitate his adjustments to those changes in the pattern of living which age forces him to make.

Types of Interests. Of the almost universally found interests among American adults of today, the following are the most important:

PHYSICAL APPEARANCE. By adulthood, most men and women have learned to accept their physiques and to make the most of them. While their height, weight, facial features, and coloring may not be to their liking, they have learned that little can be done to alter them but much can be done to cover them up or to improve them. As a result, the adult's major concern with his appearance is to improve it. This leads to interest in all sorts of beauty aids, to diets, and to exercise which will improve the figure. The adult's interest in looks begins to wane during the late twenties. But, with the first signs of aging, this interest is again revived. As signs of aging appear with greater frequency and severity, the interest becomes stronger and stronger.

The first indication of aging the young adult is confronted with is usually gain in weight. Unless careful attention is given to diet, both men and women begin to add weight in the twenties. In men, the increase is in all areas of their bodies while in women, especially those who have had children, the increase is especially noticeable in the neck and total front region [94]. Women who are poorly adjusted tend to become obese during the early adult years, often adding to the overweight condition they have carried over from adolescence [61]. In addition, other signs of aging, such as sagging chins, gray hairs, and protruding abdomens, become problems for the young adult to adjust to. Some adults accept these signs of aging without any attempt to correct them. Most, however, recognize the important role appearance plays in business, social, professional, and even family life and attack the problem both at its source and by using clothes and beauty aids to cover up the telltale signs of aging they cannot remove. Any physical defect or deformity, especially when it is facial, becomes a serious adjustment problem for adults because it may prove to be a serious handicap in getting jobs, making friends, or marrying [68].

CLOTHING. Clothing and personal adornment, one of the major interests of the adolescent years, remains strong during the early years of maturity. This is especially true of unmarried men and women. Frequently, more time and money are spent on clothing than the individual can afford, because he knows it plays a role of major importance in achieving success in whatever area of activity he is interested. Among men, clothing is important as an indication of social status and economic success. The man knows that he cannot "afford" to be poorly dressed. He is aware of the fact that his clothes tell the world not only what sort of person he is but also how successful he is. Because social relationships, in business as well as in social life, are markedly influenced by judgments people make of one another, the adult knows that his status rating by others will be affected by the type of clothes he wears [50].

For women, it is important not only to establish socioeconomic status by the clothes they wear but also to attract members of the opposite sex, to win the approval of members of their own sex, and to maintain a favorable status in the business or professional world, if they work outside the home. Because women's clothing is more individualized than men's, a woman may express her personality through the type of clothes she selects. For this reason, many women seek individuality through clothes to compensate for lack of individuality in their personality make-ups. Furthermore, the young woman knows that clothing which enhances her physical attractiveness gives her greater self-confidence and, at the same time, creates a favorable impression on others, which will give her social or professional advantages.

People select clothing to fill certain important needs. To a young adult, the following are the most important needs: *compensation,* or improving the appearance of face and figure by carefully selected clothes; *identification,* especially with a social class group that will give the individual social and business prestige; and *regression,* or making the person appear younger than he is [44]. Because all clothes affect the individual's concept of self and thus evoke some degree of ego involvement, most men and women are willing to deprive themselves of pleasures or even necessities to be in style. Professional advancement and a desire to put up a "good front" are powerful motives in determining whether men and women will spend a disproportionate amount of money on their clothes. Because clothing plays a dominant role in adjustments in all areas of adult life, interest in clothes does not lag as adulthood progresses but remains strong or may even increase in intensity if it is apparent to the individual that success in some area of adjustment that is important to him can be aided by an attractive appearance which is enhanced by stylish, becoming, and expensive clothing.

MONEY AND MATERIAL POSSESSIONS. Interest in money and material possessions generally reaches its peak during the early years of maturity. The young adult who, as an adolescent, envied those whose economic status was superior to his is motivated by a strong desire to earn enough money to have the possessions he formerly wanted but was unable to have. Many young women, even after marriage, continue to hold jobs not because they enjoy the work but rather because they want the money that will enable them to have the things they crave. Because success in the business world is generally judged by the economic and social status of the individual, as shown by his clothes, his home, his cars, and his other possessions, the typical young man of today is eager to rise as fast as possible in the business world in hopes of getting the things he and his family want. While the home and its furnishings may mean a comfortable pattern of living to older people, to the young adult it means prestige in the eyes of others [60].

Much of the unhappiness and discontent of young adults stems from the fact that they do not have the material possessions they want or that their friends and neighbors have. Many divorces stem, likewise, from the fact that young people cannot adjust successfully to deprivations, especially when they have anticipated the attainment of certain possessions when they married. Some of the adjustment problems relating to money come from lack of knowledge of how to use money wisely. Adolescents are primarily concerned with earning money or getting enough for their needs from their parents. They show little interest in the management of the family finances. They do not want to be bothered with money problems relating to the family as a whole [81]. Furthermore, they have little training in the use of money. Parents may offer advice to younger adolescents about how they are using their allowances, but older adolescents usually have complete freedom to use their money as they wish. As a result, they are ill prepared, as young adults, to budget the income they have to live on and they frequently buy on credit or on

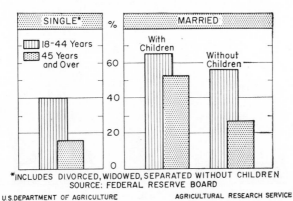

INSTALLMENT DEBTORS
By Marital Status, Age, Children, 1956

Fig. 84. Buying on installment at different ages among single and married adults. (*From E. Holmes, Who uses consumer credit? J. Home Econ.*, 1957, 49, 340–342. *Used by permission.*)

installment, thus putting themselves in a position where they are always in debt. That this is not a good solution to money problems may be seen by the anxiety it engenders in young adults and the constant fear they have of losing their jobs and being unable to pay their debts [49]. Figures 84 and 85 show how widespread the practice of buying on installment is.

Among adult criminals, one of the most common causes of crime is the desire for easy money and the attainment of possessions they would not be able to get through their own abilities. The adult criminal learned, as an adolescent, that money and material possessions play a very important role in social acceptance. His classmates who had money for clothes and recreation were sure to have friends and be included in clique activities, whereas those who lacked the money necessary for clothes and recreations were left out of the cliques and missed the fun their classmates had. To solve the problem of acceptance, the adolescent therefore turned to stealing and became a juvenile delinquent [39]. Even though this solution was not considered satisfactory in the eyes of society, to his own gangmates and to himself it was usually regarded as the easiest, if not the best, solution to the problem. As a result, he continues into adulthood to use stealing as a means of satisfying his desires for money and material possessions, hoping, as he hoped when he was younger, that this will bring the social acceptance and esteem he craves.

RELIGION. By the time the individual reaches adulthood, either he has resolved his religious doubts and formulated a philosophy of life, based

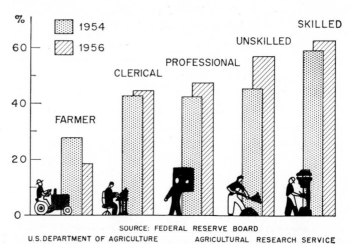

SOURCE: FEDERAL RESERVE BOARD
U.S. DEPARTMENT OF AGRICULTURE   AGRICULTURAL RESEARCH SERVICE

FIG. 85. Installment buying among adults in different occupational groups. (*From E. Holmes, Who uses consumer credit? J. Home Econ., 1957, 49, 340–342. Used by permission.*)

on religion, that will be satisfactory to him, with minor changes, for the rest of his life, or he has rejected religion as having little or nothing to offer him. In both cases, religion has less interest for the individual than it had when he was younger. The early twenties have been called the "least religious period of life" [3]. However, few young adults find indifference to or rejection of their earlier beliefs a satisfactory solution to their problem and, as a result, many develop feelings of guilt because they lack a religious faith [74].

When the responsibilities of parenthood are assumed, there is generally a return to religion. Parents of young children feel that it is their duty and responsibility as parents not only to teach their children the fundamentals of their own faith and to see that they receive proper religious instruction in Sunday school, but also to set a good example for them [3]. Consequently, religious practices which prevailed in their own homes are now revived in the home where there are children, even if these religious practices are somewhat modified to fit into the pattern of life today [18]. Regular attendance at church is now a part of the parents' life and they begin to take an active part in some of the church organizations and activities.

Strength of religious interests varies markedly in early adulthood, even more so than in adolescence. Those who have a great variety of interests and are realistic and somewhat unconventional in their thinking and behavior tend to be less interested in religion than do those who are more conventional [65]. Women, on the whole, are more interested in religion than are men, as was true during adolescence, and they take a more active part in church affairs than do men. Members of the middle class are not only more interested in religion than are those of the upper and lower classes but they participate more in church functions of all types and assume leadership roles in different church organizations. Those who achieve social and economic success in the middle class are more active than those whose status is lower [65, 66, 90]. Active participation in religious activities and a strong interest in religion have been found to be highly correlated with good social adjustments, as judged in terms of honesty and kindness [25].

The problems of adjustment to religion in adulthood are greatly complicated by *mixed marriages*. When families are of different faiths, they are less active in religious affairs than when they are of the same faith. If the father has no church affiliation, there is usually little interest in religion on the part of either parent and little encouragement to the children to become active in Sunday school or church. Lack of interest in religion on the part of one or both parents usually is accompanied by limited religious practices in the home [4]. The most difficult problem related to religious adjustments in early adulthood stems from family pressures in mixed marriages. From both sides, there are parental pressures to have the mate accept the religious faith of one side of the family and to bring up the children in that faith. Even when the young adult has limited interest in religion, he resents being forced to accept another faith; he objects to having the religious training of the children dictated by grandparents on either side; and he resents the implication that his religion is inferior to that of his mate—an implication inherent in the insistence that the change be made. Furthermore, he has to contend with the pressures of his own parents to whom adherence to the family faith may also be important [19]. Adjustment problems in religion often complicate marital adjustments and are at the basis of "in-law" problems, one of the most difficult problems in the area of marital adjustments (see pages 439–441).

RECREATIONS. By the time the individual reaches adult years, his recreational interests are fairly well formed. With the responsibilities he must assume in adulthood, the typical adult has even less time for recreation than he had in adolescence. As a result, he must narrow down the recreations to those that not only give him the greatest enjoyment but also to those that are most practical for him from the point of view of both time and money. Young unmarried people of both sexes not only have more time and money for different recreations than do those who are married but more of their recreational interests are outside the home than are those of the married group. With age, there is a marked decrease in the number of recreations outside the home. This holds true for the married as well as for the unmarried [108].

Recreational interests are markedly influenced by the social class to which the adult belongs. Up to eighteen years of age, when children and young adolescents are in school with contemporaries from different socioeconomic backgrounds, and when the recreations are influenced by the school program, there are only limited social class differences in recreation. After eighteen years, however, the patterns of life begin to change and this change will be influenced greatly by the social class to which the young person belongs. Members of the lower and lower-middle classes, who, for the most part, go to work at the end of high school or when they reach the legal minimum age for going to work, will be in environments that will necessitate the development of recreational interests that are very different from those the older adolescent in college or professional training school will have an opportunity to acquire. And, as the patterns of living in adult life are likewise influenced by socioeconomic status, it is understandable that social class differences in the use of leisure time become more marked as adulthood progresses [108].

Adults of the middle class have more time for recreation than do those of the lower, and they engage in a wider variety of recreational activities. Members of the middle class spend more of their recreational time as spectators while members of the lower and upper classes spend more time as nonspectators. Commercialized leisure activities, such as dance halls, taverns, radio, and television, appeal more to the lower-class adults, as is true also of craftsmenlike activities of the "do-it-yourself" type. Members of the upper middle and upper classes spend more of their leisure time on activities related to their work, such as reading, while adults of the lower class spend theirs on activities unrelated to their work [108]. When asked what they would do with extra leisure time if they had it, a group of higher-class adults said, "Read and study," while a group of lower said, "Rest, relax, and loaf" [26]. Family recreations, as well as individual recreations for men and women during the adult years, are influenced by the socioeconomic status of the family.

In the lower-class families, family recreations are mostly out of the home and involve commercial entertainment while those of the middle-class families are more in the home but are less organized and involve fewer family members as participants [110].

Women have fewer variations in their recreations than do men, regardless of the social class to which they belong. The reason for this is that most young adult women are housewives with children, which limits their recreations to the home. Because men are not tied down by home and children, they are free to select recreations that are congenial to them and which their friends and associates engage in [108]. For the woman, on the other hand, there are not only limitations on the types of recreation she can engage in but her time is limited by the size of her family, how old her children are, and whether she lives in an urban area with labor-saving devices to cut down on the time spent on her home duties or in a rural area lacking these aids. Her leisure time comes mostly in the afternoons and evenings and her recreations are limited to what she can engage in at home, such as reading, knitting, crocheting, radio listening, and television viewing [63]. Only occasionally can the young woman participate in any recreation away from home, as she did during her adolescence, and this is a difficult adjustment problem for many young women to make.

Types of Recreation. An analysis of the different types of recreation engaged in by American men and women today will show what marked changes there are from the interests that were dominant during the adolescent years and will emphasize the fact that this change means a difficult adjustment problem for young men as well as for young women. Giving up a recreation that has been satisfying not only because of the enjoyment of the activity itself but also because of the prestige value it may have brought to the individual is never easy, especially when a substitute recreation that fits into the limited time and family budget holds little interest for the adult. A young woman who, for example, during her high school and college days, and even during her courtship after college, found dancing a favorite recreation and must now abandon it because of the expense involved in going to dance halls, country clubs, or hotels, plus the cost of a baby sitter for the children, may find it difficult to adjust to talking to neighbors in her free time, crocheting or knitting alone in the house, or watching television after the children are in bed. For the young man who must give up a sport in which he excelled in high school or college because of limited time, the cost of joining a club where this sport could be enjoyed, or the lack of players to make up a team, it is likewise a difficult adjustment to make.

An analysis of the different forms of recreation engaged in by young American adults today will show that there are marked changes in

RECREATION FOR THE ADULTHOOD CYCLE

ADULT CYCLES		FORM OF RECREATION

YOUNG ADULT (20 to 35)
Concern for vocational skill and life work, marriage and own home responsibilities. _ _ _ _ _ _ _ ➤

Community recreation should recognize the family as a unit in its program.

MIDDLE YEARS (35 to 50)
Vocational prestige; family life established; possess social status and community recognition. _ _ _ _ _ _ ➤

Adult recreation concerns the family relationship with the teen-age world and employee recreation.

FREE YEARS (50 to 65)
Toward retirement. Increased leisure; continuity and growth in social and individual interests. _ _ _ ➤

Blending of vocation and avocation; allows time for a broader community relationship.

SENIOR CITIZENSHIP (65+)
Retirement. Longer life span gives more time to revitalize social and economic status; past experience contributes to society. _ ➤

Individual recreation: hobby activities. Organized groups: opens new ways to happiness and companionship.

FIG. 86. Changes in recreational patterns in the adult years. (*From H. D. Meyer, The adult cycle. Ann. Amer. Acad. pol. soc. Sci.*, 1957, 313, 58–67. *Used by permission.*)

activities from those commonly engaged in during the adolescent years, though these changes may be the result of necessity rather than the outcome of changed interests. While the children are still young, many of the recreations are centered around them. Even when the children become adolescent, the parents' recreations are largely family centered [79]. Changes of recreational patterns are shown in Figure 86. *Talking*, especially with those whose interests are similar, is a popular pastime of both men and women. It is especially popular with married women whose home responsibilities keep them in the home for the major part of the day and who, when there is an opportunity, enjoy talking to neighbors or friends. Much of this talking must be done over the telephone because of the restrictions placed on the young woman's activities by children in the home. Young adults, whether men or women, talk mostly about personal, day-to-day matters relating to their families, their work, social affairs, clothing, and other personal matters. Gossiping about friends, neighbors, and acquaintances is also common, especially among women [107].

When talking to members of the opposite sex, women try to discuss matters of interest to men more than men try to adapt their conversations to women's interests. Public affairs are a more popular topic of conversation among men than among women [107]. In low economic neighborhoods where interpersonal relationships lack intimacy, there is need for some superficial but universally interesting topic of conversation. Much of this need is met by talking about the newspaper comics. They are sure to bring a laugh, they serve as a source for "kidding," and they bridge the gap between those who have little or nothing in common. Men, much more than women, use this device to "break the ice" and start a conversation with their neighbors [16]. Women can generally bridge the gap by talking about their families or domestic problems, topics which are of universal interest to individuals whose patterns of life are similar.

Dancing, a popular recreation in adolescence, is engaged in only infrequently in early adulthood as home and business responsibilities are assumed. Many adults dance only infrequently during the twenties and even less during the thirties. Active participation in *sports* and *athletic events* of all sorts decreases during the adult years. While young men and women may still enjoy reading about sports, attending athletic contests, listening to them over the radio, or watching them on television, participation reaches a very low point as the individual approaches middle age. *Entertaining* friends and neighbors is far less frequent than entertaining members of the family. The major part of the entertaining in early adulthood is concentrated on relatives. When neighbors and friends are entertained, it is usually for an informal game of cards. *Play-*

ing cards is one of the most universally engaged in forms of entertainment among young adults of both sexes, especially among those who are married. It provides opportunities for social contacts on a simple scale and is a means of holding together groups whose interests are similar [30]. This type of entertainment may involve drinking but, for the most part, drinking is done away from home in taverns and bars, especially by men of the lower classes [108].

Belonging to a *club* or *lodge* is the ambition of many adolescents. By adult years, this interest wanes and most men belong to such organizations mainly for business or professional reasons. That their interest is not strong is shown in the fact that many do not attend meetings or attend only infrequently. Many young women have neither the time nor the money to belong to social or community clubs. Those who are married are able to attend only infrequently and cannot take an active part in the affairs of the organizations [71]. There are many adults who do not have *hobbies* until financial success gives them leisure to engage in them. Other adults who find their work boring and frustrating develop hobbies as a form of compensation. Men and women of high intelligence have more hobbies than those of lesser abilities. Men who are vocationally the most successful have, as a rule, more avocational interests than do those who are less successful [102]. Adult hobbies are, for the most part, of a constructional nature. They include such activities as cooking, gardening, painting, sewing, knitting, crocheting, making and repairing furniture, taking pictures and developing films, music, and making collections. These hobbies can, for the most part, be carried out in the home and do not require the companionship or help of others.

The young adult, because of his many responsibilities, generally has less time for *reading* than he had when he was an adolescent. As a result, he must be more selective in what he reads. While reading remains one of the favorite forms of recreation throughout the adult years, there are marked shifts with age in the interest value of different topics. Interest in romance, for example, decreases with age while interest in governmental and religious activities increases. There is also a rise in the quality of the material read as the individual grows older [7]. The proportion of people reading books and the time spent on them decreases with age. On the other hand, there is more magazine and newspaper reading as people grow older. While readers of all ages like short stories, humor, and continued stories, with age there is an increased interest in news, political articles, and editorials. Reading is influenced by the social class with which the adult is identified. Adults of the higher classes read more books and magazines than do those of the lower and they concentrate on the more "serious" types of books and magazines [90].

Among both men and women, newspaper reading ranks in first place, with men spending more of their reading time on newspapers than women, though single women have been found to read the newspapers more than married women. Most adults read the headlines of newspapers, even if they do not read the whole paper. Papers that are classed as "superior" are read less than the illustrated dailies by adults under thirty years of age. With advance in age, however, the better type of newspaper is read and the shift is also seen in the quality of material read within the newspaper. The range of reading interests for adults is narrower than it is for adolescents. The items of greatest interest include sports, cartoons, photographs, personal violence, disaster, finance, and trade. The items of least interest relate to state news, education and schools, church, home, gardens, and radio. Comics are read by more than three-quarters of all newspaper readers at all ages and of both sexes [104]. Adults of the higher classes are more interested in news of national and international affairs while those of the lower classes concentrate on local news [90]. People in the country read the weekly paper more fully than people from small towns read the daily papers, and the latter, in turn, read more fully than people from the city. In small towns, local news is most often read while in the larger communities, there is more interest in pictures and the comics. Economic news is the least popular with all groups [82].

The adult, far more than the child or the adolescent, likes to listen to *music*, both classical and modern. The young adult prefers modern to classical music while the middle-aged adult prefers classical to modern music. Going to the *movies* proves to be a less interesting recreation as the individual grows older. Adults, as a whole, attend movies rated as "good" or "excellent" in much greater proportions than do school children. Adults also like comedies, farces, and romantic productions. While children and adolescents are generally guided in their choice of movies by the actor or actress performing in them, adults generally are not. Adults are, likewise, less influenced in their choice by the previews and advertising than are adolescents [34].

People under forty listen to the *radio* more than do those over forty. Older adults show a greater preference for radio than reading as a recreational activity. Except as a source of news, they prefer the radio to the newspaper. Young men show a preference for sports and dance orchestra programs. Women, especially those of the middle class, like to listen to radio programs of the "soap opera" type. These are a form of folk literature, mainly of the family type, which offer the listener opportunities for identification. They stress the hopes and anxieties, the joys and sorrows of the everyday person, experiences similar to those of the listener, and put little emphasis on the world outside the home [106].

Housewives prefer radio to television because they can listen to programs while they work. Business and professional men likewise prefer radio and have little time for television watching [15]. Radio is preferred for news, popular and classical music, and for religious programs while television is preferred for sports events and comedy [85].

Television is, today, a popular form of recreation for adults, as it is for children. Middle- and upper-class families own television sets almost universally, especially when there are children in the family. While many sets are owned by families in the lower groups, they are not as widely owned as in the middle and upper classes. Women spend more time in television watching than do men, with an average of 3 or more hours daily. Because it is a form of recreation that can be enjoyed at home, it is especially popular among young adults who have children. It has a marked effect on other recreational interests, cutting down the amount of time spent in reading, going to the movies, driving, listening to the radio, talking, and playing games. At the same time, it encourages having guests in the home and brings the family members together as a unit. It has proved to be a great asset to young adults with limited access to alternative activities [27, 100].

Social Activities. The early years of adulthood are frequently lonely years for men as well as for women. When young men, because of economic reasons or because they have not yet found anyone with whom they would like to spend the rest of their lives, are living at home or are away from home, they often find themselves at loose ends during their leisure time. Their friends of earlier years and their business associates, as is true of the unmarried woman, are occupied with family activities or are preoccupied with courtship. As a result, the type of social life the young men enjoyed during adolescence, when there was always a congenial group to talk to or do things with, is no longer there and they find themselves alone many times when they would like to have companionship with their contemporaries.

Even the young adult who is married finds himself lonely at times and craves the companionship he enjoyed during the adolescent years. Tied down with the care of young children, limited by a budget that will permit little beyond the necessities of life, and often in a community away from family and former friends, the married adult may be as lonely as the unmarried and in a less favorable position to solve the problem of his loneliness. Havighurst has explained that early-adult loneliness occurs because of a "relatively unorganized period in life which marks the transition from an age-graded to a social-status-graded society." No longer can the individual count on readily available companionship in school or college. Now, in adult society, he must make his own way, form his own friendships, and establish himself through his own efforts [45].

In the process of adjustment to adult life, the individual goes through many changes in his social interests and activities. There are shifts in friendships, changes in forms of social activity, changes in dependency upon group associations and group opinions, and changes in social values. The craving for popularity and the desire to have a large number of friends wane. This is especially true of married men and women. In place of social activities outside the home, the social life centers in the home, and members of the family replace outsiders as companions. (See Figure 59, page 284, for decrease in time spent in the community and increase in time spent in the home during the adult years.) Now he relies more on relatives from both sides of the family for companionship than on outsiders, as he did when he was younger, and with them he engages in social activities. The married adult is far less dependent on outsiders for companionship than is the unmarried adult. As he reaches the thirties, the adult, whether married or single, has usually made adjustments to changes in his social life and has established a satisfactory and relatively stable social life for himself.

Social Participation. The form of social participation in adulthood will vary according to the social class of the individual, whether he lives in urban or rural areas, and many other factors. Adults of the higher *social classes* are more active and diverse in their social participation than are those of the lower classes. Members of the upper middle class belong to more community organizations than the lower classes, are more active in these organizations, and tend to dominate them and assume leadership in the life of the community. They have more intimate friends, entertain and visit more, and spend less time with relatives than do members of the lower classes [90]. Members of the working class, by contrast, have memberships in few community organizations and participate little in them except for athletic and church-affiliated groups. Their main social contacts are with family and relatives, or with cliques made up of childhood friends, neighbors, or fellow workers. They have relatively few intimate friends and what entertaining they do is mostly for members of the family and for relatives [33].

Environment has a marked influence on the type and amount of social participation. In cities, approximately three-quarters of the younger men belong to at least one formal group organization though the amount of their participation is influenced by their social-class status. Relatively few younger women in the cities belong to clubs or community organizations and even fewer are active participants. For the majority of young adults in cities, social life is limited to informal group associations, mainly with relatives. Less time is spent with friends, neighbors, or co-workers [8, 11]. The amount of association there will be with neighbors will depend on how much they have in common. This will be determined by the type of people involved, their conduct and standards, the behavior of the children, the tendency to gossip, and many other factors [70]. When families have interests in common, as in a university community, there will be more intimate relationships and, in turn, more social interaction [22].

In rural areas, there is more "neighborliness" and more social participation [73]. However, adults who have come to the cities from farm areas participate less in community activities in the cities than they did in the rural areas. They also participate less than those trained in the cities because they have not acquired the urban cultural traits and, as a result, feel inadequate to cope with the urban social life [112]. Because suburban areas are made up of individuals of similar interests and backgrounds, their social relationships are more like those in rural than in urban areas. For the most part, suburban dwellers are young married people with children and a middle-class social status. Their social life is more informal than formal, and neighborliness, based on common interests, leads to social interactions with outsiders more than with relatives. In the suburbs, women take a more active part in social and community affairs than do men who, for the most part, commute to the cities to work and have established their interests and associations largely in the cities [36, 72].

Friends. As is true of every age, friends in adulthood are selected on the basis of congeniality of interests. The adult, who in his work or social life comes in contact with people whose interests are similar to his, finds these people more congenial than those whose interests are different. As a result, a friendship is established. It is popularly believed that friendships established during childhood will persist throughout life and that the friends of one's youth, because they are "old" friends, will be one's best friends. There is no evidence to prove that such is the case. Rather, as interests and patterns of living change, old friends may have less in common than newly formed friends. In general, adult friends are mainly from the same socioeconomic group and have the same religion. Those who are popular mutually attract each other while those who are least popular tend to choose each other [69].

Young adults who are married generally have two sets of friends, those of their own sex who are congenial because of similar interests and those who are "family friends" or friends agreed upon by both husband and wife. The adult's personal friends are selected by the adult himself and the relationship is a mutually satisfying one. Family friendships, on the other hand, are generally initiated by the husband and are established on the basis of interests in common between the men, such as business, college, education, background, or recreations. When the husbands are friends, the wives are expected to be friends, regardless of how much they have in common or how congenial they are. The number of family friends varies with the presence or absence of children, the amount of social activity the families can afford to engage in, and how much money they have for outside recreation [43]. The more successful the family, the more family friends there are likely to be. Those with marital troubles have fewer family friends but more personal friends [113].

In early adulthood, much the same sort of social grouping exists as existed during the adolescent period. The social distance that marked off degrees of friendship then is operative in adulthood. There is a small group of intimate friends or confidants which frequently is made up of old friends unless the life interests of the individual have changed so that old friends are no longer congenial. Then there are less intimate friends belonging to the "crowd" whom the individual sees infrequently, for parties or other social gatherings. And on the outer rim of the friendship circle is the large list of acquaintances whom the individual knows but slightly and with whom he comes in contact infrequently. In business, there are cliques just as in social life. The younger workers are more closely knit as a group than the older. They form friendships more easily, are less discriminating in the choice of their clique members, and have more clique interactions both in business and after business than the older workers [41].

Degrees of social distance within the friendship circle change from time to time during adult years. Intimate friends may drift apart as their interests change or their places of residence change. This ebb and flow within the friendship circle results in an instability of friendships which, to an adolescent, would be very disturbing. To the adult, however, it is of little consequence. His major interest is in the family circle and, therefore, friendships are of less importance than they were in either childhood or adolescence. Forming of new friendships becomes increasingly difficult as age advances. By the late thirties or mid-forties, most men and women have a circle of friends as large as they want and, because their interests are stabilized by this time, their friends are not so likely to change as they did when the individual was younger and when there was a greater shift in his interests.

Popularity, which is so important to an adolescent, becomes increasingly less important as the adult approaches middle age. A few congenial friends mean more to him than a large group of friends with whom he has less in common. How popular the adult is will depend upon many factors, most of which are the same as those determining his acceptance in adolescence. In a study of social acceptance among women, it was found that those who were most popular had been popular and had been officers in girls' clubs during their high school days; they had had previous friendships and social experiences with women similar to those with whom they were now associated; they were interested in and had both time and energy available for social involvement with other people; and they were not only members of but active participants in a number of women's clubs, including church groups. Those who had the least acceptance were newcomers in the community; they were unhappy and uninterested in social activities; many of them were "only children"; and most had children, which made active participation in social life difficult [71].

The adult is affected in much the same way by social acceptance or lack of it as the adolescent is, but to a lesser extent. The more he is accepted by a group with which he would like to be identified, the more he conforms to group pressures. When he enjoys somewhat less than complete acceptance but sees the possibility of improving his acceptance, there will be a high degree of adherence to group standards, if he is motivated by a desire to improve his status in the group. If, on the other hand, his acceptance is low, he has little motivation to conform to group standards except in public and then only to forestall the possibility of complete rejection [32]. Adults who are discriminated against because of color, race, or religion resent it as does the child or adolescent but they are able to withdraw from the environment where there is discrimination better than the younger person can. In general, adults are more prejudiced and more discriminatory in their behavior than are adolescents, with women, on the whole, showing more tolerance than men [88].

Leadership. Studies of persistence of leadership have revealed that "once a leader, always a leader," holds true in a large percentage of adolescent leaders. Not only do these individuals attain positions of leadership in business or community affairs during their adult years but their chance of making a success in whatever line of work they enter is greater than for those who were followers during their school days. The experience gained from his leadership status in school, the prestige associated with leadership, and the self-confidence being a leader engenders in the individual all contribute to his success in adult life. However, whether he will continue to be a leader in adulthood will depend largely on his ability and willingness to adapt himself to the wishes of the group. Most leaders have learned adaptability and, as a result, are flexible enough to adjust to groups of many different structures [111]. This is especially true of very bright individuals who, during high school and college, participated in many extracurricular activities and played roles of leadership in these activities. In adult years, they have been found to hold more positions of leadership and responsibility than is true of college graduates as a group [102].

Men who hold executive positions in business and industry have been found to have many of the qualities necessary for successful leadership in the adolescent years. These include high frustration tolerance, self-evaluation, ability to express hostility tactfully, ability to accept victory or defeat without too much emotion, ability to accept authority, and ability to set realistic goals [6]. Women who become leaders in social activities in adult life show a clear-cut superiority in adjustment over nonleaders. Office holders in women's organizations are superior in dominance and self-confidence but are not significantly different in sociability and self-sufficiency from those who do not hold leadership positions [91]. Adults who have not been accustomed to being leaders find it difficult to adjust to playing a leadership role even when placed in such a role. This is shown by the fact that members of groups who are placed in leadership roles function in a nondirective manner and allow leadership to be taken over by the group. Leaders, on the other hand, when placed in a nonleadership role find this adjustment difficult and function in a less active way than do those who are unaccustomed to leadership roles [92].

Social Mobility. Some adults are satisfied with their social status but most are not. Most American adults would like to be identified with a higher social class than that of their own families, especially if they discovered during the adolescent years that those who were most popular and held most of the leadership roles were from the higher socioeconomic groups [48]. Because men and women in American society today usually achieve their highest economic and social status in middle adulthood, from thirty years of age on, the young adult is motivated to do all he can to rise above his present status as rapidly as possible to guarantee that he and his family will be in a position to enjoy the benefits of higher-class status [45]. As a result of this desire, the social status of many families today is mobile, not static. With occupational improvement comes a move to a better neighborhood and an opportunity to be identified with a higher social group.

Occupational success and advancement are the most usual methods of achieving higher social status. Other methods include marriage to a higher-status person, inheritance of wealth, association with and acceptance by people of higher status, transfer of membership to a higher-status church, purchase of a better home in a better residential district, use of money to purchase status symbols, and the acceptance and adoption of customs, attitudes, and symbols of a higher-status group. Usually a combination of several of these methods must be employed to achieve higher-status identification. In the case of women, marriage into a higher-status family is sufficient, provided she is willing to learn the patterns of life of the new group with which she is identified [46]. Higher education is especially valuable not only in bringing the individual in contact with members of a higher-status group but also in helping the individual to learn the patterns of living which are essential to acceptance by the group [76]. Geographic mobility, in that it offers the adult an opportunity to "bury his background," likewise facilitates upward mobility [35].

Adjustment to social mobility is not easy, whether the movement be upward or downward. The socially mobile person faces far more social dilemmas than does the relatively immobile one because he is torn from his social roots and must adjust to new social groups with new social values and standards of behavior. As families move upward, it means moving from poor to better neighborhoods, giving up old associations and values, choosing between associations with members of two classes, joining new social organizations, and giving up most of their social life with relatives and former neighbors. If the individual clings to his relatives and old friends, he is likely to feel superior when he is with them and this will often affect his relationships with them unfavorably. When he tries to affiliate himself with people of the higher class with whom he wants to be identified, he is likely to feel inferior. Often he is not accepted by this group or is in a marginal position. The chances of social acceptance are less if the individual's occupation carries him across major occupational lines, as from a day laborer to a white-collar worker [14]. In such a case, he has no real friends nor does he feel that he belongs to either group [13, 80].

Because upward mobility is often motivated by a series of humiliating experiences in childhood and adolescence, the mobile individual is often likely to be driven by neurotic tendencies. The difficulties involved in adjustment to the group he wants to be identified with tend to increase these neurotic tendencies, which not only leads to unhappiness but also militates against the possibility of social acceptance even after he has learned the patterns of behavior and accepted the values of that group [35]. Individuals who, for one reason or another, are forced to move downward in the social hierarchy find little in common with the members of the social class with which their occupational status identifies them. As a result, they tend to isolate themselves [14]. Furthermore, their former friends and neighbors are likely to drop them because they no longer live in the same neighborhood or have money for the social activities they formerly engaged in. Downward mobility, thus, not only brings social isolation but it also is likely to lead to marked feelings of inadequacy and inferiority.

Sex-role Adjustment. Even though boys and girls are well aware of the socially approved sex roles for the two sexes before they reach adulthood, they have not always been willing to accept these roles so completely that they can adjust their behavior to fit the roles. This is especially true of girls who, as a result of education and childhood experiences similar to those of boys, find that society expects them, after they become sexually mature, to play roles that differ markedly from those of boys. While they may want to be wives and mothers, they do not want to be wives and mothers in the traditional sense in which they play roles subordinate to those of their husbands and devote their entire time to home and children with no outside interests. College girls, when questioned about their preferred adult roles, overwhelmingly agreed that they wanted a career before and after marriage, until their children arrived, and part-time work or community activities until they reached middle age, when their children would be grown and they could resume their careers [24] (see Figure 74, page 350). While social attitudes are changing toward sex roles and social-sex relationships, especially toward the role of women, girls in late adolescence are increasingly aware of the fact that many boys and young men still cling to the concepts of the traditional role of women, just as their parents do [86].

By adulthood, men and women learn that there are certain culturally approved roles for an adult man and women, for a wife and mother, and for a husband and father. Not only are there traditional duties, rights, and privileges associated with these roles but there are traditional attitudes about the two sexes which are different. As early as high school days, for example, boys believe that a wife should be placed in a subordinate role to her husband more often than they believe that a sister should be placed in a subordinate role to her brother. High school girls, on the other hand, would place women more in a partnership role with men in both work and education than boys would be willing to do [105]. Boys, with each passing year in adolescence, have an increasingly more favorable attitude toward masculinity and the masculine sex and an increasingly unfavorable attitude toward the feminine role [83].

Concepts of Sex Roles. In every culture, whether primitive or civilized, there are certain patterns of behavior approved for women and others for men. While most cultures have rigidly prescribed roles, in America today the roles are not defined as rigidly as in the past. In fact, they vary from one social class to another and from one individual to another within different social classes, depending on past experiences, racial backgrounds, education, social contacts with individuals from different classes, and many other factors [23]. Furthermore, changes in the adult pattern of living, due to urban and suburban life where the man is away from home most of the working day, and the tendency of an increasingly large number of young women to work outside the home both before and after marriage have brought about changes in the concepts of adult roles for both men and women. These changes are more pronounced among adults in the middle and upper classes than in those of the lower classes. The *traditional* concepts of male and female roles are gradually being replaced in the upper classes by *developmental* concepts. The latter emphasize the individuality of the person whereas the traditional concepts follow a prescribed pattern, regardless of individual interests or abilities [23]. Social class differences between traditional and developmental concepts are illustrated in Figure 87.

The traditional role of the *man* in our culture is that of wage earner, head of family, and citizen. He is expected to be able to withstand physical and emotional strains without flinching, to be aggressive and strong-willed, and to be dominant in all relationships with women. In family decision making, it is the husband who does most of the talking, who contributes most of the ideas, and who makes most of the final

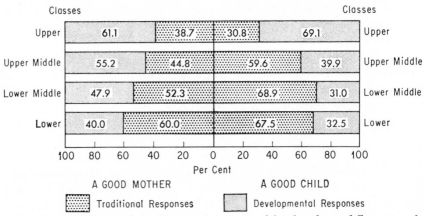

FIG. 87. Traditional and developmental concepts of family roles in different social-class groups. (*From E. M. Duvall, Conceptions of parenthood. Amer. J. Sociol., 1946, 52, 193–203. Used by permission.*)

decisions, especially when they relate to economic problems [56]. Closely related to this concept of masculine supremacy is an intolerance for any trait that hints of femininity [2]. For the married *woman*, there are three separate roles she may play: the traditional role of wife and mother, the companion role which permits her to share pleasures with her husband and enjoy individual pursuits, and the partner role with economic independence and equal authority in family matters. The traditional role is more widely accepted among adults in the lower classes while the companion and partner roles are gradually gaining more acceptance in the middle and upper classes [93]. While the unmarried woman is free to choose her own role, she is subject to severe social criticism if her behavior deviates from the traditional concept of femininity [86].

Just as there are variations in social concepts of the roles men and women should play, so there are variations in the concepts accepted today of mothers and fathers. According to the traditional concept of *mother,* the woman should devote her time to the care and training of children, molding them according to a socially approved pattern. The developmental concept of mother, on the other hand, emphasizes the guidance of the child according to his abilities, with the mother having more freedom as an individual, just as the child has. There is even more change in the social concept of *father* than of mother. Traditionally, the father was the person who provided for the family, disciplined and advised the children, and set an example of masculinity for his sons to imitate. In recent years, emphasis on the important role the father can and should play has resulted in a developmental concept of father which includes sharing in the care of the child, playing with him and teaching him how to play, and sharing in the home duties or even taking over these duties when the mother is away from home for work or pleasure [28, 101]. As with concepts of men and women, individual as well as social-class differences influence the acceptance of traditional or developmental concepts of parental roles (see Figure 19, page 112).

Adjustment Problems. Conflicting concepts of the role the individual is expected to play lead to uncertainty, confusion, anxiety, and feelings of futility, and, at the same time, interfere with good adjustments. The person who knows exactly what is expected of him will make quicker and easier adjustments, even though he may rebel against the role he is expected to play. But when rebellion is accompanied by confusion and uncertainty, not only is the difficulty of adjustment increased but feelings of futility arise and, in turn, militate against the individual's motivation to conform [109]. Because there is more confusion about the approved role for women than for men, the adjustment problem is more difficult for women than it is for men [31, 40].

To avoid being considered "unmanly" or "effeminate," the man will go to any length to prove to himself and others that he is typically masculine. This may take the form of overtaxing his strength to prove that he is big and strong, disregarding warning signals of poor health in the belief that poor health is effeminate, or devaluing feminine characteristics to the point where he tries constantly to assert his masculine superiority in his relationships with women [2, 75]. Women, as a result of being treated as inferior to men, often develop a typical "minority-group complex" which is expressed in being critical of members of their own sex, having misgivings about women's participation in business, industry, or the professions, being unwilling to work under women, and having a strong wish that they had been born men [42]. Even unmarried women who do not have to divide their time and energies between family and career as married women do often find barriers to advancement. This leads to frustrations and disappointments which, in turn, make them unhappy and interfere with good adjustments not only in their careers but also in other areas of their lives [17].

Marital adjustments are often seriously affected by conflicting concepts of the role the husband or the wife should play. The wife who, because of her childhood training and lack of emancipation from her parents, shows a greater closeness to her family than the husband shows to his, may cause resentments on the part of her husband because he feels she is too influenced by her parents or because she favors her own family rather than his [59]. Or, if the wife feels that her husband is devoting so much time to his work that he neglects her and the children, there will be discord [78]. A dominant wife will cause more discord in the family than a less dominant one unless her husband is willing to be dominated and play the role of a "henpecked" husband [98]. Marital rifts and divorce are more often the result of conflicts arising from opposing concepts of the role each partner should play than from any other single cause [51]. Only when there is agreement as to the role each should play and a willingness on the part of each to play this role will there be good marital adjustment. Among American men and women today, the best marital adjustment comes when the relationship between husband and wife is equalitarian or a "democratic partnership" [67].

How adults adjust to their sex roles as parents will have great impact on their personal and social adjustments, on family relationships, and on the happiness of every member of the family. Women of the higher socioeconomic groups are, on the whole, better adjusted to their roles as mothers than are women from the lower groups [29]. However, the role of mother is not easy and many women feel insecure because their concepts of what a mother should be conflict with the concepts held by their husbands and relatives. Furthermore, women discover that social and cultural patterns cause the role of mother to be personally unsatisfying, especially as the children grow older and become critical of the mother and look upon her role as inferior to that of the man. Being in a role that lacks prestige and is subject to criticism from those for whom she makes personal sacrifices does not add to a woman's happiness or contribute to good adjustments [96]. If the man accepts the traditional role of the father as the authoritarian head of the family, he is considered "soft and unmasculine" if he loves his sons. If he conforms to this role, he makes his sons into bullies and alienates their affection [9]. If, on the other hand, he tries to conform to the developmental concept of father, playing an active role in the care of the children, this often interferes with his advancement in his career, thus making him resentful and frustrated [78]. In addition, when this role makes him feel that he is only a "mother's helper," he is frustrated and ashamed of the role. Only when he can feel like a father within the structure of his masculinity can he be happy in this role and make good adjustments to it [55].

BIBLIOGRAPHY

1. Aberle, D. F., and K. D. Naegele: Middle-class fathers' occupational role and attitudes toward children. *Amer. J. Orthopsychiat.*, 1952, 22, 366–378.
2. Allen, D. A.: Antifemininity in men. *Amer. sociol. Rev.*, 1954, 19, 591–593.
3. Allport, G. W., J. M. Gillespie, and J. Young: Religion of the freshman college student. *J. Psychol.*, 1948, 25, 3–33.
4. Anders, S. F.: Religious behavior of church families. *Marriage Fam. Living*, 1955, 17, 54–57.
5. Anderson, J. E.: *The psychology of development and personal adjustment.* New York: Holt, 1949.
6. Argyris, C.: Some characteristics of successful executives. *Personnel J.*, 1953, 32, 50–55.
7. Austin, G. R.: Non-fiction best sellers: types and trends. *J. soc. Psychol.*, 1953, 38, 141–143.
8. Axelrod, M.: Urban structure and social participation. *Amer. sociol. Rev.*, 1956, 21, 13–15.
9. Bartemeier, L.: The contribution of the father to the mental health of the family. *Amer. J. Psychiat.*, 1953, 110, 277–280.
10. Bayley, N.: On the growth of intelligence. *Amer. Psychologist*, 1955, 10, 805–818.
11. Bell, W., and M. T. Force: Urban neighborhood types and participation in formal associations. *Amer. sociol. Rev.*, 1956, 21, 25–34.
12. Benedict, R.: Continuities and discontinuities in cultural conditioning. *Psychiatry*, 1938, 1, 161–167.
13. Blau, P. M.: Social mobility and interpersonal relations. *Amer. sociol. Rev.*, 1956, 21, 290–295.
14. Blau, P. M.: Occupational bias and mobility. *Amer. sociol. Rev.*, 1957, 22, 392–399.
15. Bogardus, E. S.: A television scale and television index. *Amer. sociol. Rev.*, 1952, 17, 220–223.
16. Bogart, L.: Adult talk about newspaper comics. *Amer. J. Sociol.*, 1955, 61, 26–30.
17. Boring, E. G.: The woman problem. *Amer. Psychologist*, 1951, 6, 679–692.
18. Bossard, J. H. S., and E. S. Boll: *Ritual in family living.* Philadelphia: Univer. Pennsylvania Press, 1950.
19. Bossard, J. H. S., and E. S. Boll: *One marriage, two faiths.* New York: Ronald, 1957.
20. Bugental, J. F. T., and E. C. Gunning: Investigations into self-concept. III. Stability of reported self-identifications. *J. clin. Psychol.*, 1955, 11, 41–46.
21. Bühler, C.: The curve of life as studied in biographies. *J. appl. Psychol.*, 1935, 19, 405–409.
22. Caplow, T., and R. Forman: Neighborhood interaction in a homogeneous community. *Amer. sociol. Rev.*, 1950, 15, 357–366.
23. Cavan, R. S.: *The American family.* New York: Crowell, 1953.
24. Christensen, H. T., and M. M. Swihart: Postgraduate role preferences of senior women in college. *Marriage Fam. Living*, 1956, 18, 52–57.

25. Clark, W. H., and C. M. Warner: The relation of church attendance to honesty and kindness in a small community. *Rel. Educ.*, 1955, 50, 340–342.
26. Clarke, A. C.: The use of leisure and its relation to levels of occupational prestige. *Amer. sociol. Rev.*, 1956, 21, 301–307.
27. Coffin, T. E.: Television's impact on society. *Amer. Psychologist*, 1955, 10, 630–641.
28. Connor, R., T. B. Johannis, and J. Walters: Parent-adolescent relationships. *J. Home Econ.*, 1954, 46, 183–191.
29. Crandell, V. J., and A. Preston: An assessment of personal-social adjustments of a group of middle-class mothers. *J. genet. Psychol.*, 1956, 89, 239–249.
30. Crespi, I.: The social significance of card playing as a leisure time activity. *Amer. sociol. Rev.*, 1956, 21, 717–721.
31. Diamond, S.: Sex stereotypes and acceptance of sex role. *J. Psychol.*, 1955, 39, 385–388.
32. Dittes, J. E., and H. H. Kelley: Effects of different conditions of acceptance upon conformity to group norms. *J. abnorm. soc. Psychol.*, 1956, 53, 100–107.
33. Dotson, F.: Patterns of voluntary association among urban working-class families. *Amer. sociol. Rev.*, 1951, 16, 687–693.
34. Edman, M.: Attendance of school pupils and adults at moving pictures. *Sch. Rev.*, 1940, 48, 753–763.
35. Ellis, E.: Social psychological correlates of upward social mobility among unmarried career women. *Amer. sociol. Rev.*, 1952, 17, 558–563.
36. Fava, S. F.: Suburbanism as a way of life. *Amer. sociol. Rev.*, 1956, 21, 34–37.
37. Folkman, J. D.: Stressful and supportive interaction. *Marriage Fam. Living*, 1956, 18, 102–106.
38. Foulds, G. A.: Variations in the intellectual activities of adults. *Amer. J. Psychol.*, 1949, 62, 238–246.
39. Glueck, S., and E. T. Glueck: *Unravelling juvenile delinquency.* New York: Commonwealth Fund, 1950.
40. Gray, S. W.: Masculinity-femininity in relation to anxiety and social acceptance. *Child Develpm.*, 1957, 28, 203–214.
41. Gullahorn, J. T.: Distance and friendship as factors in the gross interaction matrix. *Sociometry*, 1952, 15, 123–134.
42. Hacker, H. M.: Women as a minority group. *Soc. Forces*, 1951, 30, 60–69.
43. Hare, A. P., and R. T. Hare: Family friendship within the community. *Sociometry*, 1948, 11, 329–334.
44. Hartmann, G. W.: Clothing: personal problems and social issues. *J. Home Econ.*, 1949, 41, 295–298.
45. Havighurst, R. J.: *Human development and education.* New York: Longmans, 1953.
46. Havighurst, R. J., and H. Taba: *Adolescent character and personality.* New York: Wiley, 1949.
47. Hendriksen, L.: Medical report. *Today's Hlth*, 1957, Jan., p. 15.
48. Higgin, G.: The effect of reference group functions on social status ratings. *Brit. J. Psychol.*, 1954, 45, 88–93.
49. Holmes, E.: Who uses consumer credit? *J. Home Econ.*, 1957, 49, 340–342.
50. Hoult, T. F.: Experimental measurement of clothing as a factor in some social ratings of selected American men. *Amer. sociol. Rev.*, 1954, 19, 324–328.
51. Jacobson, A. H.: Conflict of attitudes toward the roles of the husband and wife in marriage. *Amer. sociol. Rev.*, 1952, 17, 146–150.

52. Jepson, V. L.: College activities and vocational success. *Occupations,* 1951, 29, 345–347.
53. Jersild, A. T.: *The psychology of adolescence.* New York: Macmillan, 1957.
54. Jones, M. C.: The later careers of boys who were early- or late-maturing. *Child Develpm.,* 1957, 28, 113–128.
55. Josselyn, I. M.: Psychology of fatherliness. *Smith Coll. Stud. soc. Wk,* 1956, 26, 1–13.
56. Kenkel, W. F.: Influence differentiation in family decision making. *Sociol. soc. Res.,* 1957, 42, 18–25.
57. Kelly, E. L.: Consistency of the adult personality. *Amer. Psychologist,* 1955, 10, 659–681.
58. Kerr, W. A., H. L. Newman, and A. R. Sadewic: Lifetime worry patterns of American psychologists. *J. consult. Psychol.,* 1949, 13, 377–380.
59. Komarovsky, M.: Functional analysis of sex roles. *Amer. sociol. Rev.,* 1950, 15, 508–516.
60. Koppe, W. A.: The psychological meanings of housing and furnishings. *Marriage Fam. Living,* 1955, 17, 129–132.
61. Kotkoo, B., and B. Murawski: A Rorschach study of the personality structure of obese women. *J. clin. Psychol.,* 1952, 8, 391–396.
62. Kuhlen, R. G.: Age differences in personality during adult years. *Psychol. Bull.,* 1945, 42, 333–358.
63. Leevy, J. R.: Leisure time of the American housewife. *Sociol. soc. Res.,* 1951, 35, 97–105.
64. Lehman, H. C.: *Age and achievement.* Princeton, N.J.: Princeton Univer. Press, 1953.
65. Lenski, G. E.: Social correlates of religious interest. *Amer. sociol. Rev.,* 1953, 18, 533–544.
66. Lowe, W. L.: Religious beliefs and religious delusions. *Amer. J. Psychother.,* 1955, 9, 54–61.
67. Lu, Y-C.: Marital roles and marriage adjustment. *Sociol. soc. Res.,* 1952, 36, 364–368.
68. MacGregor, F. C.: Some psycho-social problems associated with facial deformities. *Amer. sociol. Rev.,* 1951, 16, 629–638.
69. Maisonveuve, J.: Contribution to the sociometry of mutual choices. *Sociometry,* 1954, 17, 33–46.
70. Mann, P. H.: The concept of neighborliness. *Amer. J. Sociol.,* 1954, 60, 163–168.
71. Marshall, H. R.: Some factors associated with social acceptance in women's groups. *J. Home Econ.,* 1957, 49, 173–176.
72. Martin, W. T.: The structuring of social relationships engendered by suburban residence. *Amer. sociol. Rev.,* 1956, 21, 446–464.
73. Mayo, S. C., and C. P. Marsh: Social participation in the rural community. *Amer. J. Sociol.,* 1951, 57, 243–248.
74. McCann, R. V.: Developmental factors in the growth of a mature faith. *Rel. Educ.,* 1955, 50, 147–155.
75. McGee, L. C.: The suicidal cult of "manliness." *Today's Hlth,* 1957, Jan., pp. 28–30.
76. McGuire, C.: Social stratification and mobility patterns. *Amer. sociol. Rev.,* 1950, 15, 195–204.
77. McQuitty, L. L.: A measure of personality integration in relation to the concept of self. *J. Pers.,* 1950, 18, 461–482.

78. Mead, M.: American man in a woman's world. *The New York Times*, 1957, Feb. 10.

79. Meyer, H. D.: The adult cycle. *Ann. Amer. Acad. pol. soc. Sci.*, 1957, 313, 58–67.

80. Mogey, J. M.: Changes in family life experienced by English workers moving from slums to housing estates. *Marriage Fam. Living*, 1955, 17, 123–128.

81. Moore, D. F.: Sharing in family financial management by high-school students. *Marriage Fam. Living*, 1953, 15, 319–321.

82. Nafziger, R. O., M. MacLean, and W. Engstrom: Who reads what in newspapers? *Int. J. Opin., Attitude Res.*, 1952, 5, 519–540.

83. Neiman, L. J.: The influence of peer groups upon attitudes toward the feminine role. *Soc. Problems*, 1954, 2, 104–111.

84. Nelson, E. N. P.: Persistence of attitudes of college students fourteen years later. *Psychol. Monogr.*, 1954, 68, No. 2.

85. O'Hara, H.: Comparative preferences of radio and television programs. *Sociol. soc. Res.*, 1953, 37, 305–311.

86. Pressey, S. L., and A. W. Jones: 1923–1953 and 20–60 age changes in moral codes, anxieties, and interests, as shown by the "X-O Tests." *J. Psychol.*, 1955, 39, 485–502.

87. Pressey, S. L., and R. G. Kuhlen: *Psychological development through the life span.* New York: Harper, 1957.

88. Prothro, E. T., and O. K. Miles: A comparison of ethnic attitudes of college students and middle class adults from the same state. *J. soc. Psychol.*, 1952, 36, 53–58.

89. Reid, J. W.: Stability of measured Kuder interests in young adults. *J. educ. Res.*, 1951, 45, 307–312.

90. Reissman, L.: Class, leisure, and social participation. *Amer. sociol. Rev.*, 1954, 19, 76–84.

91. Richardson, H. M., and N. G. Hanawalt: Leadership as related to the Bernreuter personality measures. V. Leadership among adult women in social activities. *J. soc. Psychol.*, 1952, 36, 141–153.

92. Rock, M. L., and E. N. Hay: Investigation of the use of tests as a predictor of leadership and group effectiveness in a job evaluation situation. *J. soc. Psychol.*, 1953, 38, 109–119.

93. Rose, A. M.: The adequacy of women's expectations for adult roles. *Soc. Forces*, 1951, 30, 69–77.

94. Skerlj, B.: Further evidence of age changes in body form based on material of D. A. W. Edwards. *Hum. Biol.*, 1954, 26, 330–336.

95. Spoerl, D. T.: The values of post-war college students. *J. soc. Psychol.*, 1952, 35, 217–225.

96. Stoodley, B. H.: Mother role as a focus of some family problems. *Marriage Fam. Living*, 1952, 14, 13–16.

97. Strecker, E. A.: *Their mothers' sons.* Philadelphia: Lippincott, 1946.

98. Strodtbeck, F. L.: The interaction of a "henpecked" husband with his wife. *Marriage Fam. Living*, 1952, 14, 305–308.

99. Strong, E. K.: Interests of Negroes and whites. *J. soc. Psychol.*, 1952, 35, 139–150.

100. Sweetser, F. S.: *Grade-school families meet television.* Boston: Boston Univer. Press, 1953.

101. Tasch, R. J.: The role of the father in the family. *J. exp. Educ.*, 1952, 20, 319–361.

102. Terman, L. M., and M. H. Oden: *The gifted child grows up*. Stanford, Calif.: Stanford Univer. Press, 1947.
103. Thorndike, E. L.: Note on the shifts of interest with age. *J. appl. Psychol.*, 1949, 33, 55.
104. Wall, W. D.: The newspaper reading of adolescents and adults. *Brit. J. educ. Psychol.*, 1948, 18, 26–40.
105. Walters, J., and R. H. Ojemann: A study of the components of adolescent attitudes concerning the role of women. *J. soc. Psychol.*, 1952, 35, 101–110.
106. Warner, W. L., and W. E. Henry: The radio daytime serial: a symbolic analysis. *Genet. Psychol. Monogr.*, 1948, 37, 3–71.
107. Watson, J., W. Breed, and H. Posman: A study of adult conversations: sample of 1,001 remarks overheard in Manhattan. *J. soc. Psychol.*, 1948, 28, 121–133.
108. White, R. C.: Social class differences in the uses of leisure. *Amer. J. Sociol.*, 1955, 61, 138–144.
109. Wilson, P. P.: College women who express futility. *Teach. Coll. Contr. Educ.*, 1950, No. 956.
110. Wylie, J. A.: A survey of 504 families to determine the relationship between certain factors and the nature of the family recreation program. *Res. Quart. Amer. phys. Educ. Ass.*, 1953, 24, 229–243.
111. Zeleny, L. D.: Social leadership. *Sociol. soc. Res.*, 1949, 33, 431–436.
112. Zimmer, B. G.: Farm background and urban participation. *Amer. J. Sociol.*, 1956, 61, 470–475.
113. Zimmerman, C. C., and C. B. Broderick: Nature and role of informal family groups. *Marriage Fam. Living*, 1954, 16, 107–111.

Early Adulthood

Continued

Even though many boys and girls make their vocational selections, begin
to work, marry, and become parents before they reach legal maturity,
the major part of their adjustments to these areas of their lives is made
during the adult years. For others, whose education and training for a
life career go beyond the age of legal maturity or who do not marry
until the twenties or even the thirties, the entire adjustment will be made
in adulthood. The adjustments to adult patterns of living described in
the preceding chapter all have a background of previous training and
experience in the childhood and adolescent years. Such adjustments,
therefore, are mainly revisions of patterns already established.

In the adjustments to be described in this chapter, there is less foundation on which to build. As a result, the adjustments are more difficult,
they require a longer time, and the end results are often far from satisfactory. Furthermore, the adult must usually make these adjustments
without guidance and help from others. This further adds to the difficulties he must cope with. By far the most important aspect of the problem
is the fact that the success or failure of these adjustments will affect the
areas of his life most closely related to his prestige in the eyes of others,
his concept of himself as an individual, his own happiness, and that of
every member of his family. For these reasons they can justifiably be
classed as the "major adjustments" of adulthood.

VOCATIONAL ADJUSTMENT

Vocational adjustment becomes increasingly difficult for each successive generation of young adults. This is due partly to the ever-increasing

number of different types of work available from which the individual must make his choice, partly to the long and often costly preparation needed for the type of work the individual selects, and partly to the individual's ignorance of his capacities. The choice is further complicated by the unrealistic vocational aims that children and adolescents often have. When an individual has had vocational aspirations far beyond his capacities for a number of years, it is difficult, if not impossible, to make a satisfactory adjustment to the type of work his abilities and training force him into.

And yet, to the average man, adult happiness is largely dependent upon a satisfactory vocational adjustment. If he is unhappy in his work, if he feels that he is capable of a higher paying and more responsible job than he has, and if he dislikes his work associates, he will be unhappy in his home life, his social life, and every other area of his life. Much

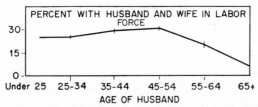

Fig. 88. Percentages of men of different ages with wives in the labor force. (*From P. C. Glick, The life cycle of the family. Marriage Fam. Living, 1955, 17, 3–9. Used by permission.*)

unhappiness in adult life today stems from vocational maladjustments. Men alone do not experience vocational maladjustments. With the increasing number of women in the vocational field, women of today are subject to the effects of vocational adjustment, just as men are. According to statistics released by the government in 1957, women work more than one-fourth of the annual total of man hours worked (see Figure 88). Six out of every ten working women are married, three out of every ten married women are working, and two out of every five married women who work are mothers of school-age children [86]. Because women find many of the lines of work in which they are interested either shut to them or so dominated by men that the woman's progress is blocked, vocational adjustments become as serious a problem for women as for men [9].

Vocational Selection. The gigantic task of finding the right niche becomes apparent when one realizes that, at the time of World War II, there were 25,000 major civilian occupations from which the soldiers came. It has been estimated that, in our country, there are at least 100,000 distinct occupations from which the individual must make the choice of his life career [87]. Each year, as new discoveries and inventions appear, new types of work are created. Only after the individual leaves school and tries to fit himself into our complex modern society does he realize how serious the task of vocational selection actually is. For these reasons, many young adults who have had little specific training for a particular line of work in high school or college go through a period of trial and error in which they try out one job after another. Even though the individual's first vocational choice has little relationship to the parental occupation, he generally finds himself in the general occupational group of his parent when the final decision is made [53].

How stable the young adult's vocational selection is will depend partly upon his job experience and partly upon his vocational values. Boys, during their adolescent years, often overstrain in their vocational ambitions, wanting a career above their abilities. This is less common among girls. In high schools and colleges, attempts are made to help students choose careers suited to their abilities by counseling and by placing the students in part-time jobs that give them opportunities to learn something about the work they are interested in and to see if they have the necessary abilities to do such work successfully. An increasingly large number of students work part time as they go through high school and college. On the basis of this *job experience,* they can make vocational choices that will be far more satisfactory than the choices made by individuals who lack job experience [89]. When vocations that follow the individual's lines of interest, as revealed in his choice of subjects in high school or college, are selected, the job experience not only helps him to make the selection more quickly but he is more satisfied with the decision he makes and is, therefore, less anxious to change [119].

Vocational values are even more important in vocational stability than is job experience. Work has different meanings for different people, whatever their occupations. It may be a source of prestige and social recognition, a basis for self-respect and a sense of worth, an opportunity for social participation, a way of being of service to others, a source of intrinsic enjoyment or of creative self-expression, or merely a way of earning a living [44]. The values an individual stresses in selecting a vocation will be influenced by the social class to which he belongs. Individuals from the lower economic groups stress the economic value and the easy nature of the job while those of the upper groups stress the satisfaction to be derived from the work and the freedom the work offers the worker [34, 76, 85]. When the work selected fits into the values the worker holds and, as a result, gives him satisfaction, he will be stable in his vocational choice and satisfied with the choice he has made [79, 91]. Vocational values vary for the two sexes. Women are interested in less active, less adventuresome, and less dangerous occupations than men. They prefer work that is social in nature and offers them opportunities to help others, such as teaching, social service, nursing, and office work. Work of this sort has little appeal for men [40]. For both men and women, there is a tendency to change vocational values as a result of experience. More emphasis is placed, as adults grow older, on independence and work in which one is more or less on his own than on interesting jobs, fame, or profit [99].

Studies of *stability of vocational choices* throughout adulthood have revealed that stability increases with age. One study revealed, for example, that twenty years after college, most of the individuals studied were in occupations of their early choice or those closely related to it. Those who had changed either had changed their interests or were in jobs of lower prestige value, showing a change to a more realistic goal [103]. Job changes within an occupation are more frequent than occupational changes. Professional workers change least while those in unskilled or the higher white-collar occupations change most. Skilled workers find it increasingly difficult to change their occupations as they grow older because of the difficulties in acquiring new skills. When skills are once learned, they can be maintained over a period of time, but learning new skills becomes difficult even in the twenties [6]. Individuals who are successful in their careers are stable in their vocational choices in adult years. When shifts occur, they are mainly in the general vocational category selected and are the result of the individual's mature appraisal of his talents and predispositions, based on experience [100]. Women often are forced to shift their vocations to fit into their home responsibilities or to adapt to changes to another community, necessitated by their husbands' jobs. Because most women do not take courses of study to fit them for specific vocations, this shift is not difficult for them to adjust to [119].

Adjustment to Work. When vocational selection has been made, the adult must then adjust to the work he has chosen. This involves adjustments to the work to be done, the hours of work, coworkers and superiors, and the environment in which the work is done. Adults who have had previous work experience during their adolescent years make these adjustments more quickly and more satisfactorily than do those who have had no previous work experience [89]. Because the status of the individual in adult society is determined largely by his occupation, he must adjust to this also. If he remains in the same community with his family, his vocational status is likely to be influenced by the general social status of his family. If, on the other hand, he migrates out of a small or moderate-sized community he is likely to rise above his parents' occupational status. This occurs mostly when the individual's intelligence and abilities are above those of his parents [92]. When the individual's abilities are above the level of his work, he will derive little satisfaction from his work or from the social group with which he is associated because of his work. By contrast, the individual whose abilities are well suited to his work makes good adjustments to it and to the people with whom he works and lives.

Vocational adjustments of women are even more difficult than those of men. The attainment of an occupational status that fits their abilities is frequently denied them because of their sex [9]. This results in frustrations which militate against good adjustment to the work to be done and to coworkers or superiors. Added to this is the problem of adjusting to two jobs, as happens when the woman worker is married. Even when it is necessary for her to work to help support the family, this may cause friction with her husband if he holds the conventional concept of a woman as wife and mother. The working wife must, of necessity, neglect

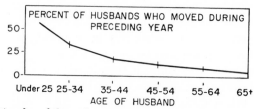

Fig. 89. Vocational mobility of men at different ages. (*From P. C. Glick, The life cycle of the family. Marriage Fam. Living, 1955, 17, 3–9. Used by permission.*)

many of the homemaking duties, with the result that they remain undone or the children are called upon to assist her. The recreational activities of the family must be curtailed and the mother is often too busy or too tired when she returns from work to take an active part in her children's interests. This they resent and, as a result, the home life is far from satisfactory for the whole family. This adds to the adjustment problems arising from the work itself [10].

Vocational advancement for men often necessitates *mobility*. If the man is to be happy in his work, he must advance to higher levels in the occupation he has chosen. Figure 89 shows ages of husbands when vocational mobility is most frequent. When occupational advancement can be achieved only by a move to another community, it means adjustments for the man and for his entire family. These adjustments include breaking off family ties and old friendships; making new friends and becoming established in a new community; adjusting to the mores and social life of a community different from the one the family has become accustomed to; and learning to be self-sufficient as a family at holiday times. When there are school-age children, their relationships with their peers and their schooling are affected by family moves and this often makes them unhappy and dissatisfied with their environment, thus increasing the adjustment problems the parents must make [105]. Even when the move results in financial improvement and higher social status for the family, it is not usually enough to compensate for the other adjustment problems [92].

Appraisal of Adjustment. How successfully the adult adjusts to his chosen vocation can be judged by his achievements and by the degree of satisfaction he and his family derive from his work and the socio-economic status associated with it. The urge to success, so strong in adolescence, carries over into the early adult years and results in a pre-occupation with the chosen work and the expenditure of tremendous energy in the hopes of winning success and advancement. This results in the peak of vocational *achievement* during the thirties, when both quality and quantity of work are the result of initiative, ambition, and hard work [9, 72]. The more education the individual has had and the more successful he has been in both academic and extracurricular activities, the greater his chances are for vocational achievements that are satisfying to him during the adult years [5]. The individual who has not made a satisfactory adjustment to his work or who has not shown at least reasonable success in it by the time he reaches middle age is not likely to do so as he grows older. By middle age, the vocational drive is replaced by a desire for security. Having a job with security back of it now means more to the individual than climbing higher on the vocational ladder [72]. Relatively few individuals, either men or women, realize their vocational aspirations. Nevertheless, they are satisfied if economically secure and they compensate for lack of vocational satisfaction by transferring their vocational aspirations to their children [91].

The *satisfaction* the adult derives from his chosen vocation is an even better index of his adjustment than is his achievement. There are age cycles in satisfaction for both men and women. In the early twenties, men are glad to have a job, even if it is not entirely to their liking, because it gives them the independence they crave and makes marriage possible. With the confidence of youth, they believe it will be just a matter of time until they are promoted to a job more to their liking or until a better job opens up. By mid-twenties, when they have not risen as rapidly as they hoped, dissatisfaction begins to set in. If family responsibilities makes it impossible for them to change, this adds to their dissatisfaction. This period of unrest and dissatisfaction lasts generally until the early- or mid-thirties, after which there is generally an increase in satisfaction resulting from greater achievement and better financial rewards. Most men in their thirties like their work but they do not "love" it [50]. They enjoy the social contacts work gives them, the feeling of being a part of the world of action, and the satisfaction from achievement [85]. Those who are most likely to be dissatisfied are the younger and less well paid workers, especially manual workers, or those who are self-employed and meet competition too stiff to compete with successfully [91].

For women, the main goal in life is generally marriage, with or without a job. As the unmarried woman approaches the thirties and sees no prospect of marriage, stress increases and this affects her attitude toward her work. After thirty, she shifts her goals and orients herself toward her work, working hard for a promotion or a change to work that will offer her more opportunities. How successfully she achieves this goal will affect her job satisfaction [66]. Women who did not originally plan to make work their life career or who married and expected to withdraw from the work world but were then forced by economic necessity to return to work are more likely to be dissatisfied with their work than are those who planned a career of work or returned to work voluntarily after marriage [91]. The degree of satisfaction the worker derives from his work not only influences the quality and quantity of his work but it may also make him accident-prone. Workers in factories who are dissatisfied with their jobs have more accidents than do the more satisfied workers [58].

The basis on which the individual selects his vocation will have a marked influence on the degree of satisfaction he derives from it. If the selection is made on the basis of a strong interest in and ability for activities related to the type of work he has chosen, he will be far better satisfied than if his interests and abilities are unsuited to the job [50, 74]. Favorable working conditions, especially when they offer independence of action and congenial associations with his coworkers, add to his satisfaction. Job dissatisfaction is usually greatest among workers who have personally experienced minority group discrimination [96]. The major source of satisfaction comes from the extent to which the job enables the worker to play the kind of role he wants to play. This, in turn, is influenced by the money he receives. When his earnings are sufficient to provide his family with living conditions that match their aspirations and a social status that is satisfying to them, while at the same time giving him membership and status in a group with which he wants to be identified, he will find satisfaction in his work, even though the work itself is not entirely to his liking [2, 106].

The *attitude of the worker's family* plays an important role in job satisfaction. This is true of women workers as well as of men. When a man's wife and children are dissatisfied with his job, because of the salary, the time it requires him to be away from home, or the prestige of the job, there are pressures on him from his family to change jobs. Family dissatisfaction greatly increases the worker's dissatisfaction [28]. Many husbands and children are critical of the working mother, not so much because of the nature of the work she does, the prestige status of the job, or the money she earns, but because it means that she cannot do many of the things for her family that the homemaker is expected to do. Even when adequate provision is made for the care of young children while the mother is at work, children often object to the mother's absence from the home. Older children and adolescents object mainly because it interferes with their social lives [10, 98].

When mothers work sporadically, because of boredom or in order to meet some financial need or crisis in the family, the adjustment problem for the children is greater than when the mothers are regularly employed. Having been accustomed to depending on the mother, they are more prone to delinquency when the mother is temporarily away from the home than they would be if the mother were regularly employed and they had learned to manage without her [38]. For the mother there are problems of adjustment too. Even though the work is to her liking and the money she earns makes it possible for the family to have many things they want and otherwise would be unable to have, these satisfactions are counteracted by feelings of guilt on her part that stem from the dissatisfactions of her husband and children. When, in addition to family dissatisfactions, the woman feels that family responsibilities make it impossible for her to compete on equal terms with unmarried women, or that her lack of advancement is due to the fact that she is a woman, her dissatisfaction with her work will be greatly increased [9].

MARITAL ADJUSTMENT

To the average young adult, marriage is the most important and, at the same time, most serious adjustment that must be made. While the adolescent thinks almost exclusively in terms of love, ignoring such important factors in marriage happiness as congeniality of interests and family backgrounds, the adult approaches marriage in a more realistic manner, facing the many problems that marriage entails before embarking upon this all-important lifetime adventure. He knows how important it is to choose the right mate for himself and then learn to get along well with that person. His happiness and that of the entire family will be affected by how well he makes this adjustment. Success in his work is likewise greatly influenced by the attitude of his family toward it [28]. And, not of least importance, the happiness of his children, as well as their attitudes toward their parents and toward marriage for themselves will be affected by the marital success of their parents [116].

Difficulties in Marital Adjustment. Marital adjustment is difficult for people throughout the world, whether primitive or civilized. However, in America today, there are certain factors that contribute to this difficulty and, as a result, intensify it. These factors are:

1. *Limited Preparation.* Unlike in most cultures, young people in America today receive little preparation for marriage. True, there is more emphasis than in the past on premarital preparation, but this is limited mainly to information related to sexual adjustments [69] (see Figure 90). However, that many adults feel the need for more preparation than they receive is shown by the fact that they turn to the "advice columns" in newspaper for this. Furthermore, there is more discussion, and of a franker sort, about such matters as sexual behavior, number of children desired, and contraceptive methods than would have been considered "proper" in past generations [63]. However, such important areas as domestic skills, child rearing, getting along with in-laws, or money management receive little attention in the preparation of marriage for people of today.

MOTHER

DAUGHTER

Fig. 90. Proportions of two married generations who sought premarital advice. (*From P. H. Landis, Marriage preparation in two generations. Marriage Fam. Living,* 1951, 13, 155–156. Used by permission.)

2. *Roles in Marriage.* As has been stressed before (see pages 362–363), modern adolescents know, in a general way, what roles members of the two sexes are expected to play in adult life. But with the trend toward change in these roles for both men and women, and with differences in concepts of the roles by different social classes, adjustment problems arise in today's marriages which were not present in the past when the roles of men and women were more rigidly prescribed and varied little from one social class to another. When the individual feels that his spouse does not perform her role satisfactorily, according to his concept of it, conflicts arise [108].

3. *Early Marriages.* In the past, marriages in the teens were common among members of the lower social classes. Today, there is a trend toward earlier marriages in all social classes, with the greatest gains among the more educated members of the middle class [87] (see Figure 91). While the tendency in the past was for the man to be older, more mature in experience, and better established in his vocation, today's trend is toward marriages where the husband's age is nearer that of his wife. The most recent statistics show that the average age at first marriage for women is twenty years and, for men, twenty-three years [37]. There are many reasons for this shift to earlier marriages, especially among individuals of the social classes where increasingly longer time is needed for

preparation for their life work. These include the widespread belief that thwarting of the sex desire is both physically and psychologically bad, widespread knowledge of how to regulate childbearing by the use of contraceptives, family help in the early years of marriage, employment of the wife, and changed concepts of the prerequisites for marriage, especially concerning financial security on the part of the husband [41].

Perhaps the most powerful factor in this change has been the change in *sex ratio* since shortly after the turn of the century. In 1910, the ratio of males to females was 106 to 100 in the early adult years. By 1940, it had dropped to 100.7 to 100, and in 1956, to 96.6 to 100 [87]. This change in sex ratio, which for the first time in the history of our country puts young women in a position of disadvantage in marriage selection, has had a marked influence not only on the courtship pattern but also on

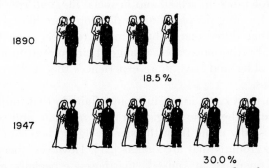

1890   18.5%

1947   30.0%

Fig. 91. The trend toward earlier marriages as shown by the increased percentage of marriages under twenty-five in 1947 as compared with 1890. (*From P. H. Landis, Sequential marriage. J. Home Econ., 1950, 42, 625–627. Used by permission.*)

the trend toward earlier marriages. That this trend has added to the problem of marital adjustments is readily apparent in the marked increase in divorces, especially among the members of the middle class (see pages 445–449). Because young adults have had little or no experience outside of school and college, and because early marriage occurs before they are economically independent and therefore leads to feelings of insecurity and inadequacy, they are ill equipped to meet the problems of marriage which they must face.

4. *Mixed Marriages.* Since success or failure in marriage depends more upon the right choice of a mate than upon any one other factor in the marriage pattern, it is important that the choice be made wisely and with complete understanding of the entire situation. In the past, the decision was largely in the hands of the parents of both young people. But since the turn of the century, there has been a gradual swing in the opposite direction. Today, young people date individuals their parents may disapprove of and they often marry against parental wishes [63].

While parents may try to control their children's dating and mate selection by providing a social milieu for "proper" courtship, by persuasion, or by threatening to withdraw economic support, they are not always successful in their efforts [107]. Not only is the choice of a mate more in the hands of the persons involved than it was in the past, but women play a more aggressive role in the choice than would have been considered sexually appropriate in the past. This change has come partly from the trend toward equality of the sexes and partly from the change in sex ratio. The competition for eligible men grows increasingly keener as the ratio becomes more unfavorable to women [87].

For the most part, the selection of a mate is greatly influenced by past experiences, attitudes formed from these experiences, and the values the individual has formed. As a result of greater independence in dating, the emphasis on tolerance in school and in social life, and experiences in the business world, young people of today develop more liberal attitudes and have values that differ markedly in many respects from the values of their parents. Furthermore, they change their own attitudes and values as they grow older and have more experiences that incline them toward liberal attitudes.

Marriage in most cases is an "in-group affair" in that individuals select as mates those of the same religious, racial, national, and socioeconomic status. They usually come from the same neighborhoods or communities and have backgrounds that are similar [21]. However, there is a marked trend toward increase in "mixed" marriages, especially among young people in the middle class. The trend is to cross class lines and marry individuals of different faiths, of different racial or national backgrounds, and of different social classes [13]. That such marriages require more difficult adjustments is shown by the greater number of separations and divorces than in marriages between people of more similar backgrounds (see pages 447–448). Furthermore, mixed marriages increase the difficulties of parenthood and in-law adjustments, two areas where satisfactory adjustment is important to family happiness [13, 107].

5. *Shorter Courtship.* With the new trend toward "going steady," the courtship period is shorter than in the past. Usually the time interval between being engaged and being married is reduced to a few months. The constant contact characteristic of modern engagements helps to reduce some of the adjustment problems to a less serious level, as shown by the fact that there is a decline in disagreement with increased intimacy. There is a slight sex difference, with women showing a tendency to disagree more than men, especially during the engagement period. This is because women expect more than men do, and they especially expect to be treated in a chivalrous manner, even though engaged [61]. Figure 92 shows the decline in disagreements with increase in intimacy

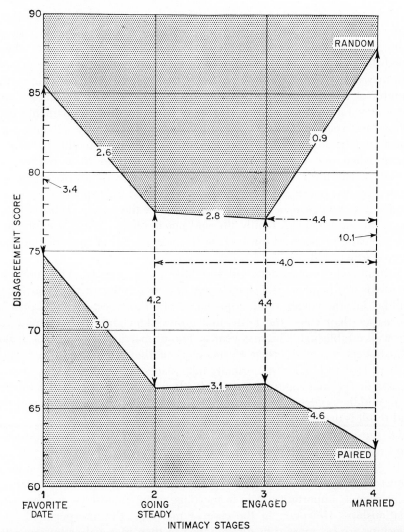

FIG. 92. Decline in disagreements with increase in intimacy. (*From C. Kirk-patrick and C. Hobart, Disagreement, disagreement estimate, and non-empathetic imputations for intimacy groups varying from favorite date to married. Amer. sociol. Rev., 1954, 19, 10–19. Used by permission.*)

(see also Figure 69, page 316). Even though the intimacy of the engagement period provides young adults with opportunities to discuss matters that may give rise to disagreements after marriage and to agree upon a mutually satisfactory solution to them, in most cases it is too short to permit the solution of many problems which will make the adjustments to marriage difficult.

Problems in Marital Adjustment. Marital adjustment is a far more difficult adjustment than most people realize. It is more than a case of falling in love and living happily ever after, as our fairy tales of childhood days intimate. And it is far more than just adjusting to one person, the marriage partner. While it is true that a person does not "marry the family" of the marriage partner, he or she automatically becomes a unit in a new family group after marriage. This involves adjustments to a whole new social group, one in which the individual may not be a welcome member. Then, too, there are marked changes in the pattern of living when one changes status from an unmarried to a married individual that must be adjusted to. A good family atmosphere can be ruined by one poorly adjusted person and a good atmosphere is essential for the psychological health of all members of the family. Tension exists rarely in one region of family life and not in others. When it exists, it is symptomatic of poor adjustment on the part of one or both of the marriage partners [54].

Adjustment to marriage will not take place quickly. The more individuals are involved, the longer and the more difficult the adjustment will be. For the young adult, adjustments of all sorts, especially to people, are easier than when the individual grows older and his habit patterns are well established. The first year or two of marriage is when the major adjustments to one another, to members of the families, and to friends of both husband and wife normally take place. This can be a very stormy period in the marriage career and it often is. Marriages in the thirties or in middle age frequently require a longer time for adjustment and the end result is usually not as satisfactory as in earlier marriages.

Of the many adjustment problems in marriage, the following are the most common and the most important for marital happiness:

1. *Adjustment to Mate.* Being in love is not enough to guarantee good adjustment to the person chosen as a life mate. Interpersonal relationships play as important a role in marriage as in friendships and business relationships. However, in the case of marriage, the interpersonal relationships are far more difficult to adjust to than in social or business life because they are complicated by factors not present in any other area of the individual's life. The more experience in interpersonal relationships both men and women have had in the past, the greater social insight they have developed, and the greater willingness to cooperate with others, the better they will be able to adjust to one another in marriage. Adults who have been popular throughout their childhood and adolescence have acquired the ability to adjust to others and the social insight necessary to make adjustments, and these experiences will go a long way toward helping them make good adjustments to marriage [29].

In selecting a mate, both men and women are guided by a concept of an *ideal mate*. Each sex will have an ideal for the mate based on past experiences, values, interests, and culturally defined roles for individuals of that sex. Women, for example, stress the importance of achievement, affection, love, and understanding from a husband while men want their wives to make good impressions on their friends and acquaintances, to be home-loving, to be good managers, to adjust to a routine that will fit into the pattern of their lives, to be even tempered, and to avoid friction [70]. The intimacy of marriage often unmasks the illusions that mates initially have about one another and then idealization must give way to reality. The more the individual must readjust his ideal to fit into reality, the more difficult the adjustment will be.

Early experiences of the adult not only influence the choice of a mate but they determine what sort of adjustment will be made to this mate. Men who, because of their inferior height, have been outsized and outdistanced by their peers, frequently select a woman smaller than they as a wife and make satisfactory adjustments in their relationships in the home because they feel dominant. Women, on the other hand, who protest against masculine domination make better marital adjustments to men equal in size or smaller than they [4]. Women who rebelled against strict discipline in their childhood days are often predisposed to play a dominant role in marriage, thus leading to conflicts when the husband feels that the dominant role should be played by the male [75]. Unfulfilled needs stemming from early experiences must be filled by the mate if good adjustments are to be made. If the adult needs recognition, achievement, and social status to be happy, the mate must help him to meet these needs if the marriage is to be happy [14].

Every married adult must learn to live with a person whose background is different from his and whose interests, values, and expectations differ from his. Even when backgrounds appear, on the surface, to be very similar, each adult has built up, from his past experiences, an outlook on life that is unique. It is popularly believed that good adjustment in marriage depends upon common *interests*. But the type of interest is more important than the number of interests held in common. Mutual interests that are *familistic* in character have been found to lead to better adjustments between husbands and wives than mutual interests that are *individualistic* in character [7]. Well-adjusted couples have been found to have more similar *values* than couples who are poorly adjusted. While similar backgrounds are likely to produce similar values, this is not always true [56]. If, for example, both husband and wife are "conforming" in the sense that they accept the values of the social group with which they are identified, or if they are both "mobile" and strive for a pattern of life better than the present, they will make more successful adjustments to one another than if they are "divergent," each having a different set of values and a different goal [80]. Each mate has a definite concept of the role a husband and wife should play (see pages 407–409), and each mate expects the other to play that role. When *role expectations* are not fulfilled, there is conflict, and unless the conflict is handled to the satisfaction of both, there will be poor adjustment and unhappiness [90].

Adjustment to a mate means reorganizing the pattern of living, revamping friendships and social activities, and changing occupational requirements, especially for the wife. Even young people whose life patterns are not fully established find adjustment to these changes difficult, and these adjustments are often accompanied by conflict with emotional storm and stress. The closer the relationship between two individuals and the stronger the personalities, the more conflicts there will be. Conflicts generally end in one of three ways: a temporary truce with no solution; one mate gives in for the sake of peace; and mutual adaptation, where each sees and understands the other's point of view. When conflicts are accompanied by physical or verbal aggression, or by avoidance of the mate, the chances of a satisfactory solution are markedly decreased. In the long run, only mutual adaptation leads to satisfactory adjustments. While quarreling in the early years of marriage is dangerous in that it can and often does lead to a breakup of the marriage, when properly handled it can lead to satisfactory adjustments by enabling both husband and wife to see limits beyond which they cannot go without meeting resistance from the spouse [90].

2. *Sexual Adjustments.* Of all the adjustments to marriage, this is unquestionably one of the most difficult to achieve and the one, if not satisfactorily achieved by both husband and wife, most likely to lead to marital discord and unhappiness. Unlike other adjustments adults must make to marriage, there has been less opportunity for either men or women to have preliminary experience related closely enough to this adjustment to enable them to make it easily and with a minimum of emotional tension. Furthermore, there are complications which are likely to increase the difficulty of the adjustment for many, though aiding others. Whether these will aid or handicap adjustment will depend largely on the personality pattern of the individual and his past experiences. The most common complications to good sex adjustment consist of attitudes toward sex, past experiences in sex behavior, and differences in the strength of sex desire.

While young adults of today have more information and more accurate information about sex before they marry than was true in past generations, this is no guarantee that their *attitudes* toward sex will be favorable [69]. How they got their information and from what sources will have a marked influence on their attitudes. Most children and adolescents engage in some forms of sex play, either with members of their own sex or with members of the opposite sex, and most engage in masturbation at some time or other in the early years of their lives. When adolescents start to date, petting becomes a common practice and often goes to the extreme of including sexual intercourse. While these *past experiences in sex behavior* increase the adolescent's information about sex, they also color his attitudes toward sex. Being made to feel guilty about sex play and masturbation can distort attitudes about the marital relationship. Petting provides both boys and girls with an understanding of a heterosexual relationship but it can, at the same time, color their attitudes unfavorably. If petting is accompanied by feelings of guilt, fear of social disapproval, or nervous exhaustion, it will leave an impression that can have far-reaching effects on sexual adjustments in marriage. While petting may help to release men from inhibitions that would plague them in marriage, this is not always true of women. Girls know that they must control how far the petting will go and, as a result, they build up inhibitions. Frequent petting before marriage may therefore establish an inhibitory pattern that will militate against good sexual adjustment in marriage [60, 81]. Studies of premarital heterosexual behavior have revealed that men more often cross class lines and date women of a lower social class than women do. Furthermore, extremes in heterosexual behavior occur when men are in the company of women of a lower class more often than when their dates are with women of their own or a higher class. This may result in the development of a proprietary attitude toward women on the part of the man and a defensive, resentful attitude on the part of the woman, which can have serious effects on sexual adjustments in marriage [31].

Among men, the peak of the sexual drive which influences the strength of *sex desire* comes in the late teens or early twenties and then begins to decline. While the number and frequency of outlets for this desire vary markedly according to the educational and social level of men, as seen in the frequency of intercourse and masturbation, there is evidence that it reaches its peak even before the average man is married, during the early twenties, and then begins to wane as he approaches the thirties. Early-maturing boys have a higher rate of sexual outlet throughout adulthood than do late-maturing boys. Sexual outlets for men of different ages are shown in Figure 93. Among women, by contrast, the peak of sexual desire does not come until the late twenties, several years after the average woman is married. This discrepancy in ages of maximum sexual desire is especially important in cases where women marry men a year or more older than they. Because the peak of the woman's sexual desire does not come until the male sexual desire has started to wane significantly, sexual adjustments in marriage are often difficult for both men and women [60].

Added to this is another matter of great significance in sexual adjustments, the *periodicity of the female sexual desire*. The cycle of this desire is regulated by the ovarian hormone, with the desire reaching a height about the time of ovulation, then waning to reach another height just before menstruation. This bimodal curve of sexual desire may vary slightly

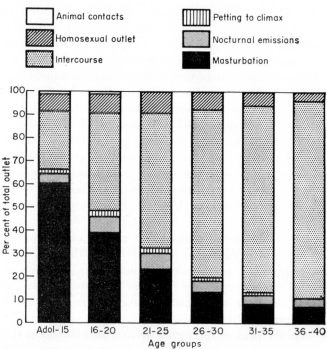

Fig. 93. Sources of orgasm for total U.S. male population. (*From A. C. Kinsey, W. B. Pomeroy, and C. E. Martin, Sexual behavior in the human male. Philadelphia: Saunders, 1948. Used by permission.*)

for different women, but it is always present. This is not true of men. While the strength of their sexual desire may fluctuate from time to time, owing to physical causes such as fatigue or poor health, to psychological causes such as worry or depression, or even to the stimuli in the individual's immediate environment such as the presence of a member of the opposite sex who excites or revolts them, these fluctuations are far less pronounced than are those among women. This further adds to the difficulties of sexual adjustments for both men and women [60]. While pregnancy usually lowers the level of sexual desire for both men and women, especially in the months immediately following the birth of the child, there is no evidence that it has any lasting effect on sexual adjustments for either men or women [67].

Because sexual relationships are new and difficult, the first marital sex experiences may be unsatisfactory to one or both mates. Furthermore, the belief that sexual relations produce states of ecstasy not paralleled by any other experience has led many young adults to be so disillusioned at the beginning of their married lives that later sexual adjustments are difficult or even impossible. Fear of pregnancy is likewise a common handicap to good adjustment in early marital adjustments. When satisfactory sex relationships in marriage are achieved, there is usually a good adjustment between husband and wife and both find happiness in marriage. Unsatisfactory sex relationships, on the other hand, may be the cause or the effect of unsatisfactory relationships in other areas of marriage. When sexual relationships are satisfactory, marital success is aided but not guaranteed. From the point of view of good marital adjustment, it is more important that sexual relationships be satisfactory to the wife than to the husband, though satisfaction to both will go a long way toward helping them to adjust to other problems that are inevitable accompaniments of marriage [59, 60, 113]. As Terman has stressed, "The wife's orgasm adequacy is only one of many factors influencing her marital happiness and by no means the most important factor." This is seen by the fact that divorce among inadequate wives does not differ significantly from the percentage among adequate wives [109].

3. *Adjustment to Parenthood.* In spite of the fact that most women, since their childhood days, have looked forward to having children, the adjustment to parenthood is not always easy for them. Men, during their youth, have been more concerned about plans for their vocations than about parenthood and, as a result, have not given serious consideration to playing the role of a parent. With the trend toward earlier marriages and earlier childbearing, the adjustment to parenthood must be made when both men and women are in their early- to mid-twenties, and often before they have successfully solved adjustment problems in other areas of their marriage or in other areas of their lives, especially vocational adjustments and adjustments to changed interests and changes in social life. How early in adulthood adjustment to parenthood must be made is shown by the fact that the average women of today has had her last child when she is twenty-six years old, as compared with thirty-two years of age in 1890 [37]. Furthermore, with the smaller families of recent generations, few young adults of today have had much experience in handling babies or young children in their own homes and few have had training in school or college in child care. Only those who have had part-time jobs in baby sitting have had much in the way of preliminary experience on which to base their adjustment to parenthood.

Adjustment to parenthood is influenced by many factors, the most important of which are:

a. ATTITUDE TOWARD PARENTHOOD. The younger the parent, the less realistic the attitude toward parenthood. *Young* parents tend to take their parental responsibilities lightly and not to allow them to interfere too much with their interests and pleasures; older parents tend to be more anxious and concerned, and this makes them place parental responsibilities ahead of their personal interests and pleasures [10]. *Marital adjustment* has a strong influence on the adult's attitude toward parenthood. High marital adjustment is usually accompanied by concentration on one another with less interest in the child. Medium marital adjustment, on the other hand, results in a more favorable attitude toward parenthood [94]. Adults who are *poorly adjusted,* unhappy, and discontented, not only have unfavorable attitudes toward parenthood but their relationships with their children are such that they cause them to be poorly adjusted too [71]. Adults of different *social-class backgrounds* have different attitudes toward parenthood. Those of the middle and upper classes regard parenthood as the fulfillment of marriage and look upon their children with possessive pride and hope; adults from the lower classes look upon parenthood as the "inevitable payment for sex relations," a point of view that does not contribute to favorable attitudes toward parenthood [10].

Men and women not only have different concepts of parental roles but their attitudes toward parenthood are also different. The man who holds the traditional concept of the role of the father will feel that his main contribution is economic and will be motivated to greater vocational achievements. The man with high vocational aims will often resent the noise and confusion children make in the home, and the demands they make on his time; he may even resent giving money that he wants for vocational advancement to the family. Men who hold the developmental concept of father will be "family men" in the sense that they devote time to their children, not only in the care of the children but in teaching, guiding, and playing with them [42]. The woman's attitude toward parenthood is colored by her physical condition during pregnancy and her attitude toward woman's biological role. When her attitude is favorable, the woman will adjust to any physical discomforts pregnancy may bring and willingly accept the role of mother when the baby is born, even when it means giving up a career that has interested her [23]. Should her attitude toward motherhood be unfavorable, her adjustment to pregnancy discomforts will be poor, she may try to bring on an abortion, and her attitude toward the baby after its birth is likely to be unfavorable [88]. There is more likely to be an unfavorable attitude toward the second than the first child, especially if the interval between the arrival of the first and second child is short [16]. In most cases, when the woman's attitude has been unfavorable during pregnancy, it improves after the baby's birth [121]. This is true even in the case of unwed mothers [114].

b. SEX OF CHILDREN. Most adults, both men and women, want their first child to be a boy. They hope that the second-born will be a girl and that, if the number of children is large, there will be an equal distribution of boys and girls [26]. However, after the birth of the child, both parents try not to be disappointed, should the child not be of the desired sex. As the children grow older, parental preferences become apparent in the treatment of the children. Women are more severe with their daughters and show a preference for their sons while men pamper their daughters and are stricter with their sons. Sex preferences thus tend to affect the adult's attitude toward parenthood. If he has a child or children of the sex he prefers, his attitude toward parenthood will be more favorable than if the children are not of the preferred sex. For most adults, parenthood is viewed more favorably if at least one of their children is a son [81].

c. NUMBER OF CHILDREN. As is true of sex preferences, most adults have a preference for a family of a given number of children. Men who believe that a large family is a sign of their masculinity prefer large to small families, especially when there is a preponderance of sons [47]. Whether or not adults want children and the number of children they want will be influenced by their religion, education, socioeconomic status, and whether or not their own childhoods were happy or unhappy. Many adults believe that one can have a happy and rewarding life only when there are children and they prefer large to small families. When families are planned, the size of the family is closely related to the adults' interest in children, the satisfaction they derive from parenthood, and whether they prefer to concentrate on a few children or get more enjoyment from a large group [17]. When the number of children in the family coincides with the adult's concept of the "ideal family," the attitude toward parenthood will be more favorable than when the number is either larger or smaller than the desired number. A family smaller than the desired size may lead to feelings of masculine inadequacy or resentment on the part of the husband toward his wife because she did not give him as many children as he wanted, while the woman's attitude may readily develop into overprotectiveness of the children, leading to anxiety and worry about their safety. A family that is larger in number than desired can put such a strain on the time, energy, and budget of a family that the attitudes of both parents toward parenthood can be unfavorably influenced. This is shown by the fact that marital tensions are greater in families with four or more children than in families with one, two, or three children. Tensions are also great in childless families if one or both parents wanted children [33]. Marital adjustment is thus not determined by family size per se but by the ability to control fertility in line with the desires of both parents. When there are more or fewer children than either parent wants, adjustment to parenthood and marriage is affected [18].

d. FEELINGS OF PARENTAL ADEQUACY. The more adequate a person feels he is to meet a situation, the better he will adjust to it. Many adults feel inadequate for the role of parenthood not only because of lack of previous training and experience in this role but also because of confusion as to the best methods of *child training* to use. Many adults who are inclined to favor the traditional methods, which emphasize parental authority and strict discipline to bring about conformity on the child's part, feel unsure about the wisdom of such training when friends, child-training experts, or their spouse maintain that more permissive methods, which allow the child more freedom for development along the lines of his abilities, will produce better results. Conflicts within the family about child training lead to feelings of inadequacy in the parental role. Men, as a rule, are more critical of their wives as parents than women are of their husbands [108]. Because the character structure of the parent influences the way the parent interprets the practices and techniques of child training, feelings of inadequacy, often accentuated by criticisms from the mate, will have a profound influence on the individual's adjustment to the parental role [3]. That many parents feel inadequate for their roles is seen in the frequency with which they seek advice and aid from relatives, friends, or child-guidance experts. Mothers seek advice more for children under nine years of age while fathers ask more for advice in dealing with the problems of adolescence [101].

e. PARENTAL OCCUPATION. Attitudes acquired in relation to work influence the adult's attitude toward his parental role. Middle-class parents, especially fathers, feel that their parental duty is to train their children for success in life and this leads them to set goals often beyond the child's ability to reach. Parental pressures on the child to live up to these expectations result in nervousness in the child and resentment toward the parent, neither of which contributes to good adjustment to parenthood on the part of the parent [45]. The mother who works carries a heavy burden which often causes her to eliminate many home duties normally assumed by a housewife, cut down on the amount of social life the family engages in, develop tensions which lead to friction with the children, and reduce the amount of time she can spend with the children. Furthermore, like the man, the working mother carries into the home habits of efficiency and expectations characteristic of the work world. In a comparison of professional with nonprofessional women as mothers, the professional women were found to emphasize discipline and independence on the part of their children while the nonprofessional women empha- sized the protective, empathetic, and understanding functions of mother- hood. Professional women have more rules and expect more from their children, justifying this on the grounds that the child should have experi- ences with reasonable and routinized behavior to prepare him for adult life. By contrast, the nonprofessional women believe that the child should enjoy himself while he is young. They recognize the child's wishes more and expect the child to perform household tasks less than mothers who are active professionally [115]. Figure 94 shows the types of relationships that exist between mother and adolescent children when the mother works full time, part time, or devotes herself exclusively to homemaking.

4. *Economic Conditions.* Money or lack of it will have a profound in- fluence on the adult's adjustment to marriage. Traditionally, the money is earned by the husband and the control of it is in his hands. Today, as a result of premarital experience in the business world, many wives resent not having control of the money needed for the home, and they find it difficult to adjust to liv- ing on their husband's earnings after being accustomed to having money from their own earnings to spend as they wish. Many men, likewise, find financial adjustments after marriage

FIG. 94. Adolescent-parent adjustment in homes where mothers work full time, part time, or not at all. (*From I. Nye, Adolescent-parent adjustment: age, sex, sibling number, broken homes, and employed mothers as variables. Mar- riage Fam. Living,* 1952, 14, 327–332. *Used by permission.*)

very difficult to make. These adjustments are made more difficult if the wife has worked after marriage and their combined incomes have pro- vided them with what they want. Then, with the arrival of the first child, the income is not only reduced but the husband's earnings must be spread over a wider area to cover the expenses of the children. That both men and women find such adjustments difficult is shown by the large number of women returning to work even while their children are still young [86].

With the modern labor-saving devices and the ease with which all the necessities for running a home can be obtained in our present culture, adjustment to managing a home would appear to be the simplest ad- justment the adult must make. If money were unlimited and if domestic help were readily available at a price the average young couple could afford to pay, this would be true. But, during the early years of marriage, when rearing a family takes the major part of the mother's time and when labor-saving devices and domestic help would be of the maximum help, the family income can usually not provide such help. The tendency is for most families to leave the burden of responsibility for the management of the home in the hands of the wife. Some women are quick and efficient with the result that they run their homes with minimum effort and need little help from the other members of the family. Other women, by contrast, are slow and inefficient. To help them carry the burden of running the home, women call on their husbands for help and this frequently causes friction, especially when the man's concept of homemaking is that it is "woman's work."

Studies of the effect of the economic factor on marital adjustments have revealed that when there is economic security in the form of savings, regular employment, and absence of debt, and when there is effective economic management in the form of good budgeting and absence of borrowing, marital adjustments are far better than when the income is insufficient to cover family needs, when there is constant debt, or when irregular employment of the husband necessitates the wife's working while her husband is unemployed. Because adults of the middle and upper classes have fewer economic problems than do those of the lower classes, there is less friction stemming from money problems [120].

Economic conditions influence the *social status* of the family by determining where the family will live, how it will live, and the level of education and occupation the different members will have. Adjustments to marriage are greatly influenced by the socioeconomic status of the family, with better adjustments in families of higher status. How good the adjustment will be in cross-class marriages will depend upon which mate comes from the higher class. If the wife comes from the higher class, the adjustments are poorer because it is the wife who must make the major adjustments to marriage, both economically and socially, and it is harder to "live down" than to "live up." When both husband and wife move ahead of their families, as a result of higher education, greater earnings, and social mobility, the adjustment is better than when only one is ahead of the families. The best adjustment occurs when both husband and wife are of the same class at the time of marriage, even if that is higher than the occupational and social class identifications of their parents [97]. Many families are able to improve their status by the mid-thirties, the beginning of the period when family income is normally at its peak (see Figure 108, page 501). By that time, the husband's earnings are reaching their peak and the family income is often supplemented by earnings from the wife as well as by those of the children [37]. A favorable income, with economic security, makes social mobility possible and eliminates the friction that arises within a family when every member suffers from money problems.

5. *In-law Adjustments.* With marriage, the adult acquires a whole new set of relatives, his "in-laws." This group varies in size but might be conservatively estimated to include an average of six people. It is made up of individuals of different ages, different interests, and often markedly different cultural backgrounds. The adult must learn to adjust to people who are not of his choosing and, as often happens in the case of in-laws, who are more critical of him than they would be of others who are not members of the "family." Furthermore, because they regard themselves as members of the family, they assume the privilege of trying to direct his life as they do with those who are blood members of the family. A number of factors, in recent years, have made the in-law problem especially serious: the housing shortage, which requires many young couples to "double up" with the family of one side; early marriages which take place before the man is vocationally established; military service which forces the young wife to return to the family; financial aid from the parents who are unwilling or unable to support two families under separate roofs; and the employment of young mothers who live with the family so their children can be taken care of while they work [27].

In-law adjustments have been made more difficult by a number of factors which are of recent origin and which members of past generations, for the most part, were not forced to cope with. There is a widespread and widely accepted *stereotype* of the "typical mother-in-law," which causes unfavorable mental sets even before marriage and increases the difficulties of adjustment on the part of both men and women. While mother-in-law jokes are of early origin in our culture, the comic element is now replaced with bitter resentments and strong defenses. Young married couples of today, as a result of the greater *independence* they have enjoyed throughout childhood and adolescence, expect complete independence with marriage and rebel against parental advice or guidance even when they must accept parental financial aid. In families where one parent, especially the mother, comes from a nationality favoring an *extended family system,* as the French, Italian, or Polish, adjustments are complicated by the parental belief that young couples should devote more time to their parents and willingly accept advice from them. *Cross-class marriages,* with their different concepts of roles and different patterns of living, complicate adjustments by leading to frictions. The increase in the number of old people, especially women, and the decrease in incomes, owing to retirement and the shrinkage of the value of money in pensions, necessitates caring for *elderly relatives* in the homes of young adults in greater numbers than ever before. While this has always been a complicating factor in marital adjustment, it is especially so today as a result of the present-day unfavorable concept of old age and the present belief that young people should be independent of relatives [1, 27, 104].

The in-law problem is largely a "woman problem" because the woman's life is more family centered than the man's in that she is more dependent, both economically and psychologically, than is the man on family relationships [104]. Furthermore, the wife is more in the home than the man and hence is more accessible to all members of the family. This is especially true when a young couple lives with the parents. Furthermore, when it is necessary to care for an elderly relative in the home, it is the wife who bears the major part of the burden [64]. With increasing age and early marriages, the family pattern is becoming elongated, with more women than men in this pattern (see Figure 115, page 526). As a result, young adults have more family relationships to adjust to and more chances for friction in in-law relationships than formerly [1]. In-law friction is mainly centered in the mother-in-law and sisters-in-law, especially those on the husband's side. Because the girl's parents exercise more control over the choice of a mate than do the boy's parents, the son-in-law is usually more acceptable to the wife's family than the wife is to the husband's family. As a result, the husband's family is not always receptive to their son's wife and this causes friction. Women, on the whole, report less favorable attitudes toward their mothers-in-law than do men. Because the husband is more acceptable in most cases to his in-laws, as they have exercised some control in his selection, they are more receptive to him and this leads to better in-law adjustments. Furthermore, the husband's work gives him more outside interests and requires him to be away from home more than the wife, with the result that he can avoid many frictions that the ever-accessible wife, with her home-bound interests, cannot escape [117].

The trend toward early marriages intensifies the problems of in-law adjustment, especially for the wife. While early marriage may be an advantage in many respects for a woman, it is likely to be a disadvantage for a man. It is especially serious when he must rely upon his parents for economic aid. This makes independence from them impossible and encourages them to try to control his life, a fact which the wife bitterly resents. The young wife, on the other hand, who has been less emancipated from her parents during adolescence than boys are, is often "homesick" for her parents, depends on her mother, and wants to live near her parents. This causes friction between husband and wife, especially when it is apparent that the wife favors her family as opposed to the husband's family. Friction is further intensified when the husband's vocation requires a move to another neighborhood or another community which the wife objects to because it will mean leaving her family [65]. In-law trouble is especially serious during the early years of marriage and is one of the most important causes of marital breakup during the first year of marriage [14, 27]. In families with no children or a few children, it is more serious than in families with many children, where in-law help is often welcome. And it is more common in the middle- and upper-class groups than in the lower, where the traditional concept of an enlarged family group, to include relatives as the chief source of companionships, is more widely held [112]. During the engagement and early part of marriage, conflicts are mainly with the husband's parents but later, because of the wife's dependence on her parents, conflicts tend to shift to the wife's parents [65].

When in-law relationships are favorable, they contribute to good marital adjustment between husband and wife and improved relationships between parents and children. There are certain factors that have been found to contribute to good in-law adjustments. These include: approval of marriage by parents of both mates; opportunities for prospective partners' parents to meet and become acquainted before the marriage; friendliness of the parental families toward each other when they meet; separate homes for the young couple and their families; marriage between persons of the same religion; marriage course before marriage, especially for the wife; happy relationships between the grandparents and grandchildren; similarities in the pattern of social activities; happy marriage of the parents on both sides and of the young couple; acceptance of the other family as their own by both husband and wife; and an intimate title of address for the in-laws, as "Mother" and "Dad," rather than "Mr." and "Mrs." [77].

ASSESSMENT OF MARITAL ADJUSTMENT

How happy or unhappy a marriage will be depends upon the degree of adjustment both marriage partners make. And, because there are many areas in which adjustments must be made, the problem of marital adjustment is a very major one. Successful adjustment in one area alone will not guarantee happiness. In the past, happiness in marriage was taken for granted. Women and men had been trained from the time they were children for their roles in adult life and they were prepared to accept the bad with the good as part of the whole marriage pattern. Moral and religious prejudices against divorce were so great that a marriage was maintained at all cost.

Today, with the new freedom for women, with the relaxed mores regarding divorce, and the opportunities women have to maintain themselves and their children after divorce, there are many more evidences of unhappy marriages than there were in the past. This does not mean that there are proportionally more unhappy marriages today than there were in past generations. Rather, it means that society is more aware of these unhappy marriages because of the legal separations and divorces. It takes time to become adjusted to marriage, just as it does to any other new situation. The less preparation there is in the form of teaching or personal experience, the longer will be the time needed to make the adjustment. That the early years are the most difficult has been shown by the fact that the highest percentage of separations that later result in divorces occur in the first year of marriage. After that, there is a progressive decline in separations, indicating a better adjustment to marriage and an increase in marital happiness [12]. Most married couples are better adjusted to marriage after four than after three years of marriage, indicating the progressive nature of marital adjustment [14, 33]. Family solidarity is increased with the coming of the first child and when the children are very young [52].

There is no one specific pattern of living that is universally favorable to marital adjustment. Success in marriage depends on whether or not the marriage provides satisfaction for the whole family. Marital failure, on the other hand, comes when the needs of one or more of the members have been thwarted. If, for example, the husband needs success in his career to be happy but family duties and responsibilities keep him from achieving this, or at least he *believes* they have interfered with his achieving the success he wanted, he will be dissatisfied with marriage [102]. The needs of the children and their parents often conflict. Parents must play the major role in solving these conflicts so that the needs of all can be met if there is to be improvement in the home climate. So long as one member of the family is unhappy, there cannot be true marital happiness [54]. While it is often claimed that children hold a family together and that good marital adjustment cannot be achieved in a childless family, there is no evidence that children are essential to marital adjustment. Only when children are essential to the satisfaction of one or both of the mates will this influence marital adjustment [83]. While evidence points to the fact that marital adjustment is more successful when there has been no premarital sexual intercourse, some do make good adjustments who have had intercourse with their future spouses before marriage [19].

Criteria of Successful Adjustment. The success of a marriage is reflected in a number of interpersonal relationships and behavior patterns. Of these, the most important are happiness of the husband and wife, good relationships between the parents and children, well-adjusted, happy children, and enjoyment of family activities by all members of the family. The *happiness of the husband and wife* in marriage comes from the satisfaction they derive from playing the roles in marriage that lead to happiness for all concerned. These are the "developmental tasks" of marriage. For the man, it means becoming "domesticated" in the sense that he is less interested in his own activities and more concerned with sharing with his wife in such areas as money, recreation, and home duties; for the woman, it means being a good wife and homemaker; for both, it means a mature and stable love for the mate, good sexual adjustment, and the acceptance of parental roles [102].

Men, as a whole, make better adjustments to marriage than do women but they become discontented with marriage sooner than women do. Members of the upper class, if they are "new" in their status, make poor adjustments as compared with those whose status is "established." Members of the middle class adjust better to marriage while those of the lower classes make the poorest adjustments of all [48]. In general, marital satisfaction is greater among religious than among nonreligious people [15]. For women especially, religion often compensates for low sex gratification and makes marriage more satisfying than it would be for a less religious person. This is not equally true of men [118]. In commenting on marital happiness, Terman has pointed out: "What comes out of a marriage depends upon what goes into it and that among the most important things going into it are the attitudes, preferences, aversions, habit-patterns, and emotional-response patterns which give or deny to one the aptitude for compatibility. In other words, . . . a large proportion of incompatible marriages are so because of a predisposition to unhappiness in one or both of the spouses" [110].

Good *relationships between parents and children* are indicative of the acceptance of parental roles and the successful fulfillment of these roles. The adult who is well adjusted to the parental role regards the child as a person with feelings and he respects the child's right and need to express these feelings; he values the unique make-up of the child; he has unconditional love for the child; and he recognizes the child's need to differentiate and separate himself from his parents if he is to become an autonomous person [94]. Because the needs and behavior patterns of children are so different from those of adults, a well-organized home suited to adult living will not suit the needs of children. If good parent-child relationships are to exist, parents must adjust to the inevitable changes in their living. Their lives will be somewhat disrupted by schedules suited to their children's needs and childish behavior; they will have to adjust to noisiness at times; privacy at times will be intruded upon; the children will sometimes fight with siblings and resist parental restraints; furniture may be broken or damaged; and the house will often be cluttered. From the adult point of view, this is far from an "ideal" home, but if parents feel that this is better for their children's development than trying to force them prematurely into adult patterns of living, they will adjust their homes and lives accordingly and take the change in their stride instead of allowing it to annoy them and lead to friction with the children [8].

Mothers are, on the whole, more acceptant in their attitudes than are fathers and, as a result, adjust better and create better parent-child relationships. This is seen in the fact that children usually prefer their mothers to their fathers. Mothers who have been married for a longer time adjust better than those married a shorter time, as is true of all areas of marital adjustment [46]. Parent-child relationships are better when parental authority is equally divided or is in the hands of the father rather than of the mother [52]. In small families, husbands often resent the mother's concentration on the children. This causes friction with the children, and leads to sibling rivalry and jealousy, none of which contribute to good family relationships. In the large family, many of these sources of friction are removed and family life runs along more smoothly with better adjustments among the different members [10]. Pressures put on the child to conform to adult expectations disrupt family harmony and lead to poor parent-child relationships more quickly than any other one thing.

When parent-child relationships have been favorable, friction is reduced to a minimum and children show a strong liking for both parents, though when they are young, they generally prefer the mother because it is she who takes care of their needs and is with them more constantly than the father. In favorable parent-child relationships, children also idealize their parents to the point of wanting to follow in their footsteps [43]. Even college students who are well adjusted to their parents use their parents as models in the selection of a life career, want to marry at approximately the ages when their parents were married, and plan to model their married lives along lines similar to their parents' lives. While their plans for the future may deviate in some respects from the patterns they have seen in their own homes, especially in the types of recreation they prefer, the major aspects of their lives will follow those of their parents [95].

Children who are *well adjusted and happy* are a proof of their parents' good adjustment to marriage and to parental roles. On the other hand, the unresolved difficulties of parents lead to poor adjustments in marriage and to difficulties for the children of that marriage. This is partly because the child uses the parent as a model and imitates the good as well as the bad, and partly because poorly adjusted parents tend to be authoritarian in their attitudes toward their children, trying to control their activities, subordinating the child's needs to their own needs, and ignoring the child's rights as a person [55]. That this type of relationship can have far-reaching effects is shown by the fact that good adjustment in marriage is closely related to good adjustment on the part of the parents, while poorly adjusted children, who feel hostile and insecure as a result of their conflicts with their parents, carry over these unfavorable attitudes into adult life and express them in their own marriages by trying to dominate their mates as compensation for their own childhood domination by their parents [75].

A final indication of good adjustment to marriage is seen in the enjoyment of *family activities* and the sharing of *common interests*. Adults who have common interests, especially when these center around the family, provide a home atmosphere where all members are happy and can share their interests [7]. Family solidarity is increased by factors that promote successful family living, such as meals together, conversations, entertaining and visiting, auto rides for pleasure, picnics, going to the movies as a family, watching television, or listening to the radio. As children grow older, they form their own circles of friends and have their own interests apart from those of the family. But when the home is a happy one, they bring their friends to their homes and they engage in some activities with family members, even though this may not be with the entire family, as was true when they were younger [22]. Even after they marry, they retain close ties with their families if they have had a happy family life.

DIVORCE AND REMARRIAGE

Divorce is an indication of poor marital adjustment. It comes only after a period of emotional tensions between husband and wife when other solutions to their problems have proved futile. Many unhappy marriages do not end in divorce because of religious, moral, familial, economic, or other reasons. *Legal separations,* or "trial divorces," where the door is left open for a possible reconciliation as time goes on, and *desertion* of the wife and children by a husband who has found his marriage intolerable are likewise indicative of poor marital adjustment. Since the turn of the century, there has been a steady and alarming rise in the divorce rate in America. In the period of 1881 to 1890, for example, there were 5.56 divorces for every 100 marriages; from 1940 to 1949, the number had increased to 25.89 out of 100, roughly one divorce out of every four marriages, or an increase of 446 per cent in the divorce rate in the latter decade over the former. In addition, there are many marriages ending in annulment, desertion, and informal or legal separation, none of which are recorded in the statistics for divorce. Approximately 2 million married people are separated, either temporarily or permanently, every year and one-fifth to one-sixth of all couples living together claim that they are unhappy [11].

The peak year for separations is the first year of marriage and for divorce, the third year (see Figure 95). Because there is always a period of separation before the granting of a divorce, judging the duration of marriage from the time of marriage to the time of divorce gives a false picture of duration. In a study of a representative sample of divorces, it has been found that there is a difference in medians of 4.6 years between legal and actual duration of marriage. The pattern of desertion is similar to that of divorce [57]. There are more divorces among childless

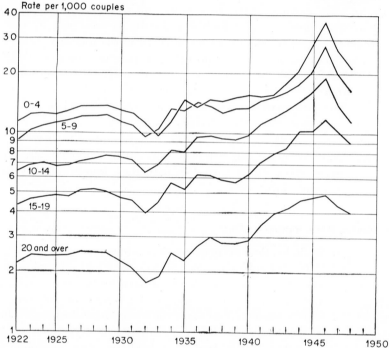

FIG. 95. Divorce rate by duration of marriage in the United States, 1922–1948. (*From P. H. Jacobson, Differentials in divorce by duration of marriage and size of family. Amer. sociol. Rev., 1950, 15, 235–244. Used by permission.*)

couples than among families with children, not because children contribute to marital adjustment but because childless couples can manage better after divorce than can those who have children to support and care for [51] (see Figure 96). Contrary to the common belief that desertion is more common in the lower and divorce in the upper economic groups, statistics for divorce by occupational class show that divorce is much more characteristic of the lower social groups, as is desertion, and much less prevalent in the upper groups. Both divorce and desertion are especially common among laborers, operatives, and craftsmen, and relatively infrequent among professionals, owners, and officials. They are also more common in urban than in rural areas [82]. Divorce is much more common in mixed marriages, whether of different cultural, religious, or socioeconomic backgrounds, than when the backgrounds are more similar. Mixed religious marriages are especially hazardous because the problems of marital adjustment are complicated by pressures from the families on both sides [13, 84].

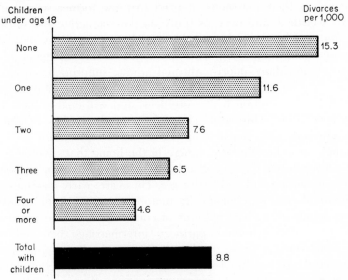

Fig. 96. Divorces per 1,000 married couples, according to size of family, in the United States, 1948. (*From P. H. Jacobson, Differentials in divorce by duration of marriage and size of family. Amer. sociol. Rev., 1950, 15, 235–244. Used by permission.*)

Just as younger adults have more difficulties in adjusting to marriage than do those who are older and more mature, so they are likely to contribute more heavily to marital breakdowns. Youthful marriages are overrepresented in the divorce rate, especially when both husband and wife are young. Furthermore "forced" marriages are more heavily concentrated in the younger groups [82]. While some "forced" or "shot-gun" marriages are successful, the high divorce rate in this type of marriage suggests that it is the most hazardous type of all. The divorce rate for premarital-pregnancy couples is much higher than for postmarital pregnancies, and the divorce is obtained sooner after marriage. Those who wait until the last minute to get married have more divorces than those who marry as soon as the condition is discovered. Premarital pregnancy intensifies conflicts and makes marital adjustment especially difficult.

Within marriage, early conceivers have higher rates of divorce than late conceivers, but less than premarital pregnancy cases. Assuming the responsibilities of parenthood before having time to adjust to marriage complicates adjustment problems to the point where divorce seems to be the only solution [19].

Causes of Divorce. There is not any one cause for marital failure that results in separation, desertion, or divorce. Studies of the personality patterns of divorced people as compared with those who were reasonably happy in their marriages showed that the former scored high on depressive, critical, and nervous traits and low on active and selfmastery traits. Men and women who are divorced have personality patterns that predispose them to make poor adjustments to life in general, not to marriage alone. Many poorly adjusted adults, suffering from emotional problems they have been unable to solve, marry in the hopes that marriage will be the solution to the problems and will enable them to "live happily ever after." This rarely happens. Not only do they become more poorly adjusted with the assumption of new responsibilities but they create such an unhealthy atmosphere in the home that divorce seems to be the only solution [73]. Bossard has given eight major reasons why marriages go wrong and end in divorce. These are: early marriage, before the individuals are psychologically mature enough for the adjustments marriage requires; modern patterns of courtship which do not make for wise choices of matrimonial partners; intermarriage between cultural groups which puts a strain on the usual marital adjustments; too much emphasis, through the movies and other forms of mass communication, on the romantic motif in marriage; attempts on the part of husband or wife or both to develop their individual personalities and interests; poor adjustment to parenthood; pressures to strive for a higher social position; and too little emphasis on the family as a group [11]. While all of these contribute to poor marital adjustment, what finally proves to be the straw that breaks the camel's back and leads to the divorce courts will vary from one couple to another, and from one period in marriage to another. Drink, for example, has been found to be the cause of divorce in only 9 per cent of the cases during the first year of marriage, as contrasted with 43 per cent after 25 years of marriage. Similarly, adultery is rarely given as the cause for separation in the first year of marriage but is the cause for one-third of the separations in the 11- to 15-year period of marriage [111].

Effects of Marital Disruptions. What happens to the spouse and children after a marriage has been broken by desertion, separation, or divorce depends largely on the type of adjustment that is made. The traumatic effect of divorce is usually greater than that of death because of the bitterness and emotional tensions preceding it and because of the social attitudes toward divorce. That these complicate postdivorce adjustment may be seen in the fact that there is a higher incidence of mental illness, as judged by admissions to mental hospitals, among the divorced and widowed than among any other groups of adults [35]. Because of changed social attitudes toward remarriage after divorce, many adults try to solve their adjustment problems by marrying again. Approximately three-fourths of those who are divorced are remarried within five years after divorce [68]. For those who do not remarry and for those who remarry only after an interval of several years, divorce often adds economic strains to other adjustment problems. This is especially true of Negro families, which are more often disorganized by separation, desertion, and divorce than are white families, and of families where the woman must become the head of the household, work, and live with relatives who can assume some of the care of the children while she works [30].

The effects of family disorganization, whether due to separation, desertion, divorce, or death, are especially serious in the case of children. The child experiences a typical grief reaction after the loss of a parent and tries to place his love on the remaining parent. If the mother finds the child a social or economic burden, this will have marked effects on his feelings of security. Or if the mother assumes an overprotective attitude, it will make the child dependent and unsure of himself. The child whose parents are not living together feels embarrassed because he is "different" and this is damaging to his self-concept [36]. However, legal divorce need not be detrimental to the child. Children suffer most from divorce when their loyalties are divided and when there is anxiety about the uncertainties that divorce brings to their lives. Children of parents who are "emotionally divorced," even though living together under the same roof, suffer even more than do those whose parents are legally divorced [25]. Negro children suffer more from family disorganization than do white children because their pattern of living is more likely to be disrupted by economic hardships [30].

Remarriage. There are fewer broken homes than there would be if remarriage after divorce were not so common. But this adds new adjustment problems and complicates life for all involved. The chances for remarriage are greater for divorced people than for those who are widowed, with peak ages at twenty, thirty, and forty-five years. For example, at thirty years of age, the divorced man's chances of marriage are 96 in 100; for the widowed, 92 in 100; and for bachelors, 67 in 100. Remarriage rates drop with age, but faster for women than for men [68] (see Figure 97). According to the most recent statistics, 1 out of every 5 marriages is a remarriage for one or both spouses, while in 1 out of every 14 marriages, both have been married before [12]. Divorced people are more likely to marry others who have been divorced than those who are widowed or single. In the first marriage, men are generally slightly older or the same age as their wives; in remarriage, the age difference is generally greater, with men older than their wives. There is some evidence that the courtship period is shorter for remarriage than for a first marriage, and that men meet their future spouses on the job more often than in public places or on blind dates, so common in the case of first marriages [49].

That remarriages are not as successful as first marriages is shown by the high divorce rate among those who remarry. The difference in duration of first marriages as compared with remarriages is 3.3 years in favor of first marriages. This suggests that individuals are conditioned toward instability after divorce. Remarriage for widows is more stable than for divorced women [57]. It has been estimated that remarriages are about 50 per cent more risky than first marriages, with women in second marriages a 10 per cent poorer risk than men. Financially, also, second marriages are not as successful as first, especially when they are between divorced persons [68]. While remarriage may provide a home for the children and two parents, the *stepparent* finds the role exceedingly difficult, just as the stepchild does.

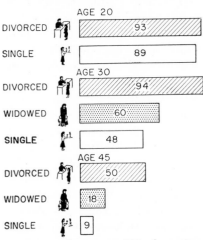

Fig. 97. Chances in 100 of marriage for single women and of remarriage for divorced and widowed women at different ages. (*From P. H. Landis, Sequential marriage. J. Home Econ.,* 1950, 42, 625–627. *Used by permission.*)

How successfully the child will adjust to the stepparent will be greatly influenced by his age at the time of remarriage. Older children have already made adjustments to one pattern of life and are resistant to change, especially when their attitude toward the stepparent is unfavorable as a result of traditional beliefs about the "cruel stepmother" or their personal experiences with the stepparent. The younger child may, on the other hand, welcome a stepparent because this gives greater stability to his life. At any age, the child who has been accustomed to the affection and attention of a parent may resent the transference of some of this attention and affection to the stepparent, and this resentment will be increased if the stepparent tries to assign new roles to the children. Furthermore, many children are embarrassed about having stepparents because of the unfavorable social attitudes toward them. All of this complicates the problems of adjustment to the new pattern of family life, especially if the stepparent has never been a parent before [93].

ADJUSTMENT TO SINGLENESS

For both men and women, marriage is the sought-after goal of maturity. When conditions prevent marriage, whether they come from within the individual or from environmental pressures, the individual is likely to be unhappy, lonely, and thwarted in his normal desires for sex expression, for parenthood, for affection from an admired member of the opposite sex, and for the prestige that marriage and family living give. In many communities there is no place for the bachelor or spinster, except as an extra man at a dinner party or a baby sitter for married relatives. The American stereotype of the unmarried woman is far less favorable than that of the unmarried man. Even the successful "career gal" is regarded almost as unfavorably as the "spinster" of past generations. A study of American novels from 1851 to 1935 reveals a derogatory social attitude toward the women who do not marry. This, as is true of other areas of mass communication, has helped to influence social attitudes toward unmarried women unfavorably [24].

In planning for their futures, especially during the adolescent years, girls stress marriage more than boys do (see pages 350–351). The adolescent boy's major concern is finding out what kind of work he is capable of doing and then preparing himself for it. Vocational interests thus take precedence over interest in marriage. Many boys in high school and college become concerned about dating that might force them into marriage before they have established themselves vocationally. They know that they want to marry eventually but want to wait until they feel ready, economically, for the responsibilities that marriage brings. College students maintain that they hope to marry at the age their fathers married, though the modern trend toward early marriages causes many of them to marry at an earlier age than their fathers did. College women, by contrast, claim that they want to marry at the age when their mothers *wished* they had married, rather than when they did marry. There is greater variation in the ages at which college men want to marry than is true of college women [95].

Many girls in high school and college, while placing marriage as their goal for adulthood, maintain that they want a year or two after graduation to work and to "look around" before they make their final choice of a life mate. Some, of course, want to marry immediately after graduation and some marry while still in school or college [20] (see Figure 74, page 350). During the twenties, the goal of unmarried women, whether working or not working, is marriage. If they have not married by thirty, the age at which unmarried women of today are thought of as "spinsters," there is a tendency to shift goals and values and to find a new life oriented in work. For unmarried women, therefore, age thirty is a "critical age" which marks the turning point of hope for marriage. As the unmarried woman approaches this critical age, her life is characterized by stress which increases to a peak at thirty and then gradually decreases as she makes adjustments to new goals and a new pattern of living. The desire for marriage and a home decreases after thirty with

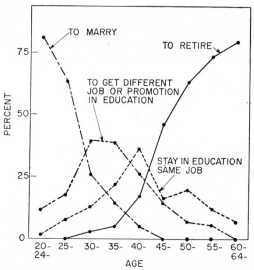

Fig. 98. Age trends in goals of single women teachers. (*From R. G. Kuhlen and G. H. Johnson, Changes in goals with adult increasing age. J. consult. Psychol., 1952, 16, 1–4. Used by permission.*)

the recognition that this goal is not likely to be achieved [66]. Figure 98 shows the typical pattern of goal changes for unmarried women. However, not all unmarried women are willing to resign themselves to spinsterhood, as is seen by the large numbers who join "lonely heart clubs" in the hopes of finding the mate they have not found elsewhere [113].

Reasons for Singleness. In spite of the fact that most boys and girls during the adolescent years, and most men and women in early adulthood, want to marry and expect to, there are large numbers of unmarried men and women at all ages throughout adulthood. According to the 1956 census report, while there has been a gradual but steady increase in the number of married people in the above-fourteen-year groups, there are approximately 24 per cent of the men and 18 per cent of the women in these groups who are unmarried. This refers only to those who have never been married, not to the widowed or divorced [87]. The increase in the number of married adults, in relation to the entire population, is caused partly by the large number of remarriages after divorce or death [11]. And in spite of the fact that the ratio of women to men has increased since the turn of the present century, especially in the higher age groups, the percentage of unmarried women is less than that of men [87].

Because the early years of adulthood are lonely years when radical adjustments must be made not only in the patterns of social life but in every area of life as well (see pages 374–377), many adults feel that marriage will help them to solve these problems. This is especially true of adults, women more than men, who are not well adjusted and who suffer from an ego deficiency which they believe will be met best in marriage [78]. In addition, there are the social pressures to marry, and to marry young, from parents and peers. Why, then, do both men and women remain single? There are many reasons, the most important of which are family responsibilities, a strong vocational drive which the adult believes cannot be satisfied if he divides his time and attention between his vocation and a family, self-sufficiency, disillusionment from unhappy earlier experiences, and lack of opportunity to meet eligible members of the opposite sex. A comparison of a group of married with a group of unmarried women in the thirty- to thirty-nine-year bracket revealed that the unmarried had had significantly less culturally approved heterosexual activity in the age period of sixteen to twenty-five; they were more variable in self-esteem than the married, with some very high and some very low; they had more family obligations up to age twenty-five years; they had had more parental encouragement to be married, which militated against their marrying; and more had come from the lower socioeconomic groups and, even though they had had a college education and had tried to move up the social scale through their scholastic efforts, had met keen competition with women of the class with which they tried to identify themselves, and this had interferred with marriage [62].

Success of Adjustment. How successfully the adult adjusts to singleness depends largely on his reason for remaining single and the strength of his desire to marry. The stronger the desire to marry, the more unhappy the individual will be if obstacles in his environment or within himself prevent him from doing so. That unmarried men and women make better adjustments to singleness than is popularly believed is shown by the fact that there are fewer single people admitted to mental hospitals than divorced and widowed, though more than among the married [35]. Of all adjustments, the most difficult the unmarried must make is to find satisfaction for the sex drive which is especially strong during the early years of adulthood. The unmarried man usually finds sexual outlets either in autoerotic practices or in intercourse with women of his acquaintance or with prostitutes. While women, as is true of men, engage in autoerotic practices, opportunities for extramarital intercourse, strongly tabooed for women, are limited and are always surrounded by the danger of loss of status for the woman [60].

Vocational success is a common substitute for marriage among both men and women. As this is often motivated by neurotic drives to "show" those who did not accept them as children or adolescents, it is not always a satisfactory substitute. A comparison of *mobile* career women, who had occupational and social levels above those of their families, with nonmobile career women revealed that because the former had suffered from community or family rejection when they were younger, they had less satisfactory group relationships and also more often engaged in a "mad hunt for pleasure" to compensate for loneliness than did the nonmobile women. Those who had moved upward either through higher education or geographic mobility to "hide their backgrounds" made less satisfactory adjustments to singleness, though they were more successful vocationally, than did the nonmobile career woman [32]. Single career women who do not strive to attain a higher social status have been found to show a better over-all adjustment than married women of the same age. This superiority is apparent in better health and emotional adjustment, a better sense of personal worth, fewer withdrawing tendencies, more social participation, better use of their abilities, more complete acceptance of social standards, and fewer antisocial tendencies than are shown in married women [78]. Thus, it is apparent that singleness, per se, is not responsible for either good or poor adjustment on the part of men or women. What is responsible for their singleness and what values they hold will be the determining factors in the success or failure with which they make their adjustments.

BIBLIOGRAPHY

1. Albrecht, R.: Intergeneration parent patterns. *J. Home Econ.*, 1954, 46, 29–32.
2. Becker, H. S., and J. Carper: The elements of identification with an occupation. *Amer. sociol. Rev.*, 1956, 21, 341–348.
3. Behrens, M. L.: Child-rearing and the character structure of the mother. *Child Develpm.*, 1954, 25, 225–238.
4. Beigel, H. G.: Body height in mate selection. *J. soc. Psychol.*, 1954, 39, 257–268.
5. Beilin, H.: The mobility and achievement of a 1926 class of high school graduates. *J. counsel. Psychol.*, 1954, 1, 144–148.
6. Belbin, R. M.: Difficulties of older people in industry. *Occup. Psychol., Lond.*, 1953, 27, 177–190.

7. Benson, P.: The common interests myth in marriage. *Soc. Problems*, 1955, 3, 27–34.

8. Blood, R. O.: Consequences of permissiveness for parents of young children. *Marriage Fam. Living*, 1953, 15, 209–212.

9. Boring, E. G.: The woman problem. *Amer. Psychologist*, 1951, 6, 679–692.

10. Bossard, J. H. S.: *Parent and child*. Philadelphia: Univer. of Pennsylvania Press, 1953.

11. Bossard, J. H. S.: Eight reasons why marriages go wrong. *The New York Times*, 1956, June 24.

12. Bossard, J. H. S., and E. S. Boll: Marital unhappiness in the life cycle. *Marriage Fam. Living*, 1955, 17, 10–14.

13. Bossard, J. H. S., and E. S. Boll: *One marriage—two faiths*. New York: Ronald, 1957.

14. Bowerman, C. E.: Adjustment in marriage: over-all and in specific areas. *Sociol. soc. Res.*, 1957, 41, 257–263.

15. Burchinal, L. G.: Marital satisfaction and religious behavior. *Amer. sociol. Rev.*, 1957, 22, 306–310.

16. Caplan, G.: The disturbance of the mother-child relationship by unsuccessful attempts at abortion. *Ment. Hyg., N.Y.*, 1954, 38, 67–80.

17. Centers, R., and G. H. Blumberg: Social and psychological factors in human procreation: a survey approach. *J. soc. Psychol.*, 1954, 40, 245–257.

18. Christensen, H. T., and R. E. Philbrick: Family size as a factor in the marital adjustments of college couples. *Amer. sociol. Rev.*, 1952, 17, 306–310.

19. Christensen, H. T., and B. B. Rubinstein: Premarital pregnancy and divorce: a follow-up study by the interview method. *Marriage Fam. Living*, 1956, 18, 114–123.

20. Christensen, H. T., and M. M. Swihart: Post graduate role preferences of senior women in college. *Marriage Fam. Living*, 1956, 18, 52–57.

21. Clarke, A. C.: An examination of the operation of residential propinquity as a factor in mate selection. *Amer. sociol. Rev.*, 1952, 17, 17–22.

22. Connor, R., T. B. Johannis, and J. Walters: Family recreation in relation to role conceptions of family members. *Marriage Fam. Living*, 1955, 17, 306–309.

23. Cooper, L.: Predisposition toward parenthood: a comparison of male and female students. *Sociol. soc. Res.*, 1957, 42, 31–36.

24. Deegan, D. G.: *The stereotype of the single woman in American novels*. New York: King's Crown Press, 1951.

25. Despert, J. L.: *Children of divorce*. Garden City, N.Y.: Doubleday, 1953.

26. Dinitz, S., R. R. Dynes, and A. C. Clarke: Preferences for male or female children: traditional or affectional? *Marriage Fam. Living*, 1954, 16, 128–130.

27. Duvall, E. M.: *In-laws: pro and con*. New York: Association Press, 1954.

28. Dyer, W. G.: A comparison of families of high and low job satisfaction. *Marriage Fam. Living*, 1956, 18, 58–60.

29. Dymond, R.: Inter-personal perception and marital happiness. *Canad. J. Psychol.*, 1954, 8, 164–171.

30. Edwards, G. F.: Marital status and general family characteristics of the non-white population of the United States. *J. Negro Educ.*, 1953, 22, 280–296.

31. Ehrmann, W. W.: Influence of comparative social class of companion upon premarital heterosexual behavior. *Marriage Fam. Living*, 1955, 17, 48–53.

32. Ellis, E.: Social psychological correlates of upward social mobility among un-married career women. *Amer. sociol. Rev.*, 1952, 17, 558–563.

33. Farber, B., and L. S. Blackman: Marital role tensions and number and sex of children. *Amer. sociol. Rev.*, 1956, 21, 596–601.
34. Friedmann, E. A., and R. J. Havighurst: *The meaning of work and retirement.* Chicago: Univer. of Chicago Press, 1954.
35. Frumkin, R. M.: Marital status and mental health. *Sociol. soc. Res.*, 1953, 39, 237–239.
36. Gardner, G. E.: Separation of the parents and the emotional life of the child. *Ment. Hyg., N.Y.*, 1956, 40, 53–60.
37. Glick, P. C.: The life cycle of the family. *Marriage Fam. Living*, 1955, 17, 3–9.
38. Glueck, S., and E. T. Glueck: Working mothers and delinquency. *Ment. Hyg., N.Y.*, 1957, 41, 327–352.
39. Golden, J.: Patterns of Negro-white intermarriage. *Amer. sociol. Rev.*, 1954, 19, 144–147.
40. Gough, H. G.: Identifying psychological femininity. *Educ. psychol. Measmt*, 1952, 12, 427–439.
41. Hajnal, J.: Analysis of changes in the marriage pattern by economic groups. *Amer. sociol. Rev.*, 1954, 19, 295–302.
42. Handel, G., and R. D. Hess: The family as an emotional organization. *Marriage Fam. Living*, 1956, 18, 99–101.
43. Havighurst, R. J.: *Human development and education.* New York: Longmans, 1953.
44. Havighurst, R. J., and R. Albrecht: *Older people.* New York: Longmans, 1953.
45. Havighurst, R. J., and A. Davis: A comparison of the Chicago and Harvard studies of social class differences in child rearing. *Amer. sociol. Rev.*, 1955, 20, 438–442.
46. Hawkes, G. R., L. G. Burchinal, B. Gardner, and B. M. Porter: Parents' acceptance of their children. *J. Home Econ.*, 1956, 48, 195–200.
47. Heath, C. W.: Physique, temperament, and sex ratio. *Hum. Biol.*, 1954, 26, 335–342.
48. Hollingshead, A. de B.: Class differences in family stability. *Ann. Amer. Acad. pol. soc. Sci.*, 1950, 272, 39–46.
49. Hollingshead, A. de B.: Marital status and wedding behavior. *Marriage Fam. Living*, 1952, 14, 308–311.
50. Inlow, G. M.: Job satisfaction of liberal arts graduates. *J. appl. Psychol.*, 1951, 35, 175–181.
51. Jacobson, P. H.: Differentials in divorce by duration of marriage and size of family. *Amer. sociol. Rev.*, 1950, 15, 235–244.
52. Jansen, L. T.: Measuring family solidarity. *Amer. sociol. Rev.*, 1952, 17, 727–733.
53. Jensen, P. G., and W. K. Kirchner: A national answer to the question, "Do sons follow in their fathers' occupations?" *J. appl. Psychol.*, 1955, 39, 419–421.
54. Josselyn, I. M.: The family as a psychological unit. *Soc. Casewk*, 1953, 34, 336–343.
55. Kates, S. L., and L. N. Diab: Authoritarian ideology and attitudes on parent-child relationships. *J. abnorm. soc. Psychol.*, 1955, 51, 13–16.
56. Keeley, B. J.: Value convergence and marital relations. *Marriage Fam. Living*, 1955, 17, 342–345.
57. Kephart, W. M.: The duration of marriage. *Amer. sociol. Rev.*, 1954, 19, 287–295.
58. Kerr, W. A.: Accident proneness of factory departments. *J. appl. Psychol.*, 1950, 34, 167–170.

59. King, C. E.: The sex factor in marital adjustment. *Marriage Fam. Living,* 1954, 16, 237–240.

60. Kinsey, A. C., W. B. Pomeroy, C. E. Martin, and P. H. Gebhard: *Sexual behavior in the human female.* Philadelphia: Saunders, 1953.

61. Kirkpatrick, C., and C. Hobart: Disagreement, disagreement estimate, and non-empathetic imputations for intimacy groups varying from favorite date to married. *Amer. sociol. Rev.,* 1954, 19, 10–19.

62. Klemer, R. H.: Factors of personality and experience which differentiate single from married women. *Marriage Fam. Living,* 1954, 16, 41–44.

63. Koller, M. R.: Some changes in courtship behavior in three generations of Ohio women. *Amer. sociol. Rev.,* 1951, 16, 366–370.

64. Koller, M. R.: Studies of three-generation households. *Marriage Fam. Living,* 1954, 16, 205–206.

65. Komarovsky, M.: Continuities in family research: a case study. *Amer. J. Sociol.,* 1956, 62, 42–47.

66. Kuhlen, R. G., and G. H. Johnson: Changes in goals with adult increasing age. *J. consult. Psychol.,* 1952, 16, 1–4.

67. Landis, J. T., and S. Poffenberger: The effects of first pregnancy upon the sexual adjustment of 212 couples. *Amer. sociol. Rev.,* 1950, 15, 766–772.

68. Landis, P. H.: Sequential marriage. *J. Home Econ.,* 1950, 42, 625–627.

69. Landis, P. H.: Marriage preparation in two generations. *Marriage Fam. Living,* 1951, 13, 155–156.

70. Langhorne, M. C., and P. F. Secord: Variations in marital needs with age, sex, marital status, and regional location. *J. soc. Psychol.,* 1955, 41, 19–37.

71. Law, S.: The mother of the happy child. *Smith Coll. Stud. soc. Wk,* 1954, 25, 1–27.

72. Lehman, H. C.: *Age and achievement.* Princeton, N.J.: Princeton Univer. Press, 1953.

73. Lippman, H. S.: Emotional factors in family breakdown. *Amer. J. Orthopsychiat.,* 1954, 24, 445–453.

74. Lipsett, L., and J. W. Wilson: Do "suitable" interests and mental ability lead to job satisfaction? *Educ. psychol. Measmt,* 1954, 14, 373–380.

75. Lu, Y–C.: Home discipline and reaction to authority in relation to marital roles. *Marriage Fam. Living,* 1953, 15, 223–225.

76. Lyman, E. L.: Occupational differences in the value attached to work. *Amer. J. Sociol.,* 1955, 61, 138–144.

77. Marcus, P.: In-law relationship adjustment of couples married between two and eleven years. *J. Home Econ.,* 1951, 43, 35–37.

78. Martinson, F. M.: Ego deficiency as a factor in marriage. *Amer. sociol. Rev.,* 1955, 20, 161–164.

79. McArthur, C., and L. B. Stevens: The validation of expressed interests as compared with inventoried interests: a fourteen year follow-up. *J. appl. Psychol.,* 1955, 39, 184–189.

80. McGuire, C.: Conforming, mobile, and divergent families. *Marriage Fam. Living,* 1952, 14, 109–115.

81. Mead, M.: *Male and female.* New York: Morrow, 1949.

82. Monahan, T. P.: Divorce by occupational level. *Marriage Fam. Living,* 1955, 17, 322–324.

83. Monahan, T. P.: Is childlessness related to family stability? *Amer. sociol. Rev.,* 1955, 20, 446–456.

84. Monahan, T. P., and W. M. Kephart: Divorce and desertion by religious and mixed-religious groups. *Amer. J. Sociol.*, 1954, 59, 454–465.
85. Morse, N. C., and R. S. Weiss: The function and meaning of work and the job. *Amer. sociol. Rev.*, 1955, 20, 191–198.
86. New York Times Report: U.S. survey urged on women power. *The New York Times*, 1957, Mar. 14.
87. New York Times Report: America in numbers. *The New York Times*, 1957, Nov. 17.
88. Newton, N.: *Maternal emotions*. New York: Hoeber, 1955.
89. Nye, I.: Adolescent-parent adjustment: age, sex, sibling number, broken homes, and employed mothers as variables. *Marriage Fam. Living*, 1952, 14, 327–332.
90. Ort, R. S.: A study of role-conflicts as related to happiness in marriage. *J. abnorm. soc. Psychol.*, 1950, 45, 691–699.
91. Palmer, G. L.: Attitudes toward work in an industrial community. *Amer. J. Sociol.*, 1957, 36, 17–26.
92. Pihlbled, C. T., and C. L. Gregory: Selective aspects of migration among Missouri high school graduates. *Amer. sociol. Rev.*, 1954, 19, 314–322.
93. Podolsky, E.: The emotional problems of the stepchild. *Ment. Hyg.*, N.Y., 1955, 39, 49–53.
94. Porter, B. M.: The relationship between marital adjustment and parental acceptance of children. *J. Home Econ.*, 1955, 47, 157–164.
95. Rose, A. M.: Parental models for youth. *Sociol. soc. Res.*, 1955, 40, 3–9.
96. Rose, A. W.: How Negro workers feel about their jobs. *Personnel J.*, 1951, 29, 292–296.
97. Roth, J., and R. F. Peck: Social-class and social mobility factors related to marital adjustment. *Amer. sociol. Rev.*, 1951, 16, 478–487.
98. Rouman, J.: School children's problems as related to parental factors. *Calif. J. educ. Res.*, 1955, 6, 110–117.
99. Singer, S. L., and B. Stefflre: Age differences in job values and desires. *J. counsel. Psychol.*, 1954, 1, 89–91.
100. Somerville, A. W., and F. C. Sumner: The persistence of vocational preference in successful individuals. *J. Psychol.*, 1950, 30, 77–80.
101. Sternberg, H.: Fathers who apply for child guidance. *Smith Coll. Stud. soc. Wk*, 1951, 22, 53–68.
102. Stott, L. H.: The problem of evaluating family success. *Marriage Fam. Living*, 1951, 13, 149–153.
103. Strong, E. K.: Validity of occupational choice. *Educ. psychol. Measmt*, 1953, 13, 110–121.
104. Stryker, S.: Relationships of married offspring and parent. *Amer. J. Sociol.*, 1956, 62, 308–319.
105. Stubbefield, R. L.: Children's emotional problems aggravated by family moves. *Amer. J. Orthopsychiat.*, 1955, 25, 120–126.
106. Super, D. E.: A theory of vocational development. *Amer. Psychologist*, 1953, 8, 185–190.
107. Sussman, M. B.: Parental participation in mate selection and its effect upon family continuity. *Soc. Forces*, 1953, 32, 76–81.
108. Tasch, R. J.: Interpersonal perceptions of fathers and mothers. *J. genet. Psychol.*, 1955, 87, 59–65.
109. Terman, L. M.: Correlates of orgasm adequacy in a group of 556 wives. *J. Psychol.*, 1951, 32, 115–172.

110. Terman, L. M., P. Buttenwieser, L. W. Ferguson, and W. B. Johnson: *Psychological factors in marital happiness.* New York: McGraw-Hill, 1938.
111. Thomas, J. L.: Marital failure and duration. *Soc. Order,* 1953, 3, 24–29.
112. Thomason, B.: Extent of spousal agreement on certain non-sexual and sexual aspects of marital adjustment. *Marriage Fam. Living,* 1955, 17, 332–337.
113. Vedder, C. B.: Lonely heart clubs viewed sociologically. *Soc. Forces,* 1951, 30, 219–222.
114. Vincent, C. E.: The adoption market and the unwed mother's baby. *Marriage Fam. Living,* 1956, 18, 124–127.
115. Von Mering, F. H.: Professional and non-professional women as mothers. *J. soc. Psychol.,* 1955, 42, 21–34.
116. Wallin, P.: Marital happiness of parents and their children's attitude to marriage. *Amer. sociol. Rev.,* 1954, 19, 20–23.
117. Wallin, P.: Sex differences in attitude to "in-laws." *Amer. J. Sociol.,* 1954, 59, 465–469.
118. Wallin, P.: Religiosity, sexual gratification, and marital satisfaction. *Amer. sociol. Rev.,* 1957, 22, 300–305.
119. West, L. J.: College and the years after. *J. higher Educ.,* 1953, 24, 415–419.
120. Williamson, R. C.: Socio-economic factors and marital adjustment in an urban setting. *Amer. sociol. Rev.,* 1954, 19, 213–216.
121. Zemlick, M. J., and R. I. Watson: Maternal attitudes of acceptance and rejection during and after pregnancy. *Amer. J. Orthopsychiat.,* 1953, 23, 570–584.

» 12 «

Middle Age

Middle age traditionally extends from age forty to sixty in the life span. The onset is marked by physical and mental changes, as is the end. Until recent years, when science has improved living conditions and medicine has contributed to better health, physical changes accompanying the cessation of the reproductive period of the adult's life came when the adult was approximately forty years old. At sixty, a decline in physical vigor and mental alertness marked the end of middle age and the beginning of "senescence," or old age. In spite of the fact that today these changes come later for many adults, the traditional boundary lines are still recognized and the adult between forty and sixty years of age is designated "middle-aged." As is true of every other period in the life span, there are marked individual differences in the ages when the physical changes marking off middle age from early adulthood at one end and old age at the other end occur. As Brozek has pointed out, "Humans vary, as apples do, some ripen in July, others in October" [8].

Scientific Interest. Middle age is one of the least explored periods in the life span because, until recently, there were few problems, other-than those of a physiological sort related to the so-called change of life, that seemed important enough to engage the attention of the psychologist who was already preoccupied with studies relating to children, adolescents, and young adults. Furthermore, until recently, too few people lived long enough to make middle age a serious problem for society to cope with. At the turn of the present century, for example, life expectancy for the total American population was approximately forty-five years and, as a result, only 10 per cent of the population was middle-

460

aged. Today, by contrast, four out of five Americans live to be sixty or more, and the average adult in the labor force today is forty-five years old. Since the turn of the century, there has been a 98 per cent increase in the total American population but there has been a 200 per cent increase in the middle-age group [19]. It has been predicted, on the basis of United States government statistics that, by 1980, 50 per cent of the total population will be forty-five years of age or older [55].

With the large increase in the number of men and women who live to middle or even old age, many personal and social problems have arisen and, as a result, the scientific spotlight is now thrown on middle age as it never was in the past. The adjustment problems in the home, the problems of employment of middle-aged men and women, mental breakdowns which occur when middle-aged people slump physically and mentally, and the realization that what happens in middle age will have a profound influence on the type of adjustment the individual makes to old age have all challenged the interest and attention of the psychologist as well as of other scientists. Not only is there scientific interest of increasing importance in this period of life but there is a strong popular interest, as is seen by the popularity of books for the layman, such as W. B. Pitkin's *Life Begins at Forty*, and the appearance of many articles in newspapers and magazines dealing with the problems of middle age and how to cope with them.

Because scientific interest in middle age is of recent origin, there has not been time to study age changes by the *longitudinal* method, tracing the course of life for groups of individuals from early childhood to death. Until now, most of the studies have used the *cross-sectional* approach in which groups of middle-aged men and women are compared with young adults or even with adolescents. These, for the most part, reveal differences that are more unfavorable than favorable to the middle-aged, but there is no indication that the differences reported are indicative of *age changes*, so much as of *age differences*, most of which may be due to differences in the educational and cultural environments of the two groups rather than to the effects of changes that occur as a result of mental or physical decline [34]. In the absence of scientific information, many traditional beliefs about middle age continue to be accepted. Unfortunately, most of these are unfavorable to middle age and, as a result, condition people unfavorably toward the period in the life span which can and should be the time for peak achievement.

Dreaded Period. Next to old age, middle age is the most dreaded period in the life span and the one the adult will not admit he has reached until the calendar and the mirror force him to do so. As Desmond has pointed out, "Americans slump into middle age grudgingly, sadly and with a tinge of fear" [19]. The many unfavorable stereotypes of the middle-aged person, the traditional beliefs of the deterioration, both physical and mental, which are believed to accompany the cessation of the adult's reproductive life, and the emphasis on the importance of youth in our culture as compared with the reverence for age in many other cultures, all influence the adult's attitudes unfavorably as he approaches this period in his life. To a woman it not only means the loss of her reproductive ability but also the loss of her sexual charms which, she fears, may result in her being replaced in her husband's affections by a younger woman. To the man, middle age means diminished physical as well as sexual vitality, the tell-tale signs of aging which make employment precarious, and the suspicion that he is losing his ability to attract women. To convince himself that these suspicions are groundless, pride forces him to show everybody that he can "take it" as he did when he was younger and that he still retains his masculine charms. That is why many middle-aged men engage in physical activities dangerous to their health and that is why husbands at this age are apt to go astray. That most adults accept the stereotypes of middle age and are influenced by them is seen by the fact that an increasingly large number of people from thirty to sixty years of age classify themselves as "middle-aged" [63].

AGE OF ACHIEVEMENT

Middle age should be the time in life when the individual reaches his peak and reaps the benefits of the years of preparation and hard work that preceded it. As Werner has stressed,

> At forty years of age normal persons should have had sufficient experience through education and human interrelationships to have developed sound judgment or values about social relationships. At this age they should have a high degree of understanding and be mellow and tolerant toward the weaknesses, frailties, and personal peculiarities of their fellow men. Their financial and social positions should be established, and they should at least begin to have a clear vision of the future and the goal which they wish to attain. If these accomplishments are complemented by good health, then life can begin at forty [64].

This should be the peak period in life not only for financial and social success but also for authority and prestige. Normally, the peak is reached between forty and fifty years, after which the individual rests on his laurels and enjoys the benefits of his hard-won success until he reaches the early sixties, whereupon he is regarded as "too old" and is usually replaced by a younger and more vigorous person [62].

The mean age of accomplishment varies according to the type of creative output, the quality of the output, the age at which the worker started his career, and many other factors. Only a small percentage of the worker's total creative output will occur in the thirties, but these are usually the most fruitful years for creative work of the greatest merit. The rate of good productivity in different fields does not change much in the middle years of life and the decline is gradual. Production of the highest quality tends to fall off not only at an earlier age but also at a more rapid rate than does output of lesser merit. However, the amount of output and the spacing of this output is influenced by the length of the life span, with those who are long-lived achieving their peak of productivity at a slightly later age than is true of those who are shorter-lived [39]. A study of the scientific activities of psychologists shows that the greatest publication rate was in the thirties and forties, with a falling off in rate in the fifties. During the sixties, the publications are only about one-half as great as in the younger age groups [18].

There are many factors responsible for the decline in productivity as individuals grow older. Among them are the following: decline in physical vigor, energy, and resistance to fatigue; diminution in sensory capacities and motor processes; serious illness, poor health, or some body infirmity; unhappy marriage or maladjustment in sex life; indifference to creativity due to the death of a loved one, as a mate or child; more preoccupation with the practical concerns of life, as earning a living; less favorable conditions for concentrated work, due to responsibilities and prestige; less hard work after gaining prestige and recognition; too easy, too great, or too early fame; apathetic effects of destructive criticism; less flexibility with increasing age; and less motivation. For those who are successful in productive work, the peak of high earnings comes between fifty and sixty years [39]. For the average worker, regardless of his fame or his achievements, the *peak of earning capacity* comes during the period of middle age and then declines. At the age when workers experience their peak earnings, those with the highest education, on the average, have the highest income. While those who leave school at the end of high school may make more money in the early years of adulthood than the college graduate, at the period of peak earnings, in middle age, the chances are greater that the college graduate will earn more than the high school graduate. There are variations, with one out of five high school graduates earning more than college graduates during the peak years [22]. The relationship of education to earnings during the period of peak earnings is shown in Figure 99.

Middle age is the period when leadership in business, industry, and community organizations is the reward for achievement. Most organizations, especially the older ones, elect presidents who are in their fifties. This means a period of approximately 15 years between the peak of achievement and the peak of recognition of that achievement (see Figure 100). The fifties are also the years when professional recognition occurs in the different professional societies [40]. Leadership in government, in the rank of ambassadors, United States senators, army officers, or justices of the Supreme Court, is generally not achieved until the late fifties or early sixties. The reason that leadership status lags behind achievement is that the older and more conservative organizations want a leader who has gained prestige through his achievements and who is able to command respect in social relationships. As Lehman has explained, "The conditions essential for creativity and originality, which can be displayed in private achievement, come earlier than those social skills which contribute to leadership and eminence and which inevitably must wait, not upon the insight of the leader himself, but upon the insight of society about him" [39].

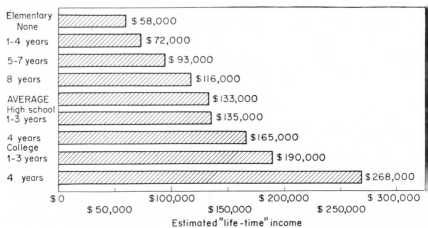

FIG. 99. Estimated "life-time" income for men of different levels of education. (*From P. C. Glick and H. P. Miller, Educational level and potential income. Amer. sociol. Rev., 1956, 21, 307–312. Used by permission.*)

Lack of Achievement. Not all middle-aged people attain success in what they do, nor are they recognized for their achievements. Many enter the prime of life with a past history of failure or mediocre success behind them, and when this is added to their dread of middle age, they "fritter away" what should be the peak years of their lives. As a result, they are unhappy and ruin their chances for usefulness and the accompanying happiness that should come with the years that are generally regarded as the "prime of life" [19]. As Billing and Adams have pointed out, "There has been an increasing awareness that middle age can bring anxiety and insecurity." This may be shown in many ways, the most frequent of which are conflicts with members of the family and a tendency to make great demands on them; excessive demands by the middle-aged person on those who work under him; glorification of youth patterns, especially in sex affairs with younger girls; and intense anxieties [6].

For most adults, the early forties are the "testing stage" when the individual examines his career to determine the extent to which he has achieved the life goals and satisfactions he had hoped to gain. Whether the outcome is entirely to his satisfaction or not, he is likely to regard the latter part of middle age, the fifties, as the time when he will concentrate on achieving the maximum gratification from what remains of a vigorous life [44]. This is the stage of "indulgence" of middle age, as contrasted with the "testing" stage of early middle age [12].

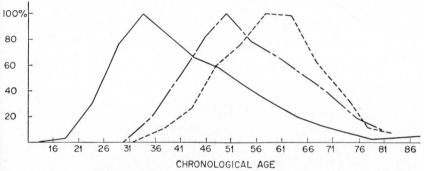

CHRONOLOGICAL AGE

FIG. 100. Age of peak of achievement and its relationship to recognition of that achievement. (*Solid line:* age versus production in science, mathematics, and practical invention. *Broken line:* age at time of first election to 671 presidencies of 13 organizations that are concerned with research in the same fields of production. *Dashed line:* age at time of first election to 1,276 presidencies of societies whose members are mostly professional practitioners. (*From H. C. Lehman, Ages at first election to presidents of professional organizations. Sci. Mon., N.Y., 1955, 80, 293–298. Used by permission.*)

During the "testing" stage of early middle age, when the individual compares his achievements with his level of aspiration, he may decide he is a success, a failure, or a partial success. Failures are of two types, acknowledged and grandiose. In the case of *acknowledged failure*, the individual recognizes that his abilities and the conditions that confront him will never permit him to achieve the goals he has set. Some react to this by revising their goals; others escape into daydreams or alcoholism, find comfort in other purposes, or develop a stoic outlook. The individual who experiences *grandiose failures* usually becomes embittered because of paranoid beliefs about the obstacles which have kept him from achieving the success he believed he was capable of. Successes are also of two types, *satisfied* and *dissatisfied*. In the case of the former, the individual feels rewarded for his efforts and is happy.

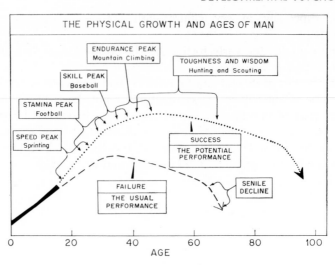

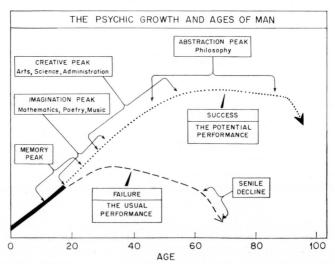

FIG. 101. Possibility and actual performance. The upper lines indicate the physical and psychological potentials of normal people with peak periods for various activities; the lower lines indicate how most people fail to measure up. (*From J. W. Still, Man's potential—and his performance. The New York Times, Nov. 24, 1957. Used by permission.*)

In the latter, by contrast, he lacks satisfaction even when he achieves his goals because he feels he has chosen the wrong goals. In such a situation, some try to escape, through daydreams, alchohol, or even suicide; others try to compensate for their dissatisfaction by enjoying pleasures; or they seek new goals to replace the ones that have not brought satisfaction [54].

The gap between the individual's potentialities and his performance is shown in Figure 101.

PERIOD OF ADJUSTMENT

After a period of approximately 20 years during which time the young adult becomes accustomed to thinking of himself in terms of a fairly definite self-concept and to playing certain roles, he finds it necessary to change his roles and his self-concept. After he reaches forty, there will be changes in his appearance, in his strength and resistance to fatigue, in his speed in doing things, and in his ability to adjust quickly to new situations. Either slowly or gradually he will become aware of the fact that he neither looks nor feels as he did when he was 10 or 20 years younger. This will mean revisions in his *self-concept*, perhaps minor at first, but gradually, as time goes on, more and more pronounced changes will have to be made. For the most part, the changes in his self-concept will relate more to his physical than to his mental abilities, though there will be changes in the latter that must be adjusted to as middle age progresses. Because he knows that he is judged in terms of his appearance and what he can do, he tries to convince himself and others that he is not as old as he appears and that he can do the things he did when he was younger.

Changes in the *roles* he plays as he becomes middle-aged must be adjusted to, and these, likewise, will affect his self-concept. As roles change, especially in the fifties, the individual must compensate for loss of one role by greater activity in other roles or by developing a new role to replace the one that no longer exists. Roles most likely to change during middle age are those of parenthood, work, spouse (in the event of the death or divorce of a mate), club membership, and the sex role in marriage. To replace these roles, or to supplement them as they gradually take less and less of the individual's time, roles hitherto neglected or given little time, such as committee membership, citizenship activities, widened family relationships, wider activities with friends, church activities, homemaking, and hobbies, can be intensified. Changing roles is never easy, especially after one has played certain prescribed roles over a period of time and has learned to derive satisfaction from them. Adjustment to middle age requires flexibility so that the individual can shift to new roles, and this, in turn, means willingness to break old habits and learn new activities which will not only use the individual's time and efforts but which will also give him the satisfaction the old roles gave. Too much success in one role is likely to lead to rigidity and may make adjustment to another role difficult. Also, a person who has played a narrow range of roles is likely to be less flexible than one who has played a wider range of roles and has learned from experience to derive satisfaction from different roles. Shifting to a new role is, thus, easier for him. To make a good adjustment to new roles, the individual must "withdraw emotional capital from one role and invest it in another one" [29].

Social attitudes about middle age influence the individual's concept of self when he reaches this period in his life. In stratified societies where roles are prescribed for different age levels and where middle age is an honored state because the individual is at his peak, there are no "middle age problems" of the sort people in America must face and adjust to. Like adolescence, the problems of middle age are not intrinsic to the phase of life but are a consequence of certain social conditions [54]. Because middle age is the least understood phase of life and because there are many misunderstandings and misconceptions about the individual's abilities and opportunities at this period of life, traditional beliefs are permitted to influence social and personal attitudes concerning middle age, and these complicate the adjustments the individual must make. At the present time, there are two different philosophies about how the person should adjust to middle age: the philosophy that the individual should stay young and keep active, and the belief that he should grow old gracefully, deliberately slowing down and taking life comfortably—the "rocking chair" philosophy. People of the middle class tend to follow the former, those of the lower classes, the latter, and members of the upper class are evenly divided between the two. Women, on the whole, are more likely to follow the "rocking chair" philosophy than men are [27]. The individual's adjustment will be determined, to a large extent, by the effect that social attitudes toward middle age have upon his self-concept.

Factors Militating against Adjustment. Adjustments to middle age are made more difficult by a number of factors. The most common and serious of these are lack of preparation for the changes in roles and self-concepts which are inevitable at this period of life; physical ailments; difficulties in learning; tendency toward mental rigidity; lack of motivation; and unfavorable home conditions. Throughout adulthood, most men and women are too busy establishing themselves vocationally, taking care of their families, and adjusting to constantly changing demands upon their time, energy, and money to be able to think ahead and prepare for the time when the patterns of their lives will be changed. What preparation they do make for middle age is largely negative in character, trying, for example, to convince themselves and everyone else that they are not aging. Preparation of a positive type, in the form of creating new interests and preparing themselves to play new roles when changed conditions within their living patterns demand this, is largely ignored. Physical ailments, either real or imagined, always complicate adjustments, and this is true of the adjustments that must be made to middle age. Few adults reach the forties and even fewer, the fifties, without having some physical problems to contend with [10]. The good health of early adulthood, which aided in the adjustments to the problems of that period of life, is usually lacking at middle age.

Adjustments often require *learning* of new motor skills. For the middle-aged person, this is far more difficult than for the younger adult. Studies of learning have shown that there is, with age, a decline in speed and accuracy, just as there are more difficulties in adjusting to new situations. As Lehman has stressed, "To learn the new they often have to unlearn the old and that is twice as hard as learning without unlearning. But when a situation requires a store of past knowledge then the old find their advantage over the young" [39]. The tendency toward *mental rigidity* is a barrier to good adjustments, especially in a culture that is subject to rapid changes. Unless the individual can and will adjust his attitudes to changed conditions, he will find himself out of step with existing conditions. It is popularly believed that mental rigidity is the result of mental decline, which is believed to set in during the middle years of life. Intelligence test scores have, for the most part, been found to decline with age but there is now reason to believe that these declines are due to sampling errors in the groups tested or to the measuring instruments themselves which, because of their emphasis on speed, are fairer to young than to middle-aged subjects [17]. Follow-up studies of the same individuals in middle age have revealed that there is a significant increase in test scores when abilities that require the use of reasoning or past experience are measured, and there is little or no change in tests where speed of mental activity is essential (see Figure 2, page 10). Thus, there is, with age, a highly significant increase in test scores and not a decrease, as is commonly believed [46]. While gains in test scores have been found for all age levels up to fifty years of age, the greatest gains are made by those with less education [1].

The tendency toward mental rigidity so often found in middle-aged people is, obviously, not the result of mental decline. A comparison of middle-aged people up to sixty years of age with college students of today revealed, for example, that the former were more conservative than the latter. But when the attitudes of the older people were compared with those of their youth, it was apparent that the older people were actually more liberal than they had been when they were younger. Thus, supposed conservatism or tendency toward mental rigidity is merely a continuation of attitudes established in youth rather than an actual increasing conservatism with age. On some issues studied, such as smoking, social-sex behavior such as flirting, and extravagance, the middle-aged group have become more liberal than they were in their youth, even though they seem conservative when compared with the youth of today. Figure 102 shows this trend. Thus, in a rapidly changing culture, as is true of America today, conservatism may merely mean clinging to attitudes established earlier, not becoming mentally rigid [47]. Conservatism, as Desmond has pointed out, is advantageous. According to him, "If middle age were as reckless as the twenties and thirties, our economic and social civilization would be catapulted toward every new panacea, every bright promise. . . . Middle age is

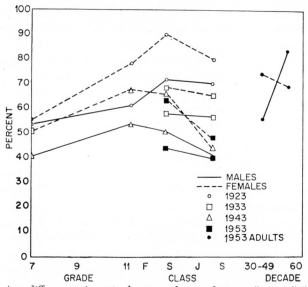

Fig. 102. Age differences in attitudes toward immodesty as "wrong." (*From S. L. Pressey and A. W. Jones, 1923–1953 and 20–60 age changes in moral codes, anxieties, and interests, as shown by the "X-O Tests." J. Psychol., 1955, 39, 485–502. Used by permission.*)

needed as a bulwark against youth's recklessness and age's conservatism. Middle age is not conservative so much as deliberate and judicial" [19]. Only when conservatism is carried to the point of rigidity does it prove to be a handicap to adjustment.

Lack of motivation to adjust to new problems as they arise increases adjustment difficulties. In a culture that idealizes youth, there is little incentive for the individual to turn his attention to the problems of middle age until he has to. Even then, admitting that the problems exist and making efforts to adjust to them mean admitting to himself and to others that he is getting old. This, he feels, is a step downward and he avoids it as long as he possibly can. Furthermore, in a culture that encourages young people to aspire to life goals that are often impossible for them to reach, the realization of failure by middle age is often a traumatic experience which saps any motivation a person might otherwise have had to try to adjust to new problems as they arise. Feelings of failure at any age are detrimental to motivation to do anything of a constructive sort. If, on the other hand, the life goals are not only achieved but are achieved early in life, the rest of life is likely to seem void and meaningless. This, like failure to achieve goals, militates against the individual's motivation to adjust to new circumstances in his life or to try to set up new goals [54].

Unfavorable home conditions, especially the attitudes of family members toward the person approaching middle age, give that person little incentive to admit his age or to try to adjust to the problems it brings. The personal problems of middle-aged men and women are complicated by the attitudes and behavior of overly critical, rebellious adolescent offspring and by older parents who are not only a burden but who remind the middle-aged constantly of their own approaching old age. This leads to a critical, intolerant attitude toward the elderly relatives which makes them more difficult to live with, thus increasing the unfavorable model the middle-aged have constantly before them. In business or social life, the increasing competition with young people who press the middle-aged to perform more actively and more efficiently adds to the unfavorable self-concepts established in the home, with the result that the middle-aged person's motivation to adjust to problems he dreads and tries to avoid is still further reduced [25].

There are marked *individual differences* in the difficulties encountered by people who are adjusting to middle age and the problems it gives rise to. *Sex differences* in adjustment are especially marked. Women whose chief role in life is homemaking and child rearing, find the adjustments especially difficult, particularly when their roles change abruptly, as in the case of the last child's marriage or departure from home, divorce, or the death of the husband, which may make it necessary for the woman to shift from her former role to that of breadwinner. With the tendency toward smaller families, earlier marriages, and earlier childbearing, the average American woman of today is usually in her early forties when her last child is grown and leaves home for marriage or to work away from home. This leaves her without the role of child rearing and drastically reduces her role of homemaking. Many women are not prepared for these changes, especially when there are cultural pressures against their assuming new roles, such as a career outside the home. Unless she makes a shift to new roles, the woman will be dissatisfied and unhappy because she feels useless and idle. The adjustment for the woman is made especially difficult when changes in her life roles coincide with the menopause, which often undermines the woman's confidence in her worth as a woman and wife. Should her roles be changed by death or divorce, she may be forced to move and get a job. To complicate matters, the emotional tensions accompanying the death or divorce militate against her psychological and social adjustment to these new roles. Often the adjustment is further complicated by the realization that the chances for remarriage are relatively slim [14, 42].

The effects of role changes on the middle-aged man are very different from those of the woman. Because the man's main role is that of bread-winner, he will continue this role through middle age, unless illness forces him to retire early. Should he lose his job and be forced to accept a job with lower pay and prestige, there will be a difficult adjustment for him to make. On the other hand, if he reaches his peak of earning power, which normally comes in middle age, he will have greater responsibility and prestige in his work, which then will compensate for the loss of his role as a father. While he may be caused greater stress by his desire to appear younger than he is in order to maintain this position of re-sponsibility and prestige, his stress will not be much greater than that of the middle-aged woman who desires to retain a youthful appearance and vigor. In the case of divorce or death, the middle-aged man's life patterns are less disrupted than those of the woman and his chances of remarriage are far greater [14].

Social class differences likewise affect the adjustment problems of both men and women. Women of the middle class find the adjustments more difficult than do men or than do women of the upper and lower classes. The increased leisure resulting from the reduction of her homemaking responsibilities leaves the middle-aged woman with few sources of satis-faction unless she develops new roles, which may, in turn, be blocked by social or family pressures. Women of the lower class who have worked for the major part of their adult lives, either through necessity to support the family or from a desire to give their children greater advantages than would be possible with only the husbands' earnings, find the decrease in their home roles satisfying because it relieves the pressure from carrying a double load and gives them more money to spend as they wish. Women of the upper classes have adequate income to enable them to spend their increased leisure in community and social activities, the prestige from which is adequate compensation for the loss of roles as homemaker and parent [50]. As for men, the effects of middle age are more serious in the lower than in the middle or upper classes. In the latter, occupational status is higher and, as a result, more satisfying. Men of the lower class, on the other hand, may find it diffi-cult to keep pace with the constantly changing methods of industry, and their slowing down as a result of physical changes may result in the loss of their jobs. Furthermore, learning new skills and getting new jobs becomes increasingly difficult with advancing age. For men of the lower classes, therefore, adjustment to middle age is complicated by the emotional tensions arising from fear of unemployment or humiliation at having to accept a job with lower wages and less prestige.

Assessment of Adjustment. How well the individual adjusts to middle age will be determined by his emotional state, his personality pattern, and the satisfactions or happiness he experiences. While stress from *emotional tensions* varies from person to person and from age to age, there is evidence that it is more common during the early part of middle age than during the latter, as is true of early adulthood. Changes to new situations, new roles, and new concepts of self are always difficult and, as a result, are generally accompanied by stress. Because changes in living patterns generally come upon both men and women suddenly, and

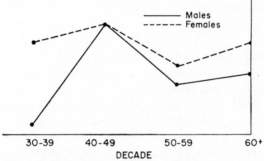

Fig. 103. Worries at middle age. (*From S. L. Pressey and A. W. Jones, 1923–1953 and 20–60 age changes in moral codes, anxieties, and interests, as shown by the "X-O Tests." J. Psychol., 1955, 39, 485–502. Used by permission.*)

because few have made adequate provision for these changes, they are disturbing and emotion-producing. Most men and women make reasonable adjustments to the physical and psychological changes of middle age within a period of time. As a result, the emotional tension subsides and emotional calm once again appears. By the mid-fifties, most individuals are fairly well adjusted to middle age and are no longer upset by it. They have adjusted their roles, their interests, and their activities to fit into the changes that have taken place in their organisms. Life then moves along smoothly for them until the onset of old age. Studies of worries have revealed that middle-aged men and women worry more about business, health, disease, weakness, dizziness, falling, helplessness, and death than do younger people [47]. Figure 103 shows the increase in number of worries with increasing age.

A comparison of college students with business and professional men forty-five to fifty-five years of age has revealed that the older group shows greater tension and greater responsiveness to emotion-creating stimuli than does the younger. The older men are less calm and easy-going than the younger. Their muscles often become tense and their stomachs feel as if they are tied in knots. They are more hurt by criticism but get over it more quickly; they are more moved to tears but fluctuate less in moods and are more reserved in expressing their feelings than are younger men. Even though they feel angry, they keep their tensions well covered up. Middle-aged men consider themselves high-strung and lose more sleep over worry than do younger men. However, younger men have more frequent periods of excitement, restlessness, and "blueness" than do middle-aged men [10]. Stress from business is especially strong among middle-aged men. If successful, they feel burdened and cannot get away from their responsibilities or enjoy life; if less successful, they are goaded on by their own ego drives or by a frustrated wife. Further-more, home life is often less stimulating. Because the middle-aged man's ego strength is influenced by his sexual potency, he finds less satisfac-tion from the companionship of his wife. As a result of this stress, he may find a wife who is younger and who "understands him better" [60].

It is commonly believed that women suffer more from stress than do men during middle age because of the physical changes that take place during the menopause. Most of the studies have been on women who have sought medical attention and whose symptoms are therefore the most exaggerated. As Kuhlen has pointed out from studies of middle-aged women who were not receiving medical treatment and who were suffering no more frequently from nervousness in the forties than in the fifties, when the menopause is usually completed, "It is even possible that the 'storm and stress' of the menopause will turn out to be the same type of will-o'-the-wisp as the traditional, but never really demonstrated, 'storm and stress' of adolescence" [34]. However, there are evidences of increased stress due to *environmental* causes during middle age. Women who find their customary roles ending, whose husbands, if successful, are preoccupied with their work, and whose children no longer need their care often do experience stress from boredom and feelings of use-lessness. Furthermore, there is the stress resulting from their awareness that they are losing their sex appeal for their husbands and may be re-placed by younger, more attractive women. The unmarried career woman is not free from stress either. She realizes that her career is in danger from competition with younger women and that her chances of marriage become slimmer with each passing year. Many women, and men too, compensate for the stresses of middle age by eating and, as a result, suffer from obesity [60].

Personality disorganization in middle age is related to poor social and emotional adjustment, much of which stems from a basis of poor adjust-ment in the earlier years. There is little evidence to indicate that middle age, per se, is responsible for the mental illnesses that occur at that time. On the other hand, there is adequate evidence that those who break under the strain of adjustments in middle age have a history of unresolved problems which have interfered with good adjustments. The stresses of middle age, then, prove to be too severe for them to cope with and mental illness of a severe enough type to necessitate their being institutionalized sets in. The involutional mental disorders found mainly in the forty-five- to fifty-five-year groups take the form of depression or apathy, anxiety states, self-pity, emotional outbursts, manic-depressive states, schizophrenia, paranoiac states, and psychosomatic disorders. While some of these conditions may be caused partly by brain deterioration, they are largely the result of feelings of insecurity and inadequacy and are especially serious when there is a history of poor adjustment. They are more common in women than in men and in the unmarried than in the married [24].

The number of *satisfactions* the middle-aged person derives from his life will determine how happy he is. The person who is well adjusted, in the sense that he is able to satisfy his needs quickly and adequately within the controls and outlets provided by the cultural group with which he is identified, will be far happier than the one who has been unable or unwilling to make the adjustments essential to satisfy his needs. The more adequately men and women prepare during the early adult years for the physical and psychological changes that are an inevitable accompaniment of advancing years, and the better they are equipped to shift roles when this is essential, the happier they will be. Success in a chosen vocation, which brings with it prestige, financial rewards, and improved social status for the family, goes a long way toward making middle age a satisfying period of life for men and helps to counteract lack of satisfaction in other areas of their lives. For women, to whom family life is the dominant role as business is for men, satisfaction in middle age is dependent mainly on the success with which they are able to adjust to the changes they must make in the role of homemaking in middle age. These adjustments will be made easier if the husband is successful vocationally and provides the money and leisure that make the changes in the woman's roles possible. Happiness in middle age, for both men and women, is thus both a criterion and a reward for a well-conducted life then and in the earlier years [28, 31].

A study of satisfactions in middle-aged women has revealed that there are certain factors that play important roles in determining how great these satisfactions will be. These factors are: (1) *Age at marriage* for both husband and wife. Dissatisfied women were found mainly among the group that married under twenty years of age while the less dissatisfied were married at thirty or later. Women who are married too young lack the education needed to change their roles in middle age and they often feel that they are unable to "keep up" with their husbands, who have advanced vocationally, socially, and educationally during the adult years, while they, because of family responsibilities, have stood still. In the case of men, there is no relationship between age at marriage and satisfaction during middle age. (2) *The age factor* between husband and wife often causes dissatisfactions at middle age when the husband and wife are the same age or when the wife is older than the husband. (3) *Intimacy of family life* causes greater satisfactions, especially for the woman. (4) *Time spent in housework* influences middle-aged women's satisfaction. Women who feel that they are "slaves to housework" or who have no paid help are less satisfied than those with paid help who may or may not have jobs outside the home. (5) *Employment outside the home* during middle age is closely associated with satisfactions on the part of women. (6) *Activity in voluntary or community* organizations is a source of satisfaction. (7) *Hobbies* also lead to increased satisfactions. (8) *Opportunities for an increase in amusements* contribute to satisfactions, especially for women, during middle age [50].

ADJUSTMENT PROBLEMS

There are certain problems of adjustment that are characteristic of middle age in our culture. Some of these problems are more difficult for men while others are more difficult for women to adjust to. There are also social-class differences in adjustment problems which, for the most part, are more serious for members of the middle- than for those of the lower- or upper-class groups. Of the many problems American men and women must meet and make satisfactory adjustments to during the middle years of life, the following are the most important:

Adjustments to Physical Changes. One of the most difficult adjustments middle-aged men and women must make is to changed appearance. They must recognize that the body is not functioning as adequately as it formerly did and may even be "wearing out" in certain vital areas, and they must accept the fact that the reproductive capacity is waning or coming to an end, only to be accompanied by a weakening of the sex drive and sex appeal. Like the pubescent child who has carried through childhood an ideal of what he wants to look like when he grows up and then must adjust to the appearance nature gives him, the middle-aged person must adjust to changes that are not only not to his liking but which, even worse, are tell-tale signs that the years are creeping up on him. At any age, adjustment is made easier by favorable attitudes and more difficult by unfavorable attitudes. Because unfavorable personal attitudes are intensified at middle age by unfavorable social attitudes

toward the normal changes that come with advancing age, the adjustment is made doubly hard. Having known, since early adolescence, the
important role appearance plays in social judgments, social acceptance,
and leadership, the middle-aged person rebels against handicaps to the
status he has won and fears he may lose as his appearance deteriorates.
For the man, there is the added handicap of competition with younger,
more vigorous, and more energetic competitors who tend to judge his
capacity to hold down his job in terms of his appearance. And, for both
men and women, there is the ever-present fear that their middle-aged
looks will militate against their ability to hold their spouses or to attract
members of the opposite sex.

Causes of Change. Middle age marks the beginning of the acceleration
of the aging process that has been going on since birth. Whether this
acceleration will start early or late in the forties or not until the fifties
will vary from person to person. But its beginning is inevitable during
this period in the life span and must be faced sooner or later by every
man and woman. It is never a precipitous drop at a certain age but rather
a slow, gradual process which, if not dreaded, would likely go unnoticed
for months at a time. However, because of the unfavorable attitudes
toward aging, each change is the source of great concern to the individual and, as a result, has an exaggerated importance to his psychological or physical well-being. Not only does the rate of aging vary for
different people, as does the onset of aging, but the rate of aging for the
different organ systems of the body varies widely in the same individual
and in different individuals of the same age. As is true of the developmental changes taking place at puberty, there is a general pattern that
all children follow but each at his own rate and in his own way. So it is
with the involutional changes of aging [51].

There are *physiological causes* for aging, some of which are now well
known while others are still to be verified. In old cells, there is an
accumulation of extracellular materials filling up the spaces where functioning cells have disappeared. The different organ systems function less
effectively, mainly because of a reduction in reserve capacity. Even
though the individual can meet his day-to-day needs, he will not be able
to meet situations as well as a younger person if called on to perform
under conditions of stress or extra load [51]. Most important of all, there
are certain endocrine changes and deficiencies which occur at this time
and which affect the functioning of the entire body. When endocrine
changes are rapid, physical changes are likewise rapid and often cause
physical and emotional stress which can be lessened by endocrine treat-
ments. Under normal conditions, the endocrine system will right itself
in time and the disturbances accompanying bodily changes will disappear [4].

Physical Changes. There are certain physical and physiological changes occurring at middle age that are so universal and so characteristic of the period that few fail to recognize them. There is a tendency to gain *weight,* especially in the area of the waistline, known as the "middle-age spread." It has been said that middle-aged people stop growing at the ends and begin to grow in the middle. Throughout early adulthood, there is a tendency for men and women to gain weight, some more rapidly than others. This gain is partly due to the accumulation of excess fat and partly to changes in body composition in which some of the muscles and other body tissues are replaced by fat. In late adolescence, the body fat is approximately 10 per cent of the total body weight of individuals who are "normal" for their height and body build; in middle age, this percentage has doubled as a result of changes in body composition. This means that even when the weight is kept at "normal" there is a greater accumulation of fat tissue than the scales tell. However, as most adults have added weight, the percentage of the body tissue that is fat is even greater than the normal 20 per cent [11]. In middle age, fat in the upper part of the body increases and that in the lower part decreases. It is greater in the trunk than in the extremities, especially in men [53].

By the late forties or early fifties, many men and women become aware of their middle-age bulges to the point where they decide to get rid of them. Furthermore, many receive warnings from doctors of the dangers of overweight. It is now a recognized fact that the mortality rate is greater in overweight people than in underweight and also that overweight people have more diseases, especially heart trouble, diabetes, arteriosclerosis, and high blood pressure, than do those of normal weight [36]. That middle-aged men and women of today are more fashion- and health-conscious than in the past is shown by the increase since the 1920s in the number of worries about overeating [47]. Concern about being overweight often leads to strict diets with quick loss of weight. In adolescence and early adulthood, the skin is quite elastic and follows the receding tissues from which excess fat tissue disappears with dieting. After forty, however, the individual may feel and act younger after dieting but he looks older. The face, arms, thighs, and abdomen present loose folds of skin which has not yet tightened up and receded to the tissues beneath from which the fat has disappeared. Flabby skin is a tell-tale sign of aging [7].

Changes in the *hair* and *skin* are as characteristic of middle age as is weight increase. In the forties the hairline begins to recede, especially in men, and the hair becomes thinner. In men, baldness at the crown or on top of the head is very common from forty on. If the first gray hairs have not already made their appearance by the time the man or woman reaches forty, they do so shortly afterward. By fifty, most men and women have a predominance of gray hair and some are even snowy white. Among men, there is a gradual growth of stiff hair in the nose, ears, and eyelashes during middle age and, among women, there is an increase in growth of hair on the upper lip and chin. Men, on the other hand, find that, after forty, they need to shave less with each successive year because of the slower and less luxuriant growth of hair on the face. In middle age, the skin on the face, neck, arms, and hands becomes coarser and begins to show wrinkles. Bags under the eyes, usually associated with dissipation, are common accompaniments of aging. They are caused by weakening of the underlying muscle and fibrous tissue, with the result that the lower lid falls in folds. Then subcutaneous fat forms through the weakened muscles and causes the redundant skin to balloon. Dark circles under the eyes are more prominent and more permanent after forty than before. They are accentuated by paleness of the skin which is common at this age and by a more sparing use of cosmetics. Many middle-aged men and women have bluish-red discolorations, often in the shape of a spider web, around the ankles or on the mid-calf. These come from dilated surface blood vessels and are made worse by pressure resulting from overweight [16].

There are other physical changes common at middle age, but not as universally found as the changes in weight, hair, and skin. The *eyes* look less bright than they did when the individual was younger and the *teeth* become yellowed. If the man or woman has done hard manual work for the major part of his life, his *muscles* will be strong at middle age, though they will have less resiliency than previously. Most men and women, however, look and act as if their muscles were soft and flabby. This is especially apparent in the areas of the chin, upper arms, and abdomen. The *bones* become gradually more brittle with a consequent tendency to break more easily and to require a longer time to heal after they are broken. Some middle-aged people develop difficulties with their *joints* and *limbs*, thus causing them to walk with difficulty and with a degree of awkwardness rarely found in younger people.

Gradual deterioration of *sensory abilities* begins in middle age, the most marked and troublesome of which comes in the eyes and ears. The degenerative and functional changes in the *eye* result in decrease in pupil size, acuity, and glare resistance, and a tendency toward glaucoma, cataracts, and tumors. Most middle-aged people suffer from presbyopia, or farsightedness (often called "old sight"), which is a gradual loss of accommodative power of the eyes resulting from a decrease in the elasticity of the lens. Between the ages of forty and fifty years, the accommodative power of the lens is usually insufficient for ordinary close work and the individual must wear glasses. There is no evidence that color vision is impaired with the normal changes in the eye at middle age [8]. *Hearing* is likely to be impaired with the result that the individual must listen more attentively than he formerly did. Sensitivity to high pitches is lost first, followed by progressive losses down the pitch scale. Because of loss in the ability to hear, many middle-aged people start to talk very loudly, and often in a monotone. The sense of *smell* grows weaker in men, because of the increase in the hairy network of the nose, and this affects the sense of *taste*.

Changes in the exterior of the body do not occur without a parallel change in the internal organs and their functioning. These changes are, for the most part, the direct or indirect result of changes in the body tissues. Like rubber bands, the walls of the *arteries* become brittle as middle age progresses and this leads to circulatory difficulties. Increase in *blood pressure*, especially among those who are overweight, may lead to *heart complications* unless radical changes are made in the individual's diet and mode of life. There is increasing sluggishness in the functioning of most of the *glands* of the body. The pores and skin glands are slower than they formerly were in ridding the skin of waste materials with the result that there is an increased tendency to body odors. The different glands connected with the digestive process likewise function more slowly with a consequent increase in number and severity of digestive disorders. To add to this problem, many middle-aged men and women must have dental plates which increase the difficulty of *chewing*. In addition, few individuals revise their eating habits to keep pace with the slowing down of their activities and this likewise adds a burden to the functioning of the *digestive* system. Constipation is very common in middle age [16].

As a general rule, *men* in our culture show signs of aging sooner than women. This may be explained by the fact that women who know that their attractiveness to members of the opposite sex depends so much upon their physical appearance see to it that signs of middle age are quickly covered up. There is also a tendency for the rate of aging to differ in different *socioeconomic* groups. In general, men and women of the higher socioeconomic groups appear younger than their years while those of the lower socioeconomic groups look older than they actually are. This may be explained partially by the fact that those of the more favored groups work less, expend less energy, and are better nourished than those who must earn their living by hard manual work. Furthermore, those who come from the less well-to-do groups are unable to afford the beauty aids and clothing that cover up tell-tale signs of growing old.

Health Conditions. Middle age is characterized by a general decline in physical fitness and some deterioration of health is common. Beginning in the mid-forties, there is an increase in disability and invalidism, which progresses rapidly from then on [52]. This trend is shown in Figure 104. Common health problems in middle age include the tendency to fatigue easily, buzzing or ringing in the ears, muscular pains, skin sensitivity to touch and itching, general aches and pains, gastrointestinal complaints such as constipation, acid stomach, and belching, loss of appetite, and tendency to insomnia [10]. How middle age affects the health of the individual will be dependent upon many factors, among them, his heredity, his past health history, the emotional stresses of his life, and his willingness to adjust his pattern of living to his

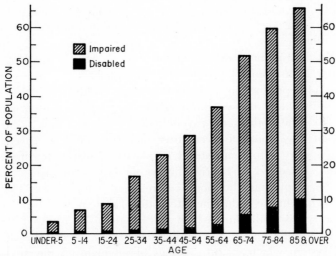

FIG. 104. Increase in disability and invalidism with advancing age. (*From N. W. Shock, Trends in gerontology. Stanford: Stanford Univer. Press, 1951. Used by permission.*)

changed physical condition. Those who refuse to adjust and try to convince themselves and others that they can "still take it," are the ones who usually suffer most from middle-age ailments.

Climacteric. By far the most difficult physical adjustment men and women must make in middle age is to the "change of life," "menopause," or "climacterium." The climacteric, from the Greek, *klimakterikos,* meaning peak or climax, is a period in the life span of men and women which is characterized by the termination of their reproductive capacity. In women, this period is commonly referred to as the "change of life" because of the physical changes that occur then in addition to the loss of the childbearing capacity, or as the "menopause" which, strictly speaking, means cessation of menstrual periods. In men, the period is usually referred to as the "male climacteric." Both the menopause and the male climacteric are surrounded by mystery for most men and women and there are many traditional beliefs which heighten the dread people experience when they approach the period in life when these physical changes occur. Science today has far more information about the causes and effects of these changes than was known in the past and there is growing evidence that these changes are a normal part of the life pattern. When marked psychological changes occur, they are the result more of emotional stress than of physical disturbances. This holds true for men as well as for women.

IN WOMEN. The *menopause* is the gradual cessation of the menstrual function, taking place during the female climacteric, which includes general bodily and emotional changes that coincide with but are not necessarily caused by the menopause or related to it. Cessation of menstruation is, therefore, only one aspect of the female climacteric. As Greenblatt has pointed out, "The menopause is . . . another rung in the ladder in a woman's progression through life. . . . She steps from the stage of reproduction into the period of 'middle life,' free from the responsibilities, the stresses, the hazards and trials associated with childbirth" [26]. The bodily and psychological changes which occur during this period may continue even after menstruation has ceased, just as they often start before menstrual regularity is markedly affected. The menopause is caused by ovarian failure, or *hypoovarianism*, though the production of pituitary hormone continues at a high level. The ovaries fall out of line in the endocrine interactional system, thus bringing about a temporary disequilibrium which will, in time, be adjusted. This temporary disequilibrium in the endocrine system affects the autonomic nervous system which, in turn, brings about many of the physical and emotional symptoms characteristic of the female climacteric.

During the climacteric, the female reproductive system goes through a process of change which, in time, makes childbearing impossible. There is a generalized atrophy of the genital tract, with the ovaries shrinking in size and becoming mere masses of connective tissue. As a result of this, they no longer produce mature ova or the two ovarian hormones, estrogen and progestin. The uterus shrinks in size and the periodic changes in the uterine lining to take care of a fertilized ovum, should conception occur, no longer take place. The lining of the vagina becomes thin and sensitive to touch, and there is a decrease in vulvar fat. As the ovarian hormones become less dominant, the male hormone secretions which have been present since birth but which have been dominated by the female hormone secretions now come to the fore. As a result, the woman is less feminine in appearance than she was during the period from puberty to the menopause. Hair develops on the upper lip and at the corners of the mouth, coarser than the fine down usually found on the woman's face, and more pigmented. The high-pitched female voice deepens, though rarely to as low a pitch as in the typical masculine voice. The curves of the body flatten out as a result of dwindling adipose tissue, though there is usually a temporary deposition of fat over the hips and breasts. Later, the breasts tend to look flabby as the milk glands atrophy. Pubic and axillary hair generally become scantier as the climacteric changes are completed [25, 45, 64].

The peak of ovarian activity comes between twenty-five and thirty years, the peak of the normal childbearing period. After that, there is a gradual decline in functioning which is speeded up as the woman approaches the climacteric. This is apparent in the lengthening of time between menstrual periods and diminished flow during the periods. The average age for cessation of the menstrual flow, or the menopause, is around forty-five years, though this varies widely among women, depending on hereditary endowment, general health conditions, and variations in climate. Early puberty usually means late menopause and vice versa. Cessation of the childbearing function is not an overnight phenomenon, any more than is the development of this function at puberty. It takes several years for the reproduction apparatus to cease its normal functioning, the rate depending on the rate of decline of the ovarian functioning. When there is a rapid decrease in ovarian functioning, the woman is likely to undergo a period of violent "climacteric storm" while slow decline is accompanied by effects that are mild and only slightly noticeable. Endocrine treatment, to slow down the speed of change, makes the transition less difficult by promoting better physical and emotional states [4].

During the transient period when the endocrine interactional system is becoming adjusted to lessened ovarian functioning, there are certain physical symptoms that normally occur. These are the result of the estrogen deprivation which comes from the decline in the functioning of the ovaries. How mild or severe these symptoms will be will depend largely on the rate of decline of ovarian functioning. The three symptoms known to have a physiological cause are: *flushes* involving the head, neck, and upper thorax; *sweats* that accompany or immediately follow the flush; and *hot flashes*, typified by tingling, which involve the entire body. In addition to these three symptoms there are others which are due in part to estrogen deprivation but are mainly the result of environmental stress and are, as a result, psychological in origin. They include headaches, fatigue, vertigo, nervousness, irritability, laryngeal spasms, choking sensations, insomnia, heart palpitations, restlessness, and frigidity. These conditions may appear before there is any marked change in glandular activity, though they are more likely to accompany the decline in ovarian functioning. Many women, in this transient period, become hostile, depressed, or self-critical, and suffer from feelings of guilt. These are a part of the syndrome of "climacteric neurosis" and are emotional, not physical, in origin [20, 32].

IN MEN. The *male climacteric* is very different from that of women. It comes at a later date, usually in the sixties or seventies, and occurs at a very slow rate. With the general aging of his entire body comes a very gradual weakening of the male sexual and reproductive powers. Just when hormonal imbalance begins in men is hard to determine because there is no definite indication of this change as occurs in the female with the cessation of the menstrual function. Testosterone secretion may begin to decline in men at any age, but the magnitude of the deficiency increases with advancing years [23]. After fifty, there is a gradual decline in gonadal activity in men but motile sperms have been found into the seventies, and men occasionally have offspring as late as the eighties. Because the decline of gonadal functioning is so slow and gradual in men, they do not suffer from the physical discomforts of a too rapid readjustment of the endocrine system, nor do they have to face a sudden crisis in their reproductive abilities as women do with the onset of the menopause [23, 33].

During the fifties, as the gradual decline in the sexual powers of the man occurs, there is a decline in the male hormone secretion which allows the female hormone secretion to come to the fore. As is true of women at the menopause, the man loses some of his typically masculine characteristics and takes on some of the characteristics of the female. The voice becomes somewhat higher in pitch, there is less hair on the face and body than formerly, and frequently the body becomes slightly more rounded due to deposits of adipose tissue. Accompanying this tendency toward a more feminine appearance is a gradual increase in feminine interests and forms of behavior. Because there is a popular tradition that hair on the face, body, arms, and legs is a sign of virility, the lessening of the hair during middle age is likely to be a source of great concern to men. Even the beginning of baldness disturbs them because they believe that it is indicative of a decline in their sexual powers. In reality *anxiety about virility* is one of the chief causes of its decline. As a result, the middle-aged man who worries about his increasing baldness or the fact that he does not have to shave as often as he did when he was younger, merely accelerates the pace of decline in his sexual powers [20].

While the climacteric in men actually comes during the period of old age, rather than during the middle years of life, many men in their forties or fifties have symptoms similar to those of the female climacteric. They complain of depression, anxiety, irritability, tingling sensations in their extremities, headaches, insomnia, digestive disturbances, nervousness, flushes, fatigue, and many minor aches and pains. These occur in the absence of any demonstrable organic change and, therefore, are not physical but emotional or social in origin. They are due to pressures from outside, in their business, social, or family lives, which lead to a waning of sexual desire, or they may result from feelings of inadequacy that stem from a normal decrease in strength and endurance, the result of a glandular deficiency that leads to waning sexual powers. The psychological effects of anticipating a decline in sexual powers are greater in middle age than are the physical effects of endocrine decline. Even testosterone therapy will not relieve the symptoms of the male "climacteric neurosis," which is further proof that these symptoms are psychological rather than physical in origin [33, 37].

Assessment of Adjustment. Adjustment to physical changes is difficult and is often met with rebellion on the part of both men and women. Were it not for the unfavorable social attitudes toward advancing age, there might be a greater willingness to "grow old gracefully." However, knowing that age is a handicap in most areas of life, it is logical that the person who sees himself growing older will do all within his power to cover up the tell-tale signs. The necessity for cutting down on their food and drink intake, giving up strenuous exercise, wearing stronger glasses or hearing aids, and taking rest during the day and going to bed earlier at night are all adjustments middle-aged people must make to their declining physical powers. These adjustments are generally made gradually and reluctantly, but once they are accepted, the individual makes better adjustments to his role as a middle-aged person. If they can cover up some of these adjustments to waning physical powers by looking and dressing as if they were younger than they are, middle-aged people make adjustments more quickly and less reluctantly. The individual who makes poor adjustments is in constant rebellion against the restrictions age places on his usual patterns of behavior. He refuses to adhere to the diet or the restrictions on activities his doctor advises and he burns the candle at both ends to show that he can still "take it." Like the pubescent child who rebels against restrictions on his behavior, the middle-aged adult rebels against restrictions, but for a different reason. His rebellion stems from a recognition of the values of youth and the knowledge that society does not recognize the values of age. As a result, he rebels against restrictions that mean he is growing old [41].

As Werner has pointed out, "Forty has been described as 'the dangerous age'; it can be dangerous for several reasons. At this age, many persons develop a desire or have an urge to stray from the beaten path in more ways than one. They seem to sense or fear that the tide of life may ebb and they want to take a last fling at new experiences; youth in the opposite sex and flattery seem attractive. This is the age at which persons of stable character remain 'hitched.' Forty can also be dangerous for reasons pertaining to health. Many persons at this age and during the succeeding decade develop disorders of the ductless glands, especially those related to sexual function" [64]. Revolt against the loss of youth, as it becomes apparent in loss of physical and sexual vigor, often develops into a *generalized* revolt against work, the spouse, friends, and former pleasures [5]. When this happens, it is apparent that the middle-aged person, whether man or woman, has not been willing to accept the inevitable changes that accompany the aging process and, as a result, has made poor adjustments to it.

By far the most difficult adjustment men and women must make to changed physical conditions in middle age is to the climacteric. For women, this adjustment is much harder than for men and is, as a result, less often made successfully. Puberty is the only other time in life when physical changes put the individual's capacity to master change to such a test, and, like middle age, puberty is harder for the girl to adjust to than for the boy. While puberty is a difficult adjustment task for many girls, a larger number of women show stress and strain in their attempts to adjust to the change in the pattern of life that comes with the menopause. While most women of today pass through the climacteric without interrupting their normal pattern of living and live an active life with much ego satisfaction, others do not. How successfully the adjustment will be made will be influenced greatly by the woman's past experiences, especially her willingness to accept the feminine sex role. For those who do not make good adjustments, many of the psychological reactions to the climacteric are similar to those of puberty, especially to the pubescent girl's reaction to menstruation and her tendency to overeat [3]. While most women are prepared for the physical changes that come with the climacteric, few are prepared for the psychological changes, especially those related to changes in their life roles. Unfortunately, these changes usually coincide with the menopause, and this intensifies the difficulties of the adjustments the woman must make to the physical changes that accompany the climacteric [13, 31].

Women who make the poorest adjustments to the climacteric are those who have idealized youth and basked in masculine admiration. When they are forced to recognize that they no longer have a youthful appearance and that they can no longer attract and hold masculine attention, they are unwilling to accept the fact that they are now middle-aged and openly rebel against it. Some try to compensate for their loss of youthful appearance by youthful dress, coyness, and flirtation; some have a last fling at childbearing or cling to the youngest child of the family; some become involved in sordid love affairs or love fantasies; and some become temporarily neurotic or even psychotic [13]. Women who have lived unwisely enter middle age with many regrets that make them depressed, irritable, remorseful, bitter, and pessimistic. These unfavorable attitudes aggravate the physical symptoms of the climacteric and thus make good adjustments difficult if not impossible. How well the individual will adjust to the menopausal syndrome will be greatly influenced by the personality pattern built up during the earlier years of life [21]. When adjustment is very poor, it often leads to mental disorders, especially those of a nervous type. Studies of women patients have revealed that approximately 80 per cent who experience nervous disorders during the climacteric have had prior disturbances which are intensified during the menopause by the physical and emotional disturbances related to the menopause. And conversely, prior disturbances intensify the physical and emotional disturbances of menopause [3, 38].

How well men adjust to the climacteric is likewise influenced by previous experiences and the success of adjustments in other areas. Men who are successful in business, who have high prestige in the community, and who are well adjusted to their families accept the changes in appearance, the lessened physical strength, and the beginning of the waning of sexual desire as a normal part of aging and adjust philosophically to it. When, on the other hand, they have glorified youth to the point where they feel that success in sports, attractiveness to members of the opposite sex, and a youthful appearance are of more importance than the satisfactions of business success and a happy home life, they will make poor adjustments to middle age and will openly rebel against the restrictions and frustrations it brings. Dread of physical and sexual decline leads to poor adjustment in men just as it does in women. At the present time, this dread is being intensified by the knowledge that business and industry are less willing to employ middle-aged men than younger men and that, as a result, the man who is not satisfied with his chosen career or the job he is in will find it difficult to shift, and is thus doomed to a situation that he has not found satisfactory. Business and economic worries often intensify the physical changes that are taking place, leading to poorer adjustments than would otherwise be made [3, 21].

ADJUSTMENT TO CHANGED INTERESTS

It is popularly believed that there are marked changes in interests with the "change of life" which comes during middle age. Experimental evidence has not borne out this belief. While it is true that there are changes, these changes are far less marked than during the earlier years of life [49]. There is a gradual diminution in the range of interests, with the result that, at middle age, there are fewer interests than there were during the adolescent years and even fewer than there were during the early years of adulthood. With changes in duties and responsibilities, in health, and in roles in life, it is logical that the middle-aged person would have some changes in interests. In men, concentration on vocational advancement plays an important role in narrowing down the range of interests they had when they were younger. The more successful the man, the more time and attention he must give to his vocation to the exclusion of a broader pattern of activities [35]. New interests may be established in middle age, but unless there are changes in the individual's environment and pattern of life, unless there are opportunities to develop new interests, or a strong motivation to do so, it is more likely that he will cling to the old interests he has found satisfying than that he will develop new ones.

This tendency to cling to old interests rather than to establish new interests as age advances is frequently interpreted as indicative of the *mental rigidity* popularly associated with middle-aged and elderly people. There is little evidence from studies of middle-aged people that such is the case. Rather, the evidence points more in the direction of *values.* Middle-aged people have discovered, from experience, what gives them satisfaction, and they see little reason to change just for the sake of change. Desmond has explained the matter thus:

> Middle age is the period of synthesis. Neither green nor overripe, middle age can weld together its past experiences into a meaningful whole. . . . Middle age is not so much "settled" as matured. It can change, but will not without good cause. . . . Middle age isn't interested in newness for the sake of newness, or in learning tricks for the sake of learning new tricks. The alleged inflexibility of middle age is really quite often a subtle protest against futile change for change's sake. Patterns of life established in the twenties and thirties can be altered if there is sufficient motivation. . . . There is less expending of self on meaningless frivolities. There is in middle life a search for satisfying relationships with others and between one's self and destiny [19].

That middle-aged people can and do develop new interests when they find the old ones no longer satisfying or possible to pursue because of the changes in health and living patterns associated with advancing age is well illustrated in the growing numbers of middle-aged men and women who enroll in adult education classes throughout the country or who join cultural groups within their communities.

Not only is there a tendency to narrow down the range of interests with age but there is also a tendency to shift the emphasis on already-present interests [57]. There is a tendency to shift from interests that require greater expenditure of energy and more social contacts to those that are not physically so strenuous and are more solitary in form. For example, interest in sports, dancing, and other active recreations decreases while interest in more cultural pursuits such as reading, art, and card games increases [24]. Interest in love, courtship, and marriage, so

strong in the latter part of adolescence and the early years of adulthood,
decreases as individuals reach the fifties. Interest in a philosophy of life,
on the other hand, is slight in adolescence but becomes one of the
dominant interests of middle age [57] (see Figure 78, page 360). There
are also less-marked *sex differences* in interests during middle age than
during the earlier years of adulthood. With both sexes, there is a

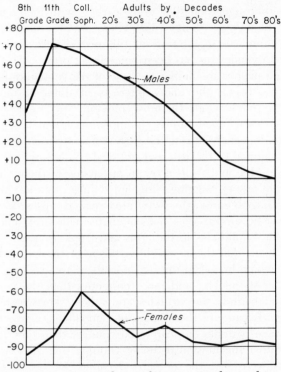

FIG. 105. Changes in interests with age, showing a trend toward increased feminin-
ity. (*Based on L. M. Terman and C. C. Miles, Sex and personality. New York:
McGraw-Hill, 1936. From F. K. Shuttleworth, The adolescent period: a graphic atlas.
Monogr. Soc. Res. Child Develpm., 1949, 14, No. 1. Used by permission.*)

tendency toward increased femininity of interests throughout maturity,
with a peak coming in the later years of life. Masculinity in men is associated with active and mechanical pursuits and with indifference to
artistic and cultural pursuits, pursuits which characterize feminine
women. With middle age, the shift to cultural pursuits, characteristic of
both men and women, is due partly to age and partly to the greater
length of married life together [58]. Figure 105 shows the shift to
femininity of interests with age. Patterns of interests are fairly well
stabilized by the mid-fifties. Approximately 50 per cent of shifts and

changes occur between thirty-five and fifty-five, with the other 50 per cent taking place in early adulthood, between twenty-five and thirty-five years. After the mid-fifties, there is little or no change in interests except a further narrowing down of interests already established [24, 56].

Areas of Interest. As is true at every age, there are marked individual differences in interests and in the strength of the same interests in different people. On the whole, sex differences in interests become less marked in middle age than they were earlier, with men's interests becoming more feminine with age [58]. There are also environmental and social class differences in interests at this period, just as is true of the earlier years. In general, as has been pointed out previously, the interests of middle-aged people are similar to those of the young adult, except for shifts in emphasis. Of the many interests of different individuals in middle age, the following are the most common:

Appearance and Clothes. Interest in appearance, which begins to wane after marriage, especially during the early years of parenthood, intensifies with the appearance of the external physical changes which accompany advancing age. Men and women try to put a stop to these changes or to hide them from others. Sagging chins are reduced by diet, massage, and chin straps; bulges under the eyes are covered up with make-up if massage or plastic surgery does not eliminate them; gray hair is touched up or dyed; flabby muscles in the arms and trunk are reduced with diet or massaged to harden them; weight is taken off by diet or by massage and exercise, which break up the fat deposits in areas where fat tells the person's age most quickly; and more cosmetics than the younger adult needs are used to hide the wrinkles and sallow skin which come with advancing age. Because of these forms of camouflage, many middle-aged men and women of today appear to be younger than they actually are. For men, creating the illusion of being younger than they are is a business asset, as is true of the unmarried career woman or the married woman who wants to work when her home duties lessen. The married woman who has no work outside the home likewise is interested in covering up telltale signs of aging to avoid looking older than her husband, to satisfy her own vanity, to ward off the hypercritical remarks of adolescent children, and to help her establish herself as a leader in community activities. Middle- and upper-class men and women are, on the whole, more interested in retaining a youthful appearance than are those of the lower classes where appearance plays a less important role in their work or social lives [28, 31].

Well-adjusted middle-aged men and women become more conservative about their *clothes,* both in style and color, than do those who are less well adjusted and who rebel against their advancing years [10]. Men recognize the importance of clothes and grooming to business success, and as they advance toward the peak of achievement in middle age, they are far more clothes-conscious than they were when they were younger and when their status in the business world was lower. Women, by contrast, are less clothes-conscious in middle age than in early adulthood though they, like men, recognize the importance of clothes and grooming to success in both the business and social worlds [57]. When adjustment to middle age is poor, as shown by constant rebellion against the changes which are an inevitable accompaniment of aging, interest in clothes is not only intensified but it is concentrated mainly on the selection of clothes which will create the illusion that the individual is younger than he is. Bright colors, extreme styles, and a large wardrobe become as important to the middle-aged man or woman who is trying to defy age as to an adolescent who is mainly interested in attracting the attention of members of his own sex as well as of members of the opposite sex [5, 14].

Money and Material Possessions. How the middle-aged person feels about money and material possessions is influenced to a large extent by how prosperous he is and how much he has had in the way of worldly goods throughout the earlier years of life. Unless there are marked demands on him from his children, relatives, or wife, the middle-aged man is less concerned about how much money he earns than he was when he was younger. Stability of work, job satisfaction, and prestige are more important to him than earnings. And because most men in the skilled-artisan field, in business, and in professional fields are reaching the peak of their achievement during middle age, many of the money worries they had when they were younger cease to exist [39, 57]. For those in the unskilled and semiskilled groups, employment is less stable as the worker becomes middle-aged; in addition, the slowing down of the middle-aged worker's speed as well as the difficulties he has in learning new techniques often make the worker in this group accept jobs at wages below those of his earlier peak years. For him, money becomes a source of real concern. Poor health, debts carried over from earlier years, or economic responsibilities for elderly relatives tend to heighten money worries for middle-aged men of all occupational groups, except those whose incomes are more than adequate to meet their needs (see Figure 84, page 391). And with worry comes a focusing of attention on money, an emphasis not found in the absence of worry.

To the middle-aged woman, money is often a source of greater interest than it is to the man. Not only does she want many of the material possessions, in the form of clothes, a car, and a home with furnishings, that will compare favorably with those of her friends or come up to her ideal, but money means security to her. Worry about financial security, stemming from the death or illness of the breadwinner of the family, or from divorce, plagues many middle-aged women of today, and this source of concern heightens their interest in money. It is one of the common reasons for middle-aged women's return to the labor force. Even if they are not worried about security, they are motivated to take jobs outside the home to enable them to have things they want and to be able to save for old age. (See pages 507–508 for a discussion of women's working outside the home during middle age.)

In middle age, there is a change in attitude toward the use of money. A comparison of college students' attitudes toward extravagance and

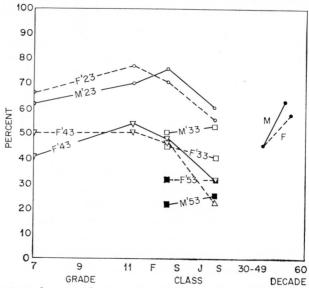

FIG. 106. Attitudes toward extravagance as "wrong" at different ages and their changes from 1923 to 1953. (*From S. L. Pressey and A. W. Jones, 1923–1953 and 20-60 age changes in moral codes, anxieties, and interests, as shown by the "X-O Tests." J. Psychol., 1955, 39, 485–502. Used by permission.*)

that of men and women in middle age has revealed that the former group considers extravagance less wrong than do members of the older group. Furthermore, the tendency to emphasize the wrong of extravagance increases with advancing age [47]. This is illustrated in Figure 106. Whether this change in attitudes is the result of the conservatism that characteristically comes with age or of a different value system that is culturally defined is impossible to say. A comparison of college students' attitudes toward extravagance in 1923, 1943, and 1953 has shown a marked decline in the number of students who regard extravagance as wrong. Since those who are middle-aged today were adolescents during the 1920s, a time when cultural values toward extravagance were markedly different from those of today, the emphasis on wrongness of extravagance by middle-aged men and women may mean that they are clinging to values learned when they were younger and not displaying a tendency toward greater conservatism in money management in middle age.

Religion. Interest in religion, as a rule, becomes stronger rather than weaker as middle age advances. The middle-aged man or woman is more interested in the church and its activities than he was when he was younger, though he may be less regular in attendance than he was during childhood or even early adulthood. Because of the narrowing of interests and the shift in emphasis on different interests that characterize middle age, religion fills a need in the middle-aged person's life to replace interests that are no longer dominant. Many middle-aged men and women find in religion a source of comfort and happiness they never experienced in the religion of their younger years. On the whole, middle-aged people are less worried by religious questions, less dogmatic in their beliefs, less sure that there is only one true religion, and more skeptical about the devil and hell in afterlife and about miracles than are college students [10]. They are not "religiously disturbed" at this time in their lives [47].

Community Affairs. Middle age is the time for service. By then, the average man is well established in his chosen line of work and the average woman's home responsibilities have decreased. As a result, more time can be given to community affairs, whether in the form of serving on committees, on church or professional boards, or in leadership roles in different community organizations. Studies of civic and political participation have revealed a pattern of emerging responsibility and activity throughout the early years of adulthood, a maintenance of activity on a plateau for a period of time, followed by constriction of activity and voluntary relinquishment of responsibility (see Figure 86, page 396). This does not come until the latter part of middle age or even as late as old age [48]. Civic participation increases in the early forties and then begins to decline. Political activity in the form of voting, reading and discussing politics, and sending telegrams increases up to the fifties and is maintained until the sixties before declining. In the case of both civic and political activity, the age at which the decline begins is related to the amount of initiative and energy involved in the activity [61].

Recreations. Interest in recreations of a strenuous type wanes rapidly in middle age and is replaced by recreations of a quieter, less active sort. For the most part, middle-aged men and women prefer quiet evenings and week ends of reading, radio, and television to sports, picnics, dancing, and other forms of recreation they formerly enjoyed. There is also a shift from interest in recreations involving groups to those involving only several people. When middle-aged people do participate in recreations of a group type, they are likely to be the driving forces [9]. As is true of other interests, there is a narrowing down of variety in recreational interests during middle age. From those that formerly were engaged in, there is a tendency to select the ones that give the greatest pleasure and to concentrate on them. While recreational interests vary from individual to individual, there are certain forms of recreation that are universally popular among middle-aged American men and women. *Reading* is a more widely engaged-in recreation during middle age than in the early years of adulthood, mainly because the older person has more time to read than has the younger. Middle-aged people spend more time reading newspapers than books or magazines [24]. Furthermore, they are more selective in what they read than they were when they were younger. More time is devoted to reading editorials in the newspapers than to reading about sports, crime, or disaster. In books, they prefer history and love stories to science and sports. There is less interest in reading or talking about sex than there was earlier. In fact, middle-aged men are often embarrassed by "dirty" stories and disgusted by sexy jokes or shows [10].

During middle age, there is less interest in *movies* and *radio* than in the earlier years of adulthood. When they attend movies or listen to the radio, middle-aged people tend to be more selective than younger people [24]. *Television,* which has become a popular form of recreation in recent years, often has greater appeal for middle-aged people than for younger people because the former have more free time to watch, and it requires less effort than going to the movies. As age advances, television watching becomes one of the favorite recreational activities. The amount of time spent in television watching, however, is markedly influenced by the educational and socioeconomic status of the individual. It appeals more to those of the lower than to those of the higher socioeconomic groups [15].

Hobbies become a popular form of recreation among many middle-aged people. For men whose work does not absorb their interest, time, and attention a hobby is a form of compensation; for those whose work is all-absorbing, hobbies are a form of relaxation. Men who fail to develop hobbies before middle age ends usually have more difficulty in adjusting to retirement in old age than do those who have developed hobbies which can fill the gap left by their former jobs. Men who are most successful in business have been found to have more hobbies than those who are less successful. Women not only have more hobbies than do men throughout the adult years but there is a greater variability in their hobbies than in those of men [59]. For the most part, the hobbies of middle-aged people are of a constructional nature, including such activities as gardening, woodwork, painting, sewing, cooking, or photography. *Collections* are a favorite hobby for those who are financially able to engage in this form of recreation. The objects collected generally have some intrinsic value, such as stamps, *objets d'art*, pictures, fine needlework, or jewelry. Another favorite hobby of middle-aged people consists of "taking courses" in subjects which interest them and which are of cultural rather than vocational value. Much of the interest in adult education on the part of middle-aged people falls into this category [19].

There are *social-class* and *sex* differences in recreational interests during middle age, as is true at other ages during the life span. Members of the upper middle class devote much of their recreational time to such formal associations as clubs and community activities, to participation in sports, to gardening, especially the raising of flowers, and to reading. Members of the lower middle class and the lower social classes, on the other hand, favor manual-manipulative activities in which they make things they can use, watching television, and fishing. Those of the lower-lower social class do little reading, spend most of their recreational time visiting relatives and neighbors. When they garden, it is usually to raise vegetables. Men of all social classes concentrate more of their recreational time on sports than do women, especially as spectators at different athletic contests; they enjoy fishing, and spend some time gardening. Women, on the other hand, have greater interest in formal and informal associations with other people than have men and they devote more time to reading than men do [30].

Social Interests. Middle age often brings with it a renewed interest in social life. As the responsibilities of the family decrease and as the economic status of the family improves, men and women are in a position to engage in more social activities than was possible during the early years of adulthood when family responsibilities and adjustment to work made an active social life impossible. In some middle-aged men and women, especially those who married young and were deprived of the social experiences their unmarried contemporaries enjoyed, there is a craving for parties and a desire to be "on the go" all the time. Popularity, as expressed in a large number of friends, in constant calls from these friends, and in invitations to do things together is as important to them as to the adolescent. Often there is a tendency to engage in flirtations with members of the opposite sex and a preoccupation with dress and grooming, in hopes of appearing younger and more attractive. For such middle-aged people, this is a "dangerous age," because at this time, the individual frequently breaks up the established pattern of family life, seeks excitement and adventure outside the home, and neglects the family. Middle-aged people who are happy in their work and home lives are more moderate in their social interests, though they, too, broaden their social contacts and engage in more social activities than was possible during the early years of adulthood.

Studies of social participation have revealed that membership in formal community, church, and business groups is low during early adulthood, reaches a peak in the late forties or early fifties, and then begins to decline as the individual reaches the sixties [19, 43]. Declining energy at that time puts a stop to a too active social life. Furthermore, popularity bought by entertaining and expenditure of money loses its appeal as the individual looks ahead to retirement and decreased income. As a result,

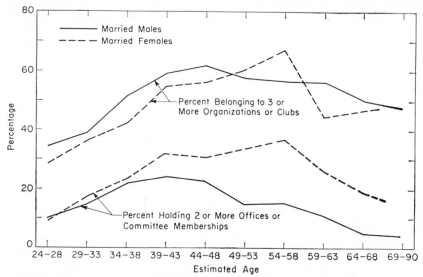

Fig. 107. Pattern of participation in formal organizations during middle age. (*Unpublished analysis by R. G. Kuhlen of Time Magazine survey data. From S. L. Pressey and R. G. Kuhlen, Psychological development through the life span. New York: Harper, 1957. Used by permission.*)

there is a tendency to settle down to the home circle and to spend most of the time with the family, the children's newly established families, and old friends [48]. Figure 107 shows the pattern of participation in formal organizations throughout the adult years, with the peak coming during middle age. The pattern of social participation is markedly influenced by the socioeconomic status of the individual. Those of higher status are more active during middle age than are those of the lower-status groups, most of whom belong to few groups and attend meetings seldom or never. They are thus "socially isolated," as is true of a large percentage of the aged [2].

On the whole, middle-aged people make better social adjustments than do those who are younger, and they depend more on people for happiness than do the younger. A comparison of college students with middle-aged business and professional men showed that the older group got along better with their relatives than did the younger, but they found loud parties and crowds less attractive than did the younger. Putting on a stunt in a group makes them uncomfortable and they often refuse to play a game in which they are not at home [10]. The older individuals are less outgoing, talk less, and express their views in group discussions less readily than do the younger. They have a tendency to keep their troubles and personal problems to themselves, and when they dislike someone, they are discreet about it. Like the adolescent, the middle-aged person is sensitive to the way people feel about him and he feels group approval or disapproval keenly [9]. Because social contacts outside the home are often a compensation for lack of social contacts in the home after the children grow up, the middle-aged man or woman has a strong motivation to make good social adjustments.

BIBLIOGRAPHY

1. Bayley, N., and M. H. Oden: The maintenance of intellectual ability in gifted adults. *J. Geront.*, 1955, 10, 91–107.
2. Bell, W., and M. T. Force: Urban neighborhood types and participation in formal associations. *Amer. sociol. Rev.*, 1956, 21, 25–34.
3. Benedek, T.: Climacterium: a developmental phase. *Psychoanal. Quart.*, 1950, 19, 1–27.
4. Benjamin, H.: The use of sex hormone combinations in female patients. *J. Geront.*, 1949, 4, 222–233.
5. Bergler, E.: *The revolt of the middle-aged man.* New York: A. A. Wyn, 1954.
6. Billig, O., and R. W. Adams: Emotional conflicts of the middle-aged man. *Geriatrics*, 1957, 12, 535–541.
7. Bram, I.: Psychic factors in obesity: observations in over 1,000 cases. *Arch. Pediat.*, 1950, 67, 543–552.
8. Brozek, J.: The age problem in research workers: psychological viewpoint. *Sci. Mon., N.Y.*, 1951, 72, 355–359.
9. Brozek, J.: Personality of young and middle-aged normal men: an analysis of a psychosomatic inventory. *J. Geront.*, 1952, 7, 410–418.
10. Brozek, J.: Personality changes with age: an item analysis of the Minnesota Multiphasic Personality Inventory. *J. Geront.*, 1955, 10, 194–206.
11. Brozek, J., and A. Keys: Limitations of the "normal" body weight as a criterion of normality. *Science*, 1950, 112, 788.
12. Bühler, C.: The curve of life as studied in biographies. *J. appl. Psychol.*, 1935, 19, 405–409.
13. Cavan, R. S.: Adjustment problems of the older woman. *Marriage Fam. Living*, 1952, 14, 16–18.
14. Cavan, R. S.: *The American family.* New York: Crowell, 1953.
15. Coffin, T. E.: Television's effects on leisure-time activities. *J. appl. Psychol.*, 1948, 32, 550–558.
16. Conley, V. L.: Common skin worries. *Today's Hlth*, 1957, Jan., pp. 31–32.

17. Corsini, R. J., and K. K. Fassett: Intelligence and aging. *J. genet. Psychol.*, 1953, 83, 249–264.
18. Dennis, W., and E. Girden: Current scientific activities of psychologists as a function of age. *J. Geront.*, 1954, 9, 175–178.
19. Desmond, T. C.: America's unknown middle-agers. *The New York Times*, 1956, July 29.
20. English, O. S.: Climacteric neuroses and their management. *Geriatrics*, 1954, 9, 139–145.
21. English, O. S., and G. H. J. Pearson: *Emotional problems of living.* New York: Norton, 1945.
22. Glick, P. C., and H. P. Miller: Educational level and potential income. *Amer. sociol. Rev.*, 1956, 21, 307–312.
23. Goldzieher, M., and J. W. Goldzieher: The male climacteric and the post-climacteric state. *Geriatrics*, 1953, 8, 1–10.
24. Granick, S.: Studies of psychopathology in later maturity—a review. *J. Geront.*, 1950, 5, 361–369.
25. Greenblatt, R. B.: Metabolic and psychosomatic disorders in menopausal women. *Geriatrics*, 1955, 10, 165–169.
26. Greenblatt, R. B.: Treatment of menopausal symptoms. *Geriatrics*, 1957, 12, 452–453.
27. Havighurst, R. J.: Old age—an American problem. *J. Geront.*, 1949, 4, 298–304.
28. Havighurst, R. J.: *Human development and education.* New York: Longmans, 1953.
29. Havighurst, R. J.: Flexibility and the social roles of the retired. *Amer. J. Sociol.*, 1954, 59, 309–311.
30. Havighurst, R. J.: The leisure activities of the middle-aged. *Amer. J. Sociol.*, 1957, 63, 152–162.
31. Havighurst, R. J., and R. Albrecht: *Older people.* New York: Longmans, 1953.
32. Hellbaum, A. A., J. B. Eskridge, and R. W. Payne: The influence of pituitary factors on the menopausal vasomotor instability. *J. Geront.*, 1956, 11, 58–60.
33. Hess, E., R. B. Roth, and A. F. Kaminsky: Is there a male climacteric? *Geriatrics*, 1955, 10, 170–173.
34. Kuhlen, R. G.: Age differences in personality during adult years. *Psychol. Bull.*, 1945, 42, 333–358.
35. Kuhlen, R. G., and G. H. Johnson: Changes in goals with adult increasing age. *J. consult. Psychol.*, 1952, 16, 1–4.
36. Kurlander, A. B., S. Abraham, and J. W. Rion: Obesity and disease. *Hum. Biol.*, 1956, 28, 203–216.
37. Landau, R. L.: The concept of the male climacteric. *Med. Clin. N. Amer.*, 1951, 35, 279–288.
38. Lazarsfeld, S., and A. Kadis: Is the "critical age" a critical age? *Psyché, Paris*, 1954, 9, 152–163.
39. Lehman, H. C.: *Age and achievement.* Princeton, N.J.: Princeton Univer. Press, 1953.
40. Lehman, H. C.: Ages at time of first election of presidents of professional organizations. *Sci. Mon., N.Y.*, 1955, 80, 293–298.
41. Linden, M. E., and D. Courtney: The human life cycle and its interruptions: a psychologic hypothesis. Studies in gerontologic human relations. *Amer. J. Psychiat.*, 1953, 109, 906–915.
42. Lloyd-Jones, E.: Women today and their education. *Teach. Coll. Rec.*, 1955, 57, 1–7.

43. Mayo, S. C., and C. P. Marsh: Social participation in the rural community. *Amer. J. Sociol.*, 1951, 57, 243–248.
44. Meyer, H. D.: The adult cycle. *Ann. Amer. Acad. pol. soc. Sci.*, 1957, 313, 58–67.
45. Novak, E. R.: The menopause. *J. Amer. med. Ass.*, 1954, 156, 575–578.
46. Owens, W. A.: Age and mental abilities: a longitudinal study. *Genet. Psychol. Monogr.*, 1953, 48, 3–54.
47. Pressey, S. L., and A. W. Jones: 1923–1953 and 20–60 age changes in moral codes, anxieties, and interests, as shown by the "X-O Tests." *J. Psychol.*, 1955, 39, 485–502.
48. Pressey, S. L., and R. G. Kuhlen: *Psychological development through the life span*. New York: Harper, 1957.
49. Reid, J. W.: Stability of measured Kuder interests in young adults. *J. educ. Res.*, 1951, 45, 307–312.
50. Rose, A. M.: Factors associated with the life satisfactions of middle-class, middle-aged persons. *Marriage Fam. Living*, 1955, 17, 15–19.
51. Shock, N. W.: The age problem in research workers: physiological view point. *Sci. Mon., N.Y.*, 1951, 72, 353–355.
52. Shock, N. W.: *Trends in gerontology*. Stanford, Calif.: Stanford Univer. Press, 1951.
53. Skerlj, B.: Further evidence of age changes in body form based on material of D. A. W. Edwards. *Hum. Biol.*, 1954, 26, 330–336.
54. Slotkin, J. S.: Life course in middle age. *Soc. Forces*, 1954, 33, 171–177.
55. Stanton, J. E.: Part-time employment for the older worker. *J. appl. Psychol.*, 1951, 35, 418–421.
56. Strong, E. K.: Permanence of interest scores over 22 years. *J. appl. Psychol.*, 1951, 35, 89–91.
57. Symonds, P. M.: Changes in problems and interests with increasing age. *Psychol. Bull.*, 1936, 33, 789.
58. Terman, L. M., and C. C. Miles: *Sex and personality*. New York: McGraw-Hill, 1936.
59. Terman, L. M., and M. H. Oden: *The gifted child grows up*. Stanford, Calif.: Stanford Univer. Press, 1947.
60. Thompson, J. L.: Stresses in middle life from the psychiatrist's viewpoint. *Geriatrics*, 1955, 10, 162–164.
61. Trumbull, R., C. R. Pace, and R. G. Kuhlen: Expansion and constriction of life activities during the adult life span as reflected in civic and political participation. *Amer. Psychologist*, 1950, 5, 367.
62. Tuckman, J., and I. Lorge: The best years of life: a study in ranking. *J. Psychol.*, 1952, 34, 137–149.
63. Tuckman, J., and I. Lorge: Classification of the self as young, middle-aged, or old. *Geriatrics*, 1954, 9, 534–536.
64. Werner, A. A.: Sex behavior and problems of the climacteric. *In* M. Fishbein and E. W. Burgess, *Successful marriage*, rev. ed. Garden City, N.Y.: Doubleday, 1955. Pp. 475–490.

Middle Age

Continued

The most difficult adjustments the middle-aged person must make, as is true of the young adult, center around work and the family. For men, problems arising in relation to work present the most serious sources of adjustment, while for women, those arising from family relationships take precedence over all other adjustment problems. In spite of the fact that most adults have made adjustments of greater or lesser success to these areas during the early years of adulthood, new problems arise at middle age which require a shift of attitude and marked changes in patterns of behavior established earlier. Even though the problems are in the same areas of the individual's life as those encountered earlier, they are different enough in their major aspects to require shifts of attitude and patterns of behavior often of major proportions. Furthermore, there is no indication that successful adjustment in the earlier years of adulthood will lead to a lessening of these problems in middle age. A woman who, for example, has adjusted successfully to her role as wife and mother will not be spared the adjustment problems to changed roles in the home as her children grow up and go into homes of their own or as her husband, whose interests change and who is, therefore, less companionable, provides her with little to compensate for her loss of the mother role. Similarly, the successful businessman is not going to be spared the problems of adjustment to change in status that comes with approaching retirement, nor will he be spared the anxiety stemming from desire to change jobs, or the constant fear that poor health, change in management, or competition with younger workers may necessitate adjustments to a new job or even a period of unemployment.

500

In addition to these areas of adjustment, the middle-aged person is faced with a totally new problem, that of adjusting to the realization that old age is "just around the corner." And, like all problems for which there has been no previous experience, the adjustment is often difficult and gives rise to strong emotional tension. How successfully the middle-aged man or woman is able to make this adjustment will determine, to a large extent, how well adjusted and how happy he or she will be during the closing years of the life span. Until recently, what emphasis was placed on this area of adjustment was largely limited to achieving financial security. Today, emphasis has shifted to psychological preparation for old age, which necessitates the recognition and acceptance of the fact that adjustments must be made and that the sooner they are made, the easier it will be. Rebellion against advancing age or refusal to recognize that one is growing old may result in a temporary adjustment of enough success to guarantee temporary satisfaction, but it will mean a major adjustment later on with little time to prepare oneself psychologically for it.

VOCATIONAL ADJUSTMENTS

Normally, the peak years for achievement come during middle age, in the forties and early fifties (see pages 462–464). Not only is the worker at the peak of status in the organization with which he is associated but

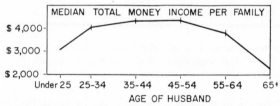

Fig. 108. For the average worker, income reaches its peak early in middle age. (*From P. C. Glick, The life cycle of the family. Marriage Fam. Living, 1955, 17, 3–9. Used by permission.*)

his income from work reaches its peak also (see Figure 108). On the surface, then, it would seem that his adjustment problems have been solved and that his vocational life should move smoothly until he reaches the age of retirement. This is, of course, sometimes true but in a majority of cases, middle age brings with it many new conditions which necessitate new adjustments. Even when they have achieved status vocationally, many middle-aged men and women are dissatisfied with their work. The greatest instability in the area of vocational adjustment has been found to be in the twenties and early forties. The early twenties are the years when the average worker is trying out different lines of work or different jobs in his chosen field and when he is becoming adjusted to the new pattern of behavior required by the world of work. (See pages 419–423 for a discussion of the adjustment problems the young adult must face in his vocational role.) Vocational instability in the early forties stems from a number of causes, the most important of which are the general restlessness characteristic of this period of life; the ending of the responsibility for the support of the children, thus freeing the worker from the burden he has carried for many years; and the realization that he must change now or never if he is dissatisfied with his work [32].

Fig. 109. Age trends in goals of married teachers. (*From R. G. Kuhlen and G. H. Johnson, Changes in goals with adult increasing age. J. consult. Psychol.*, 1952, 16, 1–4. *Used by permission.*)

Vocational unrest in early middle age has been studied in relation to goals of teachers. Married men, when asked what they would most like to be doing ten years hence, showed a peak in desire to get into other work or to get a different job or promotion in education during the early 40's. These desires waned with advancing years to be replaced by a desire to remain in the same job and then retire (see Figure 109). Married women teachers showed less desire to remain at home as housewives when they reached middle age than they did when they were younger, and they showed a decrease in desire to remain in the same job or to get into another job as middle age advanced. In contrast to the married men, the women teachers began to be anxious to retire nearly ten years earlier than the men and the desire for retirement was stronger in them than in the men [34] (see Figure 109). Much the same pattern of attitudes toward work was shown by unmarried women teachers (see Figure 98, page 452). While this study was limited to teachers, there is reason to believe that similar attitudes toward work are characteristic of most middle-aged men and women.

The vocational adjustment problems of middle age are as serious for *women* today, if not more so, as for men. In the past, relatively few women worked outside the home and those who did so were usually in domestic service, teaching, and nursing. Today, women enter almost all vocational fields and in far larger numbers (see Figure 110). Even those

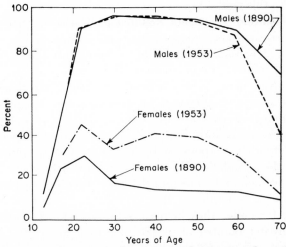

Fig. 110. Increase in percentage of women in relation to total population working now as compared with the percentage working in 1890. (*From S. L. Pressey and R. G. Kuhlen, Psychological development through the life span. New York: Harper, 1957. Used by permission.*)

who withdrew from the labor force during the early years of adulthood, to take care of their homes and children, are returning to work in increasingly larger numbers as their children reach the school age. In recent years, there has been a growing tendency for women over thirty-five years of age to work outside the home, some of whom hold a job for the first time in their lives while others return to jobs similar to those they held before or during the early years of marriage. At the present time, over 5,000,000 middle-aged women are in the nation's labor force and many of them maintain the triple roles of mother-wife-earner [18]. By 1975, it is predicted that 17,460,000 middle-aged women will be working. There are many reasons given for the growing increase in the numbers of middle-aged women who are working outside the home. Simpler homemaking and labor-saving devices make it possible for them to take care of their homes in a fraction of the time formerly needed. The trend toward earlier marriages, earlier childbearing, and smaller families means that the woman's parental responsibilities end often before she reaches middle age, thus freeing her to spend her time as she wishes. The high cost of living and the increased desire for a better standard of living mean that most families need more money than the husband can earn. And, finally, as young men spend more time in school and college to prepare for their life careers and young women marry and start their families shortly after completing their education, there is need for more workers, and middle-aged women are being used in increasing numbers to fill this need [43].

Factors Influencing Vocational Adjustment. The vocational adjustments of middle-aged men and women have been complicated in recent years by a number of factors. Most of these were not present in the past and are a result of modern life in America. These factors are:

Increasing Life Span. As was pointed out earlier (see pages 460–461), middle age is a new phenomenon for the majority of the population. Up to the beginning of the present century, the life expectancy for the average American was forty-five years and only about 10 per cent of the entire population ever experienced middle age. Today, approximately 80 per cent of the population lives to be at least sixty years old and the average age of men and women in the labor force is now forty-five years [18]. By 1980, it is predicted that over 50 per cent of the population will be over forty-five, thus increasing the vocational adjustment problems for a greater number of people than exist today [51]. This means that most men and women will be working throughout middle age, and being satisfied with the work they do will become a problem of major importance for them. If they remained in work that was not to their liking during the early years of adulthood because of family responsibilities, they will realize that with the lessening of family responsibilities they are free to change, and this change must be made soon or it will be too late to get another job or to enter a new line of work [32].

Social Attitudes toward Middle-aged Workers. The general attitude toward workers who are in their forties and fifties is unfavorable. It is believed that they are too old to adapt themselves to new methods because of the mental rigidity that is supposed to accompany aging, that they are too slow to keep up to the working pace of younger people, that they fatigue quickly and therefore not only produce less but also make more errors and increase the possibility of accident, and that they are less dependable because of absenteeism due to the more frequent illnesses that are believed to be characteristic of middle-aged people. As a result of this generally unfavorable attitude toward middle-aged workers in almost every occupational category, workers over forty-five years of

age have fewer employment opportunities than their numerical representation would lead one to expect [37]. This holds true not only for
getting new jobs but also for retaining a job during slack periods when
layoffs are frequent.

A person's attitude toward older workers has itself been found to be
related to age. The younger the person, the less favorable is his attitude
toward the older worker. The attitude is not actually antagonistic but
tends more to be neutral. As workers become older, their attitudes
toward older workers become increasingly more favorable. Married
people, on the whole, tend to have more favorable attitudes toward older
workers than do unmarried, perhaps because the former have a better
understanding of the importance of a job to a middle-aged person who
has a family to support. The person's relative age within his work group
affects his attitude toward himself as a worker and the attitudes of others
toward him [29]. The closer the worker is in age to his coworkers, the
less unfavorable will be his attitude toward the older worker. That such
attitudes are important is shown by the fact that even in periods of relatively little unemployment, unemployment for workers over forty-five
is significantly higher than for younger workers. In less prosperous times,
the unemployment of middle-aged workers is even greater [51]. Furthermore, when it comes to promotion, middle-aged workers are often rated
down on items involving promotability. This is often more a matter of
policy, stemming from the fact that they are shortly to be retired, than
a reflection of their present job worth [38]. It does, however, show how
the general social attitude toward middle-aged workers affects their
vocational lives and emphasizes their adjustment problems.

In recent years, a number of studies have been made to determine
how valid the arguments against the middle-aged worker are and to
what extent the generally unfavorable attitude toward employing or
promoting middle-aged workers is justified. For the most part, these
studies have revealed that middle-aged workers are in many respects
superior to younger workers and in other respects are equal to or only
slightly inferior to younger workers. In fact, older workers are often
undervalued [38]. Approximately 95 per cent of the men and women in
the middle-age group are not disabled and can work [18]. Furthermore,
in work where experience is important, they are superior to younger
workers. In addition, they have been found to be better in attendance,
conscientiousness, and steadiness than are younger workers [9]. For
part-time work, especially in the case of women, as in department stores
during the rush seasons, older workers are not only available for longer
periods of time but they want to work and, as a result, are happier and
shift less than do younger workers [51].

A comparison of business and professional men in the age group of forty-five to fifty-five with college students showed that the older were much more conscientious about their work than were the younger men. For the older group, work came before fun; they were rarely late for appointments; they disliked seeing others shirking on the job and they rarely did so themselves; they liked a routine and definite schedule for their work; they were less willing to put off matters that required immediate attention; they were less impatient when interrupted in work; and their attitude toward work was more stable. While middle-aged workers tend to work under greater tension than do younger men, they feel that their work ability has not decreased and they are more compulsive about doing their work than are younger men [12, 13]. As Bowers has pointed out, "Quite evidently workers should be employed and retained on the basis of merit without reference to age. Biases and misconceptions limiting the use of older persons should be replaced by facts. Oldsters can maintain productivity, thus making an extended productive life worth while, strengthening man power resources, and lessening possible economic burdens resulting from dependency of large numbers of non-productive older persons" [9]. Middle-aged workers may not show as much initiative or get along as well with other workers as do those who are younger but this is compensated for by their greater conscientiousness [38, 46]. Even in lines of work where it was formerly believed that only young men could qualify, as in the case of airplane pilots, there has been a tendency in recent years to use an increasing number who are middle-aged and whose ability to pass the rigid medical tests required for such work has been far greater than was formerly believed possible [50]. In addition, they have been found to perform on the job as well as younger pilots [39].

Hiring Policy. Since World War I, but especially since the depression of the twenties, there has been a widespread policy in business and industry to hire only younger people [16]. This is done partly to minimize the expense the organization must carry for retirement pensions and partly because of the widespread belief that maximum productivity can be achieved best by hiring and by training younger workers. Employers are reluctant to hire older people because of the heavier contributory charge for the pension funds which they must assume. It has been estimated that a single premium for a worker hired at the age of forty years may cost the employer as high as $6,823. Each year, as the worker grows older, the cost to an employer for such a premium grows larger. When the worker reaches sixty years, the cost is approximately $13,860 [24]. This situation could be corrected by transfer of pension contributions from one company to another and by amending the Social Security Act to make benefit payments after retirement uniform but, to date, this has not been done [9].

So long as a man in middle age retains his job, no matter how discontented he may be with it, he is reasonably certain of employment until he reaches the compulsory retirement age. The unions see to that. But, should a period of depression come at this time, the unions cannot keep him on the job and, because middle-aged workers are regarded as less efficient and, hence, less valuable to their employers, they are usually the first to be laid off. The possibility of unemployment in middle age, combined with the realization that reemployment at that age will be almost impossible, is a constant threat hanging over the head of a middle-aged worker. This causes job dissatisfaction and is a constant threat to the happiness of the middle-aged man.

Changing jobs in middle age, even when the change is to a closely related line of work, is almost impossible. The employment practice, mentioned above, which is designed to take new and young workers on the grounds that their days of usefulness will be greater to their employers than is true of older workers and that even though an older worker may have greater skill, he is less adjustable to new work situations, makes it almost impossible for a middle-aged worker to change jobs, no matter how unsatisfactory his present work conditions may be [18]. Knowing the difficulties in getting a new job, the middle-aged person often develops an unfavorable attitude toward himself and toward work. This hinders his getting and keeping a job. Those who have been unemployed for a long time often develop feelings of inadequacy and of being unwanted, which result either in overaggressiveness or in extreme passivity, both of which are handicaps to employment [19]. Middle-aged workers in industry generally have even more difficulty in getting jobs than have those in business. Furthermore, because salaries in the lower occupations generally reach their peak earlier, those who do get jobs are usually forced to work for less money than they received when they were younger, a condition that does not contribute to good morale or good adjustment to the work. Professional workers who find difficulties in getting jobs in middle age often work independently as consultants [16]. Difficulties in getting jobs as age advances for workers in different categories are illustrated in Figure 111.

The middle-aged woman who, after bringing up her family, may want to work to supplement the family income or to fill in idle hours, finds the situation even more difficult than men do. Because she has not been working during the earlier years of adulthood, she is unfamiliar with the new methods, even though she may have had training and experience in similar lines of work when she was younger. She finds competition with younger women far stiffer than men do and, as a result, she discovers that getting any job at all, with the exception of work in the domestic or related fields, is almost impossible. During rush seasons, women can usually get part- or full-time work in stores, but getting full-time, permanent jobs, or even part-time work on a permanent basis is very difficult [51].

At the present time, about one-third of the unemployed workers in the United States are middle-aged women. The situation has attracted the attention of the Labor Department and strong efforts are now being made to break down employer resistance to employing middle-aged women. When such women are given employment, in offices or stores,

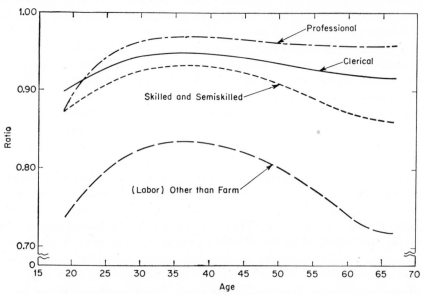

FIG. 111. The differential threat of aging for various economic groups as reflected in age trends in percentage employed in different categories at different ages. (*From S. L. Pressey and R. G. Kuhlen, Psychological development through the life span. New York: Harper, 1957. Used by permission.*)

their work measures up favorably to that of younger women [41]. The difficulty the middle-aged woman has in getting work tends to intensify her adjustment problems. This is especially true of women in the lower-income brackets. Like men, they face the problems of old age with deep concern, especially when they have children to support, owing to the death, divorce, or desertion of the husband, or when their husbands are older than they or in poor health, a circumstance which, the women know, may leave them in a precarious economic position as they grow older. Feeling unwanted in the business world is as detrimental to the morale of the middle-aged woman as to the man, and often intensifies the general feeling of uselessness that develops when her role of mother ends.

Changes in Work Conditions. Modern business and industry are in a constant state of flux. As new machinery, efficiency techniques, and new methods of mass production appear, the worker must make constant adjustments to work methods. Furthermore, with the workers' constant demand for higher pay and shorter work hours, employers are demanding more output per work hour to compensate for the higher costs. Instead of individual work, most of the work done in business or industry is becoming "team work" in the sense that workers must cooperate with each other in work that used to be done by one or several workers. This means constant change to new patterns of work, an adjustment it is believed younger workers can make better than those who are middle-aged. The widespread belief that individuals are less adaptable with age militates against the employment of older workers in many businesses and industries and it leads to the layoff of older workers during slack seasons or periods of business recession, or to lack of promotion or even to demotion to a job with lower pay and less responsibility for those who are retained [26]. Except in the professions and administrative positions in business and industry, middle-aged workers face these problems which militate against good work morale.

Studies of on-the-job learning have shown that middle-aged men and women learn more slowly than do those who are younger, even though this is partially compensated for by their greater dependability, better attendance, and conscientiousness [9]. Ratings of workers by foremen in a manufacturing company indicated that workers' ability to learn started to decline in the thirties and then fell rapidly during the forties and fifties [46]. A study of government-sponsored training of rural craftsmen in England, as blacksmiths, carpenters, and electrical engineers, revealed that difficulties in training began to be pronounced around forty years of age. While these individuals were not "untrainable," their rate of learning was slower than that of younger workers [26]. Work requiring a high degree of sensory-motor skill is more difficult for middle-aged workers to learn than that requiring less skill. Skills once acquired are maintained fairly well throughout middle age but the learning of new skills proves to be a stumbling block for many middle-aged people [4]. The degree of difficulty in learning new skills is influenced by the brightness of the worker and by the relationship of what is to be learned to skills formerly acquired [11].

Difficulties in learning are increased by resistance to learning new methods and by the speed required by the new task. The ability to adopt new methods and to adjust to new situations begins to decline in the thirties and becomes marked in the forties [11]. Workers frequently are resistant to learning new techniques and this lowers their motivation to learn [26]. This resistance is generally believed to be caused by the mental rigidity which is popularly associated with middle age, but it may, in part, stem from the belief of the middle-aged person that the new methods are inferior to the old and that clinging to the old is therefore more sensible than shifting to the new just because it is new [18]. There is no question about the fact that many middle-aged workers give the impression, through their slowness in learning and their resistance to learning new methods, that there is some truth to the saying that "you can't teach old dogs new tricks," and this impression will affect their opportunities for employment.

Stress on speed in work is difficult for the middle-aged worker to adjust to. By working under tension, the middle-aged worker can usually keep his output up to that of younger workers [13, 46]. However, he is slower in doing the work and is able to keep up to the standard required only by being conscientious about his work and being willing to work until the assignment is completed [9, 26]. The speed factor is especially serious in the learning of a new job. Middle-aged workers are not only slower in learning than are younger workers but their slowness is increased when the task they are learning requires speed. Training difficulties are especially frequent in jobs involving high-speed manual skills and these difficulties appear as early as thirty years of age, increasing as the individual becomes older [26]. Because most industries today stress time, the difficulties of the middle-aged worker are increased both by lowering the prospects of employment in a new job and by reducing the chances of continued employment in a job already held. There is a tendency for both men and women to move away from work requiring continuous activity at a set speed, especially when the worker is paced by a machine or conveyor [4].

One of the most difficult adjustments to modern methods in business and industry the middle-aged person must make is to working with a group of people. Whether there is a general tendency to be less social and less cooperative in group activities because of the mental and physical changes characteristic of middle age, or whether this difficulty in adjusting to groups is the result of less practice in group activities in childhood and adolescence is an open question. It is true that schools of today put more stress on group activities than was done in the past and that training in social adjustments in the home, neighborhood, and school is stressed more today than when the middle-aged people of today were in school. It may readily be, therefore, that the greater ability on the part of the younger worker to get along better with his superiors and his fellow workers is the result of his training, a training which those who are now middle-aged did not have [32]. Whatever the cause, comparisons of middle-aged workers with those who are younger show the middle-aged workers to rate lower on relationships with others [38].

There is also a tendency for older workers to be somewhat intolerant of younger workers, especially when they feel that the younger worker is shirking on the job [12]. The widespread belief that middle-aged people, especially women, do not get along as well with others as do younger people influences the attitudes of employers unfavorably toward the employment of middle-aged men or women for jobs where relationships with others are important for the work morale of the other workers.

Compulsory Retirement. Since the days of the depression of the 1930s, there has been a steady increase in the adoption of a rigid retirement policy for all workers. In industry, this is generally at sixty years of age for women and sixty-five for men, though in many industries where speed is important the retirement ages are lowered to fifty-five for women and sixty for men. In business, the retirement age varies from sixty to sixty-five years, with those in administrative positions being affected just as are the clerical workers. While many men and women say that they would like to retire, and this desire grows stronger as middle age progresses [34] (see Figures 98 and 109, pages 452 and 502), they are realistic enough to recognize that retirement brings with it many problems, perhaps the most serious of which is economic insecurity. With the high cost of living and the heavy taxation today, they become increasingly aware of the fact that their days of earning good salaries draw to a close as they reach the mid-forties and early fifties. These are the peak years for earning in most occupations and unless the individual is able to make adequate provision for the remaining years of his life then, he realizes that his future chances of doing so are limited.

Furthermore, middle-aged people know that their chances for advancement after middle age will be slight and that, in place of advancement, there is a likelihood that they will have to take a position in their organization with less responsibility and, hence, less pay. The realization that they are being pushed aside by younger workers as they approach the compulsory retirement age does not add to the vocational satisfaction of the middle-aged worker. An equally serious hindrance to vocational satisfaction in middle age is lack of promotion as people become older. Studies of ratings of workers in different lines of work have shown that older workers are often rated down on items involving promotability mainly because they are to be retired shortly rather than as a reflection on their present job worth. In such qualities as initiative and drive, organizing and planning, and general promotability, middle-aged workers are usually rated lower than younger workers [38]. And, as they have little chance to improve their status by taking another job, middle-aged workers must accept their lack of promotion or run the risk of being unemployed or having to take a job on a lower level and with lower pay than they are now receiving [46]. The feeling that he has been unfairly treated and that others win promotions while he is overlooked will naturally militate against a middle-aged person's good morale, his vocational satisfaction, or even his satisfaction in home life, particularly when vocational status contributes to status within the family group. For women, retirement from their principal occupation at the end of the child-rearing period often coincides with the period when they are faced with lack of promotion in their work outside the home. This intensifies the woman's adjustment problems to middle age [58].

ADJUSTMENTS TO CHANGED FAMILY PATTERNS

The pattern of family life undergoes marked changes during the period of middle age. This change is usually more difficult for the woman to

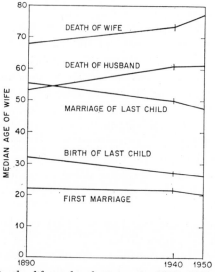

FIG. 112. Stages in the life cycle of women in 1890, 1940, and 1950, showing changes that have a marked effect on women's lives today. (*From P. C. Glick, The life cycle of the family. Marriage Fam. Living,* 1955, 17, 3–9. *Used by permission.*)

adjust to than for the man primarily because the woman's life is centered in the home. Changes in family patterns are more marked at the present time than they were in the past and this means even more difficult adjustments for middle-aged men and women of the present generation than for those of past generations. These changes are the outgrowth of certain trends, the most important of which are early marriages, smaller families, prevalence of divorce, and increase in the life span. How these trends alter the pattern of family life in middle age is illustrated in Figure 112. A comparison of family patterns in 1950 with those in 1890 shows that women of today are marrying at an average age of twenty years as compared with twenty-two years in 1890; that the birth of their last child comes when they are in the mid-twenties rather than in the early thirties; that their last child leaves home when they are in the late forties as compared with the mid-fifties; and that the death of the average woman's husband today comes when she is in the early sixties as contrasted with the early fifties in 1890. In 1950, the average woman could expect forty-one or forty-two years of marriage before the death of her husband. This means approximately fourteen years with no children at home, or approximately one-third of a couple's entire married life. In 1890, there was an average of thirty-one years of joint survival after marriage and one spouse, usually the husband, died about 2 years before the youngest child was married [21]. The average woman of today, therefore, is faced with adjustment problems unknown to women of a generation or two ago.

Adjustments to changes in the pattern of family life are complicated for many women by the fact that these adjustments must be made simultaneously with adjustments to physical changes, not only those relating to appearance but of even greater importance, those relating to the woman's childbearing function. The physical and psychological disturbances occurring at the time of the climacteric often intensify the other adjustment problems the middle-aged woman faces and they, in turn, intensify the physical disturbances of the climacteric. (See pages 482-484 for a more complete discussion of the climacteric and its effects on the middle-aged woman.) Although the male climacteric comes later than the female, sexual desire and potency begin to wane during middle age, and this change, like the female climacteric, is influenced by and, in turn, influences the male sexual and physical states. This intensifies the problems of adjustment to family relationships for the man, though usually to a lesser extent than for the woman [5]. That problems of family adjustment are difficult and not always met successfully during middle age may be seen in the fact that ratings by brothers and sisters of married couples have revealed that while happiness in marriage does not vary for men to any extent with age, for women, the forties and early fifties are a "critical period" in marriage during which time they manifest much unhappiness [8].

Even though middle age is a "problem period" in the home, most men and women prefer being at home to being away from home and they prefer associations with their families to associations with outsiders [12, 18]. Because of the responsibilities which necessitate their centering their lives around the home and family during the early adult years, parents form the habit of being at home and of maintaining family associations, a habit which, like other habits, is difficult to break. As the children grow older and need less care, especially after they have reached adolescence, parents increase the number of social activities outside the home and they take more active parts in community and social organizations. If they are able to occupy their time with activities that meet their needs and find substitute satisfactions for the satisfactions they formerly derived from family relationships, the middle-aged man and woman will be happy. However, like all adjustments, it takes time to become adjusted to the radical changes in family relationships which normally occur during middle age. As was pointed out earlier, most middle-aged women are prepared for the physical changes which occur at middle age but few are prepared for the radical changes that take place in the pattern of their lives, especially in the home, at this time [15]. This lack of psychological preparation increases the time needed for adjustments and prolongs the unhappiness few middle-aged women escape [8].

Adjustment Problems. There are many adjustment problems middle-aged men and women must face in their family lives, some of which are individual in nature while others are more or less universal and a product of the culture in which the individual lives. Of these problems, the most common are:

Adjustment to Changed Roles. Throughout marriage, both men and women must continually make adjustments. At first, they must adjust to one another and then to their roles of parenthood, when their major tasks and problems center around the home and child rearing. As the children grow older and less helpless, adjustments must be made to the new problems and demands that come with their more mature status. However, at no time until the children are grown up and leave home do parents find themselves without some problems of adjustment that must be faced in relation to their children. When the children reach maturity and leave home, for marriage or careers, parents become "deserted parents" and must face the adjustment problems of another period, one which is almost as long today as the whole period of parenthood. No longer do their lives center around their children nor are their tasks mainly related to the welfare of their children. This means a change of roles for both parents, a branching out from the family, which is especially difficult for the woman. For some adults, those who are childless, widowed, or unmarried, life patterns are different and adjustments are of a different sort. But for the average American who marries and has a family, changing family roles during middle age becomes a major developmental task, a task which is far more difficult for the woman than for the man [25].

Retirement from the role of parenthood is as difficult for most adults as retirement from work. How well they will adjust to it will be determined by the type of relationship they have with their grown children, and by how well they have prepared themselves, through the gradual development of new interests and activities, to replace parental duties as they are relinquished. Those who make good adjustments to retirement from their parental roles devote more time to undertakings with their mates, such as home repairs, dining out, entertaining friends, joining clubs, or going to concerts and movies together. When their parental duties end, they find pleasure in the greater freedom they have and in the additional money they have to enjoy it. If they are financially able, they may undertake some major venture to fill in their time and keep them interested, such as trips, building a new home or refurnishing the old home, or becoming active in community organizations. Well-adjusted women find the need for new activities to replace the home activities that formerly absorbed their time and may decide to take a job outside the home. Others who have worked, after their children went to school, to help support the family, often leave their jobs when their children marry and increased earnings are no longer necessary [21]. They spend their time doing the things they were not able to do when they carried the double load of parenthood and a job. Men often devote more time to their work to compensate for the loss of time formerly spent with their children and this preoccupation with business helps them to adjust successfully to their changed roles. When the children who are grown live nearby, and when their relationships with the parents are favorable, the parents do things for and with them, thus making it less necessary for the parents to develop new interests and activities [56].

However, many parents, especially mothers, do not make satisfactory adjustments to their retirement from parental roles. From the beginning of adolescence, children try to cut the "psychic umbilical cord" and the mother tries to prevent them. Each year, as they grow older, the children's attempts become stronger, and the mother, in her efforts to prevent them, often tries to keep them from marrying or from having careers that will take them away from the parental roof. Instead of welcoming the easing of the burden they have carried for so many years, mothers cling to it in the hope that their lives will not seem empty and futile now that their main lifework has been completed and their principal role has come to an end. For such women, the ending of the parental role is a traumatic experience and neurotic difficulties are often the aftermath [23]. Some women become temporarily neurotic or even psychotic when the need for making the adjustment to a changed parental role coincides with the need to adjust to the physical and psychological changes accompanying the climacteric [15].

Difficulties of adjusting to the departure of the children from the home and to the changed roles for the parents this departure necessitates are increased when parents, because of a lack of outside interests, center the family life, their ambitions, and their time around their children. Overly protective and possessive parents are especially prone to center their lives around the lives of their children. If the child is the partial or sole support of a widowed mother, who expects this support to continue indefinitely, the adjustment to changed roles for the mother is greatly aggravated. Should the mate selected by the child diverge in personal characteristics, status, or values from parental expectations, not only will the mother oppose the marriage but this opposition will militate against her making satisfactory adjustments to the child's departure from the home. Her opposition to the marriage generally results in a barrier between her and her child with the result that her contacts with the child after marriage are few and her relationships with the child's family are unfavorable [23]. Even when the relationships of the parent with the married child and his family are favorable, there is a "growing away" of the child from his parents as his time and attention are centered on his own family [8]. This intensifies the parents' adjustment problems, especially for the mother.

Adjustment to Spouse. Even when adjustments, both social and sexual, to the spouse have been good during the early years of marriage, before the arrival of the children and during the early years of parenthood, there is a tendency for husbands and wives to grow apart as each fulfills his life role. The man becomes more preoccupied with his business as business responsibilities become greater and as economic demands on him by his family become stronger. The woman's time and interests are centered around the home and the children and there is little time or money for her to enjoy the activities she and her husband shared during courtship or in the early days of marriage. As a result of the different roles the husband and wife must play throughout the early years of adulthood, there is a tendency for them to have less in common and to be less congenial than they were in the early part of marriage. With the ending of parental responsibilities, the husband and wife once again become dependent upon one another for companionship. Whether they will adjust successfully to this changed pattern of family relationships will be greatly influenced by how well adjusted they have been during the time of their marriage when parental roles took precedence over husband-wife roles. Because marriage is a dynamic relationship that requires continual adjustment, dissatisfaction is likely to develop in middle age when husband or wife or both have failed to make a mutual adjustment earlier in their marriage and have remained together only so long as the children were at home [52].

A close relationship with the spouse leads to happiness in marriage during middle age for both the husband and the wife, but especially for the wife whose interests are largely centered in her marriage and home. The wife who feels that she is little more than a slave to the home, who has few opportunities for amusement because of housework or care of an elderly relative, or whose husband's income is inadequate to provide the amusements and social life she was denied during the years when her children were young is likely to be dissatisfied with her marriage and, as a result, has a poor relationship with her husband [48]. For men, frustration and unhappiness in marriage often center around their occupations. Those who are successful often find that their wives have not kept pace with them in their upward climb and, as a result, they have little in common with them as they reach the peak of their careers in middle age. Those who have not come up to their earlier vocational aspirations often rationalize their failure by trying to convince themselves and others that they never had a chance to succeed because their wives were no help to them or were even handicaps. The wife, thus, becomes the scapegoat for the husband's failure. Such men find comfort in developing feelings of self-pity and animosity toward their wives, types of compensation which certaintly do not improve husband-wife relationships at any age but especially at a time when the wife is having difficulties adjusting to home situations which make her feel that her days of usefulness have ended with the end of her parental role [8].

The basic opinions the husband and wife have of each other, the concepts they hold of the roles men and women should play in marriage, both as spouse and as parent, and their concepts of sex-appropriate roles have profound influences on whether they will draw closer together as their children leave home or whether they will be separated by a spanless gulf. The success or failure of their marriage in middle age will be greatly affected by how well they adjusted to one another during the earlier years of marriage. Women often suffer from a sense of insecurity in middle age, stemming from concern about whether their husbands will still love them as they age in appearance and lose their reproductive capacity. Furthermore, women who, as girls, saw their mothers and teachers "keeping males in line," often adopt this attitude toward their husbands. While men may tolerate this during the early years of marriage, they ultimately revolt. As Clark has pointed out, "For the wife, middle-aged men are little boys with gray hair—or no hair at all—who want to be loved, but not dominated, and mothered but not smothered" [17].

Sex adjustments are important to husband-wife relationships in middle age, just as they are in the early years of marriage. While poor sexual adjustment does not necessarily lead to marital unhappiness and divorce in early marriage, it has been found to be an important contributing factor (see pages 430–433). Even when poor sexual adjustment does not lead to marital breakups, it is a serious interference to good marital adjustment. This becomes an important element in the type of adjustment that is made between husband and wife in middle age, when family ties, formerly strengthened by the responsibilities of taking care of the children, are now weakened. Middle age puts a great strain on husband-wife relationships even under the most favorable conditions, and this strain is intensified when the sexual adjustment has been unsatisfactory. Both men and women, but especially men, who feel that their sex lives have been unsatisfactory often turn to outside sources for satisfaction. This is one of the fears many women have when they realize that their hold on the husband, through the husband's feeling of responsibility toward the children, has ended. Men who have not found sexual satisfaction from their wives often feel justified in seeking satis-

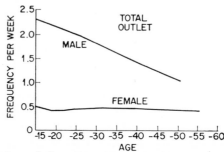

Fig. 113. Comparison of the aging patterns in the sexual interests and behavior of men and women. (*From A. C. Kinsey, W. B. Pomeroy, C. E. Martin, and P. H. Gebhard, Sexual behavior in the human female. Philadelphia: Saunders, 1953. Used by permission.*)

faction in extramarital affairs or by divorcing their wives and remarrying younger women who they believe will meet their needs better than the wives of their younger years. This is one of the reasons for labeling middle age the "dangerous age" [63].

Studies of the pattern of development of the *sex drive* have shown that the patterns are different for the two sexes, with the masculine drive stronger in adolescence and reaching its peak earlier than the female sex drive [27]. The woman's sex drive and interest, by contrast, become stronger as she approaches middle age [28] (see Figure 113). This means that, during middle age, the woman's sex pattern follows a different course than that of her husband and this, combined with differences in interest in sexual behavior, may result in marital discord [5].

Differences in the intensity of the sex drive in middle age stem from both psychological and physical causes and influence the strength of sexual desire. For the average middle-aged man, sexual desire may drop because of the earlier inhibitions of his wife or extramarital coitus as a source of substitute sex satisfaction [28]. Furthermore, the urethra may become more sensitive with advancing age and the prostate gland often gives trouble. These two common conditions lead to bladder trouble, especially at night. Erection is not as spontaneous as in younger men and there is greater difficulty in maintaining it. In addition, it takes longer to reach orgasm. If the wife is unsympathetic, this tends to increase the trouble. Men who believe they are losing their sexual vigor with aging develop feelings of inadequacy, or they may go to the opposite extreme and engage in sexual behavior with younger women to prove to themselves that such is not the case. For men who are concerned about the decline in their potency, androgen (male sex hormone) treatment is used to increase their potency [17]. It is not unusual for middle-aged men to talk less about sex and be less attracted to matters relating to sex than they were when they were younger, as has been pointed out, or they may even be disgusted and embarrassed by "dirty" stories and references to sexual matters [13].

During the forties and early fifties, many women lose their earlier inhibitions and develop more interest in sex. Because this occurs at the time when interest in sex declines for men, women are sexually unsatisfied and unhappy [8]. Some women, knowing that it is their last chance to have a child, take a last fling at childbearing and this often complicates adjustments to their husbands, who feel that a baby brings new problems at a time when they have won freedom from their parental responsibilities, or who are embarrassed at having a baby the age of their grandchildren [15]. Women who realize their husband's difficulties in erection and reaching orgasm are likely to feel that their husbands are no longer interested in intercourse or that they are no longer stimulated by their wives; women may even be embarrassed about continuing their sexual lives when they are grandmothers. The middle-aged woman who derives little satisfaction from intercourse or feels that intercourse is no longer interesting to her husband or a necessary part of marriage may take the initiative in stopping it. This adds to an already-existing belief that she is no longer needed or wanted, a belief that adds neither to her happiness nor to good adjustments with her husband [17].

Adjustment to Threats of Marital Instability. With the rising number of cases of desertion and divorce and with the changing social attitude toward divorce, marital stability is constantly threatened. Studies of desertion and divorce have shown that the most vulnerable times come within the first few years of marriage and in the forties [22] (see Figure 95, page 446). Recognizing the threat of marital breakdown, many couples seek help from marriage counselors, the usual ages for such help coming at the times when threats of divorce are greatest, between twenty-two and twenty-five years and in early middle age, between forty-one and forty-five years. The most common causes of marital difficulties in middle age are the "other woman," nagging wives, sexual incompatibility, and the claimed irresponsibility of husbands [61]. It is more often the husband than the wife who wants the divorce in middle age, though in the early years of marriage, women are often more dissatisfied with their marriages than are men and they initiate the divorce proceedings [22]. In spite of the fact that men and women, on the whole, live longer than in the past, marital stability in middle age is threatened by the *death* of the spouse, usually the husband. When the age differential between husband and wife is large, this threat is increased. In the United States census report for 1956, widowed women outnumber men by more than three to one, with about one woman in eight widowed [42]. This includes women over sixty years of age and no figures are available for the number of middle-aged widows.

Widowhood, whether due to death or divorce, presents many adjustment problems for the middle-aged man or woman, but especially for the woman. Death of a spouse in middle age means marked loneliness for the remaining spouse, and this is intensified by frustrations of the normal sex desires which are far from dormant. If the individual remains widowed for 10 or more years, he generally makes satisfactory adjustments to his single state. There is, however, a tendency to be lonely and to find the single state unsatisfactory. Those whose marriages have been happy usually react to the death of a spouse by idealizing the deceased, by escaping the loneliness through participiation in social or community organizations, or by remarrying. Those who are satisfied with widowhood are glad to be liberated from a resented mate [20]. For the man, widowhood means a disruption in the pattern of living unless he has a daughter to manage the home for him. For the woman, widowhood not only means loneliness but it often means that she is forced to give up her home, go to work, and live according to a very different pattern than she was accustomed to when her husband was alive or before her divorce [3]. There are also social complications to widowhood for the woman which men do not face. With no male escort to count on, the widowed woman may be reluctant to go out, and the problem of entertaining is likewise awkward [15].

Perhaps the most serious problem of widowhood for women, whether their widowhood is due to divorce or death, is the fact that their chances for remarriage grow slimmer as they grow older. And as women can expect to live longer than men, this means a long period of loneliness complicated by financial and social problems. Predictions based on statistics of the Metropolitan Life Insurance Company have shown that women widowed by forty years of age can expect, in 9 out of 10 cases to live for 20 more years; those widowed by fifty can expect, in 3 out of

4 cases likewise to live for 20 more years. When husband and wife are the same age, there is a 60 per cent chance that the wife will outlive the husband; when the age differential is 5 years, the chances are 70 per cent, while for a 10-year differential, the chances rise to 80 per cent [3].

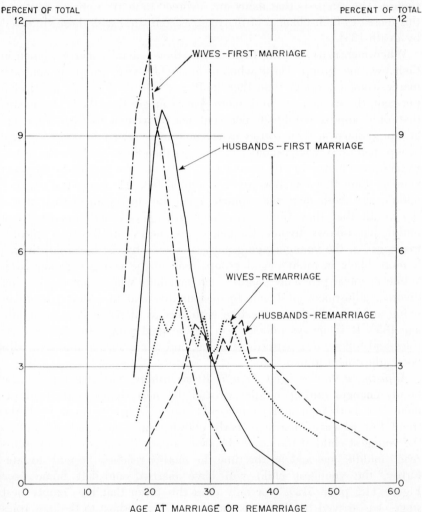

PERCENT OF TOTAL

PERCENT OF TOTAL

WIVES–FIRST MARRIAGE

HUSBANDS–FIRST MARRIAGE

WIVES–REMARRIAGE

HUSBANDS–REMARRIAGE

AGE AT MARRIAGE OR REMARRIAGE

FIG. 114. Ages of husbands and wives at first marriage and remarriage. (*From P. C. Glick and E. Landau, Age as a factor in marriage. Amer. sociol. Rev.*, 1950, 15, 517–529. *Used by permission.*)

Chances for remarriage for women who are divorced after forty-five are 50 per cent while the chances for those widowed by death are only 18 per cent [21] (see Figure 97, page 450). In Figure 114 are shown the ages of remarriage for both husbands and wives. Note how the curve drops sharply for women after forty and also for men, but less sharply for men than for women. Remarriage after divorce usually comes within the first 5 years, but one-half of the men and three-quarters of the women widowed by death have not remarried in 5 years after the death of the spouse. This suggests that many are divorced to marry someone else and this increases their chances of marriage as compared with those widowed by death [35].

When men marry during their forties, they generally marry women in their own age group. Those who are in the fifty-year group, by contrast, marry women younger than they in 76 per cent of the cases and in 3.5 per cent, the women are 30 or more years younger than they. This means that only approximately 20 per cent marry women in their own age group. Women in their forties marry men more nearly in their own age group than those who are older or younger than they. Those in the fifties, by contrast, marry mostly younger men, those who are 15 to 20 years younger than they. As Bossard has pointed out, this suggests that after middle age, both men and women "reach out to regain in their mates the youth that they themselves have lost" [7]. When remarrying in middle age follows divorce, the chances of success are less than with re-marriages in the younger age groups, as shown by the fact that divorce is more likely in middle-aged groups than in the younger groups [57]. While financial problems plague younger adults who remarry following divorce, adjustment problems to one another and to a new pattern of living are more likely to interfere with success of remarriage in middle age [35]. It is always difficult for middle-aged people to change their roles and follow new patterns of living, and this is sure to interfere with good adjustment to marriage.

Adjustment to Changed Family Relationships. The structure of the family changes during middle age and this necessitates marked adjustments for both men and women, but especially for women. With the trend toward early marriage, early childbearing, and smaller families, the youngest child of the family becomes an adolescent when his parents reach middle age, and by the time the mother reaches the mid- to late-forties, the youngest child will have married and left home (see Figure 112, page 512). Not only does this mean that the "empty nest stage" has arrived but it means the parents must adjust to the new roles of their grown children and to their in-laws and grandchildren. Adjustment to adolescent sons and daughters who are still living at home is difficult for many middle-aged parents mainly because of the marked changes in approved patterns of behavior for adolescents in recent years, especially those relating to dating. Furthermore, the marked shift from authoritarian to democratic child training in recent years means that adolescents of today, through their contacts at school, have concepts of more democratic discipline than have their parents who were brought up in homes and schools where authoritarian discipline was the approved pattern. This is especially true of rural parents and parents from the lower-middle and lower classes whose concepts of discipline, based on their own childhood experiences, conflict with those of their adolescent children, thus bringing about friction in the home [10] (see Figure 94, page 437). Even those middle-aged parents who were brought up in more democratic home environments or who have tried to keep in step with changing methods of child training often find it difficult to adjust to the new patterns of social life engaged in by the adolescents of today and this leads to friction.

IN-LAW RELATIONSHIPS. Middle-aged people who found, during their early years of marriage, that adjustments to their in-laws were difficult often find, at middle age, that their adjustments to their children's spouses are equally, if not more, difficult. There may be many reasons for this, the most important of which are living with the in-laws, expecting the same relationship to exist with one's children that existed before marriage, or expecting the same type of relationship with in-laws as with one's own children [44]. Furthermore, parents who have used authoritarian child-training methods are likely to continue to be authoritarian in their attitudes toward and treatment of their children, even after they are grown and married. While this behavior will take a new form, that of offering too many suggestions and too much advice, it is sure to lead to friction not only with the grown children but also with their spouses. It takes time for middle-aged adults to change their attitudes and patterns of behavior and this difficulty is increased when there is a strong emotional conflict involved [55]. The mother who does not want to lose her main role in life, that of parenthood, or who has a strong attachment to one of her children will find it more difficult to adjust to that child's spouse than will the mother who has other interests, who is more concerned about her child's happiness than about her own interests, or who believes that she can share love with her child after marriage by a good relationship with that child's spouse. Like any role, it takes time, effort, and motivation to learn the in-law role. Learning the mother-in-law role is more difficult than the father-in-law role because the former requires greater adjustments than the latter [44].

The type of relationship that exists between middle-aged parents and their grown children and spouses will be influenced by many factors. When the *sociocultural backgrounds* of the spouses are similar to those of the family into which they marry, especially in ethnic, religious, class, and educational backgrounds, there will be a more harmonious relationship between the parents and the in-laws than when the backgrounds are dissimilar. Under the latter conditions, relationships are likely to be strained, parents become critical of small and petty differences and tend to magnify them, and they project their personal biases into the behavior of the in-laws, often distorting this behavior and the motives behind it. Furthermore, because of the differences stemming from different backgrounds, parents are often unable to predict how their in-laws will behave and this makes them ill at ease when they are with the in-laws, a condition that does not lead to harmonious relationships. If children follow the *traditional courtship pattern*, with an engagement long enough for parents to get to know the future in-laws and their families, the relationship is usually better after marriage than when the courtship is brief, carried out without the parents' knowledge, or when the parents do not meet their future in-laws or their families until the wedding. Parents' relationships with their children's spouses are usually poor when there has been an *elopement*. The elopement may have been motivated by real or suspected parental disapproval of the proposed marriage, by the young people's objections to the type of wedding their parents want them to have, by premarital pregnancy, or other causes. But under any conditions, elopement will usually be disapproved of by the parents, it will cause them embarrassment because of gossip and will likely lower the family prestige in the eyes of others. Parents more often blame the in-law for the elopement than their own child, thus building up a resentment toward the in-law which will militate against good adjustments [55].

Residential propinquity plays an important role in determining the kind of adjustment middle-aged parents will make with their in-laws. When the married child lives in another community or another part of the same community as the parents, distance is not a serious factor in adjustment, providing the parents approve of the marriage. When they disapprove, however, distance makes it difficult to get to know the in-law better, and the disapproval usually persists or may even be intensified if there is reason for the parents to believe that residential distance was intentional, to avoid parental interference, or if they find that invitations to visit in the home of the married child or visits to the parental home are infrequent and brief. The husband who resents the amount of time his wife spends with her mother and her dependency on her mother, which often makes her resist moving away from the neighborhood in which her parents live, will antagonize his mother-in-law and cause poor relationships to exist with her and other members of the family. The husband's adjustment to his in-laws has been found to be independent of his wife's adjustment to her parents, and his adjustment to his mother-in-law negatively related to his wife's dependence on her mother. His adjustment to his father-in-law, on the other hand, is positively related to his wife's dependence on her father. The age of the married children and the number of years they have been married have been found to be unrelated to the type of adjustment middle-aged parents make to their in-laws [53].

While psychological dependency on parents may result in poor relationships between middle-aged parents and their children's spouses, *material dependency* usually strengthens family ties. This dependency may take different forms, financial help from parents, employment of sons or in-laws, helping the young people in the care of their children or in household repairs, and giving the married children and grandchildren a vacation [54]. Because many young adults marry before the husband has completed his education or has become established in business, it is often necessary to depend on the parents for help in the early years of marriage. Parents who are able to give this help feel closer to their children and in-laws than do those whose children are able to be independent. Not only does this give middle-aged parents, especially mothers, a substitute for their former parental roles but it helps to counteract any feeling they may have that their days of usefulness are over [15, 54]. Furthermore, their children's spouses are more likely to try to be on friendly terms with their in-laws when they receive help from them than when they are able to be independent. Married children with offspring of their own generally make better adjustments to their mothers and mothers-in-law than do those who have no children and who, as a result, have less need for parental help [54].

At middle age, a new in-law adjustment problem arises in many American homes, that of caring for *aged parents*. Sometimes it means bringing the parents into the home, while at other times, it means financial sacrifices on the part of middle-aged men and women to enable the parents to live in their own homes. In many cases, these aged parents need physical care as well as financial aid, or they are widowed and it is unwise or unsafe for them to try to live alone. Because women as a group outlive men, the chances are that the elderly parent who must be taken care of will be the mother of either the wife or the husband. When the elderly mother is brought into the home, the social adjustment problems are very great, not only for the middle-aged parents but also for any children who still are unmarried and living at home. If the elderly relative is the mother of one of the spouses, it means a predominantly feminine household, which many husbands find difficult to adjust to [2] (see Figure 115). A three-generation household, especially when it is predominantly feminine, is a hazardous type of family living in which the "combined virtues of a diplomat, statesman, and saint are needed" [31]. The elderly relative, having had considerable authority in his or her own home in the past, does not find it easy to relinquish this power to even a grown child, and especially not to an in-law. Middle-aged husbands and wives, freed from most of the financial burdens of caring for their own children and the restrictions placed on their activities when the children were younger, often resent the added financial burden created by the care of an elderly in-law, the extra work the care of this elderly in-law makes, and the restraints on their independence. Husbands are more resentful when the relative is an in-law than when it is a member of his own family, as is true of the wife. When husband-wife relationships are strained in middle age, the in-law problem often strains them to the breaking point [30].

Adjustments to elderly in-laws are not limited to middle-aged parents. They affect the adjustments the parents make to their own children and to the friction caused by the presence of a member of the older generation in the home. When the elderly in-law interferes with the parental

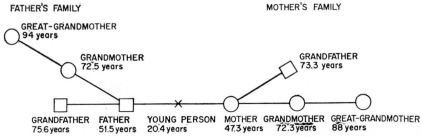

Fig. 115. Pattern of an elongated family. (*From R. Albrecht, Intergeneration parent patterns. J. Home Econ., 1954, 46, 29–32. Used by permission.*)

authority over the adolescent children or tries to use the authoritarian methods of his own generation, resentments and friction are created which intensify the difficulties of adjustment between middle-aged parents and their children. Furthermore, parents who find the care of the elderly relative difficult often are reluctant to have their children marry and leave home, thus putting all the burden of care on the middle-aged parent. While this burden may help to fill the gap created when their children leave home, the substitute satisfaction they derive from the companionship of an elderly relative may be far from adequate and may even intensify parental loneliness [2].

How well the middle-aged person adjusts to the elderly parent, whether his own or his spouse's, will be markedly influenced by the type of experiences he has had in the past with that individual. The individual who felt, in childhood or adolescence, that he was rejected by his parent, that he was forced to work too hard at home, or that he was socially handicapped by his parent's occupation and the socioeconomic status of the family, will not make as good adjustments to his parent in middle age as will the individual whose relationships with his parent in earlier life were more satisfactory. His attitude will likewise be affected by whether the parent is his real parent or a stepparent. As Albrecht has pointed out, "It is no longer realistic to take for granted that all people love their parents, or that all parents love their children" [1]. How satisfactory an adjustment is made to having to care for an elderly in-law in the home or elsewhere will be influenced likewise by earlier relationships with that in-law. Parents who approve of the marriage of their child generally get along better, both before and after marriage, with their in-laws than do those who disapprove of the marriage. Furthermore, those who learn to play the "in-law role," whether it be the mother-in-law or father-in-law role, satisfactorily in the early years of their child's marriage are guaranteed better adjustments to their children and their children's spouses as they grow older and become partially or totally dependent on them for help and support [44, 55]. In turn, middle-aged adults make better adjustments to in-law responsibilities when their attitudes toward their in-laws are favorable, just as is true of their adjustments to their own parents who require their help [1].

Adjustment to Singleness. Only about 8 per cent of the adult population of the United States today is unmarried and of this group, there are more men than women [42]. By middle age, most of this group have adjusted themselves to singleness and are reasonably happy with the pattern of life they have established for themselves. However, some of those who went through the early adult years without marrying decide to do so at middle age. A sample group of men and women who married late in life showed that among the men who married in the forties, there was an equal number of first marriages and remarriages after divorce or death of the wife; in the fifties, only one out of every six marriages was a first marriage. In the case of women, the ratio of remarriages to first marriages in the forties was two to one, while in the fifties, only one out of seven marriages was a first marriage. While men and women in the forties tend to marry people from their own age group, those in the fifties more often marry individuals younger than they. This is true for women just as it is for men [7]. If this sample study is representative of the population at large, it suggests that the middle-aged woman's chances of marriage are less than those of the middle-aged man.

Most women are realistic enough to know that after they pass forty, their chances for marriage grow slimmer every year. This is far more true for single women than for widows or divorcees. After forty-five, for example, the single woman's chances of marriage are 9 out of 100 as compared with 50 out of 100 for divorcees and 18 out of 100 for widows [35] (see Figure 97, page 450). Knowing how slim her chances of marriage are, the middle-aged single woman accepts the fact that her life pattern must be adjusted to this and, as a result, her desire to marry is replaced by vocational goals [34]. See Figure 98, page 452, for a graphic illustration of this shift. However, problems of employment and of advancement are even more serious for the middle-aged woman than for the man. Should she lose her job, her chances of reemployment are even less than those for men and, should she be fortunate enough to get a job, it usually means a cut in salary and a job with less responsibility and less prestige. Women who hold their jobs through middle age are far less often promoted to positions of prestige and responsibility than are men, and they must face an earlier retirement age in most companies. As a result of these practices, vocational goals are not always a satisfactory substitute for family and home, with the security these normally bring. Worries about economic security and frustrations arising from the realization that promotion is blocked more because she is a woman than because of lack of ability, make middle age a less happy period for women than early adulthood, when job security was taken for granted and when there was always the possibility of marriage.

To add to her adjustment problems, it is usually the single woman of the family who is expected to assume the responsibility of caring for an elderly parent who is left alone after the death of the spouse, or for both parents, if their health is such that they cannot get along alone. This often adds a financial burden to the burden of caring for the elderly while holding down a job [1]. In many families, it is assumed that the unmarried woman is financially able to carry this burden, as she has only herself to support, and that she has plenty of time, which married members of the family lack. Were it not for imminent retirement or the constant worry of losing her job and being unemployed, the financial responsibility of parental care might not mean serious adjustment problems for the unmarried woman. Were it not also for the fact that advancing age means a drain on her strength, the extra work involved in caring for elderly parents could more easily be adjusted to. Furthermore, this new responsibility generally means limiting her social life, with the result that the middle-aged woman often cuts off social contacts and activities in community organizations so drastically that when the care of the parent ends with the parent's death, the middle-aged woman finds herself far lonelier than the middle-aged widow, who usually has her children or the friends she has known during the years of her marriage to fall back on for companionship.

The role of the single man in middle age is usually more favorable than that of the woman. Because he has not had the responsibilities of a family through the early adult years, he has been able to devote as much time as he wished to his business and he has been free to move to areas where greater opportunities were available. As business success necessitates hard work and willingness to adapt oneself to new situations, should this be necessary, the middle-aged man is usually better rewarded for his past efforts than is the middle-aged woman who has followed the same pattern of hard work and personal sacrifice in the earlier years. When promotions are made, they usually go to the man [6]. The middle-aged bachelor, therefore, is generally at the peak of his career and he has little reason to be concerned about unemployment, unless his health fails [36]. If he finds himself lonely, there will be little difficulty in finding a wife and making a reasonably happy marriage. As has already been stressed, the chances for marriage for single men in middle age are greater than those for women. When men remain single, it is more often from choice than from necessity. Furthermore, the man will not be handicapped by the problems of caring for elderly parents unless there are no other family members able to assume this responsibility. When he must take over this responsibility, he usually does so by financial aid rather than by sacrificing his time and efforts to take care of their needs. Consequently, he is free to make the type of life he wishes and has relatively few problems of adjustment of the sort the middle-aged single woman must face.

ADJUSTMENT TO APPROACHING OLD AGE

Until recent years, few people lived to old age and those who did so had few adjustment problems to face. If they were in good health, they could continue to follow the pattern of life they had been accustomed to follow with few modifications. There were no compulsory retirement policies in effect and, as most men were self-employed, they could work as much or as little as they wished. They were not forced out of their jobs and cut off from doing things that interested them just because they had reached a certain age. With larger families and closer family ties than exist today, women in the past who survived middle age could expect to face old age with the feeling that their families would take care of them if they were widowed and that they would be welcome in the homes of married children. Furthermore, there was always the possibility that the "baby of the family," grown to adulthood, would still remain under the parental roof to take care of a widowed parent, whether he was single or married. Thus, middle-aged women of past generations had little to worry about in relation to approaching old age. Like the men of their generation, they could look forward to security and reasonable happiness, knowing that if they survived their contemporaries, they could always count on their children for financial help and care, if this were needed.

Most of the conditions that contributed to security and happiness during old age in the past no longer exist. And because an increasing number of men and women live into the old-age period of life today, the problem of adjusting to conditions affecting them has become a major one. In recent years, it has been recognized by many business and industrial organizations that they owe it to their employees to help them to adjust to the problems of retirement since the employers are largely responsible for creating these problems. At first, the main emphasis was on stressing the importance of saving and investing in pension funds that would guarantee an income after retirement. It soon became apparent that problems more difficult to meet than financial problems should be included in this preparation for old age and, as a result, some large corporations today run series of lectures and provide individual counseling for employees who will soon reach the retirement age. This has brought to the attention of many laymen what psychologists have stressed for a number of years, the fact that adjustment to any problem is made more quickly and with less emotional stress if one is prepared ahead of time for it. The longer the individual has to prepare and the more aspects of the situation he explores and understands, the better prepared he will be to adjust to a problem, even though it may differ in its major aspects from what he had anticipated during the period of preparation [40]. It is now agreed among experts in the areas of *gerontology* (the branch of psychology that studies the problems of old age) and of *geriatrics* (the branch of medicine that studies the diseases of old age) that preparation for old age and retirement should begin in middle age.

Because social attitudes toward old age are, for the most part, unfavorable and, as a result, old age is an even more dreaded period of life than middle age, many men and women resist any attempts to help them to prepare for approaching old age. This is a problem constantly met by doctors. Advice to a middle-aged man to "slow down and take things easy" is usually ignored until a heart attack or some other serious illness persuades the man that the doctor knew what he was talking about when he gave the advice. Similarly, the middle-aged woman often refuses to accept the advice of her husband and friends to develop interests outside the home in preparation for the time when her duties as housewife and mother will be reduced to a minimum. She believes that her children will always need her, as they have during their years of growing up. Then, when the time comes for them to leave home and establish homes of their own, she is faced with a traumatic experience for which she is ill prepared but which she could have spared herself had she been willing to face a fact which she dreaded, the fact that she was no longer as necessary to her children as she was when they were dependent children. Because far too many middle-aged men and women dread approaching old age, a dread based on their acceptance of the unfavorable stereotype so widely held in our culture, they reach old age with too little preparation to make the necessary adjustments to the problems that this age brings. As a result, they find old age one of the most, if not the most, unsatisfactory periods of life [60].

Areas of Preparation. The ability to live a happy, useful life at any age is greatly influenced by the *health* of the individual. Even the school-age child cannot do good schoolwork or make satisfactory social adjustments if he is in poor health. And because the demands of adult life are more exacting than those on the child, the adult whose strength, endurance, and general health condition are inferior to those of his contemporaries is at a disadvantage in whatever he undertakes. Medical research has shown that, as the years advance, different parts of the body show the effects of wear and tear. Preparation for old age should consist, therefore, of health measures which are not designed primarily to increase the individual's life span but rather to prevent chronic and progressive diseases which will impair the efficiency and happiness of old age. Attention to diet, pace of activity, and work load, for example, will go far to enable the organs of the body that are functioning at a lower level of efficiency than they did in the earlier years of life to continue to function efficiently throughout the remaining years of life [14]. Many of the serious and debilitating diseases of old age could be prevented or at least mitigated if they were recognized and treated during middle age. With more health education, middle-aged people would know how to live so that they could keep themselves in good health as they grow older. This would help to prevent the development of the chronic illnesses which are so common in old age [40].

Preparation for *retirement* is limited, in the case of most middle-aged men, to building up a financial reserve in the form of pensions, savings accounts, investments, or social security benefits for the time when the pay check no longer comes in. They look forward to the day when they will no longer have to work and when their time will be their own to do with as they wish (see Figure 109, page 502). Few realize that with retirement will come progressive physical handicaps, a feeling of uselessness, lack of social contacts, loneliness, boredom, and inactivity. Because, in most cases, income after retirement is less than during the working years, it often means changing the pattern of living, giving up many of the activities formerly engaged in, and even moving into smaller quarters or living with a married child. All of the changes in pattern of living that come with retirement tend to increase the feeling of uselessness and boredom which, in turn, aggravate any physical ailment that might be present. Thus the retired person is usually unhappy and he makes his wife and other members of the family unhappy too. When there is preparation during middle age for retirement through the building up of new interests and engaging in new activities which can later be substituted for work, the retired person makes better adjustments to old age and is, as a result, happier than the one who makes no preparations and whose unrealistic idealization of retirement makes actual retirement a traumatic experience for him [59].

Middle age is the time to prepare the individual for the role changes which are an inevitable accomplishment of old age. The objectives of this education include giving the middle-aged person knowledge of the physical and psychological changes which will occur so that he can understand them when they occur and make suitable adjustments to them; providing new knowledge and skills as a basis for continuing employment, volunteer services, and creative expression; education for the enjoyment of the arts, for intelligent citizenship, and the postponement of mental deterioration; upsetting the prevailing stereotype of aging and substituting for it constructive concepts with favorable social attitudes; and education to provide the specialized knowledge required by those working with older people [59]. It is recognized today that when the individual is prepared, psychologically, during middle age for what he can expect in old age, he makes far better adjustments than when such preparation is lacking. This is well illustrated in the case of community organizations planned for the elderly. In one community with a large old-age population it was found that over one-half of the elderly residents belonged to none of these community organizations and only one-third belonged to one. Very few belonged to more than one organization and those who did join attended the meetings only irregularly. Fewer women than men belonged and fewer married than single people. Because they had not learned to enjoy such activities when they were younger and had not developed interests in community organizations during middle age, they were unprepared to take advantage of these substitutes for the loneliness, boredom, and inactivity which make old age an unhappy period of life for many men and women [62].

Family plans for old age should occupy the attention of most middle-aged people but few prepare themselves realistically for where and how they will live when they are old or when they reach the retirement age. In order to determine middle-age attitudes toward the future and the plans made for it, a group of middle-aged people were asked what bothers them most about old age and what plans they have for it. Sources of concern centered mainly around lack of financial security, health, who will take care of them, being a "bother" or a dependent, and having nothing to look forward to. Of the group questioned, 17 per cent claimed that they never thought about old age and the problems it brings. When questioned about their family plans, most felt it was the responsibility of families to help older people, either wholly or in part, if they cannot take care of themselves. Most of the group objected to homes for the aged or to being cared for by the government on the grounds that this was a family duty.

Living with their married children or other relatives was contemplated by only 15 per cent of the group while 30 per cent claimed that under no circumstance would they do so. Most claimed that only in cases of disability or actual necessity would they live with their married children. Their objections were based on the belief that this would give them no privacy or independence, that it would mean too crowded living quarters, and that they would feel that they were in the way. In cases of chronic illness or disability, about half claimed that they would rely on their families, live on insurance, or hire a housekeeper, while the other half said they had no plans [49]. It is true that in this area of planning for old age, as in the case of retirement, the usual attitude of middle-aged people is to ignore the problems of the future because they are unpleasant and to wait until the problems actually arise before tackling them. Until this attitude is replaced with a constructive approach to old age, widely accepted by men and women of all social and occupational groups, few will be prepared to meet the problems of old age, to make satisfactory adjustments to them, and to look upon old age as the time when they will reap the harvest for the years of toil that have preceded old age. In emphasizing the importance of preparation for old age, Kuhlen has pointed out that

> Programs designed to foster continuous learning and broad participation in life *throughout the adult years* (in the 30's, 40's, and 50's) will promote the development of the kinds of habits and personal resources (knowledge, skills, attitudes, and appreciations) which will make for good adjustment both at present age and later in old age. . . . The most effective educational program for *old age* is a program of *adult* education which is broad and varied in scope and which is sensitive to the needs of all ages including those in the older years [33].

BIBLIOGRAPHY

1. Albrecht, R.: Relationships of older people with their own parents. *Marriage Fam. Living*, 1953, 15, 296–298.
2. Albrecht, R.: Intergeneration parent patterns. *J. Home Econ.*, 1954, 46, 29–32.
3. Alvarez, W. E.: The duration of widowhood. *Geriatrics*, 1955, 10, 297.
4. Belbin, R. M.: Difficulties of older people in industry. *Occup. Psychol.*, 1953, 27, 177–190.
5. Benedek, T.: Climacterium: a developmental phase. *Psychoanal. Quart.*, 1950, 19, 1–27.
6. Boring, E. G.: The woman problem. *Amer. Psychologist*, 1951, 6, 679–692.
7. Bossard, J. H. S.: Marrying late in life. *Soc. Forces*, 1951, 29, 405–408.
8. Bossard, J. H. S., and E. S. Boll: Marital unhappiness in the life cycle. *Marriage Fam. Living*, 1955, 17, 10–14.

9. Bowers, W. H.: An appraisal of worker characteristics as related to age. *J. appl. Psychol.*, 1952, 36, 296–300.

10. Briggs, V., and L. R. Schulz: Parental response to concepts of parent-adolescent relationships. *Child Develpm.*, 1955, 26, 279–284.

11. Brozek, J.: The age problem in research workers: psychological view point. *Sci. Mon., N.Y.*, 1951, 72, 355–359.

12. Brozek, J.: Personality of young and middle-aged normal men: an analysis of a psychosomatic inventory. *J. Geront.*, 1952, 7, 410–418.

13. Brozek, J.: Personality changes with age: an item analysis of the Minnesota Multiphasic Personality Inventory. *J. Geront.*, 1955, 10, 194–206.

14. Carlson, A. J., and E. J. Stieglitz: Physiological changes in aging. *Ann. Amer. Acad. pol. soc. Sci.*, 1952, 279, 18–31.

15. Cavan, R. S.: Adjustment problems of the older woman. *Marriage Fam. Living*, 1952, 14, 16–18.

16. Clague, E.: The age problem in research workers: sociological view point. *Sci. Mon., N.Y.*, 1951, 72, 359–363.

17. Clark, L. M.: Sex life in the middle-aged. *Marriage Fam. Living*, 1949, 11, 58–60.

18. Desmond, T. C.: America's unknown middle-agers. *The New York Times*, 1956, July 29.

19. Feintuch, A.: Improving the employability and attitudes of "difficult-to-place" persons. *Psychol. Monogr.*, 1955, 69, No. 7.

20. Fried, E. G., and K. Stern: The situation of the aged within the family. *Amer. J. Orthopsychiat.*, 1948, 18, 31–54.

21. Glick, P. C.: The life cycle of the family. *Marriage Fam. Living*, 1955, 17, 3–9.

22. Glick, P. C., and E. Landau: Age as a factor in marriage. *Amer. sociol. Rev.*, 1950, 15, 517–529.

23. Gravatt, A. E.: Family relations in middle and old age—a review. *J. Geront.*, 1953, 8, 197–201.

24. Gumpert, M.: Our "Inca" ideas about retirement. *The New York Times*, 1952, July, 27.

25. Hiltner, H. J.: Changing family tasks of adults. *Marriage Fam. Living*, 1953, 15, 110–113.

26. King, H. F.: The response of the older rural craftsman to individual training. *J. Geront.*, 1955, 10, 207–211.

27. Kinsey, A. C., W. B. Pomeroy, and C. E. Martin: *Sexual behavior in the human male*. Philadelphia: Saunders, 1948.

28. Kinsey, A. C., W. B. Pomeroy, C. E. Martin, and P. H. Gebhard: *Sexual behavior in the human female*. Philadelphia: Saunders, 1953.

29. Kirchner, W. K., and M. D. Dunnette: Attitudes toward older workers. *Personnel Psychol.*, 1954, 7, 257–265.

30. Koller, M. R.: Studies of three-generation households. *Marriage Fam. Living*, 1954, 16, 205–206.

31. Komarovsky, M.: Functional analysis of sex roles. *Amer. sociol. Rev.*, 1950, 15, 508–516.

32. Kuhlen, R. G.: Age differences in personality during adult years. *Psychol. Bull.*, 1945, 42, 333–358.

33. Kuhlen, R. G.: *Education for the aged and for the aging: background generalizations and recommendations for the subcommittees on education and recreation for the aged.* Syracuse, N.Y.: Syracuse Univer. Press, 1955.

34. Kuhlen, R. G., and G. H. Johnson: Changes in goals with adult increasing age. *J. consult. Psychol.*, 1952, 16, 1–4.

35. Landis, P. H.: Sequential marriage. *J. Home Econ.*, 1950, 42, 625–627.
36. Lehman, H. C.: *Age and achievement.* Princeton, N.J.: Princeton Univer. Press, 1953.
37. Lehman, H. C.: Jobs for those over sixty-five. *J. Geront.*, 1955, 10, 345–357.
38. Maher, H.: Age and performance of two work groups. *J. Geront.*, 1955, 10, 448–451.
39. McFarland, R. A.: Psycho-physiological problems of aging in air transport pilots. *J. Aviation Med.*, 1954, 25, 210–220.
40. New York Times Report: Planning urged to aid the aged. *The New York Times*, 1955, July 3.
41. New York Times Report: U.S. to seek jobs for older women. *The New York Times*, 1956, Oct. 3.
42. New York Times Report: U.S. reports rise in married total. *The New York Times*, 1956, Oct. 31.
43. New York Times Report: Working mothers play bigger role. *The New York Times*, 1956, Nov. 25.
44. New York Times Report: Like any role, mother-in-law takes learning. *The New York Times*, 1957, Jan. 17.
45. O'Donnell, W. G.: The problem of age barriers in personnel selection. *Personnel*, 1951, 27, 461–471.
46. Pressey, S. L.: Employment potentialities in age, and means for their possible increase. N.Y. *State Joint Legislative Committee on Problems of the Aging*, 1956, 92–94.
47. Pressey, S. L., and R. G. Kuhlen: *Psychological development through the life span.* New York: Harper, 1957.
48. Rose, A. M.: Factors associated with the life satisfactions of middle-class, middle-aged persons. *Marriage Fam. Living*, 1955, 17, 15–19.
49. Smith, W. M.: Family plans for later years. *Marriage Fam. Living*, 1954, 16, 36–40.
50. Spealman, C. R., and P. T. Bruyere: The changing age distribution of pilots holding first class medical certificates. *J. Geront.*, 1955, 10, 341–344.
51. Stanton, J. E.: Part-time employment for the older worker. *J. appl. Psychol.*, 1951, 35, 418–421.
52. Stone, A., and L. Levine: The dynamics of the marital relationship. *Ment. Hyg., N.Y.*, 1953, 37, 606–614.
53. Stryker, S.: The adjustment of married offspring to their parents. *Amer. sociol. Rev.*, 1955, 20, 149–154.
54. Sussman, M. B.: The help pattern of the middle class family. *Amer. sociol. Rev.*, 1953, 18, 22–28.
55. Sussman, M. B.: Family continuity: selective factors which affect relationships between families at generational levels. *Marriage Fam. Living*, 1954, 16, 112–120.
56. Sussman, M. B.: Activity patterns of post-parental couples and their relationship to family continuity. *Marriage Fam. Living*, 1955, 17, 338–341.
57. Tarver, J. D.: Age at marriage and duration of marriage of divorced couples. *Sociol. soc. Res.*, 1951, 36, 102–106.
58. Tibbitts, C.: Retirement problems in American society. *Amer. J. Sociol.*, 1954, 59, 301–308.
59. Tibbitts, C., and W. Donahue: Developments in education for later maturity. *Rev. educ. Res.*, 1953, 23, 202–217.
60. Tuckman, J., and I. Lorge: The best years of life: a study in ranking. *J. Psychol.*, 1952, 34, 137–149.

61. Turner, F. B.: Common characteristics among persons seeking professional marriage counseling. *Marriage Fam. Living,* 1954, 16, 143–144.
62. Webber, I. L.: The organized social life of the retired: two Florida communities. *Amer. J. Sociol.,* 1954, 59, 340–346.
63. Werner, A. A.: Sex behavior and problems of the climacteric. *In* M. Fishbein and E. W. Burgess, *Successful marriage,* rev. ed. Garden City, N.Y.: Doubleday, 1955. Pp. 475–490.

» 14 «

Old Age

Old age is the closing period in the life span, the time when the individual looks back on life, lives on present accomplishments, and begins to finish off his life course [16, 82]. With age comes a decline, a regression, or a return to an earlier pattern of behavior and a simpler level of function. While marked individual differences exist in the ages at which physical and mental decline set in, sixty years is taken as the arbitrary dividing line between middle and old age. Thus, traditionally, old age extends from 60 years of age until death. Chronological age is a poor criterion to use in marking off the beginning of old age because there are such marked differences between individuals in the age at which aging actually begins. Most men and women today, because of better living conditions and better medical care, do not show the physical and mental characteristics of decline until the mid-sixties or even early seventies, but the traditional dividing line is still used. Whether this will be a short or long period will be determined by how long the individual lives. For some, old age is one of the longest periods in the life span while for others, it is one of the shortest. Some individuals never reach old age, having died or been killed during one of the earlier periods in life.

Period of Decline. Because old age is a period of decline, whether slow or rapid, it gives rise to the belief that the individual has entered his "second childhood." Such, however, is infrequently true. Decline in mental and physical abilities is at first slight and is often compensated for by the use of past knowledge. With aging, the individual may have less strength, vigor, and speed of reaction but he compensates for this by increase in skill. In driving, his slower reactions may make him more

537

accident-prone but he compensates for this by driving more slowly, by taking fewer chances, and by not driving when conditions are hazardous [22]. The period of old age when the decline is slow and gradual and when compensations can be made for the declines that take place is known as "senescence." The individual may become senescent in the fifties or not until the early or late sixties, depending upon the rate of physical and mental decline. "Senility," in contrast to senescence, means the period of old age when a more or less complete physical breakdown takes place and when there is mental disorganization. The individual who becomes eccentric, careless, absent-minded, socially withdrawn, and poorly adjusted is usually described as "senile" [2]. Senility may come as early as the fifties or it may never occur because the individual dies before deterioration sets in. Many more people become senescent than senile. As a general rule, the senescent individual finds adjustments more difficult than does the senile person because the former is aware of the slipping, over which he can exercise little or no control, while the latter is so mentally disorganized that he is incapable of recognizing how rapidly he is slipping [48].

Causes of Decline. Decline comes partly from physical and partly from psychological factors. There are *structural changes* in the "matrix" of the tissues, the fibers and fluids through which nutrients are brought to living cells and waste products removed, rather than in the cells themselves. These changes in the matrix interfere with the nutrition of the cells and cause them to degenerate. Cell changes with aging are not due to specific diseases but to the aging process. They are of different types, the most important of which are: gradual tissue drying; gradual retardation of cell division, the capacity of cell growth, and tissue repair; gradual retardation of the rate of tissue oxidation, or lowering of the speed of living; cellular atrophy, degeneration, increased cell pigmentation, and fatty infiltration; gradual decrease in tissue elasticity and degenerative changes in the elastic connective tissue of the body; progressive degeneration and atrophy of the nervous system; and general impairment of the mechanisms which maintain a fairly constant internal environment for the cells and tissues (homeostasis) [22]. The aging process is accelerated by the accumulation of such substances as iron and calcium in the cytoplasm, the jellylike material of the cell, thus affecting the permeability of the cell material to food and waste products [87].

Psychological aging does not necessarily parallel physical changes. Unfavorable attitudes toward self, other people, work, and life in general can lead to senility just as changes in the brain tissue can. Individuals who have no sustaining interests after retirement are likely to become depressed and disorganized. As a result, they go downhill both physically and mentally and may soon die. About one-half of the mental patients in the old-age groups have been found to have functional disorders due to psychological factors rather than to brain disease [27]. Individuals who are poorly adjusted to the roles they must play in old age have been found to become senile sooner than those who make more satisfactory adjustments [2]. How the individual takes the strains and stresses of living will affect the rate of his decline. The psychological causes of aging are often more pronounced than the physical and, when combined with the physical, accelerate the aging process by speeding up the rate of decline. As Havigurst and Albrecht have pointed out, "What old age will be like appears to depend partly upon physical constitution and partly upon the kind of life that has been led" [50].

Motivation plays a very important role in decline. The individual who has little motivation to learn new things or to keep up-to-date in appearance, attitudes, or patterns of behavior will go downhill much faster than the individual of the same chronological and physical age whose motivation to ward off aging is stronger [102]. The new leisure which comes with retirement from work or lessening of home responsibilities often brings boredom, which lowers the individual's motivation [82]. The gap between the individual's potential, in terms of physical and psychological achievement, and his actual performance (see Figure 101, page 466) is largely due to lack of motivation. As Still has pointed out, in answer to the question of why do so many fail to achieve their physical and mental potentials, "It seems pretty clear that it is not because of poor heredity but because they fail to discover that they are able, if they choose, to make more of their lives. How to prevent these failures constitutes one of the great unsolved questions facing our society today" [103].

Rejuvenation. Because the sex hormones, when deficient, play such an important role in aging, attempts have been made to rejuvenate aging people by means of sex hormone therapy. Recent experiments have shown that it is impossible to rejuvenate or to make aging people young again. The administration of hormones can, however, build up the health and vigor of the individual, thus slowing down the rate of aging [62]. The new technique of *plasmapheresis*, which consists of removing whole blood, separating it from its plasma, and then immediately returning the red blood cells, is proving to be a definite check on the aging process. Because the aging body is unable to eliminate the gradual accumulation of toxic substances, the periodic "washing" of the elderly person's blood to remove toxic substances gives promise of slowing down the pace of aging [67]. At the present time, evidence points to the fact that all one can do to stave off the process of aging is to deal with its secondary causes, and to improve one's general health condition and manner of living. As Kallman and Sander have stressed, "Within the genetically controlled limits of variability, human life can be lengthened or shortened by outside factors and the degree of efficiency in utilizing constitutional potentialities, but in terms of present knowledge it cannot be prolonged beyond the present boundaries of man's vital capacity" [55].

Individual Differences. As is true of every period in the life span, there are marked differences between individuals of the same chronological age during the period of old age. Individual differences in the effects of age have been recognized for many centuries. Cicero, for example, in his *De Senectute,* stressed this in his reference to the popular belief that aging makes people difficult to live with. Thus according to him, "As it is not every wine, so it is not every disposition that grows sour with age." Just as there is no pattern of physical and mental development that will fit all, so it is with mental and physical decline. There are no traits that may be found in the aged alone nor are there any that may be described as *typical* of old age. Aging affects different people differently and takes place at different rates for the two sexes; in addition, it is influenced by different hereditary, socioeconomic, and educational backgrounds [22]. Studies of vision, hearing, muscular strength, reaction time, complex psychomotor performance, job performance, and accidents have shown great individual differences at every age, among those who are old as well as among those who are young. As a result, it is impossible to classify anyone as "typically old" or any trait as "typically that of an oldster."

Older people, it has been found, fall into three general categories, each with its own peculiar characteristics. However, within these general categories, there are individual differences, with some people having the traits characteristic of the category in more highly developed forms than others. The three categories are the autonomous, the adjusted, and the anomic. The *autonomous* are characterized by creative activity and an aliveness of spirit that keeps the body alive. They are relatively immune to cultural changes and, for them, aging brings increases in wisdom without losses in spontaneity. They are not necessarily balanced or well-adjusted individuals and, in numbers, they represent a relatively small group. The *adjusted* are those who carry out the tasks given them by the environment and are kept alert by these tasks. The environment provides a "protective surrounding" for them and they can maintain themselves only so long as the cultural situation remains favorable. The third category consists of the *anomic,* who decay as soon as physical vitality is lost because the culture no longer supports them. They are unable to function independently and must rely upon the forces that come from the cultural environment [92].

Aging progresses at *different rates* for different physical and mental characteristics, generally at diminishing rates as the individual grows older. As a general rule, physical aging precedes mental aging, though this is not always the case. Sometimes the reverse occurs, especially when the individual believes he is growing old and, as a result, lets go mentally when the first signs of physical aging appear. As Stieglitz has pointed out, there is "greater danger of wearing out from disuse than from sensible activity" [102]. The life span of the different organs or systems within the human organism are different. The ovaries, for example, function for a predictable number of years and then become dormant. Disease may hasten the menopause just as accident or disease may hasten the loss of elasticity in the lens of the eyes. Normally, however, the life span of the different organs is determined by some "peculiar and obscure physiological time clock inherent within some particular genes of the hereditary constitution" [22]. There are also individual differences in *mental aging*, with some abilities declining sooner than others. Analysis of subtests in a general intelligence test has shown that the least decline occurs in tests of information, vocabulary, and comprehension while the greatest decline comes in tests for block design, picture arrangement, and digit symbol. Judgment and comprehension generally show an increase with age. These differences in rates of decline of mental functions may, however, be the result of pressure under test conditions rather than indications of decline under normal circumstances [37].

SOCIAL PROBLEMS OF OLD AGE

In recent years, the aged have created many social problems that have never before existed to such a marked degree or had such a strong influence on the lives of such large segments of the population. The most important social problems created by the aged are as follows:

Increase in Number of Aged. How marked the increase in life span has been in recent years can best be appreciated by comparing the average life expectancy of men and women today with that of men and women of the past. In Rome, the mean length of life was 23 years, and in Greece, it was 29.4 years. The first American life tables, "Wiggleworth's Table," constructed from data gathered in several towns in Massachusetts and New Hampshire, appeared in 1789 and showed the mean life expectancy at that time to be 35.5 years. By 1850, the life expectancy had risen to 40 years, by 1940, to 49.2 years, and by 1954, to 69.6 years. The greatest increase in life expectancy has been in white females, 73.6 years, and in white males, 67.4 years. The life expectancy for nonwhite females at the present time is 65.8 years and for nonwhite males, 61.0 years [81] (see Figure 116 for life expectancy among whites and nonwhites). Because the life expectancy for males is less than for females, the ratio of males to females has changed in favor of the females. In 1900, the ratio of males to females in America was 106 to 100; now it is 96.6 to 100. In the age group of sixty-five and over, the ratio is 85.7 males to 100 females [88]. The life expectancy for people in the urban areas is greater than for those in rural areas [47].

Not only is the number of old people becoming greater but the *proportions* of old people in the total population are likewise becoming steadily greater (see Figure 117). The number of people sixty-five years of age or older has risen from 3 million in 1900 to 14 million 1955, and it is predicted that by 1975 the number will rise to 21 million [81]. There has been a quadrupling of the number of old people since the turn of the century and it is estimated that the increase is taking place at the rate of 1,000 daily. The decline in the birth rate during the past fifty years means that there are fewer individuals in the younger age groups, while a decline in mortality at all ages, due to better health conditions and better medical treatment for illness, means that there are more old people. There is, thus, an increase in the proportions of the total population in the upper age levels. These proportions are likely to continue to increase as medical science improves the treatment of heart diseases and cancer, the two

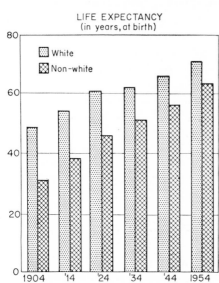

FIG. 116. Life expectancy for whites and nonwhites, according to the year of birth. Estimates based on U.S. Census Bureau figures. (*From The New York Times, Feb. 17, 1957. Used by permission.*)

most common "killers" of the aged [107]. Though the maximal length of life has not been appreciably increased, the number of individuals who live to a ripe old age has been increasing steadily for the past few generations. As Goodenough has expressed it, "The average span of life has increased not so much because the old live to be older but because a greater number of the young live to be old" [44].

Some of the important effects of the gradually increasing proportions of old people in the population have already begun to be felt. Of the effects, the most important noted to date are as follows: fall in standards of living due to the burden of old people on those of productive age, a dependency brought about by the failure of some to provide for their old age when they were younger and the inability of others among the aged to work; greater conservatism because of the larger number of old people in society and their resistance to departures from the accustomed ways; concerted action against daily risks of life because of the conservatism of age; a disturbance in the sex ratio in favor of women, which may upset the social and economic balance of life in old age; and the subjection of a large portion of the population to idleness with the resulting feelings of inadequacy and uselessness which can and often do lead to mental disorders serious enough to necessitate institutional care.

Economic Status. When a population is primarily rural, care of the

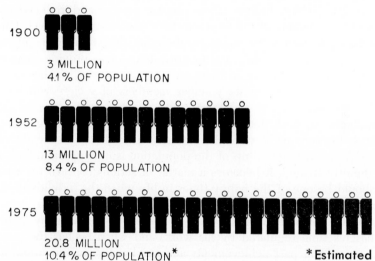

1900

3 MILLION
4.1% OF POPULATION

1952

13 MILLION
8.4% OF POPULATION

1975

20.8 MILLION
10.4% OF POPULATION*   *Estimated

Fig. 117. The percentage of the population sixty-five years and over has more than doubled since 1900 and is still growing. (*From M. Gumpert, Our "Inca" ideas about retirement. The New York Times, July 27, 1952. Used by permission.*)

aged does not present a problem of any real significance for the younger generation. But when a population becomes primarily urban, as is true in America today, and when the trend is toward smaller homes, smaller families, and simplified living, the aged become a real burden for the younger generation to fit into their lives. An extra room for an elderly parent means a dislocation of the entire family living arrangements in many cases and an added burden on the family budget to provide the necessary food for an extra family member. The role and function in society of elderly people have been greatly disturbed and lowered by the transition from rural to urban economy. Many of the problems associated with old age are thus not the result of old age per se but rather of the socioeconomic problems old age presents.

How great the economic burden of old age is may be appreciated better when one realizes that only about one-third of all Americans over sixty-five years of age are self-supporting. The remaining two-thirds must depend in part or in whole on outside help. In 1954, 5,300,000 of the 14 million people in America who were over sixty-five years of age received old age or survivor's insurance; by 1980, almost all retired people will be eligible for these benefits. Until the depression years of the thirties, half of the aged were supported primarily by relatives and friends; at the present, only about 10 per cent are [86]. This is not the result of a decrease in family affection or a sense of loyalty on the part of members of the family but is caused rather, by such factors as the high cost of living, higher taxes, smaller homes, and reduced social pressure for members of the family to take care of aged relatives. On the other hand, it means increased taxation for the younger members of society to take care of the aged in institutions or to provide them with financial assistance to live in their own homes. As the number of aged increases, the burden on the younger members of society will become steadily greater.

Happiness. In a democracy, the happiness and well-being of every citizen is the responsibility of the nation as a whole and especially of its leaders. When a large group of the population is unhappy and feels that it is unfairly treated, it becomes a matter of serious concern for all. Old age should be one of the happy times in life when the individual enjoys the results of his labors through having comforts and the leisure to enjoy them, a time of independence when he is no longer driven by ambition nor has his time regulated by his work, and when he has the prestige that comes from past achievements and the loyalty and devotion of his family. Few elderly people in our society today enjoy the closing years of life; in fact, for most, growing old is a traumatic experience [80]. While much has been done to improve the health of the aged and to provide living quarters and financial aid for the needy, far too little has been done to improve the morale of this group of the population. Many communities are aware of their responsibilities to the aged and are trying to provide opportunities for the social contacts and useful activities that old people need to be happy. However, what has been done to date has been on such a small scale that few benefit from it [85]. As a result, discontent and unhappiness are common accompaniments of old age, mental states which make all who are associated with the elderly unhappy and which predispose the elderly to mental breakdowns, thus adding to the social burden of care for this growing segment of the population. Equally serious is the fact that younger people acquire a negative attitude toward old age from their contacts with the aged, an attitude which prepares them unfavorably for their own adjustments to old age when the time comes [35].

Social Roles. The role the individual plays in the social group depends not so much upon his ability as on the social attitudes toward him and the opportunities the group provides for different roles. This is true of every age, not of old age alone. When social attitudes are favorable, the aged are permitted to play roles involving prestige and authority, but when social attitudes are unfavorable, few roles are open to the individual and these are lowly, with little authority and prestige. The status of the individual in the group and the roles he is permitted to play in old age are determined by the number of aged. If there are relatively few aged, they usually enjoy high esteem; when the number is large, the reverse is true. Old age is viewed and treated differently by different social groups. However, the "liability phase" of old age, when the individual is regarded as useless and a social burden, is usually met with uniform attitudes and social responses [100]. Regardless of the customary methods of treating the aged in different social groups, most people have a negative attitude toward the aged and there is evidence of deep hostility toward them. This is true even among the Chinese, where custom decrees that the aged be treated with homage [50]. How the aged are treated by the social group will influence their concepts of self, which will be reflected in their behavior. When social attitudes are unfavorable, this is reflected in unfavorable behavior among the aged and this, in turn, reinforces the unfavorable social attitudes [42].

Roles in History. What role old people play in society depends not upon the degree of civilization but rather upon the customs and patterns of life that have been built up over a period of time. A social group made up almost exclusively of warriors, for example, will have less use for old people than a social group where the major pursuits are those of peacetime activities. This is true of civilized as well as of primitive peoples. The economic condition of the social group is also a factor of great importance in determining the attitude of the group toward the aged and the status accorded the aged. When conditions are favorable and when the group as a whole is prosperous, each member can afford to share what he has with a nonproductive member.

The effect of the environment and of the economic status of the social group is especially marked among *primitive peoples.* When living conditions are good, the prestige of the aged is high. When, on the other hand, living conditions are poor, when food is scarce, and when epidemics strike, the aged are poorly treated. Among some tribes, the aged are killed or they are deserted and allowed to die. Among the less highly organized forms of tribal life, where there is a common store of food, all share equally, regardless of age. In still other tribes, the position of the aged is high and they are revered by the younger members. They hold sway not only as rulers but as teachers of the young. Sex differences in the status of the aged are pronounced among primitive peoples. Aged women have more nearly equal rights with men in very primitive societies than when the social structure of the group becomes more complex. In many primitive groups, aged men were regarded as repositories of knowledge and imparters of valuable information. They were looked upon as experts in solving the problems of life, such as predicting the future and controlling the weather, and they were expected to treat disease and officiate at childbirth and at all similar important events in the life of the tribal members. Rarely did the elderly women attain positions of respect and responsibility equal to those of the men [99].

The position of the aged among *civilized peoples* has varied markedly. In ancient times, because of wars, famines, and diseases, there was a high mortality rate among younger people. As a result, few lived to be old. Among the distinguished Greeks, there was remarkable vitality. Philosophers, historians, and poets lived to be 60 years of age or older. Statesmen were the oldest of all, with an average age of 78.6 years. In Sparta, the Council of Twenty-eight Men was composed of those who were 60 years of age or older, and they held great power. In Rome, old people had a higher position than in Greece. The Roman Senate, with its great power, was composed of old men. In all areas of life, even in the home, the old were revered. Much the same was true among the Jewish peoples of ancient times. The father was the head of the family with complete power over all members. The grandparents were provided for and respected, but their authority and influence diminished as age crept on.

The position of the aged in Eastern countries has been higher and more powerful than in any of the Western civilizations. While this has proved to be an advantage for the aged themselves, it has proved to be a stagnating influence on the country. Little is known about the position of the aged throughout the Middle Ages. With the Christian influence and emphasis on the care of the weak, it is logical to assume that the aged were well taken care of in all Christian countries during this time. Women, throughout the Christian era, have fared less well than men. In many European countries, as well as in Puritan America, old women were often accused of being witches and sorceresses, positions which held them in disrepute if not in actual danger [19].

Roles Today. In the American cultural pattern of today where efficiency, strength, speed, and physical attractiveness are highly valued, elderly people are often regarded as "useless." Because they cannot compete with young people in the areas where highly valued traits are needed, the social attitude toward them is unfavorable. Furthermore, it is expected that old people will play a decreasingly active role in social and community affairs, as in economic life. Elderly people are aware of the cultural values and of their falling short of them. They are aware of how society feels about them and this leads to feelings of inferiority and resentment, characteristic of members of minority groups. As Tuckman and Lorge have pointed out, "Old people are living in a social climate which is not conducive to feelings of adequacy, usefulness and security, and to good adjustment in their later years" [108]. As a result of these unfavorable social attitudes toward the elderly, there are few roles that they can perform with prestige and respect. Because they must compete with younger people for the valued roles, a competition in which they invariably lose, they must accept the roles that the younger members of society shun [113]. Under such conditions, it is difficult to be happy, and it is impossible to expect the respect and prestige which are paid to the aged in societies where old age is revered.

Unfavorable social attitudes toward old age have been fostered from childhood not only through acceptance of the stereotypes of old age from parents but also from folklore and fairy tales. While some of these picture kindly old people, many of them depict old people, especially women, as wicked and cruel. This results in an unfavorable concept, as is true of the concept of the "wicked stepmother." Throughout literature, there are frequent references to old age and they are, for the most part, unfavorable. Shakespeare, for example, has made 132 references to the senescent process, not only to the physical changes but also to changes in behavior [110]. In describing senility, Shakespeare wrote,

> Last scene of all,
> That ends this strange eventful history,
> Is second childishness, and mere oblivion,
> Sans teeth, sans eyes, sans taste, sans everything.

One of the few cheerful literary references to old age is the picture painted by Browning when he wrote,

> Grow old along with me!
> The best is yet to be,
> The last of life, for which the first was made.

SCIENTIFIC STUDIES

Because old age has created so many social problems not only for the aged themselves but for their families, their employers, and society as a whole, the spotlight of public attention and concern has been focused on this group of the population in recent years. At the same time, the spotlight of scientific attention has likewise been focused on the aged. The two new areas of scientific research which have developed recently to study the aged are *gerontology* and *geriatrics*. Gerontology is the science of aging. It is derived from the Greek *geron*, meaning "old man" and *ology*, meaning the "study of." As a science, gerontology is concerned with all facets of aging, with all forms of life, not human alone, and even with inanimate objects. Geriatrics, on the other hand, is that area of medical practice concerned with the physiologic and disease problems of those in later maturity and of the elderly. It deals with the health of the aged, just as pediatrics deals with the health of infants and of children.

While early interest was expressed in efforts to improve the lot of the elderly through providing them with economic security, the emphasis today is on emotional security. To achieve this goal, it is not only necessary for the elderly to have reasonable economic security but even more important, they must have a status in the social group where they feel wanted and needed. How to provide emotional security in a culture which emphasizes the values of youth is a problem which is occupying the attention of psychologists and sociologists. Their attack on this problem has been concentrated on gathering data to disprove the traditional beliefs about the aged which have led to the unfavorable stereotypes of old age, largely responsible for the unfavorable attitudes toward and treatment of the elderly in business, industry, social and family life. This is the main goal of the studies in the area of gerontology. To prolong the usefulness and happiness of old people through better health has been the goal of geriatrics. While improvement in the health of old people may and often does add years to their life span, this is of little value unless the individual is able to enjoy and make use of this added time not only for his own enjoyment but also to aid society. The goal of geriatrics is, therefore, to *add life to the years* of the elderly, not just years to their lives.

Studies of old age have been numerous in recent years but biased in their results. This is because the subjects have been drawn mainly from institutional cases rather than from a representative *sampling* of the aged in the total population. This sampling bias has come mainly from the practical difficulty of obtaining subjects for study. Most elderly people, aware of or suspicious of their failing powers, are unwilling to "serve as guinea pigs." Only those who are in institutions for the aged which are supported totally or in part by public funds and who feel obligated to allow themselves to be tested are willing to do so. Because the interest in studying old age has been of relatively recent origin, the approach to this study is similar to that of the early studies of intelligence among children, that is, through the use of the cross-section method. Groups of children of different chronological ages were tested, and from the averages thus received, a curve of the growth of intelligence was then plotted. The cross-section method has long since been recognized as inadequate for studying the growth of intelligence and it has been largely replaced by the *longitudinal method,* which studies the changes in intelligence in the same individuals year after year. However, since there are few records of the mental abilities of old people which trace back to their early adulthood, and even fewer, to their youth or childhood, most of the studies of physical and psychological changes with aging have used the same approach as was used in the early days of intelligence testing, the cross-sectional approach.

To the criticism of the cross-sectional approach of the growth of intelligence—that the age groups were not necessarily comparable—is added a new criticism to this method when applied to the studies of aging, the criticism that this approach fails to take into consideration *cultural changes* which always play a role of major importance in the physical and mental development patterns. The fact that the youth of today is stronger, healthier, and larger than the youth of several generations ago, owing to better pre- and postnatal care, better nutrition, and improved medical techniques, may be responsible for the fact that young adults of today are superior in size to those in their sixties and seventies, not to the fact that the elderly have *shrunken,* as the group comparisons suggest and as they are often interpreted. Similarly, the better schooling of today and the widespread use of objective tests throughout the schooling of today's youth give young adults a decided advantage over members of the older generation when comparisons of mental ability are made through the use of intelligence tests and tests of specific mental abilities. Furthermore, lack of practice in writing and even in reading during the adult years, combined with the tendency to slow down in all activities with advancing age, put old people at a decided disadvantage when their intellectual abilities are measured by tests that stress speed and what is taught in the standard curriculum of today. What have been interpreted as age changes may be only age differences due to cultural changes [50, 64, 73].

ADJUSTMENTS IN OLD AGE

When changes occur in the physical condition of the individual and in his changed status in the social group, adjustments must be made. As is true of every age, the elderly must adjust themselves psychologically before they can make the needed adjustments in the patterns of their behavior. *Psychological adjustment* is the "process by which the individual seeks to secure satisfaction for his wants and needs." The processes of adjustment and the methods available to the individual will change with age as desires, needs, and goals change. With aging, changes in structures and functional capacities may limit the methods available to the individual, as is true of the restrictions and limitations imposed on him by the cultural pattern of the society in which he lives [97]. There are two aspects to psychological adjustment, the outer and the inner. The *outer* aspect is evaluated by external observers in terms of the individual's capacity to function appropriately and efficiently; the *inner* consists of the degree to which the individual achieves a relatively integrated satisfaction of his various psychological needs and experiences a pleasurable sense of well-being, contentment, and relative freedom from unpleasant tension and anxiety [51]. While most elderly people adjust with reasonable success to changes in their environment, few adjust successfully to changes from within. If adjustment is to be successful, the individual must make the necessary adjustments to the changes that come with aging and the social group must also adjust to the needs of the elderly. However, since the world will not adapt itself to the elderly, the elderly must learn to adapt to the world and to develop their own ways of doing so. This puts a great burden on the elderly [51].

Factors Influencing Adjustment. How successfully or unsuccessfully the individual will adjust to the problems arising from changed physical and mental conditions and from the changes in status which come from aging will be influenced by many factors, some of which are beyond the individual's control. Of these factors, the following are the most important:

Social Attitudes. In a culture where the role of the elderly is clearly defined, adjustment is easier than where roles are ambiguously defined. In our culture today, there is no universally sanctioned pattern of activities for the elderly as is true of primitive societies. While specific requirements are set for retirement, there has been no attempt to define any specific functions for the individual after retirement [97]. There is, however, a general agreement on a pattern of limited and "age-appropriate" activities for the elderly, a pattern that stresses less active and less ambitious activities than the pattern approved for middle-aged people [50]. One of the greatest handicaps to good adjustment in old age is, therefore, not the individual's unwillingness or inability to adjust to changes which occur with aging but rather society's attitudes toward old age based on stereotypes of the aged. When the individual accepts these stereotypes, it stifles his motivation to adjust [34].

Personal Attitudes. Good adjustment in old age is greatly affected by the individual's attitude toward aging and the effects it has on him as an individual. When his attitude is resistant, it will be a serious obstacle to successful adjustment. Unfavorable concepts of self, based on the belief that his days of usefulness to society have ended, lead to poor adjustments and unhappiness in old age. This unfavorable self-concept is exaggerated by the aged person's realization of his lessening ability to cope with life situations and of the unfavorable attitude of society toward the aged [76]. Many old people regard old age as the "end of the line" and think of themselves as "through," as "crabby," and "hard to get along with" [36]. There are certain "insults of aging" or life changes which come with aging and which systematically "insult" the individual, thus further damaging his self-concept. No one who lives to old age can escape these "insults," though their severity may vary from individual to individual. These are *loss of physical attractiveness, lessening of physical and mental vigor,* and *loss of status.*

With age, most people are less attractive looking than they were when they were younger. Because attractiveness has high social value, loss of it is a blow to the individual's self concept. As Havighurst and Albrecht have pointed out, "We have invested a good deal of emotional capital in our physical attractiveness and this investment is going bad on us" [50]. Furthermore, old people are aware of the unfavorable social attitude toward their loss of attractiveness and the tell-tale physical signs of aging. Linden has stressed this point by saying,

> In our culture, we place a great value on the package in which an item is de livered. This is no less true of the human being. For several reasons, we tend to place a considerable worth upon physical attractiveness and youthfulness. As a rule, these are symbolic of pleasing packaging. As we grow older, the package changes, tending to deteriorate. It loses a certain freshness and desirability and thus becomes obsolescent. Therefore, in our culture, in which the package possesses a value equal to or greater than its contents, the human facade—the human package which suffers in aging—is not highly regarded [71].

Added to this are a lessening of physical health and vigor, decline in the usefulness of the sense organs and of the reproductive organs, and a slowing down of memory and other mental abilities, all of which contribute to a growing feeling of uselessness. Status-giving roles in business, the home, and in civic, social, and political life all disappear as old age sets in and are replaced by roles of minor importance which are poor substitutes for those that have been lost [50].

Unfavorable concepts of self, developed from unfavorable social and personal experiences, result in frustrations, anxiety, resentments, and feelings of helplessness. These, in turn, lead to social friction and personal unhappiness, both of which make the oldster even less capable of adjusting to the changes in the pattern of his life than he could were these factors not present [43]. In spite of the emotional disturbances that accompany the adjustment problems of old age, most old people manage to keep their equilibrium within fair balance and are reasonably happy. The individual who is financially secure, whose family status is favorable, and whose health enables him to continue to engage in activities that are enjoyable to him will have fewer emotional disturbances and will make better adjustments to old age than the individual whose status is less secure and less satisfactory.

Preparation for Old Age. The type of adjustment the individual makes to life at any age depends largely upon his earlier experiences. Studies of old age have revealed that good adjustment then is largely a product of good adjustment prior to old age [34]. In old age, difficulties in adjustment are at their peak not only because old age presents more and more difficult problems but also because the ability to make these adjustments becomes increasingly difficult with advancing age. As Menninger has pointed out, the foundations of a happy old age should be laid as early as childhood. To prepare for good adjustments in old age, children should be taught to accept reality, to take the bad along with the good, and to take it with equanimity; to plan for the future by becoming independent and by not expecting other people to do "what mother did"; to get along with other people so that they can relate themselves happily to others throughout life; and to have a capacity to love others, a measure of the emotional maturity an individual has achieved [85]. When foundations are poor, the waning physical and mental resources of the individual render the old person less capable of making adjustments to changes in his life, with the result that the adjustments are only partially made. This is apparent in the case of adjustments to retirement. Those who have not prepared themselves economically or psychologically for compulsory retirement often react to it as a traumatic experience; those who have prepared themselves or have had help from experienced counselors have been found to improve their adjustments [38].

Method of Adjustment. There are many methods used by elderly people to adjust to the problems old age brings, some of which are *rational* and make for successful adjustment while others are *irrational* and lead to poor adjustment. Of the irrational methods, many of which are unconsciously used, the following are the most common: denying the changes of age and trying to continue as before; overcompensating by becoming intolerant of younger people, pointing out all the defects of youth, and claiming many advantages for old age; giving in completely and feeling there is no use to try any further; dwelling on the pleasures and triumphs of bygone days in fantasies; regressing to infancy by becoming dependent on others for bodily care; "convenient" forgetting and "shutting" one's eyes and ears; and hallucinations in the form of talking to lost family members as the child talks to an imaginary companion. The rational methods of adjusting to aging consist of accepting the limitations of age and adjusting to the capacities one has; taking good care of one's body and being careful of clothes and grooming; finding and cultivating new friends; developing interests in community and civic affairs; learning to give up one's children; and avoiding reminiscing in the form of telling stories about the olden days [10, 50]. Any or all of the rational methods of adjusting to old-age changes and the problems they bring will result in satisfaction to the individual and good adjustments to the pattern of living old age requires.

Health Conditions. It is always easier to cope with the problems of life when one is well than when one is physically below par. This is just as true of old age as it is of other periods in life. Health conditions normally are less favorable as age progresses and this adds a burden to the adjustment problems the elderly must meet. Chronic illness, which saps the strength and energy of the individual, is a greater handicap to adjustment than are temporary illnesses, even though the latter may be more severe while they last than the former. Furthermore, how the individual feels about his health has a marked influence on his adjustments. Those who rate their own health as good or fair make better adjustments than do those who rate their health as poor [59]. The effect illness has on the individual's adjustment to old age will be influenced by the social class to which he belongs, the amount of physical care needed, family attitudes toward illness, the individual's past adjustments to life, and his attitude toward his illness, whether "hopeful" or "resigned." Those who make the best personal and social adjustments to old age when they are handicapped by illness have been found to be those with a "hopeful" attitude and those who have the resources necessary to provide for care during illness without placing too great a burden on their families [75].

Living Conditions. As has already been stressed, most of the studies of old age have, through necessity, been made on elderly people living in institutions. Because of this, the evidence pointing to the fact that old age is an unhappy period of life when adjustments are poorer than in the earlier years may be biased by the samplings used. At any age, living conditions affect the individual's concept of self and this, in turn, affects the type of adjustments he makes. When an individual is forced to live in a place that is not of his choosing, and when the place where he lives makes him feel inadequate, inferior, and resentful, it is understandable that this would affect the type of adjustments he makes. Comparisons of institutionalized elderly people with elderly people who live in their own homes have revealed that the latter make better adjustments to the problems of old age than do the former. Similarly, those living with married children, relatives, or friends make less satisfactory adjustments than those who live in their own homes. Good adjustment is thus closely associated with living arrangements resulting from choice rather than from necessity [96]. The longer the individual lives in an institution or in the home of a relative, the more unfavorable his attitude will be and, in turn, the poorer his adjustments [70].

ADJUSTMENT PROBLEMS OF OLD AGE

During the latter years of life, there are certain problems of adjustment that are the result of changes in the body, changed environmental conditions, and social attitudes toward old age that make these problems unique. In addition, there are the normal problems which all people face but which in old age have certain unique aspects, although some older people are fortunate enough to escape them. Among the problems unique to old age to which most old people must make adjustments are those resulting from physical helplessness, more serious for women than for men because women, as a rule, outlive their husbands and cannot, therefore, depend on a husband's care as the man can depend on the care given by his wife; economic insecurity, often so severe that it necessitates a complete change in the pattern of living; feelings of rejection by society, by the family, or by both; loss of a husband or wife, due to death or divorce; and loss of work due to compulsory retirement. Among the problems familiar to every age which have a unique old-age aspect are making satisfactory living arrangements in order to adjust to changes in economic or physical conditions; making new friends to replace those who have died, moved away, or are invalided; developing new activities to fill in the increased leisure time resulting from retirement or reduced home responsibilities; and treating the grown children as adults rather than as children [50]. Some individuals can adjust with great flexibility to changes in the pattern of life and, for them, the adjustments needed to be happy in old age are made with little emotional tension; but some individuals are less flexible, and for them adjustments to old-age problems are difficult and are made only with stress and emotional tension.

Of the many adjustment problems common to men and women in America today as they become elderly, the following are the most important:

Physical Changes. Because of the high social value placed on physical attractiveness, youthful appearance, strength, speed, and agility, it is difficult for the individual to adjust to the changes in appearance and bodily functioning that accompany aging. It is known to all young people that, with the passage of time, they will deteriorate in appearance and that they will suffer from some of the ailments traditionally associated with old age and believed to be inevitable. However, when the time comes for these changes to take place in their own bodies, it is difficult to accept them and to make the necessary adjustments in attitudes and patterns of behavior to fit into the changes that have taken place. The more attractive the individual's appearance has been or the greater his strength during the earlier years of his life, the greater will be the emotional accompaniments of his adjustments and the greater will be his rebellion against the changes.

While it is unquestionably true that physical changes do occur with aging and that these changes are, for the most part, in the direction of deterioration, individual differences are so marked that no two individuals of the same age are necessarily at the same state of deterioration. Chronological age is not necessarily the same as *physical age*, the assessment of the functional capacities of an individual by reference to standards derived from healthy persons of the same chronological age as the person tested [84]. Furthermore, within the same individual there are variations in the rates of aging of different structures. The organs of reproduction, for example, age sooner than the other organs [22]. Even in senility not all organs of the body have deteriorated. While senility is usually a mental, not a physical, state, it is often accompanied by physical ailments and damage of the blood vessels of the brain caused by hardening of the arteries and atrophy of the brain cells [50].

Causes of Physical Decline. The earliest recorded explanation of aging is attributed to the Greek philosophers and physicians who explained aging as the result of a decline of an "innate heat" within the body. Arabic medical writers attributed aging to a progressive loss of moisture in the body, thus causing shrinking and hardening of the tissues. More recently, biologists have suggested that when differentiated germ plasm is no longer produced, senescence ensues. Others maintain that old age is a generalized kind of disease, not one specific thing. Today, it is widely recognized that the physical condition of the elderly person depends partly upon his hereditary constitution, partly upon his temperament, partly upon his manner of living, and partly upon environmental factors. That hereditary constitution plays a primary role is shown by the fact that different species have different life spans characteristic of them and that within a species, aging appears at different ages for different individuals but, within a family, the rate of aging shows a high correlation for the different family members. Those of small build have been found to live longer than those of larger builds [89]. Even though hereditary factors are of primary importance, the secondary causes have marked influences on the rate of physical decline. The vicissitudes of living, such as faulty diet, malnutrition, infectious intoxications, gluttony, lack of repose, emotional stresses, overwork, laziness, traumata, and endocrine disorders are some of the most common of the secondary causes of physical decline. Then, too, there are environmental conditions, such as heat and cold, which influence the rate of aging [22, 89, 102].

The endocrine glands play a role of great significance in bringing about the different physical changes characteristic of old age, though they themselves are the victims of decreased blood supply because of generalized vascular sclerosis. There is a reduced output of anterior pituitary and of adrenal cortical hormones, as well as of the hormones from the thyroid and sex glands. Hormone deficiency is not the primary basic cause of physical aging, though it accelerates and intensifies the process of aging in some organs and functions. This is especially true of deficiency of the sex hormones. That deficiency of the sex hormones is an important factor in physical aging has been shown by the fact that hormonal treatment of aged persons improves their physical strength and vigor. With age, the vitality of millions of individual cells of the body tissues is affected in such a manner that their capacity to perform their normal functions is reduced. Because the various structures of the body are interrelated, a minor change in one group of cells performing a specialized function may affect the balance of the rest of the organism and thus produce changes which otherwise might not have occurred until later [62].

Bodily Changes with Aging. There are certain changes, both external and internal, which are so characteristic of old age that no one can fail to recognize them. They are tell-tale signs of aging which few individuals find easy to accept or to adjust to. The *external changes* proclaim to the world that the individual is aging and even the best beauty aids are usually incapable of hiding them. The *face* tells the individual's age more forcibly than any other part of the body, especially the lower part of the face. Due to loss of teeth or wearing down of the teeth, the jaw becomes smaller and the chin sags. The cheeks become pendulous, with wrinkles and bags, and the eyelids become baggy with the upper lids overhanging the lower. The eyes seem dull and lusterless and they often have a watery look, due to the poor functioning of the tear glands. The nose elongates in vertical dimension and, as the lower part of the face is shortened by changes in the jaw, the nose is made to appear larger than it actually is [14]. Most elderly people have lost some or all of their teeth and even with the best dentures, this is likely to change the shape of the mouth as well as the facial expression. Under the dentures, atrophic changes take place in the bones and the dentures become loose and act as irritants. This often causes speech problems, especially lisping. The supporting mucosal surfaces are likely to become inflamed and painful, thus adding to the difficulties in speech and eating [58, 66].

Changes in the facial *skin,* as well as in the skin covering the entire body, are very marked. The epidermis gradually thins and becomes more flexible and flaccid with age. Under the epidermis, the tissues are less elastic than they formerly were because of atrophy of many of the elastic fibers that make up a considerable share of the intercellular matrix. Because of loss of elasticity, the skin springs back less readily, it sags here and there, and creases or folds are fixed as wrinkles. Atrophy of the oil and sweat glands makes the skin rather dry and coarse. Perspiration is less profuse even in areas of the body where formerly it was abundant. In true senility, dark spots or white scaly plaques often appear in exposed areas of the skin. These are the beginnings of skin cancers, though many will never develop. Moles, warts, and other skin blemishes often appear as age advances.

The *hair* on the head becomes thin and gray. Gradually it becomes so thin that the head is bald or nearly bald, especially in the case of men [66]. The gray color turns into white, often with a yellowish cast. Tough, bristly hairs come around the opening of the external ear and the nose. The hairs of the eyebrows usually become coarse and more bristly, though they may not change in color as the hair on the head does. The *nails* of the hands and feet become thick and tough, with a slight increase in brittleness. The *hands* show the ravages of age not only by the toughened, rough skin that characteristically develops at this time but also by the veins that show clearly on the backs of the hands. The *arms* and *legs* are likely to be flabby and unattractive with veins showing through in the legs. The *feet* frequently grow larger because of sagging muscles and they develop corns, bunions, and other disfigurations which necessitate the wearing of larger and less attractive shoes than the individual formerly wore.

The individual's *stature* decreases and there is a stooping of the *shoulders*, thus making the individual appear smaller. Because of poor eating habits, stemming from food dislikes, difficulties in eating, or economic factors, many elderly men and women are 10 per cent or more above their desirable *weight*. Others lose weight with advancing years as a result of poor health or poor eating habits [74]. There is a gradual shrinking of the *secondary sex characteristics* with advancing age and the body does not seem to be either masculine or feminine. Loss of *muscular tone* and *stiffness of the joints* cause difficulties in locomotion. The gait of the aged shows a shortened step, lack of elasticity, a widened base, and forward leaning in a slightly flexed attitude. *Tremors* of the hands, forearms, head, and lower jaw are common among old people though not necessarily continuously present. They are usually increased by fatigue, emotions, or activity in the area involved. Restless movements, such as tapping, twitching, patting, or rocking the body are common in old age.

While *internal changes* are not readily observed, as external changes are, they are nevertheless as pronounced and as widespread. Changes in the *skeleton* come through hardening of the bones, deposits of mineral salts, and modifications of the internal structures of the bones. As a result of these changes, the *bones* become brittle and are subject to fractures and breaks which are increasingly slow in healing as age progresses. Bone fragility has been found to be more intimately related to endocrine changes, decreased activity, and loss of muscle tone than to the level of the individual's nutrition [52]. Changes in the *nervous system* are especially marked in the case of the brain. In old age, there is a loss in brain weight, the lateral ventricles tend to be dilated, and the ribbon of cortical tissue is narrowed. Central nervous system changes come early in the aging period, as is shown first in a decrease in the speed and later in the power of intelligence. The *viscera* go through a marked transformation with advancing age. Atrophy is particularly marked in the spleen, liver, testes, heart, lungs, pancreas, and kidneys. There is increased density of the solid organs. The color of the different organs changes to gray or a brownish tone, there is a change in translucency, atrophy of adipose tissue, and increased dryness and toughness of the muscles. Perhaps the most marked change of all is to be found in the heart. In the early years of life, the position of the heart is more nearly in the center of the chest than it is in advanced age. Also, its position is more erect in the young individual while later, in middle and old age, it assumes a horizontal position. It increases in bulk with age and continues to grow even after the body has ceased to do so. Therefore, the ratio of heart weight to body weight decreases gradually with age. The softness and pliability of the valves gradually change because of an increase in fibrous tissue from deposits of fat and calcium, and from changes in the quality of the elastic tissue. The gastrointestinal tract, the urinary tract, and the smooth muscle organs generally are the least and last affected by aging.

Not only are there changes in the structure of the internal organs with advancing age but there are also changes in the functioning of these organs. Regulation of *body temperature* is impaired by impairment of the regulatory devices. Old people cannot tolerate extremes of temperature, either hot or cold, because of the decreased vascularity of the skin. Reduced metabolic rate and lessened muscular vigor make regulation of body temperature difficult in cold environments. It is also difficult in hot environments because of the degeneration of the capillaries and sweat glands in the skin. On the whole, old people feel the cold more than the heat. When an old person becomes short of breath as a result of unusual exertion, it takes longer to restore breathing and heart action to normal than it did when he was younger. Pulse rate and oxygen consumption are more varied among elderly people than among the younger [63, 98]. Among elderly people, less *urine* is excreted and there is less creatine in the urine than the customary amounts for younger adults [53].

In old age, there is a decline in the amount of *sleep* needed and in the quality of sleep. By the age of sixty or seventy years, the daily amount is reduced an hour or two and brief periods of rest and sleep, "cat naps," generally replace the longer periods of sleep of the younger person. Most old people suffer from insomnia. *Digestive changes* are perhaps the most marked of the regulatory functions. Difficulties in eating come partly from loss of teeth, which is fairly universal in old age. Even with well-fitted dentures, the old person has difficulties in chewing his food. In addition, there is a decline in smell and taste sensitivity with old age and this causes even the best food to be somewhat tasteless. As a general rule, old people eat less than they did when they were younger primarily because they do not feel the need or the desire for food that they formerly did. When they do eat, it is usually in smaller quantities and at more frequent times. Old people cannot tolerate long periods of starvation because their blood sugar falls to undesirably low levels [22].

Gradual atrophy of the glands lining the walls of the stomach and bowels means a decrease in the ferments and juices that carry out *digestion*. As a result, the old person needs more fluids to lubricate and to dissolve food elements. The lower bowel, or colon, is more sensitive to irritation by roughage because it is less well lubricated with mucus. This is especially serious for old people whose loss of teeth makes it difficult for them to chew well. *Strength* and *work capacity* decrease as the ability to use the muscles as they were formerly used declines because of muscular flabbiness and general weakness. The ability for brief and violent effort diminishes with age while the ability to withstand a long, steady grind increases. Physical fatigue requires longer time for recuperation with advancing age. This is true also of fatigue from continued mental work or from nervous strain. As a result, most old people learn to cut down on any work that requires either strength or speed.

Sense Organs. There is a general but unmistakable downward trend in *sensitivity* as age progresses. All the *sense organs* function less efficiently in old age than they did when the individual was younger. However, because the decline in efficiency of use is slow and gradual in most cases, it gives the individual an opportunity to make adequate adjustments to these changes. Furthermore, modern aids in the form of glasses for impaired vision and hearing aids for impaired hearing compensate for the decline to such an extent that the adjustments can be almost perfect. Of all the sense organs, the most useful, the *eyes* and *ears*, are most seriously affected by old age. The marked decrease in the efficiency of the eyes may be due partly to poor care during the years of maturity and to generally lowered physical condition with old age, though the pupil size decreases significantly with age and this may account partially for visual changes [8]. With age, there is a consistent decline in the ability to see at low levels of illumination owing to changes in certain basic physiologic functions in the nerve cells of the brain and retina [78]. There is a decrease of color sensitivity with age and, after forty-five years of age, members of both sexes show a loss in color vision [60]. In color-matching tests, blue and green are the most difficult colors to match while less decline in this ability is found in the case of yellow and red [41] (see Figure 118). Most old people suffer from *presbyopia*, or farsightedness, because of the diminishing elasticity of the lens, which makes it impossible for the lens to change its shape adequately to accommodate for near vision.

Deterioration in *hearing* is greatest for high-pitched sounds, from the high C in the musical scale upward. Sensitivity is entirely lost for extremely high tones because of atrophy of the nerve and end organ in the basal turn of the cochlea. For tones below high C, most old people have hearing as good as younger people do. Old people as a rule regard hearing difficulties as caused by stimulus rather than by response. In other

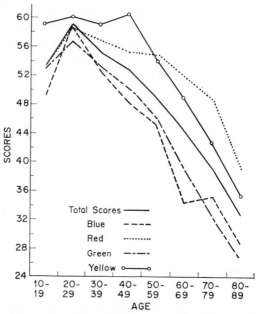

FIG. 118. Age changes in color matching as measured by a color-matching test. (*From J. C. Gilbert, Age changes in color matching. J. Geront., 1957, 12, 210–215. Used by permission.*)

words, they blame others for "mumbling" and do not in any way feel that the trouble lies within themselves. In personal conversations with just one person, the elderly individual has little difficulty in hearing because he can face the speaker directly and can read lips. In groups, on the other hand, the old person must be close to the speaker and must face him directly if he is to hear what is being said. Loss of hearing is greater for males than for females in old age, and for members of the lower socioeconomic groups than for those of the upper groups [97, 101].

Changes in *taste* are marked in old age. This is partially caused by atrophy of the taste buds, with those at the end of the tongue atrophying first and, as age advances, the atrophy extending gradually further and further back on the tongue. Taste buds likewise become fewer on the inner surface of the cheeks. The sense of *smell* becomes less acute with age and this tends to make food seem tasteless. With the drying and hardening of the skin, the sense of *touch* becomes less and less acute. Responses to tactual stimuli on the face and hands have shown that individuals over sixty-five years of age make consistently more errors than do younger people and that the incidence of errors increases with age. Individuals over sixty-five years of age respond much as do children under six years of age [46]. *Sensitivity* to pain declines with age with the result that it is less valuable as a danger signal than it is in younger people [97]. Upsets of the *labyrinthine* and *kinesthetic* sensations result in liabilities to falls, trippings, and imbalance among older people. In general, the decline in sensory efficiency that is so characteristic of old age has a marked influence on the individual's life. Diminution of sensory experiences removes for him one of the chief sources of enjoyment from life. No longer, for example, is eating as pleasurable as it formerly was nor can the individual enjoy to the same extent what he sees and hears because of poor vision or poor hearing. Declining sensitivity is likely to result in social isolation, especially when the sense organs that are most seriously affected are the eyes and ears. And, finally, personality maladjustments are frequent among old people when the use of their senses declines to the point that they are cut off from social contacts and must live within themselves. This, therefore, is one of the major areas of adjustment that comes with physical decline.

Sexual Changes. The male *climacteric* comes later than the female and it requires more time than the female. Generally there is a decline in sexual potency during the sixties which continues as age advances. As is true of the female climacteric, which comes during middle age (see pages 482–484), there is a decline in gonadal functioning, which is responsible for the changes that accompany the climacteric. The characteristic symptoms of the male climacteric have been found to be a decrease in sexual potency and, often, of libido or sexual desire. It is usual for benign prostatic hypertrophy to accompany decline in sexual potency. These sexual changes are generally accompanied by nervousness, headaches, giddiness, emotional instability with inclination to tears, increased fatigability, mental and physical lassitude, irritability, difficulties in concentration, a desire to be left alone, and insomnia. Like women, many men experience hot flushes, fits of perspiration, chill sensations, especially cold feet, numbness in their hands and feet, and tingling sensations. There is a tendency toward obesity at this time; constipation is common; the individual experiences many aches and pains; fatigability is frequent; and the skin becomes rougher, darker, and wrinkled. There is a waning of the secondary sex characteristics; the voice becomes higher in pitch; the

hair on the face and body becomes less luxuriant; and the heavy musculature gives way to a general flabbiness. In general, older men are less
"masculine" than they were in the prime of life, just as women are less
"feminine" after the changes of the climacteric have taken place [62].
This is the "third sex" or the "neuter gender" [77].

Because there are no "old wives' tales" to exaggerate the significance
of or the discomforts associated with the male climacteric, as is true of
the female, most men are affected much less than women by the fact that

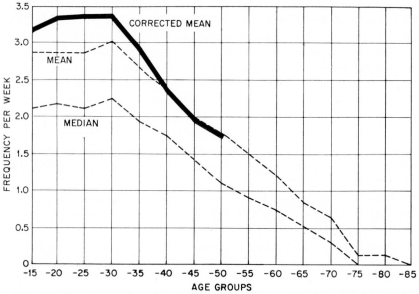

Fig. 119. Frequency of total outlet in relation to age based on total population
including single, married, and previously married groups. (*From A. C. Kinsey, W. B.
Pomeroy, and C. E. Martin, Sexual behavior in the human male. Philadelphia:
Saunders, 1948. Used by permission.*)

they no longer have the power of procreation. Even though sexual potency has declined, this does not necessarily mean a decline in sexual
desire or the ability to have intercourse. Cultural influences are more important in the waning of the sex drive than are physical changes. Cultural
influences produce anxieties which, in turn, affect sex attitudes and behavior. Men and women in old age often refrain from continuing sexual
relations or from remarriage because of the social attitudes toward sex
among older people, because of fear about their own capacities, and self-
consciousness about their power to please. To avoid having their pride
hurt, men especially are likely to refrain from sexual activity as they
grow older [77]. This is illustrated in Figure 119.

As Lawton has pointed out, to age successfully, the elderly person must retain the feeling that he is still a man or woman [68]. Because the cultural attitude is unfavorable toward sex among older people, and because this cultural attitude has a marked influence on the attitudes of elderly men and women, the sexual life of the elderly is often unsatisfactory. There is reason to believe that sexual deprivation affects the individual not only psychologically but also physically, and that it may affect longevity. Those who are married are healthier in old age than are those who are single or widowed. There is some evidence that sexual deprivation has similar effects in old age to the effects of emotional deprivation in young children [77]. How strong or weak the sex drive will be in old age will depend largely upon the general health of the individual and the type of sexual adjustments he made earlier in life. Those who made poor sexual adjustments in their earlier years have been found to have the sex drive disappear earlier than those who made better sexual adjustments when they were younger [20].

Health. Good health contributes to good adjustment and good adjustment, in turn, to good health. On the other hand, poor health interferes with good adjustment and poor adjustment is responsible, in part, for poor health. At no age does the well-adjusted individual like to be ill. Adjusting to the restrictions on activities formerly engaged in because of poor health is difficult at any age. In old age, adjustments are made with greater resistance than at earlier ages because the old person is aware of the fact that the chances of recovery are slight and that restrictions of his activities are likely to be permanent and to be increased rather than decreased with advancing age. The fact that old people resist adjusting to poor health and the restrictions it brings is evident in the tendency to complain to others about their ailments, such as digestive disturbances, difficulties in elimination, giddiness, and troublesome feet. Women, as a group, complain more about their ailments than do men but both complain more than younger people do [11]. This is illustrated in Figure 120. As old age advances, there are fewer complaints about poor health. This does not necessarily mean that individuals have made better adjustments and have accepted the fact that this is an inevitable accompaniment of old age but rather that the threshold of pain rises with age and they do not, as a result, experience as great physical discomforts as they formerly did. It may also be that they have difficulty in reporting how they feel because of the decline in mental abilities as age progresses [109].

Normally, old age is a period of increasingly poor health. Even if there is no illness, there is a tendency to feel less well than usual. In the sixties, poor general health is less common than it is when individuals live to be over seventy years of age. After seventy, fully half of all men and women can anticipate several years of invalidism before they die [48]. The marked increase in physical disability with advancing age is shown in Figure 104, page 481. There are few disorders limited to this period, but some occur more commonly in old age than at any other time. This is particularly true of constipation, hemorrhoids, digestive disturbances of all types, cancer, and the different forms of heart disease. The diseases that are peculiar to senescence are circulatory disturbances, metabolic disorders, involutional mental disorders, disorders of the joints, and tumors, both benign and malignant. Because the older organism repairs itself much more slowly than the younger, any illness or break in a bone is far more serious and is likely to incapacitate the individual for a longer time than is true of the younger individual. This tends to discourage the

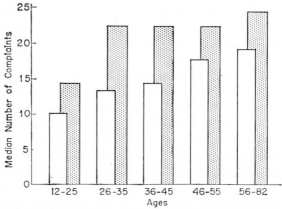

Fig. 120. Bodily complaints of men (clear area) and women (dotted area) at different ages. (*From K. Brodman, A. J. Erdmann, I. Lorge, and H. G. Wolff, The Cornell Medical Index-Health Questionnaire: VI. The relation of patients' complaints to age, sex, race, and education. J. Geront., 1953, 8, 339–342. Used by permission.*)

individual and to present special problems of adjustment [97]. In addition to actual illness, many old people suffer from *imaginary illness* and concentrate on any ache or pain they may have, thus increasing it out of all proportion. Talking about aches, pains, medicine, and doctors is a favorite pastime of many old people and serves as a means of attracting attention to themselves as well as of winning sympathy from others [39].

There are, in addition to illness, a number of physical hazards of old age, the two most common and most serious of which are malnutrition and accidents. *Malnutrition* comes more from psychological than economic causes in old age. Whether the elderly person is living in his own home, in a home of a relative, or in an institution, he is subject to this health hazard. More often he eats less than he needs for his age and general health, especially of the foods needed to maintain his physical and mental efficiency. This is shown in inadequate vitamin intake, especially a deficiency of vitamin C [56]. Malnutrition in old age comes from such psychological causes as lack of appetite due to anxiety, depression, and feelings of not being wanted; to loneliness and lack of interest in food due to having to eat alone; and to food aversions and prejudices stemming from unpleasant experiences earlier in life [91]. In addition, the dental problems of old age complicate the psychological problems as contributors to malnutrition. Because of the difficulties of eating, many elderly people not only eat less than they need but they eat too little protein, which is difficult to chew, and concentrate on the soft carbohydrates. Furthermore, chewing difficulties encourage the swallowing of larger and coarser food masses, thus leading to digestive disturbances [58].

The second physical hazard of old age is the tendency to have *accidents*. While it is true that some people are more accident-prone than others, old people, as a group, are more accident-prone than are younger people. Fatal accidents are responsible for more deaths among elderly people than any disease except cancer and the cardiovascular diseases. Even when the accidents are not fatal, they frequently leave the individual disabled for the remainder of his life. Falls are the major cause of accident mortality in old age, with women more subject to falls than men. Most of these falls occur in the home, with the bedroom, bathroom, and stairs being the most common places for accidents. Among the external factors responsible for falls, furniture, slippery floors, "throw rugs," improper lighting, and floors on different levels are the most common. In addition, many falls come from internal causes, such as dizziness, giddiness, weakness, arthritis, and defective vision. Falls outside the home are less numerous than in the home and are about equal in number for men and women [32, 54]. Motor-vehicle accidents rank second as a cause of fatal injury among the elderly, and outrank falls as a cause of death among men. In addition, many accidents that are fatal or cause permanent disability come from burns when the individual is trapped in a burning building by the infirmities of age [81].

Changes in Motor Capacities. Most studies have revealed that there is a decrease in motor capacities, in terms of strength, skill, speed of reaction time, and ability to master new skills, with advancing age. Most old people are aware of the fact that they are slower, less well coordinated in their movements, and less sure of their movements than when they were younger. These changes in motor capacities come mainly from the decrease of strength and energy that accompanies the physical changes of aging, though psychological factors play some role also. The individual is aware that he is "slipping." He knows the social values placed on skills, strength, and speed, and he is constantly reminded of his inferiority to younger people in these areas. Emotional tension stemming from

these psychological causes may hasten the changes in motor capacities
or may decrease the individual's motivation to do what he is capable of
doing. However, even under the most favorable conditions and with the
strongest motivation, few individuals can hope to keep their motor
abilities up to the peak performance achieved when they were younger.

Decline in physical *strength* begins in the mid-twenties and advances
throughout the adult years. Whatever type of strength test is used, the
results are the same. In the case of hand strength, there has been found
to be a decline in average grip strength of 17 per cent from the maximum
at sixty years and, by seventy-five years, the maximum grip strength is
approximately equal to that of twelve- to fifteen-year-olds [18]. Decline
in strength with age varies, however, with different groups of muscles.
The decline is most pronounced in the flexor muscles of the forearm and
in the muscles which raise the body. Declining strength is shown also in
the speed with which the elderly person becomes fatigued. It takes only
a short time and a minimum of use for him to complain of *fatigue* in this
or that set of muscles. There is also a *slowing down* of motor responses
with advancing age, though marked individual differences in this are
apparent [97]. Tests of *reaction time* show that the elderly subjects are
significantly slower than the younger, and that they become increasingly
slower as the difficulty of the task is increased [7] (see Figure 121).
Furthermore, older subjects require more time to organize a response
or to develop a state of expectancy than do younger subjects [9]. Fatigue,
stress, tension, and other factors affect the velocity of reaction time, thus
increasing individual differences in this aspect of aging [93].

Skills. There are age changes in motor skills learned earlier and this is
a source of embarrassment and frustration to the elderly person. Because
motor coordinations become increasingly difficult with advancing age,
there is a tendency for old people to become awkward and clumsy in
their movements, thus causing them to spill and drop things, to trip and
fall, and to do things in a careless, untidy manner. The breakdown of
motor skills proceeds in inverse order to that in which skills were formed:
the earliest-formed skills are retained longest and the most recently
formed ones are lost first. With advancing age, however, even the most
firmly established coordinations begin to break up and the individual reverts to the state of semihelplessness characteristic of the early part of
life. The tendency to be awkward, together with the greater amount
of energy needed to do things than was formerly necessary, very often
causes older people to shun motor activities whenever possible. As a result of voluntarily giving up activities, often before it is necessary, many
old people are more in danger of wearing out from disuse than from sensible activity [102]. On the other hand, continued exercise of a skill can
delay the decline of this skill [15].

Learning *new skills* in old age is an unusual experience. Not only is learning more difficult than it formerly was but lack of motivation on the individual's part further militates against the learning. When the learning is of skills that will benefit him personally, there will be the necessary motivation to put forth the effort needed, though the learning will progress more slowly and the end results will be inferior to those of younger learners. That motivation plays a dominant role in the learning

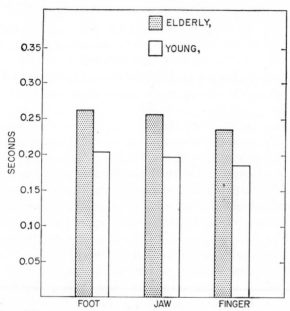

Fig. 121. Age differences in finger, jaw, and foot reaction time to auditory stimuli. (*From J. E. Birren and J. Botwinick, Age differences in finger, jaw, and foot reaction time to auditory stimuli. J. Geront., 1955, 10, 429–432. Used by permission.*)

of new skills is shown by the fact that the Balinese, who believe in reincarnation, retain the ability to learn new and complicated skills which they believe will help them in the new life after death [79]. Furthermore, measures of steadiness in the hand and arm have shown that at seventy years of age, many are as steady or even steadier than younger people. This suggests that they are capable of learning new skills and of doing good skilled work if they have the necessary motivation and the needed opportunities [33].

Decline in Mental Abilities. Elderly people become aware of their forgetfulness, their difficulties in learning new names, figures, or facts, and their emotional stress when they must solve even the simplest problem quickly. They realize that they are "slipping" mentally and this they dread because it is a tell-tale sign of aging. Older adults often refuse to be tested or to participate in any games where quick thinking is involved because they feel "threatened" by these situations and do not want to know or to have others know that they do not compare favorably with younger people [112]. As in other adjustments to changes which are traditionally associated with old age, the individual resists making such adjustments as long as possible by denying that he is "slipping" or by blaming others for his forgetfulness or slowness in learning new material. Many individuals never adjust to mental decline. Instead of accepting it as an inevitable accompaniment of aging, they avoid situations where this decline will be apparent or they rationalize any evidence there may be that they are not as mentally alert as they formerly were.

Normally, the decline in mental abilities, begun in middle age, continues throughout the closing years of life. As is true of all other areas of decline, there are marked individual variations in mental decline. There is no one age at which the decline begins and no specific pattern of decline that is characteristic of all old people. In general, among those of the higher intellectual levels, there is relatively less decrease in mental efficiency than among those of the lower intellectual levels [40]. The rate of mental decline is dependent to a large extent upon the physical condition of the individual. Lack of environmental stimulation likewise leaves its mark on the rate of mental decline. Studies of the elderly have shown that those who continue to work have more normal brain functioning and do better on intelligence tests than do others [20].

The mental decline associated with old age may not be as great as popularly supposed or as reported in earlier studies. There is a growing belief that what is assumed to be a decline in mental ability may be caused by discrepancies in the choice of groups at different age levels for comparisons and by the difference in education that exists today and at the time the elderly groups were school children [40, 73]. Most old people are not familiar with testing, are not sympathetic toward it, and refuse to be tested. This biases the samplings used for studies and usually means using institutional cases for the old-age groups, thus giving an unfair sampling of the old-age population [112]. The only true measure of the amount of decline would be to have an accurate record of the individual's intellectual abilities at their peak and then determine from this standard the percentage of decline that sets in at different ages. To date, as has been pointed out, the only studies that have been made have been cross sectional, not longitudinal [5]. In addition, since it is a known fact that speed of action slows down with advancing age, tests of mental ability that emphasize the time element are unfair to older subjects. As Lorge has pointed out, in measuring mental decline, the "power to cope with mental tasks must be considered freed from the influence of other factors or traits that may obscure it. In our opinion, speed obscures sheer mental power in older adults" [72].

Cause of Mental Decline. In the past, mental changes in old age were attributed to arteriolosclerotic brain disease or to senile dementia [20]. It has also been assumed that with physical deterioration, mental deterioration is inevitable. This, however, has not been proved, though there is no question about the fact that decline in physical strength and vigor, decrease in sensory acuity, brain changes, and diseases common to old age affect not only the physical well-being of the individual but also his emotionality, his outlook on life, and his desire to do good work [5]. That physical decline contributes to mental decline has been shown by the fact that sex-hormone treatment of elderly women resulted in improvement in ability to think, to learn new material, to memorize, to remember and in willingness to expend intellectual energy [21]. In mental as in motor learning, continuation of practice through the years slows down the rate of decline. Since many of the old people who are used as subjects for studies of old age are institutional cases with few interests and little opportunity for mental stimulation they may lack proper work habits, and this suggests greater mental decline than would be true of a more representative sampling of the old-age population [57]. Probably the most common cause of decline in mental abilities with age is the individual's *attitude.* Tradition holds that as the individual grows older, he is "too old a dog to learn new tricks." Most elderly people accept this point of view and make little effort to learn new things. In addition, society calls on them little for new adjustments. As a result, the individual has little motivation to remain mentally alert and this hastens mental decline [72].

Areas of Decline. Just as there are differences in the rate of mental decline among different individuals of the same chronological age, with those of higher intellectual ability showing less decline than those of lower ability, so there are also differences within the same individuals in the rate of decline for different mental abilities. Even when the element of speed is eliminated and the tests are given as power tests to measure different mental abilities, declines of varying degrees have been found. Whether these are true declines or merely differences in mental abilities between the subjects chosen to represent younger people and those chosen as representative of old people is still undetermined. As has already been stressed, the only sure way of knowing whether there is a decline in mental abilities in old age and how great this decline is, is to use the longitudinal approach, comparing the results of mental measurements in old age with those of the same individuals during their youth or early adulthood. This, to date, has not been done.

Tests of *general intelligence* have shown that from the age of sixty years on, there is a decline in mental efficiency as measured by these tests. An analysis of the different mental abilities measured by these tests has shown the decline to be greatest in the tests involving learning and formation of new associations and least in those stressing general information and vocabulary [97]. In *learning* tasks, older subjects are more cautious, need more time to integrate their responses, and are less capable of dealing with novel material that cannot readily be integrated with earlier experiences than are younger subjects [13, 61]. As the complexity

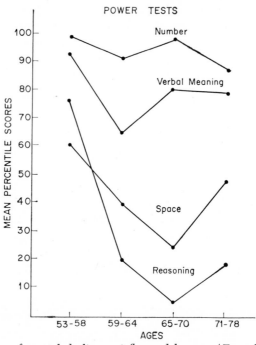

Fig. 122. Areas of mental decline as influenced by age. (*From K. W. Schaie, F. Rosenthal, and R. M. Perlman, Differential mental deterioration of factorially "pure" functions in later maturity. J. Geront., 1953, 8, 191–196. Used by permission.*)

of the task increases, older subjects require more time, are less accurate, and do not always comprehend the task. They often become confused when the task is complicated and this militates against their ability to organize their material in a logical way to correct their errors, though they are aware of their errors [26]. Even when they slow down, they continue to make mistakes as the complexity of the task is increased [6]. The ability to *reason* declines at a much faster rate than the abilities of verbal meanings and numbers, as shown in Figure 122 [95]. Old people tend to lack the capacity for *independent* and *creative* thinking [28]. They show limited ability to perform on an abstract level [106].

Forgetfulness is one of the popular criteria of old age. Tests of intellectual abilities have shown that old people have poor recent memories but good remote memories. Because motivation is important in memory, old people do not always have as strong a motivation to remember as do those who are younger. Furthermore, old people are usually not as attentive as they were when they were younger and, as a result, they do not get a clear impression of the things they see and hear, thus aiding forgetting. Deterioration in *vocabulary* is very slight in old age as compared with other mental abilities. This is because vocabulary is in constant use and the words used have, for the most part, been learned when the old person was a child or youth. Even in the late sixties, decline in vocabulary is less than in all other tests [37]. The *mental rigidity* that sets in during middle age becomes increasingly pronounced as age advances. While individuals differ in the degree of mental rigidity they experience, men as a group are more flexible than women because their mode of life gives them opportunities to adjust to new situations more often than is offered to women throughout their adult lives, and this aids in warding off mental rigidity. Part of the mental rigidity characteristic of old age comes from the fact that learning is slow and laborious as age advances. As a result, the individual takes the easiest way out by doing things in the old and tried way [23]. Old-age "childishness," often found in individuals in their seventies and eighties, is shown in forgetfulness, slowness of comprehension, emotional immaturity, and in animistic tendencies in which they attribute living qualities to inanimate objects, as children do [30].

Achievements. With decline in physical strength and energy and in mental abilities, especially the capacity for independent and creative thinking, it is logical that there would be a decline in creative achievements during old age. Significant achievements in creative work are less common among older than among younger people [97]. Quality of output has been found to decline more rapidly than quantity as age advances, and output of the highest quality declines faster than that of lesser merit [12, 69]. Among scientists, for example, there is a peak in reading scientific literature, followed by a falling off as the individual grows older. Scientists in the sixties publish about half as much as those in the thirties and forties, the peak years for productivity [29]. In spite of the fact that the individual's achievements have passed their peak in both quantity and quality by the time the individual reaches old age, he is generally not accorded full recognition and prestige until he reaches the latter years of life. Economic control of the United States, for example, is largely in the hands of bankers, capitalists, and financiers in the latter decades of life, as shown in Figure 123 [69]. By that time, the individual is literally "resting on his laurels" and is reaping the harvest of hard work and sacrifices made during the earlier years of his life.

Narrowing of Interests. This process, which began in middle age, continues as age advances. Instead of developing new interests, old people concentrate on interests acquired when they were younger and select from them the ones that give the greatest satisfaction. Even those that are satisfying often must be given up because of failing health, living conditions, money, and lack of companionship with their contemporaries. Changes in health and energy are reflected in an increase in sedentary pursuits and a decrease in activities that require strength and energy. Old people of the higher socioeconomic groups usually have a wider variety of interests, many of which are carry-overs of those developed in the earlier years of life. There is a close correlation between

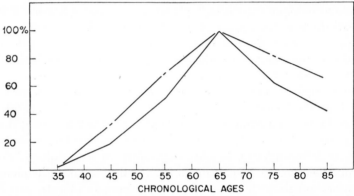

Fig. 123. Economic control of the U.S.A. at different ages. *Solid line,* bankers, capitalists, and financiers; *broken line,* trustees of private foundations and community trusts. (*From H. C. Lehman, Age and achievement. Princeton, N.J.: Princeton Univer. Press, 1953. Used by permission.*)

the number and types of interests the individual has and his happiness in old age [17]. The more interests the individual has to fill in the time formerly spent in other activities, such as work and homemaking, the better adjusted and, hence, the happier he will be. While members of the upper socioeconomic groups are, on the whole, more dependent upon themselves for their leisure-time activities than are those of the lower groups, most old people are happier if they have interests that bring them in contact with people [24]. If poor health or inadequate money makes the elderly person withdraw from contacts with others and thus further narrow the range of his interests, he usually makes poorer adjustments and is less happy than those who are not handicapped in this way [28].

Areas of Interest. Old people become increasingly more preoccupied with *self,* especially how they feel, as they grow older. Even when their physical condition is good, they are preoccupied with their health and with the bodily processes. They tend to complain about their health and to exaggerate any ailment they may have [104]. Interest in appearance wanes as age progresses. Some old people are as appearance-conscious as they were when they were younger but they are the exception to the rule. Most old people show little interest in how they look and thus do not try to make the best of their appearance through the use of clothes that hide the tell-tale signs of aging. This lack of interest in clothes is shown also in extreme conservatism about style and a tendency to cling to the styles in vogue when the individual was younger. Lack of interest in appearance in old age is often a form of compensation. The old person who is unwilling to accept the fact that he is aging often develops an "I don't care" attitude toward his appearance and frequently becomes slovenly and careless. Old men, as a rule, are more interested in their appearance than are old women. This is in direct contrast to the prevailing interests of younger people and may be explained by the fact that women use this as a compensation for the distress that failing looks bring them [3].

Interest in *money*, which starts to wane during middle age, generally is revived and becomes more intense as old age progresses. With retirement or unemployment, the elderly person usually finds himself with a greatly reduced income or with no income at all. This focuses his attention on money and stimulates an interest in the problem of how he can get more. Interest in money is not for the purpose of having more material possessions, as is true during adolescence and early adulthood, but rather to maintain independence and to be able to live where and how he wishes, free from dependency on charity or relatives [25].

While it is popularly believed that old people turn to religion as life draws to a close, there is little evidence of increased interest in *religion* with advancing age. Instead, most people carry on the religious habits formed earlier in life. As Havighurst and Albrecht have pointed out, "There is no evidence of a large-scale turning to religion of people as they grow older" [50]. While religious feelings do not increase with aging, there is usually a shift to a less strict adherence to religious dogmas and a more tolerant attitude toward the church and the clergy [20, 25]. There is also a falling off in *church attendance* and a decline in participation in *church activities*. This is not so much the result of poor health, as is popularly believed, as it is because older people have problems of transportation, they often feel they cannot dress properly, or are embarrassed because they cannot contribute financially. Furthermore, there is a strong belief on the part of older people that church activities are planned mainly for younger people, who want to run things as they please. As a result, many men and women withdraw from leadership roles in the church after sixty and are less active participants in the different church organizations than they formerly were. Dissatisfaction with the attitudes of the younger members toward them is, in many cases, responsible for their dropping out of these organizations [45].

Women, more often than men, continue to attend the meetings of the church organizations as they grow older because of the opportunities these organizations offer for social contacts [50]. Church activity in old age varies according to social class. Members of the upper class and the upper middle class are less active than are those of the lower middle class and upper lower class, for whom the church offers about the only opportunity available for social contacts outside of the family circle. Members of the lower lower class are relatively inactive in church affairs and attend infrequently because they feel they do not have the proper clothes [1].

While those who are church members are usually better adjusted to old age than are those who are not, the *quality* of membership is more important than membership per se. Those who joined voluntarily when they were younger and who have been active participants, often holding leadership roles, tend to be better adjusted in old age than are those whose interest and activity in religious organizations have been limited. Religion is only one factor in the adjustment to old age but it is an important one [83]. The relationship between church attendance and personal adjustment in old age may be affected more by the social experiences the church offers than by the religious experiences. It offers opportunities for social life and companionship, thus satisfying the older person's need to belong and to feel useful, and it minimizes feelings of loneliness. In addition, it alleviates anxieties about death and afterlife. Many old people look upon death as the "end" but those who have strong religious beliefs are more likely to think of it as the beginning of life hereafter. During the period after seventy, most people begin to fear death. This may explain why, at that time, many to whom religion was less important in their earlier years resort to a religious outlook to cope with their fears of death. Whatever the reasons for interest in religion, attendance at church, and participation in religious organizations, there is evidence that these contribute to good adjustment in old age [36, 45].

As a general rule, the *recreational* interests of elderly people are similar to those of the middle-aged, with a gradual narrowing down of interests as health fails (see Figure 86, page 396). Individuals of the higher intellectual and socioeconomic groups have, as a rule, more recreational interests, more hobbies, and are more self-sufficient about the use of their time than are those who are less bright, less well educated, and of lower socioeconomic status. Economic status and living conditions in old age likewise influence the number and type of recreational interests the individual has [17, 24, 25]. Until now, community interest has centered largely on providing recreations for the young and has left the elderly citizens to get along as best they can, providing their own recreations [82]. It is rather unusual when an old person cultivates a new recreational interest. He may, however, devote his time to an activity which interested him when he was younger but which he had to put aside because of the pressures of work and family life, or for economic reasons. For the most part, the recreations engaged in by elderly men and women are sedentary in character and require a minimum of physical strength and energy [49]. Among the common recreational interests of older people are reading, writing letters, listening to the radio, watching television, "visiting," sewing, embroidering, gardening, traveling, playing cards, going to the theater or movies, and taking part in civic, political, or religious organizations [20, 25, 50].

Old people suffer increasing *social* losses with age. Their social life is narrowed by loss of work associates, death of relatives, friends, and spouse, and poor health which restricts their participation in social activities [89]. There are three types of social relationships that are affected by aging: *close personal friendships,* as husband and wife, sister and sister, or chums from childhood days; *friendship cliques* made up of couples banded together when they were younger; and *formal groups* or clubs. Once broken, these social relationships are rarely replaced. Women, as a rule, retain their friendships longer than men mainly because their friends come from their neighborhoods while men's friends are largely from their work associates who live in scattered areas of the community and who are not brought together by their common interest in work after retirement [50]. Furthermore, as the elderly person's interest in self increases, interest in other people decreases. At first, he loses interest in acquaintances, then in his friends, then in a few intimate friends or "cronies," thus limiting his social interests to his immediate family.

To the elderly person, the family circle constitutes the nucleus of his social life. The older he is, the more he must rely upon his family for companionship (see Figure 59, page 284). His contemporaries have either died or are physically unable to do things with him. He finds it difficult or impossible to keep up to the pace set by his younger friends and, as a result, he is no longer a welcome member of a younger group. Thus, the old person must limit his social contacts to family members or to individuals of his own age. This means generally a group of intimate friends, many of whom have been friends since childhood days [1]. One of the advantages of institutional living for the elderly is that it provides opportunities for social contacts with contemporaries which are usually not available when the elderly live in homes of their own or with their relatives [89]. Social contacts with contemporaries have great advantages for the elderly, even though many elderly people resist making this adjustment and, as a result, cut themselves off from social contacts [50]. The elderly person's contemporaries have interests in common with his; he does not have to make radical adjustments in his pattern of behavior when he is with them; he moves physically and mentally at a tempo similar to theirs; he knows he is certain of acceptance because his friendship will help to eliminate their loneliness; and he has an opportunity for prestige, based on his past accomplishments, which he would not have in a group of younger people.

As age advances, *participation* in social activities declines and its scope narrows (see Figure 107, page 496). While declining health is generally believed to be the main reason for decline in social participation, this is not always true. The extent of the individual's participation when he was younger will have a marked influence on his participation in old age [50]. At every age, socioeconomic status plays an important role in the amount of participation in community organizations. Members of the upper groups dominate the organized life of the community and supply it with leadership. Because members of the lower groups usually do not belong to these organizations when they are younger, they hesitate to join them when they are older. Furthermore, because many of the community organizations are occupation-oriented, as is true of the different business clubs and trade unions, older people who are retired no longer belong to these organizations. What participation they engage in, then, is limited mainly to the nonoccupationally oriented organizations that emphasize sociability rather than occupational activities or opportunities to satisfy occupational aspirations or achieve advancement, as is true of the occupation-oriented organizations. This, in part, accounts for the dropping off of membership and participation in community organizations on the part of elderly people [105].

Married people are socially more active in old age than are those who are single or widowed, and those from the upper socioeconomic groups more than those from the lower [111]. Even when there are community organizations available that provide old people with opportunities for social contacts and activities, many do not belong to these organizations, and those who do belong attend meetings infrequently or take an inactive part when they do attend. This is not because of a lack of interest in social activities but for other reasons: most of the meetings, for example, are held at night when it is difficult for older people to go out; they cannot attend when the weather is unfavorable, as is true during a major part of the winter; they often find the dues and cost of transportation too great for their reduced incomes; they lack interest in the activities planned by the younger members who are now in leadership roles; or they feel rejected by the younger members of these organizations [50].

Many communities are trying to meet the social needs of the aged by establishing social clubs for them with activities planned to fit into their interests and capacities. These clubs are designed to offer entertainment and opportunities to form friendships with men and women of the same age level. To be successful, however, such clubs need strong leadership to plan the activities as there is a tendency on the part of those who are elderly to be passive in their approach to situations and wait for someone else to take the initiative. This is true regardless of whether the individual is living in his own home, in the home of a relative, or in an institution [31]. Those who take advantage of any opportunities they have for social participation and who make an effort to retain old friendships or establish new ones not only make a better adjustment to old age than do those who are socially inactive but they find old age a far happier period of life than they had anticipated when they were younger. As is true at every age, the social needs of the individual at that period of his life must be met and met to his satisfaction if he is to be happy [89].

BIBLIOGRAPHY

1. Albrecht, R.: Social class in old age. *Soc. Forces*, 1951, 29, 400–405.
2. Albrecht, R.: Social roles in the prevention of senility. *J. Geront.*, 1951, 6, 380–386.
3. Anderson, J. E.: *The psychology of development and personal adjustment*. New York: Holt, 1949.
4. Anderson, J. E.: *Psychological aspects of aging*. Washington, D.C.: American Psychological Ass., 1956.
5. Arnhoff, F. N.: Research problems in gerontology. *J. Geront.*, 1955, 10, 452–456.
6. Birren, J. E., W. R. Allen, and H. G. Landau: The relation of problem length in simple addition to time required, probability of success, and age. *J. Geront.*, 1954, 9, 150–161.
7. Birren, J. E., and J. Botwinick: Age differences in finger, jaw, and foot reaction time to auditory stimuli. *J. Geront.*, 1955, 10, 429–432.
8. Birren, J. E., R. C. Casperson, and J. Botwinick: Age changes in pupil size. *J. Geront.*, 1950, 5, 216–221.
9. Botwinick, J., B. F. Brinley, and J. E. Birren: Set in relation to age. *J. Geront.*, 1957, 12, 300–305.
10. Bowman, K. M.: Personality development in aging adults. *Geriatrics*, 1954, 9, 563–566.
11. Brodman, K., A. J. Erdmann, I. Lorge, and H. G. Wolff: The Cornell Medical Index-Health Questionnaire. VI. The relation of patients' complaints to age, sex, race, and education. *J. Geront.*, 1953, 8, 339–342.
12. Bromley, D. B.: Some experimental tests of the effect of age on creative intellectual output. *J. Geront.*, 1956, 11, 74–82.
13. Bromley, D. B.: Some effects of age on the quality of intellectual output. *J. Geront.*, 1957, 12, 318–323.
14. Brown, A. M.: Surgical restorative art for the aging face. *J. Geront.*, 1953, 8, 173–184.

15. Brozek, J.: Changes in sensory, motor, and intellective function with age. *Geriatrics*, 1951, 6, 221–226.
16. Bühler, C.: The curve of life as studied in biographies. *J. appl. Psychol.*, 1935, 19, 405–409.
17. Burgess, E. W.: Social relations, activities, and personal adjustment. *Amer. J. Sociol.*, 1954, 59, 352–360.
18. Burke, W. E., W. W. Tuttle, C. W. Thompson, C. D. Janney, and R. J. Weber: The relation of grip-strength endurance to age. *J. appl. Physiol.*, 1953, 5, 628–630.
19. Burstein, S. R.: The historical background of gerontology. *Geriatrics*, 1955, 10, 189–193.
20. Busse, E. W.: Studies in the process of aging: the strengths and weaknesses of psychic functioning in the aged. *Amer. J. Psychiat.*, 1955, 116, 896–901.
21. Caldwell, B. M., and R. I. Watson: An evaluation of sex hormone replacement in aged women. *J. genet. Psychol.*, 1954, 85, 181–200.
22. Carlson, A. J., and E. J. Stieglitz: Physiological changes in aging. *Ann. Amer. Acad. pol. soc. Sci.*, 1952, 279, 18–31.
23. Cavan, R. S., E. W. Burgess, R. J. Havighurst, and H. Goldhamer: *Personal adjustments in old age.* Chicago: Science Research Associates, 1949.
24. Chalfen, L.: Leisure-time adjustments of the aged. II. Activities and interests and some factors influencing choice. *J. genet. Psychol.*, 1956, 88, 261–276.
25. Chandler, A. R.: Attitudes of superior groups towards retirement and old age. *J. Geront.*, 1950, 5, 254–261.
26. Clay, H. M.: Changes of performance with age on similar tasks of varying complexity. *Brit. J. Psychol.*, 1954, 45, 7–13.
27. Clow, H. E.: Psychiatric factors in the rehabilitation of the aging. *Ment. Hyg., N.Y.*, 1950, 34, 592–599.
28. Davidson, H. H., and L. P. Kruglov: Personality characteristics of the institutionalized aged. *J. consult. Psychol.*, 1952, 16, 5–12.
29. Dennis, W., and E. Girden: Current scientific activities of psychologists as a function of age. *J. Geront.*, 1954, 9, 175–178.
30. Dennis, W., and B. Mallinger: Animism and related tendencies in senescence. *J. Geront.*, 1949, 4, 218–221.
31. Donahue, W., W. W. Hunter, and D. Coons: A study of the socialization of old people. *Geriatrics*, 1953, 8, 656–666.
32. Droller, H.: Falls among elderly people living at home. *Geriatrics*, 1955, 10, 239–244.
33. Edwards, A. E.: The myth of chronological age. *J. appl. Psychol.*, 1950, 34, 316–318.
34. Essert, P. L., I. Lorge, and J. Tuckman: Preparation for a constructive approach to later maturity. *Teach. Coll. Rec.*, 1951, 53, 70–76.
35. Feifel, H.: Psychiatric patients look at old age: level of adjustment and attitudes toward aging. *Amer. J. Psychiat.*, 1955, 111, 459–465.
36. Feifel, H.: Older persons look at death. *Geriatrics*, 1956, 11, 127–130.
37. Fox, C., and J. E. Birren: The differential decline of Wechsler subtest scores in 60–69 year old individuals. *Amer. Psychologist*, 1950, 5, 467.
38. Frank, L. K.: Aging—scope and perspectives. *Merrill-Palmer Quart.*, 1954, 1, 18–22.
39. Gardiner, L. P.: Attitudes and activities of the middle-aged and aged. *Geriatrics*, 1949, 4, 33–50.

40. Ghiselli, E. E.: The relationship between intelligence and age among superior adults. *J. genet. Psychol.*, 1957, 90, 131–142.

41. Gilbert, J. C.: Age changes in color matching. *J. Geront.*, 1957, 12, 210–215.

42. Ginzberg, R.: The negative attitude toward the elderly. *Geriatrics*, 1952, 7, 297–302.

43. Goldfarb, A. I.: Psychotherapy with aged persons: patterns of adjustment in a home for the aged. *Ment. Hyg., N.Y.*, 1955, 39, 608–621.

44. Goodenough, F. L.: *Developmental psychology*, 2d ed. New York: Appleton-Century-Crofts, 1945.

45. Gray, R. M.: The personal adjustment of the older person in the church. *Sociol. soc. Res.*, 1957, 41, 175–180.

46. Green, M. A., and M. B. Bender: Cutaneous perception in the aged. *Arch. Neurol. Psychiat.*, 1953, 69, 577–581.

47. Hart, H.: Expectations of life—actual versus predicted trends. *Soc. Forces*, 1954, 33, 82–85.

48. Havighurst, R. J.: *Human development and education.* New York: Longmans, 1953.

49. Havighurst, R. J.: The leisure activities of the middle-aged. *Amer. J. Sociol.*, 1957, 63, 152–162.

50. Havighurst, R. J., and R. Albrecht: *Older people.* New York: Longmans, 1953.

51. Havighurst, R. J., and B. E. Orr: Aging and psychological adjustment. *Rev. educ. Res.*, 1955, 25, 477–486.

52. Hayes, O. B., L. J. Bowser, and M. F. Trulson: Relation of dietary intake to bone fragility in the aged. *J. Geront.*, 1956, 11, 154–159.

53. Howell, T. H.: Urinary excretion after the age of ninety. *J. Geront.*, 1956, 11, 61–65.

54. Johnson, R. J., and M. A. Pond: Health standards of housing for the aging population. *J. Geront.*, 1952, 7, 254–258.

55. Kallman, F. J., and G. Sander: Twin studies in senescence. *Amer. J. Psychiat.*, 1949, 106, 29–36.

56. Kaplan, L., J. H. Landes, and J. Pincus: The nutritional status of non-institutionalized aged persons. *Geriatrics*, 1955, 10, 287–290.

57. Kaplan, O. J.: Psychological aspects of aging. *Ann. Amer. Acad. pol. soc. Sci.*, 1952, 279, 32–42.

58. Kessler, H. E.: Speech problems of elderly denture wearers. *Geriatrics*, 1955, 10, 339–341.

59. Kleemeier, R. W.: The effect of a work program on adjustment attitudes in an aged population. *J. Geront.*, 1951, 6, 372–379.

60. Kleemeier, R. W.: The relationship between orthorater tests of acuity and color vision in a senescent group. *J. appl. Psychol.*, 1952, 36, 114–116.

61. Korchin, S. J., and H. Basowitz: Age differences in verbal learning. *J. abnorm. soc. Psychol.*, 1957, 54, 64–69.

62. Korenchevsky, V.: Endocrines and aging. *N.Y. State Joint Legislative Committee on Problems of the Aging*, 1952, 120–128.

63. Krag, C. L., and W. B. Kountz: Stability of body function in the aged. II. Effect of exposure of the body to heat. *J. Geront.*, 1952, 7, 61–70.

64. Kuhlen, R. G.: Social change: a neglected factor in psychological studies of the life span. *Sch. and Soc.*, 1940, 52, 14–16.

65. Kuhlen, R. G.: Age differences in personality during adult years. *Psychol. Bull.*, 1945, 42, 333–358.

66. Kvorning, S. A., and E. Kirk: The correlation between the clinical appearance

of the skin lipid secretion in middle-aged and old individuals. *J. Geront.*, 1949, 4, 113–120.

67. Laurence, W. L.: Sterile blood plasmas provide new ways to attack disease and prolong life. *The New York Times*, 1957, May 12.

68. Lawton, G.: *Aging successfully*. New York: Columbia Univer. Press, 1951.

69. Lehman, H. C.: *Age and achievement*. Princeton, N.J.: Princeton Univer. Press, 1953.

70. Lepkowski, J. R.: The attitudes and adjustments of institutionalized and non-institutionalized Catholic aged. *J. Geront.*, 1956, 11, 185–191.

71. Linden, M. E.: Effects of social attitudes on the mental health of the aging. *Geriatrics*, 1957, 12, 109–114.

72. Lorge, I.: Psychology and our older people. *New York State Joint Legislative Committee on Problems of the Aging*, 1952, 62–64.

73. Lorge, I.: Gerontology (later maturity). *Annu. Rev. Psychol.*, 1956, 7, 349–364.

74. Lyons, J. S., and M. F. Trulson: Food practices of older people living at home. *J. Geront.*, 1956, 11, 66–72.

75. Mack, M. J.: Personal adjustment of chronically ill old people under home care. *Geriatrics*, 1953, 8, 407–416.

76. Mason, E. P.: Some factors in self-judgments. *J. clin. Psychol.*, 1954, 10, 336–346.

77. Masters, W. H., and J. W. Ballew: The third sex. *Geriatrics*, 1955, 10, 1–4.

78. McFarland, R. A., and M. B. Fisher: Alterations in dark adaptation as a function of age. *J. Geront.*, 1955, 10, 424–428.

79. Mead, M.: *Male and female*. New York: Morrow, 1949.

80. Meerloo, J. A. M.: Transference and resistance in geriatric psychotherapy. *Psychoanal. Rev.*, 1955, 42, 72–82.

81. Metropolitan Life Insurance Report: Accidents to aged cut 15% in 6 years. *The New York Times*, 1957, Aug. 28.

82. Meyer, H. D.: The adult cycle. *Ann. Amer. Acad. pol. soc. Sci.*, 1957, 313, 58–67.

83. Moberg, D. O.: Religious activities and personal adjustment in old age. *J. soc. Psychol.*, 1956, 43, 261–267.

84. Murray, I. M.: Assessment of physiologic age by combination of several criteria —vision, hearing, blood pressure, and muscle force. *J. Geront.*, 1951, 6, 120–126.

85. New York Times Report: Aids to morale needed for aged. *The New York Times*, 1955, Feb. 24.

86. New York Times Report: Aid to the aging termed urgent. *The New York Times*, 1955, Oct. 28.

87. New York Times Report: Body cells cited as cause of aging. *The New York Times*, 1956, Sept. 30.

88. New York Times Report: Women increase majority in U.S. *The New York Times*, 1956, Nov. 12.

89. Pressey, S. L.: Potentials of age: an exploratory field study. *Genet. Psychol. Monogr.*, 1957, 56, 159–205.

90. Pressey, S. L., and R. G. Kuhlen: *Psychological development through the life span*. New York: Harper, 1957.

91. Ranall, O. A.: The health needs of older people. *Marriage Fam. Living*, 1957, 19, 187–192.

92. Riesman, D.: Some clinical and cultural aspects of aging. *Amer. J. Sociol.*, 1954, 59, 379–383.

93. Rumnick, L. S.: Aging and pupillary response to light and sound. *J. Geront.*, 1956, 11, 38–45.

94. Ryan, E. J.: The dental problems of senescence. *J. Geront.*, 1949, 4, 326–329.

95. Schaie, K. W., F. Rosenthal, and R. M. Perlman: Differential mental deterioration of factorially "pure" functions in later maturity. *J. Geront.*, 1953, 8, 191–196.

96. Shanas, E.: The personal adjustment of recipients of old age assistance. *J. Geront.*, 1950, 5, 249–253.

97. Shock, N. W.: Aging and psychological adjustment. *Rev. educ. Res.*, 1952, 22, 439–458.

98. Shock, N. W., and M. J. Yiengst: Age changes in basal respiratory measurements and metabolism in males. *J. Geront.*, 1955, 10, 31–40.

99. Simmons, L. W.: *The role of the aged in primitive society.* New Haven, Conn.: Yale Univer. Press, 1945.

100. Simmons, L. W.: Social participation of the aged in different cultures. *Ann. Amer. Acad. pol. soc. Sci.*, 1952, 279, 43–51.

101. Simonton, K. M.: Presbycusis: the hearing loss of old age. *Geriatrics*, 1955, 10, 337–338.

102. Stieglitz, E. J.: Orientation in gerontology. *In* New York Academy of Medicine, *Biological foundation of health education.* New York: Columbia Univer. Press, 1950. Pp. 96–116.

103. Still, J. W.: Man's potential—and his performance. *The New York Times*, 1957, Nov. 24.

104. Strom, A.: An investigation into the living conditions and health of 1,389 persons aged 70 years or more in Norway. *J. Geront.*, 1956, 11, 178–184.

105. Taietz, P., and O. F. Larson: Social participation and old age. *Rural Sociol.*, 1956, 21, 229–238.

106. Thaler, M.: Relationships among Wechsler, Weigl, Rorschach, EEG findings in abstract-concrete behavior in a group of normal aged subjects. *J. Geront.*, 1956, 11, 404–409.

107. Tibbitts, C., and H. D. Sheldon: A philosophy of aging. *Ann. Amer. Acad. pol. soc. Sci.*, 1952, 279, 1–10.

108. Tuckman, J., and I. Lorge: Attitudes toward old people. *J. soc. Psychol.*, 1953, 37, 249–260.

109. Tuckman, J., I. Lorge, R. W. Steinhardt, and F. D. Zeman: Somatic and psychological complaints of older people in institutions and at home. *Geriatrics*, 1953, 8, 274–279.

110. Vest, W. E.: William Shakespeare, gerontologist. *Geriatrics*, 1954, 9, 80–82.

111. Webber, I. L.: The organized social life of the retired: two Florida communities. *Amer. J. Sociol.*, 1954, 59, 340–346.

112. Wesman, A. C.: Standardizing an individual intelligence test on adults: some problems. *J. Geront.*, 1955, 10, 216–219.

113. Willie, C. V.: Group relationships of the elderly in our culture. *Soc. Casewk*, 1954, 35, 206–212.

Old Age

Continued

Two of the most important areas of life for an adult, his work and his family, present adjustment problems common in some respects to those of other periods in life but with features that are unique to old age. Not only must he adjust to working conditions in his chosen vocation but, in addition, he must adjust to the realization that his usefulness is lessened as he grows older and, as a result, his status in the work group is lower. Furthermore, he has the problem of adjusting to retirement when it is considered that his usefulness to the work world has come to an end. In the family, older men and women must adjust to the dependency on one another for companionship, to the lack of contact with and influence on their children, and to widowhood for the remaining spouse when the marital relationship is broken by death. These two areas of adjustment are complicated by the economic factor which plays an even more important role than it did in the adjustments of earlier periods in life [51]. To be well adjusted and happy in old age, both men and women must adjust to the realization that, in the eyes of society, their usefulness and prestige have waned and they are looked upon as "has-beens." Only when they can convince themselves and others that they still are useful and that they have a status in the group that is satisfying to them are old people able to be happy in the closing years of life.

Changes in Work. Most older people, unless their health is poor, want to work and would continue if they could get employment [68]. Even women who did not work during the early years of adulthood when they were preoccupied with the care of their homes and children often return to work during middle age and find it a satisfactory substitute for the lost role of parenthood. If employment were available and if their health permitted, they, like men, would want to work as long as they were able to do so. The reasons for wanting to work are different for different people, even though they are in different occupations. Their reasons for wanting to work are dependent on what work means to them personally. To some, it is a basis for self-respect and a sense of worth; to others, it is a source of prestige; some find in work a locus of social participation where one can enjoy the companionship of other people; or it may be a source of intrinsic enjoyment or of creative self-expression, a way of being of service to others, a way of making time pass in a pleasant routine manner, a way of earning a living, or a heavy and unpleasant burden. The prevailing *cultural attitude* toward work also influences the individual's attitude. The United States used to be a work-centered society where work and achievement were highly valued. Since World War I, but especially since the depression of the early thirties, emphasis has been placed more on the value of leisure than of work. Old people who grew up during the time when the cultural attitude toward work was more favorable than it is today have a very different attitude toward work, established when they were young people, than do the young people of today. This colors their attitude toward their own work and increases the difficulties of adjusting to not being able to get employment if they are physically able to work. For those to whom work means status and prestige, there is a preference for work on a part-time basis in that line to full employment in work on a lower level and with less prestige [51].

To be happy, the individual must feel that he is *useful* to society and that his services are of value to his family and the community. In addition, he must have *status* in the group with which he is identified. The higher the prestige his status gives him in the eyes of his family, friends, neighbors, and work associates, the happier he will be. For a work-oriented individual, as are most of those who grew up in a work-centered society when work was the main source of status and feelings of usefulness, having work to do that gives him both status and feelings of usefulness is essential to good mental health. For such individuals, remunerative work with some reward is essential to good adjustment [90]. Studies of the elderly have shown that those who continue to work have more normal brain functioning and are better adjusted than those who do not work. They also do better on intelligence tests than those who are idle [21]. For those who are able and willing to work, there is no question about the fact that it is best for them to do so, especially when it is a means for them to maintain good physical and mental health and retain their self-respect [72].

Unfortunately, for those who want to work and are able to do so, there are very few work opportunities available. Most industrial plants, government bureaus and agencies, and businesses fix sixty-five as the compulsory retirement age for men and many require women to retire at sixty [68]. When the personnel departments of business and industry are in the hands of younger people, the barrier to the employment of older workers is greatly increased [1]. There is a close correlation between the existence of a pension plan in business and industry and the failure to make use of workers over sixty-five years of age. In one survey, for example, it was found that of the firms that did not have pension plans, 93 per cent kept on most or all of their employees who were on an hourly basis and 87 per cent kept on all or most of their salaried employees who were sixty-five years of age. Firms with pension plans, by contrast, kept on the employees who worked on an hourly basis in only 33 per cent of the cases and salaried employees at sixty-five in only 26 per cent of the cases [37]. Difficulties older people face when they want to work come from a decline in the importance of agriculture or the small-scale type of urban enterprise and fluctuations in the business cycle which, during periods of restricted business, lead to the laying off of the older workers who are then replaced by younger workers when business improves [25].

Vocational Opportunities. With each passing year, the individual is capable of producing less than he did when he was younger. His failing strength and energy sap his motivation, and society gives him relatively little chance to do even what he is capable of doing. As a result, the output of the older person, measured in terms of achievement and income, falls short of that of the middle-aged or younger person. (See Figure 108, page 501, for a graphic description of fall in income with advancing age.) The type of work the individual engages in determines to some extent the duration of his usefulness. In executive positions, his days of employment in large and even in some of the smaller organizations are limited by retirement policies. Several years prior to retirement, he is aware of the fact that a younger man is being groomed to succeed him and that his influence in the organization is waning. Clerical workers are usually retired at sixty-five, if they have been able to retain their jobs for that long. The skilled, semiskilled, or unskilled worker finds that as his speed and strength decrease with age, his usefulness to the organization likewise decreases and he is often laid off during a slack period, only to be replaced by a younger worker when conditions improve. In high-grade skills, a small fall in performance is noticed around the age of fifty, but there is great variability in this fall with advancing age [26]. Only when a person is in business for himself or in a profession where he is not employed by an organization can he continue to work as long or as much as he wishes without an arbitrarily set retirement age [86].

After middle age, vocational opportunities decrease rapidly. For the most part, older workers, though they engage in a wide variety of different types of work, are in dead-end, monotonous jobs far below the level of their ability or the standards they would find satisfying, while relatively few are in highly skilled or responsible jobs. In business and industry, only the poorest jobs are available to the older worker [86]. Older workers are overrepresented in vocations that are on the wane, stationary, or increasing only very slowly, and they are underrepresented in new and rapidly growing occupations requiring special and newer skills. They engage less in hazardous occupations and those requiring wide geographic mobility, much formal schooling, strenuous physical exertion, agility, and speed. Farmers, small businessmen, real-estate agents, bankers, workers at independent hand trades, and certain professional workers remain in their own lines of work longer than do wage and salary workers because they can control work loads and hours of work. On the whole, older workers are overrepresented at the bottom of the earning scale, in jobs in which the pay rate is comparatively small, and underrepresented at the top of the earning scale [68]. Under such conditions, it is not surprising that older workers find little satisfaction in their jobs.

Even though older workers are unable to compete successfully with younger workers for jobs requiring continuous bodily movement and activity, especially when the worker is paced by a machine or conveyor, or in business where speed is essential, there are many types of work where the skills and experience of the older worker can and should be utilized [13]. By transferring them to jobs suited to their age, or by changing the nature and layout of the job without making them feel inadequate, they can become real assets to their employers [101]. Part-time employment has been found to be especially well suited to older workers. In department stores or other lines of work where the cost of training makes rapid turnover a serious problem, the length of time a worker is available is important. Older workers are available for such work much more so than are younger workers and, as a result, they are being utilized in increasing numbers in organizations where part-time or seasonal work is needed [103]. The best types of work for an elderly person who wants to work and is physically able to do so are unhurried, skilled, somewhat independent types, adjusted in time and effort to the individual's energies and limitations. Being a specialist in certain fields or working part time in a field in which the individual can make use of past training and experience meets the needs of the elderly best [13].

In spite of the fact that many elderly women want to work or must work for financial reasons stemming from widowhood or the incapacity of their husbands for work, women find it even more difficult to hold their jobs or to get new ones as they grow older than do men. Figure 88, page 417, shows the sharp decline in the number of women who work after fifty-five years of age. The traditional belief that women, after the menopause, are no longer capable of doing what they did when they were younger affects their vocational lives just as it affects their sex lives. Just as is true of men, there are marked individual differences in women's abilities to hold jobs and to do the work these jobs require. For women as for men, these differences become greater with advancing age. Even those women who returned to their former vocations in middle age, after their children no longer needed their entire time and attention, or who began to work outside of the home for the first time in middle age find it difficult to hold their jobs after sixty because many business and industrial organizations have compulsory retirement for women at that age. Other organizations which do not have compulsory retirement are likely to lay off older women first when business becomes slack and then replace them with younger women as business conditions improve. For older women, part-time work in stores and offices is one of the few vocational opportunities open to them [9, 103].

Unemployment. Unemployment strikes hard at any age, but as the individual becomes older, being unemployed is a very serious problem. When a person is physically and mentally able to work and wants to do so, either because of financial necessity or for the status-giving satisfaction work brings, being laid off during a period of slack work and then being replaced later, as business conditions improve, by a younger and often less-experienced person, is a frustrating and humiliating experience. In 1952, for example, 5 per cent of the workers over sixty-five who wanted to work were unemployed as compared with 3.1 per cent of the twenty-five- to forty-four-year-old group. The average duration of unemployment for the older group was 20.5 weeks as compared with an average of 8.9 weeks for the younger group [5]. Not only is it harder for the older worker to get another job than it is for a younger, but the effects on his personality are far more serious and far-reaching than is true of the younger worker. The younger worker knows that his chances of obtaining future employment are good, even if he must take a temporary setback in wages. With the older worker, there is a far less hopeful outlook. He knows that most business and industrial organizations have a strict policy against hiring older workers and that if he is lucky enough to get a job, it will likely be far below his capacities, the pay will be much less than he formerly received, and the job may be only temporary or on a part-time basis [13].

The type of work the individual engages in determines the ease or difficulty he encounters in changing jobs or in getting a job, if he is unemployed. As a general rule, workers who are at the two extremes of the business or industrial ladders are in the least favorable positions in this respect. After fifty, stepping into an important executive position is almost impossible. The less skilled the older worker, the less chance he has of getting a new job. It is feared that he is "too old a dog to learn new tricks" and that he is not quick enough to keep up to the pace that modern business and industry demand. In general, it is more difficult for an individual who has left his job or has been released to find employment of any sort than for one who merely wants or needs a change because he finds the work he is doing too taxing on his strength or at a pace too fast for him as he grows older [8].

Studies of the *mental effects* of unemployment on older workers have revealed how serious they are. Measures of the mental efficiency and attitudes of employed and unemployed older people have shown that those who engage in regular, gainful occupation are, on the whole, superior to those who are unemployed. Lack of practice, motivation, and unfavorable attitudes are important contributing factors to the deterioration that comes with unemployment [21]. While it is difficult or almost impossible in our present cultural setup to eliminate completely unemployment among older workers, some of the unemployment could be eliminated by correcting prejudices that lead to discrimination against older workers, attempting to find work suited to the health and mental abilities of the individuals while, at the same time, making use of their past skills and experience, and by trying to prevent workers from becoming technologically and physiologically obsolete as they grow older. Among highly trained specialists, such as psychologists, use can be made of their services in work related to their training and experience, even when they have passed the retirement age [89].

Appraisal of Older Workers. Many elderly people want to work and they feel that they are capable of doing the work the jobs they have been trained to do require. They resent the lack of opportunity to work and the fact that it is not recognized that their slowing down with age is compensated for by their increased wisdom and experience [48]. Employers, on the other hand, emphasize the disadvantages to business and industry brought about by the employment of older people. They accept the popular belief that older workers are unable to work under younger supervisors, that they resist change in work methods or the introduction of new machinery, and that they are difficult to work with [111]. The older the employer or the employee, the more favorable he is likely to be toward the employment of older workers [64]. Studies of the advantages and disadvantages of older workers reveal that they differ according to the type of work to be done. Some jobs are more appropriate for older and some for younger workers. Jobs in which judgment and experience are required or in which quality is more important than speed are more appropriate for older workers. Even in work where speed and ability to adjust to new tasks are essential, as in skilled, unskilled, and clerical work, the older worker usually compensates for loss of speed and difficulties of adjustment by his steadiness, attendance, and ability to work without supervision [101]. And yet, in spite of the prevailing opinion among employers that older workers are better for certain types of jobs than younger workers, the practice of personnel officers is usually to discriminate against the older worker and to employ a younger worker [96].

Appraisals of older workers in comparison with younger workers have revealed that the older worker is equal to and, in some respects, superior to the younger worker, though in some qualities he is inferior to the younger worker. The older worker, through his experience, tends to do things with less waste motion than does the younger, less-experienced worker. As a result, he compensates for a work pace that is lower than that of the younger worker. He is less inclined to distractions from home and other outside sources than is the younger worker, whose interests are centered around his romances or his family life. He is less restless and less likely to be dissatisfied with his job or to want to change jobs than is the younger worker. While the volume of his work may fall below that of the younger worker, the quality is generally higher and he spoils less material. He makes fewer mistakes partly because his judgment is better and partly because he works at a slower pace and does not jump to conclusions without adequate study of the situation.

There is greater conscientiousness among older workers because of their more mature attitudes and their desire to keep their jobs. As a result, they can be depended on in whatever they do. Absenteeism, due to illness or disinclination to work, is a problem that plagues most employers. Absenteeism is highest among the younger workers, especially those under twenty years of age, while older workers are far less prone to absenteesim (see Figure 124). Disabling illnesses and injuries, popularly believed to make older workers less desirable employment risks, are far less frequent than believed and are less frequent than among younger workers. Even workers up to seventy-four years of age are affected by chronic disabilities in only about half the cases and these are not serious enough to militate against their working abilities. No age group over fifty years has been found to have a rate for disabling injuries as high as the thirty-five to forty-five-year group [47, 96]. Accident proneness is likewise far less among older workers than is popularly believed. In the case of professional truck drivers, for example, older drivers have fewer accidents than do younger drivers. Awareness that they are slower and less able to meet crises than they once were makes them anxious and they compensate for this by being cautious [73]. As for the argument that older workers get along less well with other workers than do those who are younger, this likewise has not been found to be true. While some older workers unquestionably make poorer adjustments to their fellow workers than do others, the percentage who do so is not appreciably greater than is true in the case of younger workers [16, 84]. In summary, the "values of older workers have actually been adequately demonstrated; the big need, now, is to develop adjustments to meet the needs of the older, and agencies to foster opportunities for them" [90].

Retirement. To the younger person whose days are so often overly crowded with duties and responsibilities, retirement or semiretirement seems like a golden period of life. By middle age, thoughts of retirement

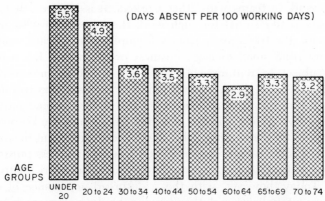

Fig. 124. Days absent from work per 100 days for workers of different ages. (*From M. Gumpert, Our "Inca" ideas about retirement. The New York Times, July 27, 1952. Used by permission.*)

grow increasingly strong not only because the individual finds the burden of work becoming heavier and heavier as his strength and energy diminish but also because he realizes that in his competition with younger workers he is waging a losing battle. He must use greater effort to complete the tasks his job requires; traveling to and from his work is now a greater strain than it was when he was younger; and he wants to do things and pursue interests he never has had time for. He, therefore, looks forward to retirement as an acceptable withdrawal from the competitive arena and as a way of eliminating the anxieties and strain of keeping up to the pace set by younger workers [116]. But when the time comes and the days of retirement arrive, the situation seems far less rosy than it did when viewed through the eyes of a younger person. For most elderly people, there is a marked difference between the expectations before retirement and the realities of retirement [99]. Relinquishing lifetime patterns and suddenly changing habits of a lifetime give rise to an "experience which can be quite traumatic" for the elderly person [68].

Since World War I, there has been a growing tendency to enforce retirement on American workers at an arbitrarily set age, regardless of the capacities of the individual when he reaches that age. This tendency has increased and has become more widespread since the depression years of the thirties and World War II. In 1955, 55 per cent of women workers over sixty-five years of age and 43 per cent of the men were retired, as compared with 22 per cent of the women and 18 per cent of the men in 1940 [81]. The trend toward compulsory retirement at a fixed age is due mainly to scientific and technological achievements which require constant readjustment to new methods and machinery, speed of work, and ability to work in teams with other workers. It is believed that younger workers are better suited for such work than are those who are older. Furthermore, the trend away from self-employment toward working for others, and from small to large business organizations, has made most workers subject to requirements set down by their employers [109]. When attempts have been made to find out how workers feel about retirement, the results have shown that most of them would rather work than be inactive. While it is true that many feel unable to keep up to the pace required by their former jobs, they nevertheless want to work, even if it means a job with less responsibility, less pay, and less prestige [38].

Until recently, retirement was a problem that affected relatively few workers. Today, however, with the widespread acceptance of compulsory-retirement policies and the growing tendency for more men and women to live longer than ever before, retirement is becoming one of the major social problems of our culture. Each year, the gap between the total life span and the span of the working life for men and women is widening. It has been estimated that a twenty-year-old male worker in 1975 may expect to spend an average of 10 years outside the labor force, in retirement, as compared with $5\frac{1}{2}$ years in 1940 and less than 3 years in 1900. Thus, with the increasing life span and the decreasing work life, the average worker in the future can anticipate an ever-increasing time in retirement [24] (see Figure 125). As Havighurst and Albrecht have pointed out, "Retirement is the greatest man-made problem in the lives of most of us" [51].

Attitude toward Retirement. Not all workers feel the same way toward retirement. What their attitude is will be influenced by many factors, the most important of which are:

ATTITUDE TOWARD WORK. The older person's attitude toward retirement is influenced by what work has meant to him. When work has a strong personal value for the individual, he will adjust with difficulty to retirement. As Michelon has pointed out, there is an inverse correlation between a person's adjustment to his job and his probable adjustment to retirement [76]. For those who grew up in an era when work had high personal values, as is true of most elderly people of today, adjustment to retirement is difficult unless substitutes can be found to provide the gratifications associated with work [52]. For those to whom work has no great psychological value, on the other hand, adjustment to retirement

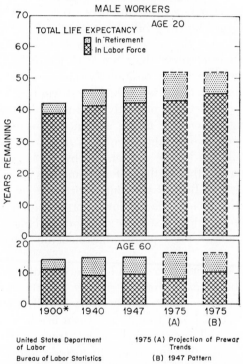

Fig. 125. Total life expectancy in relation to work-life expectancy from 1900 to 1975. (*From E. Clague, The working life span of American workers. J. Geront.,* 1949, 4, 285–289. *Used by permission.*)

is made easily, especially if the individual has a number of vital interests outside his work [40]. Attitudes toward work vary according to the type of work the individual does. In the professions, prestige affects individuals' attitudes unfavorably toward retirement. Instead of giving up work entirely, they prefer to work on a full- or part-time basis in lines where their training has given them status and prestige. Nonprofessional workers, on the other hand, want to "retire and take it easy," especially if their pensions are adequate to enable them to live comfortably. The skilled, semiskilled, and unskilled workers, on the other hand, want to continue to work, but mainly for economic reasons [40, 95].

TYPE OF RETIREMENT. While many older workers want to be free from the routines and pressures of work, they do not want to give up work completely and thus be deprived of the income, the feeling of usefulness, the opportunities for social contacts, and the other values they associate with work. The type of retirement determines to a large extent whether they will be able to satisfy most of their work desires or not. In general, there are five different types of retirement used today: complete retirement at a fixed age; tapering off of activity in the same job; slowing down and turning over the responsibility to a person being trained as a successor; a lower-level job in the same work hierarchy; and a shift to a different and less demanding position in another work situation [52]. When left to the choice of the individual, most would select the tapering-off-of-activity type of retirement partly because it does not mean loss of status and prestige, even if it means a reduction in income, and partly because it does not involve adjustment to a new work situation [88]. If the successor is chosen by the worker, not by the organization employing the older worker, this method of retirement is likewise satisfactory to most older workers. Being forced into retirement by dismissal, serious illness, or discontinuance of the employing organization, especially when there has been no warning, is so emotionally disturbing to the individual that it seriously affects the type of adjustment he makes to retirement [38].

PREPARATION FOR RETIREMENT. To adjust successfully to retirement, the individual must be prepared for the changes in pattern of living retirement will bring, and he must also be economically prepared. For the most part, the major interest to date has been in economic preparation. Large corporations and industries which put strong emphasis on pension plans are, today, enlarging their work to include individual and group counseling to help their workers, as they approach the retirement age, with their retirement plans and adjustments. This, however, is far from a universal practice; most workers are expected to make their own adjustments as best they can [110]. Because many workers do not want to retire, they resist the idea of retirement and this militates against their preparing themselves psychologically for it. For the worker who believes that retirement is the "worst thing that could happen to a person," there is little likelihood that he will be prepared to meet the problems retirement brings [18]. Then, when the time comes for retirement, or if poor health and loss of job bring it sooner than has been anticipated, the traumatic effect is even more serious than if it had been anticipated, though resisted.

ECONOMIC CONDITION. If the economic side of the picture could be eliminated, retirement might not prove to be the psychological problem for the elderly that it is. But retirement brings with it economic problems that have serious effects on the individual's concept of self, the status he holds in the family, and the prestige he has in the eyes of the community, thus leading to many emotional conflicts with their damaging effects. After retirement, many elderly people are in genuine need of money for the necessities of life. Their desire to continue working is often motivated by the need for enough money to meet the necessities of happy, healthy living. Much of the resistance against retirement stems from fear of a future in which there will not be adequate money to provide for the remaining years of life. This problem affects the wife's attitude toward her husband's retirement and intensifies the adjustment problems for both [18, 109].

Relatively few elderly people have adequate incomes from investments to meet their needs; most must depend instead on economic aid from public or private sources, such as government, churches, institutions, friends, and relatives. While some do continue to work, full or part time, most do not earn enough to meet their needs. At the present time, 8 million old people receive old-age and survivor's insurance benefits and 17,000 belong to private pension plans [80, 81]. Since 1932, there has been an increase from 5 to 60 per cent in the number of old people who receive income from old-age and survivor's insurance and an increase from less than 1 to 8 per cent in the number of those who have income from private pensions [5]. Old-age assistance, supported mainly by grants to the states by the Federal government and administered by the states, contributes to the support of approximately 2.5 million people over sixty-five years of age at the present time [81]. The average size of old-age benefits for a retired worker is $47 monthly and for a retired worker and his wife, $77, amounts which are hopelessly inadequate to meet the present high cost of living. To make matters worse, benefits are withheld if the individual *earns* more than $1,200 annually though no penalty is imposed on those who derive their income from investments or from private pension plans. Only after the individual reaches seventy-two years of age may he earn as much as he wishes and is able to without losing these benefits [47, 81]. Inflationary trends, which have been on the rise since World War II, cause great hardship not only for those who receive old-age assistance but also for those who are living on pensions. There is a growing demand for greater social-security benefits but this would be a hardship on younger workers who would be forced to pay even more out of their earnings than they now do [32]. The percentages of families in the various income groups whose heads are sixty-five years of age or older are shown in Figure 126.

SUBSTITUTE ACTIVITIES. When a person has been accustomed to working for the major part of his life, first in school and then on a job, being robbed suddenly of work and responsibility can be and often is a traumatic experience. As Alexis Carrel has pointed out, "Leisure is even more dangerous for the old than for the young." Wayne emphasized this even more forcefully when he said, "Inactivity is a catalyst for senility and death" [116]. Enforced leisure, over a period of time, often brings boredom. This is especially true when the individual has not been accustomed to leisure and has not, as a result, learned to use leisure in a way that is satisfying to him [75]. Figure 127 shows the ways men spent their time

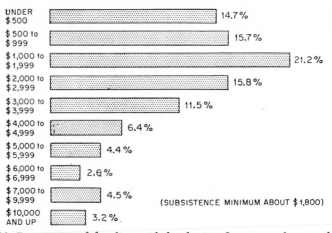

FIG. 126. Percentages of families, with heads sixty-five years of age and over, in the various income groups. (*From M. Gumpert, Our "Inca" ideas about retirement. The New York Times, July 27, 1952. Used by permission.*)

in 1885 as compared with 1950 and the predictions for the year 2000. The main difference, as this diagram shows, is in the amount of time spent in work and leisure. To meet the needs of more leisure at all ages, but especially in the period following retirement, there should be more adult education to help individuals acquire new interests and skills and to encourage more cultural interests [106].

Not only is inactivity a problem for the retired worker but his whole family suffers also. The increased hours spent at home by an unhappy and dissatisfied retired man, the lack of opportunities for social contacts with other men which he had daily in his work, and the feelings of uselessness or of "being through," which so many retired men experience, all contribute to the creation of problems for the entire family. The retired man is likely to make undue demands on the different family members, but especially on his wife, thus creating stress and friction with his wife and difficulties in his relationships with his children and grandchildren [46]. Furthermore, the younger members of the family fear that retirement and loss of income may cause them to lose their independence by the necessity of caring for an invalid or assuming the

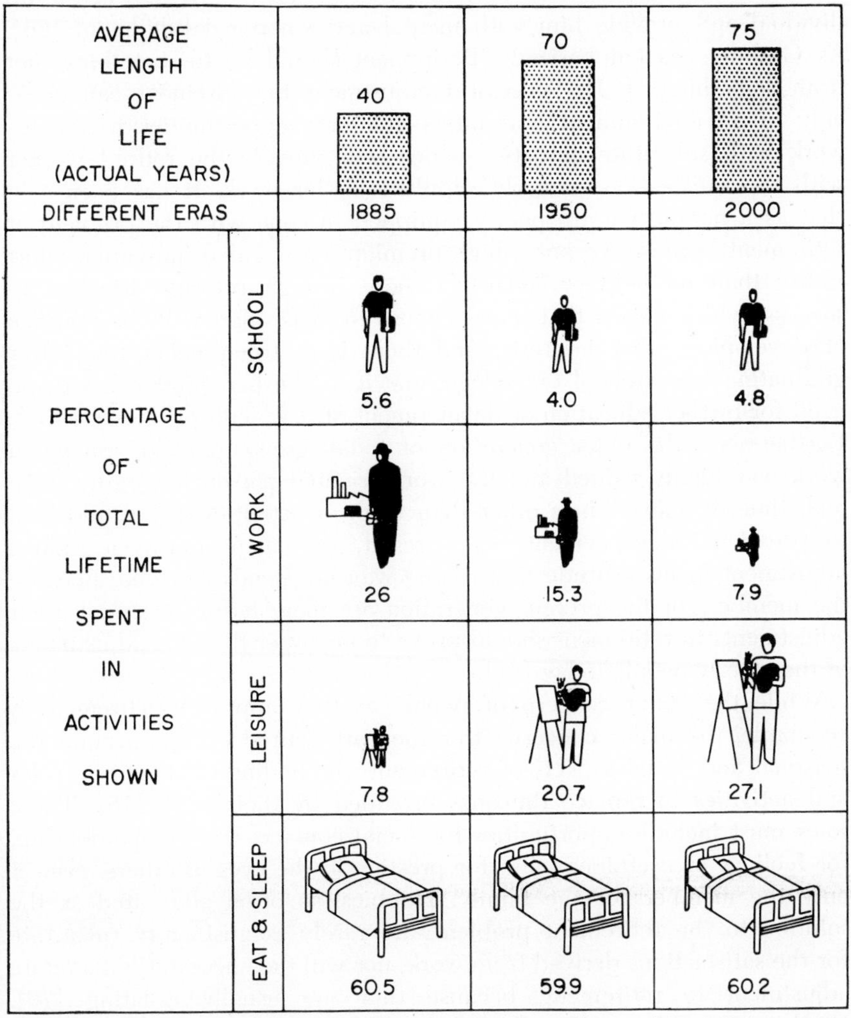

AVERAGE LENGTH OF LIFE (ACTUAL YEARS)		40	70	75
DIFFERENT ERAS		1885	1950	2000
PERCENTAGE OF TOTAL LIFETIME SPENT IN ACTIVITIES SHOWN	SCHOOL	5.6	4.0	4.8
	WORK	26	15.3	7.9
	LEISURE	7.8	20.7	27.1
	EAT & SLEEP	60.5	59.9	60.2

Fig. 127. Increase in leisure time and decrease in work time from 1885 to 2000. (*From J. W. Still, Boredom—the psychosocial disease of aging. Geriatrics, 1957, 12, 557–560. Used by permission.*)

responsibility of supporting him. The retired person knows or senses how the family feels and this causes him to feel unwanted. Such unfavorable attitudes on the part of the retired worker and his family cause many clashes which disrupt family harmony [33].

To avoid the disastrous effects retirement can and often does bring, the retired worker must discover new occupations and roles for the occupations and roles formerly held. These cannot be just "time-killing" activities if they are to be satisfactory substitutes for the activities they are replacing; they must be activities that tax all the abilities of the individual and provide him with mental and emotional fulfillment [66]. As Cushing has emphasized, "Retirement should be to something, not from something" [29]. Successful adjustment to retirement can occur only in an environment that offers adequate opportunities to replace work with substitute activities which will provide the retired worker with the satisfaction formerly supplied by his work. It has been said that as a nation, we are poorly equipped to cope with the problem of retirement because we put a high premium on unaided individual effort rather than on help or "charity"; there is high prestige attached to success, which means that many choose to make money at the sacrifice of developing other interests; and there is a strong belief that, after graduating from school or college, one is a "finished product" with no need for further education or development of new skills or interests [34]. Furthermore, the older generation of today grew up in an era when work was highly valued and the work-oriented person felt guilty if he took time to enjoy things other than work or activities that would lead to vocational advancement. As a result, retirement means a radical adjustment in his attitude toward the way he spends his time. Because the members of the present generation are more leisure oriented, their adjustments to retirement should prove to be easier than the adjustments of the elderly people today [51].

While the major concern of people as they approach retirement is economic, the major concern after they are retired centers around the personal and social aspects of retirement, the finding of substitute roles and activities to replace the ones provided by their work [18]. These roles must include opportunities for social contacts and companionship, for feelings of usefulness, and for prestige in the eyes of others, even if only the members of the family. Hobbies, so often advocated as the solution to the retirement problem, are rarely a satisfactory substitute for the satisfactions derived from work, nor will they necessarily facilitate adjustment to retirement, because they are usually isolating [76]. Furthermore, they are usually only "time-killers" for the elderly and, as such, do not contribute to feelings of usefulness, to prestige, or to the improvement of the economic status of the individual. While attitudes toward retirement vary with social class *before* retirement, there is an almost unanimous desire to return to work on the part of individuals of all social classes after the novelty of retirement has worn off. This desire may be motivated by different reasons—economic, social, or personal—

but for most who have retired, there is a desire to be active again as a means of escaping depression, self-preoccupation, inner restlessness, and loneliness, and of maintaining feelings of usefulness and status in society [38]. Even professional workers who keep themselves busy in retirement with reading, creative writing, civic and church work, club meetings, gardening, and a wide variety of other activities do not find the satisfaction from these activities they formerly found in their work [95]. Women, on the whole, adjust more easily to retirement than men because they get psychological satisfaction from their homemaking, friendships, and club activities to replace the satisfactions formerly derived from work. Men, however, have less readily available means of securing satisfactions to replace their work and, as a result, adjust less well to retirement [17].

Success of Adjustment. How successfully the individual will adjust to retirement will be largely dependent upon his financial status in retirement, because this will determine his status in the group, what activities he can substitute for his former work, whether or not he can afford to participate in social activities and join clubs that will provide him with social contacts, and how his family will feel about his retirement. If he feels that he is still useful to society, he will adjust far better than if he feels his days of usefulness are over. It is possible to predict with some accuracy before a worker retires what sort of adjustment he will make to retirement. The most important considerations are whether or not he owns his home, the reason he has for retiring, and his as well as his family's attitude toward his retirement [83]. Retirement that is voluntary is adjusted to better than compulsory retirement, especially when the worker wants to continue to work. Poor health at the time of retirement facilitates the adjustment while good health is likely to militate against it. Tapering off, for most workers, is better than an abrupt ending to patterns of work and living established many years earlier [18, 53]. Only when there is a healthy attitude toward aging and toward retirement on the part of the worker and his family can there be truly satisfactory adjustment to it.

Adjustment to retirement, like adjustment to any major change in patterns of living at any time in life, takes time. The individual who resists retirement and who, as a result, refuses to prepare himself psychologically for it by creating new interests and activities to replace those related to work will make poorer adjustments, and this will affect his health, often causing a physical decline and premature death [53]. Prolonged inactivity following work and absence of marked positive interests, especially common on the part of those who have resisted retirement, are conductive to both mental and physical ill health [98]. Not only will there be a deterioration in health and physical appearance but there will also be deterioration in emotional stability, social consciousness, and self-esteem [60]. When retirement is abrupt and adequate preparation has not been made for it, it is likely to affect the physical condition of the individual to the point where it may be fatal before adjustments can be made. Once the adjustment period has passed, the individual's chances of survival improve or become more normal [108].

Thus, it is apparent that the effects of the "retirement impact" are most serious immediately after retirement, during the period of adjustment to the changes in work routines and the breaking off of social relationships [74, 79]. The "retirement impact" is most serious for those who have resisted retirement and are unprepared for it. It affects men more than women because women have already-established interests and activities they can fall back on. And it is especially serious for men who have lost their mates after their retirement [60, 78]. Those who spend their retirement years in homes for the aged have more opportunities for social contacts and recreational activities than do those who remain in their own homes or live with relatives. However, unless the environment provides opportunities for activities that will promote a feeling of usefulness, it will not promote good adjustment to retirement [60].

Family Relationships. The pattern of family life, established in the early years of adulthood, starts to change with onset of middle age. Interest in sex, as a rule, declines and the duties and responsibilities of rearing a family gradually come to an end as the children grow up, marry, and go to homes of their own. With the diminishing family size and curtailment of income frequently come changes in living conditions. These changes are often made more pronounced by retirement with its reduced income or by the death of the spouse. At a time in life when adjustments to new conditions are difficult to make, the aging individual is frequently called upon to make radical changes in the pattern of his life. This is especially difficult for women, not because women adjust less well than men but rather because the woman's life is centered around the home much more than is that of the man.

Of the many adjustments in family relationships the elderly person must make, the following are the most important:

Sexual Behavior. It is popularly believed that with old age come sexual impotence and loss of interest in sex. Furthermore, social taboos make many aged men and women feel that showing an interest of any sort in sexual matters is "not nice" and that such interest should be limited to younger people. When the individual passes middle age, any behavior of a sexual sort is regarded by many people as a form of sexual perversion. Because according to tradition, women become sexually impotent with the menopause, their sexual lives are expected to have come to an end at that time. The reaction of young adults to the realization that their parents engage in intercourse in the fifties and sixties is often one of distress or even of repulsion. This attitude frequently carries into old age. Many individuals feel that people should be done with sex as a personal matter when they reach middle age and certainly by the time they are in the sixties [7].

In recent years, it has become apparent that sexual interest and sexual desire do not decline as early as is popularly believed and the sexual needs of the elderly are too widespread to be considered pathological. It has become apparent also that sexual impotence comes much later than was formerly believed and that interest in sex after fifty is normal, not pathological. Men and women in their sixties or even seventies have intercourse, though it is spaced further apart than in the younger years

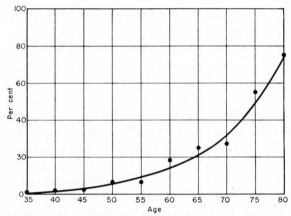

Fig. 128. Age of onset of impotence. (*From A. C. Kinsey, W. B. Pomeroy, and C. E. Martin, Sexual behavior in the human male. Philadelphia: Saunders, 1948. Used by permission.*)

and the man's preliminary orgastic phase is longer. In most cases where sexual intercourse is terminated, it is because of physical illness [49, 62]. Under conditions of normal health, there is no sudden cessation of sexual activity but rather a gradual diminishing of this activity [7]. By seventy, *erective impotence* becomes more common than earlier, though *ejaculatory impotence,* or the inability to ejaculate when in erection, is very rare. After seventy, there is a marked increase in the number of men who *believe* they are impotent though, as Kinsey has pointed out, they *expect* to be impotent and this expectation frequently leads to impotency [61]. Increase of impotence with age is shown in Figure 128.

Because of the strong social taboos that interfere with the satisfaction of the sexual needs of old people, and because of the increasing tendency to be preoccupied with bodily sensations in general, such as eating, eliminating, and sleeping, there is need for some sexual outlets, either through contacts with members of the opposite sex or through forms of sexual expression used in early adolescence, especially *masturbation*. There is evidence that this is widely practiced among those for whom there are few if any other sexual outlets. It is more common in the sixties than in the forties and fifties, and it generally is more often practiced among those who are becoming senile than among those who are senescent. Masturbation is more frequent among women than among men. This may be due to the social taboos against direct sexual expression through intercourse, which affect women in middle and old age more than they affect men. It is a type of compensation for lack of sexual activities, especially among widowed and unmarried women, though it is by no means limited to these groups. Married women in old age indulge in it also [61, 62].

The psychological effects of unfavorable social attitudes toward sexual behavior in the elderly are far more serious than is generally recognized. Feelings of guilt, emotional storm and stress from thwarted sex desires, and feelings of inadequacy may and do lead to sexual impotence or to sexual outlets more characteristic of adolescence than of adulthood. As a result, there is a decrease in the frequency of coitus and an increase in other sexual outlets. As general physical decline sets in, in the sixties or seventies, there are glandular and physical changes in the sex organs and in the body as a whole which lead to a decline in sexual interest and potency. This, however, generally comes later than declines in interest and potency due to psychological causes. In men, impotence for physical reasons alone is rare under the age of sixty years [61].

One indication of senility is sexual recrudescence, or foolish infatuations on the part of elderly people for young people of the opposite sex. This may be diffuse or localized in one love object. Among men, it usually takes the form of wanting to make love to all pretty young girls, or it may result in seduction or rape of children or adults. It is not uncommon for a man who is becoming senile to want to marry a girl who is young enough to be his granddaughter. Aged women may play with dolls, may mother children, or take a strong interest in young men. It is not uncommon for women who show this form of sexual regression to be infatuated with a man young enough to be a grandson.

Relationship with Offspring. Family roles, which underwent marked changes during middle age with the growing up of the children, the "empty nest," and the necessity to take care of elderly relatives, continue to change as illness, poor health, retirement, widowhood, and other changes in the lives of elderly people bring about changes in the roles they must play both in the home and outside. The man who, for the major part of his married life, played the role of provider must, with retirement, often play the role of a dependent. Or, the woman who has been accustomed to the role of mother, which involves authority as well as care, now finds she must relinquish this role and substitute for it the role of friend and companion to her grown children if she wishes to maintain a harmonious relationship with them and the members of their families. For elderly men, adjustment to a predominantly feminine social group within the family is an especially difficult one, coming as it does at the time of retirement, when the man is cut off from social contacts with his former business associates and thus deprived of much of the masculine companionship he formerly enjoyed. The predominantly feminine make-up of the family group in old age is due to two factors: the tendency for men to die sooner than women and the tendency for grown sons to be absorbed into their wives' families while the daughters' husbands are not always accepted as part of the family circle [49]. The trend toward the feminine make-up of the family with advancing years is shown in Figure 115, page 526.

The relationship of elderly people with their children may be a very pleasant one and it may not. Much depends upon the type of relationship that was established earlier in life. When parents are willing to shift their attitudes toward their children to suit the age and developmental level of the children, the chances are that the parent-child relationship will be a wholesome one as the years go on. As a result, it is probable that the elderly person will find much satisfaction in the companionship of sons and daughters. When, on the other hand, the parent has been unwilling, through the years, to adjust his attitude to meet the changing needs of growing children, he is likely to face a lonely old age. The strain in parent-child relationship which began in adolescence will likely grow worse rather than better as time goes on [79]. Attitudes toward filial obligations to and responsibilities for parents have been changing rapidly during the past generation, especially on the part of girls. Parents who grew up at a time when feelings of obligation toward parents, especially as they become older, were fostered are often resentful of the lack of family feeling and absence of responsibility toward the parents that is becoming so widespread in our present culture [93]. Because it is traditional for girls to assume more responsibility for aging parents than boys assume, this change in attitude on the part of girls leads to family resentments and friction, especially when grown daughters maintain that they should be just as free to lead their own lives as their brothers are and that care of elderly parents is no more their responsibility than it is their brothers' responsibility.

For the most part, elderly women are more absorbed in the relationship with their children than are elderly men. This is a continuation of the parent-child relationship that started at the time of the child's birth. Because women have a closer relationship with their grown children than men have, there is usually more friction between women and their children than between men and their children. If the parent-child relationship has been satisfactory up to the age of fifty or fifty-five years, it is unlikely that new alienations will develop after that [39]. Mother-daughter conflicts often come in old age when a mother and her aging daughter are bound together in a dependent relationship. It is usually an unmarried daughter who has assumed the responsibility of caring for a widowed mother and who, as a result, is emotionally impoverished and subjected to her mother's whims and demands. Should she marry later, she will be made to feel guilty because she has "deserted" her mother and there is usually friction between the mother and her son-in-law. Daughters bound in such relationships with their mothers usually suffer in silence or have outbursts of anger for which they later feel guilty [35]. Many parents expect their grown children, even when they are married and have children of their own, to obey them, to ask them for advice, or to respect their wishes as they did when they were children. A parent-child relationship of this sort, carried into old age, rarely proves to be a satisfactory one for the parents involved or for their children [42].

Parental Dependency. Elderly parents are of different types: some are independent, live alone, and treat their children and in-laws as adults and friends; others are dependent on their children, both emotionally and financially, and have a relationship with their children in which the roles that formerly existed are now reversed. The older the parent, the more dependent he is likely to be. This is especially true of widowed mothers [3]. Elderly parents who are happily married and have interests of their own are *emotionally* less dependent on their children than are those whose marriages have been unhappy or who have failed to develop interests to occupy the time formerly devoted to parental roles. The emotional independence of elderly parents, however, is generally less than the independence achieved by their children. *Financial dependency* on their children is a bitter pill for most parents to swallow. One of the most difficult adjustments old people must make is to play roles where they must be supported by their children. This is especially true of men who have been accustomed to playing the role of provider for the major part of their lives. Most elderly parents prefer to get along the best they can with retirement pensions, old age assistance, or other subsidies, even when this means a radical revision downward in the patterns of living, to being dependent on their children. Those who accept the role of financial dependency without resistance have usually come from countries where the cultural background differs from that which prevails in America today [39].

Relationship with Grandchildren. The role of the grandparent in the home life of modern America is less important than it was in the past.

Then families lived closer together than they do today, the social unit of family life was made up of members of the family, and the authority of the grandparents over their children and grandchildren was supreme. A tradition has grown up that the grandparent is a stabilizing influence in family life, that the grandparent understands and is more tolerant of children than parents are, and that children just "naturally" love old people. With changes in living conditions, grandparents play a less important role in family life now than they did in the past. Not only do families live farther apart today than formerly but respect for parental authority is less. Furthermore, because there have been marked changes in child-rearing practices in recent years, there has been a growing tendency to question the tradition that grandparents understand children better than parents do.

The most common relationship of grandparents with their grandchildren is in the form of active social participation in visits with the family but with no responsibility for the care of the grandchildren. In an emergency, they may be called on for help, but otherwise, a "hands off" policy generally prevails [4]. This is the result of parents' attitudes toward interference with their methods of rearing their children and the grandparents' wishes to be free of responsibility since their methods of child training will be met with criticism. This "hands off" policy has tended to build up a barrier between children and their grandparents which has been intensified by the lack of close contact children of past generations had with their grandparents. It has also tended to foster unfavorable attitudes toward old people because of their appearance and behavior, an attitude which would be less pronounced if there were a favorable attitude toward specific old people, in the form of grandparents. Antipathy for old people, fostered outside the home, in turn conditions the child unfavorably toward his grandparents and further widens the gap between them [113].

From the point of view of the grandparents, the attitude toward grandchildren is more favorable. Grandparents feel that they gain much from associations with young people: they are stimulated, become acquainted with the customs, problems, and ideas of the present generation, and find their lives enriched as a result of these contacts. The closer in age the child and his grandparents are, the closer is the relationship; the larger the age difference, especially in the case of great-grandchildren, the more remote the relationship [4]. In spite of the fact that grandparents enjoy their contacts with their grandchildren and derive emotional satisfaction as well as intellectual stimulation from these contacts, most elderly people feel that their children mean more to them than their grandchildren do. Grandfathers, on the whole, have fewer and more remote contacts with grandchildren than do grandmothers and they are far less likely to be called on for help in an emergency than are grandmothers. As a result, grandmothers generally are more interested in and absorbed in the lives of their grandchildren than are grandfathers. While the grandfather may be proud of the achievements of his grandchildren and feel that they reflect favorably on the family status, grandmothers' reactions are usually more personal and more emotionally toned [39].

Marital Happiness. Marital happiness in old age is an indication of good adjustment to family relationships not only late in life but throughout the period of marriage. Those who are unhappily married in old age, by contrast, are generally those who were unhappy almost from the start of their marriages but whose marriages were never dissolved because of moral or religious reasons or because of feelings of obligation to remain together for the sake of the children. The fate of a marriage is usually decided during its early years. It is more usual than unusual for it to follow the same pattern that was established earlier rather than to make a radical change in pattern with advancing age. Marital disharmony, for example, is frequent among elderly male identical twins because of the jealousy of the wives over the close relationship of the brothers. This is not a new pattern in old age but one of long duration [59]. Those adults who feel their marriages are happy generally find that their marriages become more satisfying to them as they grow older. With time, mutual interests are developed, their children grow up and leave home, thus drawing the partners closer together, illness or retirement of the husband gives the wife a feeling of usefulness to replace that formerly experienced when the children were young, and the death of demanding and dominating parents-in-law removes a source of potential friction between husband and wife [39].

Loneliness. Old age can be and often is the loneliest period of life. While the young adult is often lonely when he is making adjustments to a new pattern of living and is achieving independence from his family (see pages 400–401 for a discussion of loneliness in early adulthood), this period is usually of short duration and ends as he finds a place for himself in the adult world and establishes a family of his own to replace the family of his childhood days. With each passing year, as these adjustments are increased, there is a decrease in loneliness. The conditions responsible for this decrease, especially social contacts in work and in the community and an increasingly larger circle of home contacts as the family size expands to include children and in-laws, are lacking in old age. Instead of loneliness decreasing with each passing year, it is far more likely that it will increase as the family circle disintegrates with death of the mate, marriage and preoccupation with their families on the part of the children, and the death of elderly parents and in-laws. Because women, on the average, live longer than men, loneliness is a more serious

adjustment problem for them than it is for men, even though men are
faced with the loneliness that retirement brings, a problem which relatively few women find difficult if they have families and friends to fall
back on.

Studies of social-class differences in interests have revealed that members of the upper classes are more self-sufficient and better able to plan
their own activities than are those of the lower social classes (see pages
575–577 for a discussion of this). This would suggest that loneliness is
much more serious a problem for members of the lower than for those of
the upper social classes. This, however, is not the case. Family solidarity
and feelings of responsibility for aging parents are stronger among men
and women of the lower than of the middle and upper classes. Furthermore, those of the middle and upper classes are generally financially able
to remain in their own homes or to live in a simpler manner without having to become dependent on their grown children for support. As a result,
they lack the companionship of members of their family which those of
the lower classes have when they live with their children or spend the
remaining years of their lives in institutions for the aged where there is
constant companionship with others of their own ages. Loneliness in old
age is markedly influenced by where the individual lives and, in turn, it
influences his plans for where and how he will live.

Death of Spouse. Because it is customary for women to marry men
their own age or older than they, and because men, on the average, die
sooner than women, widowhood in old age is a far more common cause
of loneliness for women than it is for men. Figure 129 shows the mortality rates of males and females at different ages (see also, Figures 1 and
112, pages 3 and 512, for ages of mortality of men and women). Statistics indicate that three out of four women widowed by the time they are
fifty years old will face 20 years of widowhood unless they remarry, while
those who are widowed at sixty-five can, in 50 per cent of the cases,
expect to live for 15 more years, and one out of three, for 20 more years
[6]. It has been estimated that 50 per cent of the women at sixty years of
age are widows while, at eighty-five years, 85 per cent are widows
[14, 50]. There are no statistics available to tell how many men of comparable ages are widowers but there is reason to believe that, because
widowers at every age remarry more than do widows, the percentages
would be far less.

Young adults frequently solve the problem of an unsatisfactory marriage by *divorce.* Divorce is more frequent in the first few years of marriage than it is later, espicially when there are children (see pages 446–
448). The number of divorces decreases as age progresses until middle
age, when a second peak occurs (see pages 519–520). In the sixties and
seventies, there are divorces but they are far less frequent than earlier.

Even after celebrating a golden anniversary, couples occasionally obtain a divorce [56]. (See Figure 95, page 446 for a graphic illustration of the relation of divorce to age.) No matter how unsatisfactory marriage may be to elderly people, most of them do not contemplate ending it in a divorce court. When they do decide to get a divorce in old age, it is generally not a new decision but rather something they had contemplated since the early days of marriage but which they never did because of the children or for economic circumstances [39].

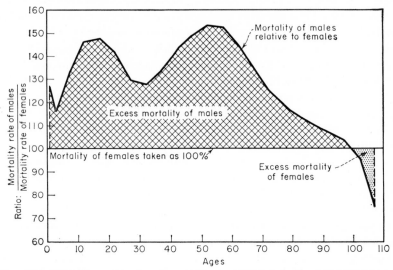

FIG. 129. Mortality rates of males at all ages relative to the mortality rates of females. On the average for the entire life span the mortality rate for males is higher than that for females by 36.8 per cent. (*From F. K. Shuttleworth, The adolescent period: a graphic atlas. Monogr. Soc. Res. Child Develpm.*, 1949, 14, No. 1. *Used by permission.*)

Adjustment to death or divorce of a spouse is difficult for men and women in old age because at this time all adjustments are increasingly difficult to make. When death of a spouse comes shortly after a man's retirement from work, it greatly increases the difficulties of this adjustment for him [60]. Furthermore, because old age is a period of contracting interests, especially social interests, being left alone cannot be compensated for by the development of new interests as readily as it can during the younger ages. For the widow, there is usually a decreased income which frequently necessitates giving up interests she might otherwise retain and which would supply her with opportunities for social contacts. Decreased income often necessitates moving into new, smaller, and less desirable living quarters, going to live with a married child, or living in an institution, any of which mean serious adjustment and further complicate adjustment to the loneliness which widowhood brings [87]. While many elderly people recognize the possibility of widowhood and make plans for it, relatively few realize the problems it brings and they are therefore not prepared to meet them or to adjust to the loneliness that is one of the major problems of widowhood [39].

Remarriage. Remarriage is one of the ways older people solve the problem of loneliness. Older women have poorer remarriage prospects than have older men (see Figure 97, page 450). This is true not only because there are proportionally more elderly women than there are men but also because women may hesitate to give up their pension rights or inheritance should they remarry. Furthermore, older men usually select women younger than they when they remarry. While relatively few marry women 20 to 30 years younger than they, the majority of men in the sixties and seventies marry women whose average age is 10 years below theirs [43]. The tendency to marry younger women reaches its maximum after seventy. Up to middle age, women usually marry men older than they or of approximately the same age. After that, a reverse trend appears. As is true of men, the tendency for older women to marry younger men increases with age. Often the men selected for a second or later marriage are 15 to 20 years younger than the women. While both men and women in the later years of their lives do marry individuals of approximately their own age, the number who marry individuals younger than they has been reported to be "surprisingly large" [15].

Singleness. The popular belief that an old person, who has never married and who, as a result, is "alone in the world," will face an unhappy, lonely old age is not borne out by real experiences. Not having had the companionship of a family of his own, he has learned through the years to develop interests and activities to compensate for this companionship. As a result, he is less likely to face a lonely old age than is the individual who married, whose interests were tied up in home and in family, and who now, in old age, finds himself widowed and with his children in homes of their own. Furthermore, the person who marries is far less likely to have made the necessary adjustments to meet old age alone than is the person who has been alone for the major part of his adult life. Consequently, old age is more likely to be lonely for the widow or widower than for the bachelor or spinster, unless the former remarry.

Those who reach old age without having married do so more often from choice than from necessity. This is especially true of men. Few unmarried men or women live alone; most live with relatives, friends of their own age, or in clubs [39]. It is commonly believed that the unmarried person faces a lonely old age. It is questionable whether such is the case. True, the unmarried woman who makes her home with a married brother or sister or an aging parent may find old age a lonely and dreary period of life. But such women are few and far between in America today. The modern woman builds up a life of her own, just as a man does. As a result, she has much to keep her happy and occupied in old age. Even though she is retired from her life career, she has the benefit of retirement pensions or old-age assistance, in addition to what she has saved from her earnings. And because her leisure time was never at the beck and call of a family, she has had an opportunity to establish many interests which will keep her from being lonely when she reaches retirement age. Even more so than men, older women who are unmarried can adjust successfully to old age and do not experience the loneliness experienced by women who have married and whose lives have been so centered in their families that they have few sources of substitute satisfaction when their husbands die and their children become preoccupied with their work and families. The adjustment to loneliness in old age is, therefore, a greater problem for those who have been married than for those who have never married.

Living Quarters. One of the most difficult adjustments for old people to make is that of changed living quarters. Having spent many years of their adult lives in saving and planning for homes of their own, it is a source of great concern to them if economic necessity forces them out of these homes. Not only are there many happy memories associated with their homes but they have become accustomed to every inch of the home and feel safe and secure there. In the past, old people, far more often than is possible today, remained in their homes until death. When poor health made it impossible for them to live alone, it was considered the duty of a daughter to move back to the parental home to take charge of things for her parents. When reduced income threatened the parental home, the children either contributed to the support of it or one of the married children moved back to the home and shared the expenses of running it. In that way, the old person was guaranteed the security of the home he had lived in for the major part of his adult life [93].

Conditions have changed so radically, not only financially but also in feelings of responsibility toward aging parents, that many old people of today are forced to move out of their homes when health or financial conditions become poor. This is presenting a serious adjustment problem for the older members of our culture. Compulsory retirement, with its accompaniment of reduced income from pensions or savings, frequently makes it financially impossible to maintain the home any longer. Statistics for 1954 showed that persons sixty-five or older who were heads of families had a median income of $2,875, as compared with a median of $4,591 for all families. For older persons living alone, and this means nearly three out of five old people, the median income dropped to $855, totally inadequate for maintaining a home of their own [27].

Because of high taxes and high cost of living, grown children have difficulties in making two ends meet in their own homes without the added burden of contributing to the support of the parental home. Furthermore, social pressures against those who do not contribute to the family home are far less severe than they formerly were, with the result that many children no longer feel they must make the personal sacrifices necessary to help their parents maintain the home [93]. In addition, there is a widespread feeling that it is unwise for "three generations to live under one roof." This has cut down on the former practice of married children's returning to the parental home with their families. The belief that children are better off in their own homes than in the home of someone else has further strengthened the tendency. Modern living conditions militate against married children's opening their doors to their aging parents. Modern homes are small and space is at a premium. As a result, the family must usually be dislocated when parents come to make their home with their married children. Then, too, the presence of an elderly person in the home adds to the already heavy burdens of the modern housewife.

Homes of Elderly. Where the elderly live depends upon their economic status, how lonely they are, what they want or need because of their age and health, and where they feel they will be happiest. Fundamentally, the living quarters of older people should promote health and happiness. Because the needs and wants necessary to their health and happiness are not the same as for younger people, nor are they the same for all who are elderly, living quarters that meet the needs of some will not necessarily meet the needs or wants of others. Some want to live in a familiar neighborhood and a familiar home; others want to get into a new neighborhood and a different home [20, 57]. Most elderly people, however, want quiet, privacy, independence of action, nearness to relatives and friends, residence among members of their own cultural group, cheapness, and closeness to transportation lines and community institutions such as churches, libraries, and shops [51].

Patterns of living vary greatly in old age, much more so than in middle age where the pattern is well standardized. There are six patterns that are common among the elderly today. These are: a married couple living alone; a lone person living in his own home; a nonmarital partnership of members of the same generation, as a brother and sister, brothers, sisters, or friends; a two-generation household with a widowed mother or father with adult children; three-generation households; and homes or institutions for the aged [51]. *Social class* and, indirectly, *economic status* influence the pattern of living chosen by the elderly. Those of the upper social class usually live in large, old, and well-built homes which they have lived in for years, though some move into a smaller, new, modern-type home. Members of the upper middle class live in less select and less pretentious homes while those of the lower middle class live in smaller homes or with their children. The pattern for lower-class, elderly people is influenced to some extent by whether or not they are working. If so, they usually live in small houses or shacks with their children, or, if they have no source of income, in old-age homes [2]. *Marital status* likewise influences the living arrangements of elderly people. Single men are found in the highest proportions in rural nonfarm areas and single women in urban areas; married men and women live mainly in rural farm areas;

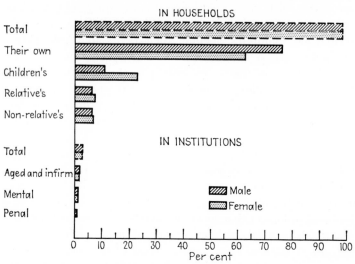

FIG. 130. Per cent of male and female population, sixty-five years of age and older, in households and institutions. "Nonrelatives" include quasi-households. (*From N. W. Shock, Trends in gerontology. Stanford, Calif.: Stanford Univer. Press, 1951. Used by permission.*)

widowed men and women in urban areas; and the divorced in urban areas [117]. Where elderly people live is illustrated in Figure 130.

When it is impossible for an old person to maintain his home, he must either live with a relative or friend or in an institution. Most old people accept such arrangements as a last resort. In the case of living with married children, they often resist the idea because they feel they are unwanted or will be in the way. They are criticized for interfering in family affairs or for their personal habits; they do not want to give up their own homes, which are symbols of their independence; and they fear the resentment of their in-laws or the restrictions on their individual freedom [39, 42]. If every effort is made on the part of the son or daughter to make parents feel wanted and if attempts are made to help them to retain a feeling of independence even if dependent financially, living with a grown child can be a satisfactory arrangement for elderly people [105]. Some elderly people prefer *institutional life* to living with their children. The institution provides for their basic needs of food, shelter, and physical care; it provides a feeling of security, for they know that they will be cared for in sickness as well as in health; it offers an escape from difficult family situations or enables them to keep on good terms with their families; and it provides companionship with their contemporaries [20].

How happy and how well adjusted the elderly person is when he lives in an institution will depend partly on the institution and partly on his attitude toward living in an institution. When the individual does not want to live in an institution but circumstances force him to do so, strong feelings of inadequacy develop and there is a tendency to show little interest in the outside world or his surroundings and to withdraw into a kind of fantasy which leads to intellectual deterioration [30]. For those who have unfavorable family relationships, the institution provides opportunities for social contacts and activities and eliminates the feeling of being unwanted which would exist if they lived with relatives [82]. When the institution is composed of fairly homogeneous groups without sharp differences along economic, occupational, or educational lines, it makes for a better social climate and this facilitates personal-social adjustments [107]. However, even though institutional living has advantages and is often preferable to living with married children, elderly people who can live in their own homes are generally happier and better adjusted than are those who must live either with their children or in institutions [30, 82].

Suitable Living Quarters. Many homes that are suitable for young children, adolescents, or adults are unsuitable for old people because they contain hazards to the health and safety of the old person. Declining motor coordinations, combined with a poor sense of equilibrium in old age, may readily result in falls which cause broken bones or other serious injuries. Provisions for physical safeguards are, therefore, not only important for the old person himself but also for the sake of every member of the family. When old people are living alone or with other older people, the provision for protection against household hazards is even more important than when they are with younger people. Many of the homes that have been occupied by the elderly since the earlier days of their marriage fall short of the requirements for safety, though they may fulfill the psychological needs of these individuals better than houses or apartments that are more suitable from the point of view of the physical needs.

There are four fundamental *physiological* needs of the elderly which should be taken into consideration if housing is to be suitable for them. First, the air temperature should be comparatively even from floor to ceiling because poor circulation and impairment of the heat-regulating system of the body make the elderly person especially sensitive to chilling in the extremities. Minimum labor should be required to operate the heating system. Second, there should be large windows to ensure more daylight because of the gradual impairment of vision in the elderly. Glare is disturbing and can be controlled by slat blinds. There should be plenty of direct sunlight because the elderly are often housebound and, furthermore, sunlight has a good psychological effect on the elderly just as it has on the young. Artificial lighting should be indirect to avoid glare, and lights should be placed near the floors and steps to avoid accidents. Third, noise should be controlled, either by locating the living quarters on a quiet street or in the back part of a building on a noisy street, because older people are less able to adjust to external stress than are younger. And fourth, there should be adequate space for indoor and outdoor recreation, a requirement best met in multiple housing developments built on a community basis. From the *psychological* angle, suitable living quarters for the elderly should provide a privacy whereby the person can avoid the tensions of daily living and find opportunities for sedentary recreation, labor-saving devices for cleaning and cooking, and provision for storage of possessions that were an important part of the individual's past life [57].

Relatively few older people, especially after retirement, live in homes that meet their needs. Those over sixty-five years of age, on the whole live in less valuable homes than the American population generally. These homes are usually in poorer locations in the community and are old and in poor condition. They have poor facilities, as absence of running water, flush toilets, and central heating, and they are often in a dilapidated condition (see Figure 131). Because they are old, they often have large rooms and more space than is needed, thus eliminating the overcrowding that younger families often have in the more modern type of home. Those who live in rented property, whether in homes or apartments, likewise are in the low-value structures in the older neighborhoods of the community and have poor facilities. Many elderly people move to such living quarters in old age for economic reasons and are forced to accept conditions inferior to those they had in their younger years [28, 97].

Migration in Old Age. Statistics have shown that older people move as often as do the middle-aged. They may move from house to house in the same community or to another community. They do so for many reasons: economic conditions, health, convenience, or to be near members of the family. Members of the upper and middle socioeconomic groups move less often than do those of the lower groups, though there is a tendency for elderly people with larger incomes and bigger retirement pay to migrate to warmer climates rather than to move within the same community. Members of the lower economic groups, on the other hand, move more within the community than to other communities and this movement is usually a downward one, to poorer neighborhoods and a lower-cost type of dwelling. People from the suburbs move more than do those from the cities and those from farms tend to migrate to towns or villages near their farms [28, 70]. Married couples among the elderly make, on the whole, the fewest moves, while widows and single people make the most. Figure 89, page 420, shows the residential mobility of elderly people as compared with that of younger and middle-aged people. As a result of this shifting around, there are today more elderly people living in nonfarm rural areas, villages, and small towns than in cities. In general,

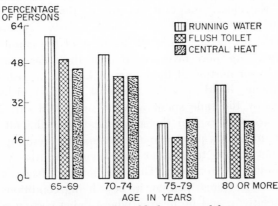

Fig. 131. Housing facilities for the elderly in rural-farm areas. (*From M. L. Cowles, Housing and associated problems of the rural-farm population in two Wisconsin counties. Rur. Sociol., 1956, 21, 239–248. Used by permission.*)

conditions in smaller communities are more favorable to the aged than in cities, especially from the point of view of social contacts.

In recent years, there has been a migration of elderly people to more favorable climates, especially to Florida and California. As a result, these states have had a proportionally greater increase in old people than have other areas of the country [96]. While this migration is not as great as is popularly believed, it is a trend that is growing. As Havighurst and Albrecht have pointed out, "The trickle of people from thousands of towns and cities becomes a fairly large stream when seen at the receiving end of the migration in Florida, Arizona, or California" [51]. There are many reasons for this new trend of migration to areas which are coming to be known as "paradises for the aged." The most important of these reasons, in addition to more favorable climatic conditions for those whose health is poor, are the breakdown of three-generation family units, a warmer climate, which eliminates the possibility of being cut off from social contacts during the winter months, improved transportation, inflationary pressures which make lower living costs necessary, and opportunities for contact with those of the same age group and similar interests [31]. In communities made up mostly of retired elderly people, there is more equal status than in other communities and this eliminates the feelings of uselessness and of being unwanted which are likely to develop in communities where members of the younger generations are in the majority and occupy most community leadership positions [55]. Furthermore, communities made up largely of elderly people eliminate the emotional tensions of large cities and this is more favorable to the physical and mental health of the elderly. Migrations are usually away from urban centers to smaller cities. State capitols and university towns are especially attractive to the elderly migrant because of the cultural opportunities they offer [102].

Some elderly people who migrate to areas of the country where climatic conditions are more favorable than in the areas where they have lived for the major portion of their lives make good adjustments to their new environments, build up a new circle of friends, and have many interests to occupy the time spent in work and child care in their pre-retirement years. Others find the adjustments too difficult and are unhappy. As Desmond has pointed out, adjustment to retirement is difficult enough without adding to it other adjustment hazards by moving to a new and strange environment. These adjustment hazards come from being with totally strange people, in new living conditions, away from friends and relatives, and in an area where living costs may be as great or even greater than they would have been in the old communities. While it is true that an environment where climatic conditions are favorable makes it possible for the elderly to have interests and hobbies they might not otherwise be able to enjoy, this advantage will not necessarily compensate for the loneliness that comes when one is cut off from friends and relatives and from the home and community that is familiar from years of association. Desmond emphasizes a cautionary approach to migration for the elderly, which consists of "trying it out" before pulling up stakes and making the move final [31].

Assessment of Adjustment. Old people's adjustments to where they live and how they live will be affected mainly by whether or not the choice of living arrangement was theirs. When an individual resists the idea of living with a married child, for example, partly because he feels unwanted and partly because of the restrictions this will place on his independence, he will make poor adjustments and be unhappy if poor health or economic conditions necessitate this pattern of living [39]. With retirement and decreased strength, the individual spends more hours in the home than he did during his more vigorous years. Restrictive living arrangements breed discontent and restlessness while living conditions similar to what he has been used to during the major part of his adult life lead to contentment.

Furthermore, life falls into a pattern as the individual grows older. Any change in this pattern means breaking habits of many years' duration with the necessity for making new adjustments. Not only is this difficult, but if satisfactory adjustments are not made the individual is unhappy. Men who remain in their own homes throughout their old age have the most advantageous position from the point of view of health, activity, and attitudes. Poorest adjustment comes when they live in rooming houses or hotels. Old women, like old men, are best adjusted if they remain in their own homes or in homes of relatives. In institutions, where the individual is deprived of the independence he enjoyed for the major part of his life, the old person makes the poorest adjustments and is the least happy [23, 82]. As Vivrett has pointed out, old people should be "an integral part of and contributory to, the main stream of community life and action" if they are to be happy [114].

ASSESSMENT OF ADJUSTMENTS IN OLD AGE

Changes in the pattern of life in old age involve relinquishing social relationships and roles that are typical of adulthood and accepting those that are typical of the later years of life. To be well adjusted, the individual must be able to satisfy his personal needs and live up to the expectations of others within the framework of life provided for him. When the individual must change his roles, especially when the changes are as radical as those necessitated by health and environmental pressures during old age, he is more likely to be maladjusted than well adjusted [85]. Financial security, late retirement, good living arrangements, and good health all favor good adjustment to the changed roles of the later years of life. Financial insecurity, unfavorable family relationships, poor health, and living in an institution that is isolated from the outside world and provides few contacts with family, friends, and young people are likely to contribute to poor adjustment in old age [52, 82]. Fundamentally, the cause of poor or good adjustment in old age is traceable to the individual's concept of self and how this has been affected by the role changes that come with old age. The more favorable the self-concept, the more favorable will be the adjustment, and the poorer the self-concept, the less favorable the adjustment [46].

The individual's *attitude* toward himself and toward the roles society expects him to play influences the type of adjustment he will make. When the individual has a resistant attitude toward growing old, it will be an obstacle to successful adjustment. How resistant the attitude is will depend not only upon society's attitude toward old people, which, in our culture, is far from favorable, but also upon the individual's own status. The individual who is financially secure, whose family status is favorable, and whose health enables him to continue activities that are enjoyable to him will adjust better to old age than will the individual whose status is less secure and less satisfactory. Idleness and the accompanying feeling of uselessness, of "being through," which comes when the individual has been retired from his life work, predisposes the old individual to poor adjustment [94].

How well the individual adjusts to life at any age depends largely upon his *earlier experiences*. In middle and old age, difficulties in adjustment are at their peak not only because these ages present more and more difficult problems but also because the ability to make adjustments is progressively reduced as one advances in age. The difficulties experienced in adjustments in old age are, for the most part, the product of earlier learning of certain forms of adjustment that are not adequate to present circumstances. When the individual discovers this, he must make new adjustments. This means a flexibility which is difficult for those who are old. Many old people react with emotional tension to their own aging, to loss of health, to loss of occupation, to loss of persons dear to them, and to financial or physical dependency. In spite of the emotional disturbances these problems present, most old people manage to keep their equilibrium within fair balance. The severity of the problems of old age, the individual's reactions to them, and their solutions are dependent on the previous life experiences of the individual. They are, as a result, predominantly individual and to a large extent different in each person [41].

It is possible to *predict*, in middle age or even in early adulthood, what sort of adjustment the individual will make to old age. This prediction is based on the type of adjustment he has made to the roles society expected him to play at different age levels, on his attitude toward old age in general and his attitude toward his own old age, and on circumstances in his life which will necessitate major or minor changes in the roles he will be forced to play in old age. There are certain *causal factors* that influence the degree of change in these roles. These include: increasing age, living arrangements, health status, economic status, social participation, upward or downward mobility, presence or absence of nonadaptive behavior, degree of wish fulfillment, and satisfaction the individual derives from the activities he engages in. Knowing which of these factors will be operative in a given individual's case and to what extent they will influence his attitudes and behavior makes prediction of his adjustments to old age reliable [82].

Criteria of Adjustment. Assessment of the type of adjustment the elderly make can be made by applying four criteria: quality of behavior patterns; emotional states; personality changes; and happiness.

1. *Quality of Behavior Patterns.* In general, there is evidence that those who made good adjustments when they were younger will make good adjustments when they are old. As Cicero pointed out in his *De Senectute* many years ago, "Those with simple desires and good dispositions find old age easy to take. Those who do not show wisdom and virtue in their youth are prone to attribute to old age those infirmities which are actually produced by former irregularities." How the individual meets the stresses of adolescence and adjusts to them will influence how he will adjust to old age, because patterns of adult attitudes and behavior are set then [92]. The cultural milieu in which the individual lived during the formative years of his life will also affect the type of adjustment he makes to old age. Because America is a young country and is youth-conscious, there are negative and unfavorable attitudes toward old age. Having grown up in a milieu in which such attitudes prevail, it is difficult for an individual to "grow old gracefully" or to accept old age gracefully in others [33]. Although the old person is a senior citizen, he has none of the prestige associated with that status in countries where the elderly are respected because of their wisdom and experience [75].

To be well adjusted, there must be a minimum of worry. Idleness at any age predisposes the individual to worry, and because old age is a period of relatively greater idleness than any other life period, there are plenty of opportunities for the elderly person to worry. Keeping busy, then, is very important to good adjustment in old age. Being busy, however, is not all that is required for good adjustment. Studies of well-adjusted and poorly adjusted old people have revealed a number of behavior patterns associated with good adjustment, the most important of which are: strong and varied interests; economic independence, which makes independence of living possible; many social contacts with people of all ages, not just with one's contemporaries; good relationships with members of the family and frequent contacts with them; some form of work which is pleasurable and useful but not overtaxing; participation in or contribution to community organizations, especially the church; delegation of responsibility and authority to others, either in the home or business, thus enabling the older person to pursue interests of his own while still maintaining a feeling of usefulness; maintaining a home where life is comfortable but not too taxing; and enjoying of present activities without regrets for the past [2, 52].

Poorly adjusted old people develop patterns of behavior that suggest they are trying to escape from situations they dislike and often find intolerable. There is a tendency to reminisce, recalling with strong emotional reactions previous successes and happinesses. They show little interest in the world of today or their role in it; instead, they withdraw into the world of fantasy and make a world of their own, colored by memories of past experiences. This is especially true of the institutionalized whose environment is usually so lacking in stimulation that they dwell more on the past than on the present or future [36]. Lack of interest in the present results in low productivity, little drive, and a narrowing of interests [30]. Other traits indicative of maladjustment in old age stem from feelings of inadequacy, of rejection, of being unwanted, and of self-pity, all of which are expressed in behavior patterns characteristic of martyrdom; hypochondria, including overvaluing genuine physical symptoms; anxiety and worry; apathy; passivity; negativism; irritability; querulousness; restlessness; boredom; tearfulness; rigidity and difficulty in adjusting to new situations; extreme conservatism; loss of social inhibitions as shown in vulgarity, untidiness, and overtalkativeness; and regressive tendencies, especially in the sex life, as autoeroticism [87]. These patterns of behavior that are indicative of poor adjustment in old age are due partly to environmental frustrations and the limited opportunities the aged have for the satisfaction of thwarted needs and partly to changes in mental and physical functions, as shown in loss of strength and energy which results in fatigue, or in rigidity which hampers adjustment to new situations [11].

That most elderly people make satisfactory adjustments may be seen in the fact that *criminality* is proportionally lower during old age than in any other age period beyond childhood. There is no evidence of increase in crime in the older ages even though the aged population has increased in recent years. In fact, from middle age on, the crime rate becomes progressively lower. The most common causes of arrest among old people are drunkenness, assault, disorderly conduct, vagrancy, driving while intoxicated, theft, and sex crimes. The decline in criminality rate among elderly people may be due in part to the greater leniency of judges and juries when dealing with older people, but it is more likely that the decline comes from an unwillingness on the part of older people to expose themselves to physical dangers, physical incapacity to undertake certain types of crime, realization from past experience that crime does not pay, and increasing conformity to the law with advancing age, an outgrowth of their greater conservatism. Some of the crimes of old age come from the individual's attempts to resist conditions influenced or imposed by old age [52, 77].

2. *Changes in Emotional Behavior.* Poorly adjusted people at all ages react to environmental conditions with more emotional tension than do those who are better adjusted. In the poorly adjusted people who withdraw from the world and live in a world of fantasy, there is a tendency to be apathetic and to show decreased emotional responsiveness. This is especially characteristic of institutionalized elderly people who, for the most part, make poorer adjustments to old age than do those who live outside of institutions [30]. However, in spite of the new problems of

adjustment that elderly people must face, regardless of where they live, there is no indication of greater emotional instability than is found in the younger segments of the population [44]. Studies of elderly people have shown that their affective life tends toward a level of apathy. They are less responsive than they were when they were younger and show less enthusiasm. Typically, the emotional responses are more specific, less varied, and less appropriate to the occasion than are those of younger people. It is not unusual for the elderly person to show signs of regression in his emotional behavior, such as negativism, temper tantrums, and excitability characteristic of a child [11]. Many elderly people have little capacity to express warm and spontaneous feelings toward others. They become "misers" in their affections in that they are afraid to invest an object or person with positive feelings because they have discovered, from past experience, that it is unlikely that such feelings will be returned and their efforts will then have been fruitless [21].

While the affective life of the old person does, on the whole, show less intensity than is characteristic of the younger years, the resistant emotions show an unaccustomed intensity. The old person is likely to be irritable, quarrelsome, crotchety, and contrary. Fears and worries, disappointments and disillusions, and feelings of persecution are far more common than the pleasanter emotional states. The old person is more likely to be belligerent than peace loving. His belligerent attitudes come from thwartings and feelings of rejection. Some of the thwartings come not from the environment but from the individual's not being able to do many of the things he did when he was younger. The old person senses society's attitude toward him and he resents this attitude. Financial dependence often makes the old person feel ashamed and unhappy, another common cause for the predominance of unpleasant emotions in old age. All in all, there are few things in our culture to make an old person happy and many things to make him cross, unpleasant, and generally disagreeable to live with [11].

Recovery from emotional experiences also changes as the individual grows older. While the child or adult may spend his energy, mobilized for emotional responses, in play or work, the elderly person is usually exhausted, less able to turn to other things, and may remain anxious and depressed for a long time. In old people, grief due to the death of a spouse or some loved one is expressed by a dearth of overt manifestations. Instead, somatic illness is often precipitated or accentuated by this grief. Furthermore, there is often irrational hostility toward living persons, especially those in the individual's immediate environment, and a tendency toward withdrawal and isolation [104]. According to Banham, "The emotions of old people are characterized by paucity rather than overabundance of affective energy. The form of their behavior tends to narrow, like a stream in a drought, into one channel rather than to brim over into general hyperactivity and tension" [11].

Old people are often accused of being *neurotic*. This accusation is based on the fact that traits indicative of neuroticism, such as feelings of inadequacy, of rejection, of depression and self-pity, hypochondria, anxiety, emotional sensitivity, irritability, quarrelsomeness, tearfulness, boredom, apathy, negativism, social withdrawal, guilt feelings, rigidity, and regressive tendencies, are more commonly found among the elderly than among the young. While these are unquestionably due in part to environmental thwartings and in part to waning physical and mental abilities, it is questionable whether, even if environmental conditions changed, the tendency toward unpleasant emotional reactions could be eliminated completely. Many old people are well aware of their tendency to be disagreeable and claim that their worst faults are irritability and quick temper [42].

3. *Personality Changes.* Changes in personality, whether they are for the better or for the worse, indicate how well the individual is adjusting to life. While personality is never static, marked changes, especially when they are for the worse, are indicative of poor adjustment. Considering the changes that come in physical and mental functions with age and the concomitant change in pattern of living that is pressed upon the older person, and considering also the prevailing concept of old age in our culture, it would be surprising if there were not changes in personality in old age. How marked the changes will be, however, depends largely on the adjustment of the individual. It is popularly believed that all old people, regardless of what sort of personality patterns they had when they were younger, will develop into ogrelike creatures who are mean, stingy, quarrelsome, demanding, selfish, self-centered, egotistical, and generally impossible to live with. Furthermore, it is popularly believed that if old people live long enough they will deteriorate into childlike personalities in the closing years of life and that they must, as a result, be treated like children. Studies of personality in old age, while limited in number and made mostly by the cross-sectional rather than the longitudinal approach, have produced enough evidence to contradict the popular concepts of senescent personality and the changes which old age are supposed to make in the personality pattern.

As long ago as the time of Plato, it was recognized that the personality of the individual prior to old age influences his reactions to old age and this, in turn, determines how much change will take place in his personality when he becomes old. As Plato pointed out, "He who is of a calm and happy nature will hardly feel the pressure of old age, but to him who is of an opposite disposition, youth and old age are equally a burden." This point of view has been substantiated by modern studies of personality. They emphasize the fact that while changes do occur, they are *quantitative* rather than qualitative; the fundamental pattern of personality, set earlier in life, becomes more set with advancing years [100]. Although the individual may become more rigid in his thinking, more conservative in his actions, more prejudiced in his attitudes toward people, more opinionated, and more self-centered with age, these are not new personality traits that have developed as he became elderly; they are exaggerations of lifelong traits that have become more pronounced with the pressure that old age has placed upon him. When pressures are too severe for him to adjust to and personality breakdown occurs, there is still evidence that the predominant traits developed earlier will be dominant in the pattern the breakdown takes [54]. As Lawton has pointed out, "Aging is like applying a magnifying glass to the personality" [66].

CONCEPT OF SELF. Changes in personality during old age come from changes in the core of the personality pattern, the individual's concept of self. How much this self-concept changes and in what direction the change occurs will determine the quality and quantity of change in the personality pattern. Changes in the self-concept in old age come from subjective awareness of aging, the acceptance of the cultural stereotype of old age, and the individual's recognition of the attitude toward him and the treatment he receives from others because of his age. As Watson has pointed out, "A person is as old as his self-concept" [115]. Those who consider themselves "old" are less well adjusted and happy than are those who think of themselves as "middle-aged" or who have a more favorable concept of "old age" than the one that is popularly accepted in our present culture [85]. Disdain for age is implanted in the minds of the young and becomes stronger with passing time as the individual realizes how society feels about old age. As he becomes older, the individual directs this attitude toward himself with the result that he ascribes to himself the characteristics belonging to the stereotype of old age. Because he expects to be rejected, he rejects himself. This is fundamentally the basis of personality deterioration in old age [69]. Many older people try to deny approaching age and prolong youthfulness to avoid having to face the acceptance of the concept they hold of old age. So long as they are able to appear and act younger than their chronological ages, they can avoid accepting the stereotype of old age as applicable to them [19].

The time at which a person begins to feel that he is getting old and the time at which this becomes a matter of concern for him differ greatly for different individuals. Some people use their chronological age as a criterion of their own aging whereas others use such physical symptoms as failing eyesight or hearing, increased tendency to fatigue, decline in sexual potency, or changes in the texture of the skin and color of the hair. Still others assess their aging in terms of their capacity for work, their output in relation to standards set in earlier years, their lack of interest in competing with others, lack of motivation to do things, or a tendency to reminisce and turn their thoughts to the past rather than dwell on the present or the future [46]. For most people, physical symptoms of aging are more often used to assess their age than are behavioral symptoms. It is not uncommon for older people, once they have accepted the fact that they are "old," to develop an "old-age complex" which is expressed in undue concern and preoccupation over the physical and mental restrictions age has imposed on them. This predisposes them to exaggerate their loneliness, to fear losing the place they formerly enjoyed in the community, to have feelings of not being wanted, of having outlived their usefulness, and of being a burden on their families, and to worry over their financial status [54]. As old people become less able to function independently, they subscribe more and more to the cultural stereotypes of old age and this further influences their self-concepts, even to the point where they believe that they, like other old people, would be better off in old-age homes because they are hard to get along with [111].

In short, then, what the individual *thinks* he is, he is likely to become. If he thinks of himself as "old," he is very likely to think and behave as an old person is supposed to, thus developing a personality pattern that conforms to social expectancy. The more change there is from the personality pattern of his younger days and the more closely this new pattern conforms to the cultural stereotype of "old-age personality," the stronger the indication that he has not made a good adjustment to old age. Because no two people age in the same way and because no two are influenced in the same way by environmental forces, there is no such thing as a "typical" personality pattern of old age. However, there are certain personality traits so characteristically found among the elderly that they might be considered "typical." In spite of the fact that the number of old people is increasing rapidly, they are still a "minority group" in our culture. They are stereotyped as such by younger people and have not yet been permitted to find a place in our present culture. As a minority group, they suffer from subordination to the younger members of society, they are discriminated against and made to feel unwanted, as is true of any minority group. Because of their minority-group status, many old people develop personality traits that are typical of minority groups, such as hypersensitivity, self-hatred, symptoms of insecurity and uncertainty such as quarrelsomeness, apathy, and regression, introversion, anxiety, overdependency, and defensiveness concerning age [12, 90].

Not all old people develop a typical "minority-group personality" nor do those who do develop this personality pattern develop all the traits characteristic of it and in equal strength. Personality differences occur in old age as at every other period of life. However, those who are institutionalized, especially when against their wishes, have poorer attitudes toward themselves and more marked characteristics of the minority-group personality than is true of those who live outside of institutions [71]. The most acute reaction to advancing age is in the area of self-esteem. When the sources of self-esteem, as success in work and community life and importance in the home, are cut off suddenly by retirement and are not replaced by other sources of self-esteem, the individual is predisposed to develop traits characteristic of the minority-group personality [65]. Unless something is done to restore this waning self-esteem, the changes in personality will increase. In an experiment with a group of elderly people placed in a stimulating environment, marked changes were found in their personalities after a year. They changed from acceptance of the stereotype for "old people" to being more alert, more emotionally controlled, and in better health, from poorly to well-adjusted individuals. This suggests that changes in personality patterns, resulting from changes in the self-concept, are due more to environmental influences than to physical causes [10].

PERSONALITY BREAKDOWN. Breakdown in the personality structure is, at every age, indicative of poor adjustment. With advancing age and its pressures comes an increase in the number of personality breakdowns and in the proportional number of individuals committed to mental institutions. In the milder forms, these breakdowns consist of such disorders as disturbances of memory, falsifications of memory, faulty attention, disturbances of orientation as to time, place, and person, suspiciousness, disturbances in the ethical domain, hallucinations and delusions—especially of persecution—and such common neuroses as anxiety, preoccupation with bodily functions, chronic fatigue, compulsion and hysterical disorders, neurotic depressions, and sex deviations [60].

Personality breakdown of a more serious sort, as shown in mental disease, increases greatly. About one-third of the patients in state mental hospitals today are people over sixty years of age, and still others are cared for in private institutions or nursing homes for the aged [54]. After sixty-five, there is a marked upward trend in serious emotional disorders. Patients suffering from mental disease show severe intellectual deterioration which makes life outside of an institution almost impossible for them [44]. In the sixties, psychoses with cerebral arteriosclerosis and senile dementia predominate and these groups increase steadily to the end of life. After seventy, senile psychoses mostly prevail. Not only does mental disease increase with advancing age but there is also an increase

in *suicides* or attempts at suicide. Men of all ages and all races have a
higher suicide rate than do women [63]. While many suicides in old age
are traceable to poverty or to economic insecurity with its accompaniment of dependency, not all suicides in old age are due to economic
factors alone. Some are due to the loss of a loved one, physical ailments,
especially those of hopeless prognosis, and mental disease [58].

Many of the mental breakdowns in old age trace their origin to personal maladjustment of long duration. "Second childhood" is not always
senility in the sense of physical deterioration but is often a case of emotional and intellectual immaturity carried over from younger years. This
is shown by the fact that old people whose behavior becomes increasingly
childish have lived lives that are extremely conventional and patterned
after the opinions of others. Then, when these social pressures are gone,
the individual reverts to childish behavior. There is evidence that most
personality breakdowns in old age are not due to brain damage but to
social conditions which give rise to feelings of insecurity. These are especially serious when there is a history of poor adjustment. Many old
people have shown similar maladaptive behavior under stress when they
were younger [118]. Then, under the pressures of such conditions as
the death of a spouse, threatened disability from physical disorders, or
problems resulting from retirement, loss of financial security, breaking
up of the home, or moving to a new environment, there is a breakdown
in the personality pattern already weakened by past experiences [54].
Thus, personality changes, especially of an extreme degree, are not necessarily inevitable as age progresses. They depend partly on the rapidity
of degenerative changes and partly on the strength of personality integration and its ability to withstand the social pressures that come with
aging. Personality breakdown is thus a clear indication of poor adjustment to the problems that must be met with advancing years.

4. *Happiness.* How happy the individual is at any age depends largely
upon the degree of adjustment attained. This, in turn, depends not so
much upon present environmental conditions as upon the success or
failure of past adjustments and upon the attitudes that have been created
by the individual's successes or failures. At no time in life do unsuccessful past adjustments make present adjustment as difficult as in old age,
and at no other life period is the adjustment to existing conditions as
hard as it is in old age. As a result, the old person's chances for happiness
are far less than they are at earlier periods in his life. The more upset the
pattern of the older person's life, the more predisposed he will be to unhappiness. The best chances for happiness in old age, on the other hand,
come from happiness in middle age. Because the individual's attitudes
and patterns of adjustment are established while he is still young, preparation for old age should be started while the individual is at the peak of

achievement if he is to have a happy old age. Healthy attitudes toward old age as a normal part of the life span, toward the abilities and disabilities of old age, and toward the activities and interests old age can enjoy should all be established while the individual is able to make adjustments easily. Waiting until he is old is often too late. Good adjustment, so essential to happiness, depends largely on how well the individual can assimilate his own past experiences and come to terms with himself, rather than on external social conditions and how well he can adjust to them [45, 51].

To be happy, then, the individual must accept himself and the conditions of his life, even if they fall below his expectations. At every age, levels of aspiration above one's abilities and unrealistic goals will mean feelings of inadequacy which, in turn, will lead to unhappiness. In old age, the individual must be realistic about himself, his abilities and disabilities, his gradual isolation from society, and all the other changes in the life pattern which old age brings. Even though these are not to his liking, so long as they are beyond his control he must accept them; otherwise, he is doomed to unhappiness. Furthermore, "happiness" shifts its meaning as people grow older. In youth, happiness means freedom from care and responsibility, gaiety and popularity with members of both sexes, setting goals and achieving them, and above all, activity. In old age, by contrast, the elements of happiness are health, economic security, acceptance by society, freedom from loneliness, feelings of usefulness, religion, and contentment. Old age cannot know the same kind of happiness as youth because it is a period when life is more passive and contemplative than the active period of youth. What a person *does* is more important to his happiness in old age than what he is. In general, happy old people are more alert and ready for new activities than are the unhappy [67, 112].

It is thus apparent that old people can be happy only if society gives them a chance. If they are permitted to be as active as their health and strength allow, and if their activity produces results that are of some use to the social group, they will be happy in the knowledge that their lives are useful until the grave claims them. Lawton has suggested a "bill of rights" for old people which, if fulfilled in every aspect, would bring both happiness and contentment to old age. The ten "rights" the old person is entitled to are [66]:

1. The right to be treated as a person.
2. The right to be treated as an adult.
3. The right to a fair chance on our merits.
4. The right to a say about our own life.
5. The right to a future.
6. The right to have fun and companions.

7. The right to be romantic.
8. The right to your help in becoming interesting to you.
9. The right to professional help whenever necessary.
10. The right to be old.

However, if the elderly are to be happy, it is not enough that society meet their physical and economic needs. As Havighurst has pointed out, the elderly will still have the "need to be needed; the need to have a function in society—to have a respected place in the eyes of others and to be doing something which is interesting and significant in one's own eyes. . . . the need for ego support" [80].

BIBLIOGRAPHY

1. Abrams, A. J.: Barriers to the employment of older workers. *Ann. Amer. Acad. pol. soc. Sci.*, 1952, 279, 62–71.
2. Albrecht, R.: The social roles of old people. *J. Geront.*, 1951, 6, 138–145.
3. Albrecht, R.: Relationships of older parents with their children. *Marriage Fam. Living*, 1954, 16, 32–35.
4. Albrecht, R.: The parental responsibilities of grandparents. *Marriage Fam. Living*, 1954, 16, 201–204.
5. Altmeyer, A. J.: Economic status of older people and their need for economic security. *Geriatrics*, 1957, 12, 201–202.
6. Alvarez, W. E.: The duration of widowhood. *Geriatrics*, 1955, 10, 297.
7. Alvarez, W. E.: Sexual life of the aging. *Geriatrics*, 1957, 12, 141–142.
8. Amulree, L.: The employment of elderly workers. *Practitioneer*, 1950, 165, 111–114.
9. Anderson, J. E.: *Psychological aspects of aging*. Washington: American Psychological Ass., 1956.
10. Andrus, R.: Personality change in an older age group. *Geriatrics*, 1955, 10, 432–435.
11. Banham, K. M.: Senescence and the emotions: a genetic theory. *J. genet. Psychol.*, 1951, 78, 175–183.
12. Barron, M. L.: Minority group characteristics of the aged in American society. *J. Geront.*, 1953, 8, 477–482.
13. Belbin, R. M.: Difficulties of older people in industry. *Occup. Psychol.*, 1953, 27, 177–190.
14. Bond, J. O.: The fragile male. *Geriatrics*, 1957, 12, 489–493.
15. Bossard, J. H. S.: Marrying late in life. *Soc. Forces*, 1951, 29, 405–408.
16. Bowers, W. H.: An appraisal of worker characteristics as related to age. *J. appl. Psychol.*, 1952, 36, 295–300.
17. Britton, J. H.: The personal adjustment of retired school teachers. *J. Geront.*, 1953, 8, 333–338.
18. Britton, J. H., and J. O. Britton: Work and retirement for older university alumni. *J. Geront.*, 1954, 9, 468–474.
19. Bühler, C.: Clinical study of the reactions of the individual to his age. *Geriatrics*, 1957, 12, 439–443.
20. Burgess, E. W.: Family living in the later decades. *Ann. Amer. Acad. pol. soc. Sci.*, 1952, 279, 106–114.

21. Busse, E. W.: Studies in the process of aging: The strengths and weaknesses of psychic functioning in the aged. *Amer. J. Psychiat.*, 1955, 116, 896–901.

22. Carlson, A. J., and E. J. Stieglitz: Physiological changes in aging. *Ann. Amer. Acad. pol. soc. Sci.*, 1952, 279, 18–31.

23. Cavan, R. S.: Family life and family substitutes in old age. *Amer. sociol. Rev.*, 1949, 14, 71–83.

24. Clague, E.: The working life span of American workers. *J. Geront.*, 1949, 4, 285–289.

25. Clague, E.: Labor force trends in the United States. *J. Geront.*, 1952, 7, 92–99.

26. Clay, H. M.: A study of performance in relation to age at two printing works. *J. Geront.*, 1956, 11, 417–424.

27. Cole, M. A.: What the aged need in their homes. *The New York Times*, 1957, Aug. 4.

28. Cowles, M. L.: Housing and associated problems of the rural-farm aged population in two Wisconsin counties. *Rur. Sociol.*, 1956, 21, 239–248.

29. Cushing, J. G.: Problems of retirement. *Ment. Hyg., N.Y.*, 1952, 36, 449–455.

30. Davidson, H. H., and L. P. Kruglov: Personality characteristics of the institutionalized aged. *J. consult. Psychol.*, 1952, 16, 5–10.

31. Desmond, T. C.: Look before you migrate. *Today's Hlth*, 1957, Jan., pp. 20–23.

32. Dickinson, F. G.: Economic aspects of the aging of our population. *In* T. L. Smith, *Problems of America's aging population*. Gainesville, Fla.: Univer. of Florida Press, 1951. Pp. 75–86.

33. Ebaugh, F. G.: Age introduces stress into the family. *Geriatrics*, 1956, 11, 146–150.

34. English, O. S., and G. H. J. Pearson: *Emotional problems of living*. New York: Norton, 1943.

35. Farrar, M. S.: Mother-daughter conflicts extended into later life. *Soc. Casewk*, 1955, 36, 202–207.

36. Fink, H. H.: The relationship of time perspective to age, institutionalization and activity. *J. Geront.*, 1957, 12, 414–417.

37. Fox, H.: Utilization of older manpower. *Harvard Bus. Rev.*, 1951, 29, 40–54.

38. Fried, E. G.: Attitudes of the older population groups toward activity and inactivity. *J. Geront.*, 1949, 4, 141–151.

39. Fried, E. G., and K. Stern: The situation of the aged within the family. *Amer. J. Orthopsychiat.*, 1948, 18, 31–54.

40. Friedmann, E. A., and R. J. Havighurst: *The meaning of work and retirement*. Chicago: Univer. of Chicago Press, 1954.

41. Frohlich, M. M.: Mental hygiene in old age. *In* C. Tibbitts, *Living through the older years*. Ann. Arbor, Mich.: Univer. of Michigan Press, 1949. Pp. 85–97.

42. Gardiner, L. P.: Attitudes and activities of the middle-aged and aged. *Geriatrics*, 1949, 4, 33–50.

43. Glick, P. C., and E. Landau: Age as a factor in marriage. *Amer. sociol. Rev.*, 1950, 15, 517–529.

44. Granick, S.: Studies of psychopathology in later maturity—a review. *J. Geront.*, 1950, 5, 361–369.

45. Gravatt, A. E.: Family relations in middle and old age—a review. *J. Geront.*, 1953, 8, 197–201.

46. Greenleigh, L.: Some psychological aspects of aging. *Soc. Casewk*, 1955, 36, 99–106.

47. Gumpert, M.: Our "Inca" ideas about retirement. *The New York Times*, 1952, July 27.

48. Gumpert, M.: Old age and productive loss. *Bull. Menninger Clin.*, 1953, 17, 103–109.
49. Harsch, C. M., and H. G. Schrickel: *Personality*. New York: Ronald, 1950.
50. Havighurst, R. J.: *Human development and education*. New York: Longmans, 1953.
51. Havighurst, R. J., and R. Albrecht: *Older people*. New York: Longmans, 1953.
52. Havighurst, R. J., and E. Shanas: Retirement and the professional worker. *J. Geront.*, 1953, 8, 81–85.
53. Hibbard, D. L., and J. P. Lee: Presbyterian ministers and their widows in retirement. *J. Geront.*, 1954, 9, 46–55.
54. Himler, L. E.: Psychiatric aspects of aging. *J. Amer. med. Ass.*, 1951, 147, 1330–1331.
55. Hoyt, G. C.: The life of the retired in a trailer park. *Amer. J. Soc.*, 1954, 59, 361–370.
56. Jacobson, P. H.: Differentials in divorce by duration of marriage and size of family. *Amer. sociol. Rev.*, 1950, 15, 235–244.
57. Johnson, R. J., and M. A. Pond: Health standards of housing for the aging population. *J. Geront.*, 1952, 7, 254–258.
58. Jones, H. E., and C. J. Kaplan: *Psychological aspects of mental disorders in later life*. Stanford, Calif.: Stanford Univer. Press, 1945.
59. Kallman, F. J., and G. Sander: Twin studies in senescence. *Amer. J. Psychiat.*, 1949, 106, 29–36.
60. Kaplan, J.: Effect of group activity on psychogenic manifestations of older people. *Geriatrics*, 1954, 9, 537–539.
61. Kinsey, A. C., W. B. Pomeroy, and C. E. Martin: *Sexual behavior in the human male*. Philadelphia: Saunders, 1948.
62. Kinsey, A. C., W. B. Pomeroy, C. E. Martin, and P. H. Gebhard: *Sexual behavior in the human female*. Philadelphia: Saunders, 1953.
63. Kiorbee, E.: Suicide and attempted suicide among old people. *J. Geront.*, 1951, 6, 233–236.
64. Kirchner, W., T. Lindbom, and D. G. Patterson: Attitudes toward the employment of older workers. *J. appl. Psychol.*, 1952, 36, 154–156.
65. Landau, G.: Restoration of self-esteem. *Geriatrics*, 1955, 10, 141–143.
66. Lawton, G.: *Aging successfully*. New York: Columbia Univer. Press, 1951.
67. Lebo, D.: Some factors said to make for happiness in old age. *J. clin. Psychol.*, 1953, 9, 385–387.
68. Lehman, H. C.: Jobs for those over sixty-five. *J. Geront.*, 1955, 10, 345–357.
69. Linden, M. E., and D. Courtney: The human life cycle and its interruptions: a psychologic hypothesis. Studies in gerontologic human relations. *Amer. J. Psychiat.*, 1953, 109, 906–915.
70. Manley, C. R.: The migration of older people. *Amer. J. Sociol.*, 1954, 59, 324–331.
71. Mason, E. P.: Some correlates of self-judgments of the aged. *J. Geront.*, 1954, 9, 324–337.
72. Mathiasen, G.: The continued employment of older workers. *Geriatrics*, 1955, 10, 137–140.
73. McFarland, R. A., A. L. Moseley, and M. B. Fisher: Age and the problem of professional truck drivers in highway transportation. *J. Geront.*, 1954, 9, 338–348.
74. McMahan, C. A., and T. R. Ford: Surviving the first five years of retirement. *J. Geront.*, 1955, 10, 212–215.

75. Meyer, H. D.: The adult cycle. *Ann. Amer. Acad. pol. soc. Sci.*, 1957, 313, 58–67.
76. Michelon, L. C.: The new leisure class. *Amer. J. Sociol.*, 1954, 59, 371–378.
77. Moberg, D. O.: Old age and crime. *J. crim. Law Criminol.*, 1953, 43, 764–766.
78. Moore, E. H.: Professors in retirement. *J. Geront.*, 1951, 6, 243–252.
79. Myers, R. J.: Factors in interpreting mortality after retirement. *Amer. Stat. Ass.*, 1954, 49, 267, 499–509.
80. New York Times Report: Widening of aid to aged mapped. *The New York Times*, 1957, Nov. 2.
81. New York Times Report: U.S. plans study of pensions: 3,000 to report for 12 years. *The New York Times*, 1957, Nov. 25.
82. Pam, J-S.: Institutional and personal adjustment in old age. *J. genet. Psychol.*, 1954, 85, 155–158.
83. Payne, S. L.: The Cleveland survey of retired men. *Personnel Psychol.*, 1953, 6, 81–110.
84. Peterson, R. L.: Older workers and their job effectiveness. *Geriatrics*, 1955, 10, 34–38.
85. Phillips, B. S.: A role theory approach to adjustment in old age. *Amer. sociol. Rev.*, 1957, 22, 212–217.
86. Pollak, O.: The older worker in the labor market. *In* M. Derber, *The aged and society*. Champaign, Ill.: Industrial Relations Research Ass., 1950, Pp. 56–64.
87. Pollak, O., and G. Heathers: *Social adjustment in old age*. New York: Social Science Research Council, 1948, Bull. 59.
88. Pressey, S. L.: Certain findings and proposals regarding professional retirement. *Amer. Ass. Univer. Prof.*, 1955, 41, 503–509.
89. Pressey, S. L.: The older psychologist: his potentials and problems. *Amer. Psychologist*, 1955, 10, 163–165.
90. Pressey, S. L.: Potentials of age: an exploratory field study. *Genet. Psychol. Monogr.*, 1957, 56, 159–205.
91. Pressey, S. L., and R. G. Kuhlen: *Psychological development through the life span*. New York: Harper, 1957.
92. Raines, G. N.: Adolescence: pattern for the future. *Geriatrics*, 1956, 11, 159–162.
93. Ramsey, C. E., and L. Nelson: Change in values and attitudes toward the family. *Amer. sociol. Rev.*, 1956, 21, 605–609.
94. Schmidt, J. F.: Pattern of poor adjustment in old age. *Amer. J. Sociol.*, 1951, 57, 33–42.
95. Shanas, E., and R. J. Havighurst: Retirement in four professions. *J. Geront*, 1953, 8, 212–221.
96. Shock, N. W.: *Trends in gerontology*. Stanford, Calif.: Stanford Univer. Press, 1951.
97. Silk, L. S.: The housing circumstances of the aged in the United States, 1950. *J. Geront.*, 1952, 7, 87–91.
98. Silverman, M.: Psychological and social aspects of psychiatric disorders in the aged. *J. ment. Sci.*, 1953, 99, 257–264.
99. Simerville, C. L., and R. R. Reichart: Pre-retirement expectancy and retirement reality. *Personnel Guid. J.*, 1955, 3, 344–346.
100. Smith, M. E.: A comparison of certain personality traits as rated in the same individuals in childhood and fifty years later. *Child Develpm.*, 1952, 23, 159–180.

101. Smith, M. W.: Older workers' efficiency in jobs of various types. *Personnel J.*, 1953, 32, 19–23.

102. Smith, T. L.: The immigration of the aged. *In* T. L. Smith, *Problems of America's aging population.* Gainesville, Fla.: Univer. Florida Press, 1951. Pp. 15–34.

103. Stanton, J. E.: *Some factors affecting employment in relation to age.* Ohio State Univer, 1955. Doctoral Dissertation No. 66.

104. Stern, K., G. M. Williams, and M. Prados: Grief reactions in later life. *Amer. J. Psychiat.*, 1951, 108, 289–294.

105. Stern, E. M., and M. Ross: *You and your aging parents.* New York: Wyn, 1952.

106. Still, J. W.: Boredom—the psychological disease of aging. *Geriatrics*, 1957, 12, 557–560.

107. Taietz, P.: *Administrative practices and personal adjustment in homes for the aged.* Ithaca, N.Y.: Cornell Univer. Agricultural Experiment Station, 1953, Bull. 899.

108. Thompson, W. E., and G. F. Strieb: *Retirement and health.* Paper read at the 10th Annual Meeting of the Gerontological Society, Cleveland, Ohio, Nov. 1, 1957.

109. Tibbitts, C.: Retirement problems in American society. *Amer. J. Sociol.*, 1954, 59, 301–308.

110. Tuckman, J., and I. Lorge: Retirement practices in business and industry. *J. Geront.*, 1952, 7, 77–86.

111. Tuckman, J., and I. Lorge: The effect of institutionalization on attitudes toward old people. *J. abnorm. soc. Psychol.*, 1952, 47, 337–344.

112. Tuckman, J., and I. Lorge: Old people's appraisal of adjustment over the life span. *J. Pers.*, 1954, 22, 417–422.

113. Tuckman, J., I. Lorge, and G. A. Spooner: The effect of family environment on attitudes toward old people and the older worker. *J. soc. Psychol.*, 1953, 38, 207–218.

114. Vivrett, W. K.: Environmental needs of the aging. *Geriatrics*, 1957, 12, 209–210.

115. Watson, R. I.: The personality of the aged—a review. *J. Geront.*, 1954, 9, 309–315.

116. Wayne, G. J.: Work as therapy, with special reference to the elderly. *Ment. Hyg., N.Y.*, 1955, 39, 79–88.

117. Webber, I. L.: *Variations in marital status of the older population in the United States according to residence and region.* Paper read at the 10th Annual Meeting of the Gerontological Society, Cleveland, Ohio, Nov. 2, 1957.

118. Zemen, F. D.: Constructive programs for the mental health of the elderly. *Ment. Hyg., N.Y.*, 1951, 35, 221–234.

Index

Early Childhood - Late Childhood

Developmental tasks - Identify
1. Motor Skills
2. Speech.
3. Emotional
4. Social

Specify what parents can do in each of these areas
to help child to surmount obstacles or hurdles
?